DONALD M. GOLDBERG

oral education today and tomorrow

ann m. mulholland, editor

**the alexander graham bell
association for the deaf
3417 volta place, n.w.
washington, d.c.**

library of congress cataloging in publication data
oral education
today and tomorrow
mulholland, ann m., editor

library of congress catalogue card number 81-65738
8104 810210
isbn 0-88200 144-2
© 1981 by the a.g. bell association for the deaf
3417 volta place, n.w.
washington, d.c. 20007

all rights reserved. no part of this book may be reprinted, or reproduced, or utilized in any form
or by any electronic, mechanical, or other means,
now known or hereafter invented, including any information
storage and retrieval system, without permission in
writing by the publisher.

10 9 8 7 6 5 4 3 2 1

printed in the united states of america

foreword

The need to study philosophies, knowledges and skills basic to the education of hearing-impaired children and youth transcends geographical borders. It has been professionally rewarding to see materialize the Symposium titled, "Oral Education: Today and Tomorrow." Now in written form, the messages of the Symposium's participants and the reactions of their colleagues are herein made available to all of us to analyze, question, and develop. The challenge to provide each prelingually deaf child the opportunity to communicate orally is clearly set forth. The decade of the 1980's should see preservice personnel preparation programs, medical schools, educational settings, scientists being capable of assuring that, regardless of place of birth on earth, oral communication is a true option for each hearing-impaired person.

Edwin A. Martin
Assistant Secretary
Office of Special Education
Rehabilitation Services
U. S. Department of Education
July, 1980

editorial board

armin löwe   jan j.m. van eijndhoven   thomas j. watson

preface

The impetus for convening the first International Symposium on Oral Education rose from the need for a forum where international leaders might engage in discourse on matters of common concern and shared interest. Current research findings, new and developing instructional strategies, techniques of assessment and diagnosis, and the status of the field internationally were topics frequently discussed by visitors to the Instituut voor Doven. That the Symposium was initiated at Sint Michielsgestel where visitors from around the world have been stimulated by necessarily brief but provocative interchanges is logical. Under the perceptive leadership of Jan van Eijndhoven, Director of the Instituut; Dr. Anthony van Uden, Scientific Adviser; J. A. C. Leijten, Chairman of the Board of Trustees; and the Instituut's Research Committee, planning for the Symposium was begun. With Director van Eijndhoven as Coordinating Chairman, the Program Committee was selected representing West Germany, Armin Löwe, Pädagogische Hochschule, Heidelberg; England, Thomas Watson, University of Manchester; the United States, Ann Mulholland, Teachers College, Columbia University; and the Netherlands, A. van Uden and Director, van Eijndhoven. The Symposium had as its objectives:
- the sharing of knowledge of research and practice in oral education of the deaf;
- the development of deeper insights into the art of teaching deaf children to use and to understand their mother tongue orally;
- determination of the role of oral education in the deaf child's personal and social development; and
- the examination of "the state of the art" of oral education internationally.

To ensure that the focus would be on prelingually profoundly deaf children, the following definition was specified to be used in the prepared papers and in the discussions.

Children in whom the onset of deafness occurred before one year six months of age, who, even with the best auditory training and the best hearing aid available, have to rely mainly on lipreading or speechreading as a means of understanding speech, and whose pure tone thresholds are not less than:

Hz	125	250	500	1000	2000	4000
dB	60	60	90	90	90	90

The incessant controvery over the communication mode for use in the instruction of deaf children has led to increasing polarization of the views of those who advocate the oral method and those who advocate total or manual communication. To overcome the effects of such dissension it was important to review, to reaffirm the principles and characteristic features of the oral development of prelingually profoundly deaf children, to search for new ways of improving oral methods of instruction, and to generate hypotheses for needed research. By examining the results of research and of practice across Western Europe and North America from the perspectives of sociology, psychology, linguistics, speech science, education, audiology, and anthroplogy, it was anticipated that the role of oral education in personal and vocational fulfillment would be clarified.

The program was designed to produce discussion by having the papers circulated for study prior to the Symposium and having an abstracted oral presentation and reaction to each paper. Forty participants, observers, and alternates were selected by the Program Committee and titles of papers assigned. The completed version of each paper is presented in this volume. To accommodate to the communication preference of the participants, general discussion followed single or, in some instances, several sequenced presentations; small group discussions and plenary sessions facilitated communication and focus.

The content of the Proceedings of the Symposium has been organized in six major sections: The Foundations of Oral Education, The State of the Art, The Essence of the Oral Method, Diagnosis and Assessment, Social and Emotional Development, and Oral Education: Today and Tomorrow.

Two features of the Symposium that were appreciated by those attending were one entire Symposium session conducted before the State Secretary of Education and Science and members of Parliament at the Hague, and the final session of the week-long Symposium held at de Huif Sint Michielsgestel before Dutch professionals, administrators, and teachers of schools for the deaf, parents, and interested persons from the community where the conclusions and summary were presented.

There may be a certain number of minor stylistic inconsistencies in these presentations since the material came from varied sources and in the interest of going to press some minor points were allowed to stand. We feel, however, that this does not in any way concern the essential value of these papers.

It is a pleasure to acknowledge the invaluable contributions of a number of individuals without whose assistance the Symposium would have been less than memorable.

> State Secretary for Education and Science Mr. A. J. Hermes, who thoughtfully arranged the meeting at the Hague and the reception which followed at the Ministry of Education and Science;

> The Board of Trustees Chairman J. A. C. Leijten of the Instituut voor Doven Foundation, who generously provided support beyond the financial, reflecting concern for deaf children and their education internationally as well as for the personal comfort of the participants;

> The sisters in charge of the conference center at Duyn en Dael, Nuland, whose gracious hospitality and personal attention ensured the well-being of the participants;

> Dr. Helen Lane who, unable to travel, prepared her reaction paper and joined the participants via her videotaped presentation;

Professor Harriet Kopp for her perceptiveness in succinctly summarizing the formal papers, the discussions, the conclusions and recommendations with logic and clarity and which she presented with humor and vigor;

The heads of the several schools of the Instituut voor Doven, their teachers, and deaf pupils who demonstrated for the participants the value of oral education in their classrooms, residences, and recreational activities;

Mrs. T. Schakenraad and Mrs. L. van Lanchot, who graciously provided secretarial, translation, and personal services beyond the expected;

The participants and observers whose enthusiasm, diligence, and patience overcame jet lag, a tightly scheduled program, and deadlines, yet managed to generate an openness of communication and personal involvement which has laid the foundation for new friendships unhampered by geographical boundaries and for future collaborative research efforts;

Dean Harold Noah and Professor Frances P. Connor, Teachers College, Columbia University, for their encouragement and support;

The Editorial Board—Jan van Eijndhoven, Thomas Watson, and Armin Löwe—for their professional concern and assistance in the preparation of this publication;

Dr. Edwin C. Martin, Assistant Secretary for Special Education and Rehabilitation Services, U.S. Department of Education, for his unswerving support, financial and otherwise, for the betterment of education of the hearing impaired;

Lucy Cuzon du Rest, Publications Manager of the Alexander Graham Bell Association for the Deaf, who took over the responsibility of moving the book through to final publication with considerable expertise and commitment;

Finally, Dir. Ton van Hagen, who with patience and zeal coordinated the organization of the Symposium and served gallantly as liaison between the committees and participants across languages and work styles in tandem with his New York counterpart to meet stringent deadlines with an unruffled spirit.

Ann M. Mulholland
Teachers College, Columbia University
June 1980

part V: social and emotional development of prelingually deaf persons during school life and afterward   453

chapter 18— the effect of oral education on the attitudes of deaf persons toward the hearing environment   george w. fellendorf   455

chapter 19— the effect of oral education on the attitudes of the family and the environment toward deafness   edgar l. lowell   473

   reactions to 18 and 19   david manning   481

chapter 20— a perspective on the mental health of young deaf adults in modern society   d. robert frisina   485

   reaction to 20   irene w. leigh   495

chapter 21— a panel of young deaf adults: experiences with oral education   toos-verdonschot-kroëf, bart bosch, p.m.a.l. hezemans, w. noom   503

chapter 22   human values and idealism   john p. hourihan   517

   reaction to 22   jan j.m. van eijndhoven   528

part VI: summary and conclusions   531

chapter 23— an oral education of the deaf   jan j.m. van eijndhoven   533

chapter 24— oral education defined   535

chapter 25— conclusions and recommendations   harriet green kopp   537

committees

program committee - chairman of the symposium
rev. jan j. m. van eijndhoven
professor armin löwe
professor dr. ann m. mulholland
rev. dr. a. m. j. van uden
dr. thomas j. watson

advisory committee
rev. dr. a. m. j. van uden
dir. jan p. m. van dijk
rev. jan j. m. van eijndhoven
dir. ton p. m. van hagen
dir. sjaak c. s. van puijenbroek
fr. norbert a. j. smulders
bro. dir. leo speth
dir. frans j. w. iJsseldijk

organizing committee
rev. j. a. c. leijten
rev. jan j. m. van eijndhoven
bro. dir. leo speth
dir. ton p. m. van hagen

participants

sr. dr. joyce buckler, director
st. joseph institute for the deaf
st. louis, missouri u.s.a.

dr. hugo w. campbell
department of psychology
catholic university of nijmegen
the netherlands

ms. morag h. clark, principal
birkdale school
southport, england

dr. bethan davies,
consultant pediatric audiologist
london, england

dr. george w. fellendorf,
executive director
hearing, educational aid
and research foundation
washington, d.c. - u.s.a.

dr. d. robert frisina,
senior vice-president
rochester institute of technology
rochester, new york - u.s.a.

sr. m. nicholas griffey, director
course for teachers of the deaf,
university college
dublin, ireland

ms. janet head,
supervisor of speech
lexington school for the deaf
new york, new york - u.s.a.

rev. dr. john p. hourihan,
assistant professor
teachers college,
columbia university
new york, new york - u.s.a.

dir. frans j. w. ijsseldijk, director
psychological department
instituut voor doven
sint michielsgestel,
the netherlands

dr. geofrey p. ivimey, lecturer
university of london
london, england

professor harriet green kopp, chairman
department of communicative
disorders
san diego state university
san diego, california - u.s.a.

professor richard r. kretschmer, jr.
department of psychology
and special education
university of cincinnati
cincinnati, ohio - u.s.a.

dr. helen s. lane, principal emeritus
central institute for the deaf
st. louis, missouri - u.s.a.

ms. irene leigh, counselor-therapist,
the lexington school for the deaf
new york, new york - u.s.a.

professor daniel ling
school of communication disorders
mcgill university
montreal, canada

professor armin löwe
college of education
heidelberg,
federal republic of germany

dr. edgar l. lowell, director
john tracy clinic
university of southern california
los angeles, california - u.s.a.

mr. david manning,
mainstream coordinator
clark school for the deaf
northhampton, massachusetts - u.s.a.

dr. andreas markides,
senior lecturer
manchester university
manchester, england

professor dr. ann m. mulholland,
coordinator of programs
for the hearing impaired
teachers college, columbia university
new york, new york - u.s.a.

dr. dónall p. o'baóill, lecturer
university college
dublin, ireland

dr. h. leslie owrid,
senior lecturer
manchester university
manchester, england

jean a. m. persoon
department of medical sociology
catholic university of nijmegen
the netherlands

ms. susan schmid-giovannini,
principal
schule fü hörgeschädigte
zollikon, switzerland

professor klaus schulte, director
research center for applied linguistics
for the rehabilitation of the disabled
college of education,
heidelberg,
federal republic of germany

dr. audrey simmons-martin,
director, early education
central institute for the deaf
st. louis, missouri - u.s.a.

fr. norbert a. j. smulders,
lecturer
instituut voor doven
sint michielsgestel,
the netherlands

bro. dir. leo speth
instituut voor doven
sing michielsgestel,
the netherlands

dir. jan p. m. van dijk,
director, departments for
multihandicapped children
instituut voor doven
sint michielsgestel,
the netherlands

rev. jan. j. m. van eijndhoven,
director,
instituut voor doven
sint michielsgestel,
the netherlands

dir. ton p. m. van hagen,
director of inservice training
instituut voor doven
sint michielsgestel,
the netherlands

dir. sjaak c. s. van puijenbroek,
director,
department of elementary education
instituut voor doven
sint michielsgestel,
the netherlands

dir toine l. m. van der sanden,
director of psychological services
instituut voor doven
sint michielsgestel,
the netherlands

rev. dr. a. m. j. van uden,
scientific advisor to the board of
trustees of the foundation
instituut voor doven
sint michielsgestel,
the netherlands

dr. thomas j. watson,
senior lecturer
manchester university
manchester, england

observers

dr. sara e. conlon, executive director,
a.g. bell association for the deaf
washington, d.c. - u.s.a.

ms. yvonne csanyi, director,
courses for teachers of the deaf
budapest, hungary

professor otto kröhnert
university of hamburg
hamburg,
federal republic of germany

part 1

the foundation of oral education

the historical development of oral education

armin löwe

It is not an easy task to present a paper on the historical development of oral education of deaf children to a symposium whose members come from about ten different American and European countries. Although I am fully aware that each of our countries has taken a considerable share in this development, it is quite impossible to do justice to it. Therefore, I shall not be able to come up to the expectations of all members. This will be even true for my German colleagues. They will miss what they consider important facts, whereas non-German members of this Symposium will perhaps argue that the development in Germany is overemphasized by me. If the last thing should be the case, Dr. Watson will help us to set it to rights in his paper on the same subject.

Oral education started more than 400 years ago. Again I am clear in my mind that it is an impossible task to do justice to each period and its special contribution to the historical development of oral education. I can only feature some names and aspects and have to omit many others. Although the decisions relating to this were made deliberately, they can, of course, be questioned. The following representations should be understood in these premises.

The "Spanish Method"

"The discovery of the oral education" of deaf children "took place in Spain in the 16th century" (Werner, 1932, p.9). The honor of having been the first teacher of deaf children is accorded to Pedro Ponce de León (1510–1584), a Benedictine monk who tutored deaf children of Spanish nobility at a monastary at Valladolid. He began with reading and writing and then moved on to speech. However, he also used a manual alphabet in instruction because he had not yet recognized the possibility of speechreading. His pupils, nevertheless, were well educated men who had a good command of language and speech and were masters of speechreading according to the report (1644) given by Sir Kenelm Digby (1603–1665) (Schumann, 1940, p. 47).

The method by which this outstanding result was achieved was very probably the same which was also applied by his countryman Manuel Ramirez de Carrión (1579–1652) and was described by Juan Pablo Bonet (1579–1633) in his book *Reduction de las letras y arte para enseñar a ablar los mudos* (1620). As the title of this first book on the education of deaf children indicates, it deals mainly with the art of teaching deaf children to talk.

The three mentioned Spanish teachers of deaf children may be regarded as a unit. Kröhnert (1966, p. 25) terms de León as the inventor, de Carrión as the real expert, and Bonet as the theorist of the "Spanish Method" which did not yet emphasize the need of speechreading and, therefore, had to start with written language and to use the hand alphabet before speech was taught. It is to the credit of John Bulwer (1648) from England that speechreading was recognized as an important prerequisite for a successful oral education: "That learning first to write the Images of words and to understand the conveyances of a visible and permanent speech, from that Hand A.B.C. you may proceed unto a Lip-Grammar, which may enable you to heare with your eye and thence learne to speak with your tongue" (Werner, 1932, p. 261). Bulwer's idea of speechreading or, as he called it, of "ocular audition" gave a great impetus to the further development of oral education in Europe.

It was Spain at the summit of her history which gave us the beginning of the first systematic oral education of deaf children. At that time the teaching situation was ideal for good results. The teacher had only a few children, from the most cultured and intelligent families. He was well paid and could therefore devote his full attention to the education of these children over a period of years and provide a consistent language environment, important factors which contributed to success in the education of these children. (Leadership in education of deaf children has been more than once related to political, economic, cultural, and military factors. It is, therefore, a good sign that this symposium takes place in a country which does not belong to the present "leaders" in the world.)

The "French Method"

The "French Method" developed by Charles Michel de l'Epée (1712–89) and his successor Roch-Ambroise Cucurron Sicard (1742–1822) could not contribute much to further development of oral education. On the contrary, it delayed it in many parts of the world for almost 100 years. Nevertheless, it would be unfair to regard Abbé de l'Epée only as the protagonist of manual education. He was the first who made the education of deaf children a matter of public concern and made it available also to the poor. His main concern was the instruction of as many deaf children as possible. To him as a priest this was especially urgent, since he believed that education for religious instruction was necessary for the salvation of their souls. Therefore, he also welcomed all who came to him for training as teachers from all over Europe and North America.

In all probability it will come as a surprise to some teachers of deaf children that de l'Epée was also convinced that spoken language is the most perfect form of communication. He had no doubt that deaf children could learn to talk if they were taught. Oral education was considered worthwhile for social reasons and achievable for all pupils if they were instructed in a school environment which was different from his institute. De l'Epée was also convinced that the speechreading abilities of deaf children could be improved if his methodical signs—which, however, he regarded as faster and more comfortable for a mutual understanding—were not used simultaneously (Schumann, 1940, p. 126).

The Recognition of Speechreading

The reference to the "silent method" of de l'Epée and Sicard must not be misunderstood. Oral education as it was practiced 200 years ago by de León and de Carrión in Spain was not yet written off. Their idea was kept alive and supplemented with the personal thoughts and experiences of men like John Bulwer (1614–84) and John Wallis (1616–1703) in England and Johannes Conrad Ammann (1669–1724) in the Netherlands. Above all, Ammann paved the way for what later was called the "German Method." He started from the very beginning with speech exercises for which he claims to have needed only two months. The children were not only expected to imitate each sound, syllable, or word which was spoken to them but also to write, to read, and to speechread them. Ammann was the first who realized speechreading to be an integral part of speech and language instruction. The title of one of his publications, namely "Surdus loquens" (1692), is perhaps the shortest description of the main aim of oral education which we can find. Unfortunately, Ammann held that the mastery of speech would also include the mastery of language. This was, however, a false conclusion.

Last, but not least, it must be mentioned that also in the days of Abbé de l'Epée oral education was applied with great success in France. Jacob Rodriguez Pereira (1715–80) taught his pupils to talk on the basis of reading, writing, and the Spanish hand alphabet. The understanding of language was acquired mainly by its practical use (Schumann, 1940, p. 89–94). As Pereira had done, so also Ernaud (1740–1800) taught his pupils to speak. He did not, however, use the hand alphabet because, according to his conviction, it would impede speechreading, spoil articulation, paralyze the organic activity necessary for speech and be useless in society (Schumann, 1940, p. 95). Etienne Francois Deschamps (1745–91) was another contemporary of de l'Epée who taught his pupils speech and speechreading, together with reading and writing. He even taught them to read letters in raised relief and to speechread by touch so that they could communicate in the dark (Walther, 1882, p. 75). He was also one of the first teachers who used special signs for the teaching of speech sounds.

The Forerunners of the Later "German Method"

"German schools of the eighteenth century became the champions of the oral method of teaching the deaf" (Bender, 1970, p. 99). One should restate this incorrect sentence and write it this way: A number of German-speaking Protestant priests living during the 18th century (some of them were parents of deaf children) became the champions of the oral method of teaching deaf children. Here we have to think of Georg Raphel, Lüneburg (1673–1740), Otto Benjamin Lasius, Burgdorf (?–1779), and Johann Ludwig Ferdinand Arnoldi (1737–83). They were all influenced by Ammann and speech and speechreading played a major part in their program. This is also true of the work of Heinrich Keller (1728–1802), a Protestant priest at Schlieren who was the first teacher of deaf children in Switzerland (Karth, 1902, p. 381). Among the mentioned four Protestant priests, Arnoldi was far ahead of his time. He

> "believed in a natural approach to language teaching. He took his pupils for walks in public places and showed them new things, then taught them how to express their experiences in words. He invented games and drills, so that repetition might "engrave on the minds" of his pupils the things he taught them. He remarked how pleased the deaf were when the words they pronounced were understood by others. Once they developed this skill, he said, they often talked to themselves alone, and even talked in their dreams. . . . Articulation and oral speech were used wherever he thought it practical, but his chief goal was to teach reading, so that his pupils might, as quickly as possible, make use of books," (Bender, 1970, p. 100).

Samuel Heinicke

Outside of Germany, Samuel Heinicke (1727–90) is the most well-known German teacher of deaf children. With the financial help of the elector of Saxony he opened the first German school for deaf children at Leipzig in 1778 after he had already achieved superb results in the oral education of a number of deaf children at Hamburg.

Heinicke's method was oral. For him, "spoken language is the hinge upon which everything turns" (Schumann, 1940, p. 155). Therefore, he was opposed to the teaching of letters before the teaching of speech, arguing that this was against the natural order of learning. Influenced by the work of Ammann, he attached a special quality to the spoken word. He argued that pure thought was possible only through speech, upon which everything was dependent. Operating from such a premise, he concluded that written language is secondary to spoken language and must follow, not precede it. For teaching speech he developed a theory that the sense of taste could substitute for hearing in the perception of sound. He developed this theory because he doubted the statement that deaf people "hear with their eyes." He also advocated first teaching words with functional meaning. Then the words were taken apart, into syllables, and finally letters, rather than teaching letters as meaningless hieroglyphics.

The last remarks made it understandable that Heinicke was not satisfied with the teaching of reading to hearing children as it was practiced at this time. He was the first of many other German teachers of deaf children who have also had a remarkable influence on elementary education of hearing children. I want to mention only Johann Baptist Graser (1766–1841), Heinrich Stephani (1761–1850), Constantin Malisch (1860–1925), Erwin Kern (1897–), Artur Kern (1900–), and Heinrich Kratzmeier (1930–).

Heinicke was convinced that the perception of the movements of the speech organs, so-called kinesthetic perception, is indispensable for the acquisition and reproduction of speech. He associated this knowledge with the important discovery of Ammann, who had described the touching of speech on the throat of the teacher as the "great secret of this art" (Schumann, 1912, p. 70). Heinicke's statement helped tactile-kinesthetic perception to become a firm component in the oral education of deaf children.

Another important component of the "German Method," is that Heinicke, unlike Ammann, did not rest content with the teaching of speech but thought also of the teaching of the meaning of language. According to Heinicke, there is no real thinking without language; only the possession of spoken language offers a human being the opportunity to gain a differentiated access to the world. Schumann (1940, p. 151) has stated that the "German Method," as developed by Heinicke, is based on the evidence that spoken language can also become for deaf people an inner factor which accompanies their thinking. Heinicke has, however, hardly played the first violin in the German orchestra of oral education of deaf children, as many professional people inside and outside of Germany believe. Even his great admirer and biographer Paul Schumann (1870–1943) states that "the life of Heinicke is a deep tragedy: everywhere is a contradiction between idea and realization" (1940, p. 147). Sadly, when he died, nobody was trained to continue his work.

Thomas Braidwood

Like Samuel Heinicke in Germany, Thomas Braidwood in Scotland (1715–1806) made his techniques of teaching deaf children to speak a family secret. At his death in 1806, his nephew and successor Joseph Watson (1765–1829) considered himself released from the family bond of secrecy and published his book on the *Instruction of the Deaf and Dumb* (1809). He began with articulation, first combining speech elements into syllables, then into words. From there he went on to writing and reading. Until oral language was established he accepted natural gestures and signs as a means of communication. He recommended also a two-handed alphabet which is still in use in England today. It is hard to believe that this book seems to have remained unknown to Thomas Hopkins Gallaudet (1787–1851), who applied without success to Thomas Braidwood at Birmingham and Joseph Watson at London for admission to their schools in 1815. It is common knowledge that he had to go to Paris and became a follower of the method of Sicard.

Johann Baptist Graser

Before the foundation of the first schools for deaf children in Europe (Paris, 1760; Edinburgh, 1760; Leipzig, 1778; Vienna, 1779; London, 1783; Karlsruhe, 1783; Rome, 1784; Bordeaux, 1786; Prague, 1786; Berlin, 1788; Naples, 1788; Groningen, 1790) only a few deaf children could receive private instruction. But however beneficial the opening of more and more special schools has been, they could by no means cope with the great number of children requiring education. For this reason, but also to draw the pattern of education and social training closer to the normal, Johann Baptist Graser (1766–1841) started a new way of educating deaf children in Germany. In 1821, Graser himself opened an experimental school for deaf children as a unit in a regular primary school at Bayreuth. His plan was to give the children about two years of special education, then incorporate them into regular classes, whose teachers were expected to be able to teach the deaf children along with the hearing.

Because teachers at that time had sometimes to cope with 80 and more pupils in one class and, therefore, not enough allowance could be made for the slower learning of deaf children, this system—called the generalization of the education of deaf children—was far ahead of its time and gradually was abandoned. The fact that the first schools for deaf children which were opened from the end of the 18th century were residential facilities must not lead to the assumption that interest in educating deaf children contiguous to hearing peers is a relatively recent phenomenon. In reality, quite a number of teachers of deaf children have long been sensitive to the desirability of having their pupils live at home and interact with hearing peers.

The "generalization of the education of deaf children" as it was practiced during the first half of the 19th century was doomed to failure. It contributed, however, to a greater awareness of the educational needs of deaf children and led to the opening of an increasing number of smaller special schools. It also had a welcome byproduct: it gave to the education of deaf children those teachers whose outstanding achievements in oral education resulted in the general acceptance of oral education at the end of the 19th century. I want to deal here only with two who have made the greatest impact on the further development of oral education, namely Friedrich Moritz Hill (1805–74) and Johannes Vatter (1842–1916).

Friedrich Moritz Hill

Friedrich Moritz Hill (1805–1874) was a teacher of deaf children at the small seminary school for deaf children connected with the teacher training seminary at Weissenfel. As far as possible he tried to apply the principles of Johann

Heinrich Pestalozzi's (1746–1827) "mother method" to the teaching of deaf children. In one of his early publications (1840) he summarized his teaching principles, which differed from those of his predecessors who still clung to the grammatical method of teaching language, in the following seven guidelines:

1. Arouse in your pupils the need of language in general and the need of our language in particular.
2. If you want to succeed in doing so, you have to demonstrate objects and actions to your pupils and to add to them without delay to our language. (Stoffers called this later [1868] "the immediate association of spoken language.")
3. During your teaching of language as well as during your introduction of new linguistic structures, you must always guide from the needs of the pupil and of his natural development.
4. In the teaching of language to deaf children you should always pursue the following four objects simultaneously: the training of cognitive skills, the acquisition of knowledge, the training of proficiency in language and speech to which also belongs the promotion of mechanical skills in speaking, speech-reading, writing, and reading.
5. Enlarge especially on the elements and return often to them.
6. Divide your entire instruction in small wholes, train completely the tasks through which you have gone and repeat them from time to time.
7. Make always and everywhere use of spoken language and demand its use in the same degree also from the pupil.

Hill summarizes his seven guidelines in the sentence: "Teaching of spoken language is in everything." Only when the teaching of language is not only a subject but also a principle of instruction, can one expect that spoken language will also become a "true organic activity of the life of a deaf child." Therefore, he wanted deaf children to be introduced into language in the same way as hearing children learn it, i.e., by constant daily use, associated with proper objects and actions. As it is with hearing children, speech should be the basis of all language. Therefore, oral language has to be taught before reading and writing, and has to be used from the very beginning as the basis for teaching and communication. The use of natural gestures was not excluded as a means of communication, but replaced as early as possible by oral language.

Hill's program of oral education took place in three steps. It started with the so-called "preparatory instruction" during which mainly the "techniques" of speech were trained. It was followed by the so-called "visual education" which aimed at the explanation of the meanings of language and by the "final instruction" during which the acquired linguistic rules should be secured. Whereas his predecessors kept to the guiding principle "Everything is in the teaching of language," Hill stuck to the reverse principle, namely "Teaching of spoken language is in everything." He was the first teacher who really offered an educational program which was in compliance with the educational needs of deaf children.

Like de l'Epée and Sicard and unlike Braidwood and Heinicke, Hill shared his experiences and his knowledge with all who were interested in his work. He received a great number of visitors and his books were translated into many languages. As far as I can judge, he did more for the expansion of oral education during the 19th century than anybody else in the world. His contemporaries called him already during his lifetime "the most outstanding teacher of the deaf of the 19th century" and "the reformer of the education of deaf children in Germany" (Reuschert, 1905).

In order to do justice to the work of Hill, it is wise to take notice of the following comment of Paul Schumann (1940, p. 322): "When Hill wants to label his method as 'that of the mother,' because it is in the main in agreement with the way observed by her, he means by it, however, only a 'naturally structured way of instruction,' he turns against the 'governess method,' he is an exponent of an empirical method of immediate language acquisition which is neither a constructive nor an imitative method."

The period of Hill and of the so-called small seminary schools for deaf children was the most fruitful in the history of oral education in Germany. At no other time in history was the education of deaf children so closely bound up with regular education as well as with teacher training programs as during the existence of these schools, which usually had no more than 30 or 40 pupils. After the German victory over France in 1871 they had to give way to larger institutions. It may be asked whether this step has not produced more new problems than it pretended to solve.

The Dutch Contribution to the Expansion of Oral Education

The influence of Hill was soon to be noticed in all parts of Europe. Much of the competency and inspiration of David Hirsch (1813–1895), principal of the Rotterdam school for deaf children, came from Hill. He was convinced of oral education and sent his teachers everywhere, carrying his inspiration to many places. Two of them were instrumental in the revival of oral teaching in England, namely Gerrit van Asch (he established the first school for deaf children in New Zealand in 1876), and William van Praagh. At about the same time, the later "Clarke School for the Deaf" at Northampton, Massachusetts, and the later "Lexington School for the Deaf" at New York were founded as the first oral schools in North America. Fifty years after the opening of the first school for deaf children at Hartford, Connecticut, it was no longer possible to ignore in the U.S.A. the success of the oral approach being utilized in England and Germany. By the way, Bernhard Engelsmann, a teacher of the Vienna Hebrew School for deaf children, was appointed the first principal of the Lexington School.

The Immediate Oral Language Association

Hill's idea of the "immediate oral language association" took more and more possession of the thinking of some of the leading German teachers of deaf children in the second half of the 19th century. They went a step further and advocated the so-called "pure oral method." They held the view not only that natural gestures should be banished completely from the education of deaf children but demanded also the exclusion of the simultaneous use of written language. With this they wanted to avoid several associations from occurring between the different forms of language and one and the same object or matter. Only one form, namely the tactile-kinesthetic one, should be allowed to function as "the immediate language-sign." Not before the pupil had achieved this association, and speech had become his "form of thinking," should the written form of language be added, and that as symbol for the spoken word and not as symbol for the object. It was typical of this way of thinking, that the kinesthetic sensation received an extraordinary appreciation. The method of teaching was based on muscle sense. Further aids were the receiving of vibrations on the body, feeling of the air breath with the hand, and speechreading.

Wilhelm Gude (1832–1901) and Bernhard Stahm (1818–1900), who had done research work on the physiological and psychological aspects in the acquisition of speech by deaf children, concluded from their findings that the articulation had to begin not only with speech sounds but even with elements of these sounds. They understood the teaching of speech as applied physiology, phonetics, and psychology.

Johannes Vatter

Johannes Vatter (1842–1916) has to be named as the most important exponent of this school of thinking. Although he is rather unknown in the English-speaking world compared with Heinicke and with Hill, he may have indirectly had some influence on the education of deaf children in the U.S.A. Some American professional people perhaps do not know that the "Association Phoneme Unit Method" of Mildred McGinnis applied for many years at the Central Institute for the Deaf in St. Louis and only recently again recommended as the last resort for teaching speech to deaf children (Calvert & Silverman, 1975), is almost congruent with the way Johannes Vatter taught speech to deaf children. Because his method was used in more or less all schools for deaf children in the German-speaking part of Central Eurpoe at the beginning of this century, it would be hard to believe that Max Goldstein (1870–1942) would not have known it during the years of his study at Vienna where he had worked together with Urbantschitsch in the use of residual hearing of the pupils of those schools for deaf children. After his return to the United States, he founded the above-mentioned American institute.

Johannes Vatter is still regarded in Germany as one of the most successful teachers of deaf children who has ever lived. He refused to accept more than about 40 pupils into his school at Frankfurt which was connected with a family boarding house. All pupils had to be boarders, for Vatter considered the daily life in the boarding house as an essential part of the teaching. He wanted his pupils to learn to think in the spoken language. Because he knew that children learn to think in that language in which their evironment succeeds to communicate with them, Vatter stressed the importance of a speaking environment for his deaf pupils. Only in a continually speaking environment, deaf children are able to connect their thoughts, feelings, and ideas with the spoken word. As the title of one of his books indicates, *The Joint Object and Oral Language Teaching* (1875), Vatter emphasized the direct association of oral language. Everything that is put in between, either signs or written words, has to be avoided.

Together with Johannes Vatter, two other German teachers of deaf children deserve to be mentioned: Georg Schibel (1807–1900) and Wilhelm Daniel Arnold (1810–79). They also had small boardinghouse schools with only about 40 pupils, and like Vatter they emphasized the oral conversation not only between teacher and pupils but also between the deaf children themselves. Their successes were great and have hardly been surpassed since then, although there was no preschool education in their time and compulsory education lasted only six years. They were, however, convinced of the truth of the following statement of Vatter and adhered to it with the greatest possible consequence: "Only the narrow path of the pure oral method leads to a language which is viable and which will meet the later requirements of life: the broad road of a combined method on the other hand will end with great disillusion" (1911).

The Second International Congress on Education of the Deaf at Milan (1880)

This was also the general opinion of the members of the second International Congress on Education of the Deaf which took place at Milan in 1880. Although only three Germans took part in this Congress (87 came from Italy, 57 from France, 9 from England, 5 from the U.S.A., 3 from Sweden, and 1 from Belgium), the overwhelming majority of its members voted for the following declaration (the 9 votes against it came from the Americans under the leadership of Edmund Miner Gallaudet (1837–1917) and from four other members):

> The Congress—considering that the simultaneous use of speech and signs has the disadvantage of injuring speech, lipreading and precision of ideas, declares—that the Pure Oral Method ought to be preferred (Bender, 1970, p. 165).

It was to the credit of the hard work of Italian teachers of deaf children that the oral method was almost unanimously accepted. Only about 12 years before they had changed from the "French" to the "German Method." Compared with the then standard of education in French schools for deaf children, their results were so impressive that the French delegation was converted to the oral method (Treibel, 1881, p. 14). The leading men who had brought forth this remarkable change in Italy were Abba Serafino Balestra, Como (1834–86), Abba Tomaso Pendol, Sienna (1800–83), and Abba Giulio Tarra, Milan (1832–89). It deserves to be mentioned that Abba Balestra had been convinced of the value of oral education by the work of David Hirsch at Rotterdam.

Criticism of the Pure Oral Method

The period of Johannes Vatter was the summit in the history of oral education of deaf children in German-speaking Central Europe. The great results which

Arnold, Schibel, Vatter, and other teachers achieved not only once in one single class of deaf children but with all pupils of their schools for many decades were ample evidence that they were on the right track. Nevertheless, there was an increasing number of teachers who for one reason or another no longer agreed with the approach of the pure oral method and with the family boardinghouse school. Reference has to be made to Georg Forchhammer, Fredericia (1861–1938) and Emil Göpfert Leipzig (1851–1906). Both of them were in favor of an imitative way of language teaching. They offered their pupils much written language. No doubt, their students learned to understand a lot in this way, as especially Forchhammer could prove (1930), but they were almost unable to express themselves. Therefore, they had to take refuge in signing. This, however, proved that their method was not, as pretended, an imitative method. The children did not imitate, they only learned to understand in a passive way. Although Göpfert as well as Forchhammer claimed to followers of Alexander Graham Bell (1847–1922), they neglected the most important part of his work, namely the conversation. They overlooked also the important fact that Bell as well as Anne Sullivan had applied their imitative method only to one child and not to a class of children.

It is understandable that Vatter raised severe objections to the initiative approach of Forchhammer and Göpfert.

From the Kinesthetic-Oral to the Aural-Oral Approach

The oral methods employed in Europe till the end of the 19th century were esentially nonauditory in that they relied upon speechreading for understanding the speech of others and the combination of visual imitation, tactile, and kinesthetic training for the production of speech. A remarkable change took place already during the lifetime of Vatter. Unfortunately, he was rather indifferent and apathetic to the ideas of Victor Urbantschitsch (1847–1921), Friedrich Bezold (1842–1908), and Karl Kroiss (1861–1945), who added a new aspect to oral education, namely the use of residual hearing. In this context two publications are worthy of mention, namely, *The Methodics of Auditory Education* by Kroiss (1903) and *The Acoustic Method* by Goldstein (1939), who had worked under Urbantschitsch during his years of study at Vienna.

Strictly speaking, the idea to make use of the residual hearing of deaf children for the development of language and speech is as old as oral education. It was already full of life in France at the time of Ernaud, Pereira, Deschamps and Perolle, who can be regarded as forerunners of Jean Gaspard Marie Itard (1775–1838). He was the first who had tried a systematic auditory education on a unisensory basis. Paradoxically, he had to do this with pupils educated in a manual school. Although his ideas were taken up here and there, almost 100 years had to pass until they found wider recognition. In Germany they fostered the opening of the first special schools for hard-of-hearing children at the beginning of this century.

The unisensory approach, propagated by Itard and by Urbantschitsch, had, however, soon to give way to the multisensory approach recommended by

Bezold and Kroiss at the turn of this century and 50 years ago by Gustav Barczi (1890–1964) in Hungary. Because there was not yet available any appropriate auditory education equipment for classroom instruction, a kind of double strategy had to be observed: speaking "ad concham" in individual sessions and the "look and listen" strategy in classroom situations.

Erik Wedenberg (1905–), who has had a great impact on the development of auditory education in English-speaking countries (Edith Whetnall, Doreen Pollack, et al.), had received his first impulse from Barczi. The latter had encouraged him to start with the auditory education of his deaf son as early as possible on an individual basis. This meant that he could take up again the unisensory or, as it was later called by Henk Huizing (1903–72), the acoupedic method. In this context I want to point also to the name of Emil Fröschels (1884–1972) who continued his auditory education program together with his later assistant Helen Beebe in the United States when he had to leave Austria in 1938. With the development of electronic means of amplification and the application of these systems to wearable hearing aids, has come the development of auditory methods for teaching the severely hearing impaired who no longer need to be educated together with profoundly deaf children and who have been the show-boys of many a school for deaf children in the past.

New Ways of Teaching Speech

Vatter was also criticized for his association phoneme unit method of teaching speech. In Germany Wilhelm Paul (1851–1927) introduced the multisensory syllable unit method instead of it, for he regarded "the mechanics of syllables as the basis of instruction of articulation" (1908). Karl Kroiss with his "natural speech instruction" (1922) and Karl Brauckmann (1862–1938) with his syllable method (1933) took similar views. Beginning with syllables plays also a part in the "initial speech training programme" (1969) of Herbert Ding (1935–) and Klause Schulte (1930–).

The Period of Erwin Kern (1897–)

Erwin Kern may be regarded as the leading expert of oral education of deaf children in Germany during the first two decades after World War II. He is the exponent of the auditory global method within the German-speaking countries. Having been responsible for the training of teachers for deaf children at Heidelberg, he could pass on his method to hundreds of student teachers. The "global initial instruction of language and speech for the hearing impaired child" (1958) of Erwin Kern was a further development of some of the basic principles of the methods of Barczi (1938) and Malisch (1925). It is, like the method of Hill, neither a constructive nor an imitative method.

Like Vatter, Kern was an ingenious teacher who was endowed with a superb mastership of teaching language and speech. Those who would judge him only on his book and not on the great creativity of his teaching would misinterpret him. How can it be explained that Kern experienced more or less the same fate as Vatter, that his method has been given up again by many teachers during the last 15 years without replacing it with a better method? There are several answers to this question. Only three shall be given here because they refer to Vatter as well as to Kern (and probably also to some other professional people in our field):

1. Many of their followers were only epigones who took over only the "body" of their method (which they had found in their books) but not its "soul," which had to be experienced through sitting in at their teaching.

2. In the same way that Vatter had shut his eyes to the need of auditory education, Kern was not ready to realize that early education can contribute much to oral education. He was such a great teacher himself that he hardly could believe that nonprofessionals could achieve something in the education of a deaf child. Therefore, he had left no place for it in his method. Additionally, he also had very strange reservations against the use of individual hearing aids before a deaf child was able to speak distinctly.

3. Vatter had never been ready to admit that the multisensory syllable unit method would be suitable for the teaching of speech to some deaf children. Kern, on the other hand, approved of nothing but his global method of teaching speech.

The Isolation of Oral Education in Germany

Such a rigid attitude was no longer understood by parents or by teachers at the end of the fifties, when a number of young teachers tried to break through this isolation into which most German teachers of deaf children had exposed themselves. But how could such an isolation come about? I want to give three reasons for it:

1. Before World War I teachers in elementary education—and teachers of deaf children were recruited from their ranks—were prepared in training colleges. These colleges trained their students only for those subjects which they later had to teach. Therefore, they did not learn foreign languages.

2. After the almost unanimous decision in favor of oral education of the International Congress on Education of the Deaf in Milan in 1880, German teachers of deaf children believed that their method of teaching was an exemplary model for the rest of the world. Therefore, they felt no need to see the work of their colleagues abroad.

3. First the financial situation after World War I and then the political situation from 1933 till 1945 and the consequences of it during the first decade after the end of World War II did not allow teachers to go abroad.

These factors make it clear that it is not an exaggeration to state that education of deaf children in Germany was isolated from influences from the non-German speaking world for at least 50 years.

The End of the Isolation in Germany

The International Congress on the Modern Educational Treatment of Deafness at Manchester in 1958 can be regarded as the end of this "splendid isolation" of the education of deaf children in Germany, an isolation which according to my observations has, however, existed also in other parts of the world and still exists here and there. I want to mention only states like the Argentine, France and Spain, to say nothing about the situation in the countries behind the Iron Curtain.

Much has changed during the past 20 years. The pioneer work of Lady Irene (1883–1959) and Sir Alexander Ewing (1896–) at Manchester and of Antonius van Uden (1912–) at Sint Michielsgestel was demonstrated in such a convincing and inspiring manner to the few German members of the above-mentioned congress at Manchester that only a few months later a well prepared program for early education of deaf infants was started by Armin Löwe (1922–) at Heidelberg. No one had given orders to anybody to do this. It simply was done, even against the declared will of their principles, by a few young teachers, something unheard of in the long history of oral education in Germany. This program soon became a model not only for the early education of deaf infants in Germany but also in other European countries including some behind the Iron Curtain.

Those who know that the first kindergarten for hearing children was opened as early as 1840 in Germany by Friedrich Wilhelm August Fröbel (1972–1852), will hardly be able to believe that the first permanent kindergarten for deaf children within German-speaking Central Europe was not opened until 1916 in Vienna. Compared with the opening of the first preschool for deaf children in England (Manchester, 1860), in the U.S.A. (West Medford, Mass., 1888), and in Russia (Moscow, 1900) this was a very late start. It is explained, however, by the fact that the method of Vatter, which was still the main method used in German schools for deaf children during the first quarter of this century, could, as Vatter himself has stated, only be applied at the age of about 6 or 7 years. And as there was no kindergarten education for deaf children, there was, of course, not yet any supervised home training program for them. This fact is a typical example of how German teachers have rested on their oars. Because they never had thought earnestly of the opportunities of preschool education, they had, of course, not seen the urgent need for the establishment of special kindergartens. At the beginning of World War II their number amounted to only ten!

Some Factors Which Hamper the Standard of Oral Education Today

It was the generation to which I belong which did everything in its power to overcome the many shortcomings which had resulted from the long isolation. That these efforts have not yet solved all problems is deplorable but not unexpected. On the contrary, the fact that we are meeting together to discuss possibilities for an improvement of the not yet satisfactory situation of oral education proves that these problems are by no means limited to my country. They are to be found in more or less pronounced form in almost all places of the world where deaf children are educated. For a number of reasons, they are, however, becoming more and more difficult. I want to point to only two of them:

1. In many German schools for deaf children almost 25 percent of the pupils come from non-German speaking families. The situation is very similar in some other highly industrialized European countries into which an increasing number of foreigners are immigrating. At this moment there are not yet any indications of commitment to provide adequate services for these deaf children from different minority groups.

2. Another factor which is hampering the standard of oral education everywhere in our days is to be seen in the increasing number of deaf children with additional handicaps. Many schools have accepted responsibility to serve also multihandicapped deaf children, many of whom would have received no services or would have been institutionalized in the past. Since a claim on education is, however, no longer denied to these children who, thanks to progress in medical treatment, survive in a higher percentage than in the past, they are challenging oral education. Unfortunately, this challenge is taken up adequately only in a few places like Sint Michielsgestel.

Some Prerequisites for Oral Education in Our Days

As history has proven again and again, oral education will achieve its aim, namely to educate the deaf child to become a person who is able to converse as an intelligently and intelligibly speaking human being within his environment, only on condition that the necessary prerequisites for oral education are fullfilled. At present, there is no school in Europe where the above-mentioned aim comes as near achievement as the institute for deaf children at Sint Michielsgestel. After having had the privilege of being allowed to attend the instruction in all departments of this institute more than a dozen times during the past 20 years, I am convinced that the following factors are above all reponsible for the outstanding results which are achieved by the teachers and educators of this institute:

- A multidimensional early diagnosis which tries to find out the strong as well as the weak points of each child;
- An early detection or identification of children who suffer from a dyspraxia in their gross and/or fine motor development;
- An early special promotion of children with intermodal difficulties;
- An early diagnosis of additional visual disturbances;
- An intensive early home training program;
- A preschool program which links closely into the home training and tries to comply with all individual needs;
- A homogeneous method of teaching language, based on oral conversation, which starts in early home training and is continuously applied throughout all classes of the school;
- A rapid extension of vocabulary;

- A permanently guaranteed sound perception;
- Daily individual speech lessons which aim at normal speed and rhythm of speech;
- A rhythmical-musical education for an improvement of all body movements including the movements of the speech organs;
- An overall education which aims at the humanization and christianization of the deaf child;
- Which can, however, not be achieved without the cooperation of the parents which is already initiated in early childhood, and
- Which, therefore, preconditions a positive attitude toward the deaf child for which they need and are offered much help;
- A systematic research program with the aim of contributing to the further improvement of oral education;
- A streaming of the pupils according to their different educational needs;
- A first-rate provision of the classrooms with necessary, and not showpiece, technical aids;
- Regular supervision of all hearing aids by a staff of hearing aid acousticians;
- A teaching staff which is carefully screened and is fighting for an optimal oral education of each single child and which was trained in an inservice course which took theory and practice equally into consideration;
- A great number of educators who are well prepared for their special task;
- A very small fluctuation within the staff of teachers and educators;
- A careful supervision of all those deaf children who could be integrated into regular programs for further education;
- Small boardinghouse groups of deaf children of the same age and of about the same level of language and speech with whom and among whom oral conversation can be the main means of communication.

This long enumeration and specification proves that we ought to know after 200 years of oral education in schools for deaf children which conditions we need for a good oral education in a large school for deaf children. We also know from history that these conditions are easier to realize in smaller schools or in small subdepartments of a school than in a bigger school, provided that cooperation takes place between neighboring schools (in the case of small schools). This was, for instance, one of the secrets of the hitherto unheard-of results of oral education of the school of Wilhelm Daniel Arnold. And this is without any doubt also an important factor in the present fine results of Susanne Schmidt-Giovannini's (1928–) small integrated school at Meggen. This school provides one of the first programs within German-speaking Central Europe which offers an answer to a question which Philipp Michels (18?–1933) from Budapest raised when he spoke on the future of oral education at the National Convention of the Association of German Teachers of the Deaf at Hamburg in 1927 when the 200th birthday of Samuel Heinicke was celebrated: "How are we to solve our task of the socialization of deaf children, if we incorporate them into signing communities, separated from their hearing fellows as natural factors of education from early childhood?" He demanded classes of deaf children in regular schools for the solution of this problem. The small school at Meggen has furnished proof of the soundness of his prophecy.

Dissatisfaction With the Results of Oral Education

Many teachers of deaf children are not satisfied at present with their results because the level of achievement of their school leavers is not only significantly below their potential but also below the level of hearing pupils, and because not only their oral communication but also their comprehension and use of written language do not suffice for a full integration into the hearing society. Better results are expected through early identification with early provision of hearing aids, through parent guidance and home training, through more application of audiovisual media, and through more communication with hearing children. Unfortunately, the early identification and educational intervention is still a hit-or-miss affair which depends so much upon the awareness of the parents, the availability of a concerned pediatrician and his knowledge of the importance of early identification and education.

Different opinions exist among teachers of deaf children above all about the methods of communication which should be applied. Very often teachers rush to conclusions and recommend manual communication as the alternative for children who fail with oral approaches. Regrettably no one of them is usually able to say what the causes of such failures were and whether the children who failed would make progress under a different application of the same method. As a rule the problem is seen only in the children, but not also in the teachers and/or in the environment.

Seldom do teachers know what other way would work for deaf children with additional handicapping conditions such as language disorders, mental subnormality, cerebral palsy, or severe visual disability. Oddly enough, there are also teachers who argue that higher education cannot be accomplished without the simultaneous use of fingerspelling. As a rule they underline their arguments by referring to the existence of Gallaudet College (since 1864). They are surprised when they are told that there is, for instance, an oral high school for deaf students in England (Mary Hare Grammar School, since 1946), that the classes for higher education of deaf students in Germany (Realschulklassen) could only be started because of the high oral standard of most of their later students who, by the way, have to learn at least one foreign language. After all, it is worth mentioning that an objective test has proved that 89 percent of the English words spoken by Dutch deaf children to English "naive" listeners were understood by them (van Uden et al., 1963, p. 141). Teachers who are working in a school in which all their colleagues observe oral methods have no reason to be faint-hearted. If the mentioned prerequisites for a good oral education are fulfilled, they cannot fail.

No Single Method Can Meet the Needs of all Deaf Children

The hitherto existing research results show that no method can be generally accepted and applied for all deaf children. The same is also true of the integrated education of deaf children. If we want to comply with the heterogeneous needs of the different subgroups of deaf children, we need, as the institute for deaf children at Sint Michielsgestel has already realized, a variety of smaller departments with different programs. In other words: as history has shown again and again and as Andreas Markides (1938–) has proved with his comparative study between an oral and a combined program (1976), we do not need a potpourri of methods as defined by the leaders of the total communication approach. Instead of such a potpourri we need clearly separated programs for different groups of deaf children. If we separate the minority of deaf children of whom we really know that we cannot expect them to profit from a pure oral program and who, therefore, need an education which depends mainly on the use of signs, on written language, or on the additional application of a grapheme, kineme, or phoneme transmitting hand system (Cornett, 1967; Forchhammer, 1923; Jussen Krüger, 1975; Schulte, 1974), we shall be able to offer the majority of deaf children a better oral education than many of them at present receive.

Last but not least, we should not forget that some of the best schools for the oral education of deaf children in our days became oral schools only a few decades ago. Because they were not satisfied with the final results which they had achieved with the combined method, as total communication was called in the past, they gave up the manual components of their programs and turned to a pure oral program. In this context I want to mention only three schools: the "Institute voor Doven" at Sint Michielsgestel (1906), "St. Joseph's Institute for the Deaf" at St. Louis (1934), and "St. Mary's School for Deaf Girls" at Dublin (1946).

References

Arnoldi, L.F. Praktische Unterweisung, taubstumme Personen reden und schreiben zu lehren. Geiben 1777. Verkürzter Nachdruck. In Wollermann, R.O. und E. (Hrsg.): Quellenbuch zur Geschichte und Methodik des Taubstummenunterrichts, 1 Band. Stettin (Teetzmann und Randel), 1911, 105–124.

Barczi, G. Hör-Erwecken und Hör-Erziehen. Salzberg: Selhstverlag, 1936.

Bell, A.G. Upon a method of teaching language to a very young congenitally deaf child. *American Annals of the Deaf*, 1883, 28, 124–139.

Bender, R. *The conquest of deafness* (Rev. ed.). Cleveland: Press of Case Western Reserve University, 1970.

Bezold, F. Das Hörvermögen der Taubstummen. Wiesbaden: Bergmann, 1896.

Brauckmann, K., und Limpricht, M. Das Silben-und Formenspiel der deutschen Sprache. Jena: Fischer, 1933.

Calvert, D., & Silverman, R. *Speech and deafness*. Washington, DC: A.G. Bell Association for the Deaf, 1975.

Cornett, O. Cued speech *American Annals of the Deaf*, 1967, 112, 1967, 3–13.

Forchhammer, G. Der imitative Sprachunterricht auf der Basis der Schrift. Leipzig: Schneider, 1899.

Forchhammer, G. Absehen und Mundhandsystem. In Blatter fur Taubstummenbildung, 36, 1923, 281–308.

Forchamer, G. Taubstummenpädagogische Abhandlunger. Leipzig: Dude, 1930.

Goldstein, M. The acoustic method for training of the deaf and hard-of-hearing child. St. Louis, 1939.

Göpfert, E. Die Stellung der Shriftform im Sprachunterrient der eigentlichen, insbesondere der schwachbefähigten Taubstummen. In: Organ der Taubstummenanstalten in Deutschland und den deutschredenden Nachbarländern, 43, 1897, 298–313.

Gude, W. Die Gesetze der Physiologie und Physchologie uber die Entstehung der Bewegungen und der Artikulationsunterrnicht der Taubstummen. Leipzig: Englemann, 1880.

Hill, F.M. Anleitung zum Sprachunterricht taubstummer Kinder. Essen: Bodeker, 1840.

Jussen, H., und Krüger, M. Manuelle Kommonikationshilfen bei Gehörlosen. Das Fingeralphabet. Berlin: Marhold, 1975.

Karth, J. Das Taubstummenbildungswesen in XIX. Jahrhundert in den wichtigsten Staavten Europas. Breslau: Korn, 1902.

Kern, E. Teorie und Praxis eines ganzheitlichen Sprachunterrichts für das gehörgeschädigte Kind. Frieburg i. Br.: Herder, 1958.

Kröhnert, O. Die sprachliche Bildung des Gehörlosen. Weinheim: Beltz, 1966.

Kroiss, K. Zur Methodik des Hörunterrichts. Wiesbaden: Bergmann, 1903.

Kroiss, K. Naturgemäber Sprechunternicht bei Taubstummen. In: Blätter für Taubstummenbildung, 35, 1922, 23–26, 41–46, 49–57.

Lasius, O.B. Ausführliche Nachricht von der geschehenen Unterweisung der taub- und stummgeborenen Fräulein von Meding. In Wollermann, R.O. und E. (Hrsg.) Quellenbuch zur Geschichte und Methodik des Taubstummenunterrichts, 1. Band. Stettin: Teetzmann und Randel, 1911, 133–192.

Löwe, A. Gehörlose Kinder in einer Regelschule. Eine erste Zwischenbiland nach vier Schuljahren. In Hörgeschadigtenpädagogik, 32, 1978, 314–332.

Malisch. C. Die Sprechempfindungen und der Sprechunterricht bei Taubstummen. In Blätter für Taubstummenbildung, 31, 1919.

Markides, A. Comparative linguistic proficiencies of deaf children taught by two different methods of instruction: Manual versus oral. *Teacher of the Deaf*, 1976, 74, 307–347.

McGinnis, M. *Aphasic children: Identification and education by the association method.* Washington, DC: A.G. Bell Association for the Deaf, 1963.

Michaels, Ph. Blick in die Zukunft des Bildungswesens Gehörloser. In BDT (Hrsg.) Samuel-Heinicke-Jumbiläumstagung. Leipzig: 1927, 164–185.

Paul, W. Die Silbenmechanik als Grundlage dos Artikulationsunterrichts. Metz: Seriba, 1908.

Pollack, D. *Educational audiology for the limited hearing infant.* Springfield, IL.: Charles C Thomas, 1970.

Paphel, G. Die Kunst, Taube und Stumme reden zu lehren an dem Exempel seiner eigenen Tochter gezeiget. Lüneburg, 1718. In Wollerman, R., O. und E. (Hrsg.): Quellenbuch zur Geschichte und Methodik des Taubstummenunterrichts. 1. Band Stettin: Teetzmann und ndel. 1911. 77-103.

Reuschert, E. Friedrich Moritz Hill, der Reformator des deutschen Taubstummenunterrichts. Berlin: Dude. 1905.

Schulte, K. Phonembestimmtes Manual system (PMS). Villingen: Neckar, 1974.

Schulte, K., Roesler, H., und Ding, H. Akustovibratorische Kommunikations-hilfe. Kettwig: Horgeschodigte Kinder, 1969.

Schumann, G., und P. (Hrsg.). Samuel Heinickes Gesammelte Schriften. Leipzig: Selstverlag, 1912.

Schumann, P. Geschichte des Taubstummenwesens vom deutschen Stanpunkt aus dargestellt. Frankfurt/Main: Diesterweg, 1940.

Stahm, B. Über den Stufengang beim Sprech-Unterricht und was damit zusammenhängt. In Organ der Taubstummenanstalten in Deutschland und den deutschrederden Nachbarländern, 24, 1875, 1–4, 17–21, 33–39.

Stoffers, Über G. das Prinzip der unmittelbaren Lautsprach-Assoziation bei Taubstummen. In: Organ der Taubstummen- und Blindenanstalten in Deutschland und den deutschredenden Nachbarländern, 14, 1868, 85–93.

Triebel, E. Der zweite internationale Taubstummenlehrerkongress in Mailand. Berlin: Issleib, 1881.

van Uden, A. et al. Dutch deaf children, speaking English to "naive" English listeners. *Teacher of the Deaf*, 1963, 61, 135–141.

van Uden, A. *A world of language for deaf children. part 1: Basic principles*. Sint Michielsgestel: The Institute for the Deaf, 1968.

van Uden, A. Johann Vatter, a German teacher of the deaf. *Teacher of the Deaf*, 1970, 68, 21–34.

van Uden, A. Dove kinderen leren spreken. Rotterdam: Universaitaire Pers., 1974.

Vatter, J. Der verbundene Sach- und Sprachunterricht. Frankfurt: Bechhold, 1875.

Vatter, J. Die reine Lautsprachmethode. Frankfurt: Bechhold, 1911.

Walther, E. Geschichte des Taubstummen-Bildungswesens. Bielefeld: Velhagen und Klasing, 1882.

Watson, T. *Instruction of the deaf and dumb, together with a vocabulary illustrated by numerous copperplates*. London, 1809.

Watson, T. *The education of hearing-handicapped children*. London: University Press, 1967.

Wedenberg, E. Auditory training of severely hard of hearing preschool children. *Acta Oto laryngologica* (Supplementum) 1954, 110, 2–82.

Werner, M. Geschichte des Taubstummenproblems bis ins 17. Jahrhundert. Jena: Fischer, 1932.

Whetnall, E., & Fry, D.B. *The deaf child*. London: Heinemann, 1964.

reaction to 1

thomas j. watson

I would first compliment Professor Löwe in compressing so much history into such little space. It seemed important to the organizers of the Symposium that we should first look at the bases of oral education as it has developed, and from the historical point of view, Professor Löwe has shown how cyclical this growth has been. It is interesting, and, I believe, significant how much has revolved around individual educators—Bonet, Amman, Braidwood, Heinicke, Hill, Vatter and so forth. Is the message that we have to look to leaders in our own time?

Two of the more recent developments which Professor Löwe mentions are the advent of hearing aids and the gradual reduction in the age at which education was begun. I would like briefly to add to his points. Some of the earliest attempts to introduce an "acoustic method" were made in the 1880's in the Nebraska and New York institutions, mainly through the work of Gillespie and Currier respectively. The latter developed a conversation tube which enabled the pupils not only to hear the teacher's voice speaking into one mouthpiece, but also their own voices as they spoke into another—an early recognition of the significance of auditory feedback. Kerr Love was the chief advocate of this work in Britain at the end of the 19th century, as was of course, Urbanschitsch in Vienna. The influence of auditory feedback was forgotten, I believe, in the work with aids during the 30's and 40's and was only revived again in the 50's. I would like to add to Professor Lowe's account of the multisensory approach rather more of the work of the Ewings and Littler at Manchester and Hudgins at the Clarke School in the 30's. Group hearing aids were built and distributed to schools and what was described as a hearing/lipreading method was developed for classroom use. To this must be added the growth, beginning in the 50's and 60's, of our greater understanding of the nature of speech sounds through work in speech transmission laboratories and its relevance to more precise knowledge of what could be obtained through hearing aids.

The early beginnings of help to parents of young deaf children began, in the United States early in this century, and in Britain through the work of Margaret Martin in Glasgow from 1910 onwards resulting from pressure by Kerr Love. The gradual miniaturisation of electronic components brought about during World War II and subsequent space programmes has made it possible to provide powerful aids that can be worn by young babies to enable them to begin their linguistic education as early as possible. The revolution in the development of hearing aids during the last 25 years has fundamentally affected the types of educational provinces that could realistically be made available to deaf children.

The only other comment that there is time for is a brief note on the present flight from oralism taking place in some quarters. De L'Epée in France and the

English institutions from about 1820 onwards were part of earlier flights from oralism. Surely one of the purposes of a study of history is to learn from our past mistakes for, as George Santayana put it, "Those who do not learn from the past are condemned to relive it."

Sister Nicholas Griffey in her paper has referred to the fact that issues that have been dealt with in the past are reasserting themselves and discussed without reference to their historical context. My analysis of these earlier flights from oralism leads me to suggest that there were six or seven underlying causes. These were: large classes, untrained teachers, a high proportion of deaf teachers whose oral abilities were very low, very mixed pupils in the classes, educational methods that were largely dependent upon rote learning, very low aspirations for deaf children, and the fact that manual methods were deemed to be easier. This, in photographic terms is the negative version of what Professor Löwe has set out as prerequisites of successful oral education!

We would also want to look at reasons why schools which had depended on manual methods of communication changed to oralism. In summary, it seems to me that in looking at the historical bases of oral education we need to consider what educators did in the past, how they did it, and, if there have been changes, why they were made. In this way we can learn from the past.

2

the philosophical bases of oral education

ann m. mulholland

To discuss the philosophy of oral education requires the delineation of the parameters and the terms employed. At the outset it is clear that oral education is the term used prior to electronic amplification systems and the extensive developmental data/research on psychological, social, physical, and linguistic development of the child—normally hearing and those with defective hearing. While proponents of oral education believe in and use the auditory modality, for some the terms "auditory vocal" or "auditory oral" more closely describe the degree of emphasis placed on training the auditory residual. It may be that the term "oral education" with the connotations applied by unperceiving professionals and by the deaf community may well have outlived its usefulness. With the accruing knowledge of speech perception, speech production, child language, and the capacities of deaf persons, to say nothing of the technological advances in sensory aids, we may wish to suggest terminology which more accurately reflects the instructional process today at the conclusion of our deliberations here.

Secondly, philosophy, literally the love of wisdom from the Greek *philos* and *sophos*, has been defined as "the science which investigates the facts and principles of reality and of human nature and conduct and comprises logic, ethics, aesthetics, metaphysics, and the theory of knowledge" (Webster, 1959). The objective of this paper, then, is to present both the facts which lead to a personal philosophy of (auditory) oral education and the reality out of which it emerges.

To be a professional implies that one has a commitment to a field and a set of ethical principles, the outgrowth of a philosophy which governs the actions within that profession. A leader is considered a guide who knows the way through the morass of obstacles inhibiting the fuller development of that discipline or the resolution of conflict within that field based on knowledge, experience, strategies for coping, beliefs, and convictions. The professional is a successful leader when he has not only a breadth of knowledge but integrity and a clear set of values. The professional is a successful leader when his decisions are based not on polemics but on reasoned choices, when he has the capacity to live by his convictions, to lead others to conclude with him that he knows the path, the best way of achieving what the group wishes to accomplish. In a sense, then, one's philosophy is a kind of map, the basis from which one operates, the set of principles which govern the decisions one makes.

To formulate a philosophy one must first consider the basic nature of man and his relationship to the environment. Decisions regarding these two determine to a large extent how one perceives the deaf child's learning. Questions to be answered refer to the basic inherited characteristics of man's moral nature. Is man naturally good, innately good? Is he innately evil or is his moral nature neither naturally good nor bad but neutral? If the answer is good or bad the goodness or badness will unfold, but if we perceive man's basic nature as neutral, then we assume that he has potential but not innate goodness or badness. The second assumption is based on our perception of how the child relates to the environment, rather where psychological reality lies. Such inborn characteristics may be active, passive or reactive, or interactive. Thus reality is centered in the child, the environment, or is a combination of the person-environment respectively. These basic assumptions of man's moral nature and of this relationship to the environment are an index of what we believe about the learning process. Thus, if one assumes that man is neutral-passive, one would adhere to an S-R (stimulus response) conditioning, or apperceptive mode of learning. If one believes that man is bad—active or neutral-active—the choice of a learning theory, then, is likely to be a form of mental discipline. On the other hand, belief in man as neutral-interactive would result in adherence, for example, to cognitive-field theory or Gestalt field theory. Thus decisions regarding how the deaf child is to be educated, and for what, reflect these basic assumptions that each of us holds about the moral nature of man, how he relates to the environment, and the learning theory which is most congruent with those beliefs. It remains that the assumptions one makes are based on beliefs for which there are varying degrees of validation and which may be crystalized into firm convictions resulting ultimately in commitment and values, inherent or overt, which in turn may be modified by the reality of changing life stages. Values and oral education will be discussed later by Dr. Hourihan.

The presentations and discussions of these days will be a graphic demonstration of our personal and professional philosophy of the education of profoundly deaf individuals. These deliberations should provide a unique opportunity for each of us to reflect upon the power of a philosophy so delineated and its impact upon the profession. It is the power of our convictions for which this symposium is providing an international forum that will be reflected in our future writings, our teaching, our counseling, and especially in our impact on and communication with professionals from other disciplines or fields.

The beliefs and convictions which follow are culled from research, from knowledge, if you will, gained through real and vicarious experience, and represent this writer's perception of the philosophy of oral education. The philosophical bases of oral education are presented from the perspective of *the deaf learner, his home, his school, and his community*. At the conclusion of each section are stated the principles which have emerged from the content discussed.

*Principle 1. Knowledge of, belief in, and adherence to a specific philosophy of the nature of man and his relation to the environment are significant components in the professional's development of a personal philosophy of education of the deaf and are reflected in the attitudes toward the hearing impaired person and his capabilities, the design of his educational program, the expectancies for his performance, and of his ultimate contribution to society.

Principle 2. Hearing impaired persons, children and adults, although profoundly handicapped, must be accorded their rightful dignity as human beings of worth in a highly communicative and competitive society.

The Deaf Learner

The congenitally deaf infant-child with profound deafness lacks the sense which

> is most deeply constitutive to our personality and our world . . . [Hearing is] the most integral form of experiencing the world and self within the world . . . in the construction of the exterior world . . . and of the interior world . . . and is decisively important in the development of personality within the individual and of the culture within society. More than any sense hearing is interwoven and integrated with human life. The deaf have the arduous task of creating and maintaining human relations and a human personality without having access to all those possibilities of human experience, cognition, expression, and contact (Snijders, 1953, p. 17).

The recognition that lack of an intact auditory system precludes the normal development of language, impedes communication, and concomitantly restricts interpersonal relations (Myklebust, 1964; Levine, 1956) has challenged educators of the deaf for centuries to devise procedures, techniques, and devices to facilitate the deaf child's learning, his acquisition and development of language, and his adjustment to the world.

Deafness is a less obvious handicap than is blindness or cerebral palsy, and the normally hearing person, unable to simulate deafness as one can blindness, is unable to appreciate fully what the lack of audition means to the developing prelingually deaf child. It is the auditory sense serving as background which during sleep shifts to foreground when a sudden, even light noise alerts the sleeper to a change in the acoustic environment. This "omnipresence of sound, the inevitability of hearing" (Snijders, 1953, p. 17) prevents the hearing person from understanding what a soundless environment is and how auditory deprivation affects the individual and his ability to maintain homeostasis.

The most obvious deviancy in the child with deafness from early life is the lack of speech, oral or spoken language, through which the child normally structures reality, organizes his experiences to understand and to control his

---

*The 30 principles are numbered consecutively and continue through the next sections.

environment, labels his experiences, and increases his discriminating and differentiating ability, thus attaining higher levels of conceptualization. Through language present experience is stored, retrieved, and differently categorized for predictive purposes. . . . The profoundly deaf child learns his language through the visual modality supplemented by [acoustic cues] and exploitation of his extant auditory residual. The task required of the deaf child in acquiring his language is unique (Mulholland, 1971).

Psychologists have tended to hold opposing views as to the effects of profound deafness on the developing organism. One school holds that the deaf child functions normally in all aspects of behavior except in acquiring a language system (Levine, 1956); the other to "an altered organism" theory of the psychology of deafness (Myklebust, 1964). With vision the primary input modality, the profoundly deaf child's perception of the world is different, his real world is restricted, organized differently, and thus deafness being all pervasive has an impact on all aspects of behavior. Restricted linguistic competency influences qualitatively information processing, cognition, personality development and social interrelationships, retards academic achievement, and subsequently vocational opportunity (Mulholland, 1971). "Deafness appears to alter brain processes . . . [and] may account for the differences in memory and other behavioral attributes frequently mentioned by those experienced in the psychology of deafness . . . ." Neyhus and Myklebust concluded that "the brain of deaf children is markedly and unduly reposed [and] when auditory stimulation and experience is lacking, the brain is remarkably quiet" (Neyhus and Myklebust, 1969, p. 91).

Twenty years ago an historic symposium was conducted at Harvard Medical School bringing together researchers from several disciplines who were studying the effects of sensory deprivation and human behavior. Sharply deviating from the Gestalt construct of perception, Hebb first conceptualized a theoretical neurophysiological model of central nervous system function. Riesen and his associates reported on the effects of visual deprivation on the structure and function of the visual system. The concepts of sensory distortion, sensory overload, and sensory deprivation were presented by Lindsley as was the role of the reticular formation in arousal and attending (Solomon, P., Kubzansky, P.E., Leiderman, P.H., Mendelson, J.H., Trumbull, R., and Wexler, D., pp. 2, 3, 193). Importantly, Bruner concluded that early sensory deprivation "prevents the formation of adequate models and strategies for dealing with the environment" (Solomon, 1961, p. 207). From this provocative symposium emerged support for applying by analogy Riesen's findings of the visual cortex to the auditory cortex, to reliance on a neurophysiological model, and support for the use of amplification for deaf infants. Since postmortem studies of deaf persons are rare, almost nonexistent, examination of auditory cortical structures in man under several conditions may provide answers to the questions which are being raised at this equally provocative symposium on oral education.

During the intervening years there has been a veritable explosion of brain research which has moved some psychologists away from a strictly behaviorist approach. New fields have emerged, one of which is psychobiology resulting from the marriage of the behavioral sciences and the brain sciences. This new discipline asks the questions formerly asked by philosophers and theologians:

"How do we know what we know?" "What is the real world?" "Who am I?" Psychobiology addresses the problem of "how the brain influences our perception of the world" based on what is known of the brain and how it works (Restak, 1979, pp. 4-5). Psychology has contributed much to education of the hearing impaired, and the hearing impaired learner has intrigued psychologists who have studied, if esoterically, the deaf child. Whether learning is solely "an inference from behavior" (Hilgard, 1966, p. 5) or a function of nervous tissue is a topic to be considered by Professor Ivimey. For purposes of this paper, learning is defined as

> the process by which an activity originates or is changed through reacting to an encountered situation, provided that the characteristics of the change in activity cannot be explained, on the basis of native response tendencies, maturation, or temporary states of the organism (e.g., fatigue, drugs, etc.) (Hilgard, 1966, p. 2).

The concept that there is an innate capacity for language as proposed by Chomsky (1965, p. 59) holds for the deaf child as well. Deaf infants do vocalize and babble, but, if not fitted with hearing aids, cease to babble by 24-26 weeks (Mavilya, 1969). Although restricted quantitatively, one could observe that these were "quiet babies" spending at least 50 percent of the time quietly, in silence. Carr (1971), in her study of the communicative behavior of 3- and 4-year-old children, found that the most frequently occurring communicative act was vocalization for both the 3- and 4-year-olds. At the 3-year level, vocalization comprised one-third of their communication, while vocalizations plus action comprised over 50 percent of their communicative acts. At the 4-year-old level, vocalization also accounted for the most frequently used communication.

> The conventional wisdom, at least with respect to oral education of deaf children, is that a child must be found and taught early lest his innate ability to acquire and use language become atrophied for lack of use and stimulation (Hirsh, 1974, p. 1).

Chomsky's postulate that there is an innate capacity for language (1965, p. 59) seems to be supported by provocative research findings within the past two years. At Harvard in 1978, anatomical studies revealed structural differences with the specialization for language in the left hemisphere—even in the fetus. Lateralization of speech "seems preset and genetically programmed" (Restak, 1979, p. 181). Restak's report on Turkewitz's work on the head positions of neonates provides further evidence of the prominence of the left hemisphere. Infants lying on their backs have their heads turned to the right 88 percent of the time, and they turn to the right to an auditory stimulus quicker than to the left.

> In the case of heard speech, infants as young as twenty-four hours demonstrate evoked electrical responses that can be recorded from the speech processing areas in the left hemisphere. With nonspeech sounds, the activity is recorded over the right hemisphere.
> Turkewitz's research is a compelling demonstration of preset biases for attention, speech, and language which can be demonstrated as early as twelve hours after birth (Restak, 1979, p. 181).

Ongoing brain research is philosophically intriguing. Kinsbourne hypothesized that some activities of the brain itself could interfere with other activities. "Since both speaking and right-hand performance use the same hemisphere [the left], Kinsbourne reasoned that the activity of one interfered with the other" (Restak, 1979, p. 185) and holds for adults and for children as young as 3 years.

> Speech, even involving something as automatic as reciting a memorized list, shifts our attention to the right side as a result of the activation of the left hemisphere. Our ability to perceive "reality," seems dependent on the mental "set" activated at a given time. If we think or speak out loud it seems that we are likely to miss something in our left visual field. Merely telling someone, "I would like to ask you a question," preferentially activates their left hemisphere, biasing them toward the detection of objects in their right visual field. How can we know what truth is if the process of asking the question biases us to perceive some aspects of our environment to the exclusion of others? (Restak, 1979, p. 189).

With the brain preprogrammed for language, it is necessary to diagnose deafness as early as possible and for psychological as well as educational concerns, confirm parental suspicion of hearing loss. Intensive programming of the deaf child to perceive linguistic information requires early fitting of hearing aids and parental education in their use, their maintenance, and the manner in which audition can become a highly useful secondary support to the visual input system. Research in speech perception and speech production reveals the capability of even defective auditory systems to detect, discriminate, identify, and comprehend the speech signal and to produce it.

Friedlander's underlying concept for his investigations of auditory-visual perceptual development is congruent with the philosophy of oral education delineated in this paper.

> . . . most vertebrates in general, and children in particular, are stimulus-seeking, arousal-seeking, experience-seeking organisms. They are *not* simply passive, experience-accepting recipients of stimulation acting upon them in one-way traffic from the outer environment. Rather, they are active and highly *interactive* with the environment in a two-way fashion, with inherent needs and motivations to pursue forms of activity that provide optimal levels of environmental stimulation they can instigate and regulate by their own behavior (Restak, 1979, p. 195).

It is clear that deaf children who interact with the environment, people and things, who develop a curiosity about relationships and functions and happenings of a physical as well as an interpersonal and imaginative nature, who ask the Why? or How? are those learners whose cognition will be enhanced and reciprocal to their linguistic competence and performance. Then given this natural state, the adults in the environment facilitate or impede the deaf child's maturation in information processing.

Assuming that diagnosis of hearing loss in infancy has occurred, how is information processed if "the auditory system is defective"? And if the belief that the development of the infant's residual hearing is important, fitting of hearing aids becomes imperative. Is it true that we are trying to "make the deaf hear when they hear nothing" as even some professionals believe? The belief in the nature of amplifying sound and of training the child to establish the acoustic cues that he perceives requires documentation. Fry (1978) elaborates on this critical point. He states as a principle that the individual with defective hearing is "free to employ any acoustic cues he likes provided they do the job of differentiating sounds in accordance with the phonemic system." These differentiations, these cues are provided by the brain as speech is fed into the system. The differences, rather the relationships between sounds, in timing, intensity, and frequency provide the cues to the listener. Analyses of the acoustic cues, in English at least, constitute a formidable literature (Hirsh, 1974; Levitt, 1978; Pickett, 1970; Boothroyd, 1978). The impaired ear is required to distinguish among the 40 or more phonemes in English, the half dozen or so intonation patterns, and the two stress variations (Fry, p. 25) and has considerable capability in phoneme and, if you will, feature recognition.

> The differentiation of vowels from consonants and consonants on the basis of voicing and manner of articulation is found in the time/intensity patterns of speech or in the relative times of occurrence of different events . . . (while) place of articulation is to be found in the frequency/time domain (Boothroyd, 1978, p. 127).

First and second formants provide information about vowels while consonants have the higher formants. While sensorineural hearing loss does limit to a degree the acoustic cues available, it is important to note as Boothroyd has summarized so well:

(1) Persons with sensorineural hearing losses use the same acoustic cues for speech perception as do persons with normal hearing.
(2) The highest statistical correlations have been found between speech recognition abilities and pure-tone thresholds around 2000 Hz.
(3) Place of articulation is the phonetic feature most affected by sensorineural hearing loss.
(4) Perception of voicing, manner of articulation, intonation, and rhythm is possible with hearing losses over 90 dB.
(5) In sensorineural hearing losses there is increased reliance on low frequency acoustic cues (1978, p. 133)

Acoustic cues alone do not account for the complexity of the speech perception process. It was stated earlier that sensory deprivation affects the internalized model of the world. The hearing impaired individual receives the acoustic information supplemented by visual information obtained through lipreading—within the contexts of language, the speaker, and the situation. To generate hypotheses required to decode the message requires considerable knowledge accessible for rapid and ready retrieval (p. 129).

That there is a close interaction between speech reception and speech production is undeniable, the former in time preceding production in both the normal and the hearing impaired child.

Ling indicates that the speech of others appears to be mediated through reference to one's own speech system (1976, p. 26), while Fry claims that if the deaf child is exposed to speech "loud enough and long enough he will develop to a remarkable degree the speech and language skills of the normally hearing child" (p. 31). The deaf child's ability to use spoken language relatively intelligibly is a goal achieved by many. Research on speech communication skills from Hudgins in the 1930's to writers in the late 70's reveals the same problems of production, the same speech errors (Levitt, 1978; Ling, 1976; and Boothroyd, 1978).

Unlike research in speech production, the impact of recent linguistic research has had a marked effect on the "teaching of language" (Menyuk, 1967; Russell, et al., 1976; Kretschmer & Kretschmer, 1978; Streng, 1972). Studies of early child language have provided insights into stages through which the normally hearing child passes in developing his language (Bloom & Lahey, 1978). Research underway of the young deaf child's linguistic development has relevance for the management of deaf children by both parents and other adults in the infant's environment (Fox, 1980).

Language develops through a complex interaction of maturation and learning. The normally hearing child by the age of 4 to 5 has acquired the rules of his language. "On the other hand the child doesn't learn to talk until he is old enough, and the language that he learns is that which he hears" (Hilgard & Bower, p. 4). For the deaf child the hearing of language is delayed and distorted, necessitating special attention by the adults in the environment. Terms have been carefully selected to indicate specifically that one doesn't teach language, the child learns it—its phonological, morphological, syntactical, and semantic systems. Every individual child learns

> the whole language system of his native community for himself and from scratch, and he does so by abstracting the information he needs from the mass of sensory inputs relevant to language by which he is surrounded . . . Any child will learn his first language only if he is continuously exposed to the relevant sensory inputs (Fry, 1978, p. 16).

If a normally hearing child is not in situations where speech is used reaching his auditory system and in the context of daily life, he will not learn spoken language.

For Liberman (1974), read language is a secondary linguistic activity superimposed on the base of spoken language. He concedes that the reading deficiency of deaf children is in itself supportive evidence for the "secondariness," if you will, of reading (p. 138). The retardation in reading in the United States population continues to be three to five years, further testifying to the need for designing research to clarify the causation of such marked deviancy in spite of increased knowledge of linguistics and technological advances.

The deaf learner although sensorily deprived has capacities, some innate, others learned, which facilitate his speech perception and production, the developing of his language and communication skills, his interactions with peers and adults, both deaf and hearing, within the environment.

Principle 3. Congenital profound deafness is all-pervasive, affecting all aspects of behavior.

Principle 4. The deaf child's brain is intact, and getting linguistic information into the central nervous system is a basic difficulty.

Principle 5. Like the hearing child, the deaf child has an innate capacity for language.

Principle 6. The deaf child has a defective but useful auditory system for processing linguistic information.

Principle 7. Early diagnosis of hearing loss and appropriate intervention through parental education programs is necessary during the crucial formative years.

Principle 8. The deaf child's first language is the language of his community which first is developed receptively.

Principle 9. Read and written language are best developed on the base of oral language.

The Home

The family as the first educator of its children is a basic tenet in the complete development of the orally communicating deaf child. Inherent are the critically important early identification of hearing loss and an appropriate intervention program designed cooperatively and maintained by the parents and by the parent guide. Parents are quick to note latent reactions and responses to auditory stimuli impinging naturally on the deaf infant. Far too often does the mother report her suspicions of the lack of hearing, only to have the pediatrician treat the parent as overanxious, emotionally ill, or incompetent in her realistic appraisal of her infant's functioning (Fellendorf, 1974; Luterman, 1979; Allen & Allen, 1979; Thompson, Thompson & Murphy, 1979). That parents continue to pursue the validation of their observations is a tribute to their perspicacity and patience in dealing with professionals and their too frequently conflicting advice. Once the diagnosis has been made, reactions of parents are initial shock, realization, defensive retreat, acknowledgment, and adjustment or adaptation (Murphy, 1979). The time delay until the last stage is reached is a variable dependent upon the support services available and the insight of the parent guide.

For the parents, as well as the teacher, the basic philosophy and belief in how children learn, what their aspirations are for the child, and the goal they have set for him will influence their attitude toward the child and his handicap, their management of the child, and how well he will relate to the extended family and to the other institutions impacting on him during the educational process. That such a conceptualization has been recognized in the early education of deaf children is apparent in the kinds of parent education programs developed in Europe and in the United States for both the 3- to 5-year-olds and for infants.

Historically, the parent as teacher and the critical role of the home in developing spoken language in providing the psychological and linguistic milieu for learning was recognized early. What has emerged are different types of programs developed to meet needs of parents and of the infant specifically. The focus has been parent-centered vs. infant-centered, with emphasis on tutoring, or demonstrations, or nurturing in general. The Ewings in England, van Uden in the Netherlands, Löwe at Heidelburg, Wedenberg and Barr in Sweden, and in the United States, Louise Tracy and the John Tracy Clinic, Central Institute for the Deaf, the Sara Fuller Home, Kansas University Medical School have validated the role of the parent as "prime educator" in Burton White's terms (1979). In the United States the precursors of these formalized programs were associated with day schools and were concerned with home instruction. It should be noted that 2 years was the entrance age for deaf children to be admitted to the Garrett Home School for Little Deaf Children in Philadelphia in 1893 (Best, p. 582). Best points out (p. 501) that "the earliest the age of entrance into the schools the better are the chances of acquiring speech." More recently established programs have focused on aiding parents to develop not only knowledge of deafness and management techniques but on developing insights into their feelings and attitudes as Luterman (1979) devised or more psychiatrically based as at the Lexington School for the Deaf (Connor, 1978).

In essence the infant-toddler period is critical, for

> the basis for higher intelligence is laid during Piaget's sensorimotor stage and is dependent upon the frequent interplay of caring and talking adults—who get *more* excited about that child's utterances, understandings, and discoveries than anybody else in the world. These adults providing good language models are required for the most successful children (White, 1979, p. 58).

Greenstein (1976) concluded that the most important result of his investigations into mother-infant communication was "the centrality of the affective aspects of mother-infant interaction to the child's acquisition of language" (p. 35).

The value of early intervention-preschool programs denied in early studies of programs including parents has been found (*New York Times* 11-3-79) to pay long-term dividends in progressing through school, in higher achievement in reading and mathematics, and, importantly, in loftier parental aspirations for their children. To judge fairly the benefits of such programs, long-term gains should be examined. Such a study has been undertaken by Levenstein (1979) employing Child's Behavior Traits (CBT) and Parent Child Together (PACT). The former was a 20-item instrument employing the categories: Task Orientation, Cognitive Orientation, Responsible Independence, Social Cooperation, and Emotional Stability. The PACT included 20 items categorized as Verbal Interaction, Nurturance, Encouragement of Autonomy, and Parental Controls. The maternal verbal interactions predicting the child's later independence, cooperation, and emotional stability were verbal language. Thus at 6 years of age the positive effects of the maternal verbal interactions were significantly correlated with the child's spontaneity, cheerfulness, and self-confidence. It should be noted that the parenting might well have been influenced by the existing program of toys, books, and "a joyous curriculum for using them" (Levenstein, 1979, p. 263). It can be concluded from these findings that the reciprocal interactions—both cognitive and emotional—which occurred between mother and child were mutually reinforcing. Bronfenbrenner (1979) hypothesized that such a relationship enduring over time

> leads to the development of a strong emotional attachment which, in turn, increases the motivation of the young child to attend to and to learn from the mother . . . and that this process should be reinforced when the child's dependency on the mother is greatest—that is, in the second year of life (p. 292).

Whatever the gains, by focusing on the parental role and the home setting as the place for intervention, maintenance or continuation is more likely. Studies of hearing children also indicate that the 2-year-olds seem most vulnerable to parental interaction at that time as a function of age (p. 293). Maternal nurturing is applicable for the deaf child as well.

Still there is a paucity of hard data to substantiate emphasis on parenting, maternal verbal interaction, and the stability of gains made in preschool intervention programs for the deaf. Logically one would assume that since there is a hierarchy of senses, the shift to vision, mandatory in profound deafness for maintenance of homeostasis, is accompanied by ascendency of the tactile mode as an input system—whether equal to or superior to audition has yet to be established. The increasing number of investigations into the tactile as a supplementary mode for linguistic input reported in the 1975 Congress in Tokyo gives rise to speculations for future aids and the kinds of information transmittable by the tactile. Hypothesizing that young profoundly deaf adults have had (1) mothers committed to increasing language competence in their deaf children, and (2) perceptive mothers who recognized the value of normal nonverbal communication and the great value of inculcating a mind geared to and enjoying reading, I conducted brief interviews with a number of oral deaf adults. They were asked to respond to these questions: What kind of family is yours? How demonstrative was it between parents? How much were you read to? By whom? There was unanimity regarding the positive role of the mother whose expectation of their performance was high and that between parents and parents and deaf child there was much demonstrativeness of caring by physical reinforcement, of touching, or cuddling, and of "being there when needed." Further, and importantly, these young adults were read to daily, nightly by one or the other parent. Similarly these parents had high expectations for their profoundly deaf child and facilitated, through usually a structured approach, the attainment of verbal oral competence. As children they were never punished by being isolated, sent off to bed, but tapped gently on the posterior prominence, physically a painless hurt. What is evident is what one has observed through case history taking and assessment of the functioning of several hundred deaf children, youth, and adults: that success as competent, integratable deaf persons depends approximately 99 percent on mothers and only 1 percent on a paternal role in child rearing—and this for male children. Autobiographical data, observations, and reports support these clinical judgments.

The observation can be made that without question it was the mother who aspired and who persevered to inculcate language receptively and expressively. In families the responsibility seemed to be divided in what might be construed to be a reasonable arrangement. While mother attended to the after-dinner functions, father read to the deaf child or children, but mother was acknowledged as the mover who made oral success possible.

Cremin (1974) has formulated a theory of the family as educator which appears applicable to the family of the hearing impaired child.

> It defines education as the deliberate, systematic, and sustained effort to transmit, evoke, or acquire knowledge, values, attitudes, skills and sensibilities (and the results of that effort) thereby assuming a certain overlap with concepts such as socialization, enculturation, and development but insisting at the same time that the several concepts are not synonymous. It acknowledges that education generally proceeds via many individuals and institutions—parents, peers, siblings, and friends as well as families, churches, libraries, museums, summer camps, schools, and colleges. It assumes, too, that the various educators in a community often relate to one another in configurations, though it cautions that such relationships may be dissonant as well as consonant, contradictory as well as complementary.

And it assumes finally that individuals come to education situations with their own temperaments, histories and purposes, that different individuals will interact with any given education institution or configuration in different ways and with different outcomes, and that in considering the interactions and the outcomes it is as necessary to examine the lives of those undergoing education as it is to examine the efforts of the educators (p. 260).

For in dealing generally with such phenomena as family structure, kinship networks, parental aspirations, and the connections between families and other institutions, the historiography has proved immensely suggestive concerning the character of teaching and learning within the family and the relation of that teaching and learning to education going on elsewhere. And in dealing quite specifically with the processes of growing up and coming of age, it has pointed us toward fresh insights into the ways in which education has been carried on in past eras and the ways in which it might be carried on in the present and in future eras (p. 251).

What has been enunciated here is that nonverbal, tactile communication plays a significant, if not critical, role in development affectively, linguistically, and cognitively because it does reflect interaction between child and adult; that the 0–4 year period is crucial in the development of auditory-oral skills, that the role of the mother is extensive while the father is less likely to be directly involved in the educational process until adolescence; and finally that parental expectations for the deaf child's performance are reflected in later linguistic and academic performance.

Parental support and guidance to be effective includes the difficult period of adolescence when parental hopes for normalcy in speaking, in learning, in coping are dashed if they have been counseled unrealistically and if their personal needs obfuscated those of the child (Mulholland, 1971). Oral education, it seems, facilitates the adolescent and his growth in independence, social competence, and linguistic and academic success.

The family as educator determines the emotional, cognitive, audiological, linguistic environment in which the deaf infant and young child are expected to mature, to develop receptive and expressive language, and to learn to cope with and to manipulate the environment, whether home, school, or community. There appears to be an innate capacity to communicate orally which is supported in part by research in psychobiology attributing a present left hemispheric functioning ready for linguistic development—apparent even prenatally. The tactile modality serves as a provider of emotional content in the natural holding of a child for a variety of purposes, for eating, for cuddling, for talking to, and especially for reading to.

Principle 10. The family is the first educator.
Principle 11. The emotional climate of the home, the techniques of child management, and the quality of the linguistic milieu have long-lasting effects on the deaf child's cognitive, linguistic, and emotional development.
Principle 12. The parents' advocacy of their child's rights and educational needs reinforces the work of the school.
Principle 13. Parental expectancies are a major influence on the deaf child's ultimate attainment of cognitive, linguistic, academic, and

communicative skills, and the degree to which the integration with the hearing occurs.

Principle 14. The independent, decision-making, orally communicating adult is prepared by parents whose basic philosophy and whose philosophy of education and attitudes toward child management may be congruent with the development of independence, reasoning, and coping necessary in childhood.

Principle 15. The family includes the extended family as well as the nuclear family in their nurturing and expectancy roles.

Principle 16. The home nurtures but frees the deaf child and adolescent to facilitate personal, academic, and vocational fulfillment.

The School

If the school as an institution consisting of qualified staff and knowledgeable and concerned leadership is to facilitate the learnings of deaf children, it must have basic beliefs adhered to by all who come in contact with the child. For example, if a cornerstone of the philosophy of the school is that integration for hearing impaired individuals is a desirable goal, then all workers affecting the child's development must believe in and have integration as their objective for the deaf child. It is similarly true that such a staff would support the concept that the deaf child has the right to an auditory-oral education from infancy or early childhood in order that the decision in the future regarding identification and life style might be his to make. Behrens (1978) expresses the problem of the relationship between early and later use of audition.

> (One) cannot ignore a child's residual hearing, require him to depend upon a visual form of communication, and then later, as an adult, give this individual the alternative to become a hard of hearing person (XVI).

Auditory education is defined as the process that fosters greater understanding of: audition and its parameters, the effects of consistent and constant training on the auditory residual, the impact of limited acoustic cues on communication and the quality of the dyadic relationship between the deaf child and the speaker, the fuller development of personality, language, cognition, and the acquisition of knowledge about the world. It is the school which fosters auditory education and, in combination with the home, enables the hearing impaired child to acquire the necessary skills in detecting, discriminating, recognizing, and comprehending verbal information presented via the auditory modality (Erber, 1979). In support of this belief in auditory education, it is essential that the qualified instructional staff and other school workers adhere to this basic belief and make opportunities available to reinforce auditory skills in comprehending linguistic and nonverbal information. In addition, the staff is qualified if their beliefs are founded on knowledge of information processing, linguistics, audiology, learning theory, child development, neurology, speech science, and organized into a curriculum which meets the child's individual needs determined through appropriate and inclusive assessment.

Within the school, the administration must provide the proper milieu, acoustic and visual, for the deaf child's learning including those instructional aids which the teacher would employ. The availability of materials, sensory aids, and other technology is a mark of administrative concern and support.

In the United States, at least, there has been a policy established during the past 10–12 years of having what originated as additional support for developing and improving speech, that is the employment of speech therapists. Unfortunately, in general this has militated against the very accomplishment intended since the classroom teacher reduced her constant attending to the individual child's speech skills and failed to reinforce appropriate production. Every teacher of the deaf is a teacher of language, speech, and listening regardless of type or level of subspecialization. There is a relationship between teacher expectancy and pupil performance within the daily in-school program.

Further, teachers who are secure themselves foster independence in their pupils. If the goal is integration when the child has acquired communication skills at a level where he is understood reasonably well and can cope academically with parental support and encouragement, the child should be integrated. Time of integration is individually determined—whether at grade one or four, or presecondary school. Association with hearing classmates and friends has been observed in the past to have positive effects on the deaf child's speech. In a recent Office of Demographic Studies of Communication Methods the highest correlation (.71) was found between the highest speech intelligibility ratings and communication situations when deaf students talked to hearing students. The inference that hearing students play a significant role in the refinement of speech production of deaf talkers lends support to integration. The data in the following table are compiled from Jensema (1978) and collapse the Very Intelligible and Intelligible speech ratings.

TABLE I
HIGHEST SPEECH INTELLIGIBILITY RATINGS OF STUDENTS IN PART-TIME SPECIAL EDUCATION PROGRAMS.

		Intelligible Speech		Non-Speakers	
Hearing Loss (BEA)	Total N	N	%	N	%
70 dB	196	169	86.2	3	– 2
71–90 dB	261	143	55.0	28	11
91 dB	448	110	23.0	86	18
Total	945	422	45	117	12.4

Of the total students in the subsample, 45 percent were rated as having very intelligible or intelligible speech while 12.4 percent were rated as "would not speak."

Speech intelligibility appears to be primarily related to the extent and quality of auditory input as reflected by the degree of hearing loss, usage of hearing aids, and the frequency of speech communication (p. 5).

One finding of particular concern is the ethnicity of the subjects (enrolled as students in schools and programs for the deaf in the U.S.) and the speech intelligibility ratings. Of the whites, 51 percent had intelligible or very intelligible speech, 40 percent of the Spanish-Americans were rated similarly, while for the blacks the ratings were 3.7 percent very intelligible and 17.4 percent intelligible. Those who did not speak were reported as whites 10.3 percent, Spanish-Americans 14.4 percent, and blacks 13.6 percent. Are these not provocative findings?

Quigley in 1968 found that those hearing impaired students who graduated from or attended regular colleges and universities came from oral residential schools or day programs or a combination of both which fostered interaction with hearing students. He believed that the secondary school level might be crucial in this regard; for those who attended combined-system residential schools were unlikely to attend regular colleges (p. 159-160).

A recently concluded study by one of his students (Ogden, 1979) of graduates of three private oral schools is relevant to our deliberations. The subjects responding by questionnaire included 144 graduates of St. Joseph's Institute, 242 from Central Institute for the Deaf, and 231 from Clarke School. Of the 617 graduates 91.4 percent were prelingually deaf, 83.5 percent had attended regular high school; 332 (54 percent) graduated from college, and 50 attended graduate school. At the high school level 64 percent were the only deaf persons, and at the college level 52 percent were the only deaf persons in their schools. During their high school years no interpreters were used by 92 percent of the students. Of the 49 students using interpreters, 31 used oral interpreters. As might be expected at the college level, 102 used interpreters of whom 71 used both manual and oral communication modes. But in graduate school only 26 (50 percent) students used interpreters. Eighty-eight percent of the subjects approved of their education in an oral school.

While each hearing impaired child and youth is an individual whose special needs the educational establishment must meet rather than forcing him into existing programs of study, the problem schools face regarding communication mode to be used has yet to be researched to determine the effects on academic progress of various modes housed in one building or if a manual system impedes psycholinguistic development. Reeves (1977), having experience as a teacher employing both communication modes, states the situation succinctly.

> I appreciated its [manual communication] application in the community setting, but I was never convinced of its use as an educational method of teaching. At its best it was a ready means for rapid communication. This distinction between an educational method and a means of communication should be emphasized. Sometimes workers with the adult deaf seem to get these confused. Because the latter is useful with adults, does not mean that it can provide an adequate technique for educating children (pp. 46-47).

Klima and Bellugi (1979) have engaged in intensive study of American Sign Language as part of their research effort, the general objective of which "is to study the biological foundations of human language" (p. v). They have concluded that "ASL is clearly a separate language, distinct from the spoken language of its surrounding community" (p. 2) and that the "morphological and grammatical processes that have developed in ASL are indigenous to the language and bear little or no mark of English" (p. 69). It should be noted that the researchers do not attempt to apply ASL or advocate its use in instruction.

I raise the question: Can it be that the thrust in auditory oral education based originally on beliefs and values of committed teachers and parents is being substantiated by psychobiologists who postulate genetic programming of the brain, a language specific left brain? Creativity is assigned to the right brain; the more concrete the language, the more the right brain is suppressed. It is the creativity which allows imagination to enter into language. Does this knowledge suggest teacher behaviors that might increase language learning?

As a clinical category deafness is too all-inclusive, too global to specify "the content of a language learning program" (Bloom & Lahey, 1978). The knowledge from linguistic research is reflected in the curricula developed by several participants at this Symposium for language development. In any educational setting there has to be a curriculum common to, developed with and by teachers for the instruction of deaf children and youth; otherwise confusion results and pupils' advancement is restricted. (The U.S. Education for all Handicapped Children Act of 1975 requires that programs be individualized to meet the specific needs of the handicapped child.) In the design of curriculum the strategies the teacher will use need to be considered. Certainly the research of Buckler (1977) and Fox (1980), among others, is relevant in determining how instruction will proceed, what the teacher says, how she phrases her utterances to pupils, how tenable her learning theory is, and what effect her language, her reinforcement, her modeling will have on the child's language and cognitive development.

The school then, in partnership with the parents and when appropriate with the deaf child or youth himself, has a grave responsibility for enabling deaf persons including adults to overcome the handicap of deafness and of being able to function academically, socially, and emotionally in the world of the deaf and in the larger world of the hearing.

Principle 17. There is a scientific basis to the art of teaching deaf children and youth which incorporates knowledge from psychology, linguistics, audiology, neurology, medicine, and psychobiology integrated into a frame of reference based on philosophy, learning theory, knowledge of information processing, and communication.

Principle 18. The profoundly deaf child has a right to an auditory-oral education in order that his inner language system will be based on the verbal language of his community.

Principle 19. Parents and teachers are partners in the design of the deaf child's educational program based on complete assessment of all behaviors by qualified examiners.

Principle 20. The leadership of the school is responsible for selecting (1) the best qualified teachers of the deaf competent in teaching oral and written language receptively and expressively within specific age levels and (2) qualified ancillary staff to assist in accomplishing the mission of the school.

Principle 21. The school with the parents has the responsibility for integrating pupils into the mainstream of education when the child and the receiving school are judged to be ready.

Principle 22. The leadership of the school in *loco parentis* has the responsibility of providing the most appropriate learning milieu for profoundly deaf children: physically, acoustically, cognitively, linguistically, academically, and emotionally.

Principle 23. Without violating confidentiality, the school has the responsibility for researching or facilitating research designed to investigate variables affecting oral education, post-school follow-up studies of graduates, interaction analyses of within-classroom effects of teacher behaviors, language, and instructional strategies.

Principle 24. The teaching staff has the responsibility for serving as child advocates and of maintaining close relationships with the home, providing guidance in parenting through adolescence.

Principle 25. The teaching staff should be committed to the philosophy of the school, to have realistically high expectations for pupil performance, to be skillful in organizing learning, and to be concerned for the mental health, as well as the academic advancement, of each child.

Principle 26. Provision for individual hearing aids and their repair is the joint responsibility of the home and of the school.

Principle 27. The staff must recognize and believe that each teacher is responsible for instruction in speech, language, and listening and that the value of intermittent training in communication unrelated to academic learnings is questionable.

Principle 28. The school has responsibility for facilitating a program of continuing or adult education to refresh the speech reception and production of its graduates.

The Community

It has been conceptually convenient to organize the philosophical bases of oral education by considering the deaf learner, his home, his school, and his community. The concept of community consists of more than a single entity. There is the world of the deaf, a minority, a subculture, and the larger community of the hearing. Ideally, deaf persons move between the two worlds, depending upon their objectives: work, religion, social activities, government, education, to name but a few (Myklebust, 1964).

If the larger community were responsive to the needs of deaf persons and of the deaf community within their borders, being deaf would be somewhat less difficult. Understandably, it is not the real situation. The child who is encouraged by his family to shop, to participate in local activities, who attends school in the community will feel part of that group when he is a young adult. And the facility with which the child communicates will be a factor in his integration (Pflaster, 1976) with the social, sports, religious, vocational, and educational life of the community. To accomplish this degree of belongingness, the family has to be supportive, assertive, at least aware of, if not involved in, local activities, programs, and events. Acceptance into community life and in the development of friends locally may be also partially a parent effort. Awareness on the part of the community of the needs of all handicapped is evidenced in the United States by the increasing number of curbs for wheelchairs and TTY's for deaf persons in agencies and some public places. The resultant ease of communication bridges makes possible the interactions within both worlds. Mutual benefits arise from increased communication, especially involvement within the educational system.

Part-time employment within the community might well be an outcome of career education and provide work experience leading to realistic knowledge of the work world, the ability to relate to adult as well as peer workers, to develop skills of intercommunication and social information leading to mature and mentally healthy adulthood.

Participation in the religious life of the community has opened doors for young and deaf adults. Developing understandings of the needs of all people—the poor, the ill, the elderly, the abused—through service groups, church or school or agency-related, enriches social consciousness and personal growth. Again, such activities may have spin-offs. For example, the oral deaf young adult might service the communication needs of hospitalized adults having had tracheotomies or damage to the larynx or vocal cords and interpret to the family in a reverse situation. We sent a deaf doctoral student to the intensive care unit of one of the large hospitals where he served as an interpreter for a normally hearing, dying woman who had Parkinson's Disease and had had a tracheotomy. With his help the patient's voiceless communication was speechread and said. Family matters were discussed and even a daughter's wedding planned in the weeks that elapsed until her death.

The Oral Deaf Adults Section of the A. G. Bell Association has been described by Jensema (1977) as a group whose members had attained a level of educational achievement far beyond that of the average of the hearing impaired and most of the normal population. Their universal mode of communication is speech and they believe that this enables them to participate more fully in society because they have options educationally. The oral deaf graduates studied by Ogden (1979) reveal again the ability of those who are deaf talkers to be integrated into the hearing world. Approximately 25 percent of these subjects had spouses who were normally hearing. More than 50 percent had graduated from college, and 40 percent were professional or technical workers; 18 percent were in clerical or sales work.

> It is easy to perceive a major division in the deaf community and a particular brand of class system. The subjects seem to consider themselves an elite. Among a minority—the American deaf—they are a minority. They can if they choose, communicate with the large, signing deaf population. But on the whole, the selectivity of birthright and the sustained rigors of training for genuine facility in oralism, create a major cultural, social, financial and attitudinal division within the deaf community (215, 216).

The community (Schein, 1968) at all levels has an impact on the deaf person; the oral deaf person may have impact on his community in a positive way. The division between the oral deaf community and the manual deaf community is realistic, but whether the larger deaf community should discriminate against the oral deaf is a matter yet to be publicly considered. Oral education does permit the deaf person options as to the social, work, and educational world of which he wishes to be a full, participating and contributing member.

Principle 29. The rights of the deaf person in his community are realized when the deaf person is able to communicate with neighbors, with agencies within the community, and participate fully when he communicates in and with the members in the language of that community.

Principle 30. The oral deaf person has the potential of serving his community in a meaningful, participatory way when he uses his skills and talents to contribute to the larger society.

The research, the concepts, and the constructs presented in this paper are intended to provoke questions and reactions, to promote discussion and decisions to be reflected ultimately in recommendations. It is predicted that from this group will emanate a clear, precisely articulated philosophy of oral education which will embrace new and broader insights into information processing, learning, speech perception and production, curriculum design, and language instruction and serve to promote renewed and enthusiastic understanding of oral education.

References

Allen, J., & Allen, M. Discovering and accepting hearing impairment: Initial reaction of parents. *The Volta Review,* 1979, *81,* 279–285.

Becker, S. Initial concern and action in the detection and diagnosis of a hearing impairment in the child. *The Volta Review, 78,* 105–115.

Behrens, T. In M. Ross & T. Giolas (Eds.), *Auditory management of hearing impaired children.* Baltimore: University Park Press, 1978.

Best, H. *Deafness and the deaf in the United States.* New York: Macmillan Company, 1943.

Biggs, M. *Learning theories for teachers.* New York: Harper & Row, 1964.

Blackwell, P. *Sentences and other systems.* Washington, DC: A.G. Bell Association for the Deaf, 1978.

Bloom, L., & Lahey, M. *Language development and language disorders.* New York: John Wiley & Sons, 1978.

Boothroyd, A. Speech perception and sensorineural hearing loss. In M. Ross & T. Giolas (Eds.), *Auditory management of hearing impaired children.* Baltimore: University Park Press, 1978.

Bronfenbrenner, U. Is early intervention effective? *Teachers College Record,* 1974, *76,* 279–303.

Buckler, Sr. J. *Interaction analysis of the discourse of teachers of hearing impaired children: Its relationship to cognitive development.* Unpublished doctoral dissertation, Teachers College, Columbia University, 1977.

Carr, M.J. *Communicative behavior of three and four year old deaf children.* Unpublished doctoral dissertation, Columbia University, 1971.

Chomsky, N. *Aspects of theory of syntax.* Cambridge, MA: M.I.T. Press, 1965.

Clark, M. Preparation of deaf children for hearing society. *Journal of the British Association of Teachers of the Deaf,* 1976, 5, 146–154.

Connor, L. New directions in infant programs for the deaf. *The Volta Review,* 1976, 78, 8–15.

Cremin, L. The family as educator: Some comments on the recent historiography. *Teachers College Record,* 1974, 76, 250–265.

Curtiss, S., Prutting, C., & Lowell, E. Pragmatic and semantic development in young children with impaired hearing. *Journal of Speech and Hearing Research,* 1979, 22, 534–552.

Erber, N. An approach to evaluating auditory perception ability. *The Volta Review,* 1978, 80, 16–24.

Fellendorf, G. *An Eduhealth delivery service index: A profile of education and health services to young hearing impaired children and their parents.* Unpublished doctoral dissertation, Teachers College, Columbia University, 1974.

Fox, D. *Adult-child interactions and the language of hearing impaired children in a preschool setting.* Unpublished doctoral dissertation, Teachers College, Columbia University, 1980.

Friedlander, B. Z. Facts of value and value in facts. In A. Simmons-Martin & D. Calvert, *Parent infant intervention.* New York: Grune & Stratton. 1979.

Fry, D. The role and primacy of the auditory channel in speech and language development. In M. Ross & T. Giolas (Eds.), *Auditory management of hearing impaired children.* Baltimore: University Park Press, 1978.

Gage, N. *The scientific basis of the art of teaching.* New York: Teachers College Press, 1978.

Greenstein, J., Greenstein, B., McConville, K., & Stellini, L. *Mother-infant communication and language acquisition in deaf infants.* New York: Lexington School for the Deaf, 1976.

Heidinger, V. *An exploratory study of procedures for improving temporal features in the speech of deaf children.* Unpublished doctoral dissertation, Teachers College, Columbia University, 1972.

Hilgard, E., & Bower, G. *Theories of learning.* New York: Appleton-Century-Crofts, 1966.

Hirsh, I. Information processing in the deaf child. In R. Stark (Ed.), *Sensory capabilities of hearing impaired children.* Baltimore: University Park Press, 1974.

Jensema, C. A note on the educational achievement of ODAS members. *The Volta Review,* 1975, 77, 135–137.

Jensema, C., Karchmer, M., & Trybus, R. *The rated speech intelligibility of hearing impaired children: Basic relationships and a detailed analysis.* Washington, DC: Office of Demographic Studies, Gallaudet College, 1978.

Klima, E., & Bellugi, U. *The signs of language.* Cambridge, MA: Harvard University Press, 1979.

Kretschmer, R., & Kretschmer, L. *Language development and intervention with the hearing impaired.* Baltimore: University Park Press, 1978.

Levine, E. S. *Youth in a soundless world.* New York: New York University Press, 1956.

Levenstein, P. The parent-child network. In A. Simmons-Martin & D. Calvert, *Parent infant intervention.* New York: Grune & Stratton, 1979.

Levitt, H. The acoustics of speech production. In M. Ross & T. Giolas (Eds.), *Auditory management of hearing impaired children.* Baltimore: University Park Press, 1978.

Liberman, A. M. Language processing. In R. Stark (Ed.), *Sensory capabilities of hearing impaired children.* Baltimore: University Park Press, 1974.

Ling, D. *Speech and the hearing-impaired child: Theory and practice.* Washington, DC: A.G. Bell Association for the Deaf, 1976.

Luterman, D. *Counseling parents of hearing impaired children.* Boston: Little, Brown, 1979.

Mavilya, M. *Vocalizations and babbling of hearing impaired infants.* Unpublished doctoral dissertation, Teachers College, Columbia University, 1969.
McNeill, D. *The acquisition of language: The study of developmental psycholinguistics.* New York: Harper & Row, 1970.
Menyuk, P. *The acquisition and development of language.* Englewood Cliffs, NJ: Prentice-Hall, 1967.
Mulholland, A. *Congruence of problems of deaf adolescents as perceived by parents, teachers, and selves.* Unpublished doctoral dissertation, Fordham University, 1971.
Murphy, A. The families of hearing impaired children. *The Volta Review,* 1979, *81,* 265–278.
Murphy, A. Counseling ways: Lessons parents have taught me. *The Volta Review,* 1977, *79,* 145–152.
Myklebust, H.R. *The psychology of deafness.* New York: Grune & Stratton, 1964.
New York Times. *A triumph of social engineering.* New York: 1979, 11–13.
Neyhus, A., & Myklebust, H. *Speechreading failures in deaf children.* Final Report, July 1969, Institute for Language Disorders, Northwestern University Project No. 6-2582, Grant No. OE G-3-7-062582-2084, Bureau of Education for the Handicapped, U.S. Office of Education.
Ogden, P. *Experiences and attitudes of oral deaf adults regarding oralism.* Unpublished doctoral dissertation, University of Illinois, 1979.
Pflaster, G. *A factor analytic study of hearing impaired children integrated into regular schools.* Unpublished doctoral dissertation, Teachers College, Columbia University, 1976.
Pickett, J.M., & Mártony, J. Low frequency vowel formant discrimination in hearing impaired listeners. *Journal of Speech and Hearing Research,* 1970, *13,* 347–359.
Quigley, S., Jenné, W., & Phillips, S. *Deaf students in colleges and universities.* Washington, DC: A.G. Bell Association for the Deaf, 1968.
Reeves, J.K. Scope for oralism. *The Volta Review,* 1977, *79,* 43–54.
Restak, R. *The brain: The last frontier.* Garden City, NY: Doubleday & Company, 1979.
Russell, W., Quigley, S., & Power, D. *Linguistics and deaf children.* Washington, DC: A.G. Bell Association for the Deaf, 1976.
Schein, J. *The deaf community.* Washington, DC: Gallaudet College Press, 1968.
Schiff, N. The influence of deviant maternal input on the development of language during the preschool years. *Journal of Speech and Hearing Research,* 1979, *22,* 581–903.
Snijders, J.T. Psychology of hearing and non-hearing. In *Proceedings of the international course in paedo-audiology.* Groningen, the Netherlands: Groningen University, 1953.
Solomon, P., Kubzansky, P.E., Leiderman, P.H., Mendelson, J.H., Trumbull, R., & Wexler, D. *Sensory deprivation.* Cambridge, MA: Harvard University Press, 1961.
Streng, A. *Syntax, speech, and hearing.* New York: Grune & Stratton, 1972.
Thompson, R., Thompson, A., and Murphy, A. Sounds of sorrow, sounds of joy: The hearing impaired parents of hearing impaired children—a conversation. *The Volta Review,* 1979, *81,* 337–351.
van Uden, A. *A world of language for deaf children.* Amsterdam: Swets & Zeitlinger, 1977.
Webster's New Collegiate Dictionary. Springfield, MA: G. and C. Merriam, 1959.
White, B. Hearing ability and the development of infants and toddlers. In A. Simmons-Martin & D. Calvert (Eds.), *Parent-infant intervention.* New York: Grune & Stratton, 1979.

reaction to 2

ton p.m. van hagen

In her paper "The philosophical bases of oral education," Mulholland wrote out *her* credo, *her* philosophy of an oral education of deaf children. Her philosophy is presented from the perspective of the student, his home, his school, his community, and is set out in 30 principles of an oral education. Just as Mulholland consulted Webster to define "philosophy," I consulted the Oxford dictionary to define the term "principle."

Principle means:
- fundamental source
- fundamental truth and basis for reasoning
- a general law as guide to action.

In the field of education it is a necessity to be explicit on the viewpoints on man and environment; or when they are not explicit it is a task to extract these views from the educational practice, the educational and/or psychological research. Facts only function within views (Peursen, L.A. van, 1965). Professionals within the field of the education of deaf children cannot avoid having to state explicitly their basic values on man and environment. According to me this is a question of "to be or not to be." It makes a great difference in the operation of the educational process if the handicap of a child is seen just as a hindrance or as an invincible obstacle (Bleidick, U., 1978).

The interpretation on which one decides is not without consequences, either for the educational method or for the viewpoints of the deaf child on his or her own expectations. With this statement I arrive at one of the undeniable features of the phenomenon of education: it is impossible to avoid choices as it is impossible to postpone them. Education is a work of both conviction and risk. Professional education is characterized by process-product arrangements. Search and re-search (please note the prefix!) ought to be done within the frames of these process-product arrangements. The advocates of an oral education of deaf children are sometimes charged with obscurity in their position (Conrad, R., 1976). For creating more clarity it will be necessary to:

- clarify and legitimize the aims and goals we want to realize;
- develop effective methods of teaching and education, to improve or to redress these methods; and
- research steadily the effects of the methods in use and to research the factors which influence the realization of the process-product-arrangements.

For this kind of research is valid: a research within the frame of oral education.

To clarify the aims and goals is one of the major tasks of this symposium-forum. The world of educators of the deaf, as well as the world of the deaf, is divided into two camps. The basic problem, after all, is not the code of communication, but the fundamental differences of the values, differences in views on man and his environment, differences in what is worthwhile pursuing, differences in the fundamental sources, differences in principles.

From this point of view the clarification of aims and goals of oral education ought to be realized. It is my intention to open the general discussion with the following questions:
1. Do you agree that a clarification of the aims and goals of oral education is necessary?
2. What is the best method to bring clarity to the fields of aims and goals?
3. What is your opinion on the principles as developed by Mulholland? With which principles do you agree; with which principles do you disagree?
4. "Oral education" does not label satisfactorily the process of education advocated by the oralists. Do you have suggestions for a better terminology?

References

Bleidick, U. Pädagogik der Behinderten. Carl Marhold Verlagsbuchhandlung. Berlin-Charlottenburg, 1978.
Conrad, R. Matters arising in "Methods of communication currently used in the education of deaf children." Royal National Institute for the Deaf, 1976.
van Peursen, L.A.: Feiten, waarden, gebeurtenissen. W. de Haan, Hilversum/J.M. Meulenhoff, Amsterdam, 1965.

3

the psychological bases of oral education

geoffrey p. ivimey

The fostering and maintenance of effective and fluent communication in profoundly deaf children involve a whole complex of interrelated psychological, social, linguistic, and experiential factors. Any serious attempt to solve the many problems in this area demands a consideration of each of these factors: to focus on one or the other will inevitably lead to the recommendation of practices that will be, at best, partial but that may be unfruitful or, indeed, may actively prevent the achievement of the desired aims.

Before these interacting factors are considered it is essential to be sure exactly what is meant by communication. In this paper it will be taken to mean the ability to participate autonomously and spontaneously in, and on occasion to initiate, conversations ranging over a wide spectrum of social, personal, recreational, professional, and other topics. These considerations may be conceived narrowly as face-to-face interactions or may, more generally, include distance-communication activities; letter-writing, reading, etc. In the earlier stages it is inevitable that the emphasis will be placed on a small range of face-to-face communications, i.e., conversation of one sort or another, but later the communication will become more complex and will include more of the non-face-to-face interactions.

The definition adopted here contrasts strongly with many so-called communication activities seen all too frequently in schools for hearing impaired children. These take several forms:

1. *Nonspontaneous, teacher-dominated exchanges.* These are of two main kinds—
(a) Lessons in which the teacher "asks"* questions:

---

*The word "asks" is placed in quotation marks since the practice can be observed in schools using a wide range of communicative media—oral, Paget Gorman Systematic Sign System, Cued Speech, Total Communication, sign.

"Is it raining today?"—and the children respond by making some minimal mechanical transformation—"Yes, it is raining today" or "No, it is not raining today."

(b) Lessons in which the teacher gives a number of orders which the children learn, often after many hours of drill, to obey:
"Put the book on the table,"
"Open the door,"
"Give the book to John," etc.

2. *Written exercises of a mechanical nature* in which the children replace, say, nouns and verbs (often underlined for easier recognition) by similar words in plural, past tense, etc.

3. *Diaries or "News"* consisting of a few simple sentences, usually written one to each line:
"I am a boy.
I am nine years old.
I am in school.
I am favorite football Arsenal."
It is not uncommon to find identical sentences repeated day after day over long periods of time.

4. *Intensive work* carried out by the teacher putting fragmentary utterances of his pupils on the blackboard in normal language. The end-product of such an activity may consist of four or five sentences which are then copied by the pupils into neat books, in a mechanistic manner.

5. *Stories and other material written on the board* by the teacher and copied by the pupils.

All of these activities can be witnessed in almost all schools for the deaf and it is probable that each may make some contribution to the communicative ability of the children involved. But, judging by the poor linguistic ability of deaf schoolleavers, the time spent on these activities is difficult to justify. What is more serious is that many teachers fail to recognize that exercise books filled with neat reproductions of this sort give no evidence of the actual communicative competence of the pupils unaided by their teacher. Yet many teachers assess the progress of their pupils on this basis. Thus when we are told that "Johnny has good language" we do not know whether the teacher is referring to Johnny's unaided efforts or those of the Johnny-teacher combinations described above. Much of the research carried out during the past 40 or so years into the language skills of profoundly deaf children (Brannon, 1968; Cohen, 1965; Fusfeld, 1955; Goda, 1964; Heider & Heider, 1940; Ivimey, 1976, 1978; Moore, 1973; Myklebust, 1964; Taylor, 1969) shows very similar defective and retarded levels of linguistic competence in deaf children being educated in different schools and countries and using different media of communication. Yet, these findings are rarely reflected in teacher assessments, suggesting that the teachers are not looking at spontaneous, unaided skills but at the results of the pupils and themselves in concert.

The inescapable conclusion of this is that the practices most frequently observed in schools for deaf children are unsuccessful and even counterproductive. Such a statement would be understood by many teachers to reflect on their professional work and would, rightly, be resented. However, the position of the author is not that teachers do not work hard enough (indeed it may be that many teachers work too hard. It is often the teachers who are exhausted at the end of the day, not their pupils), but that they spend too much time in fruitless activities and this arises because their initial and in-service training does not equip them with the knowledge to do the right things.* The central aim of this paper is to outline the rationale for more fruitful strategies, based on up-to-date psycho- and sociolinguistic knowledge, that may be of value to teachers in their daily work.

In order to achieve this we must first examine two topics:
1. The process underlying the acquisition of language by normally hearing children;
2. The processes underlying the acquisition of language by profoundly deaf children.

These topics must initially be treated separately, until it can be shown that they are identical or similar, for if they are not, there is little point in attempting to apply methods based on normality to abnormal situations. Some researchers have suggested that the cognitive and linguistic skills of profoundly deaf children are very different from those of normally hearing children (Pintner & Patterson, 1923). Furth (1973) has characterized the deaf child as "a human being without language" (p. 13), while Blanton and his colleagues are more specific:

> It is very rare that a deaf person learns to use English generatively (Blanton et al., 1967, p. 100) and:
> Rule learning is a rather weak tendency in the deaf. Most of their effort is expended in learning individual items rather than in the acquisition of rules by which further items may be learned (ibid. p. 6)

It will be shown, subsequently, that these statements are ill-founded, that profoundly deaf children do possess language skills and that, in their development, these pass through similar stages to those of hearing children, albeit with a great degree of retardation.

Contemporary models of language acquisition fall into three major groups: the behaviorist and neo-behaviorist, the nativist and the inductivist schools. There is no room in this paper to discuss these in detail, but the position of the author is that the inductivist model is currently the most satisfactory (Ivimey, in prep.). In this model innate language-specific components postulated by Chomsky, McNeill (1966), and others are rejected in favor of a more general ability to form integratory concepts on the basis of perceived regularities in experience (Ivimey,

---

*One may contrast this with the case of speech pathologists, whose professional training now includes more extensive and lengthy study of psychology and linguistics. It is noteworthy that, since this has become common, many Speech pathologists are taking over some of the traditional functions of teachers of the deaf. It is possible that, if this trend continues, pathologists may become dominant in the education of the deaf.

1973). Such a model is rather similar in essence to that of Bruner (1974) and Piaget. Its outlines are as follows:
1. (a) The learner is immersed in an environment that is typically characterized by recurring regularities;
   (b) These regularities become part of the observer's experience;
2. As the learner's experience accumulates, he comes to recognize these regularities. These that are perceived earliest are those that recur most frequently and that have the greatest stability (Ivimey, 1975);
3. These perceived regularities are internalized and from them the learner makes an inductive leap. In the words of Bruner (op. cit.) he "goes beyond the information given," taking the evidence of a finite and limited set of data as having universal applicability. Thus he constructs rules that will, at this stage, be inevitably partial and possibly incorrect. (This explains the paradox noted by Chomsky [Smith & Wilson, 1979] that young children produce language forms they have not experienced, and that has led the transformationalists to reject learning as a major element in language acquisition);
4. Although the constructed rules are partial and often faulty they allow the learner to restructure his subsequent interactions with his environment: his perceptions are more advanced than formerly (cf. Piaget & Inhelder, 1973);
5. As a result the learner will come to recognize mismatches between his personal model and the external environment. This disequilibrium will lead eventually to a reconstruction of the model at a more advanced and discriminating level;
6. Stages 2–5 will be repeated until the disequilibrium between the individual model system and the supra-individual target system disappears or becomes relatively unimportant. When this stage has been reached there will be little further change and the individual may be said to have acquired his maternal or local language.

This inductivist model accounts for all the facts of language acquisition as currently known. It has been shown that it disposes of a basic paradox of transformationalist theory, and it also accounts for changes in child language that McNeill (1966) could not account for.

It is clear that an inductivist model entails a number of points, of which the most important are:
1. Induction involves inductive ability, which varies from individual to individual. Some will make inductive generalizations on the basis of more limited evidence than others, or they will be more adventurous and wide-ranging in their inductive leaps. Inductive ability is probably linked to general intelligence, but its influence on language development seems to be rather limited. At lower IQ levels there is a positive connection between measured IQ and speed of language acquisition (Mittler, in Clarke & Clarke, 1958), but for children of average and above-average intelligence the relationship is probably indirect.
2. A more important fact is that induction demands a corpus of experienced data to which the inductive processes can be applied: the richer the experience the more rapidly, *ceteris paribus,* will rules be formed and, if necessary, subsequently modified.

In any educational setting the first of these points must merely be accepted: in the short- (and probably also in the long-run) teachers can do little or nothing to alter the level of intellectual processing of their pupils, although to assume that such processing occurs independently of other factors is certainly wrong. We shall return to this topic at a later stage. The second major constraint is, fortunately, within the power of the teacher to alter: the amount of language experience and its quality can be varied quite simply by the teacher in the classroom. This topic also will be examined later.

For the moment we must turn to the second major problem: the extent to which the linguistic development of profoundly deaf children resembles that of normally hearing children. As we have seen, some experts in the field deny this: in their opinion the population of deaf children is linguistically *sui generis*, characterized by difficulty or inability to form linguistic concepts.

In fact, little published research can resolve this problem. Most reports emphasize the performance differences between the deaf and hearing groups investigated. Typical of this approach is Myklebust (1964), who describes the proportions of various specific "deafisms" found in the written language of his subjects. Such an approach fails to recognize the essential feature of any language, that it does not consist merely of elements occurring in isolation, but that it is a system, formed of elements entering into complex and structured, i.e., lawful, interrelationships with each other. A simple enumeration of elements or a comparison between such enumerations can tell us nothing about the nature of any system these elements may constitute (Flavell & Wohlwill, 1969; von Bertalanffy, 1968). Thus we do not know whether Myklebust's "deafisms" are mere random concatenations of words (which would provide evidence for the inability of deaf children to form linguistic rules), or whether they reflect any regular syntactic and semantic relationships (evidence that deaf children can and do form ordered sets of language rules) or whether they reflect a combination of both, demonstrating that the deaf can form rules but do so with difficulty and rather slowly.

In contrast to this widespread primitive enumerative approach a rather small number of workers have examined the language of profoundly deaf children in order to detect any systemic characteristics (Ivimey, 1976, 1978, 1979; Ivimey & Lachterman, in prep.; Lachterman, 1975; Taylor, 1969). These workers have described the rules utilized by their deaf subjects to generate novel utterances, and Ivimey has shown that the rules also influence the perception of written language (Ivimey, 1978 and in press). It has been further demonstrated that the rules constructed by the profoundly deaf chldren studied are not *sui generis* but closely resemble those of normally hearing children. However, in the deaf population, there is a massive delay in development: Ivimey's 11- and 13-year-old children produced sentences identical in structure to those of hearing 2–2½-year-olds (Ivimey, 1977a). More recently Ivimey has shown that the earlier stages of syntactic development in a group of profoundly deaf children, aged between 5 and 12 years, closely resemble those of the hearing children aged 18–24 months described by Brown (1973) and Bloom and Lahey (1978). Since it can be shown (Ivimey, 1978) that the syntactic structures described systemically by Lachterman, Taylor, and Ivimey (op. cit.) are identical with those described nonsystemically by other workers, it can be asserted with some confidence that deaf children, as a group, do possess structured sets of linguistic rules and that these rules parallel in their development those of normally hearing children. Thus we cannot say that profoundly deaf children cannot acquire language, only that too many of them do not seem to acquire very much language: a very different proposition. Moreover, since they seem to pass through rather similar developmental stages it is possible that they are utilizing similar, if not identical, cognitive skills and processes of their younger hearing brothers and sisters. It appears that the major constraint upon language acquisition lies not in some characteristic of deaf children but elsewhere.

Ivimey (1976b) has argued that the solution to this problem can be found in the limited input of language experienced by many deaf children in schools. A survey was carried out in schools for deaf children in and around London some years ago. Teacher use of powerful group hearing aids was observed, and teachers were asked whether period of usage observed was typical of their normal practice. All teachers agreed that it was. In fact, the mean time of daily usage of the group aids was a little under one hour. The smallest amount of time was 20 minutes. Children also used individual, body-worn aids that were switched on for most of the time the children were in class. However, because of the poor condition of many aids used by children and because of the rapid decrease in sound energy over distance, it is probably that an individual aid has very little value over distances of 6 feet or more. The average distance between teacher and pupils was 12 feet. Thus we see that the majority of deaf children were experiencing powerfully amplified sound for, at best, only about an hour daily, yielding a total annual language experience of about 200 hours. It is possible that this low figure should be increased to include time spent in auditory training and speech remediation, together with some experience gained at home, but it is unlikely that any of the children tested had enjoyed more than about 400 hours language experience each year. During the seven years that the children had been in school they would have received roughly the same language input as a hearing child aged between 2 and 2½ years. It should be realized that in the schools observed, very little communication went on beyond what was noted. For the rest of the time the children worked mainly in silence, copying from the blackboard, doing "sums" from work cards, painting, swimming, playing, and so on. This could be seen in schools using oral methods of communication, Cued Speech, the Paget Gorman system, and pure manualism. Since the language experiences were markedly similar it is scarcely surprising that the 11–12–year–old hearing impaired children had developed syntactic, lexical, and phonological models very similar to those of much younger, hearing children.

In addition, other factors appear to be operating. Many lessons seen in classes consisted of teachers giving orders that the children obeyed. It was estimated that some 40 percent of teachers' utterances were in the imperative. The greatest majority of other utterances had verbs in the past tense. Yet imperatives give no evidence of any verbal morphology while the regular past tense ending does not change to indicate number. Presented with a majority of verbs without ending or terminating in -ed, it is not surprising that observers have noted that many deaf children produce verbs with no inflections (Bamford & Bench, 1979) or verbs all in the past tense, whether this is appropriate or not. In the case of deaf children it appears that lack of language experience delays the acquisition of linguistic concepts, while the distorted language that is experienced results in the formation of faulty concepts. Such a conclusion is not unexpected: hearing children acquire the language to which they are exposed, and the rate of acquisition seems to be related to the amounts and flexibility of language experienced, as shown by many sociolinguists in the case of children coming from poor and underprivileged socioeconomic backgrounds.

In this paper it has been argued:

1. that children appear to use inductive processes and strategies in constructing internalized linguistic models;

2. that induction demands not only general cognitive ability to form complex concepts, but also a body of data to which this ability can be applied;

3. that deaf children appear to use similar inductive processes and strategies as hearing children and, in the formation of their linguistic models, pass through similar stages;

4. but that they exhibit a massive delay in linguistic development, the direct result of very meager and distorted language experience.

The major conclusion of this argument is that to increase exposure to language would result in improved linguistic models and acceleration in their development. Where this has been attempted, even for relatively short periods, the results have been striking.

At this point it must be stated that the arguments advanced in this paper so far cannot be taken as evidence for an oral approach to language teaching with deaf children. They should be seen as a set of recommendations that would apply in the use of any medium or for the learning of any body of knowledge. However, while recognizing this, it must not be assumed that the choice of medium is entirely open. Indeed, recognition of the importance of improving and increasing the language experience of deaf children forces us to accept that this is most likely to be achieved in an oral environment. Before advancing the arguments in support of this position, an important point that is frequently overlooked must be made: failure* to acquire language through the medium of oral communication is often seen as justifying recourse to one or other form of manual or manual-assisted communication. However, children who have "failed" in an oral environment rarely develop well in a non-oral one.

During the past 15 to 20 years there has been, in Britain, a "flight from oralism" with many schools abandoning even token attempts to foster oral skills. Yet there has not been any noticeable improvement in the literacy and educational levels of the British deaf population. Similarly, the annual reports of the demographic department of Gallaudet College in the U.S.A. indicate very low standards of literacy in their freshmen students, the majority of whom have spent many (in some cases up to 18 or 20) years in schools using one or other form of manual communication, with or without ancillary speech and lipread-

---

*Many deaf children become categorized as "oral failures," yet it is probable that they should be seen as delayed language acquirers. These terms are not mere labels: different diagnoses will result in different recommendations for treatment.

ing. It seems that, simply to alter the medium of communication used in schools without also altering the frequency with which it is used and the nature of information transmitted by it, has very little value. Whatever medium of communication is used, the majority of deaf children are exposed to restricted and degenerate inputs of language. This is likely to become more serious with the introduction of non-oral media.

A number of powerful arguments may be advanced in support of this assertion:

1. Since the amount of language experienced by a young child appears to be critical for the development of language skills, it is important that parents be able to contribute fluently and frequently to this experience. It is rare for parents to know, before their baby is born, whether he is likely to suffer from auditory impairment or not. Even in developed countries with good medical and maternal support services, the majority of cases of childhood deafness seem to be diagnosed at about 2 years of age. After diagnosis many, probably most, parents go through a period of emotional upset and, even where this is of short duration, if parents are to begin to acquire a new medium of communication it is inevitable that further delay will intervene before they can begin to supply the necessary communicative environment for their child to operate on. Thus valuable time and experience is lost. More serious, perhaps, is the fact that the child is not passive during this time: he is constantly applying his inductive skills to the world that he experiences and begins to elaborate a model of which a main component will be silence and noncommunication beyond a crude level of animal cries, gross bodily responses and gestures: a deaf-mute is being created. It has been claimed that the various manual media can be learned quickly, but this has not been substantiated for the majority of parents, especially those of lower ability, from poorer homes, where both parents may be working irregular hours or who have large families demanding attention. It is not uncommon for parents, under the urging of teachers, to begin courses of instruction, but many of them seem to drop out after a short period. There are no published statistics of numbers of parents successfully acquiring skills in nonoral communication, but it is probable that the majority do not. Thus the greater number of deaf children who are being educated by non-oral media are forced to rely upon their schools for the totality of their experience. Yet, as has been shown above, schools do not currently provide either the amount or type of experience necessary. Even where teachers are prepared to change their normal practices, devoting every moment of the school day to communicative, preferably conversational (van Uden, 1979), activities, they would be unable to provide their pupils with more than five or six hours experience daily or *a little over 1200 hours annually*, far less than that experienced by hearing children as young as 3 years of age. Thus, even under optimal conditions, where schools become the main source of communicative experience, deaf children will still suffer a massive experiential deficit. This is more likely to occur where non-oral media of communication are in use.

2. A second, closely linked point is that the sort of language experience in schools is, inevitably, highly artificial, dealing as it is with a limited range of pedagogically approved and acceptable activities, frequently treated in a highly abstract manner. The children do not experience much language linked to

everyday living. Some attempts are made by most schools to overcome this deficiency, but these typically lack spontaneity, since they are based on pre-planned programs and delivered to classes as a whole. It is probable in any class of secondary age that one pupil is concerned with problems of personal hygiene, another with his relations with his parents, a third is worrying about the many problems of adolescent sexuality, a fourth with finding work, and so on. If these problems are to be satisfactorily solved they must be dealt with as they arise. The appropriate concepts and language forms will be acquired most readily when the child is motivated by his own needs, i.e., facts, attitudes, and language are best learned "at the moment of impact," not at some other time predetermined by a formal curriculum, however comprehensively planned and sensitively taught. Responses to the needs and worries of individual deaf children can be made most readily in the small family group, as they are with most normally hearing children. Yet, if parents are cut off from fluent and easy communication because they cannot make use of the medium of communication that their child has acquired, then they can make little or no useful contribution to their child's general educational, social, or language development.

3. A third argument can be found in the restricted lexicon of many manual systems (especially the Paget Gorman systematic sign language). Even where parents and teachers are fluent in the system used, it may be that a key concept demanded by a child's current needs or interests is totally missing from the official lexicon or has been forgotten (or never learned) by the adults. It may be that a young child has seen a squirrel in the park, or that an adolescent is worried about the beginnings of menstruation or about nocturnal emissions of sperm. If the requisite signs are missing from the lexicon or the adults do not know them, then a valuable opportunity for the acquisition of specific signs, for general and social education, and for an extended conversation is irretrievably lost. Furthermore there is a yet more serious, but rarely recognized, possible outcome of such a situation. We have already seen that children do not remain passive, waiting for their parents and teachers to communicate. Lack of fluent interchanges will begin to turn the child into a noncommunicator in a silent world. In addition, if his concerns are not resolved, he may come to see himself as a person whose needs and interests are ignored by others. A number of experiences like this must induce in the child a poor and negative self-image, with unfortunate consequences for general personality development.

The problems discussed above are by no means confined to schools using non-oral means of communication: they are ever-present in any situation where the onus for providing all or most of a child's experience is thrown onto teachers working in a formal school setting. Some of the worst effects may be ameliorated, however, where parents and other adults can communicate readily with the individual child, but this is less likely to occur where manual media are used. In contrast to the time needed to acquire fluency in sign and the limited nature of many manual lexicons, parents normally are fluent in their local language before their handicapped child arrives. Their knowledge of many technical terms in their language may be restricted but their own level of competence is likely to be adequate for the needs of their environment and for children growing up in that environment. Moreover, since almost every other adult in the neighborhood is also fluent in the locally accepted language, every adult that a deaf child meets is a potential provider of linguistic experience. The child may still be forced to rely on his school for the bulk of his linguistic experience, but with proper education of parents and their friends and associates the child's potential sources of communication become very much greater.

Thus we see that, although psychology and developmental linguistics cannot do more than indicate fruitful practices to achieve the desired end of enabling deaf children to become fluent in communication, the realities of social and familial situations and the limitations imposed by schools and traditional pedagogical practices force us to recognize that our aims are most likely to be achieved by initiating and fostering the development of oral communication. It is only by making use of the existing linguistic skills of each child's parents and their friends, acquaintances, and so on can we ensure that the child will be in a position to enjoy a wide experience of language. Without this he is unlikely to be able to construct the necessary internal linguistic models. This argument is not intended to minimize the difficulties in acquiring lipreading and speech skills, merely to suggest that use of non-oral media of communication, however seductive these may seem, is likely to force the deaf child into levels of very low achievement in general education, communication and literacy, i.e., that for the majority of deaf children use of manual communication is more, not less, likely to fail to meet the objectives of all educators.

References

Bamford, J., & Bench, J. A grammatical analysis of the speech of partially hearing children. In *Crystal*, 1979.

Blanton, R. L., Nunally, J. C., & Odom, P. *Psycholinguistic processes in the deaf*. Nashville, TN: Vanderbilt University, 1967.

Bloom, L., & Lahey, M. *Language development and language disorders*. New York: John Wiley & Sons, 1978.

Brannon, J. B. Linguistic word classes in the spoken language of normal, hard of hearing and deaf children. *Journal of Speech and Hearing Research*, 1968, *11*, 179–187.

Brown, R. *A first language: The early stages*. Cambridge, MA: Harvard University Press, 1973.

Bruner, J. S. *Beyond the information given*. London: George Allen & Unwin, 1974.

Cohen, S. R. Redundancy in the written language of the deaf: Predictability of story paraphrases of deaf and hearing children. In J. Rosenstein & W. H. McGinitie, *Research studies on the psycholinguistic behaviour of deaf children*. Reston, VA: Council for Exceptional Children, 1965.

Crystal, D. *Working with LARSP: Methods and applications*. London: Arnold, 1979.

Elkind, D., & Flavell, J. H. *Studies in cognitive development: Essays in honor of Jean Piaget*. New York: Oxford University Press, 1969.

Flavell, J. H., & Wohlwill. Formal and functional aspects of cognitive development. In D. Elkind and J. H. Flavell, *Studies in cognitive development: Essays in honor of Jean Piaget*. New York: Oxford University Press, 1969.

Furth, H. G. *Thinking without language: Psycholinguistic implications of deafness*. New York: Free Press, 1973.

Fusfeld, I. S. The academic program of schools for the deaf. *The Volta Review*, 1955, *57*, 63–70.
Goda, S. Spoken syntax of normal, deaf and retarded adolescents. *Journal of Verbal Learning and Verbal Behaviour*, 1964, *3*, 401–405.
Heider, F. K., & Heider, G. M. A comparison of the sentence structures of deaf and hearing children. *Psychological Monographs*, 1940, *52*, 42–103.
Ivimey, G. P. *The acquisition of language*. Unpublished paper read at UNESCO Conference of Experts, University of Illinois, 1973.
Ivimey, G. P. The development of English morphology: An acquisition model. *Language and Speech*, 1975, *18*, 120–144.
Ivimey, G. P. The written syntax of an English deaf child: An exploration in method. *British Journal of Disorders in Communication*, 1976, *11*(2).
Ivimey, G. P. The perception of speech: An information-processing approach—Part III: Lipreading and the deaf. *Teacher of the Deaf*, 1977a, *1*, 90–101.
Ivimey, G. P. The ontogeny of a deviant syntax. In *Drachman: Salzburger Beitrage* zur Linguistik, 1977b, *3*.
Ivimey, G. P. *The written syntax of a group of deaf English children*. Unpublished doctoral dissertation, School of Oriental and African Studies, University of London, 1978.
Ivimey, G. P. *The development of language skills in deaf children: The early stages*. Unpublished paper read at Salzburg Conference of the American Association of Linguistics, 1979.
Ivimey, G. P. *The production and perception of syntactic time cues in written English*. In press.
Ivimey, G. P. *Induction and language acquisition*. In preparation.
Ivimey, G. P., & Lachterman, D. R. *The written language of young English deaf children*. In preparation.
Lachterman, D. R. *The written language of a group of English deaf children*. Unpublished master's thesis, Institute of Education, University of London, 1975.
McNeill, D. Developmental psycholinguistics. In T. Smith & G. Miller, *The genesis of language*. Cambridge, MA: M.I.T. Press, 1966.
Moore, T. E. *Cognitive development and the acquisition of language*. New York: Academic Press, 1973.
Myklebust, H. R. *The psychology of deafness*. New York: Grune & Stratton, 1964.
Piaget, J., & Inhelder, B. *Memory and intelligence*. New York: Basic Books, 1973.
Pintner, R., & Patterson, D. G. *A scale of performance tests*. New York: Appleton Century Crofts, 1923.
Rosenstein, J., & McGinitie, W. H. *Research studies on the psycholinguistic behavior of deaf children*. Reston, VA: Council for Exceptional Children, 1965.
Smith, N., & Wilson, D. *Modern linguistics—the results of Chomsky's revolution*. Harmondsworth: Penguin, 1979.
Smith, T., & Miller, G. *The genesis of language*. Cambridge, MA: M.I.T. Press, 1966.
Taylor, L. A. *A language analysis of the writing of deaf children*. Unpublished doctoral dissertation, Florida State University, 1969.
van Uden, A. *Psycholinguistic foundations of teaching language to deaf children*. 1979.
von Bertalanffy, L. *General system theory*. London: Allen Lane, 1968.

reaction to 3

jan p. m. van dijk

In response to Mr. Ivimey's paper on "The psychological bases of oral education of deaf children," I would like to support his plea for a child-centered approach to language development in deaf children as opposed to a teacher-centered approach. As is shown in research, some teachers impose their own expressive behavior too much upon the children. If this is the case, the children will not get the chance to get really involved in conversation just because of the inability of his teacher to listen—what van Uden calls "the whole secret of our work." This point is well taken.

A second point in which we share the presenter's idea is the limited input of language experienced by many deaf children. The total number of 200 per year of real language experiences is embarrassing for the organization of those schools in which this figure is realistic. This information emphasizes again the importance of a good organization of the timetable. Persons in charge of the school should ask themselves over and over again whether a specific part of the curriculum is directly related to the educational aim: this is the child's need for language. However, even with the best balanced curriculum, the school is unable to do this job alone.

As with normal-hearing children, the language teaching—better to say, the conversation with the deaf child—should go on during all hours in which the child is awake. In this light we would like to stress the importance of training parents and child-care workers in conversational language and education.

A remark in Dr. Ivimey's paper which we cannot agree with is his statement that children who have failed in an oral environment rarely develop in a non-oral one. Although we do not consider our Department Eikenheuvel as "non-oral," the medium through which the child is taught at this school is writing and fingerspelling. As our figures will show, quite a group of these youngsters reach a vocabulary and reading level comparable with normal "oral" children.

More essential than the remarks just made are Dr. Ivimey's points on the following:

1. *Linguistic rules.* He says that these rules parallel in their development those of normally hearing children. I don't understand this statement. Does the author really mean that the deaf child himself, like a normal child, discovers the grammatical rules on his own? In exceptional cases there is a little systematization which can be compared with that of a hearing child; in most instances the deaf child (unless taught in the proper way) follows in his spontaneous spoken language the visual or emotional order of the words. The same is true for sign-language.

Am I correct in my assumption that it is the speaker's idea:

2. That through a *"wide experience of language"* the deaf child is able to construct the necessary internal linguistic models? And that no specific exercises (in which the

rhythm of the sentence is essential) are needed for the child in order to detect these "models"?

A last question is: What, according to the speaker, is the role of reading? Is there, in the opinion of the speaker, in the language acquisition process an analogy between the hearing-impaired child and the normally hearing child in discovering grammatical rules? If so, we should pursue this further.

4

the sociological bases of oral education

hugo w. campbell

Introduction

In face-to-face communication the use of oral language presupposes a particular relation between those who produce the language and those who receive it. The speaker tries to have control over the receiver with respect to both the sequence of information intake and the nature of social interaction to be established (Wold, 1978). Since oral language is a rapidly fading medium, the receiver does not have the time to distinguish between what is said and what is meant. Aspects of denotation, connotation and affect will be immediately present as a function of prior expectancy, context, information in memory about social structures as well as about general world knowledge (Olson, 1977). In written language, however, the reader is more autonomous in the sense that he can decode the information the way he wants to. He might go back to the beginning of the written sentence or even to preceding and following sentences in the given text. Written language permits reflection, whereas oral language induces action.

The sociological bases of oral education will be considered from two different points of view: regulation of social action and freedom of establishing social relations. Regulation of social action will be examined by considering, on the one hand, the linguistic means the speaker has in controlling interaction orally and, on the other, the information the speech receiver should have in order to accept the fact that the speaker is trying to establish a legitimate social interaction. Freedom of establishing social relations will be related to the opportunity of participants to establish a particular social interaction. The speaker has to feel free to use oral language. Equal opportunity and freedom to communicate then become important commodities.

Emphasis will be put on oral education of the deaf in terms of the difficulty a deaf person might have in establishing as a speaker the correct social control and to perform as a speech receiver the correct decoding of speech as a function of the established social relation. This might especially be the case when interaction is to take place outside the scope of the family, friends, or institutional caretakers. Adaptation to society might then gain priority over the emotional well-being of the individual.

Regulation of Social Action

Social relation presupposes social order. We cannot establish an appropriate social relation without knowing the social order that prevails. The nature of human interaction will always depend on the nature of the institution (office, company, etc.) in which the interaction takes place, as well as on the institutional roles of the interlocutors (Kasher, 1977). Pragmatic aspects of language use become relevant the moment we start using language to attain a particular goal. The question of how to do things with words (Austin, 1962) has led us to take notice of the performative or illocutionary force associated with an utterance. The illocution requires the intentional use of a conventional signal to carry out some socially recognized function. General pragmatic conventions of initiating and managing a conversation enable us to regulate the course of action. The ways of speaking reflect our ways of interacting (Hymes, 1974). Moreover, the linguistic variety used by an individual during speaking might be indicative of his age, social class, and sex (Labov, 1971; Grimshaw, 1977). Learning to speak will therefore be more than correct articulation. The speaking child becomes a member of a speaking society to which it has to adapt. This starts with the learning of formulas for speaking. Later, the incorporation of the full pragmatics of language use and ways of speaking will permit him to communicate with others as a fully integrated member of the society.

From sensori-motor signals to word-like symbols

In the family or in the company of other caretakers the very young child will experience a great deal of affection, tenderness, and intimacy. Since it is not cognitively competent enough and lacks a symbolic system to interact, it cannot communicate at an advanced level with other human beings. However, the emotional bond between caretaker and child might be sufficient to generate social interaction. This interaction will be instrumental to a system in the child consisting of a performative intention to communicate, a proposition of things to be communicated, and a presuppositional procedure for placing that proposition into a contextual frame (Bates, 1976).

This system will be constructed in the first year of life in preparation for language development. Studying prelingually hearing children, Bates finds that the child's intention to communicate is manifested in gesture, eye contact, and prelinguistic vocalization. This intention to communicate can be inferred from:

(1) a context indicating that a goal desired by the child is operating;
(2) the emission of some movement or sound in which eye contact is alternated between the object and the adult;
(3) the persistence of behavior (2) until the inferred goal is reached; and

(4) consummatory behavior confirming that the child did indeed have that goal in mind.

Actions that were originally meant for reaching a goal himself, i.e., orienting, reaching, grasping, are gradually separated from the concrete attempt to reach objects and become signals instead. These signals, which include the gesture of pointing, are produced in a ritual fashion and seem to be more appropriate for communicating desire to an adult than for those desires to be fulfilled by the child himself.

The deaf child, too, will produce this ritual pointing with an imperative function to communicate desires. Findings by Goldin-Meadow and Feldman (1975) indicate that deaf children of 1½ to 4 years of age develop both a lexicon of gestures and a rudimentary grammar for combining them, without receiving either spoken language or any language like gestural input from parents or others.

This does not mean, however, that the deaf child should remain at this level of nonverbal communication. The fact that for both the hearing and the deaf child communication by sensori-motor signal is prior to the use of vocalization, indicates only that oral education for the deaf should start after the deaf child has become able to use sensori-motor signals. That is to say, before the child has developed (around 11 months of age) a scheme for use in utilitarian sequences with objects (i.e., child uses means to cause: "Adult Do X"), there will be no basis to introduce oral education for the deaf child. This will be irrespective of the child's capabilities of being engaged in social sequences with familiar adults (cooing, smiling, touching the other's face and hair, etc.).

However, these kinds of interaction will help the child to develop the instrumental use of sensori-motor signals as imperatives, i.e., the child's ability to separate portions of causal sequences from his own subjective actions. Moreover, the stimulation of the communication intentions of the child by members of the family will be relevant for the transition from sensori-motor signals to words with conventional meanings. Especially the deaf child will need this stimulation since he has the additional difficulty of pronouncing word-like signals and words.

The development of the use of word as proposition with a referential value follows vocalization as signal and word as signal. Word-like signals like "Mm," "Ha," "Na-Na" are used in any situation of need, where adults can be instrumental. The child might, however, shift directly from the level of sensori-motor signal (pointing to an object) to the level of inserting words in the same communicative sequences. This shift is paralleled by cognitive achievements, which seem to be prerequisite to it. Bates (1976) discusses cases of the onset of symbolic behavior which were prior to the use of words with referents. She concluded that the use of words with a referential value is dependent on the capacity for internal representation. So oral education depends on both the communication intentions at the sensori-motor level and the cognitive development of the child. Symbolic behavior with the intention to be engaged in social interaction will occur in declarative sequences that serve to invoke and maintain adult attention. Such attention-seeking word-like signals are, for example, the word "Pu" ("all gone"), which has a referent, and "na-na," which has no referent (Bates, 1976). This type of word-like symbols might even occur before the use of word-like symbols in the form of imperatives as orders and expressions for desire.

The inability of the deaf child to use these word-like signals as declaratives (means to involve and maintain adult attention) and as imperatives (orders and expressions for desire), might lead to a gradual isolation of the child, for he will lack the means to control social interaction. The consequences might be that the child will develop behavioral tendencies which are categorized as impulsiveness. Altshuler (1978) suggests that language lag or absence at critical periods, doing without the evocativeness or emotional generality of sound and parent-child relationships disturbed by the presence of the handicap, might be relevant factors contributing to impulsive behavior.

The stage at which the child would normally have used word-like symbols seems to be the most favorable period to start with oral training. It might then use symbolic behavior to establish social interaction. The difference between deaf children of deaf parents who can use oral language and those of hearing parents might therefore be related to the moment at which oral training starts as well as to parental acceptance of the child's deafness.

Formulas for speaking

As the child grows older his assimilative way of interacting in forcing reality to submit to his plans will develop into a more cooperative interactional system. The child will learn to use conversational management conventions to facilitate verbal interaction. These consist of verbal expressions and interaction routines that are appropriate to a particular kind of setting or context. These formulas enable the child to interact socially with speakers of the language from whom he has to learn it. They range from simple vocatives having the function of calling attention (OH Mommie, Hey X) and interrupting (Hold it!, Wait a minute) to verbal rituals having to do with greetings (Hi, Bye, See you later), politeness (Thanks, Thank you very much, S'cuse me, You're welcome) and invitation to play (Wanna play. Let's X, Can I play?). These formulas are numerous and can be learned very easily by the child as a function of the appropriate context. The child can use them to regulate the interaction, as well as to indicate that he is able to interact despite his verbal limitations. Recent studies of second language learning have stressed the importance of verbal formulas for the learner in his attempt to initiate and maintain interaction (Fillmore, 1976). In the case of the deaf child, the formulas will be understood by his interlocutors even if phonation is bad; provided, however, that it has been used in the appropriate context. The child will then be able to regulate communication irrespective of his fluency in speaking. His increased interactional skill will lead to the possibility of verbal interaction with hearing children inside and outside his home. This will increase the verbal input which he will receive from fluent speakers as well as his motivation to speak and to lipread.

Moreover, since the deaf child who can use these formulas may take the initiative to establish interaction through conversation, parents might have less difficulty in stimulating oral interaction during "home training." In so doing, oral education will not lead to a state of affairs in which interaction in early childhood will be restricted to the small group of family members or other caretakers. The frequency of spontaneous interaction will increase as well as the degree of emotional satisfaction the deaf child will experience.

The fact that the deaf child might learn to regulate social interaction verbally is of significance for its adaptation to the requirements of society. Opportunity for oral interaction will enable him to learn in a direct manner the norms and values of the society he lives in.

Social Interaction in a Speaking Society

Sociologists and anthropologists who are working in accordance with the behavioristic models consider the individual in society as a person who has to be fully adapted to the requirements of society. This should ultimately lead them to prosperity. Immigrants or ethnic minority groups are studied in order to see how they change their original values and other cultural traits to blend into the "melting pot" of the society they now live in (Gordon, 1964). The problems a member of a minority group has are interpreted as arising from inadequate assimilation, which has to be made adequate by enrolling him in community aid programs. The success of these programs is measured in terms of the degree of disappearance of the minority group value system and the incorporation of those of the host society.

This too strict environmental control of the individual will be rejected. It will be argued that integration in society has to be considered from the point of view of "communication-acculturation," according to which the interactive relationship between individual and environment characterizes the integration process (Kim, 1979). In the case of the deaf, the interactive relationship between the deaf person and hearing people should be stimulated. On the basis of this relationship the deaf will be able to develop the necessary skills to perform according to requirements of the "speaking world." However, this "speaking world" should also have to accept or tolerate norms and values related to the deaf.

Integration will be considered within: 1. the family and 2. society as a whole. In both cases the interactiveness of the integration process will be stressed.

Integration in the family

Social groups differ as a function of the characteristics of their members. This is true irrespective of the fact that the group as a whole is more than the sum of the individual members. The baby in the family will make that family different from what it was without this child. The presence of a deaf child will make that family function as a "family with a deaf child." Its relationship with society will be different from that of a "family with a hearing child." Moreover, it might anticipate or experience a greater effort to integrate into society than the "family with a hearing child." Tension produced by anticipated or unresolved conflicts between the family and the larger community, or between the parents, might lead to select the deaf child as the scapegoat. Vogel and Bell (1961) have described the process of scapegoating in families with normal-hearing children. For the parents, scapegoating serves as a personality-stabilizing process. By projecting their serious internal conflicts onto the children, they are able to live up to their commitments to the wider society. However, the child does require special care and attention due to some dysfunction (for example: bed-wetter).

Integration of the deaf child in the family has to be based on integration of the "family with the deaf child" in the community. That is, if this family as a whole serves as a scapegoat for the community, the scapegoating of the deaf child by its parents might remain. Therefore, "home training" of the deaf child has to be preceded by activities meant to integrate the "family with the deaf child" in the community (Broomfield, 1967). This is especially necessary for hearing parents of a deaf child who might be more susceptible to scapegoating than deaf parents.

The use of oral language might enhance the chance for the deaf child to be integrated into the family. By coding or decoding messages by means of speaking and lipreading respectively, the deaf child might facilitate interaction with the family members and in so doing be accepted and recognized. According to Mead (1934) the individual has the capacity and therefore the necessity to acquire membership in the various social groups upon which he depends, solely through the identification and internalization of the significant symbols of the social unit. It does not mean, however, that the other family members will have a passive role. Their interaction with the deaf child will have an effect on both the language acquisition and the acquisition of appropriate speech styles.

Evidence with respect to the specific nature of the verbal interaction between adults and the hearing child is given in relation to the "baby-talk" hypothesis (Ferguson, 1964). Adults modify their speech to very young children by simplification (basic sentence patterns and simplified lexicon), repetition (repeat parts of or whole utterances) and redundancies (paraphrase ambiguous constructions, replace ambiguous forms with synonyms). A special feature of baby talk is the slow and careful articulation as well as exaggerated intonation contours. The special intonation contour might have the function of signaling the child that a particular utterance is being addressed to him. Baby talk might be the result of the interactive relationship between child and adult in which the child's inattention or misunderstanding will force the adult to modify and simplify his speech and in so doing may shape the language input. Therefore, mother's speech can be considered a function of the specific feedback cues (Gleason, 1977). The effect of mother's speech to language acquisition might be positive if the linguistic input matches the child's linguistic, psycholinguistic, and communicative abilities (Cross, 1977). Interaction between the child and his caretaker might also be considered in terms of the social appropriateness of children's speech. Children's caretakers provide them with information and guidance with respect to interaction (Blount, 1977). Speech style used by the caretaker may vary as a function of status, role, and social position that children occupy. Language socialization might then serve to regulate what is expected of children as well as what the forms and functions of interaction should be.

Integration of the deaf child in the family might therefore enable the parents to establish an interactive relationship with the child. This manner of socialization will prepare the child to face interaction with the wider community to which it has to adapt.

Integration in society

Integration of the deaf in society has to be considered in terms of social interaction. The fact that their hearing impairment might hamper their functioning in society makes such an approach obvious. For example, the possible apprehension of the deaf regarding communication will lead him to search for jobs with a minimum of communication requirements. This might be in accordance with the more general hypothesis that persons with high communication apprehension would be less likely to see themselves advancing in the organization (Scott, et al., 1978). Moreover, given a communication network in an organization with a high frequency of oral communication, the deaf person will be considered a misfit. The same might hold with respect to his daily face-to-face communication which relates to:
- transactional interactions (shopping, traveling, etc.);
- mass media behavior (the use of television); and
- personal encounters (talking to neighbors, friends, etc.).

The interactive process underlying the integration of the deaf in society has to evolve in and through relationships between the deaf and their social-cultural environment. We shall consider this process by using the conceptual framework developed by Kim (1979) in her discussion of the adaptation of immigrants to the host society. This enables us to regard the integration of the deaf into society as an ongoing, dynamic, and interactive process between a deaf person and the speaking society he lives in.

Kim considers the process of adaptation of an immigrant to the host social-cultural system a process of communication acculturation, i.e., acculturation occurs and evolves in and through communication. This process is approached from a functional point of view. The environmental context which is functionally significant to the immigrant's life is studied rather than "attempting to establish *the* cultural norms, values, and behavioral modes of the host society". Three components of the communication process are being distinguished:
- personal communication (or intrapersonal communication);
- social communication (interpersonal and mass communication); and
- communication environment.

We shall use the concepts that Kim related to these components in order to describe the process underlying the integration of the deaf in society.

Personal communication is used to indicate the mental processes in which an individual organizes himself in and with his milieu. The relevant constructs are: cognitive structure, image of self/others, motivation for integration, knowledge of host language. The cognitive structure refers to the ability to organize experience into a form suitable to deal with a stimulus. Memory structures as schemata (Bartlett, 1932; Rumelhart, 1975), scripts (Abelson & Schank, 1977), and frames (Kuyper, 1975; Winograd, 1975) are operating during the processing of language. The image of self/other concerns the cumulative result of dynamic interaction between the person and others, which leads to the perception of the self in relation to others as well as the image the person thinks other people have of him. The motivation for integration has to do with the willingness to integrate. This may be related to the difference between his image of ideal self and the image of the external world in which he lives. The knowledge of host language considers both the use of linguistically correct forms and the use of appropriate linguistic forms (speech styles, as a function of social status, role, age, sex, etc.). Adequate "home training" might provide the deaf child with the opportunity to develop an optimal system for personal communication. Especially the use of oral language in an interactive manner (formula for speaking and speech styles) might enable the deaf person to organize himself in order to communicate with others in an acceptable manner. It is well known that learning of the host language is an aid to acculturation (Chance, 1965; Kim, 1979).

Social communication refers to the manner in which we regulate feelings, thoughts and actions as functionally interrelated individuals. How do we relate to the people around us? How frequent are the interactions, etc? Three major concepts are distinguished: a. interpersonal relationship, b. mutuality of interpersonal perceptions, and c. mass media behavior. Using the concept of interpersonal relationship, we can consider the degree to which the deaf person has been incorporated into the social network at the community level. The amount and the nature of interpersonal encounter should be considered in terms of stages of intimacy: casual acquaintances, casual friends or colleagues, and intimate or close friends.

Communication at all three stages will indicate a higher degree of integration than communication at the stage of intimate or close friends only. Mutuality of interpersonal perception has to be considered a major aspect of the deaf person's relationship with other members of society. The social group (colleagues, neighbors etc.) to which he is related must also consider him a fully integrated member of the social system. Members of the group must be able to talk with him without being constantly aware of his deafness. They have to regard him as someone who is functioning effectively in society. Though the degree of mutuality of interpersonal relationship might depend on the degree of intimacy, it is very important from the point of view of integration that the interactive relationship will force the nondeaf person to disregard the deafness feature as an important factor during face-to-face interaction. Unless such a state of affairs has been reached, one cannot say that the deaf person is integrated into the "speaking society." Mass media behavior concerns the consumption of publications, radio, television, and film. The effect of television on the child's cognitive skills as well as on his behavior has been given a great deal of attention (Corder-Bolz & O'Bryant, 1978; Drabman & Thomas, 1977; Liebert & Neale, 1973; Murray & Kippax, 1978). If the deaf child can lipread, it might benefit from these television programs. Even in the case of the adults, television and film mediate in transmitting social values and norms. The validity of the social learning model is discussed in a few studies (Beinstein, 1977; Gerbner & Gross, 1976; Tan & Tan, 1979).

With respect to the environmental factor, Kim (1979) stresses the importance of "accessibility" to communication channels. The degree of opportunity to associate with members of the host society is referred to as "interaction potential." Interaction potential is dependent on both physical proximity and the plasticity of the interpersonal communication environment. Plasticity of the environment is considered the degree to which differences in behavior, values, attitudes, and outward appearances are tolerated or accepted by members of the host society. In the case of the deaf person, integration by adapting to the "speaking world" might increase the chance to benefit from the favorable "interaction potential" of the environment. He can use the condition of physical proximity (in his job or neighborhood) to initiate and regulate oral communication. Moreover, in terms of "plasticity of the environment," oral interaction with the deaf might be tolerated more easily than communication by means of another mode. That is, if members of the wider community have to learn another medium, i.e., sign language before being able to communicate effectively with the deaf, the degree of plasticity will be very low. Integration of the deaf will then be restricted to the immediate environment, where caretakers are willing to use whatever means they have to maintain interaction with them.

Freedom of Choice and Equal Opportunity

Interaction between the deaf person and people in his environment (home or wider community) is necessary if we do not want him to be completely isolated. The deaf person must be educated in order to function optimally as a member of the society he lives in. Therefore, the requirements which have to be fulfilled in order for him to function adequately have to be anticipated and incorporated in the child's training. Moreover, education of the deaf child must be based on general principles that are associated with the democratic society in which he will live. The basic concepts of freedom and equality are important elements of our value system, which may differ from person to person dependent on the rank ordering of the values (Rokeach, 1968). The goals of education of the deaf may then be formulated in such a way that they reflect these basic values.

Emphasis on equal opportunity might force educators of the deaf to have as their goal deaf people who are well equipped to function according to their intellectual abilities and irrespective of their deafness. Training programs that are "handicap-fair" should provide the deaf child with the necessary skills in order for him to function according to his abilities. The ability to speak and to communicate orally will be part of this "handicap-fair" training. Performance of the child will then be measured as a function of the training and not as some ability that he should have. The consequence of this approach is, however, that equal opportunity will not automatically mean equal outcome. Oral language usage (speaking, lipreading) might not reach an acceptable level, despite the training. However, by stressing oral communication, the deaf person has the same opportunity as the nondeaf to become an integrated member of society.

The nature of the integration process should, however, be "interactive." That is, the society should develop a degree of "plasticity" which will enable hearing people to be "tuned well" in order to understand the speech of the deaf as well as to enable the deaf person to lipread them (direct face-to-face interaction). The amount of exposure the public has to "speech of the deaf" should be increased. Of course, this should be done in a well planned program with supporting information from family members of the deaf, teachers of the deaf, colleagues of the deaf, experts in audiology and psychology of hearing, communication specialists, linguists, psycholinguists, and sociolinguists. Mass media (radio and television) can be used to promote "speech of the deaf," so that society may become acquainted with both the intonation and the particular nature of the speech sounds (voice quality, articulatory features, coarticulatory features, archi-phonemic features, etc.). Understanding "speech of the deaf" must be considered a manner of understanding continuous speech that has specific characteristics. The correct attitude to listen to that speech as well as the willingness to take contextual information (situation, shared background knowledge, etc.) into account might be important contributing factors to understanding. In so doing, the stress on the part of the deaf to articulate better might decrease. Moreover, research with respect to "speech of the deaf" might not only be motivated by the need to correct this speech but also by the need to make their speech acceptable to the wider community. Educational goals based on equal opportunity might then be more "child-centered" (adaptation of society to the deaf child) instead of solely society-oriented (adaptation of the deaf child to society).

Freedom of choice may be considered a powerful value in any interactive relationship. The nature of the interaction might not be adopted solely from the point of view of assimilation. The deaf may choose a manner of interaction (fingerspelling, sign language) which does not include any form of oral control. The consequence that he may only communicate to a restricted group of people might not concern him much. In fact, the oral-manual controversy boils down to a difference between the willingness to communicate with anyone in society and the willingness to communicate very effectively with a restricted group of people.

The choice of the deaf person to communicate in a non-oral manner makes him dependent on people with an absolute command of a manual language. His social control by means of language will not affect users of oral language. Though this might be a disadvantage, it is assumed that the advantages outweigh this disadvantage. The arguments in favor of manual communication range from "failure in oral development" to "a more effective manner to express emotion" as well as a better opportunity for the cognitive development of the deaf child (Siger, 1978; Stokoe, 1978). That is to say, for people in favor of manual communication of the deaf, solving cognitive and emotional problems outweighs adaptation to social norms. (Stokoe, 1978). It remains, however, that these deaf persons can only improve communicative effectiveness if they are given a responsive environment. The use of mass media (television) to teach hearing people sign language might be considered a positive attempt to increase communication possibilities for the deaf person who is using sign language. But then it becomes questionable whether the wider community is willing to adapt to this requirement of the deaf.

Equal opportunity and freedom of choice are so important for human functioning that they have to be defined at all times. Promoting oral communication for the deaf should, therefore, be based on these basic values. By indicating to the deaf person how oral language might provide cognitive and emotional satisfaction in addition to social integration, one might give him the opportunity to choose freely whether or not he wants to learn and improve his ability to use the actual language of hearing people.

Conclusion

The sociological bases of oral education should be considered from the point of view of the functioning of the individual in society. Integration in society should be defined in terms of an interactive manner of communication/acculturation. Oral language usage may then vary in terms of speech as a function of social factors (status, role, age, sex, etc.) and opportunity for interaction (caretaker-child interaction and interaction potential of the environment). However, equal opportunity for the deaf child in society has to be supplemented by freedom of choice in order to enable him to determine his own way of life.

Summary

The sociological bases of oral education have been discussed in terms of an interactive manner of social control. These have been considered with respect to the use of oral language in the relationship between the deaf child and his caretakers as well as in the relationship between the deaf person and the wider community: integration in the home and integration in society, respectively. Integration in the home has been viewed in terms of stimulating the communication intention of the child by presenting the correct formulas for speaking and by adjusting the complexity of the linguistic input. We have regarded the notion "integration in society" from the point of view of an interactive relationship between the person and the wider community. This does not mean, however, that we stress "only the world of hearing and speaking people" into which the deaf must integrate. On the contrary, we are suggesting that the degree to which the deaf assimilate to the requirements of the wider community has to be considered from a functional point of view. The degree of integration should be based on the interrelationship between intrapersonal, interpersonal, and environmental factors. Differences between deaf people with respect to their success to integrate should, therefore, be described in terms of these interactional relationships. Assimilation as complete adaptation must be rejected in favor of an interactive process of communication acculturation. The nature of this interactive process cannot be determined in advance. The deaf person himself must have the freedom to choose among alternative manners of interaction. Though oral communication might be considered the most favorable manner, the notion of freedom of choice might force one to give the deaf person the opportunity to reject oral communication in favor of another mode of interaction. But then one should be prepared to accept the minority status of the deaf.

References

Altshuler, K. Z. Towards a psychology of deafness? *Journal of Communication Disorders*, 1978, 11, 159–169.
Austin, J. L. *How to do things with words*. Oxford: Clarendon Press, 1962.

Bartlett, F. C. *Remembering: An experimental and social study*. Cambridge: Cambridge University Press, 1932.
Bates, E. *Language and context: The acquisition of pragmatics*. New York: Academic Press, 1976.
Beinstein, J. Friends, the media and opinion formation. *Journal of Communication*, 1977, 27 (4), 30–39.
Blount, B. G. Ethnography and caretaker-child interactions. In C. Snow & C. A. Ferguson (Eds.), *Talking to children*. Cambridge: Cambridge University Press, 1977.
Broomfield, A. M. Guidance to parents of deaf children, a perspective. *British Journal of Disorders of Communication*, 1967, 112–123.
Chance, N. A. Acculturation, self-identification and personality adjustment, *American Anthropologist*, 1965, 67, 373–393.
Corder-Bolz, Ch. R. & O'Bryant, S. Teacher vs. program. *Journal of Communication*, 1978, 28 (1), 97–103.
Cross, T. G. Mother's speech adjustments: the contribution of selected child listener variables. In C. Snow & A. Ferguson (Eds.), *Talking to children*, Cambridge: Cambridge University Press, 1977.
Drabman, R. S., & Thomas, M. H. Children's imitation of aggressive and personal behavior when viewing and in pairs. *Journal of Communication*, 1977, 27, (3), 199–205.
Gordon, M. M. *Assimilation in American life*. New York: Oxford University Press, 1964.
Grimshaw, A. D. A sociologist's point of view. In C. Snow & A. Ferguson (Eds.), *Talking to children*. Cambridge: Cambridge University Press, 1977.
Hymes, D. Ways of speaking. In R. Bauman & J. Sherzer (Eds.), *Explorations in the ethnography of speaking*. Cambridge: Cambridge University Press, 1974.
Kasher, A. What is a theory of use? *Journal of Pragmatics*, 1977, 1 (2), 105–120.
Kim, Y. Y. Toward an interactive theory of communication-acculturation. Paper presented at annual convention of the International Communication Association, Philadelphia, May, 1979.
Kuyper, B. J. A frame for frames: Representing knowledge for recognition. In D. G. Bowbrow & A. Collins (Eds.), *Representation and understanding: Studies in cognitive science*. New York: Academic Press, 1975.
Labov, W. The study of language in its social context. In J. Fisherman (Ed.), *Advances in the sociology of languge I*, The Hague: Mouton, 1971.
Liebert, R. M., & Neale, J. M. *The early window: Effects of television on children and youth*. New York: Pergamon Press, 1973.
Mead, G. H. Thought, communication and the significant symbol. In C. Morris (Ed.), *Mind, self and society*. Chicago: The University of Chicago Press, 1934.
Murray, J. P., & Kippax, S. Children's social behavior in three towns with different television experience. *Journal of Communication*, Winter 1978, 19–29.
Olson, D. R. Oral and written language and the cognitive processes of children. *Journal of Communication*, Summer, 1977.
Rokeach, M. *Beliefs, attitudes and values*. San Francisco: Jossey-Bass, 1968.
Rumelhart, D. E. Notes on a schema for stories. In D. G. Bowbrow & A. M. Collins (Eds.), *Representation and understanding: Studies in cognitive science*. New York: Academic Press, 1975.
Scott, M. D., McCroskey, J., & Sheahan, M. E. Measuring communication apprehension. *Journal of Communication*, Winter 1978, 104–111.
Siger, L. P. That deaf child and you: A forensic approach to the problem of hearing and speech. *Journal of Communication Disorders*, 1978, 2, 149–158.
Stokoe, W. C. Sign codes and sign language: Two orders of communication. *Journal of Communication Disorders*, 1978, 2, 187–192.
Tan, A. S., & Tan, G. Television use and self esteem of blacks. *Journal of Communication*, Winter 1979, 29, (1), 129–135.

Vogel, E. F., & Bell, N. W. The emotional disturbed child as the family scapegoat. In N. W. Bell & E. F. Vogel (Eds.), *A modern introduction to the family.* London: Routledge and Kegan Paul, 1961.
Winograd, T. Frame representations and the declarative-procedural controversy. In D. G. Bowbrow & A. Collins (Eds.), *Representation and understanding: Studies in cognitive science.* New York: Academic Press, 1975.
Wold, A. H. *Decoding oral language.* London: Academic Press, 1978.

reaction to 4

jean a.m. persoon

The interesting paper of Mr. Campbell lends itself to several discussion points. Being a sociologist myself I chose some topics that are in my opinion relevant from a sociological point of view.

In the first part of his paper Mr. Campbell gives a developmental view on language formation in young children. He stresses the importance of the family members and of "significant others" in the proximity of the child.

My first question would be: as language is typically a social class-bound variable, in what way is it important to take into account the social-cultural milieu of the origin of the deaf child?

For instance, how do possibilities, facilities, potentialities, willingness differ in families of different social class backgrounds? Would it not be preferable to use sociocultural variables in distinguishing between families of origin instead of socioeconomic variables? I think of educational attitudes and values in families, of the emotional and affective atmosphere, of their values concerning their place in society.

In the second part of his paper Mr. Campbell deals with the integration of deaf persons in the family and in the society. He writes about the importance of the plasticity of the environment. After Kim he says, and I quote, "Plasticity of the environment is considered the degree to which differences in behaviour, values, attitudes and outward appearances are tolerated or accepted by members of the host society."

I think that here we have to do with what is called in sociological theory labeling processes, stigmata, stereotypes in and by society.

There is a good example of research done by Lautmann a.o. (1972) in West Germany some years ago about existing stereotypes and labeling processes among the population with regard to *blind* people. The results are depressing: blind people are reduced people, not of full value; you have to be careful in interaction with them, they are aggressive, unpredictable in behavior, you soon get too much involved with them emotionally, their personality structure is not like that of "normal" people, there is a clearly felt social distance, there are barriers in communication; and on top of all that: knowing a blind person that does not meet those characteristics, makes her/him the exception to the rule. The stigma is fortified or corroborated. I wonder what stereotypes there are about deaf people. The danger of these stereotypes is that people orient their behavior to them and that the self-fulfilling prophecy becomes operative and effective.

Reactions to stigmata are not cognitive but emotional, affective, and evaluative. If people think it is difficult to communicate with deaf persons they will avoid them, and in that way make it difficult to communicate.

Several authors (Rogers a.o., 1975) have tried to analyze the modes of adaptation to a deviant label on the basis of individual and societal reactions. On the one hand the deviant individual can react with assent, with rejection, with exchange. On the other hand, society can react with magnification, manipulation, obliteration. It would lead us too far at the moment to work this out. I'd like to ask Mr. Campbell what is being done by mass media, by the government, by other agencies to help integration of deaf persons in society.

I understand from the paper that the author sees the possibility of more or less full integration of the deaf person in the wider society if she/he chooses for oral communication. Further on the author stresses that there should be a freedom of choice for the deaf person concerning alternative manners of interaction. Apart from the impossibility, in my view, for young children to choose, I don't see clearly what factors might induce a deaf person to prefer integration in a restricted group of people (and so prefer minority status as the author says) to integration in the wider community. Could it be that here again the plasticity or the lack of plasticity of the wider environment is the most relevant factor?

The author writes about deaf people as a minority *group*. I'd prefer a minority *category* instead of group. As far as I know it's not a minority group with its own subculture, like for instance the South Moluccans in the Netherlands, but a social category with a common characteristic, like, for instance, people in wheelchairs or people with red hair. In my opinion it's important to make this distinction.

There are different strategies one has to follow for becoming integrated in society if one has to do either with a strongly organized *subculture* with its own identity or with individuals characterized by a specific feature. There are more interesting points for discussion in the paper of Mr. Campbell, but, so far, these are my comments for the moment, Mr. Chairman.

References

Lautmann, a.o. Zur struktur von Stigma: das Bild der Blinden und Unehelichen, Kölner Zeitschrift für Soziologie und Sozial Psychologie, 1972, 83–100.

Rogers, J. a.o. Fighting back: Nine modes of adaptation to a deviant label. *Social Problems*, 22, 1975, 101–118.

part II

the state of the art

5

a survey of the present status of methods in english speaking countries
for the development of receptive and expressive oral skills

daniel ling

There are numerous methods of developing receptive and expressive oral skills in children who are hearing impaired. Factors that exert most influence upon the choice of methods include hearing levels, age, language attainments, educational placement, and the philosophy and skills of teachers and parents. These factors interact with each other and with each child's aptitudes and abilities. Such interactions have led to a complex range of treatments and outcomes.

In the following pages the writer will briefly outline some of the major strategies and program components affecting the acquisition of speech perception and speech production skills. Limitations of time and length preclude detailed examination of the various interactions mentioned above. The principal focus of this paper will therefore be mainly upon oral skills in relation to hearing levels and relevant practice and research.

If our current methods of developing oral communication were truly effective, our efforts with totally deaf and profoundly hearing-impaired children would be as successful as those with hard of hearing youngsters. In general, they are not. The one consistent finding in relation to hearing-impaired children is that, other things being equal, those with most residual audition tend to achieve the best speech reception skills, the highest levels of language development, and the most intelligible speech (Ling, 1976; Markides, 1970; Stark, 1974 among many others). Such studies indicate that the eye and the skin, as they have been generally exploited to date, are less effective than the ear for learning oral communication skills (Ross & Giolas, 1978). Two major guidelines are suggested by such data: the first, is that whatever residual audition is present must be exploited to the fullest possible extent (Ling, 1964); and the second, that more effective strategies for using the visual and tactile channels must be formulated for helping those children who have little or no useful residual hearing (Pickett & Risberg, in preparation).

Speech Reception

Over the past few decades, attempts to use residual audition have been abetted by advances in technology. These advances had led to the widespread availability of small, personal hearing aids and improved audiological assessment. It is now evident that, for the most part, hearing aids can, under favorable listening conditions, compensate well, if not fully, for mild to moderate hearing impairment. It is also evident that children with severe hearing impairment (average levels of 70-90 dB (ISO), must supplement the acoustic signal by speechreading if they are to achieve adequate speech reception in everyday communication situations. Profoundly hearing impaired children, those with hearing levels greater than 90 dB (ISO), vary enormously in their ability to receive speech through audition (see Erber, 1979, for a review). Under most circumstances audition serves children only as a supplement to speechreading. This is particularly true for children whose residual audition is limited principally or entirely to the low-frequency range. Although few in number, there are children who are totally deaf. Such children respond to vibration rather than audition when fitted with powerful hearing aids (Risberg & Mártony, 1972).

In general, binaural rather than monaural hearing aid fittings are preferable (Markides, 1977). This is true for any level of hearing impairment. Binaural hearing usually results in advantages due to loudness summation, noise rejection, and localization. However, not all children, even those with similar hearing levels, can process speech better with two hearing aids than with one. Such exceptions are, however, relatively rare. Thus the most acceptable procedure is to fit two hearing aids unless or until it can be shown that monaural listening yields superior performance (Ross, 1977).

Auditory Training and Experience

Speech reception involves four levels of processing: detection, discrimination, identification, and comprehension of the speech signal. In providing auditory training and experience for hearing impaired children, attention has to be given to all four aspects. Detection of sound is, of course, a prerequisite for the three higher level processes. Unfortunately, hearing aid selection procedures have not, so far, led to a situation in which all or even most severely and profoundly hearing-impaired children can detect the range of sounds that should be available to them. Thus many children who have hearing for 2000 Hz at, say, 110 dB are not fitted with aids that give sufficient gain for them to detect /ʃ/ or the second formant transitions of the front vowels which carry a heavy load of information. Similarly, many children with hearing levels of 90 dB at 4000 Hz may be fitted with hearing aids that do not allow them to detect /s/, which is an important grammatical morpheme. Such weaknesses in fitting can be identified by simple checks such as the five-sound test described by the writer (Ling & Ling, 1978). Increasing awareness of the importance of speech detection to spoken language development is essential if the effective use of individual hearing aids is to become widespread.

The traditional approach to auditory training featured discrimination of speech and non-speech stimuli. Until recently, it was commonly believed that progressive training should begin with grossly different nonverbal sounds such as bells, drums, and whistles and move to increasingly finer speech sound discrimination; for example, the differentiation of minimally different words such as *pat* and *bat* or *tin* and *sin*. Currently, much less emphasis is placed on such exercises. Attention is now more frequently seen to be upon comprehension. This shift reflects the view that, given adequate detection and extensive experience in the comprehension of meaningful discourse, auditory discrimination and identification skills may develop spontaneously (Ling, 1978). Discrimination training is not necessarily neglected in this type of approach. It is provided if the teacher realizes that a child does not, after extensive experience, spontaneously learn to discriminate sound patterns, some essential components of which are within his or her auditory range. As expressed by Fry (1978), this approach is based on the notions that children go from meaning to perception rather than vice versa and that to do so, they will, if necessary, learn to use acoustic cues that may not usually be employed by normally hearing listeners.

The approach outlined above is applied in different ways in different programs. In most, it involves multisensory teaching. In some, careful attention is given to the utmost use of residual audition. In others, hearing aids are worn but the teachers are not concerned with whether the child uses hearing or speechreading. In a few programs investigated by independent researchers, such lack of concern has led to the finding that up to half of the hearing aids worn by the children are inadequate because they have not been well selected or cared for (Gaeth & Lauansbury, 1966; Zink, 1972).

The finding that children were not necessarily developing their use of residual hearing in multisensory programs and not learning to receive and produce acceptable oral language, recently led Hoversten and her colleagues to develop an auditory skills curriculum (Office of the Los Angeles County Superintendent of Schools, 1979). It consists of numerous terminal performance objectives (TPOs) and intermediate performance objects (progressive steps of IPOs) in four parallel aspects of auditory processing: discrimination, memory sequencing, auditory feedback, and figure-ground. The outcome of using such a curriculum has not yet been reported. It is of interest to speculate why personnel responsible for some programs consider that there is a need for them to utilize this more structured approach. The commonly heard suggestion is that teachers in multisensory programs that are failing to develop auditory skills are inadequately trained to deal with hearing aids, teach oral language skills, or organize their work without the types of guidelines such a curriculum provides. The corollary of this suggestion is that, given more highly trained teachers, an auditory-global approach (cf. Calvert & Silverman, 1975) will develop auditory skills and develop them to an effective level. The problem is, however, that criteria for measuring program effectiveness have not yet been formulated, and the form and content of programs that are claimed to be successful have not yet been described in sufficient detail for their replication to be attempted. In the absence of evidence, it has been suggested that severely and profoundly hearing-impaired children need more extensive and intensive auditory experience than a multisensory approach can provide; that an auditory-oral approach would be preferable.

An auditory-oral approach to the teaching of severely and profoundly hearing-impaired children, as an alternative to a multisensory approach, has been advocated by numerous writers including Pollack (1970), Wedenberg (1951), and Whetnall and Fry (1971). Their view is that unless some training through audition alone is provided, children's attention to the visual patterns of speech will detract from their use of audition. This view may often be carelessly overstated or misinterpreted. No informed worker would suggest that such children's speechreading should be suppressed outside training sessions, since it is well established that, under most conditions, using audition and vision together yield performance that is superior to that achieved with either modality alone. Indeed, it is the expressed view of those who advocate an auditory-oral approach that children trained for part of their therapy through hearing alone will be better able to function in everyday situations involving the combined use of the two modalities than those who have been taught through the more traditional multisensory strategies.

The majority of oral programs do not suppress speechreading consistently during training in order to develop the use of residual hearing. They might therefore be better described as *multisensory-oral* than as *auditory-oral* even if some do emphasize the use of hearing aids at all times. But is this splitting hairs? Is a distinction between the two types of programs meaningful? Do they produce different results with the same or similar children? There is some evidence that they do. In numerous experiments undertaken by the writer, children who were trained for some years in multisensory programs learned to make new auditory discriminations when they were later trained through hearing alone (Ling, 1968; Ling & Maretic, 1971; Doehring & Ling, 1971). In a more recent study coordinated by the writer (in preparation), the reception of nonsense syllables was tested under three conditions: audition alone, speechreading alone, and audition-plus-speechreading. Subjects were 24 children aged from 9 to 16 years, all profoundly deaf from birth, who were drawn from three programs in which some training through hearing alone had been provided from early infancy over a period of several years. Their average hearing levels in the better ear ranged from 90 to 116 dB. Their mean scores for audition-plus-speechreading were 20 percent better than their mean scores for speechreading alone. Individual differences between the two scores ranged from -6 percent for a child with average hearing levels (500-2000 Hz) of 90 dB to +57 percent for a child with the same average hearing levels. Erber (1972) reported no such gains for nonsense syllable reception by profoundly hearing impaired children trained in a traditional (multisensory) program that is widely recognized as being of excellent quality. Sufficient variables cannot, however, be taken into account to be sure that the training procedures were responsible for these contrasting results.

Analysis of our data on nonsense syllable reception by children taught in auditory-oral programs is not complete. However, these preliminary findings show that most subjects made use of spectral cues in speech reception. Such gains cannot be made through interpretation of the time-intensity envelope alone (see Erber, 1979). Only four of the 24 subjects made less than a 10 percent gain when audition was added to speechreading; and one of these, as reported above, scored 6 percent less when two modalities were employed rather than one (vision alone). There is little doubt that these four were unable to use spectral information. They were not, however, the children with the poorest hearing levels, a point which will be discussed later in relation to selection of strategies and programs.

Studies involving the discrimination or identification of words in isolation and words in low-and high-predictability sentence contexts by children trained in auditory-oral programs have not yet been published. On the basis of our findings for nonsense syllable reception one might predict that they would be even better at word and sentence reception. This prediction is based on an extrapolation of Erber's (1979) review of seven word recognition studies in which gains of 1 to 15 percent were reported when audition was added to speechreading.

The obvious danger in limiting studies to syllable and word stimuli is that one is not tapping the extent to which audition can be used as a means of exploiting suprasegmental information in the comprehension of discourse. Sentence and multisentence materials are required for such measures. It cannot be assumed that scores on syllables or words can be used to predict how well children trained in any type of program will process running speech (Nicholls, 1979). Since our ultimate interest is in how well children can perceive spoken language in communication, more attention must be given not only to the reception of linguistic elements but to the parallel processing of all levels of material in both the single and multiple channels available to severely and profoundly hearing-impaired children.

Speechreading and Speechreading Aids

Speechreading by itself is a relatively weak channel for learning oral skills. Its many ambiguous or invisible elements make it so. The nature of the speechreading task will not be discussed here since it has been exhaustively documented by others (see Berger, 1972, Erber, 1979). The extent to which speechreading can contribute to the acquisition of oral skills is, however, central to the present discussion. Syllable reception is inevitably limited to about a 30 percent level by the nature of the task. About the same level of reception for sentences on the Utley test has been found by Clouser (1977). Hardick, Oyer, and Irion (1970) and Binnie (1974) have reported that their subjects received only from 5 to 7 percent of discourse materials. Some oral deaf adults who are highly skilled speechreaders can understand conversation and process visually presented discourse at much higher levels. Stoker (in preparation) found that 26 such subjects achieved scores for sentence materials ranging from 14 to 100 percent (mean 55 percent). Mean levels such as this, which are far from efficient, can never be attained by children who are in the early stages of learning language. For them, a supplement to speechreading is essential if they are to learn how to communicate orally (Ling & Ling, 1978).

The most common supplement to speechreading is audition. Increments in performance when profoundly hearing impaired children add audition were discussed in the previous section. The data presented show that those who have developed auditory processing skills will lose at least 20 percent information if their hearing aids become nonfunctional due to breakdown, inappropriate new fitting, or adverse noise conditions. Those who are severely rather than profoundly hearing impaired are usually able to supplement speechreading more effectively but can be left without an effective supplement if attention is not paid to the conditions under which hearing aids are worn. Without hearing aids they have to function as if they were totally deaf. Audition is clearly of no benefit to those children who are in fact totally deaf. For them, some other supplement, either tactile or visual, is required. Tactile aids have not yet been developed to the point where they provide a substantial amount of information in discourse (Sparks, Ardell, Bourgeois, Weidman, & Kuhl, 1979).

The traditional visual aid to speechreading has been the use of the written form. Most children taught in traditional oral programs have, in fact, learned the language that they use through reading as much if not more than through speechreading. Recently there has been a trend to postpone the introduction of reading until language has been developed through oral interaction (Hart, 1978; Ling & Ling, 1978; van Uden, 1977). The trend is not universal and tends to be followed strictly only in auditory-oral programs.

Many engineers have attempted to produce electronic devices that can be used to supplement speechreading in the teaching of speech (Pickett & Risberg, in preparation) but, so far, none of these has been shown to assist substantially in the task. Furthermore, no visual device has yet been produced that will serve as a communication aid, an instrument that, like the hearing aid, can be worn and used by the wearer to differentiate the visual signals in conversational speech. The only portable visual device produced to date, the eyeglass aid designed by Upton (1968), has not yielded benefit to children.

The visual supplement that has so far proven to be the most effective lipreading aid is the system known as Cued Speech, which was formulated by Cornett (1967). The system requires a speaker to use four hand positions to differentiate vowels and eight hand configurations to differentiate consonants that look alike on the lips. The system permits the cues for consonants and vowels to be produced in such a way that they can be presented in synchrony with the coarticulated patterns of speech. Studies by Ling and Clarke (1975) and by Clarke and Ling (1976), in Canada, provided evidence that children who had made little use of audition and had failed in multisensory-oral programs could benefit from its use. These studies were followed up by Nicholls (1979), in Australia, who obtained evidence that the system was highly effective as a means of speech reception.

Nicholls (1979) presented syllable materials and words in low- and high-predictability sentence contexts under seven conditions: Audition (A), Lipreading (L), Audition-plus-lipreading (AL), Cues alone (C), Audition-plus-cues

(AC), Lipreading-plus-cues (LC), and Audition-plus-lipreading plus cues (ALC). Her subjects were 18 children who had been taught by Cued Speech for at least four years. They were all profoundly hearing impaired with average hearing levels in the better ear ranging from 97-122 dB (ISO). The mean scores obtained under each condition are shown in Figure 1. As one would predict, scores for words in sentences were generally higher than for syllables. The lipreading (speechreading) scores and the audition-plus-lipreading scores were comparable to those reported elsewhere in the literature. The AC scores, compared with the C scores, show that these children, though trained on a predominantly visual system, could use their residual audition effectively. The LC and ALC scores were much higher than have ever been reported for speech reception by profoundly hearing-impaired children. These scores correlated highly with the children's language development which was exceptionally good.

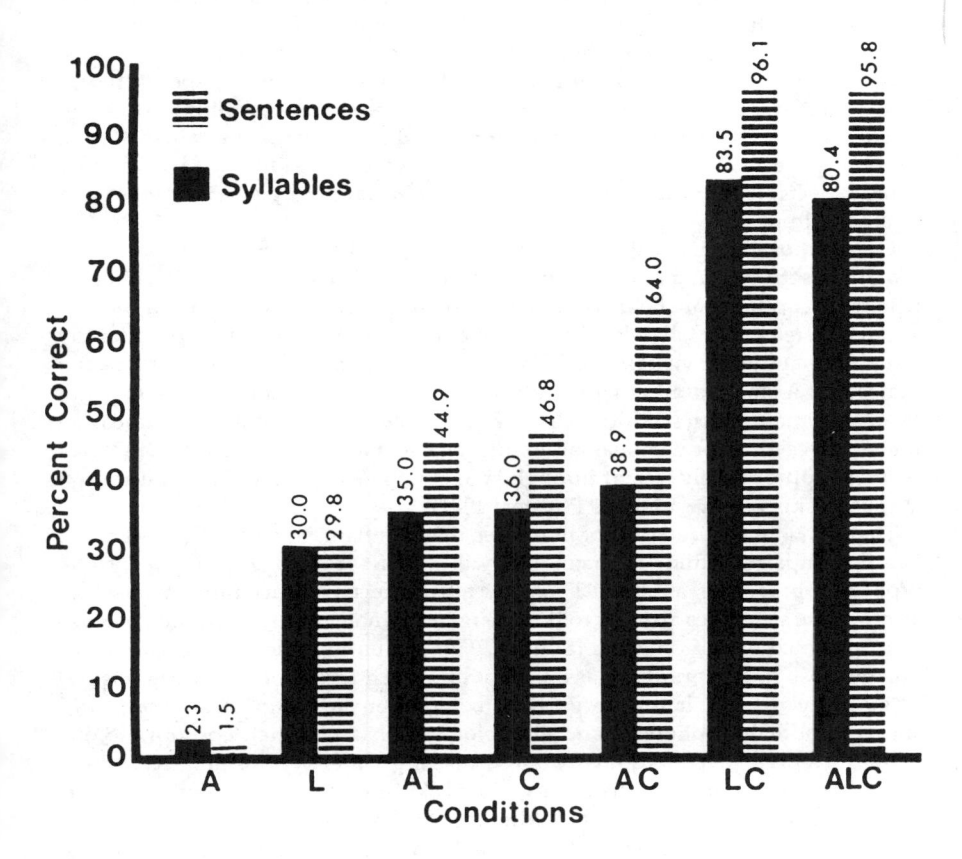

FIGURE 1.
Mean scores for syllables and key words in sentences obtained by 18 profoundly hearing-impaired children under seven conditions of presentation.

Selection of Oral Strategies and Programs

The common complaint, in all English-speaking societies, is that adequate oral skills are not acquired by many children in oral programs. Such a complaint, the essential truth of which cannot be denied, begs two questions: "What are adequate oral skills?" and "How does one define an oral program?" In this section the writer will discuss both questions and offer guidelines for evaluation of children that might lead to less frequent (and justified) charges of failure. His purpose in doing so is to focus attention on the need for individualized educational planning and a re-examination of goals that should be set by those who advocate oral education.

The oral skills acquired by hearing-impaired children should permit them to develop as happy, well adjusted individuals, to interact and learn through speech communication during their school life, and to understand and express themselves with relative ease through spoken language in most, if not all, social situations as adults. Adequacy in oral communication certainly demands no less. The three component aspects of speech communication are speech reception, linguistic competence, and speech production. Since children differ in hearing levels, as well as in many other ways, different strategies and different programs are required if they are to achieve adequate skills in each of these three aspects. It is evident that no one approach can possibly satisfy the needs of all children.

One cannot exploit audition in a child who is totally deaf. Some children have too little useful hearing to benefit from auditory-oral teaching. Certain children, fitted with appropriate hearing aids, may acquire adequate oral skills if parents and teachers simply talk with them often enough. Others may require carefully structured auditory, visual, speech and/or language training in order to master oral skills. A small number with additional handicaps of a certain type may not be able to make sufficient progress to achieve the levels of oral communication that are necessary for personal, academic, and social growth. Such children may be more appropriately taught through sign language or even fail to acquire sign language skills (Ling, Ling, & Pflaster, 1977).

There is no measure or set of measures that can be used to predict whether a hearing-impaired child, at diagnosis, will benefit from being taught by one type of approach or another. Thus the most effective procedure in selecting appropriate strategies appears to be through pragmatic assessment, i.e., evaluation in the course of ongoing training. The evaluation measures required for this purpose must permit the assessment of speech reception (auditory, visual, or auditory visual), language growth (comprehension and production), and speech production (phonetic and phonologic skills and, when appropriate, intelligibility). At present, some of these measures are well formulated; others depend almost entirely on the observational skills of the teacher/clinician (Ling, 1979). When one can show that children are making rapid progress in all three aspects, one can be satisfied that all variables affecting progress are sufficiently well in hand. When evaluation of any one of the aspects shows that a child is making slow progress, or none, then one must seek the cause among variables that are intrinsic to the child (hearing, vision, autism, dysarthria, etc.) or extrinsic to him or her (parental care, hearing aid fitting, quantity, quality, and/or type of stimulation, teacher/clinician competence, etc.). If one can thus identify obstacles to progress that are extrinsic to the child one can usually do much to overcome them. If the obstacle to progress is intrinsic to the child, then a program change is called for. Such a change may be relatively minor, as in the introduction of more structured material, or increasing the emphasis placed on audition, speechreading, or speech production. Alternatively, the results of evaluation may be seen as demanding that the child is taught not through an auditory-oral or multisensory-oral approach but through a visual-oral system such as Cued Speech.

The ongoing evaluation of the effectiveness of various strategies and programs must, of course, be a feature of provision for children of all age levels. The design and implementation of evaluation techniques is, without doubt, one of the most vitally important tasks facing oral educators. Failure to evaluate and/or to act upon the results of evaluation can be considered as the main reason why some children languish in programs without learning adequate oral skills. To ensure that evaluations are generally implemented is no mean challenge. To realize such a goal would require the design of better and more extensive evaluation procedures, and improvements in the training of teacher/clinicians and support personnel.

With widespread evaluation the strengths and the weaknesses of oral programs can be pinpointed. Only through more widespread evaluation can the complex of strategies that lead to success be better identified and taught to future teacher/clinicians and the features of provision that either do not permit optimal achievement or adversely affect children's progress be specified and eradicated. The philosophy of oral education has been and is being strongly challenged. We must specify the goals of oral education and the variety of oral programs that can be recognized as such more precisely. Programs that are labeled "oral" merely because children in them are not taught to sign cannot be allowed to go unchallenged. The effectiveness of any challenge to such programs or to those who advocate alternative modes of communication for all hearing-impaired children will depend upon demonstrable standards achieved by both the challenger and those who are challenged.

Speech Production

The speech production capabilities of hearing-impaired children, like their speech reception skills, tend to vary in relation to their degree of hearing impairment. Those who have the poorest speech tend to be those with the worst hearing levels (Markides, 1970). Up to 1975, standards of speech production had not, in general, improved among profoundly hearing-impaired children attending schools for the deaf over the past 40 years and the types of speech errors produced by such children now appear to be similar to those recorded by workers several decades ago (Nickerson, 1975). In a recent survey, Jensema, Karchmer, and Trybus (1978) found that speech skills did not improve significantly with age among children attending special schools across the U.S.A.

The findings reported above reflect an overall lack of concern with speech and the low priority generally given to speech production skills in schools rather than an intrinsic inability to learn to speak that could be attributed to deafness.

This is shown by isolated reports of profoundly hearing impaired children who can speak intelligibly. For example, in a program described by Young (1978), substantial progress was consistently made over a period of years. In a more recent paper, the writer described a follow-up study of seven of the nine profoundly hearing impaired children trained in a parent-infant program at McGill University for a period of at least three years. Their speech was not significantly less intelligible than that of their randomly selected normally hearing peers (Ling & Milne, 1979).

There has been widespread interest in the systems of speech development proposed by Calvert and Silverman (1975) and by the writer (Ling, 1976). A considerable number of research projects on speech have been implemented as a result of their publication. Implicit in the Calvert and Silverman text, and explicit in the writer's, is the notion that, in order for children to produce speech patterns in communicative (phonologic level) speech, children must first have the neuromuscular coordination to produce them. To provide such coordination, it is proposed that the orosensory-motor patterns which underlie the controlled production of speech should be established by evoking and differentiating voice, vowels and consonants in syllables at a phonetic (nonmeaningful) level. The process is akin to that followed by the normal child in babbling before speaking. The notion is not new. It was, indeed, compared by Schaffer (1942) with teaching only at a phonologic level and was found to be a superior strategy. Current studies (reported above) also indicate that it can be highly successful. Such findings are not surprising when one considers that speech is not only a rule-governed part of our language system but an activity based upon complex motor skills.

It is unfortunately common for both research workers and teacher/clinicians to emphasize one aspect of speech production (phonetic or phonologic) without sufficient regard to the other and not to read, or to ignore, the literature in order to pursue a line of thinking without undue hindrance. An example of this widespread trend to shut out fact and/or set up a straw man is provided by Moore (1979, p. 115), who has recently stated that "the teaching of speech to hearing-impaired children, has, up to now, concentrated almost exclusively on phonetic level skills, overlooking the value of an approach which recognizes an abstract level of phonology." Such statements indicate that the works of Calvert and Silverman (1975), Ewing and Ewing (1964), Haycock (1933), Ling (1976) and Vorce (1974), to mention but a few, have either not been read or not understood and general practice not observed. The purpose of speech teaching is not to evoke isolated syllables, but to permit children to communicate in words, phrases, sentences, and discourse as the occasion demands. It has never been other.

One of the main problems in teaching is to ensure that skills taught in one situation will be generalized to others. This is true in teaching speech reception, language, or speech production. A formidable effort has to be made to ensure that one aspect of oral skill is not taught in isolation. To encourage such effort, the writer has suggested ways in which speech patterns can be linked to the semantic, syntatic, and pragmatic aspects of language (Ling, 1979). Such links should help both speech and language development, in that accurate oral expression should enhance both.

Speech is not only a means of expression, it also provides a mechanism for subvocal rehearsal in memory, and an aid in speech reception. In a recent study at McGill University, 14 profoundly hearing impaired children (7 pairs) were trained on a range of phonetic level patterns. One of each pair was taught to say them and was incidentally provided with the auditory pattern in the course of the task: the other member of the pair was encouraged to share in the process by listening and watching and by making auditory discriminations involving the patterns taught (but not speaking). Both members of the pairs made significant gains in auditory discrimination over the course of training, but those who were taught to produce the patterns made the most (Novelli-Olmstead, 1979).

Speech acquisition skills are easier to measure than either speech reception or language development. This is because speech is an overt behavior. Consensus has not, however, been reached on evaluation. Phonetic level skills can be observed in young infants and evoked through imitation in older children. Four aspects of production must be assessed: accuracy, speed, economy of effort, and flexibility, or contextual variation. These four aspects are common to all motor skills (Johnson, 1961). Phonologic level evaluation and intelligibility rating are complex and time consuming. The writer suggests that it is best to base them upon a sample of at least 100 utterances, material that can also be used for language assessment. Alternatives to this have been suggested. For example, Monsen (1979) has devised a set of materials which contains sentences that can be differentiated only if the child produces minimal pairs such as "bit/beet," and "ship/sheep" sufficiently well. Such a test has the disadvantage that the phonemes involved may not be produced correctly or consistently by the child in everyday speech and it therefore lacks some face validity. Its great advantage is that it does not require the listener to have a background of phonetics.

Concluding Remarks

This survey has examined some of the methods employed in developing receptive and expressive oral skills among severely and profoundly hearing-impaired children in English-speaking countries. Readers interested in more detailed descriptions of programs are referred to Oyer (1976). The writer has limited the survey to current practice (which is often of poor quality) and the results of research studies which indicate that deafness is not an insuperable barrier to speech reception and speech production. More detailed information, which is excluded due to restrictions of time and length, is available from the references quoted.

The reader is reminded that language is more important than speech, but that the development of one should only serve to enhance the development of the other in a truly interactive oral program.

It is with some concern that the writer consented to submit a limited paper on this topic. Taking into account the interactions of receptive and expressive oral skills not only with language but with hearing levels, age, attainments, educational setting and the philosophy of parents and teachers, it can be seen that the subject matter deserves at least one book rather than a brief essay. This is particularly true if the issues involved are to be treated in sufficient depth.

References

Berger, K.W. *Speechreading: Principles and methods.* Baltimore, MD: National Educational Press, 1972.

Binnie, C.A. Auditory-visual intelligibility of various speech materials presented in three noise backgrounds. *Scan. Audiol. Suppl.,* 1974, 4, 255–281.

Calvert, D.R., & Silverman, S.R. *Speech and deafness.* Washington, DC: A.G. Bell Association for the Deaf, 1975.

Clarke, B.R., & Ling, D. The effects of using cued speech: A follow-up study. *Volta Review,* 1976, 78, 23–24.

Clouser, R.A. Relative phoneme visibility and lipreading performance. *Volta Review,* 1977, 79, 27–34.

Cornett, R.O. Cued speech. *American Annals of the Deaf,* 1967, 112, 3–13.

Doehring, D.G., & Ling, D. Programmed instruction of hearing-impaired children in the auditory discrimination of vowels. *Journal of Speech and Hearing Research,* 1971, 14, 746–754.

Erber, N.P. Auditory, visual and auditory-visual recognition of consonants by children with normal and impaired hearing. *Journal of Speech and Hearing Research,* 1972, 15, 413–422.

Erber, N.P. Speech perception by profoundly hearing-impaired children. *Journal of Speech and Hearing Disorders,* 1979, 44, 255–270.

Ewing, A.W.G., & Ewing, E.C. *Teaching deaf children to talk.* Manchester: Manchester University Press, 1964.

Fry, D.B. The role and primacy of the auditory channel in speech and language development. In M. Ross & T.G. Giolas (Eds.), *Auditory management of hearing-impaired children.* Baltimore, MD: University Park Press, 1978.

Gaeth, J.H., & Lounsbury, E. Hearing aids and children in elementary schools. *Journal of Speech and Hearing Disorders,* 1966, 31, 283–289.

Hardick, E.J., Oyer, H.J., & Irion, P.E. Lipreading performance as related to measurements of vision. *Journal of Speech and Hearing Research,* 1970, 13, 92–100.

Hart, B.O. *Teaching reading to deaf children* (Rev. ed.) Washington, DC: The A.G. Bell Association for the Deaf, 1978.

Haycock, G.S. *The teaching of speech.* Washington, DC: Volta Bureau, 1933.

Jensema, C.J., Karchmer, M.A., & Trybus, R.J. The rated speech intelligibility of hearing-impaired children: Basic relationships and a detailed analysis. Washington, DC: Gallaudet College, Office of Demographic Studies, 1978.

Johnson, H.W. Skill = Speech × accuracy × form × adaptability. *Perceptual Motor Skills,* 1961, 13, 163–170.

Ling, D. An auditory approach to the education of deaf children. *Audecibel,* 1964, 13, 96–101.

Ling, D. Three experiments on frequency transposition. *American Annals of the Deaf,* 1968, 113, 283–294.

Ling, D. *Speech and the hearing-impaired child: Theory and practice.* Washington, DC: A.G. Bell Association for the Deaf, 1976.

Ling, D. Auditory coding and re-coding. In M. Ross & T.G. Giolas (Eds.), *Auditory management of hearing-impaired children.* Baltimore, MD: University Park Press, 1978.

Ling, D. Integration of diagnostic information: Implications for speech training in school aged children. In J. Subtelny (Ed.), *Speech assessment and speech improvement for the hearing impaired.* Washington, DC: A.G. Bell Association for the Deaf, 1980.

Ling, D., & Clark, B.R. Cued speech: An evaluative study. *American Annals of the Deaf,* 1975, *120,* 480–488.

Ling, D., & Ling, A.H. *Aural habilitation: The foundations of verbal learning in hearing-impaired children.* Washington, DC: A.G. Bell Association for the Deaf, 1978.

Ling, D., Ling, A.H., & Pflaster, G. Individual education programming for hearing-impaired children. *Volta Review,* 1977, *79,* 204–230.

Ling, D., & Maretic, H. Frequency transposition in the teaching of speech to deaf children. *Journal of Speech and Hearing Research,* 1971, *14,* 37–46.

Ling, D., & Milne, M. The development of speech in hearing-impaired children. Paper delivered at the International Symposium on Amplification in Education, Nashville, Tenn., 1979.

Markides, A. The speech of deaf and partially-hearing children with special reference to factors affecting intelligibility. *British Journal of Disorders of Communication,* 1970, *5,* 126–140.

Markides, A. *Binaural hearing aids.* London: Academic Press, 1977.

Moore, D.G. An experimental approach to the phonological problems of the hearing impaired. *Teacher of the Deaf,* 1979, *3,* 113–122.

Monsen, R.B. The speech of the hearing impaired. St. Louis: Central Institute for the Deaf Research Department Periodic Progress Report No. 22, 26–28, 1979.

Nickerson, R.S. Characteristics of the speech of deaf persons. *Volta Review,* 1975, *77,* 342–362.

Office of the Los Angeles County Superintendent of Schools. *Auditory skills curriculum.* North Hollywood, CA: Foreworks, 1979.

Nicholls, G.H. *Cued speech and the reception of spoken language.* Washington, DC: Gallaudet College Office of Cued Speech Programs, 1979.

Novelli-Olmstead, T. *Production and reception of speech by hearing-impaired children.* Unpublished master's thesis, McGill University, Montreal, 1979.

Oyer, H.J. (Ed.) *Communication for the hearing handicapped: An international perspective.* Baltimore, MD: University Park Press, 1976.

Pickett, J.M., & Risberg, A. (Eds.) *Speech processing aids for the deaf.* Proceedings of the Conference held at Gallaudet College, Washington, DC, May, 1977.

Pollack, D. *Educational audiology for the limited hearing infant.* Springfield, IL: Charles C Thomas, 1970.

Risberg, A., & Mártony, J.A. A method for the classification of audiograms. In G. Fant (Ed.), *Speech communication ability and profound deafness.* Washington, DC: A.G. Bell Association for the Deaf, 1977.

Ross, M. Binaural versus monaural hearing aid amplification for hearing-impaired individuals. In F. Bess (Ed.), *Childhood deafness, causation, assessment and management.* New York: Grune & Stratton, 1977.

Ross, M., & Giolas, T.G. (Eds.) *Auditory management of the hearing-impaired child.* Baltimore, MD: University Park Press, 1978.

Schaffer, C.M. The kinesthetic method of speech development and speechreading. *American Annals of the Deaf,* 1942, *87,* 421–442.

Sparks, D.W., Ardell, L.A., Bourgeois, M., Wiedmar, B., & Kuhl, P.K. Investigating the MESA (Multipoint Electrotactile Speech Aid): The transmission of connected discourse. *Journal of the Acoustical Society of America,* 1979, *65,* 810–816.

Stark, R.E. *Sensory capabilities of hearing-impaired children.* Baltimore, MD: University Park Press, 1974.

Stoker, R.G. *The perception of speech and temporal form by oral deaf adults.* Unpublished Ph.D. dissertation, McGill University, Montreal (in preparation).

Upton, H.W. Wearable eyeglass speechreading aid. *American Annals of the Deaf*, 1968, *113*, 222–229.
van Uden, A. *A world of language for deaf children* (3rd ed.). Amsterdam and Lisse: Swets & Zeitlinger, 1977.
Vorce, E. *Teaching speech to deaf children*. Washington, DC: A.G. Bell Association for the Deaf, 1974.
Wedenberg, E. Auditory training of deaf and hard of hearing children. *Acta Otolaryngolica Supplement*, 1951, *94*.
Whetnall, E., & Fry, D.B. *The deaf child* (Rev. ed.). Springfield, IL: Charles C Thomas, 1971.
Young, B. A two-year study of speech skills. Paper presented at the A.G. Bell Association Convention, St. Louis, MO, June, 1978.
Zink, G.D. Hearing aids children wear: A longitudinal study of performance. *Volta Review*, 1972, *74*, 41–51.

reaction* to 5

a.m.j. van uden

I. We agree with the following points of this paper:

1. A multi-sensory approach, combined with challenging both hearing (in our opinion including also vibration-feeling) and speechreading, and the integration of these two functions. The gain through sound perception in the ears, even for the most deaf group of children, has been shown by us by means of P.B. lists (1956) and Eggermont by means of nonsense words (1964).
2. An emphasis on auditory training (and we would include also vibration feeling) for the control of speech, for speech perception, and for the memory of this successive function.
3. An emphasis on the differential treatment of deaf children with a need for predictive diagnosis. (See below).
4. An "evoking approach to speech training" in contrast to a mainly phonetic training. We have called these "reactive methods" in contrast to "prefab methods" (1974), although the use of the latter, more or less, is necessary for some children (See below).
5. An emphasis on speech as a communicative, interactive, and conversational function.

II. We note the following omissions, however:

1. An emphasis on rhythm of speech. Our research has shown, that accentuation should be taught to deaf children, not first of all by strength or by pitch, but by lengthening the accentuated syllable (Speth, 1957), the phonetic rules of which have been explained by us (1968, 1977). This lengthening has the effect that the children spontaneously and in the early stages still unconsciously strengthen the accentuated syllable and give it a higher pitch. This reaction can be made conscious and controllable mainly by music and dance training. The way in which the *meaning* of accentuations can be taught to deaf children has been explained by us (1968, 1977). The rhythm of speech has, in our opinion, a strong linguistic aspect and

---

*This reaction confines itself to the viewpoint of the profoundly deaf according to the definition of the Symposium.

… reaction to 5

brother leo speth

Van Uden and I studied the papers of D. Ling and K. Schulte separately. After that we compared our remarks, and it appeared that most of them were in agreement. Only in a few cases will additional information be given here, such as the following:

1. The terms used in the papers do make it difficult to understand what group of children is meant. I mean terms like:
    hearing impaired
    severe hearing impaired (70–90 dB)
    profoundly hearing impaired (90 dB and more)
    totally deaf
    hard-of-hearing youngsters.
   Will you please explain these to us?
2. Two questions need to be asked in relation to the complaint about adequate oral skills:
   1) What are adequate oral skills?
   2) How does one define an oral program?
   In my opinion another question must follow:
   3) What kind of help can be offered?
   Which means, methods, practical guidelines should be provided?
3. "Certain children fitted with appropriate hearing aids, may acquire adequate oral skills if parents and teachers simply talk with them often enough." From my own practical experience I doubt if this will be enough.
4. We also doubt why an early expert diagnosis cannot predict a well balanced educational plan and direct the special school (department) in which the child will be helped in the best way.
   A continuing evaluation in the course of ongoing training will remain valuable, of course.
5. We do not fully agree that over the past 40 years no improvements have been made in speech production among profoundly hearing-impaired children. New ways of speech teaching have improved the results, and in this connection we think of:
   —starting from babbling (progress for speech).
   —sensorimotor exercises (Speth-v.d. Hoven).
   —using contrasts (Sr. Rosa.)
   —relaxation exercises (Speth).
   —breathing therapy (Speth).
   —accent-training exercises (blowing organ; no drum); (Speth).
   —rhythmic speech (v. Uden).
   —phonetically basic words.
   —a vowel triangle (symbols for jaw and lips).
   —catching method.

requires training throughout, together with teaching of the terms "main accent," "accent of news," "accent of contrast," "pauses," "phrases," and so on.
2. The use of auditory and vibratory feedback, i.e. a cybernetic way of working, by means of closed circuit amplification and by perceiving one's own voice afterwards on a tape recording. The same holds good with speechreading, the use of visual feedback by means of a mirror and video recording (1974).
3. What kind of self control is given to the child?
4. The author seems to be rather pessimistic about the speechreading abilities of many profoundly deaf children and adults. We are not so! Most profoundly deaf children can reach a good speechreading-listening level. For the grownups we applied a "lipreading-listening-imitating-test" (See Section V in this reaction), with high significant validity correlations with daily behavior. This test shows results of good lipreading ability for the vast majority of profoundly deaf children.

The author seems to advise "cued speech" for many deaf children. We are very much opposed to this advice.
   a. Cued speech is called "the most effective lipreading aid". To me rhythmic speech, both of the speaker and of the lipreader himself, is the best lipreading aid. The research of Nicholls on a small group of 18 children is not at all conclusive. What were the findings on the speech of these children? No comparison has been made with children with good rhythmic speech in a fully oral environment which challenges their lipreading and hearing abilities to their full potential. The only fact shown by this research seems to be that these children learn what they learn! It is very astonishing and dangerous to me, that the children could identify words (36.0 percent) and even sentences (46.8 percent) from the 12 cues *only,* without speech! Which words and sentences were these?
   b. I have met personally "fluent *hearing* cuers": all of them had great difficulty in saying simple sentences in correct rhythm.
   c. The configuration of the fingers for the cues seems to lack scientific background: they are neither articulatory (See Schulte's paper) nor graphic. There are a few deaf children (See below) who need an esoteric substitute and/or supplement for an oral conversation, but this type of child needs methods which are a complete substitute for speech and may be articulatory or graphic.
   d. Forchhammer (1903, 1930) developed a similar system, called the "mouth-hand-system". One of the disadvantages of this system is the following: there are cues for instance, for /g/ and /ng/, and so when a deaf child has to say *gang*, it can suffice just to say /a/ and cue the /g/ and /ng/. Deaf children did! . . . . . Or they spoke the cued sounds carelessly. How can cued speech prevent this real danger? (See above in paragraph "a" the references to 36 and 46.8 percent.)
   e. The cues are esoteric. They tend to isolate the deaf child, which cannot be accepted apart from cases of true necessity, carefully diagnosed (See below). They will be mainly used only by those people who live with

him. But these are the people, best known to him, whom he will be able to lipread best of all! How can such a child ever develop his lipreading ability to full potential?
f. Cued speech hampers normal gesticulation.

III. Multiple handicaps

The author does not mention eupraxia and intermodal integration. He rightly mentions "neuromuscular coordination", but this is just one aspect of the eupraxia-syndrome. He says: "There is no measure or set of measures, that can be used to predict, whether . . . . a child . . . . . will benefit . . . ." etc. Thus we should try and try until a child becomes an oral failure (something that happens in very many schools for the deaf)? No! Since 1968 we have applied a set of tests, based on research, by means of which we can predict oral difficulties and prevent a delay of the correct treatment, at least at 5 years of age, and we can warn already at 2–3 years of age. See the paper of Broesterhuizen, Van Dijk, IJsseldijk.

The diagnosis of the dyspraxic or even the apraxic syndrome should be made by a psychologist or ortho-pedagogue expert in the instruction of the deaf, in cooperation with an expert teacher of the deaf. It seems to be irresponsible to leave such an important judgment just to a speech therapist, though he is ever so expert.

IV. Sign language

The author advises sign language for children "not able to make sufficient progress to achieve . . . . oral communication" etc.

We are strongly opposed to this also. There is a third way: the Rochester method and/or the phoneme transmitting manual system of Schulte which prevents signs and gives sufficient *verbal* (not the same as oral) communication. These children can be educated mainly verbally and they can reach satisfactory normal language levels, certainly not lower than those of the oral deaf children.

> Very few deaf children with *normal* intelligence need sign language, in fact only those with a pathologically poor memory and/or asymbolia for words, which very great disturbance is an aspect of a pathological intermodal integration. (See chapter 17)

V. A. van Uden's Speechreading-hearing-speech-imitation test in Dutch, 1968

The test consists of 50 words, 14 of which are monosyllabic, 11 bisyllabic, 10 three-, 11 four- and 4 fivesyllabic. These words comprise all the vowels and consonants, 25 double consonants (as in "grond", "extra") and 3 treble ones (as in "abstrakt", "arts"). —The words are not taken from the vocabulary of children; the test comprises words as "individueel", "sarkastisch", "desillusie", "minitieus" and such like.

Scoring:
- a. Direct good rhythmic imitation: 4 points
- b. Direct good phonematic imitation, defective rhythm: 3 points
- c. The experimenter has to repeat the model and/or to select one syllable (e.g. for sarkastisch, ... kas ....., he makes the child imitate kas, then the whole word sarkastisch): 2 points
- d. The experimenter has to analyse further (e.g. a loose phoneme as k, then ..... kas ..... etc., and/or ..... kas ..... and ..... sar ..... etc.) but finally gets a good phonematic imitation: 1 point
- e. Failure after 5 trials: 0 points

The maximum score is 200 points. Loose phonemes have to be subtracted. For example, a child reaches 92 points, but the experimenter had to present 6 times a loose phoneme; the score will be 92 − 6 = 86, halved to 43. Because of this halving the maximum score becomes 100.

Results and provisional standardization in rounded figures are given below.

Age	Number of children	Score	Standard deviation
5;6	9	14	6
6;6	29	24	9
7;6	29	37	14
8;6	27	62	16
9;6	31	78	11
10;6	27	71	10
11;6	31	89	6
12;6	23	94	6

References

Eggermont, J. *Taalverwerving bij een groep dove kinderen*. Groningen: J. B. Wolters, 1964.
Forchhammer, G. *On the necessity of sure means of communication in the instruction of the deaf*. Kopenhagen: Institute for the Deaf, 1903.
Forchhammer, G. *Taubstummen pädagogische Abhandlungen*. Leipzig: Taubstummen-Verlag Hugo Dude, 1930.

Speth, br. Leo, *Adem en accent,* Annual report Instituut voor Doven, Sint-Michielsgestel, 1957.

van Uden, A. M. J. *Helpt vibratiegevoel het liplezen?,* Annual report Instituut voor Doven, Sing-Michielsgestel, 1956.

van Uden, A. M. J. Lipreading from oneself. In *Dove kinderen leren spreken.* Rotterdam: Universitaire Pers, 1974.

van Uden, A. M. J. *A world of language for deaf children.* (part I: Basic principles). Sint-Michielsgestel 1968, 3rd revised edition, Swets & Zeitlinger B. V., Lisse 1977.

6

a survey of the present status of methods in continental europe
for the development of receptive and expressive oral skills
klaus schulte

Preliminary Remarks

This topic deals with the description of today's status of oral communication in Continental Europe, which comprises more than 20 countries with 15 different languages. To do justice to this comprehensive task from the point of view of content as well as form, it would have been necessary to arrange an extensive program of visits and to do some in-depth literature research.

Due to the scope of the topic, the short period of time given to deal with it, the difficulties in collecting information on the situation in the socialist countries of Eastern Europe, due to translation problems and to professional commitments to guarantee the smooth continuation of our research projects in progress here at the Research Center for the Rehabilitation of the Disabled (FST), I can only accept the topic with the following limitations:

- Structuring some *important* approaches of oral communication with the help of a short catalogue of problems (cf. Ch. 2);
- Restricting myself to those Eastern European countries which are in a leading position—the USSR and the GDR
- Necessarily a restriction to those countries, from which written or oral information were available or obtainable within the short time frame, and to those cases where necessary translations could be effected.

Therefore, the status of the oral education of prelingually profoundly deaf persons will focus on the following countries:

- The *Federal Republic of Germany* (for the German-speaking central area of Europe with Austria and Switzerland);
- The *USSR and the GDR*
- *Sweden* (for the Scandinavian countries);
- *Luxembourg and France* (for the French-speaking area);
- *Portugal* (for the Iberian Peninsula);
- The *Netherlands* (as far as the Netherlands as the host country is concerned, it is assumed that the situation will be discussed in detail by A. M. J. van Uden's presentation).

I very much regret to say that other information material that was requested on Spain, Belgium, Italy and Yugoslavia was not received here in time to be considered in this paper.

I would like to express my sincere thanks for the help provided in the collection of these data to: Jean Bohler, Director of the Logopedic Center in Luxembourg; Gérard Bourrigault, Director of F.I.S.A.F., Paris, France; Drs. A. van Hagen, St. Michielsgestel, the Netherlands; G. Hey, Research Assistant at the FST Heidelberg; Dr. L. Schwinger, Assistant Professor at the FST Heidelberg.

The unrewarding element of such an overview presentation is the emphasis on the descriptive character and thus a necessary lack of interpretation of the basis of scientific theory and methodology. Also, given the broad concept of this topic, it is hardly possible to discuss any domain-scientific reasonings relating to education science or linguistics and its subdisciplines (such as systems linguistics together with the semantics and syntax of the various languages in question, pedagogic linguistics, sociolinguistics, psycholinguistics and pragmatics; the phonetics and phonology of the various languages in question, audiometry, psychology, and diagnostics).

Supplements and corrections to this overview paper with all its limitations are, therefore, a factual necessity.

The Status of Oral Communication in Selected Countries in Europe

The education situation in Austria and Switzerland is—as far as practice is concerned—comparable, and some of the comments that I will make with regard to the Federal Republic of Germany also apply to those countries.

Status of Oral Communication in the Federal Republic of Germany

I would first like to present a critical review of the education of the deaf in Germany, for which I feel a shared responsibility as a university professor in the training of teachers for the deaf.

The objective of all the work done in this respect in the FRG is still considered to be an "intelligently and intelligibly speaking deaf person" (Singer, 1946) by the great majority of special teachers. Starting in 1958, fingerspelling and thus manual communication was also propagandized. The use of fingerspelling in the

Catalogue of Problems

relating to "The Present Status in Continental Europe of Methods of Developing Receptive and Expressive Oral Skills in Deaf Children"

Questions and Answers

(With the number of markings we try to quantify emphasis)

I. Is the education of the deaf in _____ (country)
   primarily an education
   - based on oral communication □ 1
   - based on fingerspelling and/or gestures □ 2
   - based on writing □ 3

II. Is the oral communication *primarily* oriented
   - to speech reception (receptive skills) □ 4
   - to speech production (expressive skills) □ 5

III. As far as methodology is concerned, which is *predominant factor* in oral communication:
   A. The systematic structure of language
   B. Systematic speech training
   C. The relevance of the actual world to the subjective emotional life and activity fields of the deaf child
   D. A combination of the above:

	A	B	C	D
in early education	□ 6			
in pre-school education	□ 7			
in elementary school	□ 8			
in junior high school	□ 9			
in high school	□ 10			

   - 2-4 years of age
   - 5 +6 age
   - 1-2 years of school
   - 3-4 school
   - 5-10

IV. Is the language and speech training for the deaf *primarily* synthetic—inductive—systematically constructing (as far as grammar and phonetics are concerned) □ 11

V. *primarily* analytic—deductive—subdividing—developing □ 12

   A combination of the two methods mentioned above □ 13

V. Which information system conveys *primarily*
   A Language,
   B Speech,
   C Knowledge?

	A	B	C
—Utilization of Residual Hearing				14
—Lipreading				15
—Aero-cutaneous, cutaneous-cutaneous vibrations				16
—Mechano-cutaneous vibrations with the Fonator System				17
System Suvag				18
—Phonemetransmitting Manual System (PMS)				19
—Mouth-Hand-System				20
—Cued Speech				21
—Fingerspelling				22
—Writing Skills				23
—Gestures				24
—Sign Language				25
—Visible Speech Systems— Which?				26
—Other Aids— Which?				27

VI. Particular Principles applied in speech training
   —Phonetic reductions
   —Age foci in speech training (Areas 2, III, 6-10) □ 28
   —Supplementary Speech Information Which Systems? (Areas 2, V, 14-27) □ 29

VII. Specific Objectives in the education of the hearing-and speech-impaired: □ 30 sense of the Rochester method was investigated by several scientists (Jussen, 1974, 1975; Graf, 1969) and tested in some schools by several special teachers in West and North Germany. A systematic individual testing, which can be followed up through a number of years, was done by Geisperger (1969).

At the moment there are two tendencies:
- a *reconsideration* of the *necessity of intensified speech training* and
- a certain *insecurity* with regard to the objectives of the work done so far in view of the fact that fingerspelling did not assert itself. Connected with this approach is the rise of new hopes for sign language.

The *objective* of an education in oral communication is stronger than its reality: the hopes for enhancing an earlier and more effective speech training and a larger vocabulary through a very early training—which has been systematically promoted in the past 20 years—have at least been partly destroyed, as the outstanding results have, for the most part, been due to the outstanding performance of the individual teacher and his dedication rather than to the existing systematic theories.

The fact that the success was not as great as expected may be due to:
- the segregation of kindergarten from the school framework of the schools for the deaf, which has been effected in some areas. This entailed a split responsibility as far as content of learning and approach are concerned.
- the still existing ambiguity between

| *earlier beginning of systematic language development and speech training* | vs. | an education of young deaf children that is more directed to fit their *emotional life* and is *relevant to their childhood environment.* |

As far as *didactics* and *methodology* is concerned, there is on the whole *little uniformity* with regard to the sequence and hierarchy of the efforts to solve language, speech, and factual problems. The educational work is based to a large extent on what is called "freedom of teaching," which keeps making it difficult to reach an agreement on uniform and systematic proposals (cf. Schulte, 1969, p. 45).

The *integrative education of the deaf* (e.g., Löwe, 1978, Schmid-Giovannini, 1975) is limited to a very few cases only. This may be due to the fact that we are lacking the necessary organizational prerequisites. Even the integration of the hearing impaired with hearing children is considered to be problematic. Investigations have shown that the outcome is doubtful, particularly considering the danger of the lack of socializing between hearing and hearing impaired children (e.g., Clausen, 1975, 1978).

Considering the more than 70 schools for the deaf in the Federal Republic, it can be stated that there is a predominance of the *form which attempts to combine the systematic development of language, systematic speech training,* and an *emphasis on factual knowledge.*

Twenty years ago the question as to whether more emphasis should be placed on an inductive-constructing or deductive-analytic approach would have been much easier to answer for the Federal Republic—at least with reference to certain areas. Here, too, the combination of the above-mentioned forms is predominant. This is partly due to the scientific realization that either of the two approaches—purely inductive or purely deductive—on its own bears the danger of onesidedness. On the other hand, these combined forms clearly lack a systematic basis in practice on the part of the teachers. Despite the basic recognition of the freedom of teaching in the education of the deaf, it must be considered that the combination of sign systems or methodical approaches in speech training may impair the success of the effort because supplementary speech information can only be useful to the student under certain conditions: fingerspelling, for example, is not a phoneme- but a grapheme-transmitting manual system and thus aims at manual, not oral communication. The variety of visible speech systems also has basic deficiencies as far as the intial speech training process is concerned. Their use, therefore, is problematic.

Twelve years of teaching experience at various levels of schools from early education to vocational school and 15 years of scientific work in the education of the deaf have reinforced my firm belief that in the end *those teachers will have best results who are aware of the scientific findings and combine them with the prerequisites of practice*, i.e., those who take into consideration that the hearing impaired with varying hearing losses, varying age groups, and varying developmental stages will pose *varying demands on the teacher*.

The intention of *systematically creating an awareness of the need for information* both on the side of the teacher and the student has been the underlying concern of the extensive research on the area of language development and speech training that has been conducted by the Research Center for Applied Linguistics for the Rehabilitation of the Disabled for 14 years. Experts in the field of educational science are requested to find their own way of teaching, taking into account both the limits and the opportunities of the various information systems.

Despite the development of technically very sophisticated hearing aids, teachers in the Federal Republic should make more systematic, constant use of residual hearing capabilities. Also, there is a lack of systematic training of possible residual hearing capabilities, especially in the case of the prelingually deaf; some schools are not offering any training at all, some lack the necessary didactic and methodical basis, some lack domain-specific theory and practice. The use of lipreading is a necessity which is self-explanatory; with regard to speech training, the "touch-feel-structure" (Kern, 1958), which was widely used by practitioners 20 years ago, has given way to the use of the comparable Fonator System (Schulte/Roesler/Ding, 1969; Ding, 1972) as a vibratory mechanocutaneous one-channel system and to the visuo-motoric Phonemetransmitting Manual System (Schulte, 1974; 1978; 1980), which conveys information on the place of articulation, articulatory organs, and in most cases also on the mode of articulation.

A video-"speech-training-program" (Schulte 1979) is aimed at systematically demonstrating to child-care personnel, nurses, educators, and parents the *difficulties* and the *opportunities* of *early and intensive speech training to improve speech intelligibility*. This project is scheduled for completion in 1981.

The research which we have conducted in Heidelberg aims at making us aware of the limitations of oral approach systems. It is also hoped that it will contribute to avoiding a further disintegration of the use of a great number of codes, especially with regard to visible speech or electro-cutaneous approaches with all the problems that they present theoretically and psychologically to the student.

Supplementary Speech Information (Schulte, 1978) always implies less information systems but more systematic use of systems or codes rather than many but unsystematically used codes. In the Federal Republic these are, apart from the utilization of residual hearing, which would seem to be highly desirable, the early application of the Fonator System (Mini-, Mono-, Poly-Fonator) to supplement the low feature distinction of lipreading. Both these systems should again be supplemented by the relatively high distinctive feature conveyance of the Phonemetransmitting Manual System. The Phonemetransmitting Manual System is a help in learning how to speak and does not aim at a signing but at a *speaking child*. This means that children will only use this system if their speech-motoric capabilities, skills, ideas of speech stimulation or speech control still need the phoneme signs. The yet to be developed and tested Mini-Fonator (Schulte, 1978)—a research project granted by the Federal Ministry for Labor and Social Affairs—is designed to enable the deaf who do not have enough residual hearing to make use of better speech control.

An improvement of the speech, language, and knowledge levels of the deaf does not only seem possible but also necessary. A larger turnover of speech, more directed towards the individual student, but systematically offered by the teacher, seems to be an indispensable necessity.

Oral Communication in the USSR and the GDR

The comparison between the situation as it presents itself in the Federal Republic and the objectives set forth in the USSR shows interesting contrasting elements. In-depth comparable research, especially in the field of speech training and the information means used for this purpose, has led to a quite different set of objectives which seem to be in line with the economic and social differences of the two countries. The methodology of oral communication in Eastern Europe essentially bears the stamp of the Soviet Union; other socialist states do not seem to have made any relevant contribution to the topic. Since GDR experts in this field almost exclusively orient themselves to the development in the Soviet Union, the description of the Russian system has an exemplary character also for the GDR.

Deriving from the critique on and the abandonment of the so-called pure oral approach, emphasis has now been placed on the

- **communicative aspect**, underlining the *dialog form* as the primary form of language including fingerspelling, lipreading, and speech, as well as
- **practical work**, which orients itself to the content matter of the word. This has been adopted as a *teaching principle* and even, recently, as a study subject.

According to an analysis which one of my colleagues, Gerhard Hey, prepared for this paper on the most important relevant publications (Korsunskaja/S.A. Sykow, 1954; Sykow, 1968; Sykow, 1969; Sykow, 1972; Sykow, 1976; Sykow et al., translated by Große 1979; Glawe/Pöhle, 1974; Frank 1975; Klimas, 1976), the education for the deaf developed from a—in my opinion over-enthusiastic—criticism and abandonment of the so-called pure oral communication method. It requires—in the Russian view—the total concentration of the educational process in a school for the deaf on the development of speech. Speech training is considered to be the development of the articulary component. Speech training becomes the prime object of the entire educational process; speech is replaced by articulation. All of this only defers the intellectual development of the children. Speech appears as subject to individual acquisition and should only then become a means with the help of which deaf students articulate their needs and form and maintain social relationships and contacts.

In this kind of educational approach the children are helpless as soon as they are to make themselves understood to other people. Oral communication is thus lacking its basic and primary function: the *social implication*. Insufficient differentiation of the different meanings of the actual situation ("that is a flower") and the sign function (containing the request "smell the flower") would lead to the fact that the students (in this narrow interpretation of the oral communication method) learn speech without reference to the activity that is implied and that thus the primary form of speech—the dialogue—would have to be neglected in favor of a form of speech that orients itself more to a monologue and the content of the word.

Taking this into account, there are two principles which are applied in educating the deaf:

a) *the principle of the communicative orientation of speech training*

> The basis of speech, the leading principle for language instruction and the development of the thinking process, is the communicative function of speech; the communicative language instruction is strongly interwoven with the logic thought process of the children. Deaf children who acquire oral communication and consequently a vocabulary, who understand and learn grammatical phenomena, also necessarily acquire the generalizations and abstractions contained in there. Speech is learned and used in action; this also means that the students acquire speech for the sake of others. Therefore, one does not have the individual student in mind but children who interact with others. I would like to call this aspect the *collective –communicative – Russian aspect* of the education for the deaf. This collective–communicative aspect aims at taking part in the social life and environment via oral communication.

b) *the principle of practical activity-related work*

> The second important principle of language training is the practical activity-related work. This principle is today an integrative part of the educational process in almost all schools for the deaf. In addition to this, it has become a study subject by itself after systematic testing. Having been attributed one quarter of the total subject hours offered at school, it tries to overcome the traditional spectrum of language instruction, mathematics, etc. The objectives of this practical activity-related work are:

- to promote the *intellectual development* of the students with the help of *activity-related means*,
- to prepare the students for the *acquisition of the basics of sciences* through building up and extending their *everyday vocabulary*,
- to activate the *speech development* of the children (Sykow et al., 1979, p. 1).

Frontal instruction with the acting-out teacher is to be replaced more and more by the collective activity of the students. It must be guaranteed that the students can act out a situation. The tiresome "explanations of words" which constitute part of the traditional language and reading instruction, are to be replaced by the *student's active dealing with a specific situation*, which allows the simultaneous vocabulary buildup and a systematic acquisition of terms which are related to his age group.

Extensive and systematic testing has shown that this activity-related work facilitates the development of the thought process of the children, quantitatively as well as qualitatively. The extent and sequence of physical and psychological actions determine the selection of words and the necessary speech patterns.

The materials and mechanisms used in instruction, the skills that the children are supposed to acquire, the number of terms to be developed, the application of the knowledge acquired, vocabulary and phrases, the skills of a spontaneous communication are all *systematically planned and controlled*. Modeling, paperwork, drawing with the constant parallel vocabulary buildup in the dialogue form are supposed to condition a lexicon, grammar, and articulation which naturally develops alongside the actual activities. The need for communication arises in the process of performing these activities.

Not completing sentences is regarded as a *positive factor*, since it makes it a lot easier for children to acquire the verbal communication means and *makes speech dynamics* to fit the requirements of spontaneous communication. Colloquial speech and incompleted sentences are placed on the same level.

With reference to the above-outlined principles of collective communication and activity-related training, we have to ask ourselves how the communication is actually performed. The objective of social integration of the deaf into life and the reinforcement of oral communication needs via the so-called activity-related work and its organization on a collective basis are supposed to make the use of oral communication a real need. The environment is supposed to be oriented toward oral communication; the teacher verbalizes explanations and instructions and only allows answers to be made orally. This dialogue form also explains the inevitably elliptic forms of phrases.

Early oral communication is handled on two lines of principles:
- the principle of *phonetic reductions* (especially in the USSR), and
- the principle of *fingerspelling* (dominating in the GDR).

According to Rau, the principle of phonetic reductions derives from the fact that similar phonemes with regard to the mode of production are only symbolized by one single phoneme at a very early stage of development.

Phonetic reductions as they occur in any normal speech development process are here made a principle. This principle presents us with severe problems: deaf children tend to equate difficult phonemes with simple ones if they are not corrected, which paves the way for incorrect speech patterns. At a later, more detailed stage of speech training it is then very difficult to correct those faulty patterns, especially within the context of a word. Phonetic reductions are supposed to guarantee an early articulation even on a preschool level. The phoneme system is reduced to contain only 17 of 42 phonemes at the beginning.

To guarantee early communication, the articulation process does include the so-called *dactylic form*, the signs of the Rochester system for each letter. The interaction with lipreading and writing provides for a speech training performed in four stages (Sykow, 1969) on the basis of the dactylic form of speech:

First Stage Global perception of the dactylic word;
Second Stage Analytic perception of the dactylic word and imitation; lipreading, elements of articulation;

Analytic perception and imitation of the orally expressed word with the interaction of writing;
Third Stage The fingerspelled orally expressed word in the development to the orally expressed fingerspelled word (with interaction of writing);
Fourth Stage The orally expressed fingerspelled word.

The USSR opts for fingerspelling for the following reasons:
- It is a self-contained form of language;
- It allows for a language instruction on the basis of communication;
- It can be developed separately, apart from the oral and written forms of language, and can thus occur as the initial form of speech;
- Its application as the first form of communication makes instruction more effective since a variety of speech training material can be presented;
- It does not impede the development of oral communication; with the application of the dactylic system the kinesthetics of fingerspelling are developed. This helps the deaf to memorize the structure of a word better and for a longer period of time. On the basis of the continuing neuro-dynamic interface between the kinesthetics of fingerspelling and those of the articulators the dactylic system becomes a support for oral communication;
- The application of the dactylic system facilitates the instruction in reading and writing.

The education for the deaf in the USSR and the GDR appears to be a relatively uniform, set, and self-contained structure along the lines of collective communication and speech activity-oriented principles.

With regard to the opinion that fingerspelling supports speech—a thesis corroborated in literature (Jussen, Metze et al.)—my personal experience in Moscow, the United States, and the Federal Republic of Germany has shown that oral communication with deaf adolescents who are used to signing is almost impossible to achieve. The use of fingerspelling when deaf children or adolescents communicate among each other seems to be insurmountable. The value of this nonverbal system for the formation of language and knowledge seems to be considerably higher than for the actual capability of oral communication.

Some Aspects on the Education of the Deaf in Sweden

The comments that are made on the education of the deaf in Sweden are based on the principles outlined by Rut Madebrink in her paper "Requirements of Hearing and Speech Training in Schools" at the Washington Speech Conference in 1977.

As long as a majority (of the hearing) can be the model for the so-called normalization of a minority (of the deaf), oral communication will be a vital prerequisite for the education of deaf children. The critical standpoint that Sweden has taken with regard to the education of the deaf, the strong influence of sign language, may be traced back to the fact that—on the basis of audiograms and discrimination tests as well as some fundamental knowledge of acoustical phonetics—lists of words and sentences have been compiled which can be learned by the deaf, i.e., are spoken and are even heard under more difficult conditions. However, it will be *extremely difficult* for any child to use this material in his *spontaneous communication*. Based on this insight, Madebrink requests "longitudinal research of real spontaneous conversation of deaf children and adults among themselves." Similar to the integration effort of Schmid-Giovannini in Switzerland, Madebrink requests that children that have not developed speech normally be sent to normal schools in their own communities. At the same time attention is drawn to the difficulties of the prelingually deaf children: "As we know that profoundly, prelingually deaf children, to a much smaller extent than many of us will admit, are able to interact and speak freely with hearing peers, I think it is of *utmost importance to investigate deaf people's speech and find new ways and means of teaching speech*." In contrast to the method practiced in the Netherlands, Madebrink emphasizes that differences in the speech production and the speech development of deaf people exist: "there is in reality not a great deal of speech going on between hearing and deaf people, because the entire procedure that is involved in speech production is deviating from normal speech." Madebrink's statement goes even further; according to her, people identify a deaf person's speech not with that of a foreigner, but with that of an abnormal person ("You can not identify a deaf speaker and a foreigner; he is more likely to be identified with a person with abnormal behavior."). The consequence is that speech and hearing training no longer is the primary aim in all Swedish schools; the Swedish Association for the Hearing Impaired and the Deaf and the association of parents try to solve the problem by stressing the necessity that *sign language should be learned by as many normal hearing people as possible*, in order not to make a hearing impaired person an outsider. In order to guarantee a reliable communication, students should be educated *bilingually*—in doing so, sign language can be the first or basic language.

The Swedish school system stresses individual programs with a number of opportunities for hearing impaired individuals. "For pupils with such a hearing impairment that spontaneous development of speech and language is highly restricted or is never accomplished because of profound deafness, vision is essential for the comprehension of the spoken language." These pupils "should be placed in special schools for the deaf and it is interesting that in present status of methods in continental europe **111**

Sweden those schools during the last ten years had better financial means than other programs."

Swedish linguists like Malmberg, for example, question oral communication because the "deviating speech is more likely to isolate them from hearing people." For Malmberg deaf people "constitute a minority group, which should not be forced into the society of the hearing majority." In its total approach, the Swedish education of the deaf seems to be considerably insecure as far as oral communication is concerned: "We have to admit that speech is not a natural form of language to a child born deaf. There is not yet available such a support of lipreading that natural language comprehension can be accomplished through vision."

As a logical consequence of these considerations, Madebrink states: "Today, signing is accepted by the majority group as a specific but good language to be used in the minority group of the deaf. Simultaneous use of speech and signing is supposed to function in communication between hearing and deaf people. It seems to me that in combining two modes of expressing oneself, one of them will be predominant." In that, her opinion coincides with mine: Any sign language—whatever the system may be—will have an impact on the speech performance, because the sign system aims at language, not at the spoken form of language, i.e., speech. The most outstanding feature when looking at Sweden's approach to oral communication is its lack of uniformity, not with regard to the methods used in speech training, but with the value that is placed on speech and sign language. There is no agreement among teachers or disabled as to which approach should be predominant, sign language or oral communication.

Systematic Oral Communication in Luxembourg

The objective of the Logopedic Center in Luxembourg is clearly oral communication. The diversity of languages in Luxembourg—Luxembourgian, French and German (and Portuguese for foreign children)—presents a real problem in the education for oral communication. Speech development starts at a preschool age. Systematic articulation starts at elementary school level. The attendance of high school presupposes the knowledge of the essential speech patterns.

Overall, oral communication has to be considered as a combination of the synthetic and the analytic approach, which makes extensive use of residual hearing capabilities through individually adapted hearing aids and wireless vibratory equipment. With the help of supplementary information provided by the aero-cutaneous or cutaneous-cutaneous vibrations ("touch-feel-structure") of the Fonator and the Phonemetransmitting Manual System they try to achieve a more intelligible speech and oral communication.

Analytical-Deductive Method in Oral Education in France

The primary approach in the 43 private and 7 state schools in France is oral education without gestures. Not officially, but in everyday school practice, teachers do use gestures along with speech even with more grown-up students. Speech perception has preference over speech production. Systematic speech training is predominant in the 5th and 6th years of age and obviously precedes the actual articulation training. Utilization of residual hearing, lipreading, and speech control via kinesthetics are the information systems on which France bases its oral education. In speech training, the ages between 2 and 7 years are considered to be of particular importance. Only 1 to 2 percent of the students are totally or partially integrated.

Aspects of Oral Communication in Portugal

I can only roughly outline oral communication as part of the Portuguese education for the deaf since information on Portugal was only available in the form of typewritten pages which did not identify the author. By the end of the 1960's, all hearing impaired children in the school-age group were supposed to have received an adequate school training: three years in a preschool system and 6 to 8 years in an elementary school. According to the National Institute for Statistics, 66 percent of all the hearing impaired under 20 years of age were illiterate. Visible speech equipment seems to have been widely used to "alleviate deafness" (démutisation); most of these were used with an amplifier. For example, lamps in different colors, symbolizing different frequencies, correspond to vowels and consonants. At the Lisbon institutes hearing aids are the primary medium. Since classes do not seem to be grouped in deaf-hearing-impaired or normally intelligent deaf-learning-impaired deaf, it is difficult to make any statement as to which use the applicants made by M.A. Costa, a method combining both the "méthode deductive" and "méthode inductive" has proved to have best results in speech training. In the 10 different institutes in the 6 Portuguese regions, teaching is done according to the inductive method, which corresponds to the synthetic approach, as well as according to the deductive method, which corresponds to the analytical approach. Within the framework of the actual speech training, much value is placed on correct respiration, for good respiration is the basis of a good voice, and a good voice is the basis of clear and intelligible speech. In the individual speech training, palatograms are used. Syllables are trained in groups with simultaneous rhythmic exercises. From these exercises the vowels are developed. The development of the consonants is usually initiated by presenting the opposition of voiced-voiceless phonemes which have the same place of articulation and the same mode of production: p-b, t-d, f-v, m-n-1, s-z, k-g, ch-j.

In general, it can be said that the approach that is taken by Portugal corresponds in some way to that of the Federal Republic: gestures as well as fingerspelling are discouraged or even forbidden, they are avoided wherever possible. For reading, language and speech instruction in the first three years of school, when usually a sensory education is indicated (la période d'éducation sensorielle) there are clearly formulated programs for voice and vibration, the rhythmic and auditive education and initiation of phonemes in words and sentences. With regard to the syntactical structure, nouns and verbs are separated. Much value is placed on the exercises relating to the "lecture de la parole." The program has been designed by experts. A program which would reinforce this basic program, an advanced speech training program, and the introduction of regular school subject was nonexistent in 1969, when the publication on which this paper is based appeared.

The Global-Intuitive Mother-Tongue Approach in the Netherlands: Development of Vocabulary and Grammar in Spontaneous Conversation

Similar to the Russian education for the deaf, today's education for the deaf in the Netherlands—education as it is presented by van Uden in Sint Michielsgestel—constitutes itself from the opposition to the so-called German oral communication method ("Lautsprachmethode"), which seeks to build up language with a limited number of grammatical frames. This German approach—which is also criticized by the Eastern European countries—is considered to be a hypostatic construction and is criticized for the following reasons:
- logic is given preference over emotion;
- spontaneous conversation is neglected;
- active and passive language are put on the same level;
- words and sentences are not presented as a unit;
- rhythmic sentence patterns are neglected;
- too much is being written about it; and
- normal books are not read to a satisfying extent (v. Uden, 1976, p. 73).

The Dutch education of the deaf is clearly directed toward oral communication. "Sound Perception" is interpreted as the perception of their own movements, and oral communication and dance are made conscious by vibratory sensory-motor functions which serve the aim of speech production. With regard to speech, an early onset of speech training and consistent articulatory training are considered to be necessary. The method itself is primarily deductive, and attempts to include natural behavior, emotion, spontaneity, feedback, and foresight (ibid, p. 65).

If one had to characterize this method with one term, one would have to designate it "global-intuitive mother-tongue approach for the development of vocabulary and grammar."

Fingerspelling—as in the Russian system—is strongly rejected as it is considered to be endangering to the speech progress. Gestures are considered to divide language in small segments, which would make the thinking process more difficult for the child and would be too concrete. They are not considered to be of any relevance.

The success of oral communication in the Netherlands seems, at least to the outsider, to be the consequence of:
- an *oral communication* that starts *as early as possible;*
- a *uniform "mother-tongue" approach;*
- an *early differentiated diagnosis* with consequences for individual treatment, training, and education;

- *consistent use of all necessary aids* that are adequate for the education of the deaf, i.e., hearing aids and vibrators;
- *comprehensive knowledge of system- and psycholinguistics* and the application of psycholinguistic principles by the teacher;

in short, of the *uniformity of the teaching system*.

The uniformity of content and form in the Netherlands as well as the adequate organizational structure can serve as a model for all those countries in which a greater uniformity of the system and the methods seems to be desirable. This seems to be indispensable if a relatively spontaneous communication between the hearing and the hearing impaired is the objective in the education for the deaf.

References

Claussen, W.H.: Die soziale Problematik des Hör-Sprach-Geschädigten and die aus ihr resultierende Bedeutung des Sprachunterrichts in: Psycholinguistik in der Sonderpäd. Berlin 1975.

Claussen, W.H.: Zur Frage der Integration Schwerhöriger in Bildungseinrichtungen der Sekundarstufe 2 und am Arbeitsplatz in: HörPäd. 4/77, pp. 251–261.

Claussen, W.H.: Gespräche mit Schwerhörigen Hamburg 1979.

Ding, H.: Der Fonator im Artikulationsunterricht Rheinstetten 1972.

Frank, G.: Grundpositionen der neuen Lehrpläne für die Gehörlosenschule in: SoSch, Berlin 1975.

Glawe, H./Pöhle, K.H.: Sozialistische Gehörlosenpädagogik—Eine neue Qualität in: SoSch, Berlin 1974.

Graf, R.: Fingeralphabet und Lautsprache Ber. Bodenseeländertag. Würzburg 1969, pp. 57–61.

Greulich, M.: Der Sprachunterricht in Anfangsklassen der sowjetischen Gehörlosenchule Wiss. Abschlu βarbeit Hamburg 1963.

Geisperger, F.: Ist die Lautsprache für Gehörlose noch zeitgemä β Ber. Bodenseeländertag. Würzburg 1969, S. 17.

Jussen, H.: Sprachanthropologische Überlegungen zur Anwendung eines graphembestimmten Manualsystems in der Früherziehung tauber Kinder in: HörPäd, Heidelberg 1974.

Jussen, H./Krüger, M.: Manuelle Kommunikationshilfen bei Gehörlosen-das Fingeralphabet Berlin 1975.

Kern, E.: Theorie und Praxis eines ganzheitlichen Sprachunterrichts für das hörgeschädigte Kind Freiburg 1958.

Klimas, L.: Zur Entwicklung der Unterrichtsmethodik in der Gehörlosenschule in: SoSch, Berlin 1976.

Korsunskaja, B.D./Sykow, S.A.: Die Unterrichtsstunden in der Gehörlosenschule Moskau 1954.

Madebrink, R.: Requirements of hearing and speech training in schools. Unpublished paper on the Research Conference, Washington 1977.

Löwe, A.: Die beiden Hauptaufgaben der Hörgeschädigtenpädagogik: Prävention und Integration-genutzte und ungenutzte Möglichkeiten in: Vierteljahresschrift für Heilpädagogik, 47 (3, 1978), pp. 260–271.

Löwe, A.: Gehörlose Kinder in einer Regelschule. Eine erste Zwischenbilanz nach 4 Schuljahren in: HörPäd, Heidelberg 6/78.

Metze, E.: Daktylologie und Lautsprache in: SoSh, Berlin 1964, pp. 68–70.

Schmid-Giovannini: Sprich mit mir Berlin 1976.

Srom, F.: Sprachunterricht und Daktylologie SoSch, 2, 1965.
Schulte, K./Roesler, H./Ding, H.: Akusto-vibratorische Kommunikationshilfe Villingen (Neckar) 1974.
Schulte, K.: Phonembestimmtes Manualsystem Villingen 1974.
Schulte, K.: The Phonemetransmitting Manual System (PMS), Heidelberg 1978.
Schulte, K.: The use of supplementary speech information in verbal communication. The Volta Review, 1978, 80, 12–20.
Schulte, K.: Phonemhäufigkeit and Artikulation Villingen 1979.
Schulte, K.: 'Mini-Fonator'-development of speech for deaf and hard of hearing children. International Journal of Rehabilitation Research, 1978.
Schulte, K.: Development and evaluation of speech training programs for teachers of the deaf and hearing impaired, speech therapists and students. International Journal of Rehabilitation Research, 1979, 2 (1), 106.
Schulte, K./Schwinger, L./Straub, H.-Ch.u.a.: Systemergänzte Artikulation Heidelberg 1980.
Singer, E.: Der Direktor N.Bl.f.Tb, Heidelberg 1946.
Sykow, S.A.: Neues in den Unterrichtsmethoden für die gehörlosen Kindern Moskau 1968.
Sykow, S.A.: Sprachunterricht bei gehörlosen Kindern Moskau 1969.
Sykow, S.A.: Die Anwendung der gegenständlich-praktischen Tätigkeit in der Bildung gehörloser Schüler Moskau 1976.
Sykow, S.A.: Lehrpläne für die Gehörlosenschule, Teil I u. II Moskau 1972.
Sykow, S.A.: Gegenständlich-praktische Tätigkeit gehörloser Schüler, Übers. von Grobe, Leipzig, 1. Beiheft, SoSch, Berlin 1979.
Tigges, J.: Ist die Lautsprache noch zeitgemä? Ber.Bodenseeländertag. Würzburg 1969, pp. 9–16.
van Uden, A.M.J.: Instruction of prelingually deaf children by rhythm of bodily movements and of sounds, by oral mime and general bodily expression—its possibilities and difficulties. In Proceedings of the International Congress on the Education of the Deaf, Washington, DC: A.G. Bell Association for the Deaf, 1963.
van Uden, A.M.J.: A world of language for deaf children. Amsterdam: Swets and Zeitlinger, 1977.
van Uden, A.M.J.: Psycholinguistische Begründung eines Sprachunterrichts bei Hörgeschädigten in Ber.: Bodenseeländertag. Heidelberg 1977.

reaction to 6

brother leo speth

We add a few remarks to the reactions of van Uden.

1. From the papers of K. Schulte and D. Ling it may be worthwhile to continue the studies of their topic in the future. My proposal would be to try to compare three kinds of schools in describing their problems, their success, their history:
   a. The establishment of a totally new oral school (the school in Malawi, C.A.),
   b. A school which has changed from manual to oral (the school of Sr. Nicholas in Dublin),
   c. The school at Sint-Michielsgestel.
2. For me ambiguity between "systematic language development and speech training vs. the emotional life in the education of deaf small children" is not clear. In my opinion they need each other and influence each other for the good.
3. Training often is too theoretical.
   Do teachers use freely all the possibilities? Do they use the time fully?
4. Please, can more explanation be given about the Mini- and Poly-Fonator— their sizes, their special aims, their possibilities, etc.
5. The phonetic reductions in USSR amaze me. To teach a reduced and then a full set of phonemes is double work and more. Do we interpret you correctly when we understand that in most of the countries mentioned by you there is a request for the oral method? Do they want to know better how to manage and organize it? Is it something like: "Please come and help us in our need?"
6. We should like to mention two principles:
   —The oral method provides a deaf person with the opportunity to live in a broader social field.
   —The deaf are not homogeneous.

reaction to 6

a.m.j. van uden

I. We agree with the following points, put forward by the author:

1. An emphasis on a lack of fundamental theory, of cooperation and of uniformity of treatment, as main causes of oral failure.
2. The necessity for cooperation between science and practice for a basic background of instruction and education.
3. The necessity for varied approaches for different kinds of deaf children.
4. His criticism of phonetic reduction systems.
5. Use of video recordings in the teacher training programs. We would like to hear more about this.

II. There are several problems, however:

1. How have the above-mentioned causes of oral failure arisen? We *suggest* the following possibilities: (a) The separation of teacher training from the schools themselves. The headmasters may have to appoint teachers from different training centers with different background philosophies. When professors at these centers are not themselves teachers of the deaf, the situation seems to be the more dangerous: There is much theory, completely detached from practice, and too little practical guidance. (b) A nationalization and socialization ("Verstaatlichung") including overloaded bureaucratization of both schools and teacher training centers. This very often means that people who are not themselves educators of the deaf make the final and most important decisions about the teachers' education. (c) In practice a lack of freedom of choice of school. The schools are regionalized and the parents have little or no influence on allocation, very often no choice at all.
In my opinion the law should give at least this freedom: a number of parents (for instance 5 of them) should have the freedom to appoint a teacher of the deaf for the education of their children, as a kind of continued hometraining, with mainstreaming facilities if useful.
   This freedom seems to be necessary to "run the blockades" of nationalization.
2. Nothing has been said about early diagnosis, such as of multiple handicaps.
3. Which kind of self-control of speech is aimed at?

118 oral education: today and tomorrow

　4. What about auditory and visual feedback? *How* have these means of self-control been used in order to prevent a gap between speech on the one hand, and lipreading and sound perception on the other? This gap may be one of the main causes of oral failing.
　5. What about the tempo and rhythm of speech?
　6. We miss a description of the method of Kern (Heidelberg, 1957) known as "tactile feeling structure" ("Tast-Fühl-Struktur"). Yet some elements of that method seem to be useful for some dyspraxic deaf children.
　7. We cannot accept assertions like the following: "Fingerspelling supports speech," with a "value .... higher .... than actual capability of oral communication." What about tempo? rhythm? lipreading? auditory training?

III. The author seems to be rather pessimistic about the oral abilities of prelingually profoundly deaf children. In our opinion he emphasizes "the limitations of oral approach systems" too much.

We have the following problems:
1. Is the Phoneme Transmitting Manual System (P.M.S.) meant for *all* deaf children? 2. What about the communicative means of deaf children *among themselves?*

IV. USSR

We would like to put the following questions:
1. On the one hand it is said that dialogue is neglected, on the other hand that "collective communication" is emphasized. *Which is the case*? 2. How do the deaf children communicate amongst themselves? 3. How far does their belief in a nonverbal intellectual development go? 4. Do they believe in just one method for *all* deaf children?

V. Sweden

How far is the philosophy of the deaf as constituting a "minority group" spread among the educators of the deaf?

VI. Luxembourg

How do the educators of the deaf overcome the problems of three completely different languages in the homes of deaf children?

7

a survey of present methods of developing language in deaf children
sister m. nicholas griffey

Introduction

When reviewing current methods of developing language in deaf children, one is struck by the amount of uncertainty, questioning, controversy, and heated discussion. In an age when "instant results" are the order of the day in some other fields, student teachers of the deaf are frustrated because there are no precise and failure-proof answers. This is due, no doubt, to the difficulty and complexity of communication for those whose impressions of speech from the prelinguistic stage are mainly visual. It is rather a curious situation, too, that issues which have been dealt with in one way or another over the past two hundred years are reasserting themselves today and are being discussed independently of any historical context whatsoever. The problems are further complicated when teachers of the deaf find themselves and the methods they use under attack by those who, because of lack of experience with the deaf, may have a limited understanding of the problems as a whole. Researchers who become interested in studying the linguistic and/or psychological development of the deaf, in the hope of finding answers to questions in other fields, are bound to be confused unless they have long and varied experience in developing language in deaf children. It is notable that some of those who worked in the field have moved to other areas without reaching definite conclusions. It is regrettable, too, that professionals today are tending to erect "communication barriers" among themselves. Sides are taken, and very often the welfare of the deaf child is lost sight of, in the controversy that ensues, because a particular method has become more important than the pupil. Nothing could be more disastrous for the deaf, because without open, communicating, well-informed, experienced, and well-trained teachers, they will not be enabled to reach acceptable attainment levels.

The problems are further complicated because of stereotyping of the deaf by those who have not grappled with the problem of language teaching to different types of deaf children. As a result, educational arrangements are made which are based chiefly on social development and integration, without consideration of the fact that, in the absence of adequate language development, the deaf person is really isolated in a hearing society.

Since the '60s, particularly, controversy among the adult deaf, parents, and teachers has been widespread. This is partly due to the fact that international studies in the language attainment of the deaf have indicated that despite average and above-average intellectual functioning many deaf children reach standards which are appallingly low (Wollman, 1964; Montgomery, 1968; Rodda, 1970; Hine & MacDonald, 1976; Conrad, 1977). Much of the controversy resulting from the discussions connected with low achievement levels *centers around the language code rather than the method of developing language.* The crucial area of disagreement is related to the use or non-use of supplemental manual communication. There is universal agreement that deaf children should learn to speak, but one gets the impression from the current literature (Denton, 1965; Stuckless & Birch, 1966; Meadow, 1968; Vernon & Koh, 1970), that if manual communication is used together with speech, lipreading, sound perception, reading, and writing, language attainment levels will be raised automatically. This is completely contrary to my experience. The early teachers of the deaf who used the pure manual method of communication were aware of this, as can be seen from the following, written in 1856, by an Irish teacher of the deaf who taught in a pure manual school:

> Some of the difficulties in teaching language to the deaf may seem complicated but they will appear as such, only to those who do not have an experimental knowledge of the brevity of sign language or do not know to what extent it can be simplified or do not realise that the language of signs is a language of ideas. And, is it necessary to go into such details, to analyse, to pull the language to pieces, as it were, in order to teach it to our pupils? Could they not be shown written sentences—afterwards by passages from readers—the correct expressions and then made to learn them after understanding the meaning? These are questions often put forward, and what we have got to remember in connection with them is that our questioners, no matter how earnest, have not got the whole depth of the deaf-mute's difficulty. They may be among those who rank the deaf-mute in the position of a speaker, about to acquire a new language, or with a child about to learn its first lessons from its mother. Now, the deaf-mute's position as regards the acquisition of language is unique; he has no parallel within the range of human circumstances. The teacher finds himself compelled to pass over all the methods and contrivances employed by speakers and to lay the foundation of his great work on an entirely different basis—on analysis. The aim of the teacher is to get the pupils to acquire the English language and to employ each part of speech because they know its business is to convey what they want to convey not because they saw the word used by others in writing elsewhere. They are to learn the use of language by use—to build it up, step by step, according as the understanding develops and the ideas increase. (J.B. Bourke, 1856).

While language is a complex blend of semantic, phonological, and syntactical skills, it is also the representation of an interrelated set of relationships which stem from cognitive, social, and personal experiences of the child and his parents. These experiences are linguistically encoded in situations where there is parent/child or teacher/child interaction. This dynamic process of interaction is vital if experiences are to be expressed through codes such as speech in its visual-motor form, fingerspelling, systematic sign language, speech accompanied by manual signs closely related to the speech code such as Cued Speech (Cornett, 1975; Forchammer, 1903) or the written code. Traditionally, in our field, there has been a tendency to neglect the broader aspects of language, so that, through the years, oversimplified and structured language programs based on syntax, as well as on the processes of imitation, repetition, and reinforcement, have been produced by teachers of the deaf. Some of these programs have succeeded because of the personality of a capable, experienced, and dedicated teacher. In their time, some of them were regarded as a panacea for the problems of teaching language to the deaf.

Traditional Methods of Teaching Language:

Today, there is scanty information about the didactics of language or the principles of language development, but much about the respective merits of total communication and the oral/auditory approach. In a few publications on the teaching of language one can find traces of two main approaches which have been used since the 17th century—namely, the structured or analytic method, and the natural or synthetic method. Faced with a child who could neither hear nor speak, it was natural for the early educators of the deaf to turn to the written form of language in order to help those who were dependent on visual impressions. Written patterns were supplemented by the manual alphabet or by sign language. If speech was taught, an elemental approach was used so that phonemes, syllables, and words were taught before sentences. Teachers of the deaf such as Sicard (180p), Heinicke (1778), and Vatter (1880) used a grammatical approach. Language lessons consisted of lists of nouns, verbs, adjectives, and prepositions. These were incorporated in programmed sentences which were very often divorced from the conversation and from the daily experiences of the child. The emphasis was on expressive language. Repetition and analysis of sentences were more important than communication. In the case of the natural approach advocated by Delgarno (1680), Hill (1840), and Alexander Graham Bell (1883), the aim was to follow normal language development as closely as possible. Language was regarded primarily as communication. Hill advised the teacher to develop language in the deaf child in the same way that nature does in the hearing child. He advocated the teaching of speech and language together. Delgarno said, "Let occasion be the mistress of the method." He believed that if a code which fully represents the English language to a deaf child is presented by a mother to the child as a mother does to a hearing child, then he will develop language. Alexander Graham Bell used this approach with his pupil George Saunders, but he substituted written patterns for speech. There is evidence to show that some teachers of the deaf in the past used an approach which was a combination of the analytic and the synthetic approach. In 1879 a retired Irish teacher of the deaf living in Paris had the following advice to give to the principal of the School at Cabra, Dublin, where, at the time, the pure manual method of communication or "Signed English" was being used:

> I have no hesitation in saying that the system which dispenses with grammar until children have made considerable way learning language is preferable to that which mixes up the learning of grammar with the learning of language. In this order of things the latter has precedence of the former. Grammar—what is its object? Is it not to regulate the use of language? But language to be fixed and regulated must already be in existence. It was in this order that we speaking people learned language first and grammar after and if we were required to learn grammar at the same time with language our progress in the latter would have been very slow if at all possible. The greater part of mankind dispenses with grammar in the use of language. Either they did not learn grammar at all, or, if they did, they forget it. How few are capable of applying the rules of grammar or would be able to recite the parts of speech? Yet they use language for the ordinary purpose for which it is destined.
>
> We are witness here in Paris of constant examples bearing upon this subject. A family comes to spend a year or two, chiefly on account of the young people, that they may learn French in the French capital. They have a servant or two with them. What occurs? The best teachers are employed for the members of the family, to teach them scientifically according to grammar, whilst the servants are allowed to get on as well as they can, amongst the servants of the hotel or the house. A year or two passes over and who are the most expert in speaking French? The young people of the family or the servants; those who are taught scientifically or those who are taught by the mere practice of speaking, or in other words, by use of language? Experience is there to give answer and to bear testimony in favour of the servants (McNamara, T. 1879).

Questions as to whether the approach to the teaching of language of deaf children should be analytic or synthetic or a combination of both have plagued teachers of the deaf through the years. Controversy continues. The challenge persists. And ostrich-like, we try to avoid the issue by discussing the merits of oralism versus total communication; the unisensory versus the multisensory; the residential versus the day school; or special school versus mainstreaming!

Current Methods of Developing Language:

Looking at current approaches to the development of language in deaf children we find three main methods: (1) an analytic approach; (2) the natural method; and (3) the reflective method.

1. *The Analytic Approach*

The most widely used analytic approach in schools for the deaf today is the Fitzgerald Key (1926), which is comparable to other key systems used formerly in Europe. The Key provides a visible sentence pattern so that the child can form his own acceptable sentences and recognize and correct his own mistakes. It consists of a series of interrogative pronouns and adverbs, which along with six symbols form the headings under which sentences are cast. Each work is analyzed as it is slotted into its appropriate place. Repetition and sentence drills are used constantly. Eventually children are able to write grammatically correct sentences but the language is stilted and is very often divorced from real conversation and experience. This approach is used principally when the child is admitted to school, and very often before he has developed basic language. The influence of the programmed method used by Sicard can be found in the Fitzgerald Key and before it in the Barry five-slate system (1893). In the work of Streng (Streng, 1973; Streng & Kretschmer, 1978) the influence of Chomsky's theory (1957n 1965) is evident. The method is programmed but the unity of the sentence is adhered to unlike the traditional analytic approach. Amongst others, Kreye, (1972) and Prillwitz (Claussen, 1975) use a modified analytic approach which also emphasizes the unity of the sentence. Clark (1975) refers to the "traditional vocabulary-centered, structured oralism in which the teaching of speech is separated from the 'teaching of language.' The basic vocabulary lists drawn up for use in this type of approach show a serious lack of understanding of the needs and interests of lively young children."

2. The Natural Method

Several factors combine to bring about the more widespread use of the natural method in recent years. The main ones are:

Early Diagnosis of Deafness. Probably the dominant concept in our field, in modern times, has been the emphasis on early supportive intervention in the hearing impaired child's development (Ewing, 1964). It is now realized that the early years of life are crucial in the development of linguistic skills. Happily, the age at which hearing loss can be successfully identified has shifted steadily downwards. The greater understanding of the etiology of deafness, the development of screening tests of hearing as well as advances in the field of audiology have contributed to this. Because of technological advances we now have smaller and more efficient hearing aids. In many countries today governments are making two hearing aids available to hearing impaired children. Deaf children will not hear speech but they will receive information in the form of sound cues which enable them to get information with regard to the duration and intensity of speech. They will be helped to appreciate the rhythm of speech which is now regarded as essential for language control.

The Emphasis on Parent-Centered Guidance. Today the mother, naturally endowed with the ability to facilitate language development in the child, is encouraged to use a natural approach in the preschool years. The important role of the mother in dealing with the deaf child on a daily basis is recognized, so that parents are being asked to assume increasingly active roles in education. This is a far cry from the traditional approach to parent guidance. Formerly the teachers tutored the children while parents observed. Now the mother is encouraged to adapt her behavior so that the deaf child can be helped to develop language in the normal way. The mother facilitates the development of language rather than teaches it.

The Influence of Psycholinguistic Research. Some of the current findings in the field of psycho-linguistics indicate the need for the use of a natural method or the maternal method. It stands to reason that data from normally hearing children should provide basic information against which the deaf child can be compared. While there is still much that is unsolved in the field of psycholinguistics, it is true that certain universals are characteristic of the language process. The critical period for language development is between one and five years. As already mentioned, imitation, repetition, and practice are central procedures in the analytic or structured approach but it has been shown that in terms of a mother tongue they have a considerably less important role (McNeill, D. 1971). Lenneberg says:

> There is no grammatical system available that could be used to help the essentially language-deficient person to put words together in order to form good sentences.

In the language acquisition process the child is an active agent (Lenneberg, E.J., 1967), because the use of language is a creative rather than an imitative process. The child uses language to express concepts in an original and individualistic way. He discovers the rules or structures for himself. We know this because he often misapplies them, e.g., "I hearded it", "I saw two mouses". There is not much point then in telling deaf children how to form a sentence. He must first have some language. Again professional workers are emphasizing what Bruner (1976) has referred to as "intersubjectivity" between mother and child as an important ingredient in the normal language acquisition process. Parent/child interaction leads to the building up of a world of attention between them. Mother observes the baby. She follows his attention; she automatically and instinctively assumes intention on his part as she verbalizes. She says what the child wants to say. She expands; she expatiates. She carries on an endless conversation with her baby who is beginning to talk. The response on the part of the child provides motivation for further stimulation by the mother. A mother who receives no response to her stimulation—as in the case when the baby is deaf—is under great emotional stress. She is not likely to persist in interaction unless she receives support and guidance, especially in the early post diagnostic period. Once deafness is diagnosed the mother may change in her attitude towards the child. This is one of the pathetic results in the case of early profound deafness. Accumulated feelings of anxiety and tension in parents are often the basis of poor language development in preschool children; they have difficulty in adjusting to the child's handicap and developing healthy parent/child relationships. I believe that deaf parents have more normal parent/child relationships with their deaf babies and perhaps this may account for the current evidence (Bellugi and Klima, 1972; McIntyre, 1976) that deaf children of deaf parents are more secure and in some cases more advanced linguistically. In their case, however, etiology of deafness being related to genetic factors may rule out learning difficulties associated with acquired pre-lingual deafness. If parent/child relationships are right, and if the speech input is adequate in the case of the deaf child with an intact central nervous system and no additional

present methods of developing language in deaf children 125

handicap, he will go through the normal stages of language development, though, of course, his progress will be much slower than in the case of the baby with normal hearing. Dr. Joan Tough (1976), Director of the British Schools Council Communication Skills in Early Childhood Project also says—

> Language is not learned through instruction in how to use it. The child learns language because language is part of most of the situations in which he finds himself and he learns to operate as others do, because he is involved in their talk and in their experience.

She maintains that talk is the basic form in which language is manifested and that reading and writing have their basis in talk so that ways of using language for writing and reading must first be established through talk. This is not easy with deaf children. It cannot be done without parent/child and teacher/child interaction and co-operation. Psycholinguistics has shown how the amount of language input from parents can influence their child's early linguistic maturation. More recently emphasis has been placed on the type of environmental language. We now know that normally hearing children who are learning to talk are exposed to parental language which differs considerably from family to family both in type and amount yet virtually all learn their native language easily. McNeill (1966) referred to adult speech which children have to process as being a completely random sample which is in no way designed to instruct a child in grammar. Since then, several studies have shown that, on the contrary, there is a specific style of speech which is used in addressing young children who are learning to talk. It is adopted not only by parents but by other adults with little experience of children and even by children as young as five years if they are speaking to children under three. Drach (1969) pointed out that the language everyone uses to young children has shorter, syntactically simple sentences, a smaller vocabulary and slower delivery than adult-to-adult speech. It is also more repetitive (Kobashigawa, 1969), more redundant, makes more use of concrete references, less use of pronouns and seems designed to assist the young child in identifying grammatical categories and phrase units within sentences (Snow, 1972; Philips, 1973; Frazer and Roberts, 1975). The recent findings of Howarth in the area of parent/child and teacher/child verbal interactions in the case of deaf children are similar. Formerly, teachers of the deaf and parents used very simple sentences, a slow rate of utterance as well as exaggerated speech patterns in their anxiety to get children to lipread. Now they are encouraged to use the normal adult pattern. It is essential that the rhythm of speech be present to a marked degree for children who, through their low note hearing, can perceive this important feature. The perception also of intensity as it relates to stress is possible for this type of child. In this way a lipreader is helped to know the intention of the speaker. A deaf child, in the absence of these cues perceived through sound perception, is not aware, for instance, of the different meanings attached to the following sentences:

Mary will go to the Zoo on Friday.
Mary will go *to the Zoo* on Friday.
Mary will go to the Zoo on *Friday*.

Such acoustic information is a great help to the deaf child. The environmental language has a direct bearing, too, on the type of speech production among deaf children because perception and reproduction of speech must be regarded as two processes which are closely linked. All types of hearing impaired children learn to talk by talking as well as by listening to or "feeling" and by observing the speech patterns of adults and siblings. In the case of the deaf child speech production facilitates the perception of speech when both are taught together. This is Liberman's (1962) model according to which speech proceeds via production rather than as an ordinary decoding process. Lipreading, for example, can be well nigh impossible for a deaf person who has never learned to speak. Various studies undertaken since the 1940's have shown that poor levels of speech achievement among deaf children are commonplace. The typical errors relate to respiration, phonation and the rate of utterance.

There are differences of opinion among the professionals as to the most suitable approach to the teaching of speech. One group maintains that the emphasis should be on a developmental approach without attention to the articulatory aspects. This may be due to the fact that traditionally the structural and elemental approach to the teaching of speech produced the typical "deaf speech" which was so difficult to understand. Another group favors the elemental and phonemic approach maintaining that, if in phonetic practice the child is able to produce sound patterns automatically then in phonological speech conscious attention can be directed to what the child wants to say so that with a set purpose in talking, the principal characteristics of speech such as respiration, rate of utterance, and phonation will be dynamic. In the third method of teaching of speech an approach which has been described as "natural intervention" is used (Nicholas 1977). Initially emphasis is placed on the provision of speech stimulation suited to the age of the children. As fluent patterns develop it is noted that the articulatory aspects leave much to be desired. The speech sounds are then practiced in isolation in order to perfect them but then are quickly replaced in the syllable, word, or phrase. Repetition of isolated sounds and speech drills are used to develop automaticity but never in such a way as to disrupt the natural flow of meaningful utterances. It is true that in the case of the preschool deaf child in many countries today the natural approach to the development of language is being used if suitable parent guidance is available. However, as already mentioned, when the deaf pupil enters a school for the deaf he may return to the use of a more structured approach. Clark (1978) maintains that this is responsible for the low attainment levels in reading and language among the deaf. Observing methods in various parts of the world I find two problems which militate against the development of acceptable language levels—over-emphasis on structured methods together with the use of esoteric gesture language found in oral schools (Tervoot 1968) as well as incomplete linguistic patterns where total communication is used. I agree with Brennan's (1975) description of the approach to the teaching of language currently used in oral schools.

Clark (1978) advocates the use of the pure natural method. She emphasized the speech input. She says:

> No attempts are made to get voice before a child is ready to give it or to say a word before the child has anything to say. Very little progress is therefore seen during the early years in terms of encoding language. In the case of severe and profound

hearing impairment the first sentences may not appear until the child is eight or nine years old.

3. The Reflective Approach

The reflective approach advocated by van Uden (1970, 1978) embraces what is best in both the analytic and the structured approach. He worked in a school where the natural method was used in one department and the structured approach was adhered to in another. His experience convinced him that the natural or free method was superior but that there were improvements based on psycholinguistic principles that could be introduced. He emphasized conversation and the need for the child to discover language forms and principles rather than learn them through analysis. The basis of the method is natural conversation. Like the mother of the hearing, the mother of the deaf child uses an "anticipatory device". She tries to discover what the child might want to say. She "seizes" a gesture made by the child and she then uses the appropriate language. When the child utters a one word sentence she fills it out, in other words she makes a transformation of the child's utterances. In conversation the mother plays a double role—her own as well as that of the child. She does not expect the child to repeat what she says. Later these "conversations" are written down by the mother or teacher, the ideas and sentences being written in their colloquial form. For the child it is not mere copying of the adult model; it is the provision of the appropriate pattern for what the child wants to say. The child will understand written patterns intuitively initially. The reflective method is defined by van Uden as:

> the method of teaching language by conversation, by fixing the conversations in reading lessons in normal language; by developing the ability to read books used by hearing children.

The children of school age are encouraged to detect the structure of language by the use of normal language. The discovery method rather than an analytic or structured approach is recommended. Van Uden uses an integrated approach stressing the use of sound perception, speechreading, speech, reading, writing and rhythmic training. The context in the acquisition of language for the preschool child is the context of everyday life—the daily experiences of the child in the home. In the nursery school these conditions need to be replicated. In the primary school the deductive method of acquisition of structure and syntax is applied. Great emphasis is placed on reading in order to make up for the lack of frequency of linguistic patterns in the life of the deaf child. The written language is a support to the spoken language. Such a linguistically deprived child must be helped to extract the rules of grammar from the language he has acquired through conversation and reading. For him, reading of dialogue can make up for the lack of incidental conversation in his life. For young children it is the reading of a conversation which has been understood because it is related to personal experience. For the older children it is a means of entering into dialogue with the author. Van Uden's method has been criticized (Brennan

1975) because of its emphasis on imitation, repetition and "prescriptivism" (Brennan, 1975). One does not get this impression from the actual work being done in the Sint Michielsgestel School for the Deaf. The teacher makes transformations of the child's utterances. These transformations are written down in dialogue form, so that they become a permanent record which can be consulted by the children who are gradually encouraged and guided towards a stage where the rules of language are deduced. This is guided discovery learning more than the pure analytic approach familiar to teachers of the deaf. However, in the absence of auditory impressions the child needs some definite help towards the development of language. There must be some intervention.

Looking at the progress in talking being made by some preschool children it seems to me a pity that they have to fall back if they are placed in ordinary schools without help or in special schools where the linguistic environment and the teaching methods leave much to be desired. We need to listen to the linguistic output of children who have had the right kind of stimulation. We can learn much by studying their receptive and expressive language. In this area the video-recorder is a most useful technological aid. Would that we could have an international "pool" of recorded conversations. In this way it may be shown that given the right linguistic environment a deaf child can work out the rules of language for himself. Comparisons could also be made between the pure natural approach and the reflective method. The possibilities are endless. We would learn much from such an exercise provided we are supplied with accurate audiological reports on the children concerned. It is the child's ability to converse rather than to produce vocabulary lists that really matters when language is being assessed. We need more studies of children whose parents and teachers have facilitated the development of language rather than set about to teach it in a formal way. In such an approach there is need to differentiate between the child whose hearing loss is greater than 60 dB up to 500 Hz but who has measurable hearing up to 4KHz and the pupil who fails to respond beyond IKHz. In the case of the latter, language development is always a challenge whereas the former can, with the right kind of treatment—especially in the pre-school years—make progress in language development which was never dreamed of in the past.

Children with Specific Learning Problems

So far I have been referring mainly to deaf children in whom there is no evidence of language dysfunction. However there are some children who because of central nervous system dysfunction have particular difficulty in acquiring language despite intellectual potential and ideal opportunities from the point of view of linguistic input (Nicholas Griffey, 1962; Du Bard, 1974; and van Uden, 1977). A certain amount of controversy with regard to the preferred terminology has arisen through the years but now that the existence of the condition has been established the term "language disorder" rather than aphasia or dysphasia is used. In the case of these children early diagnosis followed by a period of diagnostic teaching is recommended. There is now a consensus that such children, because of disturbed auditory perception, lack of rhythm, and the short term memory problems associated with it, will benefit from an analytic approach (Vatter, 1880; McGinnis, 1939; Nicholas Griffey, 1962; Du Bard, 1974; and van Uden, 1977). This approach may be oral or manual but in both cases the child has to depend very much in the initial stages of treatment on graphic symbols. Some of them may need manual communication.

Mentally handicapped deaf children and those with additional handicaps such as blindness or cerebral palsy will need an approach suited to their specific needs. In their cases a very broad view of language is taken; that is, the sending of messages from one person to another. This includes facial expressions, eyepointing, gestures, mime, body language, Ameslan (Stokoe, 1960), Irislan (Nicholas Griffey, 1979), fingerspelling, sign language, writing, drawing, lipreading and speech.

Future Research

Effective development of language in children, whose main impressions of speech are visual, remains a challenge to the teacher. What Chomsky said in 1966 can be applied to the approach to the development of language in deaf children:

> I am frankly skeptical about the significance for the teaching of language of such insights and understandings as have been attained in linguistics and psychology. It is possible, even likely, that principles of psychology and of linguistics and research in these disciplines may supply insights useful to the language teachers but this must be demonstrated and cannot be presumed. It is the language teacher himself who must validate or refute any specific proposal.

To do this certain research areas must be given prominence. It must be undertaken by workers who have had experience n the teaching of language to the deaf. Ideally linguists and teachers should work together in classroom-oriented research. With the increase in the number of children with neurological impairment resulting from prenatal and perinatal etiology we need to devise suitable diagnostic tests for school entrants. (Vernon, 1969). Longitudinal studies of language development in deaf children have much to offer. We can now learn from pupils whose parents through proper guidance have facilitated their language development. Future research will entail the clarification of terminology because precise definitions need to be made available to international workers. Without this there is bound to be confusion. Much of the current controversy will disappear if we can provide linguistic environments suited to the needs of different types of deaf children. This cannot be done without well trained audiologists, psychologists, and experienced teachers, who work together in ongoing research. If this research is to be fruitful comprehensive services for the hearing impaired are essential. The implications for teacher training are obvious. May I end where I began by emphasizing that in the area of professional training generally, little will be achieved if the present state of controversy and "entrenched positions" persist.

References

Barry, K. *Five slate system: A system of objective language teaching*. Philadelphia: Sherman & Co., 1899.
Bell, A. G. Upon a method of teaching language to a very young congenitally deaf child. *American Annals of the Deaf,* 1883, *28,* 124–139.
Bellugi, U., & Klima, E. S. The roots of language in the sign talk of the deaf. *Psychology Today,* 61–76.
Bourke. *Notes for teachers*. Cabra, Dublin, 1856.
Brenan, M. Can deaf children acquire a language? *American Annals of the Deaf,* 1975, *120,* 463–479.
Bruner, J. S., Jolly, J. A., & Sylva, K. *Play—The early stages*. New York: Penguin Books, 1976.
Chomsky, N. *Syntactic structure*. Cambridge: M.I.T. Press, 1957.
Chomsky, N. *Aspects of the theory of syntax*. Cambridge: M.I.T. Press, 1957.
Clark, M. A natural approach to the development of speech and language. In *Problems of deafness in the newer world*. Report of the Commonwealth Society for the Deaf seminar, Sussex, 1974.
Clark, M. Preparation of deaf children for hearing society. *Journal of British Association of Teachers of the Deaf,* 1978, *2,* 146–153.
Conrad, R. *Facts and fantasies about the verbal abilities of deaf school leavers*. Papers presented at the Triennial Congress of the British Deaf Association, 38 Victoria Place, Carlisle, CAIHU, June, 1977.
Cornett, R. O. Cued speech. *American Annals of the Deaf,* 1967, 3–13.
Delgarno, G. *Didascalocophus, or the deaf and dumb man's tutor*. London, 1680.
Denton, D. M. A study of the educational achievement of deaf children. *Proceedings of the 42nd Meeting of the Convention of American Instructors of the Deaf,* 1965.
Drach, K. M. The language of the parent: A pilot study. In *Working paper no. 14*. Berkeley: University of California, Language Behavior Research Laboratory, 1969.
Du Bard, E. *Teaching aphasics and other language deficient children*. University, MS: University Press of Mississippi, 1974.
Ewing, Sir A., & Ewing, E. L. *Teaching deaf children to talk*. Manchester University Press, 1964.
Fitzgerald, E. *Straight language for the deaf: A system of instruction for deaf children*. Austin, Texas: The Stick Co., 1926. (Republished by the Volta Bureau, Washington, D.C., 1954.)
Forchhammer, G. *The need of a sure means of communication in the instruction of the deaf—1903*. Translation available in the Royal National Institute for the Deaf Library, London.
Fraser, C., & Roberts, N. Mother's speech to children at four different ages. *Journal of Psycholinguistic Research,* 1975, *4* (1), 9–16.
Heinicke, S. Schumann. *Geschichte des Taubstummenwesens vom deutschen Standpunkt aus dargestellt*. Frankfurt: Main, 1940.
Hill, F. M. *Anleitung zum Sprachunterricht taubstummer kinder*. 1840.
Hine, W. D., & MacDonald, P. J. *The screening survey of hearing-impaired children in the Midlands and north of England*. Unpublished manuscript, University of Manchester.
Kobashigawa, B. Repetitions in a mother's speech to her child. In *Working paper no. 14*. Berkeley: University of California, Language Behavior Laboratory, 1969.
Streng, A. H., Kretschmer, R., & Kretschmer, L. W. *Language learning and deafness*. New York: Grune & Stratton, 1978.
Krye, H. von. *Grundstrukturen der deutschen sprache*. Berlin, 1972.
Lenneberg, E. H. *Biological foundation of language*. New York: John Wiley & Sons, 1967.

Liberman, A. M. A motory theory of speech perception. *Proceedings of the speech communications seminar.* Stockholm, Sweden: Royal Institute of Technology, 1962.

McGinnis, M. A. *Aphasic children.* Washington, DC: A. G. Bell Association for the Deaf, 1963.

McIntyre, M. *Signs for our times no. 43.* Washington, DC: Gallaudet College, Linguistic Research Laboratory, 1976.

McNeil, D. *The capacity for the ontogenesis of grammar in Slobin.* 1971.

Meadow, K. B. Early manual communication in relation to the deaf child's intellectual, social and communicative functioning. *American Annals of the Deaf,* 1968, *113,* 29–31.

Montgomery, G. W. G. A factorial study of communication and ability in deaf school leavers. *British Journal of Educational Psychology,* 1968, *38,* 27–37.

Griffey, N. The aphasic child. *Teacher of the Deaf,* 1962, 99–108.

Griffey, N. Perception and reproduction of speech by hearing impaired children and language disordered children. *Northern Ireland Language Forum Journal,* 1978, *4,* 10–20.

Griffey, N. *Irislan.* Irish National Association for the Deaf, 1979.

Prillwitz. In Claussen, S. H., Krohnert, O., Prillwitz, S., Schulmeister, R., & Windisch, A., *Psycholinguistik in der Sonderpadagogik.* Berlin, 1975.

Rodda, M. *The hearing impaired school leaver.* University of London Press, 1970.

Stokoe, W. C., Jr. *Sign language structure. An outline of the visual communication systems of the American deaf.* New York: University of Buffalo, 1960.

Streng, A. H. *Syntax, speech and hearing, applied linguistics for teachers of children with language and hearing disabilities.* New York: Grune & Stratton, 1972.

Stuckless, E. R., & Birch, J. W. The influence of early manual communication on the linguistic development of deaf children. *American Annals of the Deaf,* 111, 452–460.

Tough, J. *Listening to children talking—A guide to the appraisal of children's use of language.* London: Ward Lock, 1976.

van Uden, A. *A world of language for deaf children* (2nd ed.). Rotterdam University Press, 1970.

van Uden, A. Johann Vatter, a German teacher of the deaf. *The Teacher of the Deaf,* 1970, *68,* 21–34.

Vernon, M. Multiply handicapped deaf children: Medical, educational and psychological considerations. *Council for Exceptional Children Research Monograph,* Washington, 1969.

Vernon, M., & Koh, S. D. Early manual communication and deaf children's achievement. *American Annals of the Deaf,* 1970, *115,* 527–536.

section 1 of 8

linguistics and the development of the hearing child
dónall p. ó'baoill

If I were to try to characterize the postwar period in language teaching—from 1940 to the late 1960's—I would be very tempted to speak of it as *the era of linguistics in language teaching*. During that period it seemed obvious that the science of linguistics had a major role to play in language teaching, and that this discipline was indeed the backbone or basis of a sound theoretical foundation, especially for foreign language education. From the early 70's on we may view this era as coming to an end. People who were working in the fields of applied linguistics and teaching in the mid 60's were looking very much at linguistics to get insights into what might be suitable for, or applicable to, their teaching. They soon got very tired of this because what was going on in linguistics was changing very rapidly, and a lot of things that they had been expecting were not forthcoming. Why then, we may ask, has linguistics failed to influence native and foreign language teaching to any great extent?

Linguistics as Theory Building

It is a formidable task for any specialist in any area to condense the essential principles of his/her discipline or field of study, and to present them to nonspecialists in a comprehensible and undistorted fashion. One should therefore not be too critical of linguists if they have not succeeded in imparting basic insights to languageteachers. It is quite clear from a short perusal of current literature in syntactic and semantic works, that linguistics is primarily concerned with *theory building*. The questions being asked are of a very general nature and are quitebasic in their content, such as the nature and legitimacy of evidence and argument in the field. At such a moment of development it is natural for the pendulum of professional preoccupation to swing away from empirical observation to abstract theorizing, from data gathering to concept definition, from close observation of facts to arguments about theoretical constructs at the highest level of generality. It must be stressed that the high-level abstractions of theory builders are necessarily remote from the preoccupations of "applied linguists and teachers." For the mutual benefit of each, the two domains must at times be kept strictly separate and remain quite independent of each other.

Evaluation of Linguistic Influence on Language Teaching

The great *quantity* of enthusiastic work purporting to spell out the implications of this or that linguistic theory made it easy for one to assume that the flourishing science of linguistics should provide the essential theoretical input to language teaching endeavors. In recent years, however, a growing number of major restatements point to a growing gulf between linguistics and teaching and to a cautious evaluation of the desirable relationship that should exist between the two fields. Ronald Wardhaugh's address to the 1972 TESOL Convention analyzes the contribution of various academic disciplines to TESOL. In considering the contribution of linguistics, he finds little evidence of even basic linguistic sophistication in the attitudes of language teachers, and admits that the current preoccupation of theoretical linguists have little, if any relevance to language teaching.

Another paper presented at the same convention by Dwight Bolinger discusses the *organized intervention of linguistics in language teaching* and he claims that it is a relatively recent phenomenon. He fears, however, that current linguistic theory may finally turn teachers away from linguistics as a source discipline because it has very few insights to offer.

Selinker, in his *state of the art* paper (1972), seems less pessimistic than Bolinger. Nevertheless, he claims that the idea that linguistics should be the sole basis of a theory of language teaching is a discredited hypothesis because many of the problems central to the language teaching situation are of no relevance to current theoretical preoccupations in linguistics. Linguistics itself is also in a somewhat uncertain stage of development, marked by doubt, dispute, and promising hypotheses, which are nevertheless constantly under challenge.

A perusal of journals in the field of applied linguistics in the last decade will reveal a recurring assumption underlying a great deal of work that purports to apply linguistic principles to language teaching methodologies. This assumption could be summarized as follows: *what is valid in linguistic theory must also be valid in language teaching.* This is, to say the least, a dangerous hypothesis, and a great deal of valuable and sensitive work has been marred by the tacit acceptance of such a view.

Positions that are theoretically valid in any field of inquiry can be extrapolated as insights for language pedagogy. One can find applications and implications in many different fields—cognitive psychology, speech perception, anthropology, sociology and a whole host of others. The jump from theory to practice, from a principle to its application, is no easy one. An oversimplified interpretation of theory and a facile expectation that theoretical constructs must find similar counterparts in an applied field, such as language teaching, destroy the independence of the two disciplines.

The continuing popularity of some of the principles mentioned above is somewhat surprising, since Chomsky himself pointed out many of the inherent weaknesses in the principle of transfer of validity back in 1966, in his remarks to the Northeast Conference. The following quotation from his address is well worth quoting here:

> I am frankly skeptical about the significance, for the teaching of language, of such insights and understandings as have been attained in linguistics and psychology. It is possible, even likely, that principles of psychology and linguistics and research in these disciplines may supply insights useful to the language teacher, but this must be demonstrated and cannot be presumed. It is the language teacher himself who must validate or refute any specific proposal.

What Linguistics Has Not Achieved

In the spirit of the preceding comments we may mention what the organized intervention of linguistics has not achieved. Significant failure is evident in two areas:
1. Content of pedagogical grammars; and
2. Attitudes of teachers and linguistic sensitivity.

Perhaps the most startling deficiency is seen in the state of pedagogical grammars, the *content* of the language textbooks, the description of the grammatical acts underlying the program of presentation and practice. These seem to have changed remarkably little in the past decade and a half. Part of the motivation for a linguistic component in courses offered to foreign and native language teachers was an attempt to *sensitize* teachers to the nature of language phenomena, and to help them see beyond the jargon of rules and symbols to a linguistic way of thinking about language. Wilkins (1972) still maintains that such a feeling for the basic character of the human language phenomenon is the major contribution of linguistics to language teaching: "Anyone who has studied linguistics is sensitized to language and thereby to the complexity of language learning" (p. 299). Yet others do not share such optimism. Wardhaugh's negative opinion on this matter has already been mentioned.

New Fields of Linguistic Inquiry

There have been many attempts lately to restate the field of legitimate linguistic inquiry, to go beyond the competence/performance distinction, in a way that might ultimately be relevant to language pedagogy. Indeed, new branches of linguistics are developing within the transformational paradigm, but with radically different approaches that might make these fields promising from the point of view of language teaching. I mention in particular the fields of *developmental psycholinguistics, neurolinguistics*, and *sociolinguistics*.

Some of the early work in experimental psycholinguistics was vitiated by an oversimplified reliance on competence/performance distinction and on the attractive assumption that a performance model would closely reflect or resemble the competence model. Recently, however, workers in this field have been emphasizing the need to work out methods of data gathering that will enable them to answer the sorts of questions being asked. Much more attention must be paid to the communicative environment of the developing child, because we need precise answers to questions about whether parents simplify their speech to children, how parents react to failures in communication, how parents correct, elaborate or expand their children's speech, etc. We may ask similar questions about adult/child interaction. The most important thing we can learn from current work in developmental psycholinguistics may well be a set of observational techniques for measuring the contribution of the learner to language development.

Although neurolinguistics is an equally flourishing example of linguistic inquiry with an empirically firm base, its relevance to language pedagogy is not so obvious. The basic preoccupation of workers in this field is to discover physiological evidence to support postulated linguistic constructs. Much of the research is centered on data from *aphasia*. There are grounds for believing that neurological evidence will play an increasingly important role in constraining the power of linguistic theory. Some researchers in this field have felt constrained to alter radically the competence/performance distinction and have, in the process, abandoned the distinction altogether.

The last decade has seen a great deal of flourishing research into sociolinguistic questions. Lengthy studies by Labov, Gumperz, Hymes and Fishman, to mention but a few, have shown the need for a social emphasis in linguistic inquiry. In this way the notion of competence may have to be enlarged to include skill in the use of language; what is now usually termed *communicative competence*. The field of sociolinguistics holds much promise for language pedagogy and, in addition to directly applicable insights from such research, the *methodology* of sociolinguistic research will—I have no doubt—prove useful and fruitful in stimulating and facilitating research in *school language learning*.

The Prospect of Progress — A Sound Foundation in Empirical Data

I strongly believe that language teaching needs a sound foundation in empirical data. The resurgence of interest in error analysis and especially in the study of *Interlanguage* seems to be effecting a felicitous union between close observation of data (learner performance) and insights from theoretical and descriptive work in linguistics.

The study of *Interlanguage*, I believe, will have many applications for the study of the language systems of deaf children. I would like to diverge a little here in order to fill you in on the background to the development of *Interlan-*

guage studies. When applied linguists saw that the answers they were looking for were not forthcoming from linguistics, they decided that they would start doing their own research on the language of the learner. This happened around 1967, under the influence of British applied linguists and people associated with them. The new type of study that resulted is usually referred to as the study of *Interlanguage* (IL). IL means a language system which is somewhere between the *native language* and the *target language* which the learner is trying to master. It can be at a basic stage, or at an intermediate stage, or at an advanced stage. The person most associated with IL is Corder, of the University of Edinburgh. In an article written in 1967, he outlined and described what he meant by IL, and how it might be beneficial to look at IL systems, in order to see what we could find there and then build our own hypotheses, instead of depending on linguistic theory facilitating us in this direction. For the next 6 or 7 years, Corder, and others associated with him, such as Strevens and Richards, produced a series of papers dealing with IL. They also used other names to describe IL. Corder called it *Idiosyncratic Dialects,* Nemser called it *Approximate Systems,* and it was Selinker who first used the term *Interlanguage,* and this has now become the accepted term to describe the kind of language that learners, who have not yet got full command of the target language, speak or use.

The main discovery that this group made was that IL was rule-governed and, therefore, that it was describable in linguistic terms. We might ask why IL as a discipline has grown. The current approach to language treats child language learning as a progression of self-contained, internally structured systems, getting increasingly similar to the adult language system. The parallelism between this change of approach in developmental psycholinguistics and the change from traditional error analysis to the concept of IL is obvious.

If we can show, therefore, that the language used by the hearing impaired is a systematic language and not a defective version of the adult language, then research similar to that carried out on the IL systems of second language learners could be worthwhile on populations of the hearing impaired at different ages and levels of competency.

The Deaf Child's Development in the Mother Tongue

The main contribution I propose to make to this Conference will be to outline the possibilities of assistance from the discipline of applied linguistics research, and what possible future research projects would be worthwhile in light of all this information. In order to do this in a satisfactory manner, we must first look at the linguistic development of the normal child, and at some of the research carried out in this field.

Methodological Issues

The learner produces and understands a certain amount of language. This will do as a starting point. There are, however, different ways of approaching the data:

1. We must view the learner's language in time. Therefore, we need information about the state of language before the study and about its state afterwards. The best way to do this is to carry out longitudinal studies with certain controlled variables of a group of learners or of a single learner.
2. The relationship of the language system at different points in time must be outlined, and
3. We must try and relate the learner's language to a final point—the language of the ordinary native speaker or some other system agreed upon.

The next question to be raised is, what constitutes appropriate data? The usual answer to this question is that one needs a combination of *textual data* and *natural samples from speech*. By examining these two sources one can hypothesize about the learner's competence in the language. The next step is to interview the learner and question him/her about specific points of grammar, semantics, etc. We must find out what the learner really knows by designing particular techniques to elicit the type of information we are seeking.

Grammatical Morpheme Studies

Studies of this kind investigate the acquisition of grammatical morphemes. The works of Roger Brown, Bailey, Madden & Krashen, Larsen-Freeman, and many others have shown that there seems to be a certain order in the way morphemes of a certain language are acquired by native speakers, and learned by others as a second language. However, let me add a word of caution here, namely, that it must be shown that order of difficulty is the same as order of acquisition if the results of the studies mentioned are to mean anything in terms of development.

Studies of Syntactic Development

There have been many studies of the development of certain particular aspects of language. The studies of Milon (1974) on *negation,* Natalico & Natalico (1971), on *pluralization,* Cancino, et al. (1975), on *auxiliaries,* Katz (1976), on *pronouns,* and Padilla & Lindholm (1976), on *possessives*, outline certain developmental trends in the learning of English as a first language. Other areas of development have hardly been touched upon, especially *semantics.* This bias towards *syntax* leaves the study of learner's language in a curiously isolated position. It is cut off, on the one hand, from recent ideas in first language acquisition, which are more concerned with semantic, cognitive, and social development than with *syntax.* On the other hand it is cut off from recent work in *applied linguistics* which stresses communicative functions rather than grammatical form. While the grammatical data that have been brought forth are interesting in themselves, one may ask where they lead. Ultimately, insofar as learning is concerned, the learner's language and the order in which certain items are acquired are only interesting as evidence for *underlying processes at work.* The question to be answered is *why his language takes the form it does.* It is, therefore, interesting to look at some of the underlying causes of the learner's language system.

Underlying Causes and Strategies in the Learner's Language System

When a learner is confronted with language, he/she applies certain strategies, both conscious and unconscious, to what he/she hears and, in the case of the deaf child, to what he/she sees; this partly determines his/her language system (Selinker, 1972; Richards, 1971). Some of the strategies that might possibly affect the language learning of deaf children include the following:
1. Transfer of training;
2. Overgeneralization; and
3. Avoidance behavior.

The Effect of Instructional Approaches

The overall effect of a particular instructional approach on the final competence of a deaf child is very difficult to evaluate. It may be that it will have no effect whatsoever on his final competence because we do not know whether the linguistic variables we use are in any way related to the psychological processes by which certain things become part of the learner's competence. Hence, what we do psychologically with language, so that it becomes part of your competence, may not be at all the way in which it is presented to you. There are three things that can happen:
1. Interference can occur. This happens when the child is not ready to absorb some structures which are being taught to him. We all know about the futile efforts by adults to correct children's speech;
2. The learner may be psychologically ready to acquire certain structures but does not receive the appropriate structures at the correct time; or
3. The structures may be programmed in the wrong order.

It is, therefore, very important that the cognitive and the linguistic development of the child should be as closely matched as possible.

Overgeneralization and Avoidance Behavior

Another strategy that learners use is to attempt to guess the system of the language. In doing so they apply rules that they have mastered in new environments. The rules may work in certain cases but will create ungrammatical forms in other cases. This strategy is to be expected in the writing of deaf children and also in their speech since their exposure to the spoken language is severely restricted. In the learning of language by normal children, speech helps to consolidate the type of language used in writing. Shachter (1974) pointed out that learners often do not make the predicted mistakes because they can avoid using or producing a form that they are likely to get wrong.

In general, the conscious and unconscious strategies that the learner employs are of vital importance and we need to know more about them, not only in linguistic terms, but also in the cognitive and social terms that are starting to be studied (Chun, 1975; Fillmore, 1976). Another important field about which we know very little is the correction/strategies used by teachers, etc. (Cohen, 1975; Holley & King 1971). Above all, the teacher must recognize the active contribution made by the learner; regardless of what the teacher wants him/her to do, the learner adopts certain learning and production strategies. Success in learning is a product of many different factors in the learner, many of them out of the teacher's control.

Fossilized Language

All the strategies mentioned earlier produce *fossilization*, i.e., the learner reaches a stage where he/she does not want to develop his/her IL further. This is particularly true of deaf children because of insufficient exposure to language. Therefore, the teacher must evaluate the type of language being used by deaf children and decide what characteristics of it he/she wishes to eliminate or improve. In this respect it is important to remember that mothers, when talking to their children, correct only utterances *which are factually inaccurate*. This might also be applied to language learning by the deaf at the beginning. *Communication of meaning is what matters most and, therefore, a hierarchy of "errors" must be based on comprehensibility.* It will be impossible to correct all "errors," perhaps unnecessary. Current views of language/learning emphasize that language can not be taught; it must be learned by the child. So, attempts to teach language by direct imposition of an adult grammatical model seem, in some sense, psychologically inconsistent.

Future Research Projects

1. Teacher Education
In order to avoid the obvious hazards, *teachers need broad, not narrow, linguistics*. Linguists must acknowledge that they have very little to say about certain aspects of the teaching situation in the classroom.

2. Research
Much of the material that has been amassed purporting to be concerned with the teaching and learning of language, and especially of the mother tongue, does not have a close relationship with the teaching situation in the class from day to day. Thus the most fruitful line of development to follow is to have the linguist *work* with the teacher in the classroom, not simply to collect data. It is also necessary to study and describe a large number of different Interlanguage systems to be found among deaf children at all levels. Longitudinal studies of a certain number of deaf children would no doubt also produce interesting and profitable data and hypotheses.

3. *Curriculum Design*

In the preparation of curriculum materials, and especially those concerned mainly with language content, the contribution of linguistics should be obvious. However, I feel that the following conditions should be adhered to:
   a. The study *should be appropriate to the development of the pupil;*
   b. The pupils should become *guided investigators* of language and are not to be informed magisterially about it; and
   c. Such studies *are not to be dominated by grammar.*

Obviously any teaching syllabus or materials will be more effective if they pay attention to what is known about the developmental sequence the learner goes through, the comprehension and production strategies she/he uses, her/his attitudes and motivations, the type of interaction she/he wants to take part in, and so on.

I do believe that teachers and linguists must work together in spite of all the difficulties this may cause. They must both respect each other and face facts squarely and honestly and realize that each has a different job to do but that their coming together in union may prove fruitful and successful for all of us. It should be fairly obvious from what I have said—and perhaps more so from what I have not said—that our knowledge of language learning is still largely speculative, excluding the possibility of prescribing recipes for teachers. I hope that the short account of the strategies of language learning has at least suggested some of the reasons why we hear or receive the type of language that we do from our deaf children.

References

Bailey, N., Madden, C., & Krashen, S. D. Is there a "natural sequence" in second language learning? *Language Learning,* 1974, 235–243.

Bolinger, D. The influence of linguistics: Plus and minus. *TESOL Quarterly,* 1972, 6, 107–120.

Brown, R. W. *A first language—The early stages.* Cambridge, MA: Harvard University Press, 1973.

Cancino, H., Rosansky, E. J., & Schumann, J. H. The acquisition of the English auxiliary by native Spanish speakers. *TESOL Quarterly,* 1975, 9 (4), 421–430.

Chomsky, N. Linguistic theory. In R. G. Mead, Jr. (Ed.), *Language teaching—Broader contexts.* New York: Modern Language Association Materials Center, 1966.

Chun, J. Selected processes in second language acquisition. Paper presented to the Fourth AILA Congress, Stuttgart, 1975.

Cohen, A. D. Error correction and the training of language teachers. *Modern Language Journal,* 1975, 59, 414–422.

Corder, S. P. The significance of learner's errors. *IRAL,* 1967, 5, 161–169.

Corder, S. P. *Introducing applied linguistics.* Harmondsworth: Penguin Books, 1973.

Dulay, H. C., & Burt, M. K. Errors and strategies in child second language acquisition. *TESOL Quarterly,* 1974a, 8, 129–136.

Duskova, L. On sources of errors in foreign language learning. *International Review of Applied Linguistics,* 1969, 7, 11–36.

Fillmore, L. W. Individual differences in second language acquisition. *Asilomar Conference on Individual Differences in Language Ability and Language Behavior,* 1976.

Fishman, J. A. (Ed.). *Readings in the sociology of language*. The Hague: Mouton, 1968.
Fishman, J. A. (Ed.). *The sociology of language*. Rowley, MA: Newbury House, 1972.
Gumperz, J. J., & Hymes, D. (Eds.). *Directions in sociolinguistics: The ethnography of communication*. New York: Holt, Rinehart & Winston, 1972.
Holley, F. M., & King, J. K. Imitation and correction in foreign language learning. *Modern Language Journal*, 1971, 55, 494–498.
Hymes, D. Editorial introduction to language in society. *Language in Society*, 1972, 1, 1–14.
Katz, J. T. Case, gender and pronominal diamorphy in child second language acquisition. Paper presented to the First Boston Conference on Language Development, 1976.
Labov, W. The study of language in its social context. *Studium Generale*, 1970, 23, 30–87.
Lado, R. *Linguistics across cultures*. Ann Arbor, MI: University of Michigan Press, 1957.
Larsen-Freeman, D. E. An explanation for the morpheme acquisition order of second language learners. *Language Learning*, 1976, 26 (1), 125–134.
MacNamara, J. Comparison between first and second language learning. *Die Neuren Sprachen*, 1976, 75, 175–188.
Milon, J. P. The development of negation in English by a second language learner. *TESOL Quarterly*, 1974, 8 (2), 137–143.
Natalico, D. S., & Natalico, L. F. S. A comparative study of English pluralization by native and non-native English speakers. *Child Development*, 1971, 42, 1302–1306.
Nemser, W. Approximate systems of foreign language learners. *International Review of Applied Linguistics*, 1971, 9 (2), 115–123.
Padilla, A. M., & Lindholm, K. J. Development of interrogative, negative and possessive forms in the speech of young Spanish/English bilinguals. *Bilingual Review*, 1976, 3 (2), 122–152.
Perkins, K., & Larsen-Freeman, D. The effect of formal language instruction on the order of morpheme acquisition. *Language Learning*, 1975, 25, 237–243.
Richards, J. C. A non-contrastive approach to error analysis. *English Language Teaching*, 1971, 25, 204–219.
Richards, J.C. (Ed.). *Error analysis perspectives on second language acquisition*. London: Longman Group Limited.
Rosen, H. Linguistics and the teaching of a mother tongue. Plenary paper presented at the Fifth International Congress of Applied Linguistics, Montreal, 1978 (Published in AILA Bulletin, 1979.)
Sanders, C. Recent developments in contrastive analysis and their relevance to language teaching. *International Review of Applied Linguistics*, 1976, 14, 1.
Schachter, J. An error in error analysis. *Language Learning*, 1974, 24, 205–214.
Schumann, J. H., & Stensen, N. *New frontiers in second language learning*. Rowley, MA: Newbury House, 1974.
Selinker, L. Interlanguage. *International Review of Applied Linguistics*, 1972, 10, 209–231.
Sridhar, S. N. Contrastive analysis, error analysis and interlanguage—Three phases of one goal. *Studies in Language Learning*, 1975, 1 (1).
Swain, M. Changes in errors: Random or systematic? *Proceedings of the Fourth International Congress of Applied Linguistics*, Stuttgart, 1975.
Taylor, B. P. Toward a theory of language acquisition. *Language Learning*, 1974, 24, 23–35.
Wardhaugh, R. The contrastive analysis hypothesis. *TESOL Quarterly*, 1970, 4, 123–130.
Wardhaugh, R. TESOL: Our common cause. *TESOL Quarterly*, 1972, 6, 291–303.
Wardhaugh, R., & Brown, H. D. (Eds.). *A survey of applied linguistics*. Ann Arbor, MI: The University of Michigan Press, 1976.
Wilkins, D. A. *Linguistics in language teaching*. Cambridge, MA: M.I.T. Press, 1972.

section 2 of 8

applied psycholinguistics and the teacher of the hearing-impaired child
a.m.j. van uden

Outline

1. Introductory remarks.
   a. A pessimistic trend in psycholinguistic research.
   b. Wealth and poverty of psycholinguistic research.
   c. Didactics and avoiding onesidedness of viewpoints.
   d. Is a natural approach compulsory.
   e. Some limitations of this paper.
   f. Relevance of the teaching of language to deaf children for linguistics and psycholinguistics.

2. Some tendencies in modern psycholinguistic theory.
   a. What is linguistic "competence," which at we aim?
   b. Linguistic competence in psycholinguistic theories.
   c. Natural syntax?
   d. Trends of theorizing, connected with designing machines for "artificial intelligence."
   e. The influence of language (= conversation) in our thinking. Is every language a "worldview"?
   f. The "position category" (Paardenkoper, 1953) and "rhythmic closure."

3. The mother (caretaker) as a teacher of language.
   a. Avoidance of onesidedness. Some aspects of early language development still insufficiently investigated.
   b. Linguistic "symbiosis" of mother and child.
   c. Interaction of mother and baby.

4. Some evidences from modern methods of teaching a foreign language.
   a. Motivation.
   b. Passive and active language.
   c. Automatization.
   d. Discovery learning.
   e. Micro-languages.

1. Introductory remarks

a. *A pessimistic trend in psycholinguistic research.*
Especially since the high expectations from Chomsky's linguistic theory (1957) applied to psycholinguistics are fading away (± 1970), a kind of pessimism seems to have arisen, with new hypotheses for future research. It seems to be, that we are still just at the *beginning* of our knowledge about our daily psycholinguistic behavior. The hope, that there is such a thing as *a grammar from which* the correctness of all sentences can be derived, judged, or described, or even "generated", is largely undetermined, and the idea of an innate Language Acquisition Device (LAD) is rightly criticized and renounced (Levelt, 1972). The process of how we comprehend and produce sentences, never explained by Chomsky, is still essentially unknown, and we have to rely almost totally upon the so-called linguistic "intuitions", which term indicates, that no clear explanation can be given. But even these *"intuitions"* are not always reliable, sometimes even disappointing (see Kempen, 1971, 1976). Informants appear to be inconsistent, even sometimes on the same day; the judgments appear to be very dependent upon verbal and nonverbal contexts too. The so called linguistic "competence" does not seem to be always completely adequate, neither observationally nor descriptively.

It is of course possible (although not without difficulty) to compose a *"micro-language,"* say of English, as outlined (not yet fully applied as far as I know) by computer-linguistics (Wood, 1970). A corpus of words and rules is selected, resulting in a kind of "Esperanto-English." This idea is not new, has been suggested and even methodologically worked out more than one hundred years ago (e.g., Jäger, 1836; Reuschert, 1909) as a so-called "Zweck-Sprache," a "target language," for prelingually profoundly deaf children. This same idea seems to underlie some methods of foreign language teaching (See below). But apparently the line of *natural* language is lost in this way.

In the same way as there is not (yet) a complete grammar, there is not yet a comprising evident *general theory* of psycholinguistics, without onesidedness. There are only hypotheses. The optimistic sounds about the opportunities expected from "artificial intelligence" and "computer-linguistics" (See below) are just hypotheses.—On *methodology* the last word certainly has not yet been spoken. A common method of research, for example, is the following:
- From careful descriptions of the phenomenon an explanatory theory is composed;
- From that theory some predictions are derived;
- These predictions are experimentally tested;

applied psycholinguistics and the teacher of the hearing impaired   145

- If these predictions come true, these results are accepted as confirming the theory.

Although this is a helpful outline as such, it can not be accepted without caution. The big risk of a "general theory" is mainly that some *reductions* of behavior, accidentally or even purposely, are admitted. This aspect of all research must be checked continuously.

b. *Wealth and poverty of psycholinguistic research.*

Notwithstanding the difficulties of research mentioned above, there are many good results of research *in particular fields,* which may be helpful for the educational didactics of language to deaf children, especially in the field of mother-child-interactions (See below). We must be very careful, however, (and an expert teacher of the deaf who tries to follow the *spontaneous* reactions of his children as closely as possible, will do so from his own experiences) in drawing precipitate conclusions from these particular pieces of research. The following aspects of psycholinguistic research seem to be insufficiently applied:

(1) An *in-depth* phenomenologic description of linguistic behavior, especially speech as "speech-act" including integrated nonverbal aspects (See below). Video-audio-recordings of linguistic interactions are more and more used, and this seems to be promising.

(2) Conversation as a *"spontaneous* interactive exchange of thoughts", not reduced to "communication," role playing, and/or question-answer game.

(3) Intonation, *rhythm* (both of speech and of integrated bodily movements), mime, and *"body language."*

(4) *Socio*linguistics and *pragmatics.*

(5) The use of *informants* who are *not* highly intelligent, for linguistic judgments.

c. *Didactics and avoiding onesidedness of viewpoints.*

In linguistic didactics, particularly regarding the child's first language, the educator (a broader concept than just "teacher") has to work very *concretely,* i.e., with *this* child, *this* verbal and non-verbal situation, *this* interaction, *this* language.

All onesidedness and/or reduction of viewpoints can be risky and endanger good results. The educator has to watch for all aspects and to avoid both Scylla and Charybdis. Let us mention some instances of onesidedness:

(1) Onesided *physical* and quantitative spatial thinking, with a neglect of *"existential"* thinking, (e.g., a 6-year-old boy asked: "Mama, does the mouse know that it is a mouse?" (See, 1977), of orectic, social, attitudinal aspects of language.—So it may be striking, that in such an excellent textbook as Clark and Clark (1977) little if anything is said about figurative meanings, metaphors, and poetry.

(2) Onesided *structuralism,* by which language is seen too much as a system in itself, in some way detached from its code and content and from the way of using it in the situation.

(3) Onesided *functionalism,* by which language is seen too much as just a way of interactive functioning.

(4) Onesided *rationalism*, by which language is seen too much as a way of thinking, starting from innate cognitive forms.

(5) Onesided *behaviorism*, by which language is seen too much as just an external behavior.

(6) Onesided *semanticism* and/or "conceptualism," by which the study of the cultural and voluntary structure of language is overlooked. Landsberger (1977) warns against dissolving psycholinguistics into mere (cognitive) psychology.

d. *Is a natural approach compulsory?*

A conclusion from the psycholinguistic findings so far seems to be, that the educational "didacticus" has to look for an approach, in which the *spontaneous* reactions of the children are used as much as possible, for example, to look for a *natural* approach. This means, *inter alia:* He will meet existential and attitudinal thinking, much content, need for conversation, and tendencies to structures too.

"Tendencies to structures too" seems to be a law of the development of social *interactive* behavior, for example, in social *games* (Remplein, 1961). An example:

> Two children are given badminton bats with a shuttlecock; very soon they try to keep the shuttlecock in the air; this is a first rule: the game becomes structuralised; if a child cannot keep the shuttlecock in the air, it is seen as a mistake breaking that rule; one of the children hits the shuttlecock too far; a second rule arises: keep the shuttlecock between these two lines; the cases that the shuttlecock comes down between these lines in the field of Peter, is a plus point for John, beyond the line of Peter, is a plus point for Peter; thus a third rule arises. The game becomes more and more structured, etc. etc.

The same happens with language: When a *pidgin*-language, a language without flexions, word-order etc., is used as a conversational language, it develops into a *creole*-language with flexions and word-order (see Clark and Clark, 1977). This structuralization includes automatization and disambiguity. It facilitates the interaction.

It seems that these tendencies to structuralization are working also within the interactive processes of mother and child, by which a mother tongue is mastered (See below). There seems to be no reason to suppose that the behavior of deaf children will be an exception to this law, when they are taught in a conversational way (See Chapter 9).

e. *Some limitations of this paper.*

(1) We will not (directly) speak about *phonology* because this aspect comes to the fore in the papers about the teaching of speech.

(2) We will limit ourselves to those aspects of psycholinguistics, which are relevant to the *didactics* of language to deaf children, especially to the oral way of education to deaf children, especially to the oral way of education.

f. *Relevance of the teaching of language to deaf children for linguistics and psycholinguistics.*

It does not seem to be impossible that psycholinguistic theory can reap some fruits from an in-depth investigation of the growth of language in deaf children, and of the difficulties met by them, perhaps more than from machines for "artificial intelligence".

2. Some tendencies in modern psycholinguistic theory

a. *What is linguistic "competence," at which we aim?*
(1) *Linguistic competence* has to do with linguistic *"intuitions,"* as described above, which, apart from phonetic (e.g., "Is this vowel longer than that one?") and phonologic intuitions, ("Is the sound in this word a /p/ and not a /b/?") can be explained further as follows:
- Semantic intuitions, ("Is this word a homonym?")
- Morphologic intuitions ("Is this participle correctly formed?"), and
- Syntactic intuitions ("Is this a good sentence?").

(2) *Syntactic intutitions* can, according to Chomsky (1957, 1968), be summarized as follows:

(a) Is a particular sentence or phrase grammatically correct? It may be clearly correct "in the cupboard," clearly incorrect "in cupboard the" or not clearly correct "the cupboard off." In this respect competence is said to be "observationally adequate."

(b) The competence should be also "descriptively adequate," i.e., how should a sentence be interpreted:
- Which words belong to each other, in *"How many* more marbles does John have *than* Peter?"
- Is this sentence or phrase ambiguous, "The painting of Rembrandt"—"Mary is easy to please"—"Where is the salt he demanded . . ."?"
- Is this a correct paraphrase "John hit the ball" = "the ball is hit by John?"

(3) *More aspects of "linguistic competence"*

(a) *"Conversational* competence"—"Language as a guide for social reality" (Sapir, 1932), including sociolinguistic and pragmatic aspects. Oksaar (1977) rightly speaks of "communicative competence".

(b) *"Transparency"* (1968). In understanding sentences we almost never get them verbatim. We immediately grasp the content and forget the literal words (cf. Fodor, 1974). This includes a lexical skill: finding words and their groupings, interpreting them. This has to do with a very important point in the didactics: the sensori-motor *integration* and the "setting of words" (c.q. setting of groupings of words), e.g., concerning *deaf* children:
- A *flower* in its experience and reality (smelling, picking, touching it, etc.), in its variety; pictures of flowers;
- The conversational language connected with these experiences:

Through lack of this integration dyssymbolia and integrative dyslexia and dysgraphia may arise (1973). This transparency has also non-verbal aspects (See below).

Many groupings of words ask for a *direct* comprehension and/or production of the meaning as *one whole*, for example, "You were at least able to open the door for me" cannot be conceived by synthesizing or analyzing: its meaning is an

148 oral education: today and tomorrow

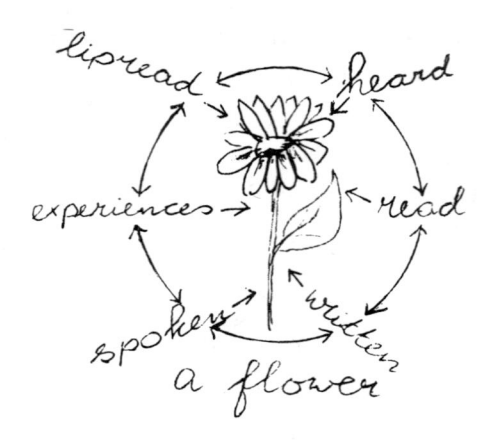

[Handwritten diagram: a flower in the center labeled "a flower", with arrows cycling between "lipread", "heard", "read", "written", "spoken", and "experiences"]

} All of this should be transparently integrated; one aspect calls forth the other ones, immediately.

"indivisible point" (1968). So we have to be cautious of descriptions like this: "sentences are composed by units of meanings, ... by a network of propositions" (Clarke and Clarke, 1977).

(c) Comprehension and production of the *intentions* in language, mainly expressed by intonation and mime—("assertion," "question," "appeal," 1968, 1977).

(d) Short Term *Memory* and Long Term *Memory*, e.g.
- "Do you like milk?"
- "What?"
- "Milk in your coffee!"
- "O yes, a little bit . . . . ."

The four elliptic sentences are connected with "Do you like . . . . . ," which has to be stored in memory. Without a good memory (conversational) competence cannot grow to its full potential (Kempen, 1968, 1971 and many others). It is clear that this points to a very important aspect of our didactics: the memory of *deaf* children for language must be trained, mainly by teaching them to "cluster" (See chapter nine).

(e) *Flexibility*.

Two examples:
- "The chair . . . . . of presidency was vacant for three years."
- "The dog's . . . . . mouth was broken."

Very often the semantic meaning and/or the grammatical meaning must be revised for a smooth comprehension ("feedback" process).

Two other examples from slips of the tongue (cf. Uylings, 1956; Cohen, 1965; Fromkin, 1973):
- "I am afraid of that b . . . . . wasp" (bee corrected to wasp).
- "Children should as much learn as much as possible" (revised groupings of words, see below).
- "I am . . . . . have been too late" (revised verb).
- "Why dó . . . . . do yóu, are yóu coming today?" (revised accentuations).

Both in comprehension and production of sentences we behave according to the T(est)-O(perate)-T(est)-E(xit) planning (Miller, Galanter and Pribam, 1960) in a scanning and screening way, rather parsimoniously. At the moment we think that sufficient features for comprehension and/or production are available we try to decide on our behavior (see Campbell, 1974) for phonologic understanding; Fodor (1974), for homonyms, and ambiguous phrases and sentences). This requires good flexibility, however, both in nonverbal and verbal thinking, as an aspect of linguistic competence.

(f) *"Syntactic eupraxia".*

Our linguistic competence operates with (brain-)*programs* (cf. Kempen, 1976), directly ready-made for use. We often do not operate logically and straight away, nor purely verbally but nonverbally too. It seems that this eupraxia is trained most of all in *conversations,* thus by interaction with other persons (See below).

A *sentence* therefore should not be defined
- as "subject-predicate-structure;"
- as "Vollständige Gedanke" "complete thought",
- but as "the smallest communicative unit" (Emons, 1978) or: "the smallest intentional say-unit in a conversation."

b. *Linguistic competence in psycholinguistic theories.*
(1) *Modern tendencies.*

After the enthusiasm about Chomsky's generative transformational grammar, according to the hypothesis of isomorphism between linguistics and psycholinguistics, some typical tendencies appear in modern psycholinguistics:

(a) A "comeback" of German linguistics, such as that of the "Junggrammatiker" [(Hermann, Paul, 1909, 6e 1959, "Syntaktische and grammatische Mittel der Wort-Sprache"), Drach (1932), Weisgerber; (1943)]. "Inhaltbezogene Grammatik" and "Wortfelder" = content-measured grammatics" and "wordfield." Instead of postulating preprogrammed mental structures the problem became how do we *use words* semantically and grammatically (1968)?

(b) "Generative *semantics"* instead of LAD and purely structural sentence diagrams (1968).

(c) *"Text*-linguistics" and "communicative linguistics" instead of too strong an emphasis on sentence-structures (1968).

(d) *Nonverbal* backgrounds of and in psycholinguistic behavior (1977, 1978).

(2) *We have to avoid onesidedness.*

Many functions are involved both in language comprehension and language production. They should be understood, however, as hierarchically ordered, which includes both interdependency and a certain amount of autonomous functioning (van Ginniken, 1929; Levelt, 1976). We may summarize this in the following diagram of four strata:

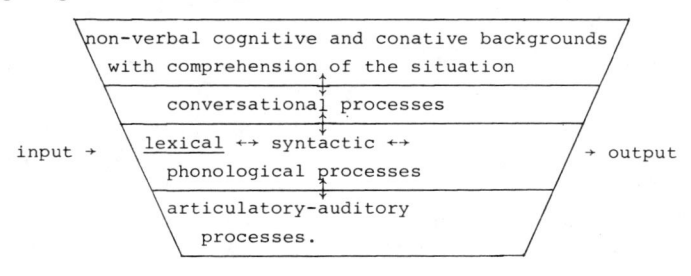

```
                  ╲non-verbal cognitive and conative backgrounds╱
                   ╲  with comprehension of the situation      ╱
                    ╲         ↕                               ╱
                     ╲   conversational processes            ╱
                      ╲         ↕                           ╱
         input →       ╲  lexical ↔ syntactic ↔           ╱  → output
                        ╲  phonological processes        ╱
                         ╲         ↕                    ╱
                          ╲ articulatory-auditory      ╱
                           ╲    processes.            ╱
```

The higher the structure the less it is automatic, the less it comprises closed circuit cybernetic processes. This may reveal itself inter alia by longer reaction-times.

This hierarchical order can be produced also in this way:

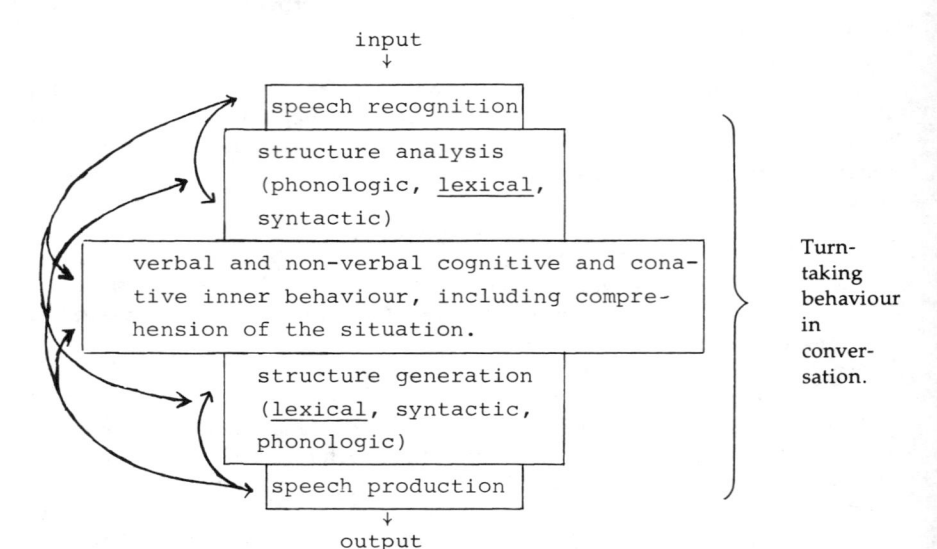

```
                        input
                          ↓
            ┌─────────────────────────┐
      ┌────→│  speech recognition     │
      │     ├─────────────────────────┴──┐
      │     │  structure analysis        │
      │ ┌──→│  (phonologic, lexical,     │
      │ │   │  syntactic)                │
    ┌─┴─┴───┴────────────────────────────┴──────┐ ⎫  Turn-
    │  verbal and non-verbal cognitive and cona-│ ⎪  taking
    │  tive inner behaviour, including compre-  │ ⎬  behaviour
    │  hension of the situation.                │ ⎪  in
    └─┬─┬───┬────────────────────────────┬──────┘ ⎪  conver-
      │ │   │  structure generation      │        ⎭  sation.
      │ └──→│  (lexical, syntactic,      │
      │     │  phonologic)               │
      │     ├─────────────────────────┬──┘
      └────→│  speech production      │
            └─────────────────────────┘
                          ↓
                        output
```

Psycholinguistic competence includes the condition that these functions— although relatively autonomous— are well integrated, cooperating, working as "Gestalts", patterns. (Davis, 1941, quoted by Lennon in Farr) pointed to *im*plicit understanding via latent meaning in our reading skill, (example, "The policeman was as patient as he could" includes knowledge about the duties of a policeman; otherwise this sentence cannot be understood). Many word-constellations such as "stone found a John" can be understood just by cognition, even if the listener or reader has too poor a syntactic competence, as happens in young deaf children, in their "vocabulary phase" of understanding and reading (1971, See appendix, See also Schlesinger, 1971). This may illustrate how non-verbal *and* verbal cognitive and conative inner behavior is working in language use.

Structure cannot be ignored. The same young deaf children can go astray in comprehension by lack of skill in structuring, for example:

> Peter has 5 apples and John 3. How many more apples has Peter than John? Answer: 5 apples. The "pincer-construction" of "more . . . . . than" and its comparative concept has not been understood (See below).

Kempen (1973, 1976) rightly has pointed out, that we, at least in the *re*production of sentences, use "grammatical retrieval plans", not only by the phrase-structure of sentences (Johnson, 1965; Kennedy, 1968), but also by congruency of conjugations and flexions, by constraints of functors and accentuations, by a kind of scanning behavior (See above).

(3) What is lexical functioning?

The reader may have noticed that we underlined the word "lexical" in the diagram of (2). *Words* seem to play a kind of pivotal part in modern psycholinguistic theories. Words are functioning both by *semantic and* by *grammatical* features (apart from phonological ones) as one whole (1968, Paul, 1909; Levelt, 1976). Context is playing a part in both aspects, for example, "The fair with all its merchandise started burning." The context shows grammatically that "fair" must be a substantive and not an adjective here, and semantically that a market-fair and not an entertainment is meant, further that it functions grammatically and semantically as a subject, not working actively or transitively, but more passively as the subject of a verb used intransitively ("burning" with a semantic feedback to "started", also to be understood passively). The 7 "grammatical means" of Paul (1909) are used here. Numbers 1, 2 and 5 the order and grouping of words including a pincer construction (see below) between "fair" and "started", and a compound construction (See below) in "with all its merchandise" and "started burning." Numbers 3 and 4 accentuation and intonation; Number 6 the functors twice "the" and "with" in a preceding position; Number 7 the flexions -s, -ed, and -ing. Several experiments have proven the correctness of Paul's approach (for example, see the "case grammar" of Fillmore, 1968; Levelt, 1976; Clark and Clark, 1977). The part played by "rhythmic closure" will be explained below. There is also non-verbal background at work. However, the knowledge (also loaded by emotional reactions) that a fair sometimes *may* start burning because of a discarded cigaret, by a short-circuit and so on, can none of it be expressed only verbally. All of this includes the ability to *understand between the lines,* for example, the shift of meaning in questions like "How *old* are you?" asked of a young child, or "This feather is *heavier,*" (see Levelt, 1976).

It may be clear that lexical functioning must be taken in a *broader* sense than is mainly done in linguistic textbooks, i.e., not just sticking to semantic content: this content cannot be fully detached from grammatical functioning (1968, See below). Actually the "lexicons" don't just indicate the meaning of the words and/or lexemes, but also their possible grammatical functions in contexts, which include "retrieval clues." We emphasize again the necessity of a good intermodal integrative functioning in learning a language (See above).

Interestingly enough the so-called "brackets-analysis," indicating the *cohesion* of the words calls back the old but much clearer analysis of van Ginniken

[((The fair)(with all its merchandise))) ((started)(burning)))]

(1922) and Reichling (1947, quoted by Tervoort 1952), which appeared to be very useful both for hearing and *deaf* children:

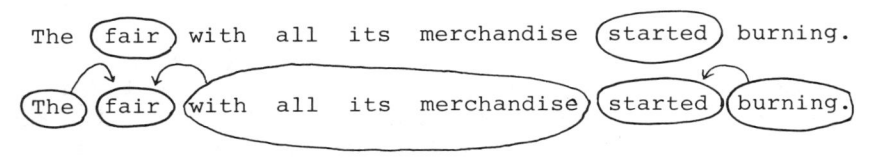

The (fair) with all its merchandise (started) burning.

(The)(fair)(with all its merchandise)(started)(burning.)

Etc. (see 1968, 1977).

The theory of the *logogen* (Morton, 1970) seems to be helpful in understanding lexical functioning both for comprehension and for production of language.

The *logogen* is a unit of a situation or of a context, which is the background from which words are understood and/or produced. It can be described, a little bit more broadly than by Morton, as a bundle of concepts, of semantic, grammatical and phonological features of words, by means of which words and their groupings are understood and/or produced. For example, a child sees a plank in the water, points to it and says impulsively: "Boat! There is a boat!" He did not exactly mean boat as such, but he first retrieved this word in his mind, although he knew the word "plank" also. The disclosure threshold of the common word "boat" is lower than that of "plank;" the phenomenon has many *semantic* and situational features in common with a "boat," perhaps phonological ones too (the labials /p/ - /b/). The *reaction-times* will be shorter when the thresholds are lower according to the cognitive system of the subject. For example, after water "cold" is recognized more quickly than "vapor" (Cf. Meyer, 1973).

The same happens very often with *deaf* children: so once a child called a brush a "bear", another one his big toe the "thumb of my foot", etc. Another deaf child said: "It bees me", instead of "The bee bites (meant stings) me" (in Dutch it was "hij bijt me", "de bij bijt me").

It is hypothesized, that we have a *logogen-system,* a *network of logogens,* a *cumulation of logogens,* evoking each other, repelling each other, grouping and combining "themselves" etc., in connection with the semantic and grammatical *combinabilities* of words (Paardekoper, 1953). The logogens *activate* words and are activated by other logogens, situations, and contexts. Homonyms seem to have different logogens (cf. Levelt, 1976). By means of the logogens combinabilities of words (*virtual combinations, 1968*) are realized into *actual combinations,* e.g., "water" and "cold" into "cold water," "the tap with cold water" (see below). The word and its logogen roots can be symbolized as follows:

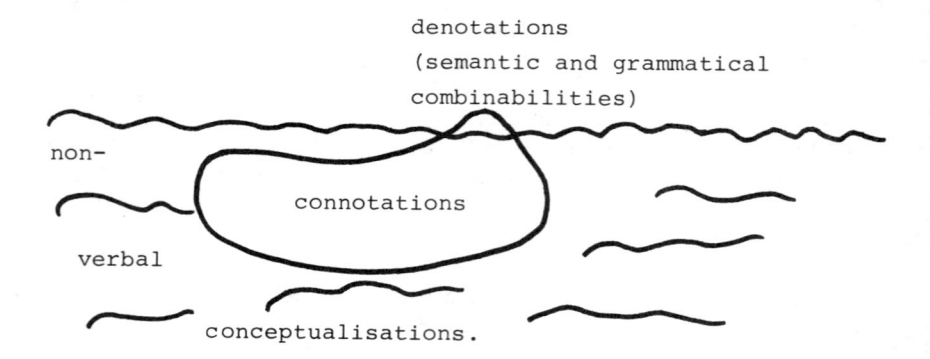

```
                    denotations
                    (semantic and grammatical
                    combinabilities)
      non-
                    connotations

      verbal

             conceptualisations.
```

(4) *The "speech-act."*

Austin, (1962 et seq., Searle, 1969 et seq.) describes the "speech-act" as "the complete speech-act in the complete situation of language *use*". It focuses on "How to do things with words." If we take this philosophy in its full deep sense, the speech-act includes:

applied psycholinguistics and the teacher of the hearing impaired 153

- Not only cognitive but also *conative* and *motor*-behavior;
- "Body language" (cf. Birdwhistell, 1960 et seq. Bullowa, 1979);
- Verbal and nonverbal face-to-face *encounter* and *coenetics* (Westcott, 1965);
- empathy, *sociocentric* behavior;
- *Human comprehension*;
- *Pragmatics*.

It may be clear that *conversation* is the most ecologic situation of the speech-act (See Chapter 9). *In* conversation speech can only be a "speech *act*." According to (van Ginniken, 1909) "conversation is the *full* form of language".

c. *Natural syntax?*

It seems contradictory to speak of a *natural* syntax, because language has been considered a largely *voluntary*, completely cultural system (Sapir, 1884–1939). It seems to be undeniable, although not yet sufficiently investigated, that there are some tendencies to typical sequences of words which mirror the programming of natural activities, for example, "John hits the ball" = agent (actor) – action – recipient (actum) = linguistically subject – verb – object. Although not in all languages, this sequence seems to be valid in most of them (Greenberg, 1968). Wundt (1895) has pointed to similar natural sequences in a series of manual signs (See also Kainz, III, 1957). In sign language it is natural to change the order "in the cupboard" into "cupboard in", because it is necessary first to draw a cupboard in the air and *then* to do something in relation to that imagined cupboard (Tervoort, 1953). This sequence rightly is called a *visual* sequence, a kind of "film-thinking."

This tendency is understandable since speech is seen as "speech act", originating from and within body language in a child 2–3 years of age (See below). Language *keeps* a function within the whole of non-verbal communication (Bruner, 1975). Even it may be said, that a child of 1–2.6 years of age is in some sense bilingual, and typical interferences between a natural and a cultural sequence of words have been found (Schaerlaekens, 1973, see below). Some typical difficulties of *deaf* children in learning language seem to originate from these kinds of interferences too (cf. Heider 1940 and others).

Other related natural sequences are those of:

- Topic—comment;
- Given—new (Clark and Clark, 1977);
- Question—answer a child of 2 years of age—"Mama? . . . sleeps!" (Leopold, 1954)

Sequences such as: "After you had opened the door, you put the box on the table" is understood by children more easily and at a younger age than: "You have put the box on the table, after you had opened the door". (See a summary of several studies in Clark and Clark, 1977; for *deaf* children see Quigley, 1975).

The same Wundt (see also, Maesse, 1933, 1977) pointed to a kind of "violation" of the visual order of signs by emotions: when the signer wants to give some prominence to a sign (a kind of "accent"), he is inclined to put that sign into the first position of a series of signs, e.g. "Hat! (I) spoke (of)!" The reason seems to be, that sign language does not have a *rhythmic* order of signs. The main means of giving a sign prominence within a string of signs is to put it in the first position of that string. This seems to be in contrast to speech, oral language, "I spoke of a *hat*". The sequence of signs arranged by emotional order, although not visual, seems to be natural too. Every teacher of the *deaf* will recognize many interferences from the above in the oral and written utterances of his children. The best way to overcome this difficulty certainly is by *rhythmic and accentuated speech*. Notwithstanding all this, the main order of spoken language is *voluntary* (e.g. "You have first to put the plate on the table, then to open the door"), although not as voluntary as has been thought before.

d. *Trends of theorizing, connected with designing machines for "artificial intelligence."*

The main topic of psycholinguistics is of course the mental processes by which utterances of language are understood, respectively produced or "formulated". Although Chomsky (1957), called his theory a "generative" one, it hardly has said anything of *how* these processes proceed. The composers of linguistic computer programs and/or of linguistic machines (machines for translating texts and finding paraphrases of sentences, so-called "within-translations," or for formulating messages or drawing conclusions or answering questions), primarily ask exactly for information about these processes in order to simulate them in a machine. Because these processes are largely unknown, however, the result of their work has just the opposite effect: they try to construct machines with programs which "understand" and/or "formulate" sentences and texts as "competently" as possible. The underlying theory of these machines then becomes a model for the real human processes, and this theory can be tested experimentally (See above. See Woods, 1970; Schank, 1972, 1975; Simmons, 1972; also surveys by Dietrich, 1974; Levelt, 1976; Kempen, 1977). Some pieces of *evidence* are suggested by these studies, which may help us to understand the linguistic difficulties of *deaf* children:

(1) The *non-verbal background* and source of linguistic behavior, both for understanding and producing language. Schank (1972, 1975) speaks of "concepts" and "conceptualizations" and "multicomplex conceptualizations," others of "encyclopedic knowledge" (see Clark and Clark, 1977). Words are interconnected not just grammatically or even semantically but also "encyclopedically." The contents of the words and their non-verbal implications (See above) must be taken primarily, instead of *empty* grammatical and syntactic diagrams, as suggested by Chomsky. The machine starts "thinking" from these contents. For example a "sentence" like this: "Hair barber too much cut my short the has" . . . will be "understood" from the contents (See above). This emphasizes the necessity of *experience* in the didactics of *deaf* children. For example, a reading lesson about a policeman may not be understood because the children have to superficially posit an "encyclopedic" knowledge of the work of a policeman. They have to go then to the police station, perhaps to the prison, to observe carefully the guidance of traffic (perhaps imitating this in role-playing), to be aware of the consequences of a police report or action etc. All of this is *not* meant as non-verbal experience (See below), but as a verbalized, equal to "conversationalized" experience with many non-verbal implications. (See chapter 9) Another example about the *feelings* of *figurative meanings*. These mainly have to be *felt* by experience, cannot be explained intellectually, cannot be poured from our mind into their minds as just another vessel.

The educator has to "seize" the right moment. For example, a preschool child observes the streams of water on a window on a rainy day and expresses, verbally or not verbally, "weeping" . . . . . At that moment the educator says: "Oh yes, what depressing weather!" These experiences are added by "a sleeping flower," "a mean nail," "a happy sun," by extending to allegories and metaphors in the course of the years.

(2) The concepts, verbal and non-verbal, and their *relationships* are expressed by nodes and arrows in the computerprograms, called *transition-networks*. These relationships or transitions easily can be made *probabilistic*, based *inter alia* on frequency of use. Typical terms, used before and elsewhere, such as *"combinabilities of words"* (1968) and *"open places* before and after words" (1968) reappear. For example, a verb such as "beat", meant transitively, has open places around it for an agent and a recipient. The agent and the recipient can be described as "case-holders," the "nominative" and "accusative" of the so-called old grammars (cf. Paul, 1909).

> A verb in a semantic network has associated with it a set of case arguments, each case argument being a relation . . . . . and a value . . . . . The value of a case relation is another concept-node, which may be expressed linguistically as either a noun-phrase or an embedded sentence. (Schank, 1975)

(3) The term "open places" calls to mind the term *position category,* as used before by Paardenkoper (1953). For example, in many languages the subject precedes the verb, a noun, marked as subject (or agent), gets a (probabilistic) mark of a position before the verb; the category subject includes a position category. The same may be true of a verb, with a direct and indirect object, an adjective, a preposition and so forth. This calls to mind the term *feedback* refuting a theory by means of which sentences are understood and/or produced from left to right (See above). For example the composition of a noun constituent as:

"a tall boy in New York"
  1   2   3

can be the result of different inputs from the "lexicon": that input could start with 3 New York, or with 2 boy etc. The arrangement can be executed 1 - 2 - 3, or 3 - 1 - 2, or 2 - 3 - 1 etc. with the same final result. Not only in children (see McWhinney, 1977) according to 5-year olds, but in adults too, there is much co-planning of sentences, *while* speaking (see Clark and Clark, 1977). We don't always plan our sentences completely beforehand, but, while speaking, the combinabilities of words, by compound- and pincer-constructions, lead us on. We follow TOTE-planning (See above). Hence so many hesitations, repetitions, revisions, retracting false-starts, slips of the tongue etc. (in writing, this TOTE eupraxia mainly happens beforehand; children can learn not to speak too impulsively but by better pre-planning. (See McWhinney, above).

Several studies, investigating reaction-times, suggest the working of these "combinabilities" from their virtual towards their actual states. Levelt (1976) rightly says, that "speech happens by favor of retrieving the right *word* at the right moment," Clark and Clark (1977) speak of *"networks* of units of meanings (of "propositions," of "ultimate constituents"), which form a new total meaning," and Labov, since 1969, wants to apply *statistical* methods to the use of the right words at the right moments based upon variabilities and relative frequencies. Kintsch (1976) measured the *combinabilities* of content-words in contexts for reading, and found that the higher the amount of combinabilities the longer the reaction times were for correct understanding. Collins and Quillian (1969) measured the *semantic "distance"*, for example between bird and duck ("a duck is a bird") and between bird and sparrow ("a sparrow is a bird"), the distance of the latter combination being smaller than that of the first (see also Clark and Clark, 1977). The longer these distances, the longer the reaction times were for the judgment of correctness of such a statement ("semantic distance effect"). Foss and Jenkins (1973) and Fodor (1974) found, that the subjects were not always aware that some sentences are *ambiguous* ("Margret is easy to tease" only understood passively). Notwithstanding that, the reaction time for such an understanding was longer than that for an unambiguous sentence. MacKay (1966, 1970, 1971) found that the completion of incomplete ambiguous sentences took longer reaction times than these of unambiguous ones, with many hesitations, repetitions, restarts and the like. Here is an example (1968, 1977), which may illustrate the importance of this theorizing for *deaf children*:

> *Situation:* John and I are walking in an avenue of oaks. Acorns are falling down. I hear this. Then: *I react* as follows:
> 1. The first word emerging in my mind may be: *acorn-s*. It is immediately put in its plural form.
> 2. *fall(ing)* immediately groups with *down*. The morpheme *-ing* is retained.
> 3. The whole phrase *acorns fall(ing) down* is stored for a moment.
> 4. *hear* had come up, which immediately groups itself to
> 5. *I hear* . . .
> 6. Then *acorns falling down* is taken from its store with the morpheme *-ing* filled in, influenced by the "feed-ahead" of *I hear,* and the sentence is uttered.
> *I hear acorns falling down.*

Schematized in this way:

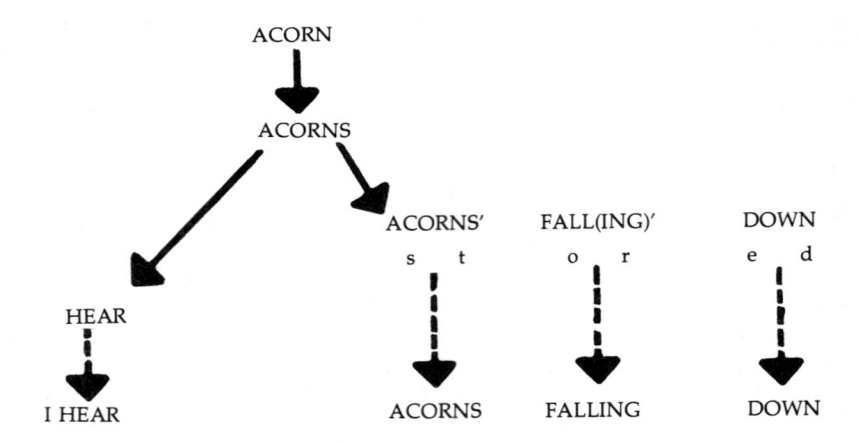

```
                    ACORN
                      ↓
                   ACORNS
                  ↙       ↘
                 ↙     ACORNS'   FALL(ING)'   DOWN
                ↙         s  t      o   r      e  d
             HEAR         ↓         ↓          ↓
              ↓           ↓         ↓          ↓
            I HEAR      ACORNS    FALLING     DOWN
```

Or schematized according to the model of Johnson (1965):

```
            3
         /     \
        /       2
       1       / \
      / \     /   1
     I   HEAR ACORNS FALLING DOWN.
```

John:
1. *Yes* as his first word . . . . . Then or together:
2. *Autumn* emerges in his mind.
3. This is immediately grouped as:
   Yes, it is autumn.

Schematized in this way:

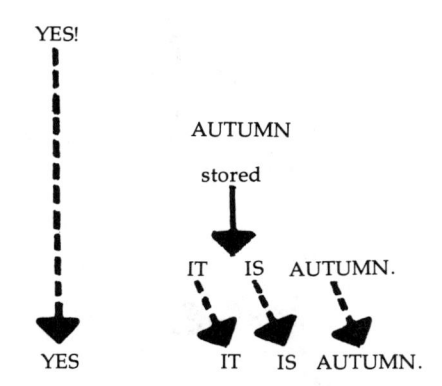

```
    YES!                AUTUMN
     |                   stored
     |                     ↓
     |              IT   IS   AUTUMN.
     ↓               ↓    ↓    ↓
    YES             IT   IS   AUTUMN.
```

Or schematized according to the Johnson's model:

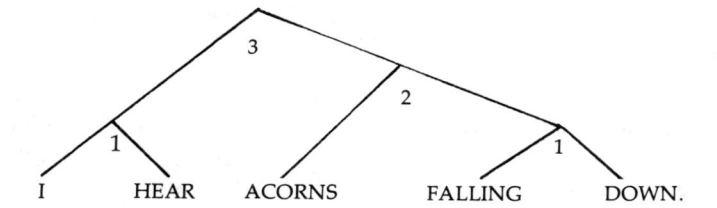

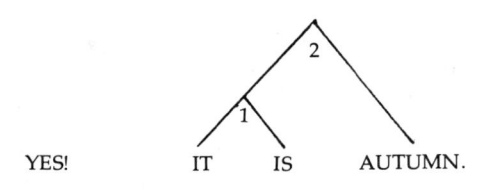

```
                  2
                 / \
                1   \
               / \   \
            YES! IT  IS  AUTUMN.
```

We see that there is continuous structuring, storing, checking, combining, mostly operating unconsciously. This needs a continuous activity of *short term memory*. If this is defective by lack of rhythmic phrasic training, it will give difficulties in language, in thinking too. If *deaf* children have not been educated in this way, we can expect a kind of unstructured *"film-thinking,"* i.e. the whole

158 oral education: today and tomorrow

story the child is telling, is running off picture after picture, in small units, almost *avoiding any burdening of their STM.*

Flexibility and selective activity.

We can schematize this, *Acorns falling down,* in another way, in order to illustrate the selective activity in speech, i.e. the need for *flexibility.* We warn against an associative concept of the grouping of words. We symbolize the words with their virtual functions, i.e. with their "combinabilities," as wheels with cogs.

Acorn: noun, singular form, plural form. The selected form is indicated by a flashing light:

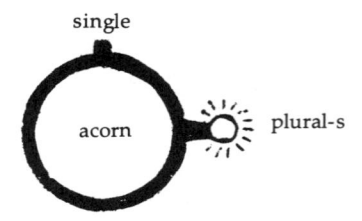

Fall: verb, intransitive, forms: falls, falling, fell, fallen; 13 meanings.—Noun, singular form, plural form, 26 meanings. The selected meaning, including form, is indicated by a flashing light.

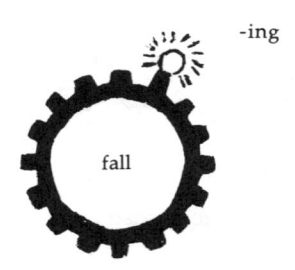

Down: adverb, 8 meanings, passing into adjective in predicative use,— preposition, 4 meanings,—verb, transitive, 1 meaning. The selected meaning is indicated by a flashing light:

applied psycholinguistics and the teacher of the hearing impaired 159

Influenced by the one *intention* of an assertion, with a general diffused intuition of the whole, this whole *differentiates* into one rhythm of a phrase in which the words appear—the wheels fit together in their selected cogs:

ACORNS — FALLING — DOWN

We see there is a big difference in the richness of combinabilities of words: *acorn* is rather poor, *fall* is very rich. This richness differs of course from person to person: in a child the 'action radius' will be smaller than in an adult, in an illiterate smaller than in a literate, in a professor of physics smaller than in a professor of literature . . . . . There must be, however, somewhere a *minimum* number of combinabilities in a mind, under which minimum the linguistic feeling of a person will be insufficient for his daily life and he will make too many mistakes. This happens in small children, in hearing impaired children, in mentally defective persons etc. In subjects having normal language, this richness must be very flexible, so that the right combinability is *immediately* actualized when needed. This immediate readiness of the words with their meanings, called by us the *"transparency"* of language, is one of the most striking features of a *mother tongue*. When we start to speak a foreign language which we have not mastered sufficiently, there suddenly appears a loss of flexibility: the words are not immediately ready in their right functions, they gear into each other very stiffly; vocabulary, expressions, and structures are limited; most words appear to be nailed down into too few combinabilities. It is clear that this will give many difficulties in receiving and expressing language.

This nailing down of words into *too few combinabilities* (contentively and functionally) is one of the consequences of programmed and limited presentation of language forms as exemplified in the constructive method. We will come back to this point later.

Groht (1958) rightly says: "The English language is so full of exceptions, that no rule seems to be absolute . . . . . No teacher . . . . . can ever give her pupils all the forms of all the principles they must know." This happens in all languages. The *only* possible way is to bring the children *to good reading* of normal language on the basis of oral conversation, as we will explain later.

It may be clear from all this that *visual diagrams,* such as the "Fitzgerald Key", are not in agreement with this way of oral thinking and behavior. Our criticism can be summarized as follows (see 1968):

(a) They are a simultaneously presented whole;
(b) They are purely visual;
(c) The rhythm of speech (see below) only plays a minor part;
(d) They suggest a language thinking from left to right.

On the contrary a large *variety of input,* of comprehension, with "guided discovery learning" of the structure *in* that variety, seems to be necessary for flexible conversations and language productions.

Some *shortcomings* in the approach of general psycholinguistic theory derived from the machines for "artificial intelligence" may be summarized as follows:

(1) There is a danger that the setting of language as a *conversational tool* is lost. The process of conversation and of the *speech acts* cannot be fully studied by means of machines.

(2) The same with the *rhythm* of language (see below).

(3) The same with *"Gestalt"* formation, which excludes a concept of "the elements before the whole," but exactly the reverse.

(4) The importance of non-verbal conceptualizations may be emphasized so much that the *influence of language in our thinking* is minimalized, which seems to be incorrect.

e. *The influence of language (= conversation) in our thinking. Is every language a "worldview"?*

This topic seems to be very important. Should we more or less *separate* education by experience from the teaching of language, as suggested by e.g. Furth and Wachs (1972) and others? Or should we *integrate* the experiences and the language as much as possible for the efficiency of both? (See above) It may be clear that we mean by "language": lively *conversational* language, not formal training of vocabulary and models of sentences and so on.

(1) *The theory: "Every language is a worldview"* (Wilhelm von Humboldt, 1767–1835) against the theory: *"Thinking without language"* (Furth 1966, 1973; Watts 1978). These are two extreme theories. The first one, advocated by (Sapir, 1944; Whorf, 1956), is that of the linguistic relativity of our thinking. The second one, advocated by Piaget (1926) and his followers, tends to postpone the main influence of language upon our thinking about 10 years of age. The computer linguists, mentioned above, do not seem to be always aware that many of the concepts that we have are formed by language, by the refining interactions of conversations. Schank is of the opinion that all natural languages can be comprised by this *language-free* conceptual system:

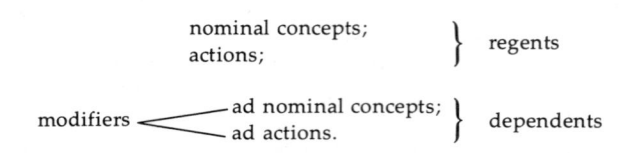

$$\left.\begin{array}{l}\text{nominal concepts;}\\ \text{actions;}\end{array}\right\} \text{regents}$$

$$\text{modifiers} \longleftarrow \left.\begin{array}{l}\text{ad nominal concepts;}\\ \text{ad actions.}\end{array}\right\} \text{dependents}$$

The arguments for large *language-free* conceptual systems are:

(a) Almost all sentences can be paraphrased by completely different words, for example:
- John is visiting the director Peter.
- The principal Peter is called upon by John.

applied psycholinguistics and the teacher of the hearing impaired 161

(b) When we understand a verbal message, by hearing or reading, we almost immediately forget the literal words and store only the content in our Long Term Memory.

(c) In our conversations and in reading we have to understand and "to read between the lines" by conceptualisations that are not at all coded verbally.

These arguments do not seem convincing for a denying of the possibility, that the concepts involved in (a) (b) and (c) are not formed by verbal coding, refined by conversations. For example, the idea of "visiting a person," or "calling upon a person" are abstracted as a field of meaning from more general experiences of "going there," in which the verbal code seems to be the "boundary" of the concept, the "social watcher" of the concept, fixing it, making it a figure against a background (1968).

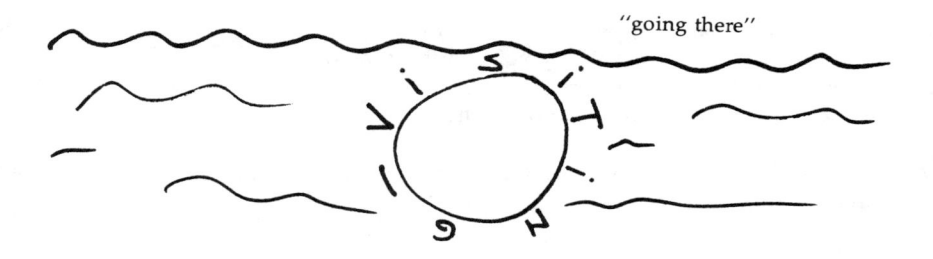

The same with words as "director," "principal," "ruler," "governor," "head" etc., which have much in common, but are not pure synonyms and may differ by sometimes small nuances, resulting into "Wortfelder" (Weisgerber, 1940) "fields of meanings," forming a kind of closed system which can be symbolized by these boundaries:

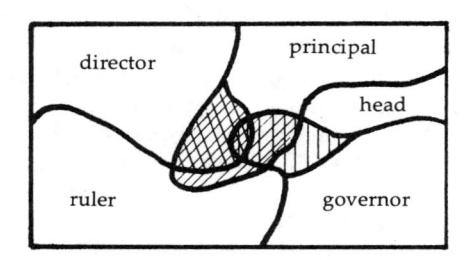

The same with many concepts related to each other, such as propelling, driving on, pushing, shoving, throwing, pitching, kicking, hitting, striking, swinging etc. As another example: *"broad;;* may be conceptualized as a modifier with a very relative content: e.g. it differs in meaning by "a broad car" and "a broad ribbon". It seems to be evident, that the content common in both experiences, difficult to describe, is singled out by verbal labeling within conversations. We can even speak of the "breadth", using the concept not as a modifier but as a nominal concept.

Still another example: *"cause"* has a different meaning

```
John cries ──────→ his scooter
                   broke                  ⎫
                                          ⎬  → = dependent from.
John laughs ─────→ Peter repaired         ⎭
                   the scooter
```

It seems to be evident, that the "commonality" of both experiences, will not be singled out without verbal labelling, originating from conversations. Most concepts seems to be shaped by language:
- As figures against backgrounds,
- Profiled by culture, by social interactions,
- Sometimes even completely voluntarily formed,
- Fenced off by co-concepts,
- Each one with its own combinabilities.

(2) *Language and the memory for experiences and conceptualisations.*
The following experience may illustrate the case:

> Uncle Louis was a visitor in a home with a small boy Freddy 2.3 years of age. The boy liked that name ("Uncle Louis," in Dutch "Ome Lowee") and sang it tens of times! After two hours Uncle Louis came back from a walk, hat and coat on. Freddy did not recognize him, was a little bit afraid. The mother said: "That is Ome Lowee!" . . . . . This word opened his eyes . . . . . .

Labelling helps us to recognize many different experiences, as has been confirmed by many researches (see Johnson, 1972). Words act as "hat racks". Leonard (1975) found, that children even use nonsense vocables as "linguistic place holders." The *rhythmic* combinations of words (trained by melodic speech, songs and dances from early childhood, see below), help us to combine experiences, to reason from one thought to another, to follow stories, to keep even long conversations going about one topic. We don't remember the spoken words verbatim, we think in language transparently (see above), but we remember some important "crests" in the strings of words, which are important as supports for our thinking.

Each teacher of the *deaf* is aware of this problem, when deeper topics of thinking have to be discussed with his children. It should be clear that the language memory of deaf children has to be trained first of all by rhythmic speech, to become a strong support for better thinking.

(3) *Piaget*
The experiments of Piaget with seriation, conservation, transitivity, class inclusion and so on are very well known. Known also is his assertion that these concepts originate in children according to a rather fixed order and are not supported by language but mainly by experience. (Furth, 1966) and (Oléron, 1972) and others have replicated these experiments on *deaf* children, supposing

applied psycholinguistics and the teacher of the hearing impaired 163

that, if it is true that these problems can be solved without language, deaf children would do as well as hearing ones. Both of them worked with deaf children who were mainly conversing in sign language among themselves. They found strong retardations of even 8 to 10 years! Furth keeps following Piaget and asserts that deaf children are behind just by lack of experiences (this thesis never has been investigated). Oléron attacks Piaget and says that this retardation only can be explained by lack of language. But how?

Sinclair de Zwart (1969), working with hearing children of low mental ability, found that those children who used in their spontaneous verbal utterances more *relative* language ("more than . . . . . ," "smaller than . . . . . ," "the same as . . . . ." etc.) solved the problems better than others. She does not recognize a facilitating influence of that language upon the problem solving, but, as a disciple of Piaget, asserts that both ways of behavior are supported by underlying cognitive growth (not explained further). Revin (1974) carried out the conservation experiments on oral deaf children in a day school and on a comparable group of largely manual (according to personal correspondence) deaf children in a residential school for the deaf. They found no backwardness in the oral children, but a large one in the manual children. They assert, following Furth, that this backwardness is only due to lack of experiences, which is not explained further.

Sign language, in its "low version" (Stokoe, 1972) as it is used by deaf children among themselves (Tervoort, 1967), lacks such comparative expressions as lar*ger than* . . . . . , *more than* . . . . . , *smaller than* . . . . . etc. It seems to be obvious that this difficulty in sign language is hampering deaf children in their thinking.

The theories of Piaget have been attacked from many sides (see Siegel and Brainerd, 1978). Other ways of instructing the children have been used, ways of operant and classic conditioning, instead of using verbal instructions, as Piaget and his followers mainly had done. Siegel definitively found a facilitating effect of language at the age of 4 years. He suggests this order of development:

1. At ± 3 years of age many problems can be solved without language. Neither the comprehension of verbal stimulation is helping the child, nor is the child able to explain his solution verbally.
2. At ± 4 years of age verbal stimulation facilitates the solving of the problems, but the child cannot yet explain the reason of his solution verbally.
3. At ± 5 years of age, both the comprehension of verbal instructions facilitates, and the child can explain his solution.

From all of this is may be concluded, how important it is to teach *deaf* children *comparative* and *relative* language. Once I heard a teacher speak to his children of 8 years of age just about a "big" and a "small" car. This is wrong. He should use relative words as "this car is bigger than that one," which is completely within the comprehension of the children, and they very often mean this by their still clumsy utterances which should be seized; at this age level the teacher can proceed with "How much bigger is it?" and so on. The relative words should be used in the preschool at 5 years of age. The children show something of these concepts guided by their experiences. Their tentative utterances should be "seized" (see below), reinforced, expanded and generalized, always of course in a conversational, even discussing way.

Beilin (1975) seems to be right according to preschool children: "Language may have a more significant role in the formation of thought than Piaget and others would allow, even though language may still not be the principal determinant." The following schema, in which all aspects are interacting, may be a conclusion:

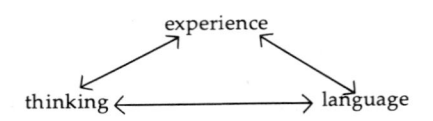

$$\text{thinking} \leftrightarrows \text{experience} \leftrightarrows \text{language}$$
$$\text{thinking} \longleftrightarrow \text{language}$$

The conclusion for our *didactics* of *deaf* children should be clear:

> deaf children need much experience, but not without language. Language in a formal way of collecting a vocabulary and building sentences? No! Language in a mainly *conversational* way. *Real* conversation *includes* experiences and contents. (See chapter 9.)

(4) *Existential thinking*.

The Piagetian studies mainly concern just physical, quantitative and "logical" (in a rather positivistic sense) thinking. There are other ways of thinking, however, studied much too little so far (see Remplein, 1963; Werner, 4é, 1959; Robinson, 1977), which we would like to call "existential thinking." This has to do with the deeper human situation: attitudes, social and individual ones, awareness of self and of the world." We mentioned above this question of a boy of 6 years of age (Fraiberg, 1963): "Mama, does the mouse know that it is a mouse?.." There are many other examples: "Why does the baby cry?", a boy putting himself before a steam locomotive: "Swanker!" . . . . . and so on (see, 1977). This way of thinking reveals itself also in pretending behavior, imaginary games, fairy tales, use of figurative meanings and metaphors, poetic thinking, religious thinking. After all a human being is a "meaning-seeking animal." Grant (1979) may be correct in saying, "Language can be thought of as a medium for creativity just as clay is the medium for the potter." It seems to be very difficult to put all of this into a language-free conceptualization system as that of Schank (1972, 1975).

Clark and Clark (1977) oppose the theory of *linguistic relativity*, mentioned above, by discussing the perception and/or judgment of colors, numbers, spaces and similar topics. Almost no relativity of such concepts has been found by cross-cultural research. It may be clear, that these findings are not at all conclusive against the thesis, that "every language is a worldview."

(5) *The difficulty of translation-work*.

Correct and idiomatic translation-work from one language to another one includes:

- a correct comprehension of both the source- and the target language according to the denotative and connotative and even of the underlying non-verbal conceptualizations of the word meanings (See above);
- a correct representation towards the target language.

This is so difficult, that Bar Hillel (1960; quoted by Landsberger, 1977) believes an automatic translation by computers to be impossible.

No expert translator or interpreter will deny that *every language is a worldview*. Therefore, a translation from English into an African language or into Chinese is more difficult than for example, from English into French or Dutch, because of the distances of the cultures. Kuipers (1977), an expert in the analysis of analphabetic languages says: "Every language is a world in itself, and that world may be different from ours."

(6) Conclusion

The theory of linguistic relativity may be incorrect in its extreme presentations. Nevertheless the thesis, that *every language is a worldview*, seems to be completely correct. Therefore the basic thesis of the great teacher of the deaf, Friedrich Moritz Hill (1805–1874), in the track of Wilhelm von Humboldt, although a little bit exaggerated, seems to be fundamentally undeniable:

> "In allem ist Sprache,
> und alles ist in der Sprache."
>
> "There is language in everything,
> and everything is in language." (See Hodgson, 1953).

f. *The "position category" (Paardekoper, 1953) and "rhythmic closure."*

"The cat is called Kitty. Who has given it that name?" The pointer word "it" is indicated to be an indirect object, not by a flexion or by a preposition, but just by its *position,* here in a pincer construction (see below) between *given* and *that name.*

Who has given it that name?

In the *Latin* language the positions of the words are very free. The reason may be, or alternatively this may be related to the fact that, the many flexions sufficiently indicate the function of the words and their belonging to each other. The same may be said somewhat of another highly flexive language as German, "In allem ist Sprache" or "Sprache ist in allem" or "(dass) in allem Sprache ist," . . "Sprache in allem ist." Fries (1940) has followed the development of the English language from the tenth through the fifteenth century, and found how the positions of the words, the parts of speech, became more and more fixed within the sentences, that is, as more and more "position-categories" were originating, the more the flexions died out. The positions of the nouns, the verbs, articles and adjectives, the adverbs and the prepositions became more and more fixed.

This position-category called "an anchoring effect" (Schwarz, 1975), seems to be a typical "bound form," in another sense than the morphemic bound forms (1968). It is a tendency, a kind of "magnetism" in a word, as part of speech, to be arranged in a stereotyped position, when used in a string of words. We have already spoken about "cohesions," "groupings" of words and about "open places" around some words (See above). This anchoring effect with open places seems to be effective already at 1 to 2 years of age in the so-called "pivot words" (See below). It is comparable with the anchoring of some phonemes: consonants ask for surrounding vowels and vice versa, combinations as mb, zt in an initial position are not English.

Concerning the *groupings*-tendencies, Behaghel (1923) formulated the "minimal distance principle" (see 1977) "What belongs together mentally is placed close together syntactically." Usually those words are spoken in "accent-groups" (1968) or phrases, connected with the "phrase-structure" of sentences. In this respect a clear isomorphism has been found between linguistics and psycholinguistics. See the research of (Johnson, 1965; Kennedy and Wilkes, 1968), the "clickology" (see 1968, 1977); Fodor (1974); and Fodor, Bever and Garret the "canonical sentoid strategy" (1974) in understanding.

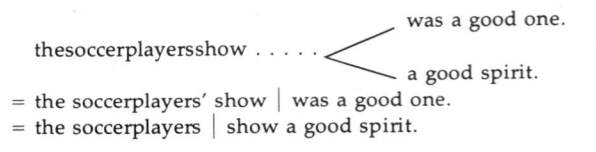

thesoccerplayersshow . . . . . ⟨ was a good one.
　　　　　　　　　　　　　　　　 a good spirit.
= the soccerplayers' show | was a good one.
= the soccerplayers | show a good spirit.

The listener scans and searches out the phrases, the accent groups.—The same in reading (See Smith, 1974). We have called these immediate constituents *compound-constructions* (1968, 1977) in opposition to *pincer-constructions*, a translation of the German term "Um-klammerung" and the Dutch term "in-klamping" (van Ginniken, 1929). This typical opposition happens in English too, although perhaps less than in German and Dutch: see the diagrams below. Drach (1963), (see also Paul, 1909) rightly points to the memory function in the pincer-constructions and to a kind of "wholistic thinking"—"ganzheitliches Denken", conditioned by this. See the examples below:

The town had suddenly acquired something really understanding . . . . .

We must not let this man get away . . . . .

The postponement of "acquired" after "suddenly" evokes a memory function, by means of which "had suddenly acquired" seems to become a stronger whole than "had acquired suddenly", which construction seems to be "looser". Not-

applied psycholinguistics and the teacher of the hearing impaired

withstanding this embedding of "suddenly" "had acquired" keep together: very often these two words have been spoken as one "accent group" by compound-construction, a kind of "deep structure" underlying the pincer-construction. Pincer-construction and compound-construction should be considered as opposite to each other, in the same way as phonemes, parts of speech, meanings are opposite to each other: "opposition" is a fundamental principle in linguistics and in information-theory. Compare the following examples:

- How do you think you will manage this?
- How will you manage this, do you think?
- How to manage this, do you think?

"Compound-constructions" and "pincer-constructions" as rhythmic oppositions.

¹ He is waiting.	‖ He is still waiting.
² The boy washes himself.	‖ The boy never washes himself.
³ He sings well.	‖ He sang that song well.
	An ambiguous sentence:
⁴ Mary washes the car.	‖ Mary asked John how to wash the car.
John washes the car.	‖ Mary asked John how to wash the car.
⁵ John wonders, how to manage this.	‖ How does he manage this?
	How do you think you will manage this?
⁶ The baby	‖ The foreigner's baby.
The mother	‖ The baby's mother.
The secretary of the director	‖ The director's secretary.
⁷ He turns off all the lights.	‖ Turn the lights off!
	‖ He always turns off the lights.
⁸ For what?	‖ What do you want a knife for?
⁹ . . . . .more than	‖ How many more marbles has John than Peter?

168 oral education: today and tomorrow

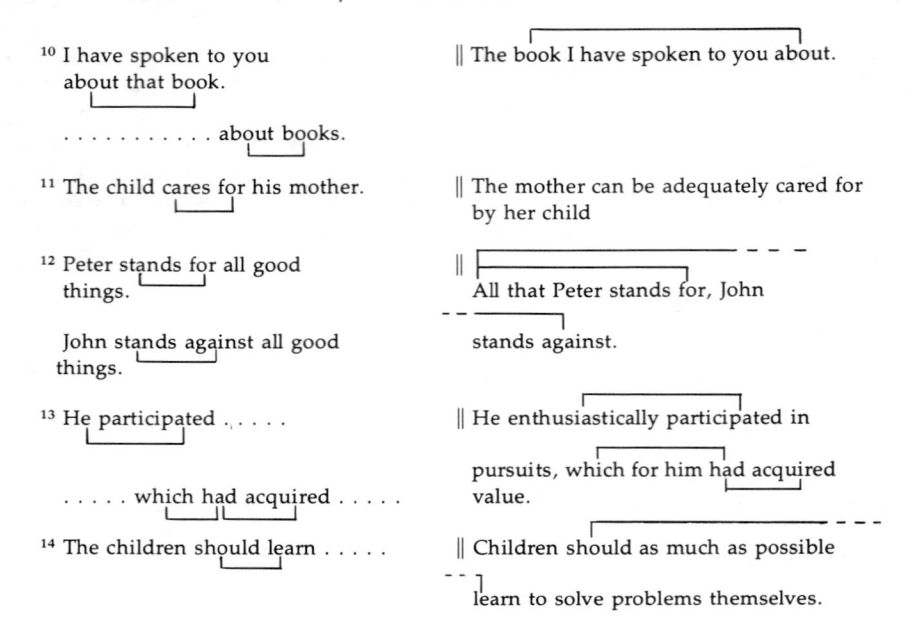

10 I have spoken to you about that book.
.... about books.

|| The book I have spoken to you about.

11 The child cares for his mother.

|| The mother can be adequately cared for by her child

12 Peter stands for all good things.

John stands against all good things.

|| All that Peter stands for, John stands against.

13 He participated .....
..... which had acquired .....

|| He enthusiastically participated in pursuits, which for him had acquired value.

14 The children should learn .....

|| Children should as much as possible learn to solve problems themselves.

This *opposition* may occasion slips of the tongue, like these:
- "That is ea ..... done not so easily done" .....
- "Children should as learn as much as possible learn" .....
- "The book I have spoken to you about" .....
  (see 1968, 1977; Fromkin, 1973).

One feels the *struggle* between the compound- and the pincer-constructions. (For more research about the "minimal distance principle" See 1977; Clark and Clark, 1977).

"What belongs together *mentally?*" ..... (See above, Behaghel). What does this "mentally" mean? Pure logic? Pure natural syntax (See above)? What then about the suggested wholistic thinking in the pincer-constructions, in the struggle with the loading upon the memory function? What *is* the positional value of words, their positional category and anchoring effect? What does the term "open places" mean? In our opinion *rhythm and melody of speech,* apart from logic and natural syntax, play an important part in the typical phenomenon of the pincer-construction in opposition to compound-construction. This phenomenon seems to be related not so much to nature but to culture, being completely different in all languages. Alas, this *important aspect* of syntax has not yet been investigated sufficiently.

There seems to be evidence enough, however. Syntactic skill and eupraxia have to do with memory. The memory for language has to do with rhythmic and melodic speech. The conclusion seems to be obvious. The following research seems to be in agreement with this suggestion:

> The "Hebb effect" (Hebb, 1961) works not only by recoding, by naming a category, but by "retrieval from the accents" too (Neisser, 1967). What happens? Subjects are

asked to memorize different series of items. But, without the subjects knowing this, some series are made identical and interpolated among the different ones, e.g.:

$$\begin{array}{cccccc} 6 & 5 & 9 & 7 & 8 & 2 \\ 8 & 3 & 2 & 6 & 7 & 5 \\ 5 & 7 & 6 & 9 & 1 & 2 \\ 3 & 2 & 7 & 8 & 1 & 6 \\ 9 & 1 & 2 & 4 & 7 & 3 \\ 2 & 3 & 1 & 5 & 7 & 6 \\ 7 & 9 & 5 & 4 & 2 & 6 \\ 5 & 7 & 6 & 9 & 1 & 2 \\ 1 & 9 & 4 & 5 & 3 & 8 \\ \end{array}$$
etc.

One may see, that the 3rd and the 8th series are identical, the same with the 13th, the 18th etc. etc. The other series are completely different. It appeared that the identical series were better memorized than the non-identical ones, even when the subjects were not aware of this identity of the "Hebb effect." Often subjects use to try to label the "unconsciously" repeated series . . . . . to categorize" or to collect them, for example "576" etc. When *objects* are presented, subjects start to categorize them as "pieces of furniture", "food" etc. Subjects spontaneously try to support their memory by coding. Neisser (1967) found that pure identical *accentuations*, rhythmic groupings, were helping his subjects also, offering them retrieval cues (see Raaijmakers, 1979).

The same effect appeared also, when pauses have been *"embedded"* in the identical interpolated series, by auditory presentation (Laughery and Spector, 1972),

		Average correct responses:
A (without pauses):	G-F-X-N-Y-Q-R-T-Z	5.1
B (with always identical pauses):	G-F-X | N-Y-Q-R- | T-Z	5.3
C (with varied pauses e.g.):	G-F-X-N | Y-Q-R | T-Z G-F | X-N-Y | Q-R-T-Z etc.	5.4

The "canonical sentoid strategy" (Fodor, Bever and Garret 1974), mentioned above, seems to suggest that the subjects *tended* to *complete* the sentences from a phrasic source as a stepping stone, such as "show," understood as a transitive verb looked for *open places* after it, not just by logic, but by "feeling" incompleteness, which had been suggested by Bever, Garret and Hurtig (1973), speaking of "perceptually incomplete clauses."

One of the few psychologists who has studied rhythmic behavior, is Fraisse in Paris (1956), following Michotte (1947) in Louvain. They use the term "structures rhythmiques." Van der Veldt (1928) and Montpellier (1935), both in Louvain, found that repeated movements become not only automatized but also more and more rhythmic, by tempo, and the other way round—that rhythmic movements tend to be automatized and to increase in tempo. For example, playing the flute, playing the piano, or the organ (with hands and feet), dancing, many kinds of skills such as knitting; wherein, an *interrupted* series of movements *tends to complete itself.* We would like to call this *rhythmic closure.* The same seems to happen in speech and language.

- Why do we feel that the words of the pincer-constructions belong to each other? Because we have spoken them thousands of times in a compound-construction.
- Why do we feel that most words have "open places" before and/or after them? Because we tend to complete the phrases we have spoken thousands of times, if not with the identical words, then with words of the same word-class.
- Why do we feel that most words have fixed positions? Because we arrange them according to the rhythmic groupings.

We have called this aspect of our psycholinguistic behavior *important*. Important for *deaf* children too? Yes, because it is a special difficulty for deaf children. In speech and composition-work they seem to avoid the pincer-constructions: they tend to keep the words, which belong to each other mentally, close to each other. Markides (1973) found that deaf children of 9 to 13 years of age limit their spontaneously *spoken* sentences to an average length of three words, in significant contrast to hard of hearing children, with an average of five words. Those strings of three words do not seem to give much place for pincer-constructions. We (1979) found that deaf children actually use pincer-constructions, but significantly less than hearing children, in their composition-work. The sentences with pincer-construction cause difficulties in *reading* too (see appendix, 1971). It seems obvious that this has to do with their limited speech memory (see 1974, 1978), and this again with their inability to hear the normal melody, with their difficulty in *rhythmic* speech and with their *lack of clustering, if* not trained well in these respects. Belmont (1976) found that deaf children show a tendency to have this lack of clustering in their spontaneous memory functioning, which correlated with the efficiency of that memory—the more they were clustering, the better was their memory function. The children could *learn* to do this clustering better and better. Kempen (1976) rightly says that normal hearing children of 2 years of age stick to sentences of two or three words not so much by lack of memory as such, but by lack of clustering. *Practice* has shown to us, that Belmont is right: one of our teachers, Miss van den Broek (1969) trained her children for one schoolyear with a pre-test and re-test design, and found a gain of 30 to 40 percent in clustering spoken sentences and their memory. Deaf children can learn the syntactical opposition of compound- and pincer-constructions (from ± 9 to 10 years of age), which helps them in controlling both language understanding and language production. It is by means of *rhythmic speech* and good phrasing that deaf children can learn to conquer this typical language difficulty.

3. The mother (caretaker) as a teacher of language.

a. *Avoidance of onesidedness.*—Some aspects of early language development still insufficiently investigated.

A complete investigation of the early linguistic development of children asks for *video-audio-recording.* This has started only recently (in the St. Michielsgestel audio-visual department at our request in 1975, Gruendell in 1977, Duchan in 1979). We have to be careful in the interpretations of the findings so far. The following aspects certainly have not yet been sufficiently investigated:

(1) *Longitudinal* aspects, not just for a few months, but for several years. Some children may show a typical behavior, which may appear to be an index of an *abnormal* development in later years. Not all investigators have been aware of this problem, and simply tested babies of normal mothers, very often their own babies. For example, Schaerlaekens (1973) remarks, that "abnormal language development can be distinguished most of all by lack of natural *intonation*." Nelson (1973) remarks, that "*echolalic* behavior at 2.0 is indicative of immature speech".

(2) The *integration* of both semantic and structural aspects. The idea of Chomsky (1968) about an innate Language Acquisition Device (see Levelt, 1972) has led many investigators astray, by looking for *structures* and bypassing much too much the content both verbal and non-verbal. Happily enough the LAD has been replaced by "*semantic* primacy" (MacNamara, 1972), with a danger of losing sight of the structures, however . . . . .

(3) It is acknowledged that the language acquisition during the interlingual period (cf. O'Boaill, 1979) does not develop linearly or by summation, but according to *stages* from one closed system to another one. But how? The children seem to differ extremely (Bloom, 1970). What is the role of their body-language, of the environment etc.?

(4) Child's *comprehension* of language. The idea of the so-called "overgeneralizations" by children has been attacked. Huttenlocher (1974) followed four children of 0.10 to 1.6 years of age. She found that children can call a cat a doggie, but when asked "Show me a doggie" etc., they only pointed to a dog, and *refused* to indicate a cat. Their comprehension was not overgeneralized at all. The so-called overgeneralizations seem to be due to lack of immediate availability of words, perhaps lack of retrieving skill, thus still deficient in "active language." A child of 1.6 to 2 years of age may have an active vocabulary of 50 words, but a "passive" one of 300 (Seligman, 1971). They understand a lot, also rather long sentences, for example, a child of 2.2 in one of my investigations: "Put that card in your pocket . . . . . No, put it in your other pocket!" did it correctly. Although the children utter sentences of two to three words at this age, their memory for series of words, investigated by a free recall experiment, is much longer (Bloom, 1973). The children understand a lot by the "crests" of sentences, that is, they distinguish "mother's baby" from "baby's mother" by pointing to the right picture (Huttenlocher, 1974). The same happens with long sentences, which has been shown by their just imitating (echoing) these crests, Mother: "How cold it was in the bus!" Child: "Cold bus!" . . . . . We already saw that Kempen, (1977) suggested that not the memory as such is lacking, but the active clustering function.

(5) *The transition from passive into active language*. Passive language = the language understood; active language = the language produced.

Nelson (1973), after a longitudinal study of 18 children 1 to 2 years of age, says: "*Comprehension* at 1.3 is correlated with *all* later language functions,

..... has a strong predictive value." It seems to be clear that active language is a fruit of passive language, to be symbolized as follows:

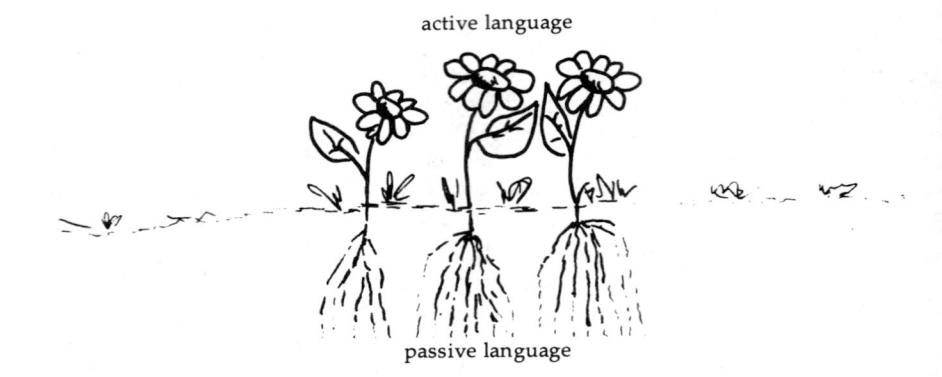

active language

passive language

But how? Seemingly not without conversation. Cazden (1965) made a comparison between two ways of influencing linguistically retarded preschool children. In one group the nurses only expanded the "telegraphic speech" of the children, for example, a child saying: "Doggy home!" was answered by, "Yes, you have a doggy at home!"

In another comparable group such an utterance would have been responded to by: "Oh? I like doggies! You do too?" This second group improved in language more than the first one. The reason seems to be obvious, more interaction. Spanish-speaking children, who daily for hours looked at English-American T.V., did *not* learn English. The reason seems to be the same, lack of interaction (See Clark and Clark, 1977). This important process is not yet investigated sufficiently.

(6) Avoidance of one-sidedness.

If we want to follow a natural approach, starting as much as possible from the spontaneous reactions of the *deaf children* we have to keep sight of all aspects:
- nonverbal, "encyclopedic," cognitive and conative backgrounds (See above);
- a large "fund" or "deposit" of language comprehension, from which language production is evoked mainly by conversation;
- not only semantic but also structural aspects and their integrations.

The following are some illustrative examples of this last aspect from a *hearing* child of 1.10 years of age (thanks to my colleague Marcel Broesterhuizen)
- "Baby auto", originating from cognitive non-verbal and verbal contexts, is pluri-interpretable and does not seem to include a special structure:
    I see the baby in the auto,
    this auto is for the baby,
    the baby is away in the auto,
    I want the baby with me in the auto
- "Where is mama? Auto away": a question-answer structure (See above).

- "Cup of tea! Cup of tea! Cup of tea! . . . . ." rhythmic structuring, auditory self-training of a word group as an "accent group".
- The same with: "Nee hoor!" (Oh no!)
  "Dát nou" (that now)
  "kijk's hier!" (look here)
- "Pivot"-constructions (See below):
  Ika boos! (Marika angry)
  Opa (grandpa) boos!
  See baby!
  See cooky!

Many soliloquies in playing, always conversational, with the three intonations of "assertions", "questions" and "calls" ("emphatic speech" Menyuk, 1969). For example, "This is for opa . . . . . Where is he sitting? . . . . . Oh here . . . . . Opa! boos! (Grandpa angry)"

b. *Linguistic "symbiosis" of mother and child.*
Although we probably cannot speak of an innate LAD in the sense of Chomsky, there are many innate functions indeed which clear the way for the cultural language of and with the environment. From the first hours after birth on, *"proto-conversation"* starts:

- body movements of the baby are coordinated both with its own vocable sounds *and* with those of the mother (see Bullowa, 1977, 1979);
- the mother tends to read her infant's expressions very well;
- body postures, intonations, facial mime etc. are understood by the baby (cf. 1978);
- turn-taking behavior, already starting with the alternative sucking and looking at the mother while being fed (Sachs, 1974), preparing the alternation of listening and speaking in conversations (for example, I—you; coming—going; giving—receiving; buying—selling; bringing—taking);
- cognitive and conative capacities with analysis and integration, preparing the integration of speech and experience;
- trial and check (TOTE strategy) behavior starts immediately;
- the symbiotic behavior achieves including more and more automatisms and structures as in a game (See above), clearing the way for more and more complex behavior;
- the child is fully aware when he is spoken to and when not (Brown and Bellugi, 1964), for example by attending less when mother is speaking to another person;
- the non-verbal babbling shows the three general kinds of intonation (assertion, question and call) very soon, seemingly also in a social way, combined with adequate mime (Menyuk, 1969).

Although this period of "proto-conversation" may be protracted in *deaf children*, most of these natural tendencies can and should be maintained, and evoked, especially "face-directedness" and "sound-awareness," turn-taking behavior and so on. Their maintenance appeared to be significantly related to future lipreading and the success of auditory training (1974, see 1978).

c. *Interaction of mother and baby*.

This interaction between mother and baby can be described as a "duet" (see the literature 1977; Lock, 1978). Labov (1969) describes the high flexibility of many mothers according to the *style* of their pragmatically linguistic behavior—towards her baby, her husband, an older child, in the shop, at the office, on the job etc. This duet can be hampered, however.

(1) *Interaction and character of mother and child respectively*.

A baby conditions his mother, as well as the mother conditions her baby. The *baby* sends clear signals to the mother, of needs, of comprehension, of agreement or disagreement and so forth, which evokes reactions from the mother (see Bohannon and Marquis, 1977). Too "passive" a baby causes the interactions to become less and less which hampers language growth (Nelson, 1973). Bohannon and Marquis (1977) found that *one* caretaker of their investigation was typically unresponsive to the activities of the baby. This hampered the interaction and the language growth. Some mothers seemingly are too dominant, don't listen sufficiently to their babies, which again hampers development. "Less intrusive mothers," says Nelson (1973) "have faster learning children." The same with acceptance and non-acceptance processes. "A general rejecting mother will probably ignore or reject many language proposals of the child," (Nelson, 1973).

(2) *"Motheresses"*

One mother in our investigations, after having seen the video-recording, said: "How much I talked!" Most mothers talk a lot to their babies. This talk shows several typical characteristics (1968), called "motheresses" (see Snow, 1972):

- It is very melodic and rhythmic, giving clear prominence to "accent groups", surrounding them by clear pauses, in a tempo of 3 ± 1 syllables per second (1968, 1974);
- It comprises many repetitions;
- It is mainly perfectly grammatical;
- It adjusts itself to, is very "conditionable" by the reactions of the baby, adjusting both length and complexity of speech according to signals of comprehension or non-comprehension of the baby, all of this completely *spontaneously*, almost unconsciously (cf. Bohannan and Marquis, 1977).

These signals of comprehension are smiling, utterances as "yeah", "uhuh" and others. By non-comprehension of the baby (question mime, "what?" "Hum?", no response) very often the mother reduces the length and complexity of her sentences, repeating them in shorter accent groups. By comprehension the mother very often makes her speech more complex sometimes within the same interaction (van der Geest, 1974). So the mother pulls up, continuously, the capacities of her child. In some way she is always "one step ahead." Seitz and others (1976) found an *average sentence length* of mother's speech to her babies of 1.2 to 2.2 years of age, of 3.8 words. The mother appears to be a good "listening teacher."

(3) *A "seizing method" and a "playing of a double part"*.

The following are mainly my own observations (1960–1963), in my opinion, in full agreement with many publications so far.

The mother accompanies her actions with her baby (or even in the presence of her baby) by *verbalizations,* "and now the potatoes . . . . . Where is the towel? . . . . . Oh no, that is not a clean one . . . . . Not a clean one, he (shows it to the baby sitting on the box) . . . . . I will look for a nice one" . . . . . These verbalizations towards a small, speechless baby, contain much orectic, social and attitudinal language, figurative meanings ("Oh see, it rains cats and dogs!" Now you are my little princess!" . . . . . , contrasts ("not clean . . . . . nicer"). While washing and clothing her baby the mother very often calls the names of the limbs, even "right" and "left," training the control of the *body-schema*. By songs and dancing the *rhythm* is trained. (See 1978.) Snow (1972) rightly observed that many mothers continue talking, even in spite of inadequate reactions from their baby.

N.B. See chapter 9 concerning the requirements for reading lessons for *deaf* preschool children.

This talking stimulates experiences, attention etc. very often, by showing the dirty towel to the baby, by saying "Look there, what a dear doggy," they look together in the same direction. The non-verbal cognitive motor-conative, social and verbal behavior become more and more *integrated*. The verbalizations set off some experiences or aspects of them, give them *figure-background* prominence, such as from the whole environment, attention is drawn only to the "doggy". This profiles the thinking in a *cultural* way.

These verbalizations are not purely accompanying, however, they are social and *conversational*. The mother *wants* to say something, and very often *makes herself understood* by manipulating the situation. The mother held a towel for her baby and said: "Seize it!" The child didn't. The mother made the towel "dance" before the eyes of the child: "Seize it!" Then the child grasped towards it, but suddenly the mother took the towel away: "You can't seize it!" The child stretched arms and hands, longing for the towel. The mother made the towel dance again before the eyes of the child: "Seize it!" Now the child seized it and held it so strongly, that the mother could not draw it back . . . . . "Now you have seized it" she said. This example may illustrate how a mother is teaching, "implanting" the meanings of the words in her baby.

These verbalizations comprise typical *dyads*. For example, the mother heard some sounds from the cradle. She approached the speechless and languageless baby who started half crying, half laughing towards the mother, and the mother said: "Are you hungry? Come here, darling!"

In the first sentence of this dyad the mother *seizes* what the child wants to say. She *puts the words in the baby's mouth,* the words which the baby, if he could, would say in this situation. The mother *plays the part of her baby*. Immediately after that she formulated her own contribution to the conversation in the second sentence, she *plays her own part*. So she plays *a double part*. The child will not understand her, but she *makes herself understood by the situation*. She picks up her baby. After a few days the child will understand this "Come here, darling!"..... This dyad comprises *a conversation*. The mother starts a conversation with her child within a few hours after birth by a seizing method and by playing a double part.

In my opinion this is a correct description of the behavior of mother and child. It is not understood by several researchers, however. On the one side the "body language" of the baby is interpreted as "just utterance," or as just "reaching contents to the mother" (van der Geest, 1974, 1977), but in my opinion very often they are really meant *"messages"* too. Also, Nelson (1973) says, "There is relatively little direct feedback given to most children." *Yet* she gives a nice example of this "seizing and playing a double part behavior," which according to my observations comprises more than one-third of the time of the verbalized interactions: Some utterances of Jane (1.2), interpreted by the mother:

>Mother: "Jane. Here's a bottle. Where is the bottle?
>   Here is a bottle."
>Jane: "Wah wah!"
>Mother: "Bottle."
>Jane: "Bah bah."
>Mother: "Bah bah."
>Jane: "Bah bah."
>Mother: "Oh, bah bah. Here is a ball."
>Jane: "Baw."
>Mother: "Ball. Yes."
>Jane: "Uh. Uh. Boo?"
>Mother: "Ball"
>............................
>Mother: "Is that a car?"
>Jane: "Bah.;;
>Mother: "Yes, car. Here's another car.;;
>Jane: "Gah."
>Mother: "Car, Yes."
>Jane: "Bah. Daddy."
>Mother: "Daddy. Daddy's car is all gone."

These dyads can be found in Stern (1909), Brown and Bellugi (1964), Spitz (1965, 1974) speaks of "exchange of affects", Vorster (1975), Berko-Gleason (1975), Carter (1975), Snow (1977) and others. For example:

> Carter in an in-depth study (1975), describes an infant, 1.2 years of age, who "went over to his mother who was holding a cup, stationed himself right in front of her, opened his mouth, thrust his chin forward and stared at her till she looked at him ..... The mother said "Do you want some juice? Show me your cup!" He held the cup out.

This is a nice example of body language, too:

> Snow (1977) tells about a mother with a baby of 0.5 awaking and the mother says, "Hello! Give me a smile then!" and gently pokes the infant in the ribs. The infant yawns ..... and the mother says, "Sleepy are you? You woke up too early today" .....

The term *expanding* seems to be insufficient. Not only are verbal utterances of the baby seized and expanded to normal sentences, but the mother is seizing already *before* the child has any verbal utterance at all. For that reason we chose the term *"seizing."* The analysis of McNeill (in Mussen ed., 1970) is quite correct, the mother is expanding, modeling, prompting and echoing, but she starts doing so already in the period of the proto-conversations.

The baby's utterances, seized by the mother, are not always put in the question-form by the mother. Laetitia, 1.3, said *non*-verbally: "The sun is too hot!" and the mother answered, "Yes, you are right. The sun is much too hot, I'll put you in the shade."

Many questions of the mother are *"seized questions,"* however, the child's behavior puts a non-verbal question by mime and some gesture: "May I have this?" The mother interprets, seizes and puts it into a verbal question-form: "Do you like to have it?" . . . . . So it is understandable that Nelson (1973) found, "A high rate of mother questions was positively related to comprehension at 20 months".

N.B. The way a normal hearing child learns *questions* seems to be important for the didactics of *deaf* children. We will explain in chapter 9 how we can start from the questions, not so much of the teacher or the mother, but from the questions put by the children themselves, following the seizing method.

The following studies, concerning the *length of oral utterances* of children, seems to be important here. Melbourne (1978) investigated two groups of infants of 1.10 to 2 years of age. Group A was given only a language *model,* "That is a blue ball". The spontaneous echoing utterances of the children were noted down, "ball" or "blue ball" etc. Group B was conditioned by *expanding.* Spontaneous utterances of the children were seized and reacted to. A child said: "Ball" and the caretaker responded, "Yes, that is a big blue ball" . . . . . The oral lengths of utterances of both groups increased significantly, but those of group B increased significantly more. Nelson (1973) found the same with children of 3 to 4 years of age, and Molauf (1972), with first graders of normal primary schools.

It seems obvious to use the *seizing* method for deaf children too (See chapter 9), and also for extending the *length* of their oral and written utterances.

(4) *"Speech acts" and word order.*

We have already seen several of these topics. So-called *"body-language"* (see 1978) precedes, penetrates, interferes with, and is conquered more and more by the cultural oral language of the environment. It must be emphasized immediately that body-language is meant here as including *facial mime* and *intonation* (assertion, question, call. See above). When a child utters his first conversational word, this immediately is a sentence with an intonation and a typical facial mime. This latter of course happens with *deaf* children too.

By speech acts, communicative behavior in its totality, the child learns first of all the *correspondences* between his cognitive growth and oral-aural skill. Many researchers emphasize the *semantic* order of the words, Hayes ed. (1970), Ingram (1971), MacNamara (1972), Slobin (1973), Schaerlaekens (1973), Brown (1973), Bruner (1975), Klein (1975), Lock (1978) and others. This would suggest then that the first *syntax* of children is a *natural* one (See above):

- Agent—action (John eats)
- Action—object (eats cooky)
- Agent—object (John cooky)
- Topic—comment (John's cooky, or cooky of John)
- Given—new (John wants a cooky)
- Question—answer—mama? Sleeps → mama sleeps (Leopold, 1954).

These child utterances (how do they relate to comprehension? Still insufficiently investigated) are completely full of many *presuppositions* from the encyclopedic knowledge of the child and his conception of the situation. Hence they usually are *ambiguous* and pluri-interpretable (See above), sometimes very, very complex. Analysis of these utterances without their intonation and facial mime, without their emotional aspects, just from written protocols, seems to be very risky. Duchan (1979) found for example, that "intonation corresponds with intentions of the (bodily) movements . . . . . in 70 percent of the utterances."

Another risky aspect of these purely semantic analyses seems to be the *exact meanings* of the words, used by the child and from his viewpoints. Huttenlocher (1974) points out that the content of many first words of the infants had already developed in their non-verbal cognitive experiential growth. These words seem to pick up these experiences, fixing them, and giving them prominence. The words give more and more precision both to comprehension and production of language, *within* a cloud of non-verbal communication. Van Ginniken (as early as 1922) has observed that most first words have an *action-based meaning*. So "ball" is not just the name of a special object, but, when the child says "ball," or "that is a ball," it means something like "There is balling something." This observation has been confirmed by modern research. See Gruendell (1977, 123 video-records!), Lock (1978). For one of the children of the investigations "ball" meant an "enclosing action." From this a child could call a bottle also a "ball," even his milk, even the mouth itself . . . . . Mother interfered a lot with these "abuses", by saying, "No, that is not a ball, it is milk!" . . . . . These action-based meanings can occasion typical "grammaticalisms" as in, "Pussy roofing" instead of "I see a cat on the roof there" . . . . .

(5) *A cultural structure and word-order.*

There seems to be more than just a natural syntax in baby's first two-word and three-word sentences: a *rhythmic grouping* with *positional effects* upon some words.

Brown and Bellugi (1964) observed that the mother usually *follows* the order of words of her child, interpreting these words as *accentuated words*, for example
- Child: "See flowers" . . . . .
- Mother: "Do you *see* these *flowers*, how nice!" . . . . .

It seems, that also the child, imitating or echoing the mother, takes over first of all the words, *accentuated* by the mother, for example,
- Mother: "I'll make a *cup* for him to *drink*."
- Child (2.7 years): "Cup drink" (Ervin-Trip 1964; see also van der Geest, 1975).

At the same time the child trains *"accent groups"* (see above "cup of tea"). Which accent groups? No rule or law has been found so far. The choice seems mainly due to chance: the child finds a word group typical or nice and "sings" it after the "model-speaker". This important phenomenon does not seem to be sufficiently investigated. Slobin (1973) mentions typical groupings (at 2.7 years of age), such as, "I know *what is it*", instead of, ... "what it is." Obviously these "mistakes" may be an effect of rhythmic auditory self-training.

Stern (1909) observed positionally fixed words in children's "dysgrammatical" speech, which later have been called *"pivot-words"* (Braine, 1963), e.g. *"Da sieh* wau-wau! . . . . ." (There see wowow).

This phenomenon has been observed by many researchers (see Fry 1977, Clark and Clark 1977). There are two kinds of pivot-words, pivot-1 with a fixed position in the beginning of a wordgroup, and pivot-2 at the end of a word group. The other words are called "open words." The child says many word groups just by "open words," without a fixed order (see above, natural syntax?), but *when* it uses a pivot-word, it uses it according to its fixed position. The child will say, within this stage of his development, "all gone milk," not "milk all gone." It will even resist, when an adult tries to make him imitate "milk all gone." *Which* words become pivot words? The same answer must be given as with the "accent-groups"—just by chance. Attention, frequency and similarity may be a cause. There is a very big difference between children. Some children do not seem to use pivot-words at all! The working of pivot-words may be based upon "rhythmic closure" (See above).

It has been suggested that a child develops a kind of pivot-open word grammar. This does not seem to be correct, however. Most sentences are open word sentences (See above). Certainly the pivot-words cannot be interpreted as "functors", and the open words as "contentors".

An important *conclusion* may be—in the beginning there seems to be not just "natural syntax," but also a cultural linguistic structural influence from the child itself and mainly due to *rhythm*. It may be clear again, that rhythmic speech is very important for *deaf* children too.

(6) *Guided discovery learning?*

That the normal young child *detects* the structure of language mainly himself between the ages of 2.6 and 4.0, has been observed by many researchers, Stern (1909), van Ginniken (1922), Lewis (1931), Leopold (1947), and Kaper (1959). The child "plays" with grammatical rules, and children even correct children,
- Phonologically: "not pussy but pushe" (Dutch);
- Semantically: "not papa but uncle!"
- Gramatically: phrases, suffixes, infixes, prefixes, "Umlaut."

Only imitation and/or conditioning do not seem to be sufficient to explain adequately the detection of language "rules" or "laws," nor can *TOTE behavior* or "putting hypotheses" and testing them (See Clark and Clark, 1977). *"The* granddad is not coming?" asked Peter, 2.7 years of age, disappointedly. Mother: "Do you like granddad?", she left out the article. Peter: "Granddad is . . . . . is coming?" He immediately dropped his hypothesis of the definite article (See Schaerlaekens, 1973). *Interaction* tends to develop rules of behavior (See above). Interestingly enough the child very often imitates conversations in his soliloquies, while playing with blocks, with his puppet (sometimes his "puppet-fellow"), in bed, often by singing . . . . . He obviously seems to *look for* rules! Alas, this has not yet been investigated sufficiently.

This detection of the structure of language presupposes *comprehension*. This comprehension again presupposes much non-verbal conceptualization. The conversion from passive into active language very often, if not always, happens *during* the interaction periods, as we have seen above with some choices of words and with "(*the*) granddad." It is astonishing how a child of 2.6 to 3 years of age already has the conceptualization behind the definite and indefinite article: at that age he learns to use it almost perfectly. The correct use of the tenses of the verbs (although the irregular verbs keep on causing troubles through 5 to 6 years of age) presupposes the conceptualizations of time, which are mainly conquered at 3.6 to 4 years of age. (See Schaerlaekens, 1973). Alas, all of this has not yet been investigated sufficiently.

The structure first discovered by the child seems to be the rhythmic-melodic "*phrase-structure.*" This is presented to him by his mother most clearly. He picks it up first in his own way of structuring, but adjusts himself very soon to the word order and the accent groups of the mother. Some researches suggest that a child of at least 4 years of age is able to take over "position rules" of nonsense words (See Moeser in MacNamara, 1977).

We have seen how *question-words* are presented to the baby and learned very soon by the "seizing method" of the mother who puts the question-words into his mouth *at the moment he* has a real question, a need for an answer.

The same seizing method teaches the child the correct use of the *pointer-words* (deixes), combining them with the gestures of pointing. This gesture, to be distinguished from just reaching or grasping, very often originates already before the first birthday (Buytendijk, 1954; Lock 1978). It seems to be typically human, not found in animals. It is combined *synchronously* with "there," "over-there," "here," "that," "this" etc. The following conversation may clear up the development of pronouns, which are a kind of pointer-words (See van Ginniken, 1922), he rightly calls the pronouns the "jumping words" because they jump from speaker to listener.

John, 2.1, approaches a chair and wants help to sit on it. He beats the chair and points to it, and says:
John: "John sit on!" . . . . .
Mother: "You want to sit on that chair? . . . . . Sit there, that is a lower chair for you! This is my chair . . . . . daddy's chair . . . . ."
John: "My chair . . . . . *my* want sit on!"

This *"my* want" very soon became "I want" . . . . . and "I myself" *pointing* to himself. The same with "you" *pointing* to the mother and others. This learning of the pronouns seems to develop very strongly during the child's "obstinacy period," (see Remplein, 1959).

There are three kinds of *discovery learning* (See Cronbach, 1977), which may be illustrative by this example. We get the child to play in a sand box and after having made a "ditch" in the sand, and put three small planks each of which is too small to bridge the ditch somewhere in the sand, we say, "Can you make a bridge?"

  I. We only give the child the material, mentioned above, and let him try.
  II. We make the child play with the planks in whatever ways he wants . . . . . "What could you do with these planks? Make a wall? Make a floor? . . . . ." We point to the ditch, from one bank to the other one.

III. We do the same as in II, but put one plank in the center of the ditch as a pier . . . . .

This last way is called "guided discovery learning" or "meaningful reception learning" (Klerk, 1979) or "ruleg" (= rule and example) system (Gagné, 1970). This way of learning is in contrast to "expository learning" (See Ausubel, 1962), if we build the whole bridge for the child and make him imitate this.

The *mother* is clearly following a method of "guided discovery learning" with her child, which method seems to be the most efficient according to several studies (See Cronbach, 1977). Expository learning, giving just models and making the child imitate them is very inefficient and seems to be even impossible: the child simply does not do it! (See Clark and Clark, 1977). The success of this guided discovery learning of language in babies is known!

4. Some evidences from modern methods of teaching a foreign language.

a. *Motivation* plays a major part. If one wants to make a trip to Spain and likes its culture, this motivation has a strong predicting value for success in learning the Spanish language (See Kadler, 1970; Carpay, 1975). Carpay found significant motivation effects by the use of loose-leaf systems, used in such a way that the student sees his growth of vocabulary (feedback).

b. *Passive and active language*. Passive language should precede active language as the primary source of the latter. According to Carpay (1975) this active language usually is not higher than 10 percent in foreign language speakers. This *conversion* should be realized by conversation.

Conversation is the crucial point. How to make conversation in a foreign language spontaneous and real? The Language Laboratories of the University of Louvain (1970, 1975) seem to have developed courses of "mediator-exercises" by creating situations and by role-playing, which are said to be promising. The "seizing method" and the "playing of a double part," see above, have not yet been applied as far as I know.

c. *Automatization* of grammatical-syntactic schemes should be realized by:
 (1) Rhythmic clustering.
 (2) Logic rules like those of question-answer, subject-predicate and similar, i.e. by completion exercises.
 (3) Conversation.

d. *Discovery learning*. Carpay (1975) made his subjects detect *word-derivation-rules*, that is to teach, teachable, teachability, teacher, teaching, teacherdom, teachership etc. He made them apply these rules to reading comprehension. He found that the *memory* for those words was significantly stronger in this group than in another comparable rote-learning group. He found also, that when the ratio of unknown words in a reading piece is higher than 5 percent, the derivation of the meaning of the word-*stems* becomes impossible.

e. *"Micro-languages," "Target-languages"*. These have been composed for stewards and stewardesses on world-flights, who are taught some basic words, idioms and sentence-structures in such an amount that they can help people in

182 oral education: today and tomorrow

airplanes. (See van Ek, 1976). No transfer from these reduced languages to the natural languages has been found so far.

The following points may be noted for our didactics of language to *deaf* children: the importance of motivation, of large language comprehension, of conversation, of rhythmic speech and of discovery learning.

Suggested conclusions

1. For outlining a *didactics* of language, as naturally as possible, that is, as closely as possible to the spontaneous reactions of the children, all one-sidedness of a special psycholinguistic theory and all reduction of the phenomenon "linguistic behavior" should be avoided,
   - one-sided cognitive and one-sided structural approaches,
   - a one-sided view of language as just a way of thinking and forgetting that it is primarily a conversational tool,
   - one-sided analytical approaches with a forgetting of the transparent global intuitive understanding,
   - detaching language as a system from its code and actual use.

2. A one-sided physical, quantitative and logistic way of thinking should be avoided, and a human *existential* thinking promoted, by orectic, attitudinal, social and metaphoric language didactics.

3. "*Conversation* is the full form of language" (van Ginniken, 1909), and should be the center both of language research and of language didactics.

4. The *memory* function, both Short Term Memory and Long Term Memory, is a basic one in psycholinguistic behavior.

5. A large fund of varied language *comprehension,* among other things, based on *flexible* combinabilities of words according to their semantic and grammatical aspects, is basic in language growth. Language *production* is a spontaneous selection from this basis, achieved mainly through conversation.

6. A *natural* (See 1 above) approach for the teaching of the structure of language should as much as possible include the methods for "guided *discovery* learning".

7. Because a language includes a *worldview,* the experiential education of a child should be as verbal as possible, for a social integration into the culture of the environment.

8. The conversational method of the mother (caretaker) in her *interactions* with the baby, by following a "seizing method" and "the playing of a double part", is necessary for the integration of experiences and language in the child, for his transparent thinking in a language, and for his control of language structure.

9. A conversational method presupposes well-developed *acceptance processes* from the mother, educator, towards the child, a disturbance of which may hamper language growth dangerously. These acceptance processes should be the main concern in all parent guidance services.

10. *Rhythmic melodic* speech, both for comprehension and for production, is not only a support for memory for language, but is basic for the learning of its structure too, by means of a "rhythmic closure" effect.

11. In-depth investigations of the language growth in deaf children may be a help for developing a *psycholinguistic theory.*

References

Austin, J. L. *How to do things with words.* Oxford: Oxford University Press, 1962.
Ausubel, D. P. *The psychology of meaningful verbal learning.* London: Grune & Stratton, 1963.
Bach, E. & Harms, R. T. (Eds.) *Universals of linguistic theory.* New York: Academic Press, 1968.
O'Baoill, P. *Linguistics and the development of the hearing child.* Dublin: Catholic University, 1979.
Behaghel, O. *Deutsche Syntax.* (I, II, III und IV). Springer-Verlag, Leipzig-Berlin 1923–1932.
Beilin, H. *Studies in the cognitive basis of language development.* New York: Academic Press, 1975.
Belmont, J. M., Karchmer, M. A., & Pilkonis, P. A. Instructed rehearsal strategies, influence on deaf memory processing. *Journal of Speech and Hearing Research,* 19, 1, 1976, 36–47.
Bever, T. G., Garret, M. F., & Hurtig, R. The interaction of perceptual processes and ambiguous sentence. *Memory and Cognition,* 1973, 227–286.
Birdwhistell, R. L. *Introduction to kinesics.* Louisville: University Press, 1952.
Bloom, L. Why not pivot-grammar? *Journal of Speech and Hearing Disorders,* 1971, 40–50.
Bloom, L. M. *One word at a time: the use of single word utterances before syntax.* The Hague: Mouton Incorporated, 1973.
Bohannon, J. N., & Marquis, A. L. Children's control of adult speech. *Child Development,* 1977, 38 (3), 1002–1008.
Borke, H. Piaget's view of social interaction and the theoretical construct of empathy. In Siegel & Brainerd (Eds.), 1978.
Braine, M. D. S. The ontogeny of English phrase structure: The first phrase. *Language,* 1963, 1–13.
Braine, M. D. S. On learning the grammatical order of words. *Psychology Review,* 1963, 323–348.
Brown, R. *A first language: The early stages.* Cambridge, MA: Harvard University Press, 1973.
Brown, R., & Bellugi, U. Three processes in the child's acquisition of syntax. *Harvard Educational Review,* 1964, 131–151.
Brown & Halon. Derivational complexity and order of acquisition in child speech. In Hayes, J. R. (Ed.), 1970.
Bruner, J. The ontogenesis of speech acts. *Journal of Child Language,* 1975, 2, 1–17.
Brus, B. T., & Bakker, J. Schoolvorderingen-tests voor het lezen. Een verantwoording. Nijmeegse bijdragen. L. C. G. Malmberg, 's-Hertogenbosch, 1966.
Bullowa, M. Linguistics—Infant Speech: From nonverbal communication to language. *Journal of Learning Disabilities,* 1977, 10, (6), 354–355.
Bullowa, M. (Ed.). *Before speech: The beginning of interpersonal communication.* London: Academic Press, 1979.
Buytendijk, F. J. J. Algemene theorie der menselijke houding en beweging. Het Spectrum, Utrecht 1957.
Campbell, H. W. Phoneme recognition by ear and eye. Doctoral dissertation. Catholic University, Psychological Department, Nijmegen, 1974.
Campbell, R., & Smith, P. (Eds.). Proceedings of the psychology of language conference, Stirling, June 1976. New York: Plenum Press, 1977.
Carpay, J. A. M. Onderwijspsychologie en leergangontwikkeling in het moderne vreemde-talen-onderwijs. Rijksuniversiteit, Groningen 1975.

Carter, A. L. Development of presyntactic communication system: A case study. *Journal of Child Language*, 1975, 2, 233–250.
Cazden, C. B. Environmental assistance to the child's acquisition of grammar. Unpublished doctoral dissertation, Harvard University, 1965.
de Cecco, J. P. (Ed.). *The psychology of language, thought and instruction*. New York: Academic Press, 1967.
Chomsky, N. Syntactic structure. The Hague: Mouton & Co., 1957.
Chomsky, N. *Language and mind*. New York: Harcourt, Brace & World, 1968.
Chomsky, A. *The acquisition of syntax in children from 5–10*. Cambridge, MA: M.I.T. Press, 1969.
Clark, H. H., & Clark, E. V. *Psychology and language*. New York: Harcourt, Brace, Jovanovich, 1977.
Cofer, C. N. (Ed.). *The structure of human memory*. San Francisco: Brace, 1976.
Cohen, A. Versprekingen als verklappers van het proces van spreken en verstaan. Instituut voor Perceptieonderzoek, Eindhoven 1965.
Cole, P., & Morgan, J. L. (Eds.). *Syntax and semantics* (volumes I, II & III). New York: Seminar Press, 1975.
Collins & Quillian. Communication between deaf children of preschool age and their mothers. Unpublished doctoral dissertation, University of Pennsylvania, Pittsburgh, 1969.
Cronbach, L. J. *Educational psychology* (3rd ed.). New York: Harcourt, Brace, Jovanovich, 1977.
Dietrich, R., & Klein, W. Computer-linguistik. Verlag Kohlhammer, Stuttgart 1974.
Drach, E. Grundgedanken der Deutschen Satzlehre. Killiger-Verlag, Darmstadt, 1932, 1937, 1963.
Duchan, J., Oliva, J., & Lindner, R. Performative acts defined by synchrony among intonational, verbal and nonverbal systems in a one and one-half year old child. *Sign Language Studies*, 1979, 75–88.
van Ek, J. A. *The 'threshold level' for modern language learning in schools*. Strasbourg: Council of Europe, Committee for General and Technical Education, 1976.
Emons, R. Valenzgrammatik für das Englische. Eine Einführung. Niemeyer Verlag, Tübingen 1978.
Ervin-Trip, S. An analysis of the interaction of language, topic and listener. *American Anthropologist*, 1964, 86–102.
Estes, K. W. Nonverbal discrimination of more and fewer elements by children. *Journal of Experimental Child Psychology*, 1976, 21, 393–405.
Farr, R. (Ed.). *Measurement and evaluation of reading*. New York: Grune & Stratton, 1970.
Fillmore, C. J. The case for case. In Bach & Harms (Eds.), 1968.
Fodor, A., Bever, T. B., & Garrett, M. F. *The psychology of language: An introduction to psycholinguistics and generative grammar*. New York: McGraw-Hill, 1974.
Foss, D. J., & Jerkins, C. M. Some effects of context on the comprehension of ambiguous sentences. *Journal of Verbal Learning and Verbal Behavior*, 1973, 577–589.
Fraiberg, S. H. The magic years. New York: Charles Scribner's Sons, 1964.
Fraisse, J. J. Les structures rhythmiques. Editions "Erasme" S.A., Paris 1956.
Fries, C. C. *The structure of English*. New York: Harcourt Brace, 1952.
Fromkin, V. (Ed.). *Speech errors as linguistic evidence*. The Hague: Mouton, 1973.
Fry, D. *Homo loquens: Man as a talking animal*. New York: Cambridge University Press, 1977.
Furth, H. G. *Thinking without language*. New York: The Free Press, 1966.
Furth, H. G. A comparison of reading test norms of deaf and hearing children. *American Annals of the Deaf*, 1966, 461–462.
Furth, H. G., & Wachs. *A school for thinking*. London: Oxford University Press, 1974.

Gagné, R. M., & Smith, E. C. A study of the effects of verbalization on problem solving. In de Cecco J. P. (Ed.), 1967.
van der Geest, T. *Evaluation of theories on child grammars.* The Hague: Mouton, 1974.
van der Geest, T. Some aspects of communicative competence and their implications for language acquisition. Assen: Van Gorcum, 1975.
van Ginniken, J. Het gesprek. Nieuwe Taalgids, 1909, 86–96.
van Ginniken, J. De roman van een kleuter. L. C. G. Malmberg, 's-Hertogenbosch 1922.
Grant, J. M. Experience: The foundation of language acquisition. In Simmons-Martin & Calvert (Eds.), 1979.
Greenberg, J. *Universals in language.* Cambridge, MA: Harvard University Press, 1963.
Groht, M. A. *Natural language for deaf children.* Washington, DC: Alexander Graham Bell Association, 1958.
Gruendell, J. M. Referential extension in early language development. *Child Development,* 1977, 48 (4), 1567–1576.
Hayes, J. R. (Ed.). *Cognition and the development of language.* New York: Academic Press, 1970.
Hebb, D. O. *A textbook of psychology.* Philadelphia: W. B. Saunders, 1961.
Heider, F., & Heider, G. M. A comparison of the sentence structure of deaf and hearing children. *Psychology Monographs U.S.A.,* 1940, 232, 42–103.
Hill, F. M. Anleitung zum Sprachunterricht taubstummer Kinder. Assens Verlag, Essen 1840.
Hodgson, K. W. *The deaf and their problems: A study in special education.* London: Watts & Co., 1953.
von Humboldt, W. Über die Verschiedenheit des menschlichen Sprachbaues. In Über die Kawisprache auf der Insel Java. Springer Verlag, Berlin 1836–1840.
Huttenlocher, J. Children's language: Word phrase relationship. *Science,* 1964, 264–265.
Ingram, D. Transitivity in child learning. *Language,* 1971, 47, 888–910.
Jäger, V. A. Anleitung zum Unterricht taubstummer Kinder in der Sprache und dem anderen Schullehrgegenständen nebst Vorlegeblättern, einer Bildersammlung and einem Lese- und Wörterbuch. Bed & Fränkel, Stuttgart 1832–1836, 1845.
Johnson, N. F. The psychological reality of phrase-structure rules. *Journal of Verbal Learning and Verbal Behavior,* 1965, 4, 469–475.
Johnson, D. M. *Systematic introduction to the psychology of thinking.* London: Harper & Row, 1972.
Kadler, E. H. Linguistics and teaching of foreign language. New York: Van Nostrand Reinhold, 1970.
Kainz, J. Psychologie der Sprache. Vol. I, II, III und IV. Ferdinand Enke Verlag, Stuttgart, Wien 1957.
Kaper, W. Einige Erscheinungen der kindlichen Spracherwerbung erläutert im Lichte des vom Kinde gezeigten Interesse für Sprachliches. J. B. Wolters, Groningen 1959.
Kempen, G. De taalgebruiker in de mens. H. D. Tjeenk Willink, Groningen 1976.
Kempen, G. Syntactic constructions as retrieval plans. *British Journal of Psychology,* 1976, 67, (2), 149–160.
Kempen, G. Sentence construction by a psychologically plausible formulator. In R. Campbell, & P. Smith (Eds.), 1977.
Kennedy, A., & Wilkes, A. Response times at different positions within a sentence. *Quarterly Journal of Experimental Psychology,* 1968, 20, 390–394.
Kintsch, W. Memory for prose. In C. N. Cofer (Ed.), 1976.
Klein, R. Word order. Dutch mothers and their children. Instituut voor Algemene Taalwetenschap, Amsterdam 1975.
de Klerk, L. F. W. Inleiding in de onderwijspsychologie. Van Loghum Slaterus, Deventer 1979.

Kuipers, A. H. Wat is descriptieve linguistiek. In Tervoort (Ed.) 1977, 22–33.
Labov, W. The logic of non-standard English. In W. Labov, 1972.
Labov, W. *Language in the inner city*. Philadelphia: University of Pennsylvania Press, 1972.
Labov, W. *Sociolinguistic patterns*. Philadelphia: University of Pennsylvania Press, 1972.
Landsberger, S. P. J. Wat is computer linguistiek? In Tervoort (ed.) 1977, 47–65.
Laughery, K. R., & Spector, A. The roles of recording and rhythm in memory organization. *Journal of Experimental Psychology*, 1972, 94, 41–48.
Lennon, R. T. What can be measured. In R. Farr (Ed.), 1970.
Leonard, L. B. On differentiating syntactic and semantic features in emerging grammars: Evidence from empty form usage. *Journal of Psycholinguistic Research*, 1975, 357–364.
Leopold, W. F. Speech development of a bilingual child. Evanston, IL: Northwestern University Press, 1949.
Leopold, W. F. Patterning in children's language learning. *Language Learning*, 1953–1954, 1–14.
Leopold, W. F. Das Sprechen lernen der Kinder. Sprachforum, 1956, 117–125.
Levelt, W. J. M. What became of L.A.D.? The Hague: Peter de Ridder Press, 1972.
Levelt, W. J. M., & Kempen, G. Taal. In Michon e.a. (eds.) 1976, 492–519.
Lewis, M. M. *Infant speech*. London: Basic Books, 1936.
Li, C. N. (Ed.). Word order and word order change. Austin: University of Texas Press, 1975.
Lipps, T. Leitfaden der Psychologie. W. Engelman Verlag, Leipzig 1909.
Lock, A. (Ed.). Action symbol and gesture: The emergence of language. New York: Academic Press, 1978.
Löwe, A. Gehörlose und Schwerhörige. In Stadler H. (ed.), 1979.
MacKay, D. G. To end ambiguous sentences. *Perception and Psychophysics*, 1966, 426–436.
MacKay, D. G. Spoonerisms: The structure of errors in the serial order of speech. *Neuropsychologica*, 1970, 323–350.
MacKay, D. G. The structure of words and syllables: Evidence from errors in speech. *Cognitive Psychology*, 1972, 210–227.
MacNamara, J. Cognitive basis of language learning in infants. *Psychological Review*, 1972, 79, 1–13.
MacNamara, J. *Language learning and thought*. New York: Academic Press, 1977.
Maesse, H. Das Verhältnis von Laut- und Gebärdensprache in der Entwicklung des taubstummen Kindes. Neckar-Verlag, Villingen-Schwenningen 1977.
Markides, A. The speech of deaf and partially hearing children with special reference to factors affecting intelligibility. *British Journal of Disorders of Communication*, 1970, 5, 126–140.
McNeill, D. *The development of language*. In H. Mussen (Ed.), 1970, 1061–1162.
McWhinney, B. Pragmatic patterns in child syntax. In *Papers and reports on child language development*. Stanford: Stanford University Press, 1975.
Meadow, K. P. Early manual communication in relation to the deaf child's intellectual, social and communicative functioning. *American Annals of the Deaf*, 1968, 29–41.
Menyuk, P. *Sentences children use*. Cambridge: Harvard University Press, 1969.
Menyuk, P. Cognition and language. *The Volta Review*, 1976, 78, 250–257.
Meyer, D. E. Correlated operations in searching stored semantic categories. *Journal of Experimental Psychology*, 1973, 124–133.
Michon, J. A., de Klerk, L. F. W., & Eijkman, E. G. (Eds.). Handboek der Psychonomie. Van Loghum Slaterus, Deventer 1976.
Michotte, A. *Miscellanea psychologica*. Louvain: University Press, 1947.
Miller, G. A., Galanter, E., & Pribam, K. H. *Plans, and the structure of behavior*. New York: Holt, Rinehart & Winston, 1960.

Moeser, S. D. Iconic factors and language word order. *Journal of Verbal Learning and Verbal Behavior*, 1975, 43–55.

de Montpellier, G. *Les altérations morphologiques des mouvements rapides.* Leuven: Institut Supérieur de Philosophie, 1935.

Moore, T. E., & Harris, A. E. Language and thought in Piagetian theory. In Siegel & Brainerd (Eds.), 1978, 131–152.

Morton, J. (Ed.). *Biological and social factors in psycholinguistics.* London: Logos Press Ltd., 1970.

Mussen, H. (Ed.). *Carmichael's manual of child psychology* (Vol. 1). New York: John Wiley, 1970.

Nanninga-Boon, A. Het denken van het doofstomme kind. J. B. Wolters, Groningen 1934.

Neisser, U. *Cognitive psychology.* New York: Appleton Century-Crofts, 1967.

Nelson, K. Structure and strategy in learning to talk. *Monographs of the Society for Research in Child Development*, 1973, 38 (Serial No. 149), 104–106.

Oléron, P. Appréhension de différences perceptives et présentation simultanée ou successive par des enfants sourds. *Revue 'Defectologie'*, 1972, 45, 18–23.

Paardekoper, P. C. Syntaxis, spraakkunst en taalkunde. L. C. G. Malmberg, 's-Hertogenbosch 1955.

Paul, H. Syntaktische und grammatische Mittel der Wortsprache. M. Niemeyer Verlag, Halle 1909, 1959.

Piaget, J. Le langage et la pensé chez l'enfant. Delachaux et Niestlé S.A. Editeurs, Neuchatel 1923.

Quigley, S. P. *The influence of fingerspelling on the development of language, communication and educational achievement in deaf children.* Urbana: University of Illinois, 1969.

Raaijmakers, J. G. W. Retrieval from long-term store. A general theory and mathematical models. Psychological Department, University of Nijmegen, 1979.

Raviv, S., Sharan, S., & Strauss, S. Intellectual development of deaf children in different educational environments. *Journal of Communication Disorders*, 1973, 6, 29–36.

Remplein, H. Die seelische Entwicklung des Menschen im Kindesund Jugendalter. Ernst Reinhardt Verlag, München 1958, 1961, 1963.

Robinson, E. *The original vision.* Oxford: Manchester College, 1977.

Ruffieux, Fr. Lesen und Sprechen. Des taubstummen Kindes Sprach-werden, Lehrgang in 5 Heften. Gehörlosenschule Wuppertal 1929–1933.

Russel, W. K., Quigley, S. P., & Power, D. J. *Linguistics and deaf children: Transformational syntax and its applications.* Washington, DC: Alexander Graham Bell Association, 1976.

Sacks, H., Schegloff, E. A., & Jefferson, G. A simplest systematics for the organization of turn taking for conversation. *Language*, 1974, 696–735.

Sapir, E. *Language: An introduction to the study of speech.* New York: Harcourt Brace, 1922.

Sapir, E. Grading: A study of semantics. *Philosophy of Science*, 1944, 93–116.

Schaerlaekens, A. M. *The two-word sentence in child language development.* The Hague: Mouton, 1973.

Schank, R. C. Conceptual dependency as a framework for linguistic analysis. *Linguistics*, 1969, 28–50.

Schank, R. C. (Ed.). *Conceptual information processing.* Amsterdam: North-Holland Press, 1975.

Schank, R. C., & Colby, K. *Computer models of thought and language.* San Francisco: Brace, 1973.

Schlesinger, I. M. The grammar of sign language and the problems of language universals. In J. Morton (Ed.) 1971, p. 98–121.

Seitz, S., & Marcus, S. Mother-child interactions: A foundation for language development. *Exceptional Children*, 1976, 42, (8), 445–449.

Siegel, L. S., & Brainerd, C. J. (Eds.) *Alternatives to Piaget: Critical essays on the theory.* New York: Academic Press, 1978.

Simmons, R. Semantic networks: Their computation and use for understanding English sentences. In R. Schank & K. Colby, *Computer models of thought and language.* San Francisco: Brace, 1973.

Simmons-Martin, A., & Calvert, D. R. *Parent-infant intervention: Communication disorders.* New York: Grune & Stratton, 1979.

Sinclair-de Zwart, H. *Acquisition du langage et développement de la pensée: Sous-systèmes linguistiques et opérations concrètes.* Paris: Presse Université France, 1967.

Slobin, D. I. The more it changes . . . . . On understanding language by watching it move through time. *Papers and reports on child language development.* Stanford: Stanford University Press, 1973.

Snow, C. E. Mothers speech to children learning language. *Child Development,* 1972, 549–566.

Snow, C. E. The development of conversation between mothers and babies. *Journal of Child Language,* 1977, 4, (1), 1–22.

Spitz, R. A. *No and yes: On the genesis of human communication.* New York: International Universities Press, 1957.

Stadler, H. (Ed.). Handbuch der Behinderten Pädagogik. J. A. Barth Verlag, München 1979.

Stern, W. L. & C. Sprache des Kindes. Springer Verlag, Berlin 1905.

Stuckless, E. R., & Birch, J. W. The influence of early manual communication on the linguistic development of deaf children. *American Annals of the Deaf,* 1966, 452–460; 499–504.

Tervoort, B. Th. Structurele analyse van visueel taalgebruik binnen een groep dove kinderen. N.V. Noord-hollandsche Uitgevers Maatschappij, Amsterdam 1953.

Tervoort, B. Th. Taalstructuur en taalonderwijs aan doven. Jaarverslag (Annual Report) Instituut voor Doven, Sint-Michielsgestel 1955, 3–15.

Tervoort, B. Th. (Ed.). Wetenschap en taal. Coutinho, Muiderberg 1977.

van Uden, A. M. J. De ontwikkeling van het tijdsbegrip bij jonge en debiele dove kinderen. Pedagogische nota over zgn. lichtklokken en lichtweken. Annual report Sint-Michielsgestel 1960, p. 19–28. (The development of the concept of time with young and with retarded deaf children. *The Australian Teacher of the Deaf* 1963, 5–11.)

van Uden, A. M. J. A maternal reflective method of teaching an oral mothertongue to deaf children. In *A world of language for deaf children, part I: Basic principles* (3rd rev.) Lisse: Swets & Zeitlinger B.V., 1977.

van Uden, A. M. J. Taalverwerving door taalarme kinderen. Universitaire Pers, Rotterdam 1973.

van Uden, A. M. J. Composition-work. Provisional report. Sint-Michielsgestel 1979.

Uylings, E. Praat op heterdaad. Rijksuniversiteit, Utrecht 1956.

van der Veldt, J. L'apprentissage du mouvement et l'automatisme. Unpubl. Doct. Diss, Leuven 1928.

Vorster, J. Mommy linguist: The case for motherese. *Lingua,* 1975, 37, 281–312.

Watts, W. J. Deafness, thought and language and the influence of Piaget. *Teacher of the Deaf,* 1978, 2, (4), 117–123.

Weisgerber, L. Von den Kräften der Deutschen Sprache: Band I. Grundzüge der inhaltbezogene Grammatik. Schwann, Düsseldorf 1962.

Werner, H. Einführung in die Entwicklungs-psychologie. J. A. Barth, München 1959.

Wescott, R. W. Introducing coenetics: A biosocial analysis of communication. *American Scholar* 1965, 35, 342–356.

Whorf, B. L. *Language, thought and reality.* Cambridge, MA: M.I.T. Press, 1956.

Wood, B. S. Children and communication: Verbal and non-verbal language development. Englewood Cliffs, NJ: Prentice-Hall, 1976.
Woods, W..A. Transition network grammars for natural language analysis. *Communications of the ACN*, 1970, *13*, 591–606.
Wundt, W. Die Sprache. In Völkerpsychologie I und II. Singer-Verlag, Leipzig 1908–1911.

Appendix

An in-depth investigation of special difficulties in reading by prelingually profoundly deaf children, 1967.

Twenty-four prelingually profoundly deaf children, in the age group of 10 to 15 years, with outstanding reading difficulties have been investigated throughout and individually, in order to find the background of their misunderstandings and mistakes. They were all children with normal, nonverbal intelligence and technical reading difficulties did not appear phonematically they could say what was written or printed down. When they made a technical reading mistake, by making them reading aloud the text, this mistake has been corrected immediately. The following is based on the analysis of these difficulties.

The reading material used was:
   (1) The verbal part of HAWIK (German "Wechsler Intelligence Scale of Children," Dutch translation by me);
   (2) "Written Tasks," another reading test by Brus-Bakker (1964): the children are presented with a picture and then have to follow some instructions, for instance "Cross out the animal that does not eat;"
   (3) "Paragraph Reading Test" by Brus-Bakker (1966).

These tests consist altogether of 1,471 reading exercises, of which in all 832 were executed incorrectly. All the children were examined individually. The results were as follows: first I picked out *those* mistakes which were mainly due to lack of vocabulary: the child just did not know certain words. For instance: "The wick was still smoking." The child did not know what a wick was and mainly because of that it could not solve the reading problem. Then there were still 582 mistakes left whereby the child at least knew all the essential words more or less or thought that it knew them. Only these real reading mistakes are analysed here.

A. I could head these 582 reading difficulties under 4 categories, which I arranged according to the percentage of the reading-mistakes made:

1. *Wrong interpretation of words,* connotative and denotative: 53 percent of the mistakes.

The interpretations can not only be too concrete but too indefinite too; and also completely wrong.

It is certain that what is most primitive is that which I would like to call *idiosyncratic reading,* i.e. the child mixes his own individual experiences into his reading. For instance

You want to buy sugar. To what sort of shop would you go?

Answer: Yes, to the department store, mummy, we both eat sugar-loaf!

Further, *"chance-reading,"* for instance "whether" is understood as "weather," "swine" as "swim," "prince" as "principal," etc. These are not technical or dyslectical reading mistakes, but the child interprets these words which are unknown or little known to him in a superficial way or just by guessing, out of his own, too little "profiled" vocabulary.

Further the wrong interpretation of the *pronouns, interrogatives,* etc. For instance "Whom did you call?" was not understood because "who(m)" was only related to a subject.

The same happened with regard to many *content-words.*

For instance "You have lost the ball" was not understood because "lost" was related to a game (See below). The child also made a sign: thumb down!—Or "The baker has no more bread" was met with: "Nonsense": the child simply could not imagine that a baker did not have bread.

Nanninga-Boon called these incorrect interpretations, "complex-ish" interpretations" (1934).

2. *Incorrect grouping of words:* 24 percent of the mistakes. The words were too often taken on their own without taking the whole context into account.

Most primitive here is—what I would call—*"pre-school reading."* When a deaf pre-school child, who cannot yet pronounce all the words, is asked to read a correctly understood sentence, it only reads the words it can pronounce and simply misses the others out. For instance a child read the sentence: "Yesterday I took out a milk tooth" as follows: "Yesterday . . . I . . . out . . . milk . . . ," while it pointed at the words. There are older children who have got into the habit of looking for only the well known words and to miss out the others. This leads to another sort of "chance reading." For instance when told "Cross out the numbers that are bigger than 8" only the 8 was crossed out. The child only read "cross out" and "8," and simply overlooked the rest. Another child crossed out all the numbers, it did not read any further than "cross out the numbers" and assumed the rest!—Or for instance "What animal gives us milk?" The answer given was: "The cat!"

This also happens in a complete piece for reading. Instead of reading the grouping of the words the child picks out some words and then tries to find out what or what story it is meant to be. This is a good thing in as far as the child orients itself primarily on the whole and tries to understand the details from the whole. It can, however, deteriorate into a "venture-game" in which a lot of words are simply not taken into account.

How it is possible that the children understood words or word-groups too much in a separate entirety, is made clear in—what I should like to call—*"summarized reading."* The child does not see any connection. For instance this sentence "John is walking on the roof" is pictured in two pieces: on the left John walking on the ground and on the right, a house with a roof. The child had understood: Draw "John walking," and "a roof"!

Especially when the words are not immediately connected ("mediate constituent elements"), this often gives difficulties for a correct understanding. I should like to call this *"successive reading."* The child only groups words immediately succeeding each other. For instance, to the question "How do you think he managed it?" he answers "With my brains". . . . The child had connected "how-do-you-think" instead of "How he managed it." Often the child only reads from left to right and tries to find an interpretation for each word that comes along. As soon as it has found an interpretation step by step, it interprets the whole in a fixed way and abandons the other words. For instance "Draw the moon and three stars!" The child drew three moons! It had simply stopped after "three," had found something it understood and did not read any further. When asked to draw the stars as well, it drew a whole lot! At the same time this shows a lack of flexibility in the interpretations, as in so many other examples (See below).

These difficulties often occur in the *constractions,* where the child imperfectly connects them, precisely because the grouping word is not there. For instance when given the numbers 5 4 7 2 9 with the request "cross out the fourth number and draw a square under the third one," the child crossed out the number 2 but drew three squares under *that* number!

The imperfect reading or non-reading of *accents,* and thus the rhythmical grouping, is a source of many difficulties too. For instance "Why do people build their houses of bricks?" was answered as follows "To live in." The contrasting accent on "bricks" was not understood.

This "successive reading" instead of taking in the whole is in my opinion connected with the lack of *short term memory* of the deaf child and especially of these multiply handicapped (Uden, 1968). However, the long term memory also often plays a part in the wrong interpretation of a piece for reading: at the end of the reading piece the child has already forgotten an essential element of the whole, that was said at the beginning. This happens of course to hearing people too. However it can be a very small word that is taken in by us correctly because of the accent, but which escapes the deaf child.

3. *Inability to understand pretending, the figurative meaning, the conjugative meaning: 14 percent of the mistakes.*

For instance this summarized reading piece:

> The teacher in a class was telling a tense story, but Peter kept interrupting. Suddenly the teacher said to Peter: "Do you know Punch?" Peter: "Yes, Miss!" Teacher: "I think Punch is very nice, but not today!" All the children laughed!

One child reacted by saying: "I always find Punch nice!" It had not understood that here Punch was meant to be Peter. Other examples are: the irreality "I would have put the letter away, if I had known you were so curious," Or "wish-forms" like: "Let him operate on you!"

This category was a hazardous difficulty for my testees. The difficulty occurred 95 times and was wrongly identified 81 times. This is 85 percent of the cases.

4. *Inability to reorganize the (chrono-) logical order: 9 percent of the mistakes.*

Quite often the order of the sentences or words does not coincide with the chronological or logical order of the story or the problem. For instance "Three boys have between them 72 pennies, each of them an even number. How many has each boy got?" The child could not find the answer after many calculations. However, when I turned the order and said: "There were 72 pennies, and there were three boys, how many pence had each boy," the problem was soon solved. This difficulty occurred 78 times in all, and 52 times my 24 subjects in this experiment answered it wrongly, i.e. in 67 percent of the cases. We can conclude that this is a hazardous difficulty too.

B. *Difficult words.*

I should like to pick out a few words or combinations which seemed exceptionally difficult. These are:

1. "Relative words" such as: still, also, to there, the last but three, right-left, too big, big enough, so much the less, even, only, at least, except, etc.

2. Indefinite words. The words: all, nothing, nobody, complete, always, never, everywhere—are easier than: some, many, somewhere, somebody, now and then, etc.

3. The "substitute-words" like the pronouns, interrogatives, the verbs "to do" and "to happen" etc.

> N.B.—We should say that these interpretations do not present as many difficulties in compositions nor in general in constructive work when active language is used: one already knows what they substitute. This, however, is not the case in reading, in understanding, in passive language.

4. The modal words, especially the modal auxiliaries, for instance "It *must* be too late, as the children are already coming out."

C. *Basic difficulties*

There are a few more basic difficulties, which are peculiar to all the categories mentioned. They probably concern more the entire education. I should like to mention two of them.

1. *To put oneself in the place of someone else.*

In order to be able to read, one should be able to detach oneself, to step out of one's ego-centrism into hetero-centrism, i.e. to think from somebody else's point of view.

The children should be brought up to think and to feel more from someone else's experience. This is not realized by vocabulary or grammar, but by play, by co-operation, by experience, and most of all by *conversing*.

2. *Flexibility, agility in thinking and imagination.*

The children should not be tied down in too severe frames of thought, but stay open or be opened to many possibilities, and "combinabilities" of fellow people, thoughts, feelings, things. One should try to prevent as much as possible the development of "fixed complexes," both in language as in behavior.

Consequently experience and creativity should be as rich as possible. The passive language, the maneuverable understanding, should be far ahead of the active language, and the active language should more and more grow from a flexible, rich understanding. The reverse is not possible in my opinion: it tends to tie children down.

For instance they did not understand a story about a gentleman, who exploited his servants. "Gentleman" was interpreted as a "gentle man." Even after some explanation they still did not entirely get away from this latter interpretation; when some of the servants rebelled the servants who stood by him were still the good people.

Especially one should not forget the function of being able to *postpone* the full interpretation of the words. Often the children clung to a certain interpretation and did not switch over. For instance: "He had omitted to read the last letter, so that he took the word as being singular." The meaning of the word 'letter' is not clear until the second part of the sentence is read. Often the child whose language is poor interprets 'letter' as a written form of communication and clings to that, instead of switching over to the meaning of 'letter' being a sound of speech, *even when* they know that 'letter' has these two meanings. To the sentence 'More than 100 years ago Watson invented the steam engine' came the reaction 'An old man!' *in spite of* the fact that the child really knew what was meant by 'ago' (3 days ago etc.). A number in combination with years was too fixedly related to age.

It will be clear that here we encounter the basic difficulty in learning to read, too much thinking in pictures, too concrete thinking, a way of thinking that is even more fixed by signs. It is not surprising that Stuckless and Birch (1964) and also Meadow (1968) did not find a very high reading level—as a matter of fact an arrears—in very intelligent deaf children who were not multi-handicapped, of deaf parents, who from the start had been brought up in sign-language. Quigley's research (1969) concerning the use of finger-spelling in the education of the deaf had as a result, which was in my opinion the most important, that signs are disadvantageous for learning to read.

reaction to 7 and 8

richard r. kretschmer

In reviewing the papers presented during this session and those throughout the remainder of this week, several points have been consistently made which require emphasis:

1. The concept of linguistic competence does need to be discarded in favor of the more comprehensive concept—communicative competence. Language can no longer be seen apart from its larger context of communication. The demands imposed by communication shape the use and appearance of linguistic forms as they occur in specific conversational exchanges.

2. Sentence production is most productively viewed as the result of an intersection of linguistic forms, cognitive structures/experiences, and social/communicative intentions rather than a hierarchical development. When producing sentences, individuals formulate syntactic forms that encode semantic/cognitive information for specific communication purposes. Thus, it is necessary to talk about syntax, or even semantics, as each relate to communicative intent or purpose, while being careful not to fall into the trap of looking exclusively at communicative purposes apart from their interaction with syntax and semantics.

3. Language acquisition processes are developmental, both in a cognitive and experiential sense. As children hear the code used by significant communicators in their environment, they begin to understand how to use language for their own cognitive and social purposes. It is important to remember that children learn about syntax, semantics, and communicative purposes simultaneously although there are some data to support the idea that communicative/interactional framing may be the most important aspect of communication in the initial developmental stages (Snow and Ferguson, 1977; Markova, 1978; Ochs and Schieffelin, 1979; and Schaffer, 1977).

I would like to spend the remainder of the time available discussing these three assertions ending with some questions for consideration by the group.

Through the efforts of sociolinguists such as Cazden (1979), Ervin-Tripp (1977), Erickson and Shultz (1977), Cook-Gumperz (1978), and Hymes (1974), it has become increasingly clear that the position articulated by theoretical linguists such as those of the Chomskyian persuasion failed to consider at least one vital issue, specifically, sentences occur in conversational contexts and these contexts shape the appearance and use of particular syntactic forms as they occur in dialogue. Research by Scallon (1979), by Garvey (1977), and by Keenan (1974), suggest that conversations entail a building process. Each participant in a conversation responds to the others involved as they utter sentences; consequently, when a speaker produces a sentence in a conversation, he/she must consider what has transpired in the conversation, what he/she hopes will transpire, and what the social conventions are that can be used to regulate conversation exchanges (Schenkein, 1978). Stated differently, the speaker must decide what is appropriate at a particular point in time to say and recognize how to use the linguistic code to deliver the message he wants, in the best way possible, given the constraints of the conversation and setting.

In my opinion, it is critical that those of us concerned with education of the hearing impaired understand fully information available from research in developmental psycholinguistics/sociolinguistics. It is clear from the developmental literature that there is no discontinuity from infant behavior to mastery of full adult forms (deVilliers and deVilliers, 1978). It is also clear that children are engaged by caretakers in conversations from the moment of birth; that as the child matures, his contributions become greater and greater (Snow and Ferguson, 1977; Waterson and Snow, 1978). In recent research conducted by Saporito (in preparation) at the University of Cincinnati, we have observed one mother engaging her normally hearing infant in conversations where she assumed both the speaker and listener role (referred to by van Uden as the double role phenomena). What is of particular interest is that her utterances tended to be approximately 1.5 seconds in duration, and were coupled with precise non-verbal body positions. That is, when she talked for the infant, she moved away from her baby. When she addressed the baby, she moved toward her. At 4 months of age, there was a dramatic change in the mother's response, due to a significant change in the baby, namely, the infant had learned to smile appropriately at her mother. At this point, the mother's vocalizations altered into "contentless forms," (see Snow, 1977, for additional support of this phenomenon) or nonsense syllables, but still clustered into vocalizations of 1.5 seconds in length. In addition, the mother began to wait for responses from her daughter rather than talking for her. The infant's contributions initially were smiles, but soon became vocalizations coupled with body movements, eye gazes, and/or grasping gestures. By 6 months of age, the daughter had established true conversations with her mother since she only began her response when the mother moved away, the previous "body-positional" cue by the mother that it was the infant's turn to speak.

Of particular significance with regard to this study, is the importance of non-verbal systems as they interact with verbalized strategies. And, these verbalized strategies include exposure to both linguistic structures *and* intonational parameters of oral communication. This theme has been well documented in the literature on normal developing children's patterns of communication/language by Bates and her colleagues (1979) and others. Verbal language emerges in a communicative milieu of pointing, body positioning, and ritualized gestures which serve as frames for the mastery of verbal forms (Bruner, 1975). Recent studies have also suggested that the non-verbal infant performatives identified by Bates (1976) and by Bruner (1975) reflect not only communicative intent, proto-imperative, proto-declarative, proto-question forms (Bates, 1979; Carter, 1975), but also an infant's cognitive understandings such as manifesting what is known about the role of "agent" in connected language (Olswang and Carpenter, 1979).

It has been suggested by O'Baoill that the study of interlanguage has considerable validity in examining language-learning issues. Such attempts by a variety of researchers have suggested that children do learn language in stages and that these stages are reflections of cognitive growth, experiential learning, and increased social awareness (Bates, 1979; Bloom and Lahey, 1978; Snow and Ferguson, 1977; Ochs and Schieffelin, 1979; Waterson and Snow, 1978; Minifie and Lloyd, 1978). For instance, growth in question patterns seems particularly tied to cognitive understandings the child has about the new information being requested by the speaker. Question forms involving who, where, and what are more easily mastered than question-forms involving why and how answers (Ervin-Tripp and Miller, 1977). In addition, acquisition of syntax seems tied to the kinds and amounts of experiences provided the child. deVilliers and deVilliers (1979), for instance, found that the first stage of negation development negative tagging (Bellugi, 1967) was directly related to parental use of negation. When parents used negation as a transition from the previous sentence to another alternative, such as, "No, that's a bird, rather than a cow," children tended to use negative tagging rather than the *late*-developing negative embedding rule. This type of study emphasizes the importance of examining language within the communication milieu in which it occurs.

The normal language development literature has shown an increase in the number of longitudinal studies of the type recommended by the previous papers. Unfortunately, such efforts have not been directed toward study of hearing-impaired children. Several studies have been reported such as those by Juneke (1973), Hess (1974), and Ivimey (1976) which suggest that hearing-impaired children display normal, but delayed developmental patterns. Unfortunately, the focus of these approaches has been on syntactic development, not on semantic acquisition and/or conversational adequacy.

With these statements in mind, let me then conclude this presentation with the following questions for consideration by the group:

1. If the hearing-impaired child like the normally hearing child learns language through communication interactions and if this is best achieved through mother-child interactions, how do we deal with families where linguistic/communication patterns do not correspond with language/communication patterns of the dominant language reflected in the society and indirectly by the school?

2. In those instances, where the school must become the primary linguistic input agent for the child, what types of alterations in traditional school formats need to be made in order to facilitate "normal" language/communication growth? Or are these alterations impractical, if not counterproductive to the school's overall goal of "education"?

3. Can we not use the developmental literature as guidelines for the types of "conversations" to engage hearing-impaired children? Also, with older deaf students who display gaps in their linguistic/communicative behavior, is it not possible to frame meaningful conversations that naturally expose and encourage the use of these missing behaviors?

4. Given the possible importance of nonverbal framing in normal language/communication development, what implications does this have for unisensory versus multisensory approaches?

5. Finally, is there a role for more analytic approaches to language teaching? If so, what is it?

References

Bates, E. *Language and context: The acquisition of pragmatics*. New York: Academic Press, 1979.

Bates, E. *The emergence of symbols: Cognition and communication in infancy*. New York: Academic Press, 1979.

Bellugi, U. *The acquisition of negation*. Unpublished doctoral dissertation, Harvard University, 1967.

Bloom, L., & Lahey, M. *Language development and language disorders*. New York: John Wiley & Sons, 1978.

Bruner, J. The ontogenesis of speech acts. *Journal of Child Language*, 1975, 2, 1–19.

Carter, A. The transformation of sensorimotor morphemes into words: A case study of the development of 'more' and 'mine'. *Journal of Child Language*, 1975, 2, 233–250.

Cazden, C. Peekaboo as an instructional model: Discourse development at home and at school. *Papers and Reports on Child Language Development*, 1979, 17, 1–29.

Cook-Gumperz, J., & Gumperz, J. Context in children's speech. In N. Waterson & C. Snow (Eds.), *The development of communication*. New York: John Wiley & Sons, 1978.

de Villiers, J., & de Villiers, P. *Language acquisition*. Cambridge: Harvard University Press, 1978.

de Villiers, P., & de Villiers, J. Form and function in the development of sentence negation. *Papers and Reports on Child Language Development*, 1979, 17, 57–64.

Erickson, F., & Shultz, J. When is a context? Some issues and methods in the analysis of social competence. *Quarterly Newsletter of the Institute for Comparative Human Development*, 1977, 1, 5–10.

Ervin-Tripp, S. From conversation to syntax. *Papers and Reports on Child Language Development*, 1977, 13, 11–21.

Garvey, C. The contingent query: A dependent act in conversation. In M. Lewis & L. Rosenblum (Eds.), *Interaction, conversation, and the development of language*. New York: John Wiley & Sons, 1977.

Hess, L. *The development of transformational structures in a deaf child and a normally hearing child over a period of five months*. Unpublished master thesis, University of Cincinnati, 1972.

Hymes, D. *Foundations in sociolinguistics: An ethnographic approach*. Philadelphia: University of Pennsylvania Press, 1974.

Ivimey, G. The written syntax of an English deaf child: An exploration in method. *British Journal Disorders Communication*, 1976, 11, 103–120.

Juenke, D. *An application of a generative-transformational model of linguistic description of hearing impaired subjects in the generation and expansion stages of language development*. Unpublished master thesis, University of Cincinnati.

Keenan, E. Conversational competence in children. *Journal of Child Language*, 1974, 1, 163–185.

Markova, I. (Ed.). *The social context of language*. New York: John Wiley & Sons, 1978.

Minifie, F., & Lloyd, L. (Eds.). *Communicative and cognitive abilities—early behavioral assessment*. Baltimore: University Park Press, 1978.

Ochs, E., & Schieffelin, B. (Eds.). *Developmental pragmatics*. New York: Academic Press, 1979.

Olswang, L., & Carpenter, R. *The ontogenesis of agent: From cognitive notion to semantic expression.* Paper presented at the 1979 National Convention of the American Speech and Hearing Association, Atlanta.

Saporito, D. Book in preparation.

Scallon, R. A real early stage: An unzippered condensation of a dissertation on child language. In E. Ochs & B. Schieffelin (Eds.), *Developmental pragmatics.* New York: Academic Press, 1979.

Schaffer, H. (Ed.). *Studies in mother-infant interaction.* London: Academic Press, 1977.

Schenkein, J.(Ed.). *Studies in the organization of conversational interaction.* New York: Academic Press, 1978.

Snow, C., & Ferguson, C. (Eds.). *Talking to children.* Cambridge: Cambridge University Press, 1977.

Waterson, N., & Snow, C. (Eds.). *The development of communication.* New York: John Wiley & Sons, 1978.

part III
the essence of the oral method

9

the conversational method and the control of language
a chapter of the didactics of language for deaf children

a.m.j. van uden

Outline

Introduction.
1. General aspects of conversations.
   a. Spontaneity.
   b. How then to come into conversation?
   c. Linguistic aspects of conversations.
2. Conversational lessons "heart to heart" and their "deposits."
   a. Two different kinds of conversational lessons.
   b. Typical phenomena in group-conversations with deaf children.
   c. Is this way of teaching compatible with preprogrammed language?
   d. Avoiding interruptions of the heart-to-heart conversations.
   e. The "deposits" of the conversations.
3. "Linguistic conversational lessons".
   a. Sources of the structure.
   b. A preprogrammed "target-language"?
   c. Guided discovery learning and motivation.
   d. Guided discovery learning and reflecting.

e. Guided discovery learning and linguistic terms.
  f. Some examples of guided discovery learning of language structure.

Conclusion: Openess.

Appendix 1.
Evoking conversations, illustrated by some practical examples.

Appendix 2.
Some more records of conversations to be used as reading material.

Introduction

The theory and the practice of the conversational way from early childhood through 5 years of age, i.e., for home-training and preschool, is described in our paper given in St. Louis (van Uden, 1978): "How to come into conversation with a speechless and languageless child?" We refer the reader, looking for that aspect of our work, to that study.

The possibility of completely oral-aural conversation, individually and in a small group of a class and/or residential home, is shown elsewhere (see 1968 verbatim representations of eight oral lessons with 4–5 year-old through 10–12 year-old deaf children, with analysis of same, 1970, 1977). This basic fact originating from continuous challenging of both speechreading and "sound perception" (auditory and vibratory) from early childhood is presupposed here.

It is also presupposed that deaf children don't use esoteric signs among themselves. This would imply strong interfering influences from a kind of compound bilingualism (1968), hampering the normal process of language acquisition, apart from deleterious effects upon speechreading and auditory potential. There is in our opinion an essential difference between esoteric signs and body language. Esoteric signs are understood by none except members of a deaf community, including some hearing people living day by day with the manual deaf. Body language is understood by everybody. For more details see the St. Louis, 1978, study. The development of the vast majority of deaf children in our institute can be described as follows:

Home training through 5 years: The way of communication of the deaf child with hearing adults and among themselves is mainly "body language" with the support of speech.

6–7 years of age: The main way of communication with the hearing is mainly oral with the support of body language. The communication among themselves seems to be still mainly by body language, changing little by little into mainly oral communication.

9–10 years of age: The communication of deaf children among themselves becomes mainly oral with a support of body language.

13–14 years of age: Body language is reduced to mainly just gesticulation. How esoteric signs, especially in the residential homes, can be provided, is explained elsewhere (Brussels, 1979).

Motivation plays a very important part. It has been said in our first paper that the acceptance processes of the mother (caretaker) are basic for language acquisition. The same must be said of the teacher of the deaf and of the houseparents. If they don't believe in their own method, are defeatist according to the real oral-aural opportunities of deaf children, they will not develop them to their full potential. Actually a kind of rejection process is originating which is very dangerous both for the language growth and for the education of deaf children. This acceptance process includes the acceptance and esteem of the deaf person as a complete and equally worthy member of the hearing community, who must be given every opportunity for normal human development.

The art of conversation is, first of all, *the art of listening* (1968, See below). This is incompatible with an authoritarian attitude. Of course this does not include loss of discipline; on the contrary, an open ear and eye to what the children want to say, to their need for communication, to what interests them, and, further, a skill to evoke their interest in something which it is necessary to teach them contribute to this art. The teacher should show a very sociocentric attitude and in this way be able to put interaction in the forefront.

By conversation the parent/teacher/educator *meets* the individual needs of the children (McKeachie, 1962): Assertive, expansive children learn best by *discussions*, which challenge their inventiveness; children with need of contact learn best by friendly encounter, and a *confirming* attitude; withdrawn and shy children with a fear of failing learn best by small steps, more directions and *immediate rewards* (see Cronbach, 1977). The able teacher, therefore, will know his children and be flexible in the style of his conversations with them. Basic to all this is that he evokes in deaf children an atmosphere of trustfulness toward the hearing with a desire to learn their language.

General Aspects of Conversations

Spontaneity

Spontaneity is the core of a real conversation. It is impossible to come into conversation without the creative spontaneity of the conversational partners, both in comprehension and in production of communication.

A conversation is an exchange of thoughts. This definition includes several presuppositions:
- There must be real *thoughts*. Otherwise an exchange of them is impossible.
- Real thoughts are *creative*, spontaneous, and intuitive.
- *Questions*, problems, are thoughts too, "seeking thoughts."
- The same with *appeals*, calls, with attitudes, feelings, etc.
- Many thoughts are presupposed, have to be *"read between the lines"* (see Chapter 8), *verbal* and *nonverbal* ones, consciously and unconsciously, sometimes even actively hidden and/or repressed.
- There are thoughts with an "intention," i.e., purposely functioning usually as a message toward the partner (which are the most direct ones). Other thoughts are *not intentional,* but may be very important for the conversation, too.
- There is *"body-language"* also: oral utterances in conversations must be seen as operating within a cloud of nonverbal communication. Several investigations have revealed that conversations are "danced duets".
- *"Exchange"* includes pragmatic behavior, "molding" the thoughts and their utterances so that they may be understood, which presupposes an amount of *empathy* from all partners, both in production and in comprehension of

communication. There are people with whom it is is (almost) impossible to develop a real conversation, because they are so full of their (idiosyncratic) own thoughts, that they don't *listen:* they suffer from a lack of empathy. This may happen with teachers, too, who only can "lecture," who are not able to come into conversation with their children: they have "closed eyes and ears." Real conversations always are *"pluri-sided,"* e.g., if the children are not putting *spontaneous* thoughts "into the field," there is no real conversation at all, but just "lecturing" or "question-answer" play and suchlike.

Not only should the pupil or student be *empathic,* but first of all the teacher and educator. Otherwise the latter will not be able to *seize* correctly what the child wants to say or which kind of presupposed thoughts it has. He also will be unable to find the conversationally right words in a *pragmatic* sense, or to manipulate the situation so that he *makes himself understood* (See chapter 8, 1978). Further, the educator must know his children throughout, as individually as possible, not only their character and feelings, but also their verbal and nonverbal cognitive "world" (their "conceptualizations," their "encyclopedic knowledge," see chapter 8). Without that, and/or without giving attention to it, he can make the most stupid errors. In our book (1968, 1977) we have given several examples, e.g.:

> A teacher of children 6–7 years of age brought a box in the classroom and put it on the table. He says and writes on the blackboard:
> "The box is on the table,"
> assuming that the children will understand this (nonseized, nonconversational "baked") sentence in the same way as he meant!

> Another teacher put a ball into the hands of Mary, and said and wrote:
> "Mary has a ball",
> which properly is not true at all. Has Mary really a ball?

The teaching of language without real conversation and correctly checked verbalizations (see first paper, 1978) will stick to a kind of "algebra" and will serve no useful purpose.

There are ways of teaching which lead both teachers and children astray. Some of the following practices may be sometimes useful, in addition to conversation. But if they replace conversation or if they take up too much time, they are, in my opinion, didactically completely wrong.

- The teacher shows a picture or some objects (e.g., a farm) and makes the children *name* or label the objects, the actions, etc.: what do you call this? What is its name? He may react to some spontaneous remarks of his children, but does not use *that* for language growth: it is "outside the program." E.g., a child says (by body-language), that a cat may scratch you; this may be reacted to with: "Yes, that would be bad," but then it "evaporates into the air," will be forgotten very soon, and remains outside the "language." Yet *such a remark* is much more important than the programmed exercises. It should be noted and if not spoken, then at least written and as much of it as possible spoken, e.g.

the conversational method and the control of language

> Willy: *The cat may scratch you!*
>
> Teacher: *Yes, that would be bad!*

Certainly the other children will react with more thoughts, seeing that they are rewarded and accepted.

Once I asked a teacher, putting the questions mentioned above about some very nice pictures, to say nothing and simply wait and see what the children would say about a new picture. She expected "no reactions," but after a minute of astonishment (the children were not accustomed to the absence of questions) these children "exploded" with a lot of (nonoral and/or clumsily oral) thoughts. These could be seized, and that day the children learned more language than on any other day. A week later the same thoughts and their written "deposits" (see below) were still very much alive.

- *Storytelling.* The teacher tells sentences, comprising a story, e.g., about a pig. Maybe the children have seen that as a picture story before. The children have to lipread, listen to every sentence, and then dramatize its content. Usually these sentences are mainly statements. After the "story" and sometimes even before it, the (written) sentences are attached to the pictures, or pictures are drawn for every sentence. It should be clear that this is more of film-thinking than of language. In this way the children will never achieve real reading of normal language.

- *Question-answer play.* This may be done with pictures, at a reading lesson with a story (line after line, see below), after an excursion to the post office, etc. It must be noted immediately, that these questions asked by the teacher are not *real* questions, because he already knows the answer. They are more like commands or directions (see below, 1977). The reaction of the children seems to be mainly similar to those they would have in an examination. So this activity is no real exchange of thoughts.

- *Verbalizations of experiences.* This was the way of teaching in the so-called "Belgian Method" (± 1930), built upon methods used for normally hearing mentally retarded children (Décroly, Herlin, see 1977).
  The teacher has many sentences prepared beforehand, written on sheets of paper, as:

> I am washing my hands.

> I am entering.

Etc.

The teacher trains his children as follows. When he gives the sentence

> I am entering.

the child learns to read it just globally and to match it with this action:

> he leaves the classroom, shuts the door behind him, opens the door again, and enters, showing his "sentence": I am entering! . . . .

Almost the same is done by many other methods: doing something and labeling every new action. Several times I have observed a way of teaching as follows: the children had to speak chorally to the teacher, when he was acting:

> You are entering the school.
> You are taking off your hat.
> You are putting the hat on the hatrack.
> You are taking off your coat.
> You are putting the coat on the hatrack.
> Etc., etc.

Together with this, many programmed *matching exercises* of pictures or objects with words are on the market and used for deaf children.

It may be questioned whether the children understand the pictures and actions in the same way as the teacher and the composers of the "method" suppose. Some investigations (e.g., van Dongen, 1948) have shown that children who could not yet read but had normal language often "saw" completely different "things" in these pictures, e.g., the picture of an *arm* (according to the programmed matching exercise) was interpreted as "Halt! Stop!" by one child, as "fighting!" by another, (see 1978).

We will see below how meaningful matching exercises that are not confusing can be drawn from *conversations*. It may be clear that this way of working hardly can be termed "teaching of language." Which language?
- *"Role playing programs"* not composed from real conversations held before (see, e.g., Voit, 1976).
By means of pictures or videofilm, situations and activities accompanied by language are shown to the children:

"Good morning, barber!"
"Good morning, John. How do you want your hair to be cut?"
"A curly head, Sir!" . . . .
"Sit down, please!"
Etc. etc.

The children learn to act these sketches. The mistake, in my opinion, is not in this role-playing as such (it may be very helpful indeed), but in its preparation without conversation, without *using* the *spontaneous* reactions of the children.

A teacher who wants to start most of all from the spontaneous reactions of the children, i.e., who wants to follow an essentially *natural* method, will feel himself "harnessed" if someone else, or a manual made obligatory by authorities, prescribes which vocabulary and which sentence-forms he has to teach from week to week or from month to month, as a kind of book of "recipes." A teacher following such a program certainly will become program-oriented and not child-oriented. In my opinion—and we have sad experiences of this—it breaks down the conversations, because *spontaneity is largely lost*. The teacher very often just forgets to seize the spontaneous reactions of his children, as we have seen above.

An objection: Do the *mothereses* (see first paper) not contain a hint for a program of teaching language to deaf children? The same as with the natural growth of language in a normally hearing child? It must be said that the mothereses originate completely *spontaneously*, not only in the mother but in other caretakers too, even in the father, older children, etc. (Clark & Clark, 1977). We see the same happening with our teachers. They *spontaneously* will not use, e.g., long embedded sentences or structures with "the more . . . the more . . . " etc., with preschool deaf children or first graders. One really can trust the teachers! The only thing some of the teachers have to learn is, to behave as *naturally* as possible, notwithstanding hearing losses. Two kinds of programs, however, are useful. We will see below how it is possible, notwithstanding a continuous use of normal colloquial language, to teach deaf children the *structure* of language, namely by "guided discovery learning."

How then to come into conversation with a deaf child?

(1) The "How" . . . .

Many textbooks *say* that conversation is very important for teaching a language to both normally hearing and deaf children, but don't explain *how* to develop it, and don't put the conversation into the center of the whole work.

This *how* has been explained in 1968, 1977, 1978: it is the "seizing method" and the "playing of a double part," i.e., by *listening* to and *viewing* the spontaneous reactions of the children, and by *making oneself understood* through the situation. In the beginning this *situation* is mainly nonverbally social and objective (see first paper) and becomes more and more verbal-oral; however, i.e., by contexts, the more language is acquired and reading is developing. These two functions, *listening* and *making oneself understood*, are basic for *all* conversations, also among the hearing, *for our whole life*. They seem to grow with age and with the occasion of conversations. They may be hampered by lack of conversations.

(2) The memory.

Deaf children may suffer from multiple handicaps. We will not treat them here, but *all* of them suffer from *a weak memory* for language, both spoken and written language (see 1977). Yet by many teachers and textbooks this memory function is simply taken for granted! It must be a continuous concern of the teacher, however. In addition to that: *the frequency of language* is lessened terribly. It easily can be calculated that the language offered to a deaf child from his birth through 6 years of age is only one millionth of the language offered to a normal-hearing child.

Three points should be emphasized for making the most of that memory function:
- motivation;
- clustering, mainly by rhythmic speech;
- repetitions.

(See Chapter 8)

Memory is basic not only for the *semantic* and *grammatical* functioning of words and for the control of language structure, but also for continuing a *long conversation* on one topic, for reading *long reading-pieces,* and so on. We will see below, how the *written* form of the words is a necessary support for prelingually profoundly deaf children in this respect.

Linguistic aspects of conversations.

(1) Semantic aspects.

We have already seen, that, ecologically speaking, the *speech act* is most at home in the conversations. An oral conversation emphasizes the *need for words* in the children. The *hunger for names,* so striking in normally hearing children of 2 years of age, is often absent in deaf children. It can be evoked, however, (as it is done in normally hearing children, too) by teaching them expressions like these:

— "How should I say that?"
— "What should I call that?"
— "What is its name?", etc.

On the other hand, words become more and more *transparent* toward their meanings, and these *meanings* are shaped more and more, exactly by the "TOTE game" of conversation. E.g., a child said: "I have no towel," meaning his handkerchief. By conversation this error is detected and corrected.

A typical difficulty appears in *telling news,* a useful didactic means. Very often the children (both normal-hearing and deaf ones) leave out very important aspects, so that the educator cannot understand and follow the child. Actually a child will start from a large background of nonverbal conceptualizations. E.g., a child says: "Big tree," spreading out his arms. He wants to tell that the group of six children had embraced the tree by holding each others' hands. The teacher did not understand this. Another child filled in the gap by saying "round" with a gesture and holding the left hand of the first child. So by conversation the idea was understood and it became a long reading lesson (as a "deposit" of the conversation, see below), because the children had a lot to tell. The children can be made *conscious,* more and more, of what they have left out, and how to make their statements more complete with the effect of being understood by the listener as a reward.

(2) Structural aspects.

We will explain below how the structural aspects of language are *discovered* in a conversational way, and how the rules, once detected, are applied more and more. An important aspect of language structure, especially meaningful in conversation, is its *phrase structure.* A word group such as "in the cupboard" is not a correct sentence, except in a conversation, e.g.,

Mother: "Where did you put the butter, Mary?"
Mary: *"In the cupboard."*
Mother: "Why *in the cupboard?* Why not *in the refrigerator?"*

By conversations we can make the children aware of "complete" and "incomplete" sentences, the complement of the latter being said by the other partner: "(did) you put the butter . . . . ."

In the same conversation it is clear how a question-word (here "where?") can act as a substitute for a whole phrase, as "in the cupboard," "in the refrigerator." We see how the phrases work as the "accessories" of the conversation: they are "transplantable," "exchangeable." Very often the children show an *overt* TOTE-behavior, e.g.,

John (9 years): "Mother buyed . . . . . ?? it" . . . . .
Teacher: "Mother *bought* . . . . . John!"
John: "Mother bought the watch (for) uncle's birthday."

Indeed, if the children have developed an attitude of *wanting to learn language,* they very often ask for help in building correct structures. Interaction spontaneously tends to structures in deaf children, too. (See chapter 8).

(3) "Conversion-loss".

We saw in our first paper how passive language is converting itself into active language, the latter mainly *being evoked* from the first *by conversation.* E.g., the expression "to cope with . . . . ." had been only understood in the reading-lessons, twice (11-year-olds):

"The brigade-general thought his army could not cope with the situation in Antwerpen" (1940 war).

"Mary had been ill twice. Nevertheless, she coped with her French examination."

John, in the conversation, "I can't cope . . . that problem, I can't cope *with* that problem" . . . . . He was rewarded by his teacher immediately.

Actually a conversation is a real *balance* between passive and active language control because the partners take their turns in *listening* and *speaking*.

(4) "As much as possible correct words, groupings of words and forms".

Time is short for deaf children. Teaching deaf children is a race with time, the frequency of completely correct language use is low, and the memory for language is low.

For these reasons we think it is necessary not to pass incorrect language forms (semantically and grammatically) given by deaf children, *if they are able* to express themselves correctly. For example:

Peter (11 years old): ". . . . . because I stumbles . . . . ."
Teacher: "You can say it better: 'because I stumbled' . . . . ."
Peter: "Because I stumbled gym hall ". . . . . .
Teacher: "Say: 'Because I stumbled *in the* gym hall'". . . . .
Peter: "Because I stumbled in the gym hall". . . . .

We make children repeat the correct forms, (especially in the "linguistic conversational lessons"), in order to support their memory and to shorten the learning process. A mother with a normal-hearing child will not do so; she does not need to, because the frequency of language use is so high that the child will find his way soon enough. We will see, however, that there are two different kinds of conversations:

"conversational lessons heart-to-heart" with as few interruptions as possible, and
"linguistic conversational lessons."

Conversational Lessons "Heart to Heart", and their "Deposits"

Two different kinds of conversational lessons.

By an analysis of 12 conversational lessons with deaf children by different teachers (1970) we found two kinds of these lessons:

- Conversational lessons in which a *topic* (prepared before and evoked, or appearing by chance during the conversation itself) is more central. In these lessons the attitude of teacher and children is more that of *personal* thinking and feeling from within. Their main effect, apart from developing knowledge and language, is growing *empathy*. We have called these lessons "lessons heart-to-heart".

- Conversational lessons in which the *structure of language,* semantically and grammatically, is the main topic. In these lessons the *discovery* of the structure of language is more central. We have called these lessons "linguistic conversational lessons."

N.B. Perhaps lessons in mathematics have much in common with these linguistic lessons.

the conversational method and the control of language

An example of the start of a "lesson heart-to-heart" from a class of 7-year-old deaf children follows:

> Marijke to teacher: "Where you yesterday?"
> Teacher: "In my room! But I saw all of you!"
> Some children together: "We danced ..... dancing ..... snowmen ....."
> Teacher to Franka: "Can you tell me what you have done?"
> Franka: "We made snowman!"
> Teacher: "We made *a* snowman ..... Look at Franka, all of you!"
> Franka: "We made a snowman" .....
> Some children together: "Not one snowman, three snowmen!"
> Etc.

This lesson resulted into a "reading-lesson" as a "deposit."

> Thursday February 19, 1970.
>
> Three Snowmen.
>
> We had a free afternoon yesterday. I asked: "What did you do all that time?"
> Franka said: "We made a snowman!"
> "No, not one snowman, but three snowmen!"
> Judith said: "One big one!"
> Kitty said: "As big as sister!"
> Mieke made a big head.
> Marijke and Franka put a grey hat on the snowman.
> Kitty said: "I snatched the cap from Gerry!"
> That was for the small snowman.
> Franka, Mieke and Gerry made the smallest snowman.
> We danced around the snowmen together with Miss Ann.
> "Yes, I saw you from the window of my room, on the second floor."
> Marijke asked: "At what time?" "At three o'clock."
> "Yes, that is right!"
> "What did you make these snowmen from?" "From snow."

212   oral education: today and tomorrow

A start of a "linguistic conversational lesson" The teacher has written the "deposit" of the "lesson heart-to-heart" on the blackboard (the children had a photocopy in their diaries, too):

Teacher: "Who can change the date?"
Mieke: "I" . . . . .
Teacher: "Say 'I can'" . . . . .
Mieke: "I can" . . . . . She does so.
Teacher: "Now we go on to underline the *verbs*! Find them . . . . ."
All children: "Had . . . . ." ". . . . . asked" ". . . . . did" ". . . . . do" etc . . . . .
Judith: "Snowman" . . . . .
Teacher: "Do you call snowman a verb?" To all children: "Judith thinks snowman is a verb. Is that correct?" . . . . .
Several children: "No!"
Kitty: "Article" . . . . .
Teacher: "Fine, Kitty, say it correctly: 'Snowman has an article: *a* snowman . . . . . Look at Kitty all of you!" . . . . .
Etc. etc.

This lesson resulted in an arrangement

[Handwritten text follows:]

~~Thursday~~ February ~~19~~, 1970.   Underline the verbs!
Friday   20

Three Snowmen.
                what?   (the day before)   you asked
We had a free afternoon yesterday I asked: "What did
you do all that time?"
          said   what?
Franka said: "We made a snowman!"
            howmany?   howmany?
"No, not one snowman, but three snowmen!" (a contrast)
     who? I   howmany?
Judith said: One big one!   One / big one!
    I   you
Kitty said: "As big as sister!" (a comparison)
         I   what?
Mieke made a big head.
   I   who? WE I   what?   him
(Marijke and Franka) put a grey hat on the snowman.
    I   your cap
Kitty said: "I snatched the cap from Gerry!" */
              for what? for whom?
That was for the small snowman.
  I   I   whatdid we do?   what   (a comparison
(Franka, Mieke and Gerry) made the smallest snowman.
who? whatdid we do?   with whom?
We danced around the snowmen together with Miss Ann.
       you   from where?   where?
"Yes, I saw you from the window of my room, on the
  where?
second floor."
       I
Marijke asked: "At what time?" ("At three o'clock")
"Yes, that is right!"
                who? WE   from what?
"What did you make these snowmen from?"   "from snow."

*/ Or: Kitty said, that she snatched the cap from Gerry. (Without inverted commas It is no "say-sentence".)

the conversational method and the control of language 213

The children have *notebooks,* in which the following entries are noted down, left page for vocabulary, right page for grammar:

Note book.

From the lesson "Three snowmen"   7 year old deaf children.
notes for the note-book:

Vocabulary: Grammar:

a free afternoon.   contrast: "not one but three".
                                     accent of contrast.
All that time.
At what time?   What did you do?
What time was it?   We made a snowman.
                                       We danced.
difficult to look-listen:
     head – hat.   One big one
                                       a numeral.
I snatched the cap.

                               Comparisons:
                                   as big as sister.
                                   the smallest one.
                                   the biggest one.

                               Pointerwords:
                                   I   you   we

                               Say-sentence:
                                   "I snatched the cap".
                               Not a say-sentence:
                                   Kitty said, that (she snatched the cap.)
                               (from the window) (of my room)
                               (of my room) belongs to (from my window)
                               At what time? (At three o'clock.)

Typical phenomena in group conversations with deaf children.

The same analysis (1970) revealed these phenomena, which may be typical of a school for the deaf.

- *Broadcasting behavior.* Very often a child has said something, which has not been picked up by the other children. The teacher repeats it—or still better, makes the child repeat it for all the others (see above) so that all the children follow. This is necessary for a real *group* conversation among the deaf, who have to understand each other mainly by speechreading. The children learn to *listen* to each other's thoughts.

- *Controlling the exact understanding of the children*, all of them, and from one child to another, too. The teacher very often asks: "What did I say?" ..... "What did John say?" ..... "Did you pick up the word *energy*? Can you write it for me?" ..... He has taught his children to let him and each other know when they don't understand: "What did you say? I don't understand you. What did you mean?" etc. The teacher tries to keep in touch with *all* his children. The scheme of his work can be symbolized as follows:

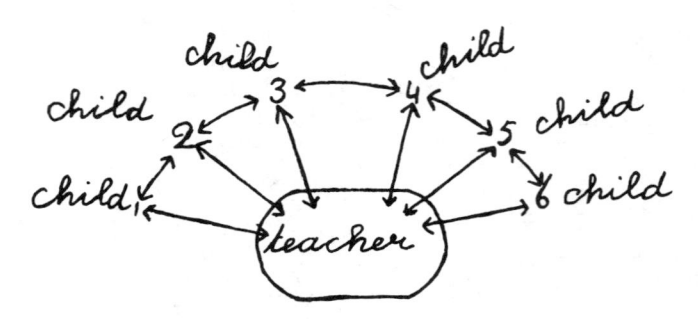

[Diagram: teacher connected bidirectionally with six children numbered 1–6]

The following phenomena may not be typical of a school for the deaf as such, but nevertheless seem to be typically prominent:

- *The teacher follows the "cooperative model"* (Flanders 1970), not only between him and the children and vice versa but among the children also. He is almost continuously listening to the spontaneous reactions of the children, and develops a listening attitude in his children, too. Sometimes he shows his sorrow that he has been unable to make use of the children's reactions. He seems to be aware of the problem of socialization and cooperation in the deaf (cf. Herren & Colin, 1972). His attitude has something "Rogerian" about it (Rogers, 1956). Many feelings, attitudes, social expressions are used both by teacher and children. His thinking is mainly "existential."
- *The teacher continuously makes his children think*. He very seldom presents a solution, but evokes "brainstorming," makes his children discuss, saying, e.g.: "Now, what do *you* think? Who can find a solution?" etc.

Is this way of teaching compatible with preprogrammed language?

No! We have already given a negative answer to this problem. Yet two kinds of "programs" may be helpful:
(1) **A program of topics** the teacher has to discuss with his children, e.g.:

for 7-year-olds: "What is happening in a barbership?"
"Rules of the road," etc.
for 14-year-olds: "A TV studio," etc.

the conversational method and the control of language

The way of treatment should be *conversational*, e.g.,
- by challenging and evoking reactions from the children,
- by catching the right moment, e.g., "If I were you, I would give it to him" . . . . . ,
- by manipulating the situations, e.g., bringing with him a washing glove in the classroom for 6-year-olds, or for 13-year-olds drawing the map of Pennsylvania on the blackboard without cities and towns, just with the rivers, the woods, the mines, etc. and asking: "Where do you expect cities will be founded and grow?" "What kind of connections do you expect?" etc.,
- by looking for good contexts and examples, e.g., for explaining a concept such as "short-sightedness": "You, John, have gone to the shop to buy a big ice cream at $1, but you appear to have only 10 cents . . . . . ." etc.

The *treatment* of *reading lessons* is especially important. Very often we have seen that teachers were just putting questions to the children line by line. It is much better to say something provoking, straight to the heart of the matter, in order to find out whether the children have got it, and much more to start a *conversation* about the reading-lesson, and to make the children read between the lines. After that general treatment the teacher will go over to more and more of the details. The same must be said about the treatment of special themes or topics.

How the treatment of reading lessons and of special themes should be *prepared* by the teacher may be illustrated by some examples: see appendix 1.

Reading-programs by using reading series written for normally hearing children in regular schools. Many schools for the deaf rightly use reading programs, written for regular schools. This *must* be done according to our reflective method too, but in such a way that *conversation* always keeps its central position. Therefore some *cautions* are indicated:

(a) We warn against the use of *too many pictures*. One often can look just at the pictures and grasp the whole story, more or less, without reading the text! There is, of course, a danger that deaf children will do the same. We try therefore to make the deaf children depend as little as possible upon pictures.

(b) Those printed reading booklets are treated first of all by *discussion*, conversation, e.g. a story about an Indian boy: "Baih with the Tiger," "Good and Bad Things" (U.S.A.). We can evoke a conversation by "What a strange tiger!" or "How stupid Baih was!" . . . . . Otherwise the teacher may become more program- than child-oriented: forgetting to listen to the *spontaneous* reactions of his children, and/or to evoke them: in doing so the most precious moments of teaching may be lost!

(c) This discussion—a "heart-to-heart conversation"—may result in a *new reading lesson* composed by the teacher (to be collected with the deposits of other conversations) again with its own *linguistic* conversation. So we get parallel-reading lessons with the two kinds of conversations running along the printed reading program.

(d) The language forms are taught in the linguistic conversations about the printed reading booklets mostly by "reflecting", i.e., by making the chil-

dren *detect* them, not just by presenting these to them. The printed manual may give rise to just a presenting method.
(e) We *avoid lists* of nonsubstantives, thus lists of verbs, of adjectives etc., keeping these parts of speech *within the context,* at least within phrases, certainly below ± 10 years of age. Only substantives may be categorized into lists, if necessary or useful, and those in the preschool years.
(f) We emphasize *notebooks* for the *children.* The teacher has his own notebook too (which may be compared with the printed guides or manuals, but for the deaf he is supposed to make his own notebook in addition to these printed manuals). The effect of the *children's* notebooks is *feedback:* they see how their language is growing.

(2) **A checking of the vocabulary and the sentence-forms** used by the children (passively, c.q. actively) *afterwards,* e.g. by applying a "language Thesaurus" (Ling & Ling, 1977). Verbakel (1951) made an investigation into the language growth of deaf children at 13-16 years of age, taught by natural methods. He checked whether Basic Dutch was known to these children. His method was thus a checking afterwards. He found that Basic Dutch had been taught at least sufficiently. This result is what would be expected since by the natural method always normal Dutch is used; this normal Dutch comprises Basic Dutch, which is used by all hearing people *spontaneously.* A good teacher will not avoid common words and idioms; on the contrary he will use them on the normal occasions offered by the situations.

Avoiding interruptions of the heart-to-heart conversations.

This is a typical problem in following a conversational way of teaching: on the one hand it seems to be unwise to allow to pass incorrect language use (see above); on the other hand, these corrections of speech and langauge-forms interrupt the conversation.
The teacher has to balance his behavior, keeping in mind that the first aim of "the heart-to-heart conversation" is the developing of empathy.
Much depends upon the *attitude* of the children. If they have an attitude of longing for learning language, they will fully accept correction, even be thankful for it; if not, they become upset. This problem is mainly an *educational* problem.
Thus: if a correction is quickly done, it should be done and will hardly interrupt the conversation; if a correction would take too much time (e.g., correcting the pronunciation of "scratches" or a form such as "You had conceived it" etc.) the teacher will keep it in his mind, put all these difficulties in the reading lessons and notebooks, and treat them either individually or in the linguistic conversational lesson.

(1) In the hometraining and preschool, up through 4 years of age.
The teacher very often has to be satisfied with rather clumsy utterances of his children and a rather global intuitive understanding by speechreading and reading. The oral-aural understanding will succeed mainly through the situations. E.g. in our hometraining in the case of a deaf child 2½ years of age, the family was living next to a shoemaker. Two shoes needing repair were standing

the conversational method and the control of language 217

under the cupboard. Mother said to her child: "Will you bring these shoes (pointing to them) to the shoemaker?" The child did it promptly! Did it understand word by word? Of course not. It had understood just by the talking and pointing of the mother in this situation.

In this period the mother/teacher will hardly ever interrupt his conversations by corrections.

(2) Language use in the "vocabulary phase" through the "structural phase."

In our research on *reading* (1969, 1971) we found three stages of reading intelligently in deaf children:

"Ideovisual reading": the child already has the *ideas* and finds them again in the *visual*-graphic forms (globally intuitively). This happens up through 5 years of age.

"Receptive reading in the vocabulary-phase": the child understands ideas, *new* to him, from the visual-graphic forms, mainly by his knowledge of the words and his "encyclopedic knowledge" (See chapter 8), but the *structure* of the language does not yet play a part, e.g., "Throw a ball, John" will be understood as well as "John throws a ball," both as assertions. This may lead to misunderstandings, however; e.g., "This is a nice flowerpot. Jean has given it to her mother" was understood as *mother* gave the flowerpot to Jean, the most obvious situation for a child. Or, "The cup is full" will be understood just literally. This phase starts at about 6 years of age.

"Receptive reading in the structural phase": the structure of the language (semantically and grammatically) is playing a part more and more. E.g. the sentence mentioned above: "This is a nice flowerpot" . . . . . etc. will be understood correctly. Figurative meanings will be understood more and more and savoured too. This phase starts at about 9–12 years of age but has to grow during the years.

The same phases seem to appear in the oral conversation of the children. Speechreading-listening detaches itself more and more from the immediate situations, the vocabulary becoming more and more flexible. At the same time, from about 5–6 years of age, the children learn to discover the structure of language, both in reading and conversation, and to use it for better and better comprehension and production of language. (Carpay, 1975, observed the same stages in normally hearing people learning a foreign language.)

The more skillfully the children are mastering both oral-aural and structural aspects of language, the more quickly a correction is made during "the heart-

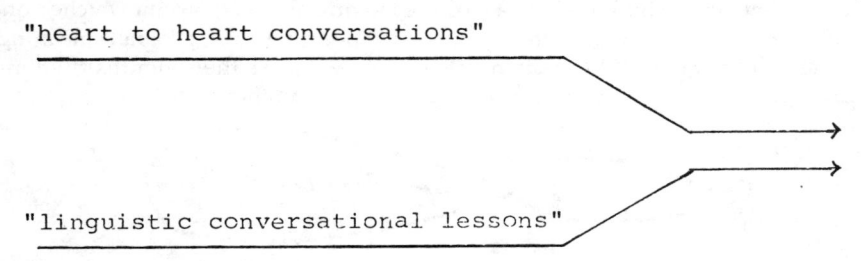

"heart to heart conversations"

"linguistic conversational lessons"

to-heart conversations." Thus the two kinds of language lessons grow nearer and nearer to each other:

The "deposits" of the conversations.

(1) Are reading and writing dangerous for the oral way? That developing reading and writing before speaking may be dangerous for the oral way, has already been emphasized by Vatter (1842–1916) of Frankfurt. He certainly is right when the written form is used in such a way that the *challenge* to speechread-listen is fading. He rightly says that the deaf children first have to imitate a new word directly by speech, and that it should be written only afterwards (see "mouth to mouth procedure" 1968, 1977).

N.B. There is, however, an exception, namely for some deaf children with dyspraxia of speech (1970): In my experience about 20 percent of the deaf children suffer from this multiple handicap so greatly that the "mouth to mouth procedure" very often is not possible. This does not mean that the purely oral way is always impossible, but quite the contrary if the handicap is detected and treated in time.

The Ewings (1951) rightly have said that the first words written down should be those words which the children already can lipread and/or speak. They further emphasize the integration of hearing, speech, and reading in their L(istening)-R(eading)-S(peaking) approach (1964). See also Dale (1968).

We don't think that reading and writing from early childhood (3–4 years of age) is dangerous for the development of the purely oral way, *if* applied as follows:

- It should be started completely connected with speechreading and listening and at least attempts to speak, so that the child is fully aware that reading and writing have to do with speech.
- This last idea—"what is written down there is the same as what is spoken"—easily can be evoked by using "speech-balloons" (see below). The evoking of this idea is the typical function of this didactive means.
- In the beginning, reading (later writing, also) is only used globally-intuitively, in a completely meaningful fashion.
- Graphic and phonetic analysis and integration (see above) can and (in my opinion) should be started at about 5½ years of age (or earlier according to the capacities of the children). This can and should be done in a playful, discovering way.

(2) How to start the written "deposits" of conversations?

The following examples from hometraining children may be helpful (see 1978). One day a child of 2½ years of age looking at the aquarium watched one fish very attentively, and after a time said, pointing to it: "Papa!" meaning: "The fish says papa!" Very often fishes open and close their mouths rhythmically, indeed . . . . . This had been seized by the mother in this way:

the conversational method and the control of language 219

Another child (again 2½ years of age) babbled mmmm very often, and this babbling had been made conscious as a game. Once she felt at the engine of the car, humming very softly, and said: "Mmmm" . . . . . meaning: "The car says mmmm". This could be seized in this way:

Many utterances can be seized from the child itself, saying: "Ooh!" or "Brrr" etc., and soon also "Hello!" or "I like ice cream!" etc. etc.

Very soon small "visualized conversations" can be written down, see above and below.

(3) "Deposits" and memory.

We have chosen this typical term purposely. One of the most difficult aspects in learning a language by deaf children is their *memory function*, emphasized by us already very often. It must be said here, that in the long run the memory for series of signs and for fingerspelled words is even more limited than for oral-aural words, if spoken rhythmically (see research 1974, 1977).

At the beginning of hometraining, in preschool, and in the lower grades the oral-aural words will just "evaporate into the air," if not kept in the fixed form of writing (see above). From the written form they will be stored in memory better, as some of my research suggests (see 1978).

Moreover, the *turn-taking behavior* of conversation is expressed and made very clear to the children by the "visualized conversation," the alternation of listening and speaking.

Even words and groupings of words can be introduced, which the child can *not yet* pronounce or even lipread. Yet these words and their groupings, seized from the children, were *fully adjusted* to their minds and interactions. Why leave them out and let the occasion pass?

A "deposit" (de Saussure, 1916, speaks of language as a "depôt psychique") is a *treasure* and a fund in a bank, well kept, from which "fruits" originate. In the same way the written "deposits," understood by the children and usually very well kept in their minds, are their language treasure and a fund from which more and more "fruits" of language originate, both for language comprehension and production, *by conversation*, but also by telling, and even (from 5–6 years of age on) by writing.

In *the higher grades* the support of *memory* by reading and writing becomes more and more necessary, especially when a *long piece of reasoning* has to be followed (apart from a long conversation on one topic or a long reading piece, see above), e.g.

the symbolic meaning of the gown, worn by judges and lawyers in court, by clergymen, by university professors, symbolizing their independency from politics; the parable of the seed as the word of God; the probability-range from completely true, through completely uncertain, to completely untrue, etc. etc.

Also when the *grammatical structures* become more and more complex, the written form can't be omitted as a means of explaining them (Can it be missed by hearing students?), See below.

(4) The composition of a "visualized conversation" and of a reading lesson. The lesson should meet these requirements:
    (a) Only *normal* language is used, not preprogrammed and not too simple in relation to the capacities of the children.
    (b) It should include direct quotations (so-called "say-sentences") and *colloquial* language.
    (c) It should be "reading-language," too: i.e., include some sentences which are a little bit more *complicated* than in everyday speech.
    (d) Not always the logical or chronological *order* should be kept.
    (e) The *feelings,* attitudes, exclamations, contrasts, doubts, social relations, etc. should be included as much as possible.

Let us first give an example of a "heart-to-heart conversation" with somewhat older children, reported verbatim, with its "deposit" and the notes for the notebooks: *An audiotaped piece (10 minutes) of a lesson of an hour to prelingually profoundly deaf children 9–10 years of age:*

U. "Look!" He takes a pre-shave bottle out of his pocket. Strong reactions from the children! . . . . . Some children: "For the beard!" Others don't recognize it.
U. (S = *seized*) "Yes, this is for the beard! . . . . . Is it for your beard, Dorien?"
Dorien: "No! You!" Several children: "You!" and "For your!"
Elly: "For father!"
U. (S) "That is for my beard. For father's too! Do you know what this is called? . . . . . No? . . . . . This is called: pre-shave." Dorien repeats it. All the children repeat it now, in turn, from mouth to mouth (= without its written form). U. writes it now on the blackboard.
U. "All of you say 'that is for the beard,' but why?"
Elly: "To grow the beard" (child uses the Dutch pincer construction correctly, literally translated: the beard to grow; Dutch *to grow* cannot be used in a transitive way,— then it has to be changed into: to make grow; this difference will be explained to the children later on, e.g., on the basis of the text in the diaries, see below.)
U. (S) "Say: To make the beard grow." (Dutch pincer construction).
Elly: "Make the beard grow."
U. "To! . . . . . Again! Look at Elly, all of you!"
Elly: "To make the beard grow" . . . . .
U. "All right! . . . . . You think so, but it is not true!"—Elly makes some plucking gestures on her chin and cheeks saying: "Grow, grow" . . . . .
U. (S) "This is stubble." (It was already afternoon so U's chin was rather dark) . . . . . "Say it: stubble!"—*Elly:* "Stubble."

the conversational method and the control of language 221

U. "I have stubble. Say it all in turn . . . . ."—All the children repeat in turn: "You have stubble," from mouth to mouth.
U. "But this is not to make the beard grow, but the beard better to . . . . . ?" (Dutch pincer construction).
Bernie: "Grow!"—U. "No, not grow! . . . . . Better to . . . . . ? The beard better to . . . . . ?"
Lea: "There off(" (In Dutch this is a good adverbial phrase.)
U. "Marvellous! . . . . . Now a verb! . . . . . In order the beard better there off to . . . . . ? (Dutch construction literally taken over.)
Cora: "Pulled" . . . . .
U. "What do you say? I don't understand you!"
Lea: "Pulled" . . . . .—U. "Oh yes . . . . . , to pull? You mean to pull?"—Lea and several children: "pull!"
U. (S) "To pull . . . . . That is the infinitive. Not pulled . . . . . To pull? How would you like it?" (He makes a gesture with his elbow) "Go on!" . . . . . Shall I pull your hair?" . . . . . All the children laugh.
Alice: "Does pain you!" (Dutch expression, literally translated).
U. (S) "Yes, that does pain!" (Dutch pincer-construction). "Do you like that, Cora?"
Cora: "Nooo!"—U. "Al right! Say: Go on!" with an elbow movement.—Cora: "Go on . . . . ."—U. "Say it nicer!" He shows how to do it with a gesture of his elbow and facial mime: "Go on!!" with the correct feeling.—Cora: "Go on" very well. All the children laugh.
U. "You will pull my beard? Go on! . . . . . That means: I don't like it! Stay away!" U. writes the new expressions on the blackboard.
U. "All right, we will go on! . . . . . This pre-shave is for the electric shaver . . . . ."
Elly interrupts: "Pain! When . . . . . does pain!" (Dutch "does pain" = hurts).
U. (S) "That is very good, Elly . . . . . You are clever! . . . . . Say: "Otherwise it will do pain" (Dutch expression in pincer-construction).
Elly: "Otherwise it will do pain." All the children imitate her from mouth to mouth.

It is the art of the teacher of the deaf to be aware, *while teaching*, which *typical points* are important for the development of language in his children. These typical points which he will (have to) remember, are indicated:

U. "Look!" He takes a pre-shave bottle out of his pocket. Strong reactions from the children! . . . . . Some children: "For the beard!" Others don't recognize it.
U. (S = *seized*) "Yes, this is for the beard! . . . . . Is it for your beard, Dorien?"

a kind of . . . .

Dorien: "No! You!" Several children: "You!" and "For your!"
Elly: "For father!"
U. (S) "That is for my beard. For father's too! Do you know what this is called? . . . . . No? . . . . . This is called: pre-shave." Dorien repeats it. All the children repeat it now, in turn, from mouth to mouth (= without its written form). U. writes it now on the blackboard.

U. "All of you say 'that is for the beard,' but (why?)

222 oral education: today and tomorrow

Elly: "To (grow) the beard" (child uses the Dutch pincer construction correctly, literally translated: the beard to grow; Dutch *to grow* cannot be used in a transitive way,—then it has to be changed into: to make grow; this difference will be explained to the children later on, e.g., on the basis of the text in the diaries, see below.)
U. (S) "Say: To make the beard grow." (Dutch pincer construction).
Elly: "Make the beard grow."
U. "To! . . . . . Again! Look at Elly, all of you!" — *transitive* . . . . .
Elly: "To make the beard grow" . . . . . *intransitive* . . . . .
U. "All right! . . . . . You think so, but it is not true!"—Elly makes some plucking gestures on her chin and cheeks saying: "Grow, grow" . . . . . *homonym* . . . . .
U. (S) "This is stubble." (It was already afternoon so U's chin was rather dark) . . . . . "Say it: (stubble!)"—*Elly:* "Stubble."
U. "I have stubble. Say it all in turn . . . . ."—All the children repeat in turn: "You have stubble," from mouth to mouth.
U. "But this is not to make the beard grow, but the beard better to . . . . . ?" (Dutch pincer construction).
Bernie: "Grow!"—*U.* "No, not grow! . . . . . Better to . . . . . ? The beard better to . . . . . ?"
Lea: ("There off") (In Dutch this is a good adverbial phrase.)

contrasts   *U.* "Marvellous! . . . . . Now a verb! . . . . . In order the beard better there off to . . . . . ? (Dutch construction literally taken over.)
Cora: "Pulled" . . . . .
U. "What do you say? I don't understand you!"
Lea: ("Pulled"). . . . . —*U.* "Oh yes . . . . . , to pull? You mean to pull?"—Lea and several children: "pull!"
U. (S) "To pull . . . . . That is the infinitive. Not pulled . . . . . To pull? How would you like it?" (He makes a gesture with his elbow) ("Go on!") . . . . . Shall I pull your hair?" . . . . . All the children laugh.
Alice: "Does pain you!" (Dutch expression, literally translated).
U. (S) "Yes, that does pain!" (Dutch pincer-construction). "Do you like that, Cora?"
Cora: "Nooo!"—*U.* "Al right! Say: Go on!" with an elbow movement.—*Cora:* "Go on . . . . ."—*U.* "Say it nicer!" He shows how to do it with a gesture of his elbow and facial mime: "Go on!!" with the correct feeling.—*Cora:* "Go on" very well. All the children laugh.
U. "You will pull my beard? Go on! . . . . . That means: I don't like it! Stay away!" U. writes the new expressions on the blackboard.
U. "All right, we will go on! . . . . . This pre-shave is for the electric shaver . . . . ."
Elly interrupts: ("Pain!") When . . . . . does pain!" (Dutch "does pain" = hurts).
U. (S) "That is very good, Elly . . . . . You are clever! . . . . . Say: Otherwise it will do pain" (Dutch expression in pincer-construction).
Elly: "Otherwise it will do pain." All the children imitate her from mouth to mouth.

Reading lesson as a deposit of this conversation:

To pull the beard?

O my! Finally we had found the answer!
Mr. U. brought Fresh-up in the classroom, a kind of pre-shave. We had to guess what is was. He did not tell it . . . . . It was for the beard. That was clear. Men use it. But *why?* Elly guessed: "To grow the beard!" She had observed that Mr. U. had stubble! Did this come from the Fresh-up? No! The beard grows by itself. Lea had a correct guess: "To take the beard off!" But she looked for the right verb . . . . .
"To pull off!" guessed Cora. Oh, no! That hurts you! Go on!!
Elly had another correct guess: "Otherwise it will hurt your chin".
The correct verb is: *to shave.*

Why do men use pre-shave? Men use pre-shave, not to grow the beard, not to pull the beard, but to shave the beard better, without pain.

For the notebook after the linguistic conversation:

Vocabulary:
Fresh-up is a *kind* of pre-shave.
Pre-shave is a *general* word.
Does pre-shave *grow* the beard? No.
The beard *grows* by itself. (homonym)
Men get *stubble*.
Go on! = I don't like it! Stay away!
To shave.

Grammar:
To *grow* has a double meaning:
 a. Transitive: does pre-shave grow the beard?
 Rain grows the wheat, the grass.
 b. Intransitive: the beard grows.

More examples in *appendix 2*.
In the preschool 3½–5 years of age, two kinds of "deposits" are used:
a "visualized conversation"
a reading lesson.

Some examples from several teachers:
Preschool St. Michielsgestel. (From an audiorecording.)

Deaf children:
4;0–5;0 years.
1st child: "Cars!" ..... with a gesture of bumping.
2nd child: "Mama" ..... and points to Mireille (3rd child)
3rd child: "All car ..... Mama all ...."
4th child: "Walk you ....."
etc.

Sr. Margret:
"Yes, bumper cars at the Fair" .....
"Yes, Mireille's mama was at the Fair too."
"Yes, all of you were in your mama's car."
"I walked. What a pity. The car was full!" ..

224 oral education: today and tomorrow

"Deposits":

Visualized conversation:

Paul: Bumper cars at the Fair!
Margriet: Mireille's mama was at the Fair too
Mireille: all the children rode in my Mommy's car
Joost: You had to walk!
Sr. Margret: Yes, I had to walk. The car was full.

At the Fair.

We drove bumper cars.
Mireille's Mommy has a car also, but it's not a bumper car!
Mireille said: "All the children were in my Mommy's car."
All the children rode in the car of Mireille's Mommy.
What a pity! Sr. Margret had to walk.

Some *more examples* of reading lessons in the preschool (5-year-olds) (Miss Bos):

Oh my Ball!

John has a new ball.
"Where's your ball, John?"
"In the water" . . . . .
"Who threw it in the water?"
"Caroline and Rocky" . . . . .
A big boy took it out of the water.
He walked very carefully through the high grass! . . . . .

the conversational method and the control of language 225

Where was John?

We were in the swimming pool.
Miss Margret had to look for John.
He had run away.
Miss Emmy had seen him.
Where?
He was standing looking at the tipcarts.

Simon was ill.

Simon isn't in the hospital anymore.
He's at home now.
On Monday he'll be back in school.
Everybody is glad. We will celebrate!
We will go to the store and buy lemonade and cookies.
For Simon!

The Mended Sweater.

Oh, Hans has torn the sleeve of his sweater.
How naughty!
Hans went to Aunt Rosé and Uncle Claus.
Aunt Rosé mended the sweater.

Carnival.

All of us have a mask.
We are going to have fun at the Carnival.
We will wear costumes and masks.
We will dance.
Willy will be Pipo, the clown.
Ellen will be a cat.

226 oral education: today and tomorrow

Into the basket.

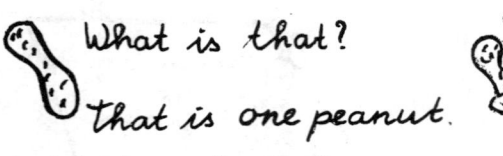

What is that?
That is one peanut.

a handful of peanuts.

Let's break open the peanut!
Ellen says: "Bite the peanut."—"No!"
Willy says: "Cut the peanut with a knife."—"No!"
"We will break open the peanut with our fingers."
Mark tries, but can't do it. Will can do it.
Oh . . . . . the shell is empty!
Throw it in the basket!

Some matching exercises from these lessons

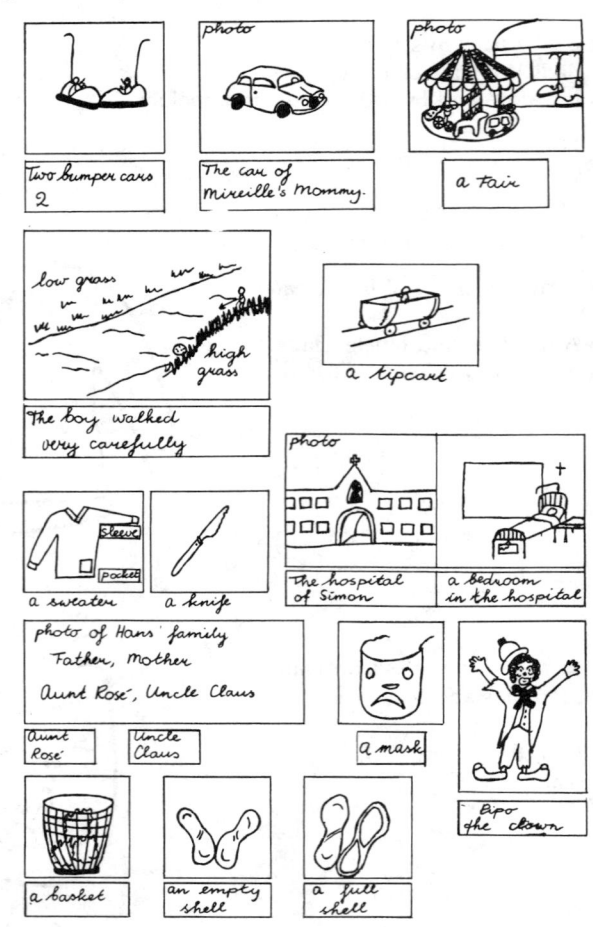

| Two bumper cars 2 | The car of Mireille's mommy. | a Fair |

| The boy walked very carefully | a tipcart |

| a sweater | a knife | The hospital of Simon | a bedroom in the hospital |

| photo of Hans' family Father, mother Aunt Rose, Uncle Claus | | |
| Aunt Rose | Uncle Claus | a mask | Pipo the clown |

| a basket | an empty shell | a full shell | |

"Linguistic Conversational Lessons"

Sources of the structure.

We have already said, that the "written deposits" of the "heart-to-heart conversations" are a necessary fund, from which the structure of language can be derived more and more by "guided discovery learning".

The same must be said about the reading books for normal hearing children. Our institute begins with these at about 9 years of age using reading books for 8-year-old children in the regular schools.

Also the oral conversations themselves and their interactions very often are a "finding place" for this discovery learning. For example, a child speaks of "the Mary," to which the teacher reacts with "we never use an article before first names or proper names".

The *"phase of understanding by vocabulary,"* mentioned above, is a necessary phase. The children understand the content globally intuitively. Only in those language pieces do they learn to detect the structure. *After that* it will happen more and more that the structure helps them to comprehend sentences not yet understood. This example, taken from an experiment on learning to read in Dutch deaf subjects. The Dutch text has been translated literally.

> Question:
> "Je hebt de bal van je vriend verloren."
> (You have the ball of your friend lost.)
> "What should you do?"
> Answer (9 year-old): "Then that friend is mean!"
> The child had understood:
>   *My* ball, *he* has lost it.
> The teacher's reaction: "Read the sentence aloud! Group the words! Which words belong to each other?"
> The child first reads:
> "Je hebt de bal / van je vriend verloren," understood as:
> I have a ball / and my friend lost it.
> This way of grouping was corrected in:
> "Je hebt / de bal van je vriend / verloren."
>   your friend's ball

By means of the right grouping, the right understanding came to the fore. There were two grouping difficulties in this Dutch text:
> the compound construction "de bal van je vriend" and the pincer construction "hebt . . . . . verloren."

The child tended to a kind of compound construction between "friend" and "lost," overlooking the pincer construction, something which happens very often in deaf children (See Appendix, chapter 8).

Very often the children ask the teacher to read aloud a reading piece, which looks difficult to them. Once a girl, 14 years of age, asked the teacher: "Can you read it aloud to us via the microphone? The grouping of the words will clear up the whole."

"The child cried. The big dog had barked at her on a walk. Quickly her mother brought her home." Question of the teacher: *"Where* did the child start crying?" Answer of a child (10 years old) "At home!" . . . . . The form *had* as past perfect could be used to make him reorganize the chronological order.

We see reading and the teaching of the structure of language as one integrated whole. So we don't understand what we have seen in several schools for the deaf, that there is a teacher for language and another teacher for reading.

The teaching of *reading* seems to be more important and also *primary* in comparison to *composition-work,* the first being the fund and the source of the latter. See below.

Both the teaching of reading and the guided discovery learning for the structure of language should be done, in our opinion, by one teacher, and first of all by the *teamwork* of the whole class. The interaction between the students, evoked by the teacher (See above), seems to be very important for a deep understanding in reading. Only in some cases of multiple handicaps— especially of dyslexia and dyssymbolia—individual treatment seems to be necessary *in addition* to the classwork.

A preprogrammed "target-language"?
(1) The concept of a target-language.

No grammar is "generative" in the full sense of the word. A grammar cannot be called the blueprint of a language. It is impossible to learn the comprehension of language in the full sense of this word, from a grammar and/or even from a dictionary.

We have already spoken about so called "microlanguage," "English reduced to a microlanguage," "threshold level language," used as a "target language" for the instruction of the deaf (See chapter 8). Most language programs, written for the deaf, start from this concept.

• These language programs are very akin to foreign language teaching in contrast to the teaching of a mother tongue as a mother does.

• They mainly and primarily aim at a correct production of language in speech and composition-work.

• The idea that this production or the active language should be as much as possible a spontaneous selection by the speaker himself from a large fund of comprehended or passive language, evoked and challenged by conversation, is not followed. The language the speaker has to use is *presented* to him.

• The language presented is a *reduced* language. The forms are readymade. There is nothing of a real discovery of structure possible, because there is no large fund of normal, varied language used as a background. Properly speaking, nothing is left to be detected.

• Some of these programmed methods limit even the *reading* lessons, according to the vocabulary and sentence models completely kept within the frame of the "language" lessons. That real reading never will be attained in this way may be obvious. Take the first normal reading book for children of the regular schools that comes along and you will find entirely different language to which the children are not accustomed at all. On a test (pre-test and re-test, etc.) the children show good results, just because that test is fully adapted to the program! I once saw a teacher working with such a reading program: a series of lessons with multiple-choice questions was treated for a whole year. He was not aware of the fact that he was teaching his children just a *trick:* how to choose a good answer from the given paragraph-text. The children actually could choose many good answers *without* having comprehended even the core of the text! Other methods don't mention the development of reading and seem to use *reading texts in normal colloquial language.* This way of working, which seems to be halfway between a full programmed method and the natural method that we are advocating, is the basis of the following criticisms.

(2) Criticisms.

Ervin (1961, 1964) has pointed out that in many *foreign-*language speakers there is something of a reduced area of productive language (both for speaking and writing), operating *separately* from a much larger and more flexible field of language comprehension, especially for reading. Can this finding be applied to first language learning, the learning of a mother tongue in profoundly deaf children? We don't think so.

- *Spontaneous conversation is lagging.* This is, to me, the most shocking aspect of this programmed way of working. What some of these teachers call "conversation" is question-answer play at the most. It seems to be dangerous to diminish conversation in learning a language, certainly a first language. This may be concluded from what we have said above at considerable length.
- Also in such a target language *the nonverbal conceptualizations* in the minds of the children (and of the educator) play a big part. How does the teacher know them, if not in continuous interaction with his children? What do the children think in "The box is on the table?" "Mary has a ball?" "We will go out, *even if* it will rain?" "John will be persistent, *even if* the task is difficult?" and so forth. It seems to be risky to "bake" sentences, outside real conversations, just for teaching "language."
- *Concepts and structures will be "nailed home"* in too narrow a meaning and flexibility. To give just one example from my experiences with formal methods, 20 years ago: After training in sentences with *if* (see above), the following sentence was not understood at all "Behold, I have just arrived, and what will please, if not surprise you, is that I sit down to write you first of all this letter" . . . . . There are many, many *interferences* from the "target language" in the understanding and reading of normal language. Besides, very often words are interpreted erroneously because only a special linguistic form was known, such as, "distinguished" only understood as a participle, "kindly" only as an adverb, "potter" only as a man, or a comparative, not also as a verb, and so forth.
- *What about the motivation?* I have seen deaf children very eager in these programs of target language learning. Because the steps are small, they have a good view of the situation. They know exactly what to do and are rewarded by almost continuous successes. But are we not fooling ourselves by being satisfied with this? This eagerness seems to be akin to that of just ciphering in mathematics, sometimes going so far that children can make a long "tail-division" correctly without a real knowledge of what division means.

Guided discovery learning and motivation.
"Discovery learning" or "explorative learning" is to be distinguished from "directive teaching" or "expository teaching" (Ausubel, 1963, 1968) and "receptive learning."

What is meant by "guided discovery learning" (See Shulman & Keislar, Eds. 1966; Cronbach, 1977, and Chapter 8).

Bruner (1961, 1975) seems to be right in asserting that real thinking is a search process with hypothesis-test procedures (TOTE), working with symbols and codes, postponements, revisions of interpretations, in a dialogue with oneself, that only what is discovered is really "learned," that transfer-processes are to be expected most of all from self-discovered rules, laws, structures, models and concepts. This seems to be true not so much about "free nondirective discovery," but more about *"guided discovery."* (See De Gecco readings, 1972; article of Gagné R. M., & Smith E. C., 1967). We saw that the mothers teaching the mother tongue to a normally hearing child may be characterized as such.

Motivation seems to play a big part in these didactics (See Kersh & Wittrock, 1962; See literature in Cronbach, 1977).

From two sides:
- If the children can be motivated to be *curious,* the discovery learning process is facilitated.
- Discovery has a strong and long-lasting *effect* upon both transfer and application of the concepts learned.

It is even so that many authors ascribe the "learning effect" of the didactics not so much to the method itself, but more to its motivation.

Guided discovery learning and reflecting.
"Reflecting" means

(1) Understanding, comprehending deeper *what one has done already before.* That is we are not aware how we pronounce an /f/: we have learned that from early childhood, completely unreflectively. But by reflection we learn to know what we do, we discover something in ourselves.

(2) *Comprehending from an interaction* with another, by TOTE behavior, one returns his reaction towards the other and one causes the other to rebound. Both activities happen in language learning (See chapter 8).

We have already said that the reading lessons especially are our "deposit" in which we search for the structure. Let us say we have to teach the children (for example, 10-year-olds), according to the program of "linguistic topics" (See below), sentences with "conjunctions." The point is now *not to introduce* such a sentence form by "baked sentences," but first of all *to make the children detect them* in the reading material already understood. The reading lessons composed by us with the children from the conversations, the reading books, etc., contain a lot of such complex sentences. We ask the children to look for them and by trial and check, as a game in the classroom, we find the following (See Appendix 1):

. . . . . cried Peter *while watching television. When the snow melts,* there is a lot of slush and dirt, father said *as he thought of his car.* John had peeked *just as the flash went off* . . . . .

These sentences are written on a corner of the blackboard, or, better, on a separate card on the wall.

The children may become aware that there are two *verbs,* that two sentences *belong to each other* (these terms are already known to them, see below). The words *while, when, as, just as* are underlined by the teacher within the sentences kept in the context, and termed: *"conjunctions,"* "these sentences contain a conjunction, and usually we have then two verbs," "the sentence with the conjunction is called a *clause"* etc. These new terms are written on the blackboard or on the card. Notes are written in the notebooks. So far so good. No formal teaching is done. But on every *occasion* that a conjunction occurs in the linguistic conversations of the following days, in the reading pieces etc., it is picked out by the teacher to make the children aware of the many conjunctions we use. In this way the *concept* of "conjunction" is built up in the minds of the children. A few days later the following happens:

> John says: "I was on the street with a croquette and a dog came" . . . . .
> Teacher: "The dog wanted that croquette too, I think!" To all children: "Can you say the same sentence now *with a conjunction?* You said: 'I was on the street with a croquette and a dog came'?" . . . . .
> John (trial): "I was on the street with a croquette when a dog came" . . . . .
> Teacher: "Who can say it in another way?"
> The teacher continues till he gets: "When I was in the street with a croquette a dog came" . . . . . "That is better".

The teacher does not explain this last assertion. He writes the correct sentence down on the "conjunction-card" on the wall and waits for another occasion. A short time later one of the children, Peter, has to write a letter to his uncle, coming back from a long journey:

> Peter writes: "How was it in London? Foggy there?"
> Teacher: "Can you use a sentence with a conjunction? Can you fill in: . . . . . foggy, when . . . . . there?"
> Peter tries: "Was it foggy, when you were there?"

After a time the teacher gives homework: *"Find* the sentences with a conjunction on page 35 of our class-reading book." The main point is, that the children learn to comprehend, to understand and to *abstract* the language forms *from many examples:*

- first of all for a better and better comprehension,
- second for a more and more flexible production.

It is not the aim to make the children find a model, and than "bake" sentences after that model. First of all, the model itself (the sample of sentences detected, written on a card on the wall) must be a flexible one. Second, the application for production must be occasional, *in the experiences,* thus leading to creativity and spontaneity and flexibility. (See 1977.)

Guided discovery learning and linguistic terms.

Has a normal-hearing child of 4 years a concept of a verb? Certainly he has! He shows he has it by his ability and competency in using that part of speech.

He has conquered that concept *without the term,* however. If you ask him: "Tell me some verbs" or "what is the verb in that sentence?", he will stare at you amazedly! A child (also a deaf child) has many unlabelled concepts, such as, dinner-service, or mammals, so also with linguistic concepts such as adjectives, substantives, conjunctions, articles, definite article and indefinite article, past tense, plural forms, phrase, accent, and so forth.

A hearing child can form these linguistic concepts by the enormous frequency of language use. A deaf child lacks this frequency. In my opinion we have to use and to teach him *appropriate terms,* in order to shorten the abstraction process. Gagné & Smith (1967) found that labelling supports discovery learning. The label, the term, acts as a *hat rack,* by means of which the abstract concept is formed.

Several researchers (see Rosenstein & McGinitie, 1969) have shown that a normal-hearing child seems to find out for himself the difference between a syntagmatical analysis of sentences and a paradigmatical one (analysis by parts of speech). Experiments with word associations have shown that a young child up to ± 7 years of age associates words mainly syntagmatically, e.g. by reacting on "horse" with "riding," on "big" with "house," after 7 years of age paradigmatically, e.g. on "horse" with "dog," on "big" and "small," etc. But the researchers mentioned above found two kinds of reactions in *deaf* children, both groups being pupils of very good oral schools:

- one group of children reacted as *older* normal hearing children, paradigmatically;
- another group in another school for the deaf reacted normally, first syntagmatically, later paradigmatically.

The reactions of the first group may look very mature, but it seems better to call them *artificial:* these children seem to have learned long lists of paradigmatically arranged words in a programmed method of language teaching. We prefer the reactions of the second group. The reactions of the first group showed a high degree of "commonality," that is there were many of the same words, in contast to the second group. Does this not show a kind of rigid thinking as a consequence of too formal a teaching of language?

A program of terms will be necessary in our reflective method. This program has been worked out for our Dutch language, for our Institute (1957, 1964, 1970, see 1977). It is impossible to explain this program here at full length, we have to limit ourselves to some anecdotal examples (See below). This program should not be misunderstood, however. For example, at the age of 6–7 years the children learn the term *verb* (see below), but lists of verbs are avoided. The verbs are kept *within the contexts* of the sentences: they are "endocentric" words (see 1977). Only substantives can be collected in lists (if one wants to do so; we don't see this as very useful, unless for some categories as fruit, furniture, etc.) without linguistic harm. See above.

The terms, which should be known to children at 7 years of age, are shown here:

TERMS

Grammatical, conversational and phonologic terms more or less to be known at ± 6–7 years of age:

1. sentence ("That is a long sentence!"—"That is a nice sentence" a.s.o.).
   word—syllable (how many syllables are there in *lemonade?*)—letter.
   order (sequence)—accent.
   accentgroup ⎫
   phrase   ⎬ = "Yes" / "The day after tomorrow".
   verb.   ⎭

2. question—{interrogative / questionword} —to put a question—yes-no-question—answer.

   statement   ⎧ "John made a statement" ⎫
   assertion   ⎨ "John asserts" . . . . .   ⎬ —direction (task)—
               ⎩ "John says" . . . . .   ⎭   call (exclamation).

   period (point)—comma—question-mark(?)—exclamatory-mark(!).

3. Conversation (to converse)—"take your turn!"—"What do you *mean?*"—"I think, that" . . . . .—"That is right, that sit, OK!"—"That is a mistake, a misunderstanding."—"How do you call that?" "What is the name for that?" "How should I say that?"

4. What belongs to what?—Pointerword—That refers to . . . . .

5. Phonological terms: vowel (long, short, monophthongh, diphthongh), consonant, fricative, plosive, nasal.—On which syllable is an accent in lemonade? On the third: lemonade.

Some examples of guided discovery learning of language structure.
(1) Phrase-structure.

This certainly is the most important aspect of language structure, which deaf children have to learn, mainly by rhythmic speech. "Compound constructions" and "pincer constructions" are its implications. See above, and first paper. It may be clear that rhythmic speech has to do with a *total rhythmic education of the deaf child* by learning play-songs and dance (1947, 1952, 1963, 1972).

Discovery learning mainly aims at finding the right pauses in sentences, the right accentuations, both accent of news and accent of contrast. See above and below.

(2) Questions.

A question is a need for an answer. The main focus of our discovery didactics is not the questions of the educator towards the children, but the real questions of the child himself, by means of the "seizing method." It seems to be that a normal-hearing child is learning questions mainly in this same way (See chapter 8). Already in hometraining and in the preschool, the deaf child puts many questions, Yes-No-questions and Wh-questions (also why- and how-questions, although this has been denied by some researchers). These proper questions of the children themselves are noted down in their diaries, preferably together with their answers, in the preschool on "question-cards" on the wall, etc. It will not take a long time (usually within a few months) for hundreds of questions to be collected. At about 6 years of age these questions are *categorized* in the classroom with the children together, by means of which the children quite easily learn the meaning of the question-words. How these question-words are used for giving the phrase-structure new prominence may be seen in the "linguistic conversation lesson" mentioned above. How "question-work" is developing through the highest grades, has been published elsewhere (1977).

(3) Pointer-words.

Pointing is very normal behavior in both normally hearing and deaf children. We have seen the role played by this pointing for learning the pointer-words (including the pronouns) in normal-hearing children (See chapter 8). By means of this, following the "seizing method," it is quite easy to teach deaf children the pronouns, for example, a photo of the child has been taken and the child points to it and to himself. This is immediately "seized" by the mother, and written down in a speech-balloon:

[illustration: child pointing with speech balloon "I am that!" and handwritten note "a photo would be very helpful."]

The speech-balloons appeared to be very helpful in teaching the pronouns and all pointerwords.

It must be remembered that, typically enough, the pointing must be executed completely *synchronously* with speech. A deaf child may point to you, without speaking, or speaking "you" without pointing (which is not necessary, but in the beginning very helpful), or saying first "you" and then pointing to you, or first pointing to you and then saying "you," etc. This must be corrected, because it is not the normal behavior. The same with "there," "here," etc.

(4) Accentuations.

The *meaning* of the accents (from about 6 years of age) easily can be taught, again by the seizing method. It is of course not sufficient to tell a child that a special word or syllable has an "accent." This will be meaningless to him. The

the conversational method and the control of language

seizing method works here as follows: a child comes to the teacher and dramatizes excitedly: "Dog there bow wow!" The teacher seizes this into:

The dog there barked at me!

At that moment, for the child the accent is on *barked*. We have explained elsewhere (1977) how to teach rhythmic speech to deaf children mainly by the temporal accent, by lengthening the accentuated syllables. The children learn the rhythmic movements of the hands, the "phrasing waves" in their music lessons (see above, see 1977). As soon as an *accent of contrast* appears, it is seized immediately and used, in this way (See above):

No, not one snowman, but three snowmen!

(5) The verbs.

The normally hearing child learns the concept of verb (without the term) mainly by the continuous changes of this part of speech. The verb is namely that word that continuously changes according to its congruency with the subject and according to the event (the tenses, the moods, the voices, etc.). Very often deaf children detect some of these changes in the preschool. For example, once the teacher wrote in a speech-balloon:

How happy is Willy! — Judith

A clever child (5-years-old) did not agree, added "Riet," and changed *is* into *are:*

How happy *are* Willy (and) Riet!

The changes of the verbs according to the tenses are mainly discovered from the calendarwork, following.

MAKING THE CHILDREN DETECT THE VERB.

The verb is that part of speech, which always is changing according to the subject and to the event. The change according to the event is most striking, but at the same time most difficult. This can be thought by means of the calendar-work, to be started at 5–6 years of age. Especially *expectations* towards the future get a chance here. This is a very important aspect in the education of deaf children.

A "lightweek" is used, as depicted below. *It is Thursday*, the window of which is kept lighted the whole day. The Sunday, Monday, Tuesday and Wednesday are gone, and one may see how the *tenses* of the verbs have been changed every day, *after* the event. Thursday is going on, Friday and Saturday have to come yet.

LIGHTWEEK

	~~Sunday~~	Margriet ~~is coming~~ CAME back from Germany.
We'll ~~write~~ have written a card home.	~~Monday~~	Simon ~~is coming~~ has come back in school.
The mommy of Mireille has visited ~~is visiting~~ us	~~Tuesday~~	We ~~are going to~~ have been at the Fair
We ~~'ll get~~ had doughnuts.	~~Wednesday~~	We'll ~~go~~ went for a swimm
We'll get lemonade instead of milk.	Thursday	
Joost will go home by bus	~~Friday~~	Mireille will be fetched
Joost will go to grandma	~~Saturday~~	Margriet will go to Germany again.

It can be expected that, if the work has been done carefully, at 6½ years of age at the latest, the children become aware of these typical words, which are then labelled "verbs," "That is a verb, and that too", etc. Of course the children will still make many errors, but the concept has started and it grows.

The most difficult verbs certainly are *to be* and *to have*. The discovery learning of *to be* happens as follows:

At about 7-years-of-age, the teacher, together with the children, starts to collect sentences from the diaries like these:

- How *are* you?
- Don't *be* long!

- How *is* it that you *are* so late?
- We *were* in the town last week.
- How happy *is* Willy!
- How happy *are* Willy and Riet!
- It *is* my turn!
- I *am* the keeper.
- My father and mother *have been* in Paris.
- I *have been* in Amsterdam.

The teacher writes them on a card on the wall with as a label on top:

Be happy!

Every time that a child has to use the correct form, he makes him look at the card in order to find it himself, e.g.

John: "Judith not there" . . . . .
Teacher: "Look at the 'be happy card' . . . . . Judith . . . . . ?"
John looks for the right form and finds: "Judith is not there" . . . . .

The same with *to have,* a month later, when *to be* has been trained somewhat sufficiently, or just for a change, keeping the children flexible. When *to be* and *to have* are taught sufficiently, a similar seizing way is followed for the comparison of both,

a table *is* 4 legs and 1 table top.
a table *has* 4 legs.
a table *has* 1 table top.

Of course all this is noted down in the notebooks too.

(6) Subject-predicate.
Leopold (1954) rightly has pointed out that the first sentence of a normally hearing child, which may be termed as "subject predicate structure," very often originates from question-answer structure:
Mama? Sleeps . . . . .
He describes the typical intonations the child is using in this "feat."
We take the same starting point for deaf children at about 8 years of age, by discovery learning.

John did not sleep well this night.

What is the verb: *Did* . . . . . *sleep.*
What is said about John? *Did not sleep well this night.*
We call this the predicate (Dutch: "Het gezegde" = "the said").
We call John the subject.
After training with some simple sentences, seized from the children, or selected from the reading lessons, more complicated sentences are explained, as: "Why are you coming so late?" The ideas of "What belongs to what?" is of course very important in this didactics, (See above.)

Conclusion: Openess.
The word openness may be called a key word in the education of the deaf: an openness of the educator towards the deaf child;
an openness of the deaf child towards the world of meaning and the society of the normal hearing.

One of the most striking characteristics of the behavior of deaf children in a good oral school is their *trustfulness* and openess towards the hearing. Did not Our Lord, when sighting, curing and redeeming a deaf mute man by giving back speech, hearing and language, say:

"Ephphatha!" = be open!

References

Ausubel, D. P. *The psychology of meaningful verbal learning.* London: Grune & Stratton, 1963.
Ausubel, D. P. Symbolization and symbolic thought: Response to Furth. *Child Development,* 1968, *39,* 997–1001.
Bruner, J. The act of discovery. *Harvard Educational Review,* 1961, *31* (1), 21–32.
Bruner, J. The ontogenesis of speech acts. *Journal of Child Language,* 1975, *2,* 1–17.
Carpay, J. A. M. *Onderwijspsychologie en Leergangontwikkeling in het Moderne Vreemde-Talen-Onderwijs.* Rijksuniversiteit Groningen, 1975.
de Cecco, J. P. (Ed.). *The psychology of language, thought and instruction.* New York: Academic Press, 1967.
Clark, H. H., & Clark, E. V. *Psychology and language.* New York: Harcourt, Brace, and Jovanovich, 1977.
Cronbach, L. J. *Educational psychology.* New York: Harcourt, Brace Jovanovich, 1977.
Dale, D. M. C. *Deaf children at home and at school.* London: University of London Press, 1968.
Décroly, O., & Dégany, J. Contribution à la pédagogie de la lecture et de l'écriture. *Archives de Psychologie,* 1907, 308–344.
van Dongen, Br. Ach. *Hoe verstaan doofgeworden kinderen met normaal taalbezit onze identificatie-oefeningen?* Sint-Michielsgestel: Instituut voor Doven, 1948.
Ervin, S. M. Correlations of associative frequency. *Journal of Verbal Learning and Verbal Behavior,* 1962/1963, 422–431.
Ewing, A. W. G., & Ewing, E. C. *Teaching deaf children to talk.* Manchester: Manchester University Press, 1964.
Ewing, I. R., & Ewing, A. W. G. *Speech and the deaf child.* Manchester: Manchester University Press, 1954.
Flanders, N. A. *Analyzing teaching behavior.* Reading, MA: Addison-Wesley, 1970.
Gagné, R. M., & Smith, E. C. A study of the effects of verbalization on problem solving. In J. P. de Cecco (Ed.), *The psychology of language, thought, and instruction.* New York: Academic Press, 1967.
Herren, H., & Colin, D. Language implicite et coopération chez l'enfant; étude comparative de sourds et d'entendants dans une tache à deux. *Enfance,* 1972, *25,* 325–347.
Kersh, B. Y., & Wittrock. The motivating effect of learning by directed discovery. *Journal of Educational Psychology,* 1962, *53,* 65–71.

Leopold, W. F. Patterning in children's language learning. *Language Learning*, 1953–1954, 1–14.
Leopold, W. F. Das Sprechen Lernen der Kinder. Sprachforum 1956, p. 117–125.
Ling, D., & Ling, A. H. *Basic vocabulary and language thesaurus for hearing impaired children.* Washington, DC: Volta Bureau, 1977.
McKeachie, W. J. Procedures and techniques of teaching: A survey of experimental studies. In N. Sanford (Ed.), *The America College.* New York: Heath, 1962.
Rogers, C. R. *On becoming a person.* Boston: Houghton Mifflin, 1961.
Rosenstein, J., & McGinitie, W. *Verbal behavior of the deaf child: Studies of word meanings and associations.* New York: Teachers College Press, 1969.
Sanford, N., (Ed.). *The America College.* New York: Heath, 1962.
de Saussure, F. *Cours de linguistique générale.* Paris: Payot, 1964.
de Saussure, F. *Course in general linguistics.* New York: The Philosophical Library, 1959.
Shulman, L. S., & Keislar, E. R. *Learning by discovery. A critical appraisal.* Chicago: Rand McNally, 1966.
van Uden, A. M. J. *Voelmuziek en dans voor doofstommen.* Sint-Michielsgestel: Instituut voor Doven, 1947.
van Uden, A. M. J. *Een geluidsmethode voor zwaar en geheel dove kinderen.* Sint-Michielsgestel: Instituut voor Doven, 1952.
van Uden, A. M. J. *Oefenboek bij de Nederlandse Spraakkunst i.v.m. de reflecterende methode.* Sint-Michielsgestel: Instituut voor Doven, 1964.
van Uden, A. M. J. *A maternal reflective method of teaching an oral mothertongue to deaf children.* With a preface by A. Ewing. In *a world of language for deaf children,* Part I: Basic principles. Lisse: Swets & Zeitlinger B.V., 1977.
van Uden, A. M. J. The pure oral method in the light of new realizations. *Volta Review,* 1970, 524–537.
van Uden, A. M. J. Waarop reageert de leerkracht in zijn leergesprek met dove kinderen. Doct. scriptie Sociale Psychologie, Universiteit Nijmegen, Psychologisch Laboratorium, juli 1970 (The teacher of the deaf and his reactions in his conversational lessons.)
van Uden, A. M. J. Psycholinguistics and the teacher of the hearing impaired. Paper Symposium Sint-Michielsgestel 25th November–1st December 1979.
van Uden, A. M. J. A purely oral school for the deaf: How to achieve a situation, where no esoteric communicative means are used? Paper read in Brussels 1978, Instituut voor Doven, Sint-Michielsgestel 1978.
van Uden, A. M. J., Zr. Vincentio, & Zr. Joanni. *Nederlandse Spraakkunst bij de toepassing van de reflecterende methode.* Sint-Michielsgestel: Instituut voor Doven, 1957.
Vatter, J. *Die Ausbildung des Taubstummen in der Lautsprache. I, II, III.* Frankfurt: Stock Verlag, 1891–1899.
Verbakel, Br. *Basis Nederlands en doofstommenonderwijs.* Sint-Michielsgestel: Instituut voor Doven, 1951.
Voit, H. *Sprachaufbau beim gehörlosen Kind aus der Perspektive gestörter Beziehung.* Rheinstetten: Schindele Verlag, 1977.

APPENDIX 1.

Evoking conversations, illustrated by some practical examples.

The Teaching of Reading

Reading is a "conversation with the writer." In principle, good reading should be taught by conversation in order to develop the ability of the children to read between the lines with comprehension.

A treatment of a reading lesson should not start by explaining the content line by line, word by word (this may be done afterwards for stronger precision), but by *evoking a conversation* about the reading material. In the following reading examples it is presupposed that the teacher knows that his children more or less understand the meaning of all the words used in the lesson sufficiently. As the teacher *prepares* his lesson, two questions should be kept in mind:
1. Which provoking or challenging question, assertion, or command can be given to the children which may evoke a conversation, and at the same time, get to the heart of the matter?
2. What are the probable difficulties which may be experienced by language-deficient children?

With the above in mind, here are some examples of how to prepare a reading lesson:

•For children ± 9 years of age:
Change of Heart
1"Look, Mom, it's snowing there,"
cried Peter while watching television.
3"I hope we will have snow here, too!"
"Oh, no! I hope not! It's a lot of trouble, and when it melts,
5there's a lot of slush and dirt,"
father said as he thought of his car.
7"But I want it!" Peter and Mary cried together.
"Let it snow! Let it snow! Let it snow!"
9Next morning snow had fallen. It was very deep.
10And who do you think was the first one outside throwing
11snowballs?
It was father!

(1) Provoking questions, assertions, commands . . . . . some examples (related to the kernel "change of heart"):

"I think father was silly!"
"or: "What about mother?"
or: "Were Peter and Mary teasing their father?"
And similarly.

(2) Special reading difficulties which may be expected:

In line [1] "there" (what is meant?), and "while." Take care of the contrast between "there" and "here" in line[3], which gives an "accent of contrast." The same accent of contrast can be found between "I" in line [4] and "I" in line [7]. "When it melts" introduces thinking towards the future, expectations: take care that the children get this. "A lot of slush and dirt" and "he thought of his car" *presuppose* many conceptualizations, even non-verbal ones. The child has to read between the lines.

In line [7] the meaning of "I" should be checked, because it means both Peter and Mary, indicated by "together".

In line [9] the verb form past perfect "had" is typical with a reversal of the chronological order.

In line [10] the meaning of "the first" should be checked, because of its comparative meaning with Peter and Mary.

● *For children of ± 10 years of age:*
"It is not nice at all?"
[1]"Don't be afraid, John!" Mother said. But John didn't like being at the photographers; so he stayed close to his mother
[3]Clinging anxiously to her.
How that flash frightened him! The photographer was busy taking
[5]a picture of a man and his wife in the next studio. John had peeked just as the flash went off . . . . . Now it was John's
[7]family's turn to have their picture taken.
But no, John refused to be photographed! Finally Father said:
[9]"It doesn't matter, we'll have it done without John." So the photo was taken.
[11]Two days later everyone at home gathered around to admire the beautiful, big, colored photo. "And where are you in
[13]this picture, John?" Mary teased. "What a dumb picture! It's not nice at all!" John grumbled.

(1) Provoking conversation, e.g.:

"John was a good boy!" . . . . .
And similarly.

(2) Special reading difficulties:

The chronological order: see the lines [1] through [7], and the form "had peeked" in the lines [5/6].
The meaning of "so" in line [2] is typical, it is not so much a pointer word but something of a conclusion.
The situation at the photographers with "studio" etc. includes many presupposed conceptualizations. The meaning of "just as . . . . ." in line [6] too.
The same must be said about "finally" in line [8]. Further, the meaning of the pointerword "it" in line [9] must be checked, ditto "so."
Take care of the accent upon "you" in line [10] (accent of contrast, the contrast of which has to be found out).
In line [13] the words "teased" and "dumb" need special care.

● *For children of ± 12 years of age:*
At the Barber.
[1]"That rotten barber cut off all my hair!" cried John when he got home.
[3]"Oh, no!" Mother said with a laugh, "That's a neat haircut. You look much nicer now."
[5]"Here's the dollar!" John exlaimed as he slammed his mother's money on the table.
[7]"I don't pay him one cent!"
"Oh, I'll pay him," Mother said. "I called and asked him to
[9]cut it short. I didn't want you to have a nest of lice" . . . . .

(1) Provoking conversation

"John was a clever boy, I think!"
"Was Mother not a little bit mean?"
And similarly.

(2) Again: the reversal of the chronological order.

The emotional meaning of "rotten barber" and the exaggeration of "all my hair" (including a kind of figurative meaning).

The meaning of "cried", compared with "said with a laugh" should be well checked. Ditto the comparative "much nicer."

The definite article in "the dollar" presupposes a conceptualization: the children have to read between the lines.

The conjunction "as . . . . ." asks for special consideration.

Take care of the figurative meaning in "one cent" in line [7]. Ditto the accent on the first "I" in line [8]. Ditto the figurative meaning of "a nest of lice" in line [9].

●*For children of ± 13 years of age:*
All in the family.
[1]The butterfly filled itself with delicious honey from the
flower as it swayed in the breeze. Then it fluttered away and
[3]alighted on a branch in the sun. Along came a caterpillar
creeping across the same branch.
[5]"Get out of here, you pest!" the yellow lady said haughtily.
"Do you know that we're from the same family?" the caterpillar
[7]growled as it hid itself under a leaf.

(1) Provoking conversation:

"The butterfly is afraid of the caterpillar, I think" . . . . .
"Is the caterpillar jealous of the butterfly?"
And similarly.

(2) Special reading difficulties:
Of course, the situation of a fairy tale and its personifications.

The reflexive pronouns in line [1] and [7] ask for special consideration.

Perhaps the meaning of the first two lines must be dramatized by the children, to be sure that they get its meaning.

Take care of the figurative meanings in "yellow lady" and "haughtily."

The meanings of "family" (not meaning here Father, Mother and children), and of "growled" ask for special consideration.

Evoking Conversations for the Explanation of Themes

The teacher must be thoroughly familiar with the interests and personalities of his students. After they are 7 years of age, he cannot depend on what the children will bring into class as his sole source of conversation. Though children's interests remain the most important origin of discussions and reading-lessons, the teacher must be aware of *flexibility* and *variety* in avoiding repetition of similar experiences. It is recommended that the teacher keep a notebook which includes a collection of useful and necessary topics. This is also valuable in reinforcing concepts which need to be repeated for easy recall and application and to prevent forgetfulness.

The point now is *how* to introduce these topics in such a way that the teacher can arouse the children's interest and evoke spontaneous *conversation,* that is, not just simply present the topic like a lecture. The teacher should not even do this, when he just repeats what already has been learned some time ago: repetitions, too, must be made as lively as possible. The art of devising *provoking or challenging* questions, assertions, or commands is the essence of this type of teaching. This holds true even when the teacher uses pictures, filmstrips, slides, or other audio-visual or tangible materials, dramatizations, and role playing. His goal is always to evoke *thinking,* determining attitudes, social and emotional reactions. Otherwise he will not enter into true *conversation* with his children.

Some examples:
(1) 7 year-old children, topic:
   "Your parents have given you the name, Mary."
Start: By drawing a puppet or having the children draw one.
"He does not have a name. What shall we call him?"
(2) 8 year-old children, topic:
   "The deeper meaning of the fairy tale, Cinderella . . . . . 'Simplicity gains the Victory'".
Start: "The prince was stupid to marry Cinderella".
(3) 10–11 year-old children, topic:
   "The composition of the air: oxygen, carbon dioxide and vapor."
Start: "Did you ever inhale water?"
(4) 13 year-old children, topic:
   "There are poor (!) people who have only their riches." (cf. "That poor man has only his rags"). ("Poor" in a figurative and in a literal meaning.)
Start: "You have won $100,000 in the lottery. What would you do?"
(5) Examples of meaningful *repetitions*.
The teacher has had a lively discussion with 7-year-olds about a hole in a stocking, with a lot of useful colloquial language. Next week he puts an old sweater with two holes on a table somewhere in the classroom, to make his children detect it and to evoke curiosity: by means of this he can repeat almost unconsciously the whole discussion of the last week, in which discussion the children feel rewarded by knowing how to utter themselves spontaneously. In the same way:

"To give a name" can be repeated by telling that your sister-in-law got pregnant;

"Simplicity gains the victory" by comparing—according to the mind of the children—a tasteful cheap suit with an expensive awful one. (This topic asks for more repetitions in variety.)

"The composition of the air" by a story about a diving dress;

The idea of "poverty" in a figurative sense by a story of a spoiled child, by "riches" in a figurative sense, and so forth.

APPENDIX 2.

Some more records of conversations to be used as reading material.

Monday, September 17th, 1979 (Boston Spa, School for the Deaf, 11–12 years of age.) Who really went for a walk? Who was rich?

A couple of children had a boring weekend, because nothing happened at home.

Maria did not agree. She said: "My sister had a birthday. For me the weekend was not at all boring. It was exciting!"

Miss Andrews asked: "What did you purchase for your sister?"

Maria replied: "A bracelet."

Miss Andrews misunderstood: She thought Maria had bought a wristwatch. The reason for the misunderstanding was that Maria made the sign for a wristwatch! . . . . .

Maite asked how expensive the bracelet was. Maria could not remember . . . . .

Miss Andrews was astonished! She said: "You must be very rich!" . . . . . Then, she laughed. Some children laughed, but others remained without a clue. The children did not really understand. Therefore, Miss Andrews explained about this again at the end of the lesson.

Maite guessed that the bracelet cost £5. Miss Andrews said: "Ask a proper question!" Maite asked Maria: "Approximately how much did the bracelet cost?"

Maria replied: "About £3."

Martin also did not agree that it was a boring weekend. He told everyone he had been for a three-mile walk. . . . . . There was a visitor in our classroom, Mr. U. He claimed: "I went for a walk too! I went for a thousand-mile 'walk'." He wrote the word "walk" on the blackboard with quotation marks around it. However, the children did not yet notice the speech marks. . . . . They had dozed off!

The children did not believe him. They said: "It's not true!"

Maite said: "I don't believe you!" Simon said: "You're pulling our legs!"

Mr. U. insisted, but pointed to the quotation marks. . . . . The children did not understand the difference between Martin's walk and Mr. U.'s "walk."

One of the children suggested: "You traveled by boat."

Another child said: "Perhaps you came by airplane?"

Mr. U. said: "Yes! I "walked" by airplane." Mr. U. put inverted commas around "walk" because it was not a "walk" in the literal sense of the word, but in a figurative sense. "Walk" between inverted commas meant "flight" here. The flight was as easy as a walk! It was an amusing way of telling everyone about the flight.

Now we return to talking about Maria being rich. Do you think rich people worry about the cost of things? Maria did not worry about the cost of the bracelet. So, Miss Andrews exclaimed: "You must be very rich!". . . . . Kevin Keegan is rich in the literal sense of the word. However, Maria is not literally rich. Miss Andrews was teasing her.

the conversational method and the control of language

Notebook.

Vocabulary:

We were *clueless*.

Approximately how much?

We had *dozed off*.

"You are *pulling our legs*" = you are deceiving us jokingly (this expression has not a *literal* sense).

Mr. U. *claimed, insisted*..... He called a flight a "walk": an *amusing way of telling*.

Maria is *not literally* rich, she behaved *as if* she were rich.

You *must* be very rich = I *conclude*, that you are rich.

Grammar:

The weekend was not at all boring, it was exciting = accent of contrast.

approximately how much . . . . . ?
an adverb at an adverb.

How much did the bracelet cost?
an adverb at a verb.

How much did the bracelet cost?
pincer construction

Wednesday October 3rd, 1979 (Pittsburgh, De Paul Institute for the Deaf, Class of Sr. Francis-Louise and Mr. Borello, 9 to 10 years of age).

Oh, you lazy watch!

On Wednesday October 3, Mr. U. visited our classroom. It was about 8:45 a.m. Sister Francis-Louise asked him to teach us a lesson.

Guess what! U. questioned us by looking at his wristwatch. He frowned and said: "What's that! My watch shows something! Can anyone tell me about my watch?" Then still looking at his watch he scolded: "Watch, you are sleepy!" "You are lazy!" "I'll teach you!"

All the children looked at U. They were wondering why he said that to his watch!

Then U. said: "Come here! Look at my watch! What is the matter with my watch? Why is my watch sleepy? Why is my watch lazy?"

One by one, the children took turns looking at his wristwatch. Maria looked puzzled. Tony didn't know! Gretchen frowned! After Mike looked at the watch, he whispered: "I know why your watch is lazy. I think you have to change it. *The date is wrong!* The watch is sleepy!" U. came close to him and said: "Sh, sh! Don't tell!"

When U. showed the watch to Traci, she smiled and replied: "I think I know why the watch is sleepy! It's wrong! It's the wrong date! It's October 3rd, not October 2nd." Again U. said: "Sh, sh . . . . . Don't tell! Don't tell anyone!"

After everyone had a chance to examine the wristwatch, U. asked: "What shall we do with it? How can we change it?" Then U. invited Tony to operate the wristwatch. Tony looked puzzled. He was not sure what to do. He asked: "What do you mean?"

246 oral education: today and tomorrow

Then U. explained: "First, pull out the button on the side of the watch. Then turn the button, turn it slowly and carefully. Be careful when you turn it!"

Tony turned it slowly. The hands began to change! Then U. let each boy and girl help to change the hands on the watch. Each one had a chance to turn the button on the wristwatch. As they did so, they noticed that the hands on the watch moved also: The "time" of the watch changed. Each child moved the hands to exactly *one more hour ahead*. The watch changed from 10 o'clock to 11 o'clock and then to 12 o'clock.

At that point, U. asked: "What time of the day is this?" Some children still looked puzzled. They did not know what U. meant. But Traci quickly replied: "It's midnight. It's night time!" And Mike answered: "The people are sleeping. It's night time!"

As the hands on the watch moved, so did the tiny number on the watch that showed the date. It began to change, too! U. said: "Hey! Take care! You see the 3 is coming. Turn slowly!"

All the boys and girls had a chance to see the tiny number as it began to change from 2 to 3. First it looked like this: [2] and then like this: [⅔] and then like this: [⅗] and at last like this: 3 .

U. asked Tony about the date. But Tony wasn't sure what U. meant. Then U. said: "Tony, you are not yet ready!"

U. asked again: "What time is it *now?*" Mike said: "It's 9:40 a.m. *now*".

U. noticed the electric clock on the wall of the room and he looked at his own watch. He said: "Let's *compare* my time with the time on the electric clock. What time is it on the clock? Is the time on my watch correct?" . . . . . The children had to change the hands of the watch further: until 9:40 a.m.

"Yes, it is right!" said Kelly. "It is 9:40 a.m. It's morning!"

U. questioned again: 'How else can we *compare* the time?"

Almost all of the children looked puzzled again. They didn't understand what to do. But U. kept asking: "Are there other ways to find out if the time on my watch is correct? How else can we find out *in this room?"*

The children kept thinking! At last Jimmy spotted Sister Francis-Louise's wristwatch and pointed to it and said: "We can look at her watch." U. said: "Yes, we can *compare* the time. We can see if our watches are the same." After looking at Sister's watch, Jimmy exclaimed: "It's the same time!" U. said: "Yes, it's the same time." He questioned again: "How *else* can we find out about the time in this room?" Traci pointed to Mr. Borello's wristwatch and said: "He has a watch, too!" "Yes," said U., "Let's *compare* the time on his watch." By this time, everyone wanted to see the time on Mr. Borello's watch! They noticed that it was the same time, too.

Soon nearly everyone noticed Sister Philomena's watch (also in this room). But it did not have the same time! It was 5 minutes fast! Sister Philomena said: "My watch is running too fast! It is 5 minutes fast!"

U. asked: "Is my watch *lazy!* Is it *sleepy* now? No, my watch is not *literally* sleepy or lazy. That is only a *figurative* meaning. Now it is *obedient* and *loyal* again!"

the conversational method and the control of language 247

Can you answer the questions about the story you just read?
1. We spoke about 4 wristwatches, which watches were these?
2. One watch was too fast. Which watch was that?
3. Which watch was 24 hours too slow?
4. How did we "teach" the slow watch?
5. What is midnight?
6. What is p.m.?
7. How many hours are a.m.? How many are p.m.?
8. The watch is *too slow*. Is this a figurative or a literal meaning?
9. How did we *compare* 1 clock and 4 watches?
10. Which words have a literal or a figurative meaning:
    a. The watch is *loyal*. What does this mean? _____
    b. One watch was *too fast*. What does this mean? _____
    c. "Oh, you are sleepy, lazy!" What does this mean? _____
    d. "Watch, I'll *teach* you!" What does this mean? _____
    e. This calendar *says* October 3rd. What does this mean? _____
    f. "No, Tony, you are *not yet ready!*" What does this mean? _____

Notebook.

Vocabulary:

"Watch, you are *sleepy, lazy*" = slow.

"Lazy" and "sleepy" don't have a literal but a figurative sense here.

The same with: "Now is my watch *loyal* again."

To examine the wristwatch.

We have 12 o'clock at noon, and 12 o'clock at midnight.

We *compared* the times of 4 clocks.

As the hands on the watch moved, so did the tiny number. = a *comparison*.

As we turned the button, we noticed that the hands moved.

We saw the tiny number *as* it began to change.

= No comparison.

a.m. = 12 hours.
p.m. = 12 hours.

First . . . . . then . . . . . then . . . . .

Grammar:

Something ⎫
Anyone   ⎬ indefinite words.
Everyone = a definite word.

Why is my watch lazy?

We were wondering, *why* he said that.

I know, *why* your watch is lazy.

He was not sure, *what* to do.
  A questionword can be used as a conjunction.

Inversion:

  2   1   3
Why is the watch sleepy?
       1   2   3
I know, why the watch is sleepy.
       2   1   3
What shall we do with it?
    2   1   3
How can we change it?
 1   2   3
We can change it.

The (watch) is slow. adjective.
(Turn) it slowly. adverb.

Suggested conclusions:
Conversation must be put in the center of the didactics of language for deaf children:
For developing empathy,
For oral-aural skill,
For learning to understand and to read
For learning the structure of language, and
For correct language production.

The conversational method *basically requires* in the educators an attitude of accepting the deaf child and of respecting him as a person, able and called upon to be a worthy and complete member of the hearing society.

A method without or with too little conversation cannot meet *the communication need* of the deaf child. It will leave him to his "body language" much too much, and essentially hamper a real oral-aural education.

It is important for a teacher of the deaf to know *how* to enter into conversation with a still speechless deaf child; this *how* implies "the playing of the double part."

The conversational didactics of language requires first of all: the art of *listening* to the child, viewing his spontaneous utterances and reactions, in order to follow the "seizing method," that is, to seize first of all what the child *wants to say*, and to offer him the appropriate words (to play the part of the child), and second: the art of *making oneself understood to the child by the situation*, that is of playing ones own part in giving a real contribution to the conversation, or the art of manipulating the situation (including contexts) in such a way that the child will understand.

The *memory function* for language (both Short Term Memory and Long Term Memory) must be a point of continuous concern for the teacher of the deaf. This requires rhythmic speech, developing clustering behavior, much lively repetition and the support of reading and writing.

Reading and writing can be used from early childhood in such a way that they are not hampering, but on the contrary supporting the oral-aural method of education.

Language production should be primarily a *spontaneous* selection by the deaf child himself, from a large fund of nonverbal and verbal comprehension (active language derived from passive language). This conversion process is evoked especially by conversation, because conversation balances both aspects of language use, by the turn-taking behavior of listening and speaking.

A method of language teaching which mainly *presents* preprogrammed language structures to the child to be used by him, *without* making allowance for the *spontaneous* nonverbal and verbal comprehension of the child, and without giving him the chance of selecting his own utterances from his fund of comprehension results in rigid thinking and can hardly be acknowledged to be real language teaching.

The *only method* which makes full allowance for the nonverbal and verbal comprehension of the child, making him understand more and more and read *between the lines*, is the conversational method.

The method of teaching a preprogrammed *target-language* breaks down *spontaneity* and, with that, of real conversation. *Interferences* with fluent understanding and reading are to be expected. Such a method hardly can be acknowledged as a real method of lively language teaching.

The only way of combining the exclusive use of *normal*, not preprogrammed language, with the learning of the *structure* of language, is the way of *guided discovery learning*.

Reading lessons should be seen as "deposits" of language, that is, as treasures gathered from conversations, and understood in a conversational way (reading is a way of conversation), and as a fund *from which* active language can reach fruition, and *in which* the structure of language can be detected by guided discovery learning.

The teaching of language comprehension both by conversation and reading, the teaching of the structure of language by guided discovery learning, and the application of the detected semantic and grammatical rules for language production and composition-work, should be seen as *one whole*, to be taught by *one teacher*, preferably in a "moving-up" system, so that one teacher keeps his children at least for several years.

The teaching of *reading* is more important and primary in comparison with *composition-work*. The first should be seen as the fund of the latter.

It is impossible to teach a language, certainly a first language, just in school hours. The work of the parents and of the houseparents (in residential schools) is as important as the schoolwork. This requires training courses both for parents and houseparents, and intense cooperation between "school" and "free time." Unqualified houseparents cannot be accepted in residential schools for the deaf, because they are not able to meet the communication needs of the deaf children in the right way.

reaction to 9

janet head

The conversational method as presented by Father van Uden has some unassailable strengths. Much of the model parallels the documented verbal behavior between normally hearing mothers and babies, which has a high rate of success in producing language competent children. Another strength I see is the use of written forms of actual classroom conversation as early level reading material.

Further, the identification of two types of conversations provides a clear guide regarding the much debated question in oral circles about the advisability of correcting deaf children's conversational speech. "Heart-to-heart" conversations are those in which personal thinking and feelings are the central focus and the goal is the development of empathy. They should be interrupted as little as possible, for any reason. "Linguistic" conversations are those in which the child's discovery of the semantic and grammatical structure of the language is the goal. Interruptions for correction are appropriate and facilitate language learning.

The conversational method provides more focus and more repetition over a longer period of time, which I believe are appropriate compensations for the difficulties imposed by profound deafness. In addition, the employment of conversation as the foundation for communicative development neatly incorporates the three major areas of parental responsibility in the child's early years:

- The fostering of healthy development in the affective area;
- The development of and practice in the use of a verbal communication system; and
- The provision of a wide range of life experiences that will generate the meanings brought to both spoken and written language and set the stage for the learning of principles and rules as opposed to item-specific learning.

The conversational interchanges mandated by the method will, in addition, facilitate short-term memory function and competence in producing the more complex language structures.

In the years since Father van Uden first wrote of the Maternal Reflective Method, he has become increasingly more specific regarding the behaviors that constitute this conversational method in practice. However, the fact remains that no matter how clearly upper echelon educators, psychologists, and linguists see the dynamics of a developing communication system and describe adult behaviors that facilitate the process, the power to make changes in what happens to children is ultimately in the hands of those who deliver direct services to those children—the teachers (and of course the parents). The gap between what is understood at the mountaintop and what is delivered on the front line can be devastating.

Father van Uden has expressed doubts regarding the merit of several teaching activities that are commonly conducted in "oral" education settings. Among these are:

- Teachers doing most of the talking in the classroom with the result that the children themselves have little opportunity to verbalize (van Uden, 1977).
- Teachers using short, syntactic structures without normal variations in talking to their students (van Uden, 1977).
- Teachers using questioning procedures that involve no real quest for information, but rather an exercise in matching question words with paradigmatic word types (van Uden, 1979).
- Teachers setting up various kinds of role-playing exercises in which a context is presented through videotape or pictures; appropriate language is modeled; and the students are then expected to play through these contrived situations (van Uden, 1979).
- Teachers methodically using pictures and diagrams to illustrate the meaning of each written item in a story, letter, chart, etc. (van Uden, 1979).
- Teachers reacting to a child's spontaneous speech try by simple expansion as opposed to a conversational comeback (van Uden, 1979).

Father van Uden has observed these teaching behaviors, assessed them within his framework, and found them lacking. I would like to look at them in another way—as products, in part, of individual personal differences among teachers. Such a concept regarding children is both familiar and comfortable, and since the advent of U.S. Public Law 94-142, also a legal mandate. Somehow, the issue of individual differences in teachers is a much more sensitive issue. Attention has been focused largely on overt behaviors and much less on the underlying sources of these behaviors.

In addition to the obvious sources, such as the quality and range of training the teacher received, and the kind of teaching models that were presented, a less often discussed source is that of the individual teacher's personality, cognitive structure, and interactive needs. These aspects constitute a powerful force in shaping both the style and content of speech-language teaching interactions and merit examination.

Teachers' synthetic thinking abilities will determine how effective they are in translating theory into activities, materials, and personal interactions. This applies equally to the technical information involved in the sciences, to the patterns of growth in the area of linguistic competence, and to the psychological foundations of behavior management approaches. Managing information and translating it into behaviors is an important part of the teaching task, and good teachers display this competence.

Teachers' needs to nurture will color their interactions with students in many ways. One of the major conflicts children experience in their growth toward adulthood is that between their drive toward independent functioning and their need to be cared for. Teachers with strong needs to nurture will find it difficult to urge their students toward independence and the risks, discomfort, and compromises that it often brings. In the process of fulfilling this need to nurture, teachers are likely to behave in ways that encourage students to lean on them in a variety of ways, when it would be more age- and stage-appropriate for them to be functioning independently. This can present a major interruption in student growth.

Teachers with a high need for immediate reinforcement may be motivated to employ communicative practices that do not contribute toward a long range growth pattern, although they may indeed serve in the immediate situation.

Teachers' predispositions toward verbal or concrete expression can impel them toward favored forms of communication. There are talkers, dancers, and mimers; it may well be that teachers with leanings toward physical expression are more strongly drawn toward manual support systems.

I would like to propose that these teacher variables can make the difference between success and failure in implementing the conversational method and other oral approaches. Because self-awareness regarding these aspects is seldom well developed, and standard teacher evaluation formats do not directly address them, they are not presently being dealt with adequately from my point of view. I have no answer today to the question of how best to address these critical teacher variables, but I believe that it may be possible to more effectively modify teacher behavior in positive directions if we do take this deeper look.

References

van Uden, A. *A World of language for deaf children, part 1: basic principles,* **Amsterdam**: Swets and Zeitlinger, 1977, *113,* 226.

van Uden, A. Psychological foundations of teaching language to deaf children, (paper) Instituut Voor Doven, 1979, 39.

van Uden, A. The conversational method and the control of language, (paper) Instituut Voor Doven, 1979, 6–8.

10

acquisition of language by under-fives including the parental role
audrey simmons-martin

A fundamental starting point in the exposition that follows is to invert the sequence of ideas explicit in its announced title, i.e., "including the parental role." This thought is suggested by the central thesis of this presentation—namely, that without parents, there is likely to be very little of the kind of language acquisition that we seek and of which children are capable.

Studies of understimulation during the early childhood of hearing children suggest convincingly that among its more baneful results is impoverished language. The data indicate emphatically that children need help in naming the things they see and feel, in recognizing similarities and differences, in classifying and categorizing perceptions, in learning the word for an object and the phrases needed to express feeling and reacting (Deutsch, 1965; Hunt, 1973). The prominent role of environmental variables on both cognitive and linguistic development has been increasingly documented.

The crucial role of sensory experiences in early development is supported by neurophysiological evidence that points to an optimal period to exploit the plasticity of the maturing nervous system, a notion that is not unfamiliar to the members of this conference. The studies in vision, in particular, lend validity to the slogan about the sense modalities, "use it or lose it." (Webster, 1977).

Psycholinguists point to an optimal period for language acquisition. By age 3, a normally hearing child given reasonable stimulation exhibits language behavior that is functional; by 5 years he is a skillful speaker. He has adequate grammar to sustain him throughout adult life; his syntax is quite complete; his vocabulary includes over 2,000 words; his phonologic skills of intonation, phrasing, and stress are established and his articulation is fairly intelligible. He is thus well on his way in linguistic *form*. Furthermore, he knows when to use the form and what to say when he uses the form. He has learned about his world, hence he has *content*. He has, that is, learned to recognize different kinds of circumstances which require an ability to *function* with or use language and has a sophisticated *form* intelligible to most people. In short, his communication has form, substance, and purpose.

Unfortunately a hearing impaired child does not have this three-dimensional view of language. At age 5 years, far too many are just beginning their linguistic acquisition and formal cognitive development in programs "tooled" for focus on the *form* of language, particularly words, syntax and, perhaps, less frequently, phonology.

What we currently know about the ways in which humans learn to communicate drives us to the conviction that we should no longer play the "word game" with young deaf children. Neither can we afford to water down the drills and skill tasks we use with the *plus* fives and by doing so avoid the development of strategies appropriate to the child's linguistic level. Young deaf children are not miniature deaf students.

Parents' Role

In real life it is the members of the family, and particularly the mother, who introduce the child to learning language. They are the significant models and sources of external feedback that are essential to the child's acquisition of a communication system. He needs the warm, constant, and expanding reciprocal activity that is the basis of an effective and affective system of interaction. For the deaf child, even more for the hearing infant, the need for a strong interpersonal parent interaction system demands diligent, consistent, and concentrated emphasis. He needs to sense the emerging surface structure or linguistic form from his deep structure or thought.

Even though the deaf child needs this experience from his parents more, he is less able to elicit it. Since the hearing impairment places distinct limitations on the child, the parents must therefore assume more responsibility within the dyad. Parents must be more sensitive and more responsive but not necessarily more active, lest they thwart initiative (Goldberg, 1979).

At the outset, simply programming parents to provide language is insufficient and perhaps premature, for they need assistance in adjusting to both the handicap itself and to their role as the parents of a handicapped child. Their ability to assume this role may hinge on their ability to accept the reality of the handicap (Greenstein, 1976). I have addressed this problem elsewhere (Simmons-Martin, 1978).

In more than 20 years of professional experience at Central Institute for the Deaf, observation, and cumulative record-keeping of parents and their children from varied economic levels and cultural contexts, our empirical data suggest strikingly that effective "parenting" during the hearing impaired child's early years determines the quality of his cognitive, social, and, most importantly, his linguistic development. The single most significant factor in the child's development of competence is the interaction between the parent and child. Areas such as emotional acceptance, ease in relating to the child, encouragement, independence, and parents' sensitivity to the child are all correlated with his development.

While language competence is the goal we have for each child, the dominant competence we seek in the parents is reciprocity with their child. The strength of the mutually harmonious interaction depends upon the parents' understanding of their child and his problems, along with sensitivity to his needs. With hearing impairment, interaction is obviously severely impeded. Because the child does not readily respond to verbalization or meet the parent's expectations, the necessary bonding between child and his parent is disrupted or, fundamentally, nonexistent. In most cases intervention is needed to prevent or repair the break in reciprocal action.

It has been our experience that patterns of communication manifest themselves in prelinguistic stages; the compatibility between the child and his parent with respect to communication and its topics can be fostered; the natural reciprocity of parent and child behavior provides each member of the dyad with frequent opportunities to feel effective; and language behavior can be enhanced by appropriate experiences.

There is still speculation about the actual process by which the parent-child relationship develops, but we have outlined some items that are in the repertoire of successful parents. Four areas seem to stand out as influencing the child's development the greatest. And within each area there are subgroups of important behaviors.

General Parent-Child Behavior

The notion that parents are important is not new, but in recent years the parents' role in shaping children's development has assumed even greater importance and has been more clearly specified. The overwhelming abundance of current studies points prominently to the shift of view from parenting as doing things to and for the child, to parenting as a process of reciprocal interaction— an active dialogue between parent and child (Lewis & Rosenblum, 1974). Furthermore, parent-child relationships in which parents influence and are influenced by their children, must be maintained over time although the reciprocal relationship changes in balance and characteristics as the children grow older (Clarke-Stewart, 1973).

Of all the interactions between parents and child which foster development, we believe the role of parents is of particular importance in: (1) establishing compatibility within the dyad—dyadic compatibility; (2) utilizing nonverbal clues for initiation and follow through in communication—patterns of communication; (3) seizing opportunities for inspiration of affection—affective dyadic feedback; and, (4) demonstration of competence relative to general behavior as well as linguistic—behavioral competence.

Dyadic Compatibility

Early reciprocal interactions between parent and child essentially constitute a turn-taking system. In visual interactions, parent and child alternate regularly between eye-to-eye contact and gaze aversion (Stern, 1974). It is a Ping-Pong-like pattern in which children display bouts of bursts and pauses and mothers alternate with physical stimulation (Kaye, 1977).

Since this turn-taking model is a forerunner of verbal conversation we believe it is a necessary context for language acquisition. Therefore, we help parents perform in this fashion with their hearing impaired child by encouraging the parent to watch the child, responding to the child, demonstrating that his activities are interesting, tuning in, as it were, to his signals. Newson (1977), in particular, stressed how mothers act as though the infant were already an active communicator. We want the mother of a hearing impaired child to develop and practice this set. We want her to allow herself to be paced by the child, reading his signals and using intonation to signal her passing of the turn to the child.

Patterns of Communication

The content of most communication with young children concerns their objects, their actions, and their possessions. These items, which are "here and now," elicit interest. The interest needs structure. Topics can be initiated by the child's gaze, which mother follows, or it can be the parent who may call attention to the topic on which she wants to focus. The mutuality of interest in external objects provides the content and the framework for exchange.

Parents of hearing impaired children need to be shown that they must follow the child's gaze and immediately label the objects or persons which attracted the child. They must notify the child that he is being addressed. They need to know the importance of making eye contact, offering an object or pointing to it, and then talking about it. It might be toys the child can play with, food he may eat, or clothing he puts on.

Affective Dyadic Feedback

There is no general agreement about what are the most desirable parental traits; we are still very far from being able to specify which particular aspects of maternal behavior are likely to foster cognitive and linguistic development (Dunn & Richards, 1977). However, maternal responsiveness was found by Clarke-Stewart (1973) to be related to measures of the child's overall competence. The child's optimal, secure attachment to the mother was significantly related to high maternal scores on dimensions of affection, stimulation, and responsiveness. Others often refer to this area as the social realm and go so far as to state that it can be considered the vehicle for cognitive and linguistic development (Lewis, 1979; White, 1975).

The findings of the Lexington School for the Deaf study on mother-infant communication (Greenstein et al., 1976) stated emphatically that:

> affective aspects of mother-infant-interaction were more highly correlated with the child's language acquisition than were technical aspects of the mother's language. The discovery of the child's handicap severely damaged the mother-child bond. p. 35

Brown (1977) described and organized the features of early communication to babies as those concerned with affection and those concerned with communication competence. Those concerned with affection are tenderness-inspiring, affection-inspiring, and intimacy-inspiring. The features concerned with communication competence are verbal production, verbal comprehension, and cognitive competence. It is the combination of affection and communication competence that constitutes a superior set of language lessons (Cross, 1977).

We generally find that the affective condition between parents and hearing impaired children is less than ideal. Therefore, one of our concerns is to help parents establish or reestablish their role as loving parents. We frequently must route the parent through the stages from physical control of situations to visual control and finally to linguistic control. Parents of hearing impaired children need to know the power of a hug, a pat, a smile, positive vocal tones, rich intonation, expressions of praise and affection, as well as the need to interpret the child's mood and respond accordingly.

It often happens that we provide the reinforcement to the mother for the child, because he may not look, smile, or vocalize. But we need to recognize that the mother will suffer because of lack of reinforcing behavior from the child, and we must assist her to develop the necessary reciprocal influence. Who reinforces whom in the parent-infant dyad is a question of considerable magnitude, but we know that it is rare that a profoundly deaf child can provide much feedback early in his training.

Behavioral Competence

It is a well-established fact that maternal rejection leads to negative behavior, whereas positive attitudes enhance performance on comprehensive measures of intellectual development and motivation (Clarke-Stewart, 1973). Mutually unsatisfying early interaction between a mother and her child may lead to a continuing pattern of difficulty. While difficulties at one period cannot be assumed to reflect an underlying insensitivity on the mother's part from which continuing difficulties will occur, the best predictions indicate that they most probably will increase without intervention (Stern, 1971).

The parental strategy of accepting the child's behavior, both nonverbal as well as verbal, were shown to facilitate the child's progress in language acquisition (Nelson, 1973). Discipline and self-control, based on communication whereby the parent assumes a role of authority but not that of a disciplinarian, are traits of a "super parent" (White, 1973). As Altshuler (1976) stated, "no one comes through childhood unscarred, unbent, and without idiosyncratic molding experiences. On the other hand, the child is a resilient little creature who can bounce back well if stresses are not too severe and persistent." p. 114

Sound is an important part of the child's bond with his mother. A mother's voice with the important vocal nuances which indicate control is obviously not as available to the hearing impaired child as to the hearing infant. Therefore, intervention must teach the important role of authority. Deaf children need to know what realistic limits are. Parents need to set them and see that they are followed. Parents may have to learn that consistency from day to day and person to person in varying environments is important. They need to become aware of intonation patterns that govern behavior, and employ them. Tones of control need to be sensibly balanced, however, by tones of endearment. Who would like a hearing aid if all it amplified was "No" and "Don't do that!"?

Speech Perception — Auditory

A hearing child's speech perception is linguistically relevant. Evidence attesting to the auditory discriminative capacities and to the importance of listening in phonological development is being accumulated by several investigators (Eimas, in press; Kuhl, 1976; Kaplan, 1971). It has been demonstrated that infants make discriminative responses between consonant-vowel combinations (Morse, 1972) and between vowels.

Friedlander (1979), studying babies in the 8- to 15-month range, has shown that they make discriminations and exhibit preferences for vocal factors of familiarity, intonation, rhythm, and loudness and for message factors of length, redundancy, and amount of information. His work suggests the presence of an experiential continuum on which these variables can be placed (Friedlander, 1970).

Facts and even speculation about theoretical characteristics of the auditory system should not intrude on the practical, demonstrable facets of parent-child interaction. Rather, parents need to recognize the difficulty involved for their profoundly deaf child. For these children, amplification provides gross time and intensity patterns and may even allow them to detect and distinguish acoustic speech signals through vibrotactile receptors in their ears (Risberg, 1977). Erber (1979) summarizes by saying:

> that profoundly hearing-impaired children are those whose ability to distinguish spectral features in speech is extremely poor, and for whom the gross variations in the acoustic pattern (waveform envelope) are the principal acoustic cues. p. 257

Therefore the principle we employ is to alert the parent to the contribution auditory capabilities make to reception of the spoken form. The key point is that the child receives acoustic speech information through a hearing aid whether it complements or only supplements the articulatory cues available to him through lipreading.

Counseling parents as to their important role in auditory management centers around: (1) hearing aid usage, (2) structuring the situation, (3) awareness of sound, (4) awareness of speech, and (5) auditory recognition.

Hearing Aid Usage

Obviously parents need to understand the child's audiogram and the value of the hearing aid. Their role, however, includes providing amplified speech at all times. Therefore, the child must wear the hearing aid regularly. Parents need to calibrate the aid daily, using their own ear, in order that the speech signals are consistent over time. They need to maintain the aids by checking cords for knots or chewing, cleaning and inspecting ear molds for fit, and protecting the microphones from cereal, jelly, and chocolate milk as much as possible (Simmons-Martin, 1975).

Structuring the Situation

While the child's auditory perceptual system may be seriously impaired, thereby permitting speech to be analyzed only as gross patterns, he must not be limited in the quality or quantity of his daily auditory experiences. A noisy home can make it very difficult to learn any language through his ears. Hence, it becomes the parents' role to structure the situation in order to provide the ideal setting. The tasks here range from judging the home for "quietness," keeping unnecessary noises to the minimum, judging proximity necessary for listening, working to increase the distance, and finally to humming, singing, and otherwise playing with sound in the quieter rooms of the home.

Awareness of Sound

Attending to sound is an early stage of auditory training. The signals can be either nonlinguistic or linguistic. Certainly the informal training provided by the parent in the home is not sufficient but is in keeping with our global approach to child development. We do not believe that the parent should have to provide "listening activities" that require full-time involvement (Erber, 1976). In order to maintain the child's interest and motivation, we suggest the listening experiences in ongoing daily schedules. These include calling attention to environmental sounds, associating all sounds with their source, reinforcing the child's response to sound, repeating sounds that please the child, and playing with noisemaking toys.

Awareness of Speech

The auditory signal of greatest importance is the human voice. Therefore, the primary job of the parent of the hearing-impaired child is to assist the child in attending and responding to speech. Parents communicate with children in a manner which reflects their belief that the child is capable of reciprocal communication. This attitude is the basis of the turn-taking model. From this model, the foundation for reciprocity is created and the context for learning is provided.

Therefore, the first task in the parent's role is calling the child by his name. Even though the profoundly deaf child may never recognize this acoustic pattern, he needs to substitute whatever auditory cues he receives for that important signal. Zeiser and Erber (1977) did some interesting research in this area and found, for example, that a name like "Marianne" was heard by deaf subjects as one very long syllable rather than the correct 3 syllables. Nevertheless, that one very long syllable must, in time, be the signal to Marianne that her name is the one being called.

Intonation patterns play an important part in language development and they are available to profoundly deaf children. It is the most salient feature in language behavior addressed to the child. It may indicate the semantic aspect because the emotional content of communication is so marked. The syntactic signals are also thus identified. In fact, it has been said that intonation is the vehicle a child rides to syntax. Most importantly, intonation serves in a social function. One must pay attention in a conversation in order to know when it is one's turn to speak, and the turn termination is indicated by the drop in voice (Garnica, 1977).

The tone of the parents' voices should be rich in rising and falling contours appropriate to the message as well as tones that are of positive affective nature. The early years are not the time for punitive, negative, harsh, angry tones regardless of their auditory availability. Vocal play can be connected with just talking or with babbling imitation or spontaneously articulated structure for his behavior with terms such as, "What a good boy!", "I like that!"

Auditory Recognition

Auditory recognition, though not involving comprehension, is a preliminary step in auditory training. It proceeds from the general to the specific as does all learning in small children and may always be very gross for some profoundly deaf children. While ideally we would like to think of auditory recognition as a unisensory event, in reality it may be through looking as well as listening that a child recognizes the parents' verbal stimulus.

There are children who, when they have only a small number of easy, familiar words to choose from, are able to recognize a very few. These profoundly deaf children typically respond to low-frequency pure tones; nevertheless, they generally have great difficulty distinguishing the low-frequency spectral features of speech. Instead they tend to perceive speech through their ears as though they were merely perceiving rhythmic vibratory patterns (Erber, 1974).

Therefore, the role of the parent is to provide auditory stimulus but not insist upon its recognition through hearing alone. She/he may playfully give him vocal play with intonation, babble with him, and present prolonged long vowels for enjoyment. She may have a set of nursery rhymes which the child recognizes when the cards are in front of him. The mother needs to do this only *after* he has had many opportunities to hear and lipread her speaking the rhyme while showing the picture. Objects may be asked for in a closed set situation, e.g., they are getting dressed to go out and mother may say, "Get your coat," turning her face away at the last word. Scrapbooks of meaningful experiences can provide other "closed sets" for auditory recognition. Other times parents may ask the child in the natural situation for a toy, a utensil, or to do something, e.g., "Throw a kiss", "Wave bye-bye", or "It's time to go to bed."

Speech Perception — Visual

For the profoundly deaf child who is the focus of this conference, vision is the main compensatory sense used for speech perception. These children will need to lipread in order to successfully participate in oral communication. In addressing this ability, Erber (1979) recently wrote:

> Messages conveyed through lipreading constitute an optical language, encoded in the muscular changes that accompany production of acoustic messages. As such, the process often is difficult because numerous speech elements look alike even to a careful observer, and the lipreader must extract meaning from the situation and language context. p. 264

Because of the context influencing the particular word or words, we have in the past addressed the "global" aspect of language (Simmons-Martin, 1977). A child needs the information about the whole or the Gestalt of language in order to prepare him to use Information Theory to predict the nonavailable word (Fry, 1963).

However, Clouser (1976) found that a deaf child's ability to recognize sentences through lipreading seems to diminish as a function of the length and syntactic complexity of the material. In the earlier data many hearing impaired children seem to have the least difficulty with subject-verb-object sentences (Davis & Silverman, 1970). Since this is the traditional basic sentence pattern and is introduced early in their educational experience, I believe it makes a case for a wider variety being presented early and often. Similarly, question forms are reported to be difficult for older children.

It should be noted, nevertheless, that older profoundly hearing impaired children can categorize spoken consonants on the basis of the points of articulation (e.g., labial, alveolar, velar), although consonant recognition is affected to an extent by vowel context (Pesonen, 1968; Erber, 1971). Hence the young child needs opportunities to receive place-of-articulation speech information while receiving complementary voicing, manner-of-articulation, time and intensity cues, and possible vowel-formant information through their distorted but useful low-frequency hearing (or feeling). (At no time are we addressing lipreading as a silent activity—always there is complementary voicing.) To the parent falls the role of obtaining attention and developing effective strategies for maintaining it. The tasks cluster in three areas: (1) managing the illumination and speaker position within the environment; (2) providing good speech patterns; and (3) holding the child to some speech recognition.

Environmental Management

Environmental factors can enhance or diminish lipreading ability. Good illumination, closeness to the speaker, and absence of distractions are all conditions which enable the best lipreading to take place. The parents' role, then, is to provide the optimal conditions in their own home and see that others observe them when speaking to the deaf child. This includes attention to such matters as seeing that the shades are up and the best light is provided in the areas of child activity. It means that the parents learn to place themselves in such a position that the light is on their faces. They need to automatically get to the child's eye level while giving a face-to-face view. They must also prevent optical competition in the way of distracting gestures and actions. This includes eliminating distractions such as dangling jewelry or background movement in the environment.

Parents' Speech Patterns

As has been pointed out, the profoundly deaf child can get categories of place and manner of articulation information from the lips. This is a critical point because the data raise questions about the amount of content that is available in the optical realm. We do not really know how and what children lipread but we do know that visual recognition of consonants is possible through lipreading, and this recognition is closely related to general lipreading ability (Heider & Heider, 1940).

Of course we must not overlook the contribution of the visual form to speech development. Therefore, parents must present the best speech patterns possible to their deaf child to assist him in his eventual speech production. This includes speaking clearly without exaggerating. It means speaking slower than to the older children or adults, which has been found to be true of the speech of mothers of hearing children (Nelson, 1973). It means parents should stress the content words, which is what parents of young hearing children also do (Blount & Padgug, 1977). It should be noted that this appears to be a natural device used to develop lexical and referential information which, after all, is one of the tasks of lipreading. The emotional and attitudinal features of speech should be marked by appropriate pitch, stress, duration, and intensity cues so that the child can perceive the Gestalt of speech.

Speech Recognition — Visual

The parents' role in this area is seeing that the child has language input and then holding the child responsible for lipreading it. In this task a parent may simply talk directly to the child about a common referent. She talks when he gives her his attention. She may give him labels for objects which she holds beside her face or gets for him. She asks questions which require a "yes" or "no" response and eventually asks questions which involve choices. She gives expressions in which the setting is not a clue and expects the child to comprehend and respond. She gives labels for a closed set of objects and plays the game of identification.

Language Behavior

Language behavior is communication, the transmission of an idea emanating from the mind of the speaker, to be decoded in the mind of the listener. This obligates the sender and the receiver to be familiar with the same code. The act of encoding requires the speaker to recall and combine the elements of the code to represent information in a spoken message. In decoding, the listener recognizes the segments the elements of the code in order to extract information from the message. The same forms of language convey the message that is to be either "de" or "en" coded.

Language, then, consists of some aspect of content or *meaning*, that is coded or represented by linguistic structures in order to function for the exchange of ideas. The important catalyst is *not the child's experience with language*, but rather his experience and interaction *with his environment*. Stated this way, the implication is obvious that children need experiences, which, in turn need labels—language. It is *the thought* in the language learner's mind that needs language form. It is the child's own experiences, his own ideas, that need structure. It means "tuning in" to the child and matching his thoughts with language.

All children learn language gradually. They acquire the "bits and pieces," as it were, over time as a result of exposure to linguistic data in meaningful situations (Brown, 1977). Somehow hearing children relate the data to significant objects and events around them. They understand the *meaning* and thus attach significance to the linguistic form (Macnamara, 1972). They observe and learn, and eventually they begin to produce utterances. The child's task is seen as being that of matching the organization of language with the cognitive organization drawn from his experience. This is made possible, Wells (1974) argues, as does Cromer (1976), because the organization of meaning within the language system is closely related to the universal categories of early experience.

Two fundamentally different strategies may be employed by very young children in learning the form of language. Most of the basic assumptions underlying the study of children's language development, however, have provided means for dealing with only one of these strategies: that which proceeds from the parts of the whole (analytic). Like Peters (1977), I would argue that children proceed from the whole to the parts (Gestalt) in producing much of their early language. Further evidence for a Gestalt strategy exists in the literature (Bloom, 1970; de Villiers, 1978; Ferguson & Farell, 1975; Nelson, 1973). Language behavior is furthermore heavily influenced by external forces. It appears to be the result of a fine process of interaction between child and caregiver which begins at birth. The first language teacher, who is the parent, purposely or not, presents the linguistic data to the child. She provides carefully circumscribed kinds of data and presents them selectively in correspondence with his language growth. The most striking characteristic of parental speech is its relevance to the child, his needs, and his environment. Thus the child understands the meaning behind the early utterances.

There is still another important area of concern in language behavior—its function. Historically, vocabulary was the first interest of students of child language; they soon moved to structure, syntax in particular; and currently there is a realization that you cannot divorce structure from content. While we have in the past decades learned much about the form of language, we are only very recently paying attention to its functions. We have been distracted from concern with how language is used, that is, the pragmatic or sociolinguistic component as it relates to early stages of language. I believe, as does Bruner, (1975) that linguistic concepts are first realized in action.

The very young infant uses vocalization to get people to come to him and provide for him. These early contingent interactive experiences provide a powerful motivation for language development. The child orders his world successively by vocalizations, verbalizations, words, and ultimately sentences. The interaction is only perceived by the infant as contingent if the parent plays her role.

Parents need to recognize their role as responders, providers, expanders, and sources of utterances while interacting with their child. They serve as reinforcers of the linguistic behavior of their child in terms of responding and, thereby, stimulating vocal and verbal productivity and shaping his responses.

We believe these goals are best attained through procedures designed to enhance the functioning of parents as parents, and not as substitute teachers. Rather, the task for the parent is to be sensitive to the child's experiential background as it provides stimuli for language acquisition and for reinforcing the vocal and verbal productions accordingly.

We see the training of parents of hearing impaired children for the role, proceeding in the direction of fostering (1) function, (2) content, (3) form, and (4) language behavior.

Language Function

The child's first step in speech production is not language learning *per se*. Rather, he learns to communicate in order to control and manipulate actual people and objects in his environment to satisfy his own needs. To achieve this he will seize any device, linguistic or otherwise, that enhances his ability. He learns, that is, the function of communication before he learns the language itself. He acquires language as a means of getting attention and regulating activity.

Recent work such as that reported by Halliday (1975), Dore (1975), Bates (1976), and Bruner (1978) has moved deliberately into the pragmatics of child language. This apparently stems from dissatisfaction with approaches limited to syntactic or semantic consideration and from a concern to explore early communicative behaviors and cognitive abilities that might precede or accompany language behavior. Francis (1979) asks that while we are studying the form of children's utterances we look at both the intentional and conventional aspects of children's linguistic behavior as well.

It is my belief that children learn language in order to use it to manipulate people. Slobin (1971) agrees and adds that the child also uses language to describe his world. Vygotsky (1962) saw primary function of speech in both children and adults as communication and social contact.

Several statements by Watts (1964) about language use are worthy of serious consideration:

> The functions of language cannot be summed up in a sentence or two . . . . Indeed, language has been devised and developed for all kinds of uses; for exciting attention, for the expression of feeling, for graphic description, for conveying instructions, for service in stipulation, for rhythmic delight, for gossip, and for abuse. p. 24

> The difficulty, as children encounter it, is that the language required for general discussion comes easily only to those accustomed to comparing freely with one another the ideas which they have separately experienced, so that when experience is scanty and discussion rare, this kind of language is not readily acquired. As long as children need language merely for telling what they have seen or heard done, without attempting to summarize it briefly or to express any judgment about it, they will have little or no need for words, other than those which call up pictorial images of concrete things and events. p. 35

It was the function of language that prompted Moog (1979) to plead with parents and teachers to listen to their child and so motivate him to talk. Two decades ago Groht (1958) wrote that the child talks because he is motivated to tell something, to find out something, to express an idea or desire, to promote companionship, or sometimes just to hear himself talk.

Listening is another role that parents must acquire. Only then can the child discover that people in his immediate environment can be responsive to his indication of needs. It is also the parent's role to help the child consciously learn to make his needs known.

The needed skills of parents range from interpreting the child's vocalizations as signals for actions, differentiating among vocalizations as indicators of needs, listening to his jargon, and interpreting it, to asking questions and getting vocal responses.

Language Content

The three components of language—content, form, and function—begin as essentially separate threads of development early in the child's development. They become increasingly coordinated as linguistic ability develops. Progress comes not from instruction but from the child's increasing contact with language examples in interactions from which he begins to abstract commonalities. Words tag the processes by which the child deals with his environment. The dealing with the environment—the content—comes first.

The precursors of language content or meaning have to do with what children learn about objects and relations between objects. These concepts become progressively more complex as the child experiences more, but they originate in actions which should be fulfilling, bonding, and pleasurable for both parent and child.

Language content is composed of words, labels; as Bloom (1978) likes to call them, *topics*. The topics may be objects (cookies, toys, Mommy, etc.); or they may be actions (throw, eat, hit, etc.); or they can be possessions (Johnny and his shoe, dog and his bone). "Johnny's shoe" may be a label within the topic, but the *content* represented in the message has to do with the concept of possessive relation as well as "shoeness" and Johnny.

Content is the totality of the process in which the child is engaged. It is the *what* of communication and should be considered as different from how people talk or why they do it. While language may not be necessary in order to develop concepts, language behavior, nevertheless, is entirely dependent upon having the content. The important catalyst is not the child's experience *with language*; rather, it is his experience and interaction *with his environment*. Language serves to mark the cognitive distinctions made by a child.

Labeling must accompany experiences. For a child to incorporate a verb, as "wash," into his language behavior, he needs multiple experiences with washing—his face and hands, his clothes, the breakfast dishes, the dog, the windows, the floor, the car. In order to be able to talk about washing at some time hence, he needs to store the implements, the actions, as well as the efforts. "Wash" applied to a pantomime of washing hands does not give children either the perceptual or conceptual construct of the cleansing experience.

Simply identifying "cookie" as different from "ball" or "fish" does not provide the child with the necessary content that is contingent. Cookies may be something the child wants, or wants more of. Beyond the eating, he needs to experience that cookies may be baked, broken, crumbled, stacked, counted, iced, offered, bought, carried, etc. They may be chocolate, vanilla, peanut butter, with or without nuts, frosted or not; square, round, or double; in the cookie box or a bag; brought by grandma or headed for sister's lunch box. The objects, agents, actions, possessions, relations, locations, all are based on the content—the experience. The language only aids in categorizing it.

The parents' role is obvious. They must convey to the hearing-impaired child the timely and pertinent linguistic "data" for the experience. They need to tailor their speech so that he accumulates the necessary input for later rule extraction. Comprehension does exceed production, and with the shared experience the task is just that of comprehending the language, not the conceptualization.

I believe that the child needs to store the perceptual aspects as well as the global language in his memory along with the experience. While the labels for the experience may not be clearly received the first time, he should have many opportunities with similar experiences in order to later be able to sort and interrelate them. Conceptual and linguistic development interact. A parent must provide opportunities for the child to categorize on the basis of perceptual, functional features. The repetition of daily home events, so monotonous to many mothers, is the necessary environment for conceptualizations and language interaction to take place.

Linguistic Form

The current view that language learning is a result of the environment in which parents present the important linguistic information to the child, strongly counters Chomsky's (1957) theory that language learning is heavily influenced by forces within the child. While the ability to learn language may be innate, the data he receives are presented in a relatively orderly way. The child is not at first confronted with all of the complexity and variety of natural language. It is asserted, on the contrary, that mother introduces forms in a more or less principled way (Lovelt, 1975). She uses different forms and speech than she uses with adults and older children (Phillips, 1973). She uses simpler sentences which tend to be short until the child lengthens his. She is redundant and repetitious. She repeats nouns rather than using pronouns, but uses "we" instead of "I". She uses value words heavily marked with exaggerated intonation (Gleason, 1973). The mother, in general, uses a greater range of pitch, and gives longer duration to speech than with older children with pronounced segmentation (Garnica, 1977).

The role of the parent of the hearing impaired child is no different. She, too, needs to provide language forms in her model. The results of our training for the role can be seen in the Anderson (1979) study. When she compared the data on parents of hearing impaired children to those of Snow (1977) who used normally hearing children, Anderson concluded that maternal speech to the two groups was "strikingly similar." This conclusion was based on measures of the percentage of questions and commands in the mother's speech, the referential features, the extent of content repetition, and the number of occasions on which the mothers attempted to elicit responses.

Fostering Language Behavior

Language addressed to young language-learning children has been shown to be significantly different from ongoing language directed to adults. Nevertheless, the determinants of the differences are not well understood. Cross (1979) believes that maternal speech is adjusted to the communicative, and particularly the receptive, maturity of the child. Snow (1977), however, challenges the linguistic feedback hypothesis. She believes mothers make changes in their language model on the basis of reciprocity. They perceive the child's turn in the "conversational" system to be smiling, laughing, or vocalizing. Both agree that the parents' adjustment is not to the child's chronological age.

In either event, the mother's performance is highly tuned to the child's level of performance. Bruner (1978) has pointed out, for example, that the less receptive the child is, the more the mother checks by expanding on what the child said as if to confirm, resulting in a negatively high correlation between receptivity and expansions. Greenbam and Landau (1973) found the forms of discourse used by mothers tend to disappear to a minimal point the moment the child begins to respond to them. Then parents use purposeful speech which is a match of what they believe the child wants to say.

A deaf child can complicate mother's speech. He is less receptive and can be inattentive to mother's input. However, I believe that the task of training parents for this role requires understanding of procedures used with language-learning hearing children and adapting it to the hearing impaired. I concur with Brown (1977) who concluded his chapter in Snow and Ferguson's (1977) text by answering the question, "How can a concerned mother facilitate her child's learning of language?"

> Believe that your child can understand more than he or she can say, and seek, above all, to communicate. To understand and be understood. To keep your minds fixed on the same target. In doing that, you will, without thinking about it, make 100 or maybe 1000 alterations in your speech and action. Do not try to practice them as such. There is no set of rules of how to talk to a child that can even approach what you unconsciously know. If you concentrate on communicating, everything else will follow. p. 26

While this is the ideal spot at which to stop, I was assigned the task of addressing language acquisition by the Under-Fives.

Language Acquisition of the Under-Fives

The role of the parent is essentially that of providing receptive language, but when we shift the focus of the child we more often address the production factor because it is unknown how to measure competence. Instead we, like everyone else, measure performance.

We notice that the first words of the children are basically what Ricks (1975) calls "dada words." They have loose referents and may even appear to have babble-like qualities with no referent at all. Our children tend to use the obvious lip movement "bababa" type of utterances. Frequently the parents interpret these utterances and read into them meaning, but often it is a case of being prone to read too much into the child's endeavor. Unlike Ricks' description, these children do not move quickly into the second type of word which he calls "label" words. With his subjects he found the label word occurring along with the event for which it was the label. For some of the children, who move into the Central Institute for the Deaf preschool, there is a need to teach the initial "label" words in a more or less structured setting. For all of the children, however, the concept behind the "label" usually has been experienced. In addition to the structured speech, lipreading and auditory training sessions, the children participate in class activities which follow a global approach (Simmons, 1973).

Instructional objectives for each child are established based upon the observation and description of the child's communication abilities. *The Scales of Early Communication Skills for Hearing-Impaired Children* (Moog & Geers, 1975) is a criterion-referenced instrument which is used to help the teacher precisely describe her observations of the communication skills of a particular child. Using these observations as a basis, the teacher then establishes speech and languages objectives for the child and selects appropriate techniques for reaching these objectives. The child's response to particular techniques and content is used to guide the teacher in planning future instruction.

Since the Scales will be described in the section on Language Testing, I shall report on the findings of Dr. Geers when she analyzed the language of the young children at Central Institute for the Deaf for an Office of Education, Bureau of Education for the Handicapped validation report. In the interest of accuracy, I shall quote directly from her report (Geers, 1977):

> The following profile characterizes the growth of the average child enrolled in the CID early education program for 2½ years or longer.
>
> The average 2-year-old in this program comprehends and expresses himself at level I on the scales. He demonstrates his awareness that the mouth and voice convey information, although he cannot understand or produce spontaneously any real words. He is, however, beginning to imitate a few syllables or words with considerable effort.
>
> At 3 the child understands and uses a few words or expressions (e.g., "bye-bye" or "mama") in natural situations. He is able to imitate a variety of words fairly easily when they are presented in isolation. By the time he is 4, the average child in this sample is rated as having "caught on" to learning new words. However, the acquisition of new words is still rather slow and labored. He is beginning to express his ideas verbally in one-word utterances, mostly nouns. He is able to imitate two- to three-word phrases, although he does not yet use them in his spontaneous speech.
>
> The 5-year-old is able to acquire new comprehension vocabulary in the context of phrases and sentences. At this point he begins learning new words after only a few presentations. He understands more than 20 different words in almost any context. He is now combining words into two–three word phrases to express his ideas and is able to imitate both the noun and the verb together in a sentence-like manner in his spontaneous speech. He is beginning to use a variety of verbs, either preceding (verb-object) or following (subject-verb), a variety of nouns. He is able to imitate at least four words of a sentence, including a noun, the verb, and a modifying word or phrase.
>
> Further development of oral language beyond this level involves increasing the length and complexity of sentences and acquiring facility with connected discourse. The steady linear increase in the scores of this group of children leads one to extrapolate that the average child will reach this level of fluency before he is 9 years old. Many of the children in this sample reached the highest level of fluency on some scales at a considerably younger age.
>
> In general, the longitudinal evaluation of language scores of 54 hearing impaired children at Central Institute for the Deaf supported the validity of the project for hearing impaired children.

Conclusion

Nevertheless, we believe we have established a solid empirical base of the attitudes and procedures discussed in this paper. The evidence from the achievements and adjustments of children who have experienced our program encourages us to continue our efforts as described and also, of course, to improve our procedures. Our continuing search for objective measures of results should contribute to this end.

References

Altshuler, K. Psychiatry and problems of deafness. In Brian Bolton (Ed.), *Psychology of deafness for rehabilitation counselors*. Baltimore: University Park Press, 1976.

Anderson, B. Parents' strategies for achieving conversational interactions with their young hearing-impaired children. In A. Simmons-Martin & D. Calvert (Eds.), *Parent-infant intervention: Communication disorders*. New York: Grune & Stratton, 1979.

Bates, E. *Language and context: The acquisition of pragmatics*. New York: Academic Press, 1976.

Bloom, L., & Lahey, M. *Language development and language disorders*. New York: John Wiley & Sons, 1978.

Blount, B., & Padgug, E. Prosodic, paralinguistic and interactional features in parent-child speech: English and Spanish. *Journal of Child Language*, 1977, 4, 67–96.

Brown, R. Introduction to *Talking to children: Language input and acquisition*. Cambridge: Cambridge University Press, 1977.

Bruner, J. The ontogenesis of speech arts. *Journal of Child Language*, 1975, 2, 1–21.

Chomsky, N. *Syntactic structures*. The Hague: Mouton, 1957.

Clarke-Stewart, K. Interactions between mothers and their young children: Characteristics and consequences. *Monographs of the Society for Research in Child Development*, 1973, 38 (153), 6–7.

Clouser, R. The effect of vowel consonant ration and sentence length on lipreading ability. *American Annals of the Deaf*, 1976, 121, 513–518.

Cromer, R. The cognitive hypothesis of language acquisition and its implications for child language deficiency. In D. Morehead & A. Morehead (Eds.), *Normal and deficient child language*. Baltimore: University Park Press, 1976.

Cross, T. Mothers' speech adjustments: The contribution of selected child listener variables. In C. Snow & C. Ferguson (Eds.), *Talking to children: Language input and acquisition*. New York: Cambridge University Press, 1977.

Davis, H., & Silverman, S. *Hearing and deafness*. New York: Holt, Rinehart & Winston, 1970.

Deutsch, M. The role of social class in language development and cognition. *American Journal of Orthopsychiatry*, 1965, 35, 78–88.

de Villiers, J., & de Villiers, P. *Language acquisition*. Cambridge, MA: Harvard University Press, 1978.

Dore, J. Holophrases, speech acts, and language universals. *Journal of Child Language*, 1975, 2, 21–40.

Dunn, J., & Richards, M. Observations on the developing relationship between mother and baby in the neonatal period. In H. Schaffer (Ed.), *Studies in mother-infant interaction*. New York: Academic Press, 1977.

Eimas, P. Developmental studies of speech perception. In L. Cohen & P. Salapatek (Eds.), *Infant perception*. New York: Academic Press, in press.

Erber, N. Auditory and audiovisual reception of words in low-frequency noise by children with normal hearing and by children with impaired hearing. *Journal of Speech and Hearing Research*, 1971, *14*, 496–512.

Erber, N. Effects of angle, distance, and illumination in visual reception of speech by profoundly deaf children. *Journal of Speech and Hearing Research*, 1974, *17*, 99–112.

Erber, N. The use of audio tape-cards in auditory training for hearing-impaired children. *The Volta Review*, 1976, *78*, 209–218.

Erber, N. Speech perception by profoundly hearing-impaired children. *Journal of Speech and Hearing Disorders*, 1979, *44*(3), 255–270.

Ferguson, C., & Farwell, C. Words and sounds in early language acquisition. *Language*, 1975, *51*, 419–439.

Francis, H. What does the child mean? A critique of the "functional" approach to langaage acquisition. *Journal of Child Language*, 1979, *6*, 201–210.

Friedlander, B. Receptive language development in infancy: Issues and problems. *Merrill-Palmer Quarterly*, 1970, *16*, 7–51.

Friedlander, B. Finding facts of value and value in facts. In A. Simmons-Martin & D. Calvert (Eds.), *Parent-infant intervention: Communication disorders*. New York: Grune & Stratton, 1979.

Fry, D. Speech. *Proceedings of the International Congress on Education of the Deaf*, 1963, 183–191.

Garnica, O. Some prosodic and paralinguistic features of speech to young children. In C. Snow & C. Ferguson (Eds.), *Talking to children: Language input and arquisition*. New York: Cambridge University Press, 1977.

Geers, A. *Early education for the handicapped*. Unpublished validation report, 1977.

Geers, A. Evaluation of educational effectiveness at the pre-school level—is it possible? In A. Simmons-Martin & D. Calvert (Eds.), *Parent-infant intervention: Communication disorders*. New York: Grune & Stratton, 1979.

Gleason, J. Code switching in children's language. In T. E. Moore (Ed.), *Cognitive development and the acquisition of language*. New York: Academic Press, 1973.

Goldberg, S. Premature birth: Consequences for the parent-infant relationship. *American Scientist*, 1979, *67*, 214–220.

Greenbam, C., & Landau, R. Mother's speech and the early development of vocal behavior: Findings from a cross-cultural observation study in Israel. In *Cultural and social influences in infancy and early childhood* (Burg Wartenstein Symposium No. 57). New York: Wenner-Gren Foundation for Anthropological Research, 1973.

Greenstein, J., Greenstein, B., McConville, K., & Stellini, L. *Mother-infant communication and language acquisition in deaf infants*. New York: Lexington School for the Deaf, 1976.

Groht, M. *Natural language for deaf children*. Washington, DC: A.G. Bell Association for the Deaf, 1958.

Halliday, M. *Learning how to mean: Explorations in the development of language*. London: Edward Arnold, 1975.

Heider, F., & Heider, G. An experimental investigation of lipreading. *Psychology Monograph*, 1940, *52*, 124–153.

Hunt, J. *Intelligence and experience*. New York: Ronald, 1961.

Kaplan, E., & Kaplan, G. The prelinguistic child. In J. Eliot (Ed.), *Human development and cognitive processes*. New York: Holt, Rinehart & Winston, 1971.

Kaye, K. Toward the origin of dialogue. In H. Schaffer (Ed.), *Studies in mother-infant interaction*. New York: Academic Press, 1977.

Kuhl, P. Speech perception in early infancy: The acquisition of speech sound categories. In S. Hirsh, D. Eldridge, I. Hirsh, & S. Silverman (Eds.), *Hearing and Davis: Essays honoring H. Davis*. St. Louis: Washington University Press, 1976.

Levelt, W. *What became of Lad?* The Hague: Peter de Redder Press, 1975.
Lewis, M., & Rosenblum, L. *The effects of the infant on its caregiver.* New York: Wiley & Sons, 1974.
Lewis, M. Emerging perspectives in infant and toddler development: Implications for the young handicapped child. Unpublished presentation made at conference, Columbia University, 1979.
Macnamara, J. The cognitive basis of language learning children. *Psychological Review,* 1972, *79,* 1–13.
Moog, J., & Geers, A. *The scales of early communication skills for hearing-impaired children.* St. Louis: Central Institute for the Deaf, 1975.
Moog, J. Listening: A critical aspect of communication. In A. Simmons-Martin & D. Calvert (Eds.), *Parent-infant intervention: Communication disorders.* New York: Grune & Stratton, 1979.
Morse, P. The discrimination of speech and non-speech stimuli in early infancy. *Journal of Experimental Child Psychology,* 1972, *14,* 477–492.
Nelson, K. Structure and strategy in learning to talk. *Monographs of the Society for Research in Child Development,* 1973, *38*(149), 1, 2.
Newson, J. An intersubjective approach to the systematic description of mother-infant interaction. In H. Schaffer (Ed.), *Mother-infant interaction.* New York: Academic Press, 1977.
Pesonen, J. Phoneme communication of the deaf. *Annals of the Finnish Academy of Science,* 1968, *2*(series B), 151.
Peters, A. Language learning strategies: Does the whole equal the sum of the parts? *Language,* 1977, *53*(3), 560–573.
Phillips, J. Syntax and vocabulary of mother's speech to young children: Age and sex comparison. *Child Development,* 1973, *44,* 182–185.
Ricks, D. *The beginnings of vocal communication in infants and autistic children.* Unpublished doctoral dissertation, University of London, 1972.
Risberg, A. *Hearing loss and auditory capacity.* Unpublished paper presented at the Research Conference on Speech-Processing Aids for the Deaf, Gallaudet College, Washington, DC, 1977.
Simmons, A. Content subjects through language. In H. Kopp (Ed.), *Curriculum, cognition and content.* Washington, DC: A.G. Bell Association, 1975.
Simmons-Martin, A. *Chats with Johnny's parents.* Washington, DC: A.G. Bell Association, 1975.
Simmons-Martin, A. Natural language and auditory input. In F. Bess (Ed.), *Childhood deafness: Causation, assessment and management.* New York: Grune & Stratton, 1977.
Simmons-Martin, A. Early management procedures for the hearing-impaired child. In F. Martin (Ed.), *Pediatric audiology.* Englewood Cliffs, NJ: Prentice-Hall, 1978.
Slobin, D. *Psycholinguistics.* Glenview, IL: Scott, Foresman & Co., 1971.
Snow, C. Mothers' speech research: From input to interaction. In C. Snow & C. Ferguson (Eds.), *Talking to children: Language input and acquisition.* New York: Cambridge University Press, 1977.
Stern, D. A micro-analysis of mother-infant interaction. *Journal of the American Academy of Child Psychiatry,* 1971, *10,* 501–517.
Stern, D. Mother and infant at play. In M. Lewis & L. Rosenblum (Eds.), *The origins of behavior* (volume I). New York: John Wiley & Sons, 1974.
Vygotsky, L. *Thought and language.* Cambridge, MA: M.I.T. Press, 1962.
Watts, A. *The language and mental development of children.* Harrap, 1964.
Webster, D. Neonatal sound deprivation affects brain stem auditory nuclei. *Archives of Otolaryngology,* 1977, 103.
Wells, G. Learning to code experience through language. *Journal of Child Language,* 1974, *1,* 243–269.

White, B., & Watts, J. *Experience and environment: Major influences on the development of the young child.* Englewood Cliffs, NJ: Prentice-Hall, 1973.

White, B. *The first three years of life.* Englewood Cliffs, NJ: Prentice-Hall, 1975.

Zeiser, M., & Erber, N. Auditory/vibratory perception of syllabic structure in words by profoundly hearing-impaired children. *Journal of Speech and Hearing Research,* 1977, 20, 430–436.

reaction to 10

susan schmid-giovannini

If we consider parents as appropriate therapists for youngsters with impaired hearing, we have to think about the possibilities of training them as early as possible so that they may function as the first teacher of their child. Most of the educational centers have already been doing this task for some time or have started recently. It is known and can be found in literature, what kind of support we have to ask parents to give to their children. We are able to give them examples about how to teach their child to use his voice and his hearing, and how to develop his skills and different talents. There are many experienced therapists who give such advice, together with material needed for this training, to parents and youngsters. There are already many places where early detection and parent training are being carried out in practice and not just "on paper" as directed by different government authorities. Still we meet with many difficulties in encouraging parents to work with their child in an appropriate way from the very start. There are many reasons why the teamwork: parents-therapist-doctor-psychologist doesn't function the way it could. I would like to talk about two reasons which I think are the most important in respect to the development of a deaf child: gaining knowledge and accepting advice and practicing both of them in daily life; and the education of the public.

I'm not one who believes in theoretical instructions to parents (the closest environment of the child) and community. Neither the intellectual nor the social level of parents is the important point in starting their education in the training of their deaf child. Parents can read about different methods, comprehend them thoroughly and finally find one suitable for their child and themselves. They can learn to use their skills and talents completely for the benefit of the child and still find themselves asking one day: "How on earth can I explain to my child the meaning of a special word or phrase, a situation or a thought?" Very often they search high and low getting further and further away from their normal daily life in order to find a solution for their problems. Frequently the only results are a lot of trouble, uncertainty and, finally, giving up.

If teachers claim that professional literature is nothing to confront parents with, that idea is not so absurd as one may think. But one must take into consideration that the same difficulties can be expected if advice is given only orally to parents, and professionals as well, and not demonstrated in an appropriate situation.

Even if parents are able to understand the professional literature pretty well, they still may have difficulty in transferring their theoretical knowledge into practice in situations in their daily life. It is not easy, even for professionals to accept advice, given in a book or by a therapist, and use it as a basis of instruction for their child and for themselves. There is a difference between reading or hearing about a method used for the education of deaf youngsters, and using the same method, or giving the same treatment to your own child. For a professional to use a certain method and treatment for a pupil doesn't involve his or her privacy, but to educate your own child in this way means that you yourself have to deal with the thoughts given to you, the actions asked from you, at every hour of the day, in every situation of your daily life. There is no way of forgetting that you have a handicapped child. In such a situation parents, teachers, therapists and, of course, the child, need an understanding environment. Parents are in a crisis. What is the parent's reaction to this special crisis and what is the reaction of the environment? Dr. Shontz, Professor of Psychology at the University of Kansas, found that the impact of the knowledge of a child's deafness may be a traumatic event for the parents—and they may experience some or all of the phenomena described by him and his colleague, Dr. Fink. Why is it such a shock? Why do parents not have the remotest notion or expectation of having a deaf child? There is no doubt, for example, that, in the life of a community a tornado, a flood, or an earthquake denotes a crisis. But somehow these crises are expected whereas deafness is never expected by parents with normal hearing. There are so many reasons that we can hardly touch on the problem. But one of the many I think we may be able to discuss during this conference, is: informing society.

Murphy said in 1962:

> We can say that the child creates his identity through his efforts in coming to terms with his environment in his own personal way. Parents are part of this environment and before they become parents of a deaf child they are as unaware of the needs of a deaf person as anyone else in their community. Everything which will be said about the behavior of that community towards the deaf child and his parents could, in most cases, be said about the parents, too. Thus, in my opinion, the training of parents has to be started even before they know that they have a deaf child. It should be some kind of basic education given, not only in words, but together with practical examples.

We should try to discover a way of explaining to the public better than has been done before, that any couple could have a deaf child. It doesn't depend on where his ancestors came from nor how much his father earns. Also, the public should know that a deaf child is nothing to be ashamed of; he is neither contagious nor evil, but can be educated and grow up as loving, talented, and skilled as any other child. In my opinion, if the public no longer looks down on such a child anymore—nor on its parents, the crisis will become *less traumatic* for parents and child, the facts less hard to bear for parents confronted with the knowledge of the deafness of their child. As it is, parents have not only to overcome the shock of dealing with a deaf child, but also to see themselves confronted with a society which still believes more in *charity towards,* than in *association with,* the handicapped. There are two sides of the coin: spending some money and visiting institutes and schools for the deaf or spending a day together with a handicapped person as a partner. There is an even larger gulf between being a companion for a day and true friendship, between listening to something a deaf person has to say and asking him and answering his questions, and the sharing of thoughts and feelings. There is a difference for many a teacher in talking to and with their pupils and accepting them out of school, and later, as adults, as an equal partner, a fellow creature who can handle his own business.

# 11

the development of language by deaf children, ages 6 to 16 years

sister joyce buckler

Introduction

To speak to the subject of language development by deaf children 6 through 16 is to span, in my analysis, three stages of language development. The 6 and 7-year-old profoundly, prelingually deaf child is, in many instances, still developing a sense of language. He continues to require a great deal of adult modeling, in conjunction with somewhat structured language forms in order to express his thoughts in appropriate and correct language. Between the ages of 8 and 12, the profoundly deaf child, who has developed a sense of language structure, has the need and the capability for more complex language to express his more complex levels of thought and to deal with the increased variety of his daily interests and experiences both receptively and expressively in speech and in writing. At this time in his life, the child's experiences are reaching beyond himself and his family into the broader world of the newspaper, television, and independent reading. By age 13, a child who has a command of the natural flow of language and is able to express his thoughts in well-ordered language, is at the stage of extensive vocabulary enrichment, advanced levels of reading and writing, of literature, and of creative written composition.

The challenge to the deaf child is to move, as naturally and painlessly as possible, through these stages of language growth. The responsibility of his teachers is to be knowledgeable of the rules of linguistic structure, to be aware of the sequence of language development, and to be able to provide the child at his readiness periods the required input, modeling, rules and resources for his growth in expressive oral language independence and richness.

Philosophy of language. How this challenge of richness in linguistic expression is met by profoundly deaf children varies with individual school systems, depending on the sophistication of the staff and the basic philosophy of language development followed. As described by Kretschmer & Kretschmer (1978) and by Dr. Ling at this Symposium, approaches to language teaching range from apparently non-structured, non-directive language programs to formalized, developmental, linguistic-based language curricula.

The task of this Symposium is not only to meet the challenges of language development in profoundly, prelingually deaf children, but to achieve this task within a specific philosophy, that of oral language. In assisting children to understand and use oral language, we must also develop the auditory potential of children, in order to bring them to a sufficiently sophisticated level of spoken and written language with a speech quality understandable to the 'man on the street.'

Our goal is to determine how best to prepare these deaf children to become an integral part of society, to enable them, by age 15 or 16 at the latest, to mainstream successfully into regular educational programs. We need to make it possible for our graduates to have choices as adults, to have the option of becoming full participators in our hearing society, or to move in and out of the "hearing" and "deaf" worlds. That a deaf adult might choose to live in the isolated "world of the deaf" is a possibility, but that our lack of quality oral education forces this choice on young deaf men and women must not occur.

Assumptions. This presentation on the development of language from ages 6 to 16 is based on specific assumptions:

(1) That the children are from caring families—families who have had some type of support in living with and communicating with their deaf youngster;

(2) That the children are of normal intelligence and above;

(3) That they have had, and continue to have, appropriate binaural amplification;

(4) That the children spend 100 percent of their lives in a truly oral environment;

(5) That the children have had early education no later than 3½ years of age;

(6) That no other handicap is more dominant than the hearing impairment;

(7) That teachers have received their teacher education in a program having an auditory-oral philosophy, and that these teachers have a knowledge and understanding of normal language development as well as the knowledge and awareness of the language development of profoundly deaf children;

(8) That the teachers' practicum centers were those based on the oral philosophy of education;

(9) That the teachers are at ease with an eclectic approach to teaching;

(10) That the staff and families of the children are united in their commitment to oralism as an appropriate, successful approach in assisting children in their task of language development;

(11) That the staff is knowledgeable of the relationship of language and thought, the relationship of oral and written language, the relationship between

receptive and expressive language, and the role of vocabulary development and reading in the development of language;
 (12) That the children are expected to use their oral skills at all times;
 (13) That there is a consistent approach to language teaching at all levels; and
 (14) That each person on the staff has realistic, yet high expectations of the children.

Decision. When teachers are met with the responsibility of planning a language program for children, a basic framework of approach is required, a philosophical orientation is necessary. This framework and orientation are an outgrowth of experience, of past successes and failures, and of reading and study in the area of language, as analyzed and defined by experts in and students of the field of language such as Bloom (1970), Menyuk (1971), Simmons (1968), Blackwell, et al. (1978), Quigley, et al. (1976), van Uden (1977), Russell, et al. (1976), and the Kretschmers (1978).

A staff is forced, appropriately so, to make decisions, based on this experience and study, as to the language approach to be used. Not to come to such a decision and to carry it out on a daily basis in the classroom is to be a victim of 'changing winds' and to deny deaf students a sense of direction in their language development. This tendency to continually change one's approach to language teaching is, I believe, a partial cause for the less than adequate linguistic competence and performance in profoundly deaf children across the United States. Experienced, successful teachers of deaf children have often been heard to say that "Any approach to language teaching will work, if you believe in it and you are consistent in using it." I support this statement.

An equally detrimental practice in language teaching, however, is to become so rigid and so inflexible in one's philosophy of language teaching that the "new winds" are disregarded and looked upon as having no value, as having no impact in an already established program.

An openness to new ideas, and flexibility in searching for better ways to teach our children supports the concept that language is a dynamic process and suggests that a language program is never finished, that each year finds a staff reanalyzing and reorganizing its language curriculum.

Language learning environment. Take a few moments to imagine a teacher and a student teacher or aide with a class of 6 to 8 deaf pupils. They are seated in a semi-circle facing the teacher and are wearing either earphones or individual hearing aids. The children are listening or listening and speechreading. They are interacting orally with the teacher and with one another. The teacher, if the children are using group amplification, is holding a microphone and the children have easy access (one between every two pupils) to a microphone. The teacher has definite objectives written in behavioral terms for it is the children's performance, not the teacher's, which is the goal of language teaching.

The teacher, though this fact is invisible to the children, is in reality a juggler and/or a clown for she must be able to "balance" all aspects of language in any one lesson; she must be able to automatically and with ease produce "many balloons of different colors and sizes" in order to reach her language objectives while at the same time be sufficiently flexible to allow the language lesson to take unexpected turns as the children's needs and interests indicate. She must, in fact, use the *seizing method* described by van Uden (1977, p. 29). Visualize, too, that the children are doing most of the talking, for it is they, not the teacher, who need the practice. That this oral practice does occur at St. Joseph's was shown in an analysis of classroom interaction by Buckler (1977).

Bases for a developmental language program. To develop a language program today and not take into account the works of Streng (1972), Blackwell (1978), and the Kretschmers (1978) would be to ignore exciting and extremely valuable contributions to our profession.

To insist, in face of research to the contrary (Quigley, et al., 1976; Kretschmer & Kretschmer, 1978) that no changes in language teaching are needed, even in the reportedly successful oral schools in our country, would be to deny painful facts and, even more seriously, to negatively affect the language progress of the children to whom we are responsible.

On the other hand, to discard without sufficient analyses an approach to language teaching which has been successful, which has resulted in a correct, natural flow of language in one's pupils, would be equally irresponsible. What is expected of us as professionals is that we take what is new, study it in all its aspects and implications, and accept or reject what would seem appropriate.

The majority of oral schools in the United States would best be described as using The Natural Approach (Groht, 1958) as the basis for language teaching, and supplementing or enhancing this approach with more formal systems such as The Fitzgerald Key (Fitzgerald, 1949). The Pattern (d'Arc, Sr. J., 1958; Buckler, 1968), as developed and used at St. Joseph Institute for the Deaf in St. Louis and at other schools in America and Australia, offers, in my experience, a dynamic approach for establishing and expanding the natural language of deaf children.

A Linguistic-Based Language Program. The following presentation is an approach to language teaching following the outline developed by Kretschmer & Kretschmer (1978). The use of this outline does not, however, imply an unnatural, stereotyped approach to language teaching, but is a guide for the teachers for the expressive language of the deaf child. To bind oneself to these stages would be to interfere with the unique, day-to-day language needs of the child. However, it is the experience of teachers that a general guide to the developmental stages of language is necessary. I propose that the Kretschmers' outline provides this guide.

In conjunction with the outline, therefore, the more natural approach to language is presented, namely, Show and Tell, daily news, experiences and trips, conversational language, incidental language, letter writing, composition, literature and vocabulary development. Suggestions as to content, materials, media, strategies, and levels of expectations of the 6- to 16-year-old child are also made.

Integration of conversational and formal approaches to language. Teachers of deaf children have often been heard to say: "Just tell me *what* to teach in language and I can figure out how to do it." The "Outline of Developmental Language Teaching Sequences" (Kretschmer & Kretschmer, 1978.), selected portions in Table 1 responds to that need and does so in a developmental, sequential manner. It is assumed that the participants in this symposium are familiar with *Language Development and Intervention with the Hearing Impaired* by the Kretschmers (1978). It is thus not included in the text in its entirety, but is placed in the appendix. Selected portions only are presented.

Having analyzed the Kretschmers' (1978) outline of language teaching, it is felt that children in the three age groups, 6–7, 8–12, and 13–16 would be able to deal with the sentence frames, modulations, and modalities across stages. The following outline indicates the stages found to be, in my experience, within the competency of these three age groups, Table 2. It is obvious, however, that the ages at which children achieve the various stages will be dependent on a number of factors, such as their native intelligence, their academic history, their unique talent for language development, and the levels of expectation within a particular school system.

Application of Language Outline/The Natural Approach

The application to this outline and these sequences is based on many years of classroom teaching experience by the author of this paper, ideas shared with numerous fellow teachers, and on the writings of well-known and long-respected persons in the field of education of the deaf, such as Groht (1958), Buell (1953), Fitzgerald (1949), Simmons (1968), Hogan (1968), and van Uden (1977).

The ongoing language program in its three divisions of 6–7, 8–12, and 13–16 year-olds is not rigid, nor is the Kretschmer outline the basis of the total program. See Table 3. In most programs, only a portion of the child's day is devoted to the more formal teaching of language principles. I propose that principles be developed following the sequential approach of the Kretschmer outline in conjunction with the language needs of the children, as indicated throughout the day, e.g. during Show and Tell, experiences and news, and as revealed by the child's conversational language and the incidental events continually occurring. These latter aspects of language development are dictated by the children's needs and are responded to in a global, natural, conversational manner. However, it is my experience that an overall language outline is necessary in order that the teacher, not the child, have specific developmental goals toward which he/she is working.

STRATEGIES/IDEA BOOK

Recommended for any program plan for language development is a companion book or section. Included in this second section would be strategies and/or ideas. Such a book, developed by the entire staff, would include the compilation of shared ideas and experiences and would, therefore, contain the richness derived from years of successful language teaching as well as ideas gathered from the many resources available, e.g. research by linguists, ideas from persons such as Groht, Buell, Fitzgerald, Hogan, d'Arc, and Buckler. This Idea/Strategy Book allows for the unique and creative approach of the individual teacher, who not only draws from this resource but adds to it. (At St. Joseph's, we have an idea box in the various teacher lounges.) New ideas for *how* to assist children in their language development are continually added, creating an ongoing, dynamic approach to language teaching.

TABLE 1
OUTLINE OF DEVELOPMENTAL LANGUAGE TEACHING SEQUENCES (SELECTED PORTIONS).

	Stage I	Stage II	Stage III	Stage IV	Stage V	Stage VI
Basic sentence frames						
Transitive verb frames	Agent, action-causative, patient (irreversible relationship): The boy ate the cake. Agent, action-causative, patient (reversible relationship): Mary hit Carolyn.	Agent, action-causative, complement: The boy painted a picture. Experiencer, process-causative, patient: John thought about Mary.		Experiencer, process-causative, complement: Barry thought up the idea. Lesli had a dream.		
Modulations						
Prepositions	In, on	At, from, into, onto, to, up, with	Above, across, at (time), away from, below, by, down, in (time), like, near, of, off of, on (time), out, over, over to, through, under, for	During, within, without	After, around, back of, before, behind, beside, between, beyond, except, except for, from (time), front of, to (time)	About, after (time), along, among, before (time), over (time), until
Modals		Modals indicating wish or intention: gonna, hafta (have to), lemme (let me), wanna	Modals indicating certainty and possibility: can, will, could, shall, let's	Modals indicating necessity and obligation: gotta (got to), would, might, should, better, ought to	Must (indicating obligation)	

TABLE 1
OUTLINE OF DEVELOPMENTAL LANGUAGE TEACHING SEQUENCES (SELECTED PORTIONS, CONT'D).

	Stage I	Stage II	Stage III	Stage IV	Stage V	Stage VI
Modalities Imperative (request or directive)	Requests indicating possession: That mine (Give it to me). Direct imperatives: Read the book.		Yes-no questions as request forms, usually to indicate permission to perform a task: Can I go to the movie?	Questions used as a request for clarification of previous statements or questions: Mother says: Did you go to the store? Child says: What?	Pretend directives: Pretend that is my doll. Obligation (has to) directives: You have to go. Conditional directives: If we are good, we will go outside.	Directives indicating willingness to perform: Do you wanna sit here? Directives indicating need to adjust performance: Will you move over, please? Directives indicating reason for performance: Why don't you eat supper? Directives indicating don't forget something: Don't forget to pick up the books.
Embedded questions Direct/Indirect discourse					Use of factive verbs to encode imperative messages: He told him to go. Use of factive verbs to encode declarative messages: I know that he will go.	Use of factive verbs and negation to encode imperative messages: He didn't tell him to go. Use of factive verbs and negation to encode declarative messages: I didn't know that he would go.

TABLE 2
LANGUAGE DEVELOPMENT OUTLINE BY STAGES RELATED TO AGES
Kretschmer & Kretschmer (1978)
(As adapted by Sister Joyce Buckler)

Frames/Nodes	Ages 6–7	Ages 8–12	Ages 13–16
Transitive Verb Frame	I, II	(I, II) IV	(I, II, IV
Intransitive Verb Frame	I, II	(I, II) III	(I, II, III)
Copulative Verb Frame	I, II, III	(I, II, III) V, VI	(I, II, III, V, VI
Indirect Object Frame	II, IV	(II, IV) V, VI	II, IV) VI
Passive Frame			(V, VI)
Optional Verb Nodes	I, II, III	(I, II, III) IV, V, VI	(I, II, III, IV, V, VI)
Modulations			
Prepositions	I, II, III, V (selected)	(I, II) III, IV, V	(I, II, III, IV, V) VI
Plurality	II	(II)	(II)
Tense/Auxiliary	I, II, IV	(I, II) III (IV) V, VI	(I, II, III, IV, V, VI)
Modals	II, III	(II, III) IV, V	(II, III) IV, V, VI
Determines	I, II	(I, II) III, IV, V, VI	(I, II, III, IV, V, VI)
Modalities			
Negation	I, II, III	(I, II, III) IV, VI	(I, II, III, IV, VI)
Imperative (request or directive)	I, II, III	(I, II, III) IV, V, VI	(I, II, III, IV, V, VI)
Question forms	I, II	(I, II) III, IV, V, VI	(I, II, III, IV, V, VI)
Conjoinings			
Coordinating conjunction	I	(I) II, III, IV, V	(I, II, III, IV, V) VI
Subordinate conjunctions		III, V, VI	(III, V, VI)
Elaborated Nodes			
Possession	I, II	(I, II) VI	(I, II, VI)
Embedded adjective	II, III	(II, III) IV, V, VI	(II, III, IV, V, VI)
Relative clause		II, III, IV, V, VI	(II, III, IV, V, VI)
Nominalizations: Infinitive	II, III, IV, V	II, III, IV, V (VI)	(II, III, IV, V, VI)
Nominalizations: Participle		IV, V, VI	(IV, V, VI)
Embedded questions		III	(III)
Direct/Indirect discourse		V, VI	(V, VI)
Factive clause			VI
Transformations			
Pronominalization	I, II	(I, II) III, IV, V, VI	(I, II, III, IV, V, VI)
Do-support		III, IV	(III, IV)

TABLE 3
APPLICATION OF LANGUAGE OUTLINE/THE NATURAL APPROACH
(As developed by Sister Joyce Buckler)

Ages 6–7

Language Period	Content	Materials	Expectations of the Child	Media
News	Self, home, school, world events	Objects, letters from home, newspapers, pictures, reference materials	The child will be able to: respond orally to questions, e.g., "Who wants a turn?" "Who wants to be first?" etc. repeat the language model of the teacher. answer questions in words, phrases, or sentences as demanded by the question. tell the teacher sentences to write on the board. identify the sentences through listening only. identify the sentences through listening and speechreading. copy the sentences. memorize the sentences. say the sentence from memory. write the sentence from memory.	Amplification system(s) Chalkboard Overhead projector Language Masters Tape recorders Filmstrip projectors Slide projectors Movie projectors Record players
Trips	Units, seasons, holidays, reading stories, local events, local sites, content subjects, information	Objects needed for trip, e.g. picnic lunch, baskets to collect apples, etc.	Before a trip, the child will be able to: participate in the discussion in preparation of a trip by verbalizing recognition of the experience and expressing questioning behavior. repeat the model of the teacher for the above.	

286 oral education: today and tomorrow

TABLE 3
APPLICATION OF LANGUAGE OUTLINE/THE NATURAL APPROACH (CON'D.)

Ages 6–7

Language Period	Content	Materials	Expectations of the Child	Media
Trips (cont'd.)			share in making preparation for the trip, e.g. making lunches, etc. During the trip, the child will be able to: be an active participant in the activity. express his ideas orally. repeat the models of language given by teacher.	
Experience Chart	Trips, planned activities, seasons, holidays, content areas, incidental happenings	Chart, illustrations and/or pictures, objects related to the experience	The child will be able to: respond orally to auditory input of trip/experience with the chart not in view. indicate understanding of the trip/experience as a whole by initiating ideas about the trip/experience. discriminate auditorially and/or through speechreading among sentences on the chart by repeating the sentences; pointing to it and repeating the sentences through immediate recall. model correct sentence. answer questions and auditorially and/or speechreading using the short form of the answer. identify on the chart the specific answer to the questions. discriminate and identify auditorially and/or through speechreading sentences from past charts.	

the development of language by deaf children 287

TABLE 3
APPLICATION OF LANGUAGE OUTLINE/THE NATURAL APPROACH (CONT'D.)

Ages 6–7

Language Period	Content	Materials	Expectations of the Child	Media
Calendar	Special events occurring during the month and on specific days	Calendar (monthly and/or yearly)	The child will be able to: identify important dates of the month. verbalize ideas about those dates and/or repeat the model of the teacher. identify the specific day on the calendar. express information orally e.g. Today is _____. cross off past day and express orally e.g. Yesterday was _____. identify future days and express orally e.g. Tomorrow is _____.	Amplification system(s) Chalkboard Overhead projector Language Masters Tape recorders Filmstrip projectors Slide projectors Movie projectors Record players
Weather	Unusual weather; weather that affects the children's lives	The weather	The child will be able to: notice changes in the weather. verbalize about weather conditions.	
Structured Language Period	Animals Food Rooms Furniture Body parts Classroom vocabulary Containers Sports Games	Actual objects, toy-type objects, pictures, vocabulary cards, sentence strips, charts, games, filmstrips, slides, movies, records, tapes	(Based on animal unit) The child will be able to: categorize animals according to habitat. name the animals. describe the animals orally. answer riddles about animals auditorially and/or speechreading. make up animal riddles. answer questions about animals auditorially and/or speechreading.	

TABLE 3
APPLICATION OF LANGUAGE OUTLINE/THE NATURAL APPROACH (CONT'D.)

Ages 6–7

Language Period	Content	Materials	Expectations of the Child	Media
Structured Language Period (cont'd.)	Occupations Places Clothing Holidays Seasons Toys Tools Transportation		ask questions about animals.	
Specific Vocabulary Development	Reading, content areas, e.g. science, math, religion, etc.	Actual objects, toy-type objects, pictures, vocabulary cards, sentence strips, charts, games, filmstrips, slides, movies, records, tapes	The child will be able to: match the written word to the object or picture. identify auditorially and/or speechreading words to picture and then picture to words. use vocabulary in appropriate situations and language structures.	
Incidental Language	Events as they occur	As required	The child will be able to: comment on or question about incidental happenings. use appropriate language and/or model appropriate language.	

TABLE 3
APPLICATION OF LANGUAGE OUTLINE/THE NATURAL APPROACH (CONT'D.)

Ages 6–7

Language Period	Content	Materials	Expectations of the Child	Media
Conversational Language	As this need arises	As required	The child will be able to: comment on or question about any topic. use appropriate language and/or model appropriate language. develop skills for the "turn-taking" of conversation.	Amplification system(s) Chalkboard Overhead projector Language Masters Tape recorders Filmstrip projectors Slide projectors Movie projectors Record players

Ages 8–12

Language Period	Content	Materials	Expectations of the Child	Media
News	Self, home, school, world events	Personal belongings, gifts, etc. Newspaper Weekly Reader, Sprint Reference books	The child will be able to: express himself orally in correct simple structure. express himself in writing in simple sentences. get ideas from the newspaper. comprehend the expanded language and vocabulary of the teachers. correct his oral and written language by referring to The Pattern and/or the Fitzgerald Key.	Amplification system(s) Chalkboard Overhead projector Language Masters Tape Recorders Filmstrip projectors Slide projectors Movie projectors Record players

TABLE 3
APPLICATION OF LANGUAGE OUTLINE/THE NATURAL APPROACH (CONT'D.)

Ages 8–12

Language Period	Content	Materials	Expectations of the Child	Media
News (cont'd.)			copy and memorize the developed news (4–6 sentences). answer questions about the news. write the news from memory. identify sentences from news through listening and/or speechreading. ask and answer questions about the news.	
Composition	Sequence stories Pictures Summaries of content units, films, filmstrips Human interest stories Famous people, holidays, content subjects	Composition cards (Hogan) Jack & Jill sequence pictures Family circus pictures Films Filmstrips Newspaper stories Pictures (especially Norman Rockwell prints)	The child will be able to: arrange pictures in proper sequence. write a simple sentence about each picture. correct his language by reference to The Pattern, patterned structures, and/or The Fitzgerald Key. maintain a simple idea in a paragraph. initiate and/or choose appropriate titles, beginning and ending sentences for stories/compositions. use synonyms and antonyms for enriching his composition. comprehend the expansions of language structures and vocabulary of the teacher. copy and memorize the composition developed (7–9 sentences). answer questions about the composition	

the development of language by deaf children

TABLE 3
APPLICATION OF LANGUAGE OUTLINE/THE NATURAL APPROACH (CONT'D.)

Ages 8–12

Language Periods	Content	Materials	Expectations of the Child	Media
Composition (cont'd.)			auditorially and/or through speechreading. write the composition from memory. identify sentences from composition through listening and/or speechreading. develop original composition.	
Trips	As they relate to content subjects, seasonal, holidays	Map, Leaflets Reference materials Sentence strips Markers Notebooks	The child will be able to: write to companies requesting tours, etc. identify what might be seen on a trip. follow the explanation of a tour guide. complete some type of written exercise during a trip. illustrate descriptions of trips. answer questions about a trip. ask questions of peers about a trip. complete written assignment resulting from a trip. make a scrapbook of written materials and souvenirs of a trip.	Amplification system(s) Chalkboard Overhead projector Language Masters Tape recorders Filmstrip projectors Slide projectors Movie projectors Record players
Letter Writing	Weekly letters to parents/relatives/friends	Notebooks, stationery, pens	The child will be able to: organize a letter in proper form. write a letter relating to personal, school events.	

TABLE 3
APPLICATION OF LANGUAGE OUTLINE/THE NATURAL APPROACH (CONT'D.)

Ages 8–12

Language Periods	Content	Materials	Expectations of the Child	Media
Letter Writing (cont'd.)			discriminate between appropriate news to share with parents. respond to questions and statements in letters received. use a variety of greetings and closings in letters. determine amount of postage needed for letters. write thank you letters and invitations.	
Formal Language Period	Trips and Treats (Numbers & Kennedy) Language Round-Up Language outline Language principles in content materials Seasonal sports, holidays, events (language required)	Texts for Trips & Treats Texts for Language Round-Up Textbooks: Reading Science Social Studies Religion etc. Pictures Newspaper	The child will be able to: comprehend language stories. dramatize and/or illustrate language stories. complete the written exercises in texts. use language principles in oral and written language. initiate correct original language and/or correct original language by use of The Pattern, Patterned structures, and/or The Fitzgerald Key. do written assignments applying principles of language presented.	
Specific Language Development	As related to reading stories and other content	Textbooks Thesaurus Dictionaries	The child will be able to: define known vocabulary. identify vocabulary unknown.	Amplification system(s) Chalkboard

TABLE 3
APPLICATION OF LANGUAGE OUTLINE/THE NATURAL APPROACH (CONT'D.)

Ages 8–12

Language Periods	Content	Materials	Expectations of the Child	Media
Specific Language Development (cont'd.)	materials. Lessons based on specific areas of need, e.g. sports, seasons, etc.	Pictures Reference books	illustrate and/or dramatize vocabulary. refer to a Thesaurus and/or a Dictionary for determining the meaning of words. apply learned vocabulary in new situations. memorize meanings of vocabulary words contained in content subjects.	Overhead projector Language Masters Tape recorders Filmstrip projectors Slide projectors Movie projectors Record players
Incidental Language	As the need arises	As required by the situation.	The child will be able to: express in simple structures his ideas about ongoing events. repeat language models of the teacher. refer to The Pattern, Patterned structures, and/or The Fitzgerald Key when necessary.	
Conversational Language	As the need arises	As required by the situation.	The child will be able to: interact with adults and peers in the "taking turns" of conversational situations. determine appropriateness of what is said in a conversation.	

TABLE 3
APPLICATION OF LANGUAGE OUTLINE/THE NATURAL APPROACH (CONT'D.)

Ages 13–16

Language Periods	Content	Materials	Expectations of the Child	Media
News	Self, home, school, world events	Objects of interest Newspapers Weekly Reader	The child will be able to: comprehend newspaper/Weekly Reader articles. refer to and use the various parts of a newspaper/Weekly Reader. find specific information in a newspaper/Weekly Reader. summarize newspaper/Weekly Reader articles orally and/or in writing. write independently of personal, home, school, world events (2–3 paragraphs). discuss with the teacher and/or peers personal, home, school, world events. answer questions orally and written about the above through listening and/or speechreading. ask questions orally and written about the above through listening and/or speechreading.	Amplification system(s) Chalkboard Overhead projector Language Masters Tape recorders Filmstrip projectors Slide projectors Movie projectors Record players
Composition	Summaries of content materials Human interest stories Famous places, persons, events as related to content, holidays, etc.	Text of content subjects Newspapers, television stories Films Filmstrips Pictures	The child will be able to: write compositions containing a variety of sentence structures and vocabulary (2–3 paragraphs) develop appropriate titles, beginning, and ending sentences for his compositions. summarize stories and/or units from content subjects.	

the development of language by deaf children **295**

TABLE 3
APPLICATION OF LANGUAGE OUTLINE/THE NATURAL APPROACH (CONT'D.)

Ages 13–16

Language Periods	Content	Materials	Expectations of the Child	Media
Composition (cont'd.)	American and European literary works Trips		summarize literary works read and/or seen in filmstrips and movies. ask and answer questions on the above through listening and/or speechreading.	
Letter Writing	Self, home, school, world events Letters from home, friends, relatives	Notebooks, stationery, pens Letters	The child will be able to: compose personal and business letters. compose letters containing personal, school, home, and world news. respond to questions and react to statements in letters received. organize a letter in appropriate form.	
Grammar/Formal Language Period	Language Round-up (McCormick-Mather) Language outline Language principles of content material	Language Round-Up text Texts of content subjects	The child will be able to: complete the exercises in a grammar book. identify the various parts of sentences. identify the form and the function of words in sentences. use sentences in oral and written form using specific language principles. use a variety of sentence structures to express the same thought. apply specific language structures to a variety of situations. ask and answer questions, orally and	Amplification system(s) Chalkboard Overhead projector Language Masters Tape recorders Filmstrip projectors Slide projectors Movie projectors Record players

TABLE 3
APPLICATION OF LANGUAGE OUTLINE/THE NATURAL APPROACH (CONT'D.)

Ages 13–16

Language Periods	Content	Materials	Expectations of the Child	Media
Grammar/Formal Language Period (cont'd.)			written, of adults and peers about the above.	
Vocabulary Development	Content materials Seasons, holidays, specific events, e.g. sports, trips, etc.	Texts of content subjects Pictures Reference books Thesaurus Dictionaries Films Filmstrips	The child will be able to: define known words. use a Thesaurus and/or a dictionary for identifying unknown words. use an extensive number of meanings of one word. determine meaning of words in context. do exercises in vocabulary work through listening only. do a variety of written and oral exercises involving new vocabulary. apply new vocabulary in new information in oral and written language.	
Incidental Language	As the need arises	Demanded by the need	The child will be able to: express, orally and in written form, ideas about the incidental events in his life. answer and ask questions of adults and peers about these events.	
Conversational Language	As the need arises	Demanded by the need	The child will be able to: carry on a conversation with peers and adults on a variety of topics. answer and ask questions appropriately in a conversational situation.	

the development of language by deaf children

Samples from the Idea/Strategy book are given below.

Use of *The Pattern*
- The Pattern consists of seven basic imperative forms and an almost infinite number of supplementary forms.
- As children indicate a need for these types of language structures, they are introduced.
- The initial use of The Pattern by the child is that of imitation, i.e. as she/he attempts to verbalize certain ideas, the teacher models and the child repeats. For example:

    Child: Open box (indicating a desire to open a package from home)
    Teacher: (Models) I want to open the box.
    Child: I want to open the box.
    Child: See (indicating a desire to see)
    Teacher: (Models) I want to see.
    Child: I want to see.
    - - - -
    Child: (on seeing a jump rope) I know how.
    Teacher: (Models) I know how to jump rope.
    Child: I know how to jump rope.

- As situations continue to occur showing the child's need for structures such as the above, the teacher displays patterns in the room:

    I want to [＝]
    I know how to [＝]

    These patterns, understood by the child, are then used by him to express ideas requiring such structures.
- The teacher adds to the imperative forms as they occur. For example:

    I want to [＝]
            open the box;
            go outside;
            read a book;
            be first;
            etc.

    I know how to [＝] .
            jump rope;
            ride my bike;
            play tennis;
            etc.

    When subsequently attempting to express themselves in such linguistic structures, the child is expected, if necessary, to refer to The Pattern displayed.
- Once a child is using these structures independently, reference to The Pattern is not required.
- Since the need for each expression occurs spontaneously and happens, for the most part, in conversational and/or incidental language situations, an analysis of the language is made. It is a matter of providing the child with appropriate language expressions at all times.

298 oral education: today and tomorrow

- As children move into the Middle School (ages 7 and 8 to 12), The Pattern can be developed more formally. An example is sports. The language/vocabulary involved in sports is of three types—the appropriate vocabulary, comments made by a player, comments or commands given by a coach and/or the spectators. Children involved in a particular sport need a command of all three areas. The following suggestions are made for developing these areas:
  (Basketball)

    - Take the children to the gymnasium.
    - The teacher has a set of sentence strips and pens.
    - The teacher asks the children what they know how to do in basketball.
    - They respond: I know how to bounce the ball, and demonstrates this.
    - The teacher writes: I know how to [=======] . and on a separate strip of paper writes: |dribble the ball|
    - The children then tell and demonstrate all the basketball skills they have.
    - Developing in a very natural manner will be such structures as:
      I don't know how to [=======] .
      I don't like to [=======] .
      I like to [=====] .
      It's a foul to [=====] .
      It's against the rules to [=======] .
         etc.
    - The command forms, such as:
      Dribble the ball.
      Make a basket.
      Shoot.
      Guard him.
      are the natural language of the coach and/or spectators.
    - Developed in this approach, also, is the correct vocabulary of the specific sport.

Following such a lesson, other sports can be covered. If desired, the teacher can then develop a unit on all types of sports or she/he may wish to leave such development until the appropriate season, e.g. during soccer season, baseball season, football season, etc. Each of the areas can be developed in similar fashion.

A teacher may choose, however, to develop lessons around various sports, using pictures, to assist the children in developing language, e.g.
  I like to [==========], but I don't like
       play basketball
  to [========].
     play baseball
  It's fun to [======] , but it's not fun to
          play soccer
  [=======] .
  play football

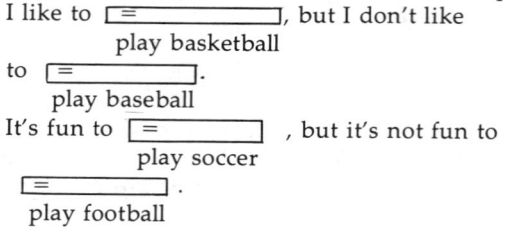

I'd rather [=] than _____
          play football   basketball
If you want to [=]
               be a good basketball player
you have to [=]
            practice;
            run fast;
            know the rules;
            obey the coach;
            grab the ball;
               etc.

In this approach to language/vocabulary development, the children must indicate a need and/or an interest. It is this need and/or interest which dictates to the teacher the extent to which such lessons should be developed.

Conclusions

The receptive language ability of children at all ages from 6 to 16 is at a much higher level than that of their expressive language. Though a teacher interacts orally with her class in language and with the variety of vocabulary at *its* level of understanding, she/he needs to be cognizant of the child's continual growth in receptive skills. Just as the normal hearing child hears language long before he is able to express himself, so the deaf child needs this exposure repeatedly before he is expected to, or in fact is capable of, expressing his thoughts in the more complex structures and the more sophisticated vocabulary.

Reading competence, though not the topic of this presentation, is directly related to a child's language and vocabulary development and with the richness of his experiences.

No presentation on language, if language is viewed from its developmentally rich potentiality, is exhaustive; language, as a dynamic process, cannot be isolated into its parts. The awareness and knowledge of the overlapping of language principles and the interlocking of linguistic constructions need to be an integral part of the style of any teacher who is dedicated to the full language growth of profoundly, prelingually deaf children. Unless this knowledge and the creative skills are present in the teacher, and are a basic philosophy of a school system, no outline, no strategy, no sequence of presentation, will succeed. If we continue our goal of preparing this creative, knowledgable kind of teacher, our dreams, our hopes, and our visions for our deaf youngsters will be realized more fully in the years ahead.

References

Blackwell, P., Engen, E., Fischgrund, J., & Zarcadoolas, C. *Sentences and other systems.* Washington, DC: Alexander Graham Bell Association for the Deaf, 1978.

Bloom, L. M. *Language development: Form and function in emerging grammars.* Cambridge, MA: M.I.T. Press, 1970.
Buckler, Sr. M. S. Expanding language through patterning. *The Volta Review,* 1968, 70, 89–96.
Buckler, Sr. J. *Interaction analysis of the discourse of hearing impaired children: Its relationship to cognitive development.* Dissertation, Teachers College, Columbia University, New York, 1977.
Buell, E. *Outline of language for deaf children* (books I, II). Washington, DC: The Volta Bureau, 1953.
d'Arc, Sr. J. The development of connected language skills with emphasis on a particular methodology. *The Volta Review,* 1958, 60, 58–65.
Fitzgerald, E. *Straight language for the deaf.* Washington, DC: Alexander Graham Bell Association for the Deaf, 1949.
Groht, M. *Natural language for deaf children.* Washington, DC: Alexander Graham Bell Association for the Deaf, 1958.
Hogan, Sr. J. *The what? when? and how? of teaching language to deaf children.* St. Louis, MO: Fontbonne College, 1968.
Kretschmer, R., & Kretschmer, L. *Language development and intervention with the hearing impaired.* Baltimore: University Park Press, 1978.
Menyuk, P. *The acquisition and development of language.* Cambridge, MA: M.I.T. Press, 1971.
Quigley, S., Wilbur, R., Power, D., Montanelli, D., & Steinkamp, M. *Syntactic structures in the language of deaf children.* Urbana, IL: Institute for Child Behavior and Development, 1976.
Russell, W., Quigley, S., & Power, D. *Linguistics and deaf children.* Washington, DC: Alexander Graham Bell Association for the Deaf, 1976.
Simmons, A. Content subjects through language. In H. G. Kopp (Ed.), *Curriculum, cognition and content.* Washington, DC: Alexander Graham Bell Association for the Deaf, 1968.
Streng, A. *Syntax, speech, and hearing.* New York: Grune & Stratton, 1972.
van Uden, A. *A world of language for deaf children.* Amsterdam: Swets & Zeitlinger, 1977.

APPENDIX 1
OUTLINE OF DEVELOPMENTAL LANGUAGE TEACHING SEQUENCES FROM KRETSCHMER & KRETSCHMER

	Stage I	Stage II
Basic sentence frames Transitive verb frames	Agent, action-causative, patient (irreversible relationship): *The boy ate the cake.* Agent, action-causative, patient (reversible relationship): *Mary hit Carolyn.* Recipient, action-causative, patient: *Connie got a present.*	Agent, action-causative, complement: *The boy painted a picture.* Experiencer, process-causative, patient: *John thought about Mary.* Possessor, Process, Patient: *Diana has a hat.*

APPENDIX 1 (CONT'D.)

	Stage I	Stage II
Basic sentence frames Transitive verb frames (cont'd.)	Experiencer, process-causative, patient/phenomenon (using no-verbs like *hear, look at,* and *see*): *I saw a ball. Ken heard the bell.*	
Intransitive verb frame	Mover, action-affective: *Dominic ran.* Patient, action-affective: *The glass broke.* Experiencer, process-affective: *Jerry slept.*	Mover, action-affective, locative-source: *Peter came from school.* Mover, action-affective, locative-goal: *Peter went to school.*
Copula verb frame	Entity, stative-static, locative-stative: *The ball is on the table.* Entity, stative-static, entity-equivalent: *John is a boy.*	Entity, stative-static, attribute (adjective): *The apple is red.* Entity, stative-dynamic, attribute (adjective): *The fire is hot. The boy became sick.*
Indirect object frame		Agent, action-causative, patient, to + recipient: *Milt gave a present to Betty.*
Passive frame Optional adverb nodes	Locative-action: *The boy put the cake in the box.* Time-action (present): *The boy is eating the cake* now. Time-action (immediate past): *I ran* already.	Instrument: *John cut the tree* with an axe. Manner: *John ran* rapidly.
Modulations Prepositions	In, on	At, from, into, onto, to, up, with
Plurality		Regular plurality: *Two boys.* Irregular plurality: *Two children.*

APPENDIX 1 (CONT'D.)

	Stage I	Stage II
Modulations (cont'd.) Tense/Auxiliary	Present progressive: *I going.*	Uncontractible copula: *This is a ball.*
	Regular past (immediate past): *I painted a picture* (just now).	Regular past (remote past): *I painted a picture* (yesterday).
	Irregular past (immediate past): *I ran* (just now).	Irregular past (remote past): *I ran* (yesterday).
		Future (immediate future): *I have to go* (in a few minutes). *I will go* (in a few minutes), *I am going* (in a few minutes).
Modals		Modals indicating wish or intention: gonna, hafta (have to), lemme (let me), wanna
Determiners	Uh, (a): *See uh ball.*	These (indicating nomination): *See these balls.*
	That (indicating nomination): *Want that ball.*	Those (indicating nomination): *See those balls.*
	This (indicating nomination): *Want this ball.*	Some, another, other (indicating the same kind of object)
	Ordinal numbers: *Want two ball.*	
	More (indicating recurrence or addition to a set): *More swing. More apples.*	Lots (indicating more than one or an unspecified quantity): *Lots of apples. Lots of fun.*
Modalities Negation	Use of negation as an affirmation of following sentence: *No, Mary fix it* (meaning Mary can fix it, not someone else).	Not, don't, can't (indicating non-existence, disappearance, nonoccurrence)
	Early usage of the semantic notions of non-existence, disappearance, nonoccurrence, rejection, prohibition, and denial: *No bananas*	Negative determiner, no (indicating non-existence or disappearance)

APPENDIX 1 (CONT'D.)

	Stage I	Stage II
Modalities Negation (cont'd.)	(There are no bananas in the bowl.) *No girl* (The girl is gone.) *No swing* (He is not swinging.) *No play* (I don't want to play.) *No play* (You can't play.) *No truck* (That's not a truck; it's a car.)	
Imperative (request or directive)	Vocative requests: *Mommy!* Desire statement requests: *Sally want dolly.* Goal object or location requests: *Up.* Requests indicating possession: *That mine* (Give it to me). Direct imperatives: *Read the book.*	Interrogative requests: *Open it?* Problem statement requests: *Mimi hungry.* Use of "please" with requests and directives.
Question forms	Yes-no question with copula. Verb frame sentence and sentence with auxiliary, cued intonationally: *That a boy? Jimmy running?* *What is* question: *What dat?*	*Who is* question: *Who is dat?* *What* as a subject question: *What is jumping?* Yes-no question with copula preposing in copula verb frame sentence: *Is this a ball?*
Conjoinings Coordinating conjunction	*What* as an object question: *What is the boy riding?* *What do* question: *What is Mary doing?* *Where* question: *Where is Tad going?* *And* (indication enumeration or addition): *Gene eat apple and pear.*	*And* (indicating temporal sequence): *Me go town and then eat.* *And, but* (indicating opposition): *This truck go and this truck no go. This girl big but this girl not big.* Forward subject + verb sentential conjoining: *Mommy clean and Mommy cook.*

APPENDIX 1 (CONT'D.)

	Stage I	Stage II
Conjoinings Coordinating conjunction (cont'd.)	Forward and backward verb + object sentential conjoining: *Drink water and drink orange juice. Fold paper and cut paper.* Backward subject + verb sentential conjoining: *Doggy jump and kittycat jump.* Forward verb + object conjunction reduction: *Drink water and orange juice.*	Backward verb + object conjunction reduction: *Feed and kiss the dolly.* Forward and backward subject + verb conjunction reduction: *The dolly talk and sing. The girl and the boy cry.* Forward and backward subject + verb + object sentential conjoining: *Mommy cook dinner and Mommy set the table. Baby want bottle and baby want toys. Mommy gave toys and baby play toys. The cow jump fence and the dog jump fence.* Forward and backward subject + verb + object conjunction reduction (deletion of two nodes): *Harry ate the apples and the pie. Mommy and the baby played a game.*
Subordinate conjunctions		
Elaborated Nodes Possession	Use of the semantic notion of possessor, object of possession: *Mary('s) dress*	Possessive markers /'s/ and of + N: *Mary's dress. Window of the house.*
Embedded adjective		Expanded noun phrases to include size, color, condition, material, or quantity modifiers (They are used to identify a specific item, not to distinguish it from other similar items). Big, little (indicating amount): *Diana has the big bag of candy.*

APPENDIX 1 (CONT'D.)

	Stage I	Stage II
Elaborated Nodes (cont'd.) Relative clause		Attaching basic sentence frame onto an indefinite form such as thing, one, or kind: *Thing I got. One Mother made. Kind I need.*
Nominalization: infinitive		Using early forms such as *wanna, gonna,* and *hafta.*
Nominalizations: Participle Embedded questions		Attaching early wh-question forms onto an indefinite form, such as place, way, thing, one, or kind: *Nancy want the thing what is eating.*
Direct/Indirect discourse Factive clause		
Transformations Pronominalization	Personal pronouns: I, *it* as object, *it* as subject, them, my, and your	Personal pronouns: *you* as subject, she, we, they, mine, me, and *you* as object Indefinite pronouns: there, here
Do-support		

	Stage III	Stage IV
Transitive verb frame		Experiencer, process-causative, complement: *Barry thought up the idea. Lesli had a dream.*
Intransitive verb frame	Ambient-action: *It is raining.*	
Copula verb frame	Entity, stative-static, time-static: *The party is on Tuesday. The race was yesterday.* Entity, stative-static, reason: *The cupcakes were for the party.*	

APPENDIX 1 (CONT'D.)

	Stage III	Stage IV
Copula verb frame (cont'd.)	Entity, stative-static, recipient: *The dress is for Barbara.* Ambient-static: *It was fun.*	
Indirect object frame		Agent, action-causative, recipient, patient (the patient consists of D + N): *Marty gave the girls some dolls.*
Passive frame Optional adverb nodes	Time-action (remote past): *I ran yesterday.* Time-action (future): *I am running tomorrow.* Reason: *Andy made the cupcakes for the party.* Comparison: He ran like a rabbit.	Time-duration: *I cried* all week. Inclusion: *I am going* too.
Prepositions	Above, across, at (time[a], away from, below, by, down, in (time), like, near, of, off, off of, on (time), out, over, over to, through, under, for	During, within, without
Plurality Tense/Auxiliary	Future (remote future): *I will run* (tomorrow). *I have to run* (tomorrow). *I am running* (tomorrow). Contractible copula: *He's nice.* Second and third person plural and singular copulas: *You are, he is, she is, it is, they are.* First person plural copula: *We are.* Uncontractible auxiliary: *The children are running.*	First person singular copula: *I am happy.*

APPENDIX 1 (CONT'D.)

	Stage III	Stage IV
Plurality Tense/Auxiliary (cont'd.)	Contractible auxiliary: *They're running.* Regular third person singular: *He runs all the time.* Irregular third person singular: *He has no money. He does nothing.*	
Modals	Modals indicating certainty and possibility: can, will, could, shall, let's	Modals indicating necessity and obligation: gotta (got to), would, might, should, better, ought to
Determiners	*A* and *the* (indicating a member of a class of objects) Pronominals: somebody, something	*A* and *the* (indicating the difference between specific and non-specific objects) Any, both, each, every, few, last, many, most, much, next, several, cardinal numbers: *I saw the first one.* That/those (indicating position with the child as the reference point) This/these (indicating position with the child as the reference point)
Negation	Can't, don't, won't, not gonna to (indicating rejection and prohibition) *That's not* (indicating denial) *Why not* question	Couldn't, wouldn't Never
Imperative (request or directive)	Yes-no questions as request forms, usually to indicate permission to perform a task: *Can I go to the movie?*	Declarative sentence frames containing modals as request forms: *You could give . . . You can give . . .*

APPENDIX 1 (CONT'D.)

	Stage III	Stage IV
Imperative (request or directive) (cont'd.)		Questions used as a request for clarification of previous statements or questions: Mother says: *Did you go to the store?* Child says: *What?*
Question forms	Yes-no question with auxiliary or modal preposing in transitive or intransitive Sentence frames: *Are the children running? Will Don run?* Yes-no question with do-support preposing: *Do girls sleep?* Who as a subject question: *Who is running?* Why question: *Why he sick?* How come question: *How come he sick?* What for question: *What for he sick?* How question: *How he go?* How about question: *How about me going?*	Who as an object question: *Who is Mary hitting?* When question.
Coordinating conjunction	And (indicating causality): *I stay at home and I sick.* But (indicating exception): *I put it in box, but it don't go there.* Or (indicating choice): *I want an apple or a peach.* Forward and backward subject + verb + object conjunction reduction (deletion of one node): *Jane made the*	Backward adjective + subject + verb sentential conjoining: *The happy boys danced and the brown bears danced.* Forward adjective + subject + verb conjunction reduction: *The big boy jumped and ran.* There transformation sentential conjoining and conjunction reduction using verb + subject sentences:

APPENDIX 1 (CONT'D.)

	Stage III	Stage IV
Coordinating conjunction (cont'd.)	cookies and cooked some water. Mom petted and Daddy feed the Kittycat. Forward adjective + subject + verb sentential conjoining: *Big boys jump and big boys run.*	There is a ball and there is a bat. There is a ball and a bat.
Subordinate conjunctions	Because, so (indicating causality)	
Possession Embedded adjective	Expanded noun phrases to include size, color, condition, material, or quantity modifiers (They are used to contrast one item from other possible items that it could be confused with). Big, little (indicating size): *I have a big house.* Expanded noun phrases that contain more than one modifier	Big, little (indicating tallness): *The big man is a giant.* The following unmarked-marked pairs: tall-short, long-short, high-low: *The marked form different.*
Relative clause	Attaching a relative clause to the end of a sentence, where both the wh-word and the definite form it modifies are objects in their respective propositions: *I like the ball that I got.*	Inserting a relative clause medially into a sentence where both the wh-word and the definite form it modifies are subjects in their respective propositions: *The boy who is running helped me.*
Nominalization: infinitive	Using infinitive forms where the subject is the same for the two propositions: *I want to go. I need to pee-pee.*	Using infinitive forms where the subject is different for the two propositions: *I want Bill to go. I watch Bill run.*
Nominalization: participle		Use of periphrastic causative verb relationships: *I dyed the egg red.*

APPENDIX 1 (CONT'D.)

	Stage III	Stage IV
Nominalization: participle (cont'd.)		Use of simple causative verb relationships: *I made the door open.*
		Participle forms as part of expanded noun phrases: *Washing machine. Fighting men.*
Embedded questions	Attaching wh-question forms onto definite forms (indicating certainty or uncertainty about a particular state of affairs, object specification, and notice): *I know how to cook dinner now. I see the room where Norman sleeps. See what I'm doing.*	
Direct/Indirect discourse		
Factive clause		
Pronominalization	Personal pronouns: its, her, he, his, him, us, our, their Anaphoric *it*: *There is a box with six balls. Give it to me.*	Indefinite pronouns: everything, everyone, everybody, anything, anyone, anybody
	Indefinite pronouns: something, someone, somebody	Reflexive pronoun
		Use of intrasentential pronominalization (indicating old information): *Tom slapped Sarah and she cried.*
		Use of pronominal co-reference in sentence when the pronoun refers to the object of the first proposition: *Marvin kicked Max, and Louise slapped him (Max).*
		Use of pronominalization in contingent pairs to signal old information: Mother: *What did Jane do?* Child: *She went home.*
Do-support	Emphatic *do*: *He does work.*	Support *do*: *He didn't go.*

APPENDIX 1 (CONT'D.)

	Stage V	Stage VI
Transitive verb frame		
Intransitive verb frame		
Copula verb frame	Entity, stative-dynamic, entity-equivalent: *The boy became a man.*	Entity, stative-static, content: *The story is about Bambi.*
Indirect object frame	Agent, action-causative, recipient, patient (The patient consists of ϕ + NP): *Marty gave the girl dolls.*	
Passive frame	Truncated passive (irreversible relationship): *The cake was eaten.* Truncated passive (reversible relationship): *Mary was hit. Mary got hit.* Full passive (irreversible relationship): *The cake was eaten by the dog.*	Full passive (reversible relationship): *Mary was hit by Jane. Mary got hit by Jane.*
Optional adverb nodes	Time-frequency: *Larry goes home every Friday.*	Time-beginning: *Al began the game at one o'clock.* Time-end: *They boy stopped at two o'clock.* Time-beginning, end: *John worked from one o'clock to two o'clock.* Intensifier: *Laura was very good.*
Prepositions	After, around, back of, before, behind, beside, between, beyond, except, except for, from (time), front of, to (time)	About, after (time), along, among, before (time), over (time), until
Plurality		
Tense/Auxiliary	First, second, and third person singular and plural auxiliary forms	Perfect tense: *I have eaten my breakfast.* Attracted tense in multipropositional sentences

APPENDIX 1 (CONT'D.)

	Stage V	Stage VI
Modals	Must (indicating obligation)	
Determiners	Some, another, other (indicating the same object)	*A* and *the* (indicating new and old information)
		That/those (indicating position with others as the reference point)
		This/these (indicating position with others as the reference point)
Negation		Negative passive
		Negative tag questions: *We went to the movie, didn't we?*
Imperative (request or directive)	Hints without explicit imperatives: *That's where the dolly goes. Put it over there.*	Directives indicating ability to perform task: *Johnny, can you hold the money?*
	Pretend directives: *Pretend that is my doll.*	Directives indicating willingness to perform: *Do you wanna sit here?*
	Obligation (has to) directives: *You have to go.*	Directives indicating need to adjust performance: *Will you move over, please?*
	Conditional directives: *If we are good, we will go outside.*	Directives indicating reason for performance: *Why don't you eat supper?*
		Directives indicating don't forget something: *Don't forget to pick up the books.*
Question forms	*Which* question: *Which cow is eating?*	What did (subject) (verb) question: *What did the girl hit?*
	Auxiliary preposing in all non-subject wh-questions: *What is Penny hitting?*	Who did (subject) (verb) question: *Who did the boy hit?*
		Which (object) *did* (subject) (verb) question: *Which boy did the girl hit?*

APPENDIX 1 (CONT'D.)

	Stage V	Stage VI
Question forms (cont'd.)		*Where did* (subject) (verb) (object) question: *Where did the girl hit the boy?* *What if* question: *What if we go home?* Tag questions: *We didn't go to the movie, did we?*
Coordinating conjunction	Or (indicating inclusion): *You can take one or all of them.* Backward adjective + subject + verb conjunction reduction: *The big boys and the little girls are playing.* *There* Transformation sentential conjoining and conjunction reduction using verb + adjective + subject sentences: *There are little dishes and pretty napkins. There is chocolate cake and cold pop.*	But first (indicating condition): *You can go, but first tie your shoe.* Either-or, neither, nor
Subordinate conjunction	Before, after (indicating a logical relationship): *Mary fills the bottle before she feeds the baby. Before Mary cried, she peeled the onions.*	Before, after (indicating an arbitrary relationship): *Mary fills the bottle before she washes her face. Before Mary cried, she went outside.* As, as long as, as soon as, although, even though, however, if, if not, if only then, since, therefore, though, unless, unless not, when, while
Possession		With: *The man with the hat is nice.*
Embedded adjective	The following unmarked-marked pairs: *thick-thin, deep-shallow, wide-narrow.*	The following unmarked-marked pair: *old-young.*

APPENDIX 1 (CONT'D.)

	Stage V	Stage VI
Embedded adjective (cont'd.)	Comparative and superlative forms with absolute adjectives: *This apple is redder than that apple. This apple is the reddest.*	Adult adjective ordering rules in expanded noun phrases *more than, less than* with discrete and mass substances: *He has more apples than John. He has more water than John.* *More, less* in question forms (indicating amount): *Which box has more?* *Most* in question forms (indicating amount): *Which boy has the most?* Double comparative forms: *Which box is wider than it is deep?* Comparative and superlative forms with relative adjectives: *John is bigger than Tom. Benjamin is the biggest.* Comparative and superlative forms with contrastive adjectives: *Joan is sadder than Norma. Marion is the saddest.*
Relative clause	Attaching a relative clause to the end of a sentence, where the wh-word is the object of its proposition and the definite form it modifies is the subject of its proposition: *I like the cow that is eating.*	Inserting a relative clause medially into a sentence, where the wh-word is the object of its proposition and the definite form it modifies is the subject of its proposition: *The horse that the boy is riding is a mustang.* Double embedded relative clauses: *The boy that kissed the girl that petted the dog is my brother.*

APPENDIX 1 (CONT'D.)

	Stage V	Stage VI
Relative clause (cont'd.)		Relative clause with deletion: *The boy playing in the park hit Joe. The boy behind the door is a scaredy-cat.*
		Apposition: *Mr. Barker, my teacher, gave me a present.*
Nominalization: infinitive	Use of event-causing causative verb relationships: *She tied the ribbon on Barbie's pigtail.*	Use of infinitive of purpose: *We went in order to get some apples. We went to get some apples.*
		Use of infinitive with adjective: *He was clever to go.*
		Use of minimal distance principle with respect to infinitive with adjective constructions: *John is easy to see. John is eager to see.*
		Iteration: *I asked him to go to get some apples. I asked him to go and get some apples.*
		Infinitive as a subject in a proposition: *To be a good boy is hard.*
Nominalization: participle	Participle forms as objects in propositions: *He likes playing with toys.*	Use of negative causative verb relationships: *John kept him from falling off the ledge.*
		Participle forms as subjects in propositions: *Playing with toys is not fun.*
		Participle forms embedding transitive and intransitive sentence frames into other propositions: *John's destruction of the painting was very sad. Mark's running in the race upset his mother.*

APPENDIX 1 (CONT'D.)

	Stage V	Stage VI
Embedded questions Direct/Indirect discourse	Use of factive verbs to encode imperative messages: *He told him to go.* Use of factive verbs to encode declarative messages: *I know that he will go.*	Use of factive verbs and negation to encode imperative messages: *He didn't tell him to go.* Use of factive verbs and negation to encode declarative messages: *I didn't know that he would go.* Use of non-factive verbs to encode declarative message: *He said that Bill was sick.* Use of non-factive verbs and negation to encode declarative messages: *He didn't say that Bill was sick.* Use of counter-factive verbs to encode declarative messages: *He pretended that it was hard.* Use of counter-factive verbs and negation to encode declarative messages: *He didn't pretend that it was hard.* Use of *ask* plus infinitive to encode yes-no question messages: *He asked to go.* Use of *ask* plus *if* subordinate clauses to encode yes-no question messages: *He asked if he could go.* Use of *ask* plus embedded questions to encode wh-question messages: *He asked who could go.*

APPENDIX 1 (CONT'D.)

	Stage V	Stage VI
Direct/Indirect discourse (cont'd.)		Use of minimal distance principle with respect to *ask* and *tell*: *Ask Bill about the story. Tell Bill about the story.*
		Direct quotes
Factive clause		Factive clause: *The fact that he is sick didn't stop him. That he was sick didn't stop him.*
Pronominalization	Use of pronominal co-reference in sentences when the pronoun refers to the subject of the first proposition: *Marvin kicked Max, and Sarah slapped him (Marvin).*	Appropriate use of number and case features with personal pronouns
		Use of intersentential pronominalization (indicating old information): *Jason went to the store. He liked going very much.*
		Conjoining of nominal personal pronouns: *He and I wanted to go.*
Do-support		

[a]Some prepositions can be used as locative or temporal indicators.

Kretschmer, R. & Kretschmer, L. *Language Development and Intervention With The Hearing Impaired.* Baltimore: University Park Press, 1978, Reprinted by permission.

reaction to 11
morag h. clark

I am glad to have this opportunity of reacting to Sister Joyce's paper because we have a lot in common, and yet differ in several respects in our practical handling of the subject under discussion. We are both committed to the maximum use of hearing through appropriate binaural amplification in a completely oral environment from the earliest possible age. We share the common aim of developing deaf children's language in such a way that they will have the opportunity to choose whether they will spend their lives in deaf or hearing society.

I would, however, take issue with Sister Joyce on the first two assumptions listed in her paper. If we are to offer an oral way of life to deaf children, in the face of the claims of those advocating Total Communication, we must be very cautious about setting limits and listing prerequisites for the population who will benefit from it.

While it is highly desirable that children coming into our programs should do so from caring families who have had support during the preschool years, we must not lay this down as a prerequisite for their success. Twenty-four percent of the present school population at Birkdale comes from one parent families. Some had very young mothers so involved with their own personal and social problems that they could scarcely benefit from the preschool guidance offered during the child's early years.

Our experience shows, too, that normal or above average intelligence is not a prerequisite for the development of fluent oral communication skills in profoundly deaf children. Twenty percent of the whole population of the school has below average intelligence when tested on the WISC Performance Test, Table 1.

This brings us to the realization that, within wholly oral educational systems, committed to the use of good, binaural amplification, there are different approaches, and there is, in fact, no one oral method. Some of the approaches used are suited only to children with average or above average ability because their analytic or deductive nature excludes less able children. Others, by placing emphasis on the written word in the early language program, may well cut out another whole group of children, or may, at least, further handicap them. A considerable number of normally hearing children, who have a good command of spoken language, never become really proficient readers. Those deaf children, then, who may have specific reading difficulties, are further handicapped if the program relies heavily on written back-up.

If, then, the maximum number of deaf children is to be offered an oral way of life, those concerned with developing oral communication skills must seek to follow the pattern of the linguistic development of the normally hearing child. For me this excludes the use of terms like *language teaching* and *language lessons*.

TABLE 1. CHARACTERISTICS OF DEAF GROUP ATTENDING BIRKDALE SCHOOL*

Characteristic Factors	Percent
One parent family	27.8
Significant additional handicaps	32.9
WISC performance IQ <90, age 7 and above	16.4
Non-oral deaf homes	4.4
Low social class (Registrar General's Scale)	42.8

*60% of total school population

Teachers committed to such a philosophy see themselves, not as teachers of language, but as those there to provide an environment in which children will be motivated to communicate, and within which they have ample opportunity to develop oral communication skills as they learn about the world. Scheffler (1965) clarifies the distinction between the concepts of learning and teaching when he says,

> Teaching normally involves trying, where learning does not . . . . to say of a child that he is learning to walk, learning several new words each day . . . . does not in itself convey that he is *trying* to accomplish these things.

One feature of the approach following the pattern of hearing children is just the lack of conscious effort on the part of the deaf child as he develops his oral communication skills.

While agreeing with Sister Joyce that an effective school program should grow out of experience, a study of past and present successes and failures, and out of reading and study, I must confess that we have been reading different books—many of them outside the field of deaf education. In the literature from the field of normal education there is a growing awareness of the importance of the child's linguistic competence. Bernstein (1971) has suggested that educational failure is often due to language failure. As Halliday develops this theme he sees the problem as:

> a limitation on the child's control over the relevant functions of language in their adaptation to certain specific demands.

The work of Joan Tough on the Schools Council Project (1976) has further advanced this theme, and we find her classification of the uses of language most helpful as we seek to assess the linguistic development of deaf children in a functional way.

Our curriculum and timetables are planned in such a way that situations appropriate to these uses of language arise frequently. Since this classification arises out of normal language usage we find that little adaptation has to be made to normal timetables.

These really are exciting times. Not only are we learning more and more about linguistic development, but also technological advances mean that we can reach more children than ever before through more powerful hearing aids with better frequency responses. It is amazing to see the use that profoundly deaf children can make of minimal residual hearing if they have lots of exposure to normal, natural language, rhythmically presented, at a normal rate of utterance.

It is important to realize, however, that the help received from good amplification may well be considerably reduced if too many visual cues are given. Deliberate drawing of attention to the lips, manual cues, or too heavy a reliance on the written word can reduce the benefit of the hearing aids. Pollack leaves us in no doubt here when she claims:

> There can be no compromise. Once emphasis is placed on looking there will be divided attention and the unimpaired modality—vision will be victorious.

Have we taken enough account of individual learning styles? Two children with identical audiograms may place different weighting on the auditory or visual cues they combine in order to decode the messages in communication situations. Do our systems allow deaf children enough freedom to find their own best learning style?

Language develops with social maturity and we believe that there is much to be said for placing deaf children, whose educational need is felt to be best met in a special school, in classes of 10–12 children so that they benefit from interaction in the larger group. Aware, however, that a child learns to talk by talking, it must be realized that the frequency of opportunity to respond is reduced in a larger group. This has led us to provide individual back up programs for children, according to individual needs, and so some children may have as many as four individual sessions per day.

Language is looked upon, not as a subject to be taught, but as a vehicle of thought through which ideas are shared. As Wiener (1954) reminds us:

> Speech is the greatest interest and the most distinctive achievement of man ....
> A semantic receiving apparatus neither receives nor translates the language word by word, but idea by idea.

Language is the means we use to operate a curriculum similar to that operating in our ordinary schools for hearing children. In our experience, as oral subject teaching goes on with individual back up, children acquire the capacity to formulate the sentences they want to use at the moment they want to use them. From audio-tapes of conversations with profoundly deaf children I recently extracted a few examples; these illustrate the children's searching for the language system rules.

Errors in the speech of profoundly deaf children approximating those of young hearing children:

> Mummy *goed* to the shop.
> Yesterday nobody at home, today *allbody* at home.
> Auntie Mary *comed* today.
> *Not nobody there.*
> I *thinked* for a long time.

Although initial results in terms of expressive language may apparently develop more slowly than those achieved in systems providing direct teaching of models, our children develop a spontaneity of language which lacks the rigidity of many oral deaf children brought up on more structured systems. Moreover, their academic achievements, in relation to their innate ability, in open examinations for hearing children are evidence of their ability to use language as a means of acquiring knowledge. Socially we find that children so educated have reached a level of oral communication skill which enables them to function in hearing society—not necessarily with completely accurate syntax or articulation, but with sufficient confidence to relate to and share orally in the environment of their homes and local areas.

In the light of the different types of oralism represented at this seminar, it would seem appropriate for some research to be done on the end products of the various systems. It could be nothing but profitable to study groups from different educational environments to find out how they are coping in after-school life as people in society, in their spheres of work, and in their own family lives.

References

Bernstein, B. *Class, codes and control 1: Theoretical studies towards a sociology of language,* 1971.
Halliday, M. A. K. *Explorations in the functions of language.* London: Edward Arnold, 1973.
Pollack, D. *Educational audiology for the limited hearing infant.* Springfield: Charles C. Thomas, 1970.
Scheffler, I. *Conditions of knowledge.* New York: Scott Foresman, 1965.
Tough, J. *Listening to children talking.* Ward Lock Educational in conjunction with Drake Educational Associates, 1976.
Wiener, N. *The human use of human beings; Cybernetics and society.* New York: Doubleday, 1954.

12

the further development of language by adolescents and young adults

sjaak c. s. van puijenbroek

You all might agree with me that the title of this paper covers a wide range of problems. Thinking about the subject, I found that, first, a number of questions had to be answered before a decision could be made whether a specific problem should be dealt with in this paper or not. I'll mention some of these questions together with my answers. This clarifies the reasons why I had to make a choice of topics in my lecture; at the same time I hope to put forward some points for further discussion.

1. "Further development" implies that something is achieved already. It is not laying the foundation, nor raising the first floor. The title suggests the assumption of building further on a noncompleted work.

Some of our prelingually deaf adults have acquired language skills commensurate with their abilities, which were not equal for all of them. Others did not come so far. In some cases this might be due to educational failure; in others to the poor stimulation of their environment; in others still to their own "faults" as human beings. In other cases they were more or less the victims of wrong educational decisions in the past. Their typical learning disabilities were discovered too late or even not at all and so, too, were the appropriate answers to their specific problem. Within the framework of this paper I have restricted myself to the students who fit in a program for "normal" continuing education, at the same time making some references to the other groups.

A number of schools have to deal with the problem of late enrollment. The students knock at the door, and schools are faced with a difficult decision because they are responsible, too, for the youngsters who have been attending the school for years. We cannot ignore the needs of these "latecomers", but we don't have the facilities for proper help, without adversely affecting the students who are attending our school.

2. Should we discuss here the older students, whether they are in a school for the deaf or not; or the young industrial workers, who left school at the age of 16? In my opinion, for most of our youngsters there are good opportunities for further education at school at the age of 15–16 years. If this is so, they have the right to be enabled to explore this opportunity. In this paper I consider them as students in a specific school program. I would like to present for discussion the conditions for deaf students to participate in secondary school programs for normal hearing students. We should consider whether this is a more urgent problem for the boarding schools, since their students live more apart from the normal social world? To summarize: We have restricted ourselves in this paper to deaf youngsters who are in a special school program of continuing education.

Preliminaries

Before I focus on language, I want to make some preliminary statements:

1. Development at a certain age-level presupposes a building-forward on what is already achieved. This has been mentioned before.

2. This secondary program is final as far as intensive education is concerned. Some students will not be able to take their part in normal social life and will stay for a shorter or a longer time (perhaps for their whole life) in a sheltered environment—special half-way houses, for example. We have to prepare them for this life, especially regarding communicative and social ability. Others will continue their education in schools for the normally hearing. A great number will find a job, whether or not combined with a vocational training program. These groups have to be prepared for their future life, of course, but their new environment should be prepared to receive them as well. Very often a continuing form of special help is needed after they have left school.

3. Since the intention of oral education is to enable deaf persons to cooperate in our society, this will influence all phases and aspects of our work; especially during the last years at school, this educational goal must color all activities.

4. In the development of personality, self-identification—discovering your own self in meeting others; assuming your individuality in experiencing relations with other persons—especially plays a big role, in the period of puberty and adolescence. More and more our students need to become aware of their own responsibilities. This means to me that programs should be set up in cooperation with the students themselves. This will motivate the young adolescent to participate fully in the program rather than the situation where the teacher develops educational strategies on his own. In the first instance the youngster will be motivated intrinsically; in the latter only external motivation will be the case.

5. All educators who have met deaf persons of this age group know that the struggle they have at this stage to accept their handicap is more intense than

ever before in their lives. This is not surprising, for this period is marked by exploring relationships. Social contact means for the deaf youngster a deep confrontation with his problem of communication. In discovering his identity as belonging to a community, he discovers his deafness as a severe handicap; he becomes aware of it as something that threatens the possibility of his growing up as a full, mature member of that community, to which he should belong.

Language Development

We want to consider conversation as the starting point for acquiring language. This is true for a program of secondary education as well.

1. All lessons—not only in language—should be based upon this principle because this formula for teaching and learning is helpful in stimulating thinking, in deepening the student's knowledge, and in giving him the opportunity to discover the facts themselves. This model of teaching also provides opportunities to deal with other aspects of teaching the subject than the cognitive ones: it involves feelings of admiration, wondering, doubt, beauty; it encompasses references to events of daily life and their emotional color. Parts of the classroom-discussion will be annotated because of the specific language problems: e.g., worthwhile expressions to be remembered, terms and sentences which are typical of a specific field of science (i.e., math, physics, geography etc.). Very often the results of the discussion are written down as notes in order to be studied together with the textbook. We meet a special difficulty in teaching where the motoric activity of the student has to be accompanied by language (the same problem holds for all ages!). He has to keep his eyes on the material, on the tool, on his hands, and is therefore unable to look *at the same time* at the face of the instructor or his classmates. We stress here the fact that handling the material and the language which goes along with it should not be separated, but integrated as a total activity. Explaining things through nonverbal means (e.g., gestures) is the easiest way when the student is carrying out some activities. Nevertheless, this is the best opportunity to teach and to learn language, because the person is really involved with head, heart, and hands.

2. In our secondary education program, language teaching is an important subject, and the conversation lesson is an important part of this subject. Such a conversation lesson results in blackboard notes, or in a blackboard lesson. The best blackboard lessons are the ones in which the language is not used in its descriptive form, but as it is used in normal conversation. As a means of learning a more descriptive type of language, the reading paragraph is used. This text is composed by the teacher (after the blackboard lesson) and offers opportunities to introduce new words, expressions, and grammatical structures for appropriate colloquial language. The blackboard lesson and the composed paragraph are used for homework. Important elements are:

- Finding of word groups and their rhythm. This can be done in order to prepare for the reading of a text aloud.
- The material offers the opportunity for collecting words or word groups which have an analogous meaning with the language used in connection

with the subject. The student is asked to discover similar grammatical structures to those used in the composed paragraph; he is requested to explain the elements of the word, etc. Very important are those questions which ask for the meaning of the pointer words in the given context.
- Figurative meaning should not be avoided.
- Last but not least, the student should be given the opportunity of applying the learned grammatical rules.

Before discussing other topics for the conversation lessons mentioned above, I would like to draw attention to a very special one: language itself, as a subject. In teaching deaf youngsters we have to allow time for reflection on language itself. A compensation—although an insufficient one—for the lack of frequency can be found in the intensity of the way language is offered to the student. This intensity is achieved partly by using the written form—a visual form which "stays" as it were—partly by repeating and working out the language in the exercises described above. Important, too, is reflection on the acquired language. When the child grows older, he is more capable of doing this. This can be explained as follows: grammar offers the possibility to talk about language, to label word categories and structures and so far as it is an adequate description of language, it is very helpful. It is indeed helpful for language development as long as the teaching of grammar is used in meaningful situations. Reflection on the meaning of words, or better still on the intention of the speaker or the writer, is the most important of all. (Grammar may be helpful for this, but is subservient to it.) Some examples may serve as an illustration:
One may ask the pupil:
- What is common and what is different in the meaning of the word "new," e.g., what is the opposite in the following uses of the word: a new book, a new day, a new friend, a new experience? (Those units are collected before in notes from various sources).
- Why is this verb used in the present and not in the past tense?
- You used the word "happy"; what about "lucky"? Wouldn't that fit your intention better; would it say what you mean?

Language always refers to something (even if we have a chat, just for some social contact). In our lessons we have to be careful about the choice of the subject. It does not only depend on the momentary interest of the students. We have the task of widening the interest of the youngsters and of motivating them to consider valuable matters. They will be more interested and more deeply involved if they find that the lessons have helped them to achieve a more meaningful life. I will mention five subjects of conversation:

1. Social behavior. We learned how to behave and what to say in different situations by seeing and hearing other persons, by noting their reaction to our utterances, and by being told about social behavior. It is important for our deaf adults to know about socially expected behavior patterns and about the normal social language.

2. At certain times there are topics about which almost everybody is talking. This may be the boat refugees or a much discussed television series or a disaster read about in the newspaper. If we discuss these themes with our adolescents,

we enlarge their world and enable them to take part in daily life communications.

3. Pupils in a vocational training program are interested in topics related to their work. All are interested in their future, and children undoubtedly have a future! Very often we talk with deaf children about the past. They learn the language; we repeat what happened and let them read it again. Is this really necessary? Yes, but we have to be aware of the danger of this one-sidedness and make the most of every opportunity to focus on the future.

In their training program they meet materials, tools, and machines which they have to use in a specific manner. If we are able to link up with those subjects in language lessons, we can be assured of their interest and teach them a useful vocabulary at the same time. Such talks can have links with social life: cooking in school, cooking at home, in a restaurant; working at a lathe in school or in a factory; their future: (Why do you learn those things?)

4. Another important subject for conversation lessons is "human feelings." In the education of the deaf, great emphasis is put on "objectivity." We teach them words for objects, we describe situations, we discuss what happened, but we forget to teach the language of emotions. However, subjective experience has to be put into words as well. We have to develop a balanced emotionality in the child and teach him to understand the feelings of his fellow man. This goal holds for all ages, but especially for our adults. They find themselves in a process of self-discovery, self-identification. They have to talk about the things of life, about themselves and other human beings, and the network of relations between them. They become aware of the complexity of feelings, reasonable and unreasonable, which underlie human behavior. They need language to get a grip on this aspect of their world, to be able to talk about themselves and to enable other people to discuss with them the field of the emotions.

5. Closely connected with the above mentioned, even more essential for human beings, are so-called "life values". Freedom means being able to make choices. We make choices in life, because we believe in a certain value. Our way of life is based on the attachment of a value to our behavior, to relationships, and to things. The life of a handicapped person has its specific restrictions. Comparing himself with others, he may feel inferior and unhappy because of this. The deaf person should be made aware that some values are more important than others. Therefore, insight into the relativity of values and in their real importance is indispensable. Although language and conversation are not sufficient conditions for a personality to be established, they are necessary to develop personal insight.

Ways of Teaching and Learning

We do not intend to discuss all possible ways of teaching and learning a spoken or written language. Some have been mentioned already. We will however, single out three of them: group work; rôle-playing (both subjects being discussed briefly); then we will elaborate further on the third way, reading.

1. Group work, achieving a task as a group, as distinct from individual work, is important; no one will deny that. Society is based upon common activities. These are carried out at distinctive levels:
- We play in a free way with other people.
- We take part in a game according to the rules.
- We make something together. Sometimes every individual contribution to the whole is identifiable, mostly it is not.
- We endeavor to clarify ideas together, to obtain better insight. (We take part in a social gathering called a symposium!)

In all cases, communication is required: the higher the level of cooperation, the greater the demand for refined communication. From this one may draw the conclusion that real group work is a difficult task for deaf people. Difficult because of the absence of hearing: one cannot use one's eyes for two things at the same time, keeping them on the work object and getting information from colleagues. Your eyes don't tell you who is speaking until you see him. Difficult because of lower ability in verbal communication. Nevertheless, difficulties don't diminish the requirement for the development of the special skills needed for cooperation in a group.

2. Rôle-playing—In discussing topics for our lessons, social behavior and the language of feelings were mentioned. An excellent way to bring in topics like these is found in rôle-play:
- A situation is played (e.g., how to apply for a job); the proper language is learned and exercised.
- The text can be composed by deliberating together. This offers a good opportunity to discuss the topic on which one is focusing.
- The capability to participate in somebody else's feelings or ideas is developed.

Group-work and rôle-play ask for:
- An attitude on the part of both teachers and children to work in this way. It should be begun at the preschool level and continued as part of the total school program. It should have its own didactics.
- A room to perform it; the management of the class and the equipment in the room must allow this lesson form.
- Optimal hearing aid equipment is also required for this kind of work.

3. Reading constitutes a special place in the language development of deaf children and an important one! All hearing children start to learn reading with a well developed ability: they know the spoken language. They learn the technique of reading, which enables them to read this spoken language. Deaf children have to learn to read in combination with learning the language itself. This is achieved by using reading right from the beginning. This "double-didactics" has its special problems. I am afraid that we don't know enough about the process in order to make our didactics sufficiently well founded. This is especially true for dealing with deaf children suffering from learning disabilities. Obviously this remark is not related to the youngsters about whom we are speaking, but we have met the problem of an unsatisfactory reading technique so often with older students that we cannot ignore it here. If this backwardness appears, a special program to improve reading skill is necessary.

Low frequency of language has already been noted as one of the reasons for delay in language development. Compensation was found in intensifying the input of language. Another compensation is to be found in reading, since this offers more language to the youngsters.

When one is unable to take part in conversation, to hear radio or television, then this decreases information considerably. Without this information how can one discover the way others live, think and feel, how can one keep up with daily events, the things of interest in one's own community? Being capable of reading solves this problem to some degree, certainly if the reading gives enjoyment. Both the ability to read and the ability to enjoy it, are basic principles for a reading program and they must be seen together. To continue, I want to make some distinctions in reading, each followed by a few didactical remarks.

Reading aloud. This is not a demand for the future, but it is a good lesson form:
- The teacher should observe the student's manner of reading and give directions for improvement.
- It is useful to control speech.
- It allows the teacher to discover whether a text is understood or not.

The reading text can be prepared by the students as homework:
- The paragraph has to be divided into right word groups.
- One has to look for the longer and shorter pauses.
- Rhythm has to be found.
- One has to pay attention to the pronunciation.

The reading text, following the blackboard lesson. This text supplies a number of activities such as:
- Reading aloud, prepared as described.
- Auditory training, because it ought to be a well known text.
- Exercises in grammar and vocabulary.

Text analysis. This is an intensive way of reading. It forces the students to find out the intentions of the author in detail. Very often the comprehension is tested by questions, either multiple choice or open.

Studying. Reading as described above is very much related to studying. Study means asking oneself questions. Making up questions about a text is therefore a good exercise, as is asking each other questions about a text. In studying it is difficult but essential to make a distinction between the main points and matters of secondary importance. Consequently it is worthwhile to have a program for teaching how to summarize a text. It is clear that the kind of texts necessary are easily found in the student's study books.

Books. Various types and styles flood the market. We find that the quality of children's books has improved during the last decade in respect to context, illustrations and layout. As soon as possible we try to make our children "lovers of books." Picture books are used to start with, and text is added more and more. Most effective are educators with an infectious enthusiasm for books: if children don't meet people who like books, how can they become enthusiastic readers? Our youngsters have to become convinced of their duty, their obligation, to read. This duty arises from tasks given by the teacher. But, if this is all they feel, it will cause a strong dislike for books and all things associated with reading.

Therefore, be careful with the choice of the proper book for this child or this class or group (this implies that a teacher has to know about juvenile books and has to read them). Can they manage it because of the language, the story, the ideas? Does the book provoke curiosity or excite their interest? The first pages are usually the most difficult ones. Help the children to make a good start; teach how to do this. We may start the book together in the classroom (with some preparatory lessons to avoid all difficulties). When the children are anxious enough to know how the story will continue, they are invited to read the book on their own.

Presents, awards, are things of intrinsic value. Books might be considered for these purposes. The appreciation of a book by one of the students can be welcomed as a recommendation for others or as a stimulus to read other books by the same author.

I would like to make some final remarks on reading as an extension and summary of the above mentioned points:

1. When we turn over the leaves of our newspaper, we see headlines, some of which attract our attention. We skim through some articles, we start reading one, but finish half way, we pay great attention to others. We read one book rather quickly, dwelling only on some passages; we study another one, struggling forward page by page. We glance at an advertisement in the station hall. It is convenient indeed to be able to change our attitude in reading. Teaching different styles of reading is a task; it might be learned by tasks suited to varying texts.

2. What about the following kinds of texts that we meet more in practice than in schoolbooks?
- Directions for use, e.g., on an article or in a laundry.
- Directions for the construction of a model.
- Instructions on how to fill out a form.

3. If a person is dependent on written information for a great deal, it is important to know where and how to find it. This implies that part of language development includes the skill to look up words in a dictionary, the skill to gather information from appropriate sources. This holds good not only for the language lessons. To teach where and how to find the information about a specific topic belongs to the instruction in each subject. Tasks for homework beginning with words such as: "Try to find out . . . . ; look up in two different books . . . . "; are very fruitful.

Each school for the deaf needs a well-provided library: an attractive room, where reading is publicized and encouraged. It should have departments where the different categories of books are recognizable. This is one of the ways of helping our students to find their way in the public library.

Remarks

So far we have paid attention to language as subject matter. Its communicative value and its significance for personal development were not ignored, or at least not intentionally. I'll use a little more of your time to comment on three points.

1. Communication is based upon understanding. Language competence is a constituent of communication and an important factor in understanding. Intelligibility of speech and lipreading skills are other important factors. Both attract great attention. They seem to be difficult for our youngsters to show improvement. However, it is too easy to pass on our responsibility for speech and lipreading to a child's earlier teachers. It has been proved that improvement is possible.

2. For everybody it is worth while to know his own limits and restrictions. As to language, it is important for our deaf students and for others as well to be aware of their limits. It is unwise to write an official letter on your own, a letter of application, for example, or a request to authorities. It is never a disgrace to ask for help, nor for assistance in putting things into correct language. The education of handicapped children includes making it clear to them that everybody needs help and pointing out that they need special help in accordance with their handicap.

3. In a small country like the Netherlands, secondary education includes the study of a second (and often a third and more) foreign language as well. To deaf children the acquisition of a mother tongue, a first language, is difficult enough. Should we tease them with a second one? In my opinion the answer is as follows: not all of them. If it hampers the development of that first language, then certainly not. For a number of them, an elementary confrontation with a second language—in our case English—will do. It is useful because their hearing friends are fairly familiar with that language as well and some knowledge of it is a prerequisite to be able to read the newspapers, television texts, etc. For most of our students it is a requirement because it is an integral part of secondary education. It is not an easy study, but it appears that it gives good opportunities for further development of their first language as well. Obviously, the study of a second language achieves the best results by using a "conversational method" as well (using the knowledge of your first one).

To end this paper I go back to language again and to what I said about it before. Our task regarding the development of language is too wide only to be accomplished in school. This means that we try to involve all persons who have to do with the child. We set students a task which must be fulfilled after school hours and which can only be solved by talking to other people. We urge parents, educators, and other people to sit down and take time to talk with these youngsters. We explain to them that these deaf boys and girls have the right to know about all those things which can be picked up incidentally if one can hear, but that those deaf children only "hear" what is directly spoken to them, face to face. This may seem self-evident but it appears to be necessary to repeat again and again the consequences of deafness for communication. This is true even for educators of the deaf, even for ourselves. As a matter of fact, shouldn't we consider society as being handicapped as well because some of its members cannot hear? If we, experts as we pretend to be, promote oral education for the deaf, we also have a duty toward their hearing fellow citizens. We have not ignored it this week.

References

Argyle, M. *The psychology of interpersonal behavior*. Harmondsworth, Middlesex: Penguin, 1967.

Dale, D.M.C. *Language development in deaf and partially hearing children*. Springfield, IL: Charles C Thomas, 1974.

Griffioen, J. *Zeggen-schap*. Groningen: Wolters-Noordhoff, 1975.

Malmquist, E., & Brus, B.Th. *Lezen Leren—Lezend Leren*. Tilburg: Zwijzen, 1974.

Maslow, A.H., *Toward a psychology of being*. New York: Litton Educational Publishing, 1974.

van Uden, A. *A world of language for deaf children*. Amsterdam: Swets & Zeitlinger, 1977.

Watzlawick, P., Beavin, J.H., & Jackson, D.D. *Pragmatics of human communications*. New York: W.W. Norton, 1978.

reaction to 12

sr. nicholas griffey

Mr. van Puijenbroek refers specifically to the pupil who is in a full-time special school program of continuing education. It was no surprise to me to find that his paper showed a deep insight into the linguistic and educational problems of the deaf adolescent, because he has had a wealth of experience of teaching at post-primary level. In the professional literature we find comparatively little regarding the teaching of language—or more correctly, the further development of language—but much concerning the development of language in the young child. It is presumed that by the end of the primary school, language has been established. In the majority of cases this is not so. This year I encountered four deaf adolescents who had practically no language. All four had been in educational programs which were quite unsuited to their needs.

Generally speaking, today children are assessed at the end of the primary school and are "streamed" according to their abilities. The pupils referred to in the paper were selected on such a basis. It is noted that they have a considerable amount of information. They have ideas but they have an inefficient means of expression. They may not have yet extracted the rules of language, but they are expected to expand their knowledge of many subjects. They may have to embark on the learning of a second or even a third language when they are still having difficulty in acquiring a mother tongue. Confronted with such a class for the first time, a teacher is very often perplexed because he does not know where to start. Without undue delay he must be able to discover each pupil's educational and linguistic standard. For one reason or another there may be serious gaps in his lexical and syntactic abilities, with the result that he may have acquired faulty concepts. It may be necessary then to teach linguistic skills that should have been acquired at primary school level. If the pupil has failed to acquire language naturally, then, I believe, he must be taught analytically. However, the study of new subjects can provide opportunities for clarification of and practice in spoken and written language as well as in reading.

The van Puijenbroek paper emphasizes the need for verbalization. To me this is crucial. At the secondary stage we are so busy imparting knowledge that we may accept imcomplete sentence patterns with faulty structure in our desire to meet the demands of an expanding curriculum. I can remember a lesson in which a secondary-level pupil described a chef as: "man work kitchen, tall hat" (the last two words were accompanied by an appropriate gesture). Another member of the class gave the following definition: "A chef is a male cook." There is a vast difference between the individual needs of these two pupils, and yet they were in the same group. This is the dilemma of many a teacher of deaf adolescents. However, it is possible to develop language through curriculum content. The pupils need to be guided in verbalizing the concepts inherent in the subject matter being taught. It is important, too, to verbalize when visual aids are being used; otherwise, concepts may be vague or even faulty.

How important is communication between teachers at primary and post-primary levels?

What are the needs of the post-primary pupil in the integrated setting?

How are we to prepare teachers who have to supervise students in the integrated setting? Do they need special skills?

13

continuing education and language development
thomas j. watson

Education does not end with the termination of compulsory schooling. Indeed, it is conceived of "as a process continuing throughout life" (Russell, 1973). This is as true for deaf persons as for all other members of our society, but, as the report quoted above reminds us, they are amongst the large groups of people whose needs in this area have been largely unmet. The purpose of the paper that follows is to indicate ways in which this need is beginning to be met, particularly in Britain, and some suggestions about how continuing education and language development interact and how they can further be encouraged to do so. Apart from its general importance to the whole field of education for deaf persons, the topic has particular relevance to the present meeting for it is in this area that the greatest integration into normal educational provision has taken place and the needs and opportunities for improved language development and communication are equally powerful.

Development of Post-elementary and Continuing Education.

The belief that deaf children could proceed beyond an elementary form of education was slow in developing. Indeed it was not until the second half of the 19th century that the earliest attempts to provide a post-elementary education were provided. The first attempt in Britain was that made by Thomas Arnold in the school which he established in Northampton, England, in 1868. He prepared deaf pupils for the Cambridge Local Examinations and London University Matriculation Examinations and published his methods in a number of books and pamphlets dating from 1881. He had shown that pupils were capable of reaching high educational standards by means of oral methods. These methods were based on a systematic approach to the development of language and a very careful training in lipreading as the main basis of understanding. He believed that speech had to be closely integrated with thinking, as opposed to the current attitude that regarded it more as an accomplishment to be acquired after language had already begun to be established, and that therefore it was a natural means of communication for the deaf.

At about the same time that Arnold began his work in Nottingham, the Columbia Institution for the Deaf, in the District of that name in the United States established a National Deaf-Mute College, later to be known as Gallaudet College. Established by an act of Congress in 1864 as an institution of higher education, it was given powers to grant degrees. The intention was to receive selected pupils from institutions all over the United States and give them a college education. Instruction was carried out mainly by a "combined" system, using speech and lipreading mainly with a few promising pupils. The professed aims of the course were "to secure the advantages of a rigid and thorough course of intellectual training in the higher walks of literature and the liberal arts" (Fay, 1893). On the whole, these limited objectives were achieved, as evidenced by the careers of those who completed the course. Over the first 30 years of its existence, there were 388 admissions of whom 58 became teachers, 4 ministers of religion, 6 involved in journalism, 15 entered the civil service, 4 were architects, while others engaged in a wide variety of occupations. How many were unable to complete the course is not stated.

In order to prepare students for the course at Gallaudet College, a number of large state institutions instituted what were described as "High Classes" where the main study was English language and arithmetic, supplemented by some history, geography, and elementary science. Teachers of the deaf in England also began to call for the establishment of more advanced classes in the existing schools. The first outcome of this proposal took the form of prevocational courses, beginning in London in 1903 with a school for older deaf boys at Anerley. The pupils were transferred from the elementary schools at the age of 13, but as half their time was then occupied in trade training, the education they received was little beyond the elementary level. A corresponding arrangement was made for deaf girls with the opening of Oak Lodge in 1905, and in the same year an Industrial Training School was founded in connection with the Manchester School for the Deaf. However, shortly before World War I a number of schools in England and Scotland began to prepare a few of their brighter pupils for examinations taken by normally hearing youngsters, particularly those set by the College of Preceptors.

Another interesting line of progress toward the provision of post-school education was the establishment by the London County Council in 1907 of evening classes for deaf students. In the first year there were 307 enrollments. Such classes spread to other cities and by the 1920's and 1930's evening classes for deaf pupils were being held in Bradford, Burnley, Castleford, Leeds, Leicester, Nottingham, and Sheffield as well as London.

In an endeavor to raise educational standards in schools, plans were drawn up for the establishment of a secondary school for deaf pupils in 1930. Despite the fact that the project had the blessing of the then Board of Education, the economic climate of the period made the establishment of the school impossible.

It was not, therefore, until after World War II that further and higher education really began to take its place in the overall provision for the education of deaf adolescents and adults in the United Kingdom and indeed in most European countries. The first type of provision began with the establishment of separate schools for the education of deaf pupils at the secondary level. These initially followed the tripartite philosophy that was current in post-war British educational circles—grammar schools for the academically able, technical schools for able but technically minded pupils, and secondary modern schools for the average and below average pupils (i.e., about 70–75% of the post-primary age group). The Mary Hare Grammar School, opened in 1946, aims at preparing its pupils, who are of both sexes and have impairments ranging from profound deafness to a partial hearing loss, for public examinations, mainly the General Certificate of Education (G.C.E.) at O (Ordinary) and A (Advanced) levels. This objective has been most successfully attained and the school continues to provide a cadre of well educated students eligible for admission to universities, other colleges of higher education, and professional associations. The second type of post-primary school has been represented since 1955 by the Burwood Park School for boys, where there have been opportunities for pupils to follow C.G.E. courses of a more technical nature and to attend local colleges of higher education for specialized training in subjects such as art. The other secondary schools have varied in the level of education provided because they have had to provide for virtually the whole range of ability. Some have provided a limited number of G.C.E. courses and, since its inception, courses leading to the Certificate of Secondary Education (C.S.E.), a lower level examination.

This growing emphasis on the preparation of pupils for external examinations has had both good and bad effects. One good effect has been that the abler pupils have had incentives to improve their linguistic skills so that they could cope with the requirements of these examinations, especially in subjects of a nontechnical nature. For the less able pupils another good effect has been the satisfaction of obtaining a qualification in a practical subject equivalent to that obtained by their hearing peers. One bad effect has been when no real attempt has been made to match that practical skill with an equivalent knowledge and use of the appropriate language with a consequent assumption that standards are identical, despite the lack of an adequate linguistic back-up.

Apart from the Grammar School and, to a lesser extent, Burwood Park, pupils have tended to leave school at the age of 16 years, so that for a very large majority this was their terminal education. It was this fact that led to the next forward movement, which was an attempt to make provision for students handicapped by deafness within the various institutions providing further and higher education. Additionally, of course, students were encouraged to remain at school beyond the statutory minimum age of 16 years. Section 41 of the Education Act of 1944 had proposed compulsory further education between the ages of 16 and 18 for all who left school, and in accordance with this it was proposed to open a special college of further education for deaf students, to be situated in Sheffield. This proposal came to naught, perhaps fortunately, and the orientation changed toward the provision of tutorial and other help for deaf school leavers within ordinary colleges of further education and other higher educational establishments.

Present Provision of Further Education for Deaf Persons

The main establishment of special help and/or courses for deaf students within the field of further education has been of fairly recent growth. Until the 1960's it took the form of special schools sending the occasional pupil for additional course work to a nearby college on a part-time basis and giving part-time help and support to this at school. One of the earliest colleges to appoint a teacher of the deaf as a full-time member of the staff was Brixton College of Further Education in the Inner London Authority (ILEA) in 1964. Since then the number of appointments has grown to the present total of eight or nine teachers of the deaf in full-time employment in colleges of further education. Colleges which hearing impaired students have attended to take courses now number at least 55, and in most cases these students are given some part-time help or supervision through the peripatetic service. It is difficult to assess the number of students attending these courses, but in 1972 it was reported that in 15 schools for the deaf in the Midlands and North of England, 12.3 percent of deaf school leavers over the previous five years had been in full-time further education. A survey in 1978 of 41 schools for the deaf in England and Wales indicated that the number of pupils leaving school in full-time higher or further education was now 24 percent (Raw, 1978).

The present types of provision appear to follow three patterns:

(a) Students live in a central hostel attached to a special school and attend courses at local colleges of further education, polytechnics, etc. Teachers of the deaf visit the colleges for liaison with the lecturers and provide tutorial help to the students at the hostel. This type of arrangement is provided at schools in Derby, Doncaster, Tewin Water, and Burwood Park (Norfolk House), the last-named also providing a sixth-form college.

(b) A teacher of the deaf is attached to a hearing-impaired group in a College of Further Education and gives tutorial help to all the hearing-impaired students and acts in an advisory capacity to the College staff. This is provided in about seven colleges at present.

(c) Full-time and part-time courses in specialist colleges for the deaf, at present only in the Center for the Deaf, City Literary Institute, London. A further experimental project within the field of higher education has been the support and tuition, at least for the first two years, of a very small group of deaf adults working for degrees from the Open University. This help was based on City Literary Institute, London, and Whitebrook School for the Deaf, Manchester.

With regard to the teachers involved in this work, it should be said that they are all qualified and experienced teachers of the deaf. As yet there are no courses of special preparation for this work in the adult education field, and those involved have had to adapt their previous experience, often at the secondary level, and build on techniques and approaches that have been found to be successful.

The Warnock report on "Children with Special Needs" published in 1978 recommended that day or block release courses should be organized by colleges of further education for children with special needs (Warnock, 1978), but that, "wherever possible" young people with special needs should be given the necessary support to enable them to attend ordinary courses of further education. The committee also felt that it was important that each college of further education should designate a member of staff as responsible for the welfare of students with special needs in the college and for briefing other members of staff on these special needs. They suggested that in each region of the country there should be at least one special unit providing special courses for the more severely handicapped. This might take the form of, say, a unit for profoundly deaf, linguistically retarded, young people, with the dual role of acting as a supporting base for these students attending ordinary colleges. The committee believed that all teachers involved in further education should receive some training, either by means of short part-time courses or as an element in their initial training, to enable them to recognize and respond to the special needs of their handicapped students. Obviously these proposals would be extremely helpful if and when implemented, but the recommendations of Warnock and other reports may have been overtaken by economic events. In any case, many of the proposals are already being implemented in some parts of the country so that what is required is a more widespread application of the best existing practices.

Objectives and Their Attainment

Continuing education can be divided into two main types—vocationally oriented and nonvocationally oriented. The latter might also be sub-divided into that directed to personal self-fulfillment in the artistic, physical, or mental senses, and that directed to the growth of the individual's place in society and ways in which mutual understanding can develop. Most of the college based courses which we have been describing are aimed either directly or indirectly at vocational goals. These include courses leading to certificates designating certain educational standards that have been achieved, as, for example, in English or mathematics or courses of training for specific jobs such as engineering, printing, catering, typewriting, or fashion design. Nonvocationally-oriented courses are more frequently followed on a part-time basis as evening classes or, as in the case of studies relating to developing higher mental powers, in institutions of higher education. These studies which affect a deaf individual's social development must clearly be undertaken in specialist centers and provided by teachers who have an understanding of the problems of deaf people. They would include communication as an important subject and also consider psychological and sociological aspects of deafness.

How can these varying objectives be attained, or indeed how far are they being attained at present? It is evident that perhaps the most attention is being paid to achieving the goal of providing adequate further education for vocational purposes. This is understandable and certainly not undesirable. A satisfying job is an essential for every person, not least for a deaf person, and a continuing education that will prepare for this is equally essential. The main concern here is what this training should comprise. It seems to be generally agreed that as far as possible it should take place alongside hearing peers whose vocational goals are the same. This principle has been established in the vast majority of courses being provided in ordinary departments of ordinary colleges. Because of constraints on normal means of communication in these situations and because of retarded language ability in the great majority of cases, something additional is necessary. Problems of communication are the more easily solved by means of appropriate hearing aid equipment, arrangements for notetaking, overhead projection, suitable reading material, extra tutorials, etc.; improvement in language ability is more difficult and, of course, is also an important determinant of communication ability. Obviously it is hoped that children, by being educated in ways already described in this symposium, will have reached higher stages of attainment in the understanding and use of language by the time they reach the stage of continuing education. Clearly this is the essential and critical issue: many skills can be developed without much language being involved, but if education is to continue in a real sense—be it related to science or humanities, to morality or religion—it must be based on a modicum of understanding and use of language. We have already been discussing how to bring this about at the school stage, and my task is to consider what must happen thereafter. This is in part exemplified by some existing problems. These have been brought to light through investigations made by a recently formed English body—the National Study Group on Further and Higher Education for the Hearing Impaired. This group has looked in considerable depth at courses of further education which have a vocational or quasi-vocational goal, although, of course, their interest is not confined to this aspect of continuing education. They have found that within the field of college based further education many deaf students are deficient in technical vocabulary specific to their particular courses; general vocabulary; and carrier language. (Sutton, 1978). They believe that students need some special training in the more common synonyms of the technical or jargon expressions used by textbooks, lecturers, and in examinations; e.g., that "utilize" means "use"; that "uniform" as an adjective means "regular"; that "locate" means to find; that "complex" may mean a group of buildings, etc. The group has also suggested that college lecturers and examiners could, with advantage to all their students whether deaf or hearing, eliminate unnecessary words and phrases in the interests of clarity and simplicity; e.g., instead of the question "What steps can be taken to ensure the protection of the steel from rust?", there should be substituted "How can the steel be protected from rust?" A further modification which many deaf students find helpful is an alteration in the grouping of words in complex sentences, e.g., "He altered the length of the window cord because it did not fit" might be changed to "It did not fit so he altered the length of the window cord," explaining that the pronoun "it" stands for the window cord and "so" takes the place of "because." Similarly, it is easier to understand question forms when the question comes at the end of the sentence, e.g., "Which of the following materials would you choose if you wished to put a new cover on a chair?" would be changed to "If you wished to put a new cover on a chair, which of the following materials would you choose?"

All these linguistic patterns and the new vocabulary have to be practiced with students so there is clearly a need for the support help of a teacher of the deaf even when the students are integrated into ordinary courses. Moreover, the specialist tutor needs to advise college lecturers on the desirability of using the kinds of patterns described above in written exercises, notes, and examinations. He also needs to help students to acquire vocabulary of the occupation if the course is highly specific, such as cake decorating, printing, or welding; but the explanation of technical terms is something that is needed by all members of a course and should be given by the appropriate lecturer. The National Study Group makes the point that where the course is related to a practical activity, as very many of them are, the student needs to show evidence of competence in the practical sessions before beginning the additional work that will inevitably be required in order to satisfactorily complete the theoretical sections. If the student is either poorly endowed with the appropriate skill or poorly motivated, it seems unlikely he will be capable of successful completion, and therefore the time spent on language teaching is rather fruitless. While this comment may be true when support is in very short supply, one cannot help but feel that any response to efforts to improve language ability is worthwhile and should be encouraged when support services are available to do so.

So far, I have concentrated mainly on continuing education as it is provided at colleges of further education or similar colleges offering courses of a vocational nature, or upgrading the general educational standards of students who need to attain these standards before proceeding further. Such education provision is certainly the most common form of continuing education for young deaf people, and, as has already been noted, is showing an encouraging increase. The second type of formal continuing education is that which is chosen on a voluntary basis. This consists of higher education, as exemplified by attendance at university degree courses, or part-time leisure occupations as provided through adult evening classes organized by local education authorities, or courses for deaf persons organized by the British Deaf Association (B.D.A.) The first two types of courses involve attendance at ordinary courses, frequently without special help; the B.D.A. courses are highly specific and make use of manual methods of communication. For the courses of higher education at universities and similar institutions, it is generally found that the linguistic standards and academic qualifications of candidates are, and require to be, within the range normally expected of entrants to the courses. The main difficulties here relate to communication, and various expedients and experiments have been tried out and adopted to help with such problems, e.g., help with notetaking, special handouts, use of appropriate textbooks, special individualized tutorials, transcribed audio-tape recordings, etc. At the College of St. Hild and St. Bede attached to the University of Durham, a qualified teacher of the deaf has been appointed as a tutor to the deaf. His role is to provide support teaching for hearing impaired students attending any course at the University of Durham. In 1974 a National Bureau for Handicapped Students was established. It is financed by the Department of Education and Science, by the Inner London

Authority, and by membership subscriptions. The aims of the organization are to provide information, coordinate work, arrange specialists' advice, and initiate study and research into the education and employment of handicapped young persons.

Voluntary part-time evening classes covering subjects such as English, handicrafts, dressmaking, foreign language learning, auto maintenance, etc. are either practically based, in which case the deaf student attends a regular class, or are specially provided for deaf adults. The emphasis placed on the correct use of normal language patterns and the methods of communication used tend to vary from center to center and course to course. Nevertheless, the provision of such courses is important if deaf adults are to be given opportunities to develop skills and interests in the same way as non-deaf adults. Courses relating to development of communication skills such as lipreading, speech, aided hearing, tend to be directed mainly to the needs of deafened adults. No doubt individual tutorial help is often directed to improvement in the above skills in the profoundly, prelingually deaf adult, but they are not often listed as areas to which specific attention will be drawn, either by means of courses or through support work. Yet, in a conversation with a very able prelingually deaf lady recently, she described how she had taken special lessons in auditory training during the previous winter since she felt she was not benefiting from her wearable hearing aid as much as she believed she might! For most deaf persons attending integrated classes the motivation to improve communication skills in addition to the language content of the communication act should surely be great and capitalized upon to as great an extent as possible.

It is the belief of many teachers of the deaf that in taking college or external examinations, such as G.C.E., a large number of deaf students are penalized through their retarded linguistic skills although their knowledge of a subject (botany, mathematics, craft subjects, etc.) may be considerable, and in practical areas their work is more than satisfactory at the required level, although some associated linguistic areas cause problems. Other teachers, while recognizing the presence of these problems, feel that it is misleading to the public, to the pupils themselves, and to their parents if the pupils are given a certificate or other qualification which implies that they have met identical criteria to those met by the hearing pupils obtaining the same qualification when, in fact, they have not. In other words, the latter group of teachers believe that no concessions should be made or be seen to be made; the former group would welcome some adjustment to procedures. The present position is that, mainly through the efforts of the National Study Group (referred to above), some bodies responsible for the arrangements for public examinations have been willing to grant concessions to deaf students. Some of these are as follows: The City and Guilds Examinations of the London Institute (mainly related to craft subjects) allow up to 50 percent extra time to a handicapped person, but require a note to be added to the certificate awarded specifying the additional time that was allowed in the examination. Other examination bodies are prepared to grant a short period (10–15 minutes) of additional time for reading carefully the examination questions. Yorkshire and Humberside Council of Further Education are prepared to allow a teacher of the deaf to sit with a candidate to insure his understanding of the questions. Some G.C.E. Boards agree simply to "give special consideration" to the answers of the candidates, and the Open University allows an extra 45 minutes in a 3-hour paper for deaf students.

An area of continuing education quite outside any kind of formal provision is the need for deaf persons to find out about themselves as persons and how they fit into a world of hearing people. One way of tackling this problem was the establishment of the Oral Deaf Adults Section (ODAS) of the A.G. Bell Association for the Deaf in the United States. This was formed by a group of 20 deaf adults in June 1964 (Breunig, 1965b) as a means to "encourage, promote and help in the development of speech, speechreading and residual hearing among those who have a severe loss of hearing." It is "a program to help deaf people help themselves" (Masters, 1965). They are perhaps, as their objectives show, more concerned with communication than with furthering the education of young deaf adults although the latter is partly implied in the former, and the group is also concerned with encouraging parents of young deaf children and demonstrating to teachers the potentialities of some of their pupils.

Another and rather different pattern is that which has evolved into "The Breakthrough Trust" in Britain. This consists of a group of deaf and hearing people whose object is mainly integration. It has a very strong element of deaf initiative ("self-help" the members call it) but clearly depends for the achievement of its objective on hearing participation. The relationship and communication are developed through meeting together for social and leisure-time activities. In the early stages of its growth, the movement succeeded mainly in achieving a "physical integration," i.e., they sat at the same table, they shared the same activity, but the group recognized that more than this was needed and have tried to work toward a sharing of minds and thinking, through working at communication techniques. These are almost entirely purely oral, but take into account lipreading difficulties, etc. and try to work out an acceptable modus operandi, as to how often a phrase should be repeated, how to cope with tiredness and strain, how to communicate in group situations, how to deal with people who are shy and embarrassed (Kenyon, 1978). Accordingly, with real communication taking place, deaf and hearing persons are coming to understand each other's viewpoints, feelings, and problems more adequately, and learn what integration, or rather assimilation, really means. The Trust is clearly endeavouring to expand their work through involving older children at school in their projects, "workshops," and programs so that the next generation of deaf adults will be better prepared to cope in a hearing world. Work has also begun in colleges again with the objective of assimilating the students into the life of the college community rather than simply attendance at ordinary courses.

In the sense of education continuing through life and not being restricted to any formal pattern or attendance at an institution, this attempt to enrich the lives of deaf people through greater assimilation into the community at large and to overcome the feelings of isolation which are so commonly a concomitant of deafness, is clearly of major importance. We would be wrong to think of education as being confined to cognitive aspects of learning, important though they are; the old three-fold division of learning which included cognitive and affective aspects also is still, I believe, valid. Any attempt to develop continuing education without taking all three aspects into consideration is too narrowly based. Moreover, without verbal ability, the inner language on which thinking is most effectively grounded is manifestly inadequate.

Conclusions

To summarize the main points of this paper, I would suggest that the education of profoundly deaf young people should not terminate with the conclusion of compulsory schooling. Already there are a variety of full-time and part-time opportunities for these young deaf persons to continue their education for a considerable time after their school days. There is evidence that an increasing number of them are interested in these facilities, and are making use of them. The existing facilities are, however, too limited for all deaf school leavers to have access to them. Courses, therefore, need to be provided much more widely throughout most countries, and on more flexible bases. For example, in some areas full-time courses are available, but not part-time ones; in other areas the reverse is the case.

Perhaps the most encouraging aspect of this development has been the fact that the greatest growth in provision has been in what might be called the integration or assimilation of young deaf students into ordinary courses, or "mainstreaming" as our American friends would describe it. This seems to me to be a highly motivating factor for oral education in school, especially in the upper classes of school, when, as seems to be increasingly the case, the pupils recognize that they will shortly be faced with the requirement of attending classes alongside their hearing peers.

This emphasis on the tertiary education of young deaf adults in ordinary institutions, of whatever level or type, must be encouraged both among the providing authorities and the students themselves. At the same time it must be recognized that many, if not most of the students, are going to require some form of support. This may be quite limited—ranging from receiving a copy of another student's notes—or it may involve a great deal of additional help, such as the provision of regular tutorials. Whatever the need may be, it should nevertheless be provided to the full, in economic terms alone the cost effectiveness of support in attending ordinary courses is much greater than the provision of specialist institutions, while in social terms the value is immeasurable especially in terms of breaking down barriers of isolation. The keys to success are communication skills, based on linguistic abilities, and character. The same opinion was expressed by a group of American deaf students attending colleges with their hearing peers who considered that personal integrity (defined as courage, optimism, stamina, perseverance, etc.) and communication skills were the most important qualities making for success at these colleges (Breunig, 1965a). In a letter to his former schoolmates a Dutch boy who had left a school for the deaf at 16 years and was attending an ordinary college wrote "You will need will power and perseverance to follow instruction in a school for the hearing . . . . You must take the initiative and show you are one of them and want to communicate." (Bosch, 1976). Obviously all these qualities need to be developed in the preschool and school years, but perhaps more can be done before admission to college, or during the early college years, to help the growth of these communication skills. Should we not, perhaps, consider the establishment either of a pre-college preparation course, based not only on improving the reading and writing of language, but also including the improvement of speechreading, speech, and the use of residual hearing, or alternatively a similar type of course, but one taken after admission to college and concurrent with other studies? Not all pupils will require the same amount of help in every aspect of the course suggested, but elements could be included according to need. Such a course, provided outside the school system and therefore likely to be more acceptable at this stage, might well prevent some of the later course failures as well as contributing to the general educational development of the students.

Whatever the practicalities of establishing a preparatory course of this nature, there is no doubt of the existence of a gap that needs to be filled if the majority of profoundly deaf children are going to obtain the maximum benefit from continuing education. At the same time, paradoxically, continuing education in the environment of ordinary institutions can have the greatest possible impact on the language development and communication skills of profoundly deaf children.

References

Bosch, B. A letter to former schoolmates. *The Volta Review*, 1976, 78, 44-46.
Breunig, H. L. An analysis of a group of deaf students in colleges with the hearing. *The Volta Review*, 1965a, 67, 17-27.
Breunig, H. L. The first milestone. *The Volta Review*, 1965b, 67, 502-504.
Gallaudet, E. M. Columbia Institution for the Deaf and Dumb. In E. A. Fay (Ed.), *Histories of American schools for the deaf* (Vol. II). Washington, DC: Volta Bureau, 1893.
Masters, J. C. ODAS is service. *The Volta Review*, 1965, 67, 580.
Kenyon, D. *Integration*. Unpublished paper presented at Conference of Heads of Schools and Services, Department of Audiology and Education of the Deaf, Manchester University, 1978.
Raw, J. *Career education in schools and units for the deaf*. Unpublished paper presented to National Study Group on Further and Higher Education for the Hearing Impaired, 1978.
Russell, L. *Report of a committee of enquiry—adult education: A plan for development*. London: Her Majesty's Stationery Office, 1973.
Sutton, J. *Teaching language to deaf students*. Paper presented to National Study Group on Further and Higher Education for the Hearing Impaired, 1978.
Warnock, H. M. *Report of a committee of enquiry—special educational needs*. London: Her Majesty's Stationery Office, 1978.

reaction to 13

norbert a.j. smulders

My first reaction to Watson's paper is, that it is one of the few of the requested size.

The second remark is, that in our Institute the age of leaving school is higher than in England and that the range of possible secondary and tertiary education shows a big difference, so that comparison of school types is almost impossible. In our Institute almost all of the children stay until age 18, 19, or sometimes 20. *Some of them* have then completed the training for specific jobs, for instance metalworking, woodwork, painting, typography, business training (*kantooropleiding*). These types of training are concluded with an examination by the teachers of their own school. Others follow an advanced elementary education (Mavo) which is concluded by public examination. Both groups are taught by trained teachers of the deaf. Concerning the first group, it must be said as Watson noted: that learning a job does not always equal learning the language of that job. The second group are the youngsters who almost all go on for further education in schools for normally hearing.

Attending schools with hearing classmates is an inspiring challenge, but there are some prerequisites (*vereisten*). Watson enumerates as the keys to success: communication skills, linguistic abilities, and character, courage, optimism, perseverance and stamina. I would add that good parents are needed. Elisabeth Kindred, in her article "Integration at the secondary school level" (*Volta Review,* 1976, p. 40), states: "The most successful students have parents who began to motivate and challenge their interests at an early age, and continued to do so." In *The Volta Review,* 1966, attention is paid to Jan, a former pupil of the Central Institute for the Deaf, who entered Junior High School. Her mother wrote: "*Parents* must be available to assist with *language.* We have found that we can't just say, 'Look it up in the dictionary.' Often there are several meanings to a word and she doesn't know how to apply the sense of the word. . . . It is up to the parents to correct speech, language usage, and to help with the speech of new vocabulary. . . . Parents may do much to pave the way,' but in the final analysis, it is *the child himself* who has to assume great responsibility and initiative in order to succeed." And it is only two days ago that Ann Mulholland stated in her paper, "The philosophical bases of oral education": "that parental expectations for the deaf child's performance are reflected in later linguistic and academic performance."

But they need guidance, for the textbooks have too complicated language, the teachers are not all or not at all aware of how to speak to the deaf student and are not accustomed to a conversational method which is so essential, and the students have personal problems. Study guidance may be intended as a help for studying, but it will turn out to be personal guidance. Henk Eykman, who is the principal of the study guidance in the Institute of Sint Michielsgestel, told me that he stimulates the students to keep a diary or to write him letters about their experiences. This cuts both ways: they put their feelings in order (which is the beginning of a solution of the problems) and they experience what language is good for. They learn to express themselves and to understand themselves.

- Question 1: In this respect the study guide is a counselor. Should not he be prepared for that task?

- Question 2: Are the teachers of the receiving school sufficiently prepared for their task?

- Question 3: For the former pupils of a school for the deaf, who do not reach so high a language level, must there not be the possibility of additional language courses and/or courses in general education?

- Question 4: What about books in simplified language or a magazine of that type that uses only the 10,000 most frequently used words of English?

part IV

diagnosis and assessment

14

audiological and pediatric diagnosis and assessment
bethan davies

The question posed is whether those children who can be educated orally can be identified by audiological and pediatric assessment. Given the present state of knowledge, the answer must be "no." However, working with our teacher and psychologist colleagues and looking at the results of our combined assessment, we may well feel either very optimistic or very pessimistic about the child's development of speech and speechreading skills. We can certainly identify some of the significant positive and negative factors present. Some, e.g., adverse social conditions, minimal residual hearing, or the presence of other handicaps, may not be remediable. Other factors, such as a treatable conductive hearing loss or a visual defect, may be amenable to treatment.

It cannot be disputed that there are deaf children in whom the prognosis for speech development and speechreading skills is so poor that some sort of manual communication is needed. However, the present situation in the United Kingdom is confused, with many different systems being used without careful evaluation either of the child's needs or the effectiveness of the methods. Each method has its enthusiastic supporters who proclaim the superiority of their method over all others; but scientific evaluation is hard to find.

Some manual methods are by their very nature inimical to the development of speechreading skills. When teachers of the deaf meet together there is no subject which provokes such emotional fervor; but the time has surely come for scientific evaluation of the methods used instead of emotional arguments based on our own particular theories. What is best for the child? This symposium will, I hope, lead the way toward the answers.

I would like to discuss some of the factors involved which may be identified in the process of audiological and pediatric assessment. First, I wish to comment on the team approach to the child and to discuss the problems of identification of the deaf child which must obviously precede all assessment.

Over the last 30 years the patterns of child health have changed considerably in Western countries. Mortality and morbidity resulting from many of the major infections have fallen dramatically. In addition, greatly improved standards of prenatal and neonatal care, at least in major centers, have improved the outlook for many high-risk babies (Reynolds, 1978).

As a result of the changing health care needs of the child population, many pediatricians are now able to devote greater resources to the care of handicapped children. The concept of comprehensive assessment of these children is widely accepted although by no means universally practiced. The comprehensive assessment of the deaf child requires close collaboration of doctors, teachers, psychologists, and others who may be involved. Such a team can only succeed if the professionals concerned recognize each others' skills and roles in the diagnostic team. The main advantage to the parents of this approach is that they are not exposed to conflicting advice from different professionals seen in different centers. The distress caused to parents when conflicting advice is given is often neglected, and the professionals themselves may realize the conflict is trivial. To the parents such conflict may imply that none of the professionals concerned is competent; the parents' trust is severely undermined, and their cooperation in a guidance program may be threatened. In the United Kingdom the audiological services for children and adults are being developed following the Danish model, and the speciality of audiological medicine has been established (Stephens, 1978).

The ideal team for pediatric and audiological assessment consists of a teacher of the deaf, preferably trained in audiology, an educational psychologist specializing in the assessment of the deaf child, an audiological physician with a pediatric background, and a speech therapist. The siting of such a team within a hospital service allows the full use of other specialities and ancillary services. The presence of a pediatric audiology team working alongside both pediatric and otological colleagues has the advantage of increasing awareness among these other doctors of the problems of hearing impairment in children and of the need for careful audiological assessment. As a result, pediatricians and otologists will refer children more readily for audiological assessment; in return, hearing impaired children identified by the audiology team may benefit from the care and increased understanding of the pediatricians and the otologists.

Most doctors in general practice (family doctors) and in the speciality of pediatrics, however, have had little or no experience in the management of hearing impaired children and often no training in the screening of hearing. In addition, the training of ENT surgeons often includes very little work in the field of pediatric audiology.

In the United Kingdom, screening tests of the hearing of babies in child welfare clinics began to be introduced over 20 years ago and are recognized now as a vital part of the community pediatric services. However, a deaf child with no other problems is still occasionally labeled mentally retarded, or aphasic, or autistic without the benefit of audiological assessment. Occasionally one sees a child with a sensorineural loss who has been subjected to repeated myringotomies without audiological assessment, and referral to audiology has been unnecessarily delayed. All children delayed in speech and language development should have a full assessment of their hearing. No child should be subjected to myringotomies without pre-operative audiology so that a surgical decision can be made on the basis of accurate audiological information and the results of surgery can be evaluated subsequently.

Early Identification

The existence of critical or sensitive learning periods for language development is widely accepted, and the implications of this for the deaf child are self-evident. The need for early identification of the deaf child has been stressed by many workers, from the Ewings in 1954 to this day (Ewing I.R., & Ewing A.W.G., 1954).

The responsiveness of the normally hearing baby to sound, and particularly to the human voice, is well recognized by parents who so often identify their hearing impaired baby in the very early months of his life because of his lack of these normal responses. Even so, there is often a long delay before the deafness is confirmed.

The European Economic Community Study in 1977 was of all the children born in 1969 in the EEC countries who had been shown to have a hearing loss of 50 dB or more in the better ear (average of frequencies 500 Hz, 1 K, and 2 K) by the age of 9 years (see also Appendices A and B). The results are about to be published (Martin & Moore, in press). The United Kingdom section of the study showed an average age of suspicion by the parents at 2 years, average age of confirmation at 2 years 11 months, and average age at which a hearing aid was supplied, 3 years 5 months. The percentages of children who were identified by 2 years of age and by 5 years of age are shown in Table 1.

TABLE 1

	Under 2 years	Under 5 years
United Kingdom	36%	81%
The Netherlands	30%	81%
Belgium	18%	67%
Denmark	30%	90%
France	15%	58%
Germany	26%	77%
Ireland	34%	71%
Italy	15%	63%

The indications from some of the American studies are that similar problems exist in the United States. A study (Luterman & Chasin, 1970) based on a questionnaire to parents of children with profound or severe hearing losses found that in their 89 families (children with a mean age at the time of 4:6 and a scatter 1:10–7:4) there was a reported mean age of suspicion at 12.3 months, and confirmation at 19.7 months. These writers found that some 50 percent of parents felt that they had had good advice on their first consultation with a pediatrician while 43 percent felt the advice was poor. The writers commented on the need for pediatricians to know the presenting signs of deafness in children, and to understand the need for accurate diagnosis of hearing loss.

In a small unpublished study in 1978, looking at 84 children who were hearing aid wearers in our own clinics, we found the following ages of identification:

TABLE 2

	N	Hearing Loss	Average Age of Identification
Group I	(18)	25–40 dB	6 yrs 0 months
Group II	(26)	41–55 dB	5 8
Group III	(15)	56–70 dB	2 8
Group IV	(13)	71–90 dB	2 8
Group V	(12)	91 dB +	1 9
Total	84		3 8

There was an expected tendency for much earlier identification of the more severe hearing losses, but there were several children in these groups with severe losses who were not identified until very late. It must be pointed out that this particular population contains a high proportion of very deprived families who make poor use of the services, and also a very high proportion of immigrant and other non-English speaking families. In these groups there is often a problem of persuading the parents to bring the children for audiological assessment. An additional problem is that professionals may have ascribed the children's failure to acquire speech and language as due to exposure to two or more languages, without adequately assessing their hearing. Of this group of children, 60 came from the inner London area; of these, one-third came from either non-English speaking or bilingual homes.

In the United Kingdom all families have free access to a general practitioner of medicine, i.e., family doctor. Also most mothers take their babies to a child welfare clinic where developmental screening tests are carried out by community pediatricians and health visitors, i.e., public health nurses. It should therefore be possible to provide accurate early identification of the majority of hearing impaired children using the conventional distraction test techniques at an age of 7 to 9 months. However, the logistics of providing such a screening service are difficult. Because severe sensorineural deafness is a relatively uncommon condition (i.e., 1–2 per 1,000 being the usually accepted figure), many doctors will very rarely come across such a child and their enthusiasm for careful screening may thus diminish with time. The results of late identification of the hearing impaired child are only too well known to those responsible for the education of the deaf, but such results and the need for much improved identification services are often not well known to doctors. This problem can only be solved by improved training facilities at all levels, both undergraduate and postgraduate, but it is particularly important that family doctors and pediatricians should be aware of the presenting signs of the child with severe hearing impairment and aware of the need for careful audiological assessment. They also need to be trained to competently carry out screening tests of hearing.

The development of tests of hearing in neonates over recent years holds out promise that many hearing impaired children will in future be identified in the early weeks of life. The automatic Crib-o-Gram developed in the United States (Simmons & Russ, 1974; Simmons, 1977) and the Auditory Response Cradle in the United Kingdom (Bennet, in press) both monitor motor and other physiological activities of the baby in response to high-intensity sound. Such techniques will identify babies who need careful audiological followup. However, long-term and large-scale evaluation of these techniques will continue to be necessary before they can be introduced as routine procedure. So far as electric response tests are concerned, the use of acoustic brain-stem electric responses in neonates holds out considerable promise but gives no information about the hearing for low frequencies. The main advantages of this test are that it is noninvasive and that the results are not affected by sedation. It may well be a valuable tool, especially in the area of audiological assessment of very high-risk babies. Another technique which is being used on neonates is the postauricular muscle response test (Douek et al., 1973), but again long-term and large-scale evaluation of this technique is going to be necessary before widespread use can be recommended. It is known that many babies will fail screening by the auditory response cradle or by postauricular muscle response test due to neurological problems other than auditory deficit. At the present stage of knowledge there seems no doubt that the various screening tests of hearing in the neonatal period currently being developed will identify a population which needs particularly careful audiological investigation. We do not yet know to what extent such tests may fail to identify children with significant hearing losses. For the time being, neonatal screening of these types will remain a facility at major centers of research.

In the United Kingdom, some 95 percent of babies are born in hospitals, so a reliable test of hearing in neonates, if generally available in obstetric units, would mean that the majority of neonates could be tested. Prior to compulsory age of school entry, the neonatal period is the only time at which one has a largely captive population.

Conventional screening tests of hearing by the distraction method at 7 to 9 months of age will continue to be necessary for the foreseeable future. Such screening tests need to be carried out on the whole population and not be restricted to a high-risk population. There is abundant evidence from studies of etiology of congenital sensorineural deafness that as many as 30 percent of cases may be due to autosomal recessive inheritance. In the first child in the family with this condition, the baby will by definition be excluded from any high-risk register. The personnel carrying out the distraction testing must fully understand the underlying principles and must be aware of the common pitfalls in testing. In particular they must be informed of the typical behavior of the deaf baby in the distraction test situation so that they realize the necessity of excluding all possible visual clues to the child. They also need to understand clearly the results of late identification to the child and his family so that their own motivation to perform the tests accurately is increased and maintained.

Early identification of the deaf child could be improved by increasing the sensitivity of all the professionals in the child health field to whom parents may turn when in doubt about their baby's hearing. Such professionals should also be encouraged to ask parents directly at appropriate times, e.g., at 6 or 12 months developmental screening, for the parents' own opinion of the child's hearing. The professionals concerned should be encouraged to refer all babies for audiological assessment when parental anxiety about hearing is present. In addition, all child health personnel need to learn the skills of evaluating the vocalizations of babies and the early speech development of young children. To the experienced ear the diagnosis may be evident on hearing the deaf child's vocalization pattern, but little attention is paid in the training of doctors and health visitors to the evaluation of early vocalization and to early speech and language development.

If the deaf baby has not been identified in the first year of his life and presents for diagnosis later, at about 2–2½ years of age, it becomes imperative that his lack of speech and his possibly difficult behavior pattern is not then mistaken for evidence of mental retardation.

Diagnosis

Full audiological examination by tests appropriate to a child's mental age is necessary so that the appropriate prescription of hearing aids can be made and teachers can be provided with as much information as is possible about the child's residual hearing. By using play audiometry or performance techniques, skilled testers can obtain a reliable pure tone audiogram in most children who have reached a mental age of 2½ years. Time and a suitably relaxed atmosphere are needed, and it is always worthwhile to persist. In case of failure to obtain reliable results, resort has to be made to distraction type testing from which much less valuable information will be available. There is an increasing tendency now to suggest that electrophysiological tests will replace conventional methods; this occurs particularly in centers where skilled testers are not available. Electric Response Audiometry (ERA) of various kinds provides a most valuable tool in testing the severely retarded and/or disturbed child or when confirmation of results obtained by other methods is essential. ERA carried out by personnel experienced in its use and in their interpretation can be of invaluable assistance in children who have proved difficult or impossible to assess by other means. This tool should not, however, be seen as a replacement for established methods of behavioral audiometry (Gibson 1978).

In the children who prove most difficult to test by conventional methods, electrocochleography is so far providing the most useful information. But, as this is an invasive technique and requires anesthesia, its use is somewhat restricted.

The Etiology of Deafness

TABLE 3

	Etiology by Percent		
	FRASER	FISCH	TAYLOR
Familial	32	26	24
Nongenetic causes	31	49	48
Unknown	36	25	28
Total	99	100	100

Table 3 indicates the distribution of different etiologies as shown in three studies (Fraser, 1976; Fisch, 1955; and Taylor et al., 1973). It now seems likely that many of the cases previously identified as of unknown etiology are in fact of genetic origin (Taylor et al., 1975). It does not seem likely that a further major infection causing deafness is likely to be found. However, cytomegalovirus infection has been shown to be a cause of deafness in recent years (MacDonald & Tobin, 1978). Haeomolytic disease of the newborn due to RH (rhesus) incompatibility has largely disappeared, although severe jaundice from other causes remains a significant problem. In looking at all surveys of etiology, one must take into account the types of investigations that have been done to establish the etiological factors present. It is probable that in the past many cases of rubella were not identified correctly. Often the child had only the single defect of deafness, without any of the other stigmata of congenital rubella infection, particularly so in cases where the infection took place after the twelfth week of pregnancy. Confirmation of the presence of rubella infection by the identification of the rubella retinopathy frequently is neglected. In addition, serological confirmation of rubella infection has only been possible in recent years. The isolation of the virus and successful measurement of the rubella antibody occurred in 1962 (Parkman et al., 1962; Weller & Neva, 1962). It was not widely known until recent years that many rubella-affected children were born after pregnancies in which the mother had subclinical rubella and was therefore unaware of the risk to her baby. This problem has been largely solved in the United Kingdom with the routine introduction of serology studies during pregnancy. In 1978 there was an epidemic of rubella in the United Kingdom, and the results of that epidemic are now appearing in the audiology clinics. It is, however, pleasing that as a result of accurate serological diagnosis in mothers, these babies are being presented at a very early stage, even in the first few weeks of life.

Retrospective studies of etiological factors in any population of deaf children are difficult and unreliable; in the case of rubella, for example, the serological studies need to be done at an early age. The most difficult differential diagnostic situation is often between the possibility of an autosomal recessive deafness and a rubella with no other stigmata but deafness. The investigation of possible etiological factors should be carried out as soon as diagnosis of deafness has been confirmed.

Taylor et al. (1975) studied a group of children of unknown etiology. From their statistical analysis of audiometric patterns of the unknown group and a comparison with other audiometric patterns, it was suggested that the majority of the unknowns were probably of genetic origin. Adding these to the cases previously known to be of genetic origin, the total figure for cases of genetic origin is then over 50 percent.

In countries or towns where there has been a considerable immigration of people from cultures where first-cousin marriages are the rule, more cases of genetic deafness are occurring, as well as other diseases which have an autosomal recessive type of inheritance. The question of the cause of a child's deafness is invariably the first question asked by the parents of the deaf child. The identification of the etiology is of the utmost importance in suggesting to us other problems which the child may have, in establishing the prognosis for the child, occasionally for his life and health, and usually for his hearing levels. Lastly, no genetic counseling can be given before the etiology has been fully investigated. A most careful family history has to be taken in order to establish whether there is any evidence of a genetic cause. A full general examination is required to identify the stigmata of the syndromes associated with deafness. Blood and urine examinations must be done to identify the possible infective causes, particularly rubella, toxoplasmosis, cytomegalovirus infection, and syphilis. In some cases relatively rare metabolic disorders have to be excluded, e.g., the mucopolysaccaridoses. The ophthalmologist may well be able to provide useful information about the etiology and should always be asked to comment on the fundi. There are very few data available in the literature on the incidence of rubella retinopathy. Its presence confirms rubella as the cause of the deafness, although the absence of rubella retinopathy is by no means proof of the absence of rubella infection (Davies, 1974).

Additional Conductive Hearing Problems

The widespread use of acoustic impedance measurements in recent years has shown that middle ear dysfunction due to serous otitis media is a very common condition in young children. Impedance measurements done in the first year of school life have indicated as many as 30 to 35 percent of children showing middle ear dysfunction (Brooks, 1973; Ferrer, 1974). There is no reason to suppose that middle ear dysfunction is less common in children with sensorineural hearing defects than in children with no such deficit. One study (Brooks, 1975) of children at schools for the deaf showed an incidence of middle ear dysfunction equal in deaf and normally hearing children at 5 years of age, but considerably higher in deaf children above 11 years of age. There is anecdotal evidence that middle ear dysfunction is also very common in much younger children. In babies referred to our clinics who have failed screening tests of hearing and who are often seen in the latter part of their first year of life, the majority are found to have a middle ear problem. In addition, we find that very large numbers of our toddlers who are in day care facilities are prone to very frequent upper respiratory tract infections, and many of these children have severe middle ear dysfunction and associated conductive hearing losses.

When a child has an underlying sensorineural deficit, and especially when the sensorineural loss is very severe, it is obviously essential to ensure that any additional conductive problem is treated promptly by medical means, or, if this fails, by surgical intervention. In my own practice we regard the presence of a sensorineural hearing loss as an indicator for urgent myringotomies in the case of persisting middle ear dysfunction. The operation of choice is adenoidectomy, myringotomies, and the insertion of grommets. It is clear that all children with sensorineural hearing losses should have regular monitoring of their middle ear function by acoustic impedance measurements and then appropriate management. Regular otoscopic examination will, of course, identify some of these children, but numerous studies have shown that impedance measurements are a much more sensitive indicator of middle ear dysfunction than otoscopic examination (Ferrer, 1974).

Visual Defects

Normally hearing children and adults depend to some extent on the visual modality in discriminating speech but are clearly largely dependent on the auditory modality. The deaf child who with even the best possible amplification can only receive a very limited amount of acoustic information will obviously be dependent upon the visual modality in discriminating speech. It seems strange, therefore, that relatively little attention has been paid to the visual problems of deaf children. Several studies have indicated that there is a higher incidence of visual defects in deaf children than in a normally hearing population. Stockwell (1952) reported that nearly half of a sample of 760 children in schools for the deaf needed glasses for correction of their visual defects compared with 15 percent in normally hearing children. An earlier study by Braly (1938) identified 38 percent of children in schools for the deaf with defective vision compared with 22 percent in normally hearing children. In some etiologies—for example, in rubella-deafened children and in post-meningitic children—the need for careful ophthalmological assessment is obvious. Nevertheless, it is not routine practice in many centers for a child with a sensorineural hearing loss to have routine examination of the eyes by an ophthalmologist or even an assessment of his visual acuity. In the United Kingdom there is routine screening of vision in all schools, including special schools for the deaf and schools and units for the partially hearing. But except in a very few centers, no special measures have been taken to date to ensure that each deaf child is seen by an ophthalmologist soon after the time of diagnosis. One of the problems is that there are relatively few ophthalmologists who specialize in the assessment of handicapped children. A deaf child recently seen in my own clinic for advice and further assessment prior to subsequent educational placement at 16 years was discovered to have a severe degree of myopia previously undiagnosed. Not surprisingly, his lipreading skills were very poor. The child with a severe hearing loss who is also partially sighted may well be mistakenly identified as mentally retarded because of the synergistic effect of the two defects. The care taken to identify all types of visual problems in children at St. Michielsgestel is a model of the care which, I feel sure, should be followed in all schools for the deaf.

Neurological Defects

All children who are identified in the audiology clinic as having a severe hearing impairment need to have a full pediatric assessment to identify signs of general developmental delay, evidence of other physical defects, and particularly neurological defects. The information we are able to obtain about neurodevelopmental function is relatively crude compared with the detailed work going on at St. Michielsgestel. The identification of the so-called dyspraxic child (van Dijk & van Uden, 1976) suggests that we should attempt to introduce a battery of neurodevelopmental tests into the pediatric diagnostic situation.

As part of a general medical study of a small group of deaf children (Davies, 1974), a short battery of neurodevelopmental tests was used. This study was of 12 rubella-deafened children compared with 12 matched controls who were deaf due to some other cause. In this very limited part of the study it was noted that many of the children in both groups showed very poor fine motor skills. No statistical significance between the two groups was demonstrated, and the poor scores were found in not only the rubella children and the post-meningitic ones but also in the children with deafness of undoubted familial origin. The tests used were a shortened form of the Oseretsky test (Rutter et al., 1970).

Work on the development of speechreading skills both in deafened adults (McCormick, 1979) and in congenitally deaf children (Erber, 1974a; Erber, 1974b; van Dijk & van Uden, 1976) suggests that we need to look more carefully at the integration of auditory and visual input and, in the case of the deaf child, at the integration of auditory, visual, and motor/kinesthetic information. Further analysis of the nature of this integration may well shed light on the differences in skills and speechreading so readily observed in both the hearing and the deaf population. We need to develop diagnostic measures for such integration and also to look at the pediatric assessment for the neuropathological correlates of the failure of integration. The usual methods of assessing the child's speech discrimination levels using his hearing aids and then looking separately at his speechreading skills without amplification deny us the opportunity to observe how well the child integrates acoustic and visual information.

In relation to the assessment and development of speechreading skills, a problem arises with some of our clinic patients who are from particular ethnic minorities: that is, the cultural pattern of eye avoidance between individuals who are speaking to each other. While this is inimical to the development of good speechreading skills in the child, one is aware of the problems being created in encouraging the child to watch faces for information when this is counter to the normal and approved pattern of behavior in this particular group.

Management After Diagnosis

Early and adequate amplification must obviously be provided for the child. The EEC figures show an alarming and unexplainable delay between the confirmation of the child's hearing loss and the provision of hearing aids, in the United Kingdom, an average of 6 months (see Appendix C). The audiological assessment should always include measurements of acoustic impedance. The necessity of prompt identification by this procedure of additional conductive hearing loss has already been discussed.

It is not relevant at this point to discuss in any detail the provision of aids, but it is of note that in the United Kingdom the range of National Health Service aids is now considerable; in addition, high-powered commercial hearing aids can be prescribed at no cost to the parents, if there is no suitable aid available in the NHS series. Such aids have to be prescribed by a consultant otologist or a consultant audiological physician. Consultants have freedom to prescribe two aids without question if they feel the child needs them; in the majority of cases, binaural aids are prescribed for the young deaf child.

Neither is it relevant to discuss at this point in any detail the role of the peripatetic teacher of the deaf, but I would like to comment on his or her role in the immediate post-diagnosis stage. In the United Kingdom the usual practice is that the peripatetic teacher of the deaf is responsible for all the preschool children in the area. She visits the family at home at the earliest possible opportunity, and in our own clinic we try to arrange this visit to occur within two or three days of the diagnosis. The immediate role of the teacher in this situation is essentially to listen to the feelings expressed by the mother, answering her questions, and endeavor to reassure her in a realistic way about the outcome for her child. Ideally this teacher of the deaf should be a member of the diagnostic team, becoming involved with the family at the time of diagnosis. The skills and personality of the teacher of the deaf working with the very young child and his family can influence very considerably the attitude of the parents toward the child's progress and his educational future. The teacher needs to be sensitive to the reactions of the parents at all times and to be skilled in understanding the emotional processes through which the parents come to terms or fail to come to terms with their situation.

Patience and skill are required in dealing with the grief situation that frequently occurs following diagnosis. Many professionals find grieving difficult to deal with and tend to react by over-reassurance. One has to accept that a period of grief for the hearing and talking child that was hoped for must invariably take place before the deaf child with his problems, but with all his good points too, can be accepted for what he is. A familiar stage of denial—the case of parents who seek more and more different opinions on their child's hearing in the hope of a different diagnosis—needs sympathetic handling.

The teacher's role in the guidance situation dealing with all these problems and many others requires the utmost skill; most teachers in guidance work accept that the present training for this work is not adequate. Given that he has colleagues in medicine and psychology to whom he can turn for advice on particular points, the teacher must be regarded as the key worker with the family. He will, of course, in some situations have to seek supportive help for the family from a social worker.

The contribution of the pediatric and audiological services to the deaf child's future educational progress lies, I think, in laying the foundations of a situation with the best possible prognosis for him by:

(a) Early identification of the deaf child;
(b) Efficient and comprehensive assessment;
(c) Appropriate amplification; and
(d) The early introduction of a good guidance program.

The handling of the child and his parents throughout all these processes needs to be sympathetic and skilled and realistically optimistic for the child's progress in an oral education system.

Unfortunately our own clinic situation is not akin to this, in that in spite of good preschool guidance our deaf children go to schools where manual communication is introduced at a very early stage. The population which we serve is one with a high degree of deprivation. Many of our children come from one-parent families and live in poor housing; there are financial problems and often overwhelming social problems of a variety of types. In addition, a large number of the families are non-English speaking so that the guidance situation is made doubly difficult and early admission to school is the only solution.

In our experience, children who do well in oral education tend to have the following characteristics:

(a) They come from families without overwhelming social problems;
(b) They are identified early;
(c) They have been provided with and use appropriate hearing aids;
(d) The parents have cooperated fully in a guidance program, and there are no language barriers to providing such a program; and
(e) There is reasonable residual hearing across the speech frequency range.

The adverse indices are the reverse of all these factors, especially if combined with minimal residual hearing.

In conclusion, I believe that the contribution of audiological and pediatric assessment, both at the diagnostic stage and in ongoing assessment, is optimal if such assessment is done in close collaboration with colleagues from the educational field; then there is a constant interchange of information and ideas which must be in the best interests of the children who come for assessment.

References

Bennet, M. H. *Trials with the auditory response cradle.* In press.
Braly, K. W. A study of defective vision among deaf children. *American Annals of the Deaf,* 1938, *83,* 192–193.
Brooks, D. N. Hearing screening: A comparative study of an impedance method and pure tone screening. *Scandinavian Audiology,* 1973, *2,* 67–72.
Brooks, D. N. Middle ear effusion in children with severe hearing loss. *Impedance Newsletters,* 1975, *4,* 6–7.

Davies, B. *Rubella and deafness in children.* Unpublished master's dissertation, University of Manchester, 1974.

Douek, E. E., Gibson, W. P. R., & Humphries, K. N. The crossed acoustic response. *Journal of Laryngology and Otology,* 1973, *87,* 711–726.

Erber, N. P. Auditory-visual perception of speech. A survey. *Scandinavian Audiology Supplement,* 1974a, *4,* 12–30.

Erber, N. P. Visual perception of speech by deaf children. *Scandinavian Audiology Supplement,* 1974b, *4,* 97–113.

Ewing, I. R., & Ewing, A. W. G. *Speech and the deaf child.* Manchester: Manchester University Press, 1954.

Ferrer, H. P. Use of impedance audiometry in school children. *Public Health London,* 1974, *88,* 153–163.

Fisch, L. *Journal of Laryngology and Otology,* 1955, *69,* 479.

Fraser, G. R. *Causes of profound deafness in childhood.* Bailliere Tindell, 1976.

Gibson, W. P. R. *Essentials of clinical electric response audiometry.* Churchill Livingstone, 1978.

Luterman, D. M., & Chasin, J. The paediatrician and the parent of the deaf child. *The Paediatrician,* 1970, *45,* 115–116.

Martin, J. A. M., & Moore, W. J. *Childhood deafness in the European community.* In press.

McCormick, B. Audio-visual discrimination of speech. *Clinical Otolaryngology,* 1979, *4,* 355–361.

MacDonald, H., & Tobin, J. O'H. *Developmental Medical Child Neurology,* 1978, *20,* 471–482.

Parkman, P. D., Buescher, E. L., & Artenstein, M. S. *Proceedings of the Society for Experimental Biology and Medicine,* 1962, *111,* 225.

Reynolds, E. O. R. *Neonatal intensive care and the prevention of major handicap.* Ciba Symposium (number 59), 1978.

Rutter, M., Graham, P., & Yule, W. A neuropsychiatric study in childhood. *Spastics International Medical Publications,* 1970, 230–237.

Simmons, F. B., & Russ, F. N. *Automated newborn screening: The crib-o-gram in hearing loss in children.* Baltimore: University Park Press, 1977.

Stephens, S. D. G. Existence and role of audiological physicians. *Hospital Update,* November 1978, 701–707.

Stockwell, E. Visual defects in the deaf child. *American Medical Association Archives of Ophthalmology,* 1952, *48,* 428–432.

Taylor, I. G., Hine, W. D., Brasier, V. J., Chiveralls, K., & Morris, T. A study of the causes of hearing loss in a population of deaf children with special reference to genetic factors. *Journal of Laryngology and Otology,* 1975, *79,* 899–914.

Van Dijk, J., & van Uden, A. Problems of communication in deaf children. *The Teacher of the Deaf,* 1976, *74,* 70–90.

Weller, T. H., & Neva, F. A. *Proceedings of the Society for Experimental Biology and Medicine,* 1962, *111,* 215.

Appendix A
Other Handicaps in Deaf Children

C.E.C.: 861 children (28.8% of the total) are reported as having a handicap additional to deafness.

The three major handicaps (either alone or in combination with others) are:
  i) Mental retardation
  ii) Visual deficits
  iii) Cerebral dysfunction (including cerebral palsy, epilepsy, hydrocephalus, etc.).

Interpretation of the differing prevalences of other handicaps between countries is made uncertain owing to the lack of information on the level of assessment in each country.

	Number	Percent of Total Number
C.E.C.	861	28.8
Belgium	34	32.4
Denmark	24	22.9
Germany	222	31.4
Ireland	18	31.0
Italy	186	21.6
Netherlands	98	43.2
United Kingdom	276	30.0

Appendix B
Percentages of Types of Handicaps by Countries

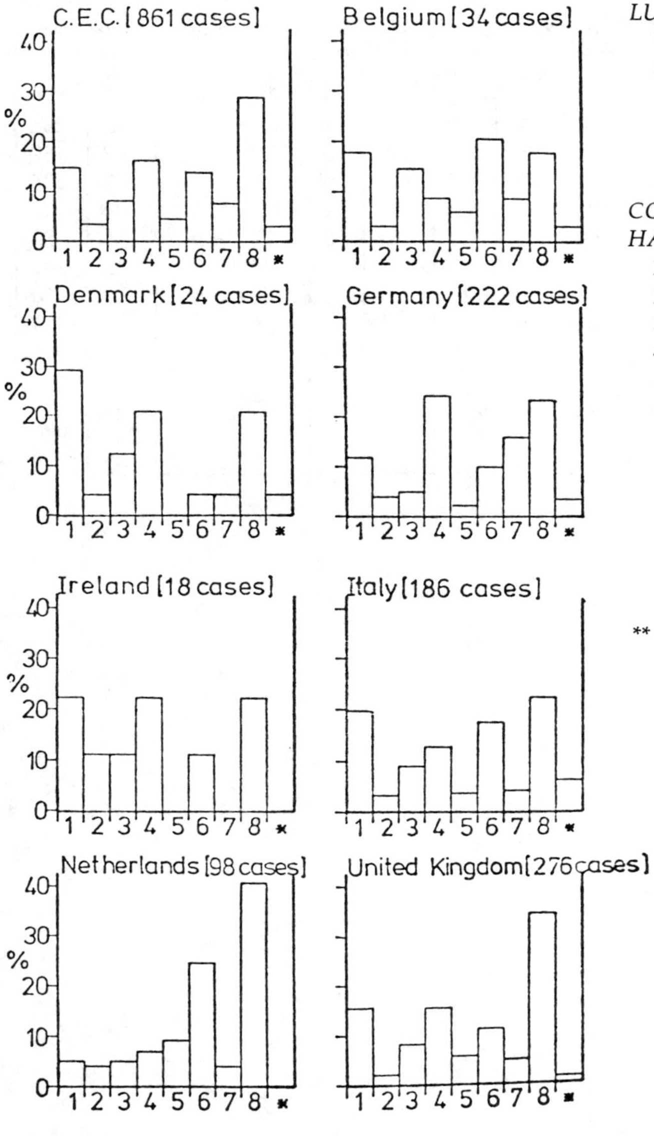
C.E.C. [861 cases]
Belgium [34 cases]
Denmark [24 cases]
Germany [222 cases]
Ireland [18 cases]
Italy [186 cases]
Netherlands [98 cases]
United Kingdom [276 cases]
%
0
10
20
30
40
1 2 3 4 5 6 7 8 *

LUXEMBOURG
(No. of cases)
3 cases - 8
1 case - *

CODE FOR HANDICAPS:

1 = Mental only
2 = Mental + Visual
3 = Mental + Other
4 = Visual only
5 = Visual + Other
6 = Cerebral Dysfunction
7 = Behavior Disorder
8 = Others**
* = Missing data

** Others include: Language, Cardiac. Renal, Stature. Skeletal, Skin. Blood. Combinations.

Appendix C
Age at which Hearing Loss Was Confirmed — Broken Down by Countries

Years	CEC including France	CEC excluding France	Belgium	Denmark	France	Germany	Ireland	Italy	Luxembourg	Netherlands	United Kingdom
0	234	218	7	7	16	56	6	28	0	15	99
1	622	569	12	24	53	130	14	105	0	53	231
2	731	641	27	35	90	165	8	176	0	48	182
3	550	476	16	18	74	111	9	153	1	32	136
4	363	320	8	11	43	81	4	85	1	36	94
5	292	248	11	4	44	55	6	73	0	16	83
6	173	150	4	4	23	31	7	49	1	13	41
7	88	76	1	1	12	10	1	47	0	0	16
8	26	22	0	0	4	8	0	9	1	0	4
Missing Data	383	268	19	1	115	60	3	138	0	14	33
Total	3462	2988	105	105	474	707	58	863	4	227	919

reaction to 14

george w. fellendorf

I am delighted to have this opportunity to comment on Dr. Davies' paper though I only received this privilege a day ago when I was asked to take the place of Mr. Veeger, who was suddenly taken ill. In particular, I am sorry that I did not have the chance to have at hand my own doctoral dissertation which I completed in 1974 (Fellendorf, 1974). This study treated in some detail the subject of education and health care service delivery to some 400 Swedish families and 600 United States' families, all of whom were included in my study because they had at least one hearing impaired child between the ages of 0 and 6. Not only did that research report on the experiences of these 1,000 families in receiving services for themselves and their hearing impaired children, but it also demonstrated the use of a statistical technique known as policy capturing or judgment analysis which provided a basis for the evaluation of the effectiveness of delivery of a wide variety of services to families with young hearing impaired children.

Dr. Davies asserts that there are no audiologic or pediatric assessment techniques to identify those children who can be educated orally. If this is the case (and Van Uden has suggested that there may well be such a technique available even now), then it would appear that the most wise route would be to approach each child as though he were going to learn the language and communication modes of his family and, until proven differently, assume that he will succeed. The alternative is to make assumptions as to the child's capacity to learn as other children do, and thereby incur the responsibility for diverting him for his entire lifetime toward a communication form and a lifestyle which must be viewed as less than normal.

In the area of early identification, I think we can agree internationally that there is great need for improvement. The most profitable short-term approach, however, may be in the area of sensitizing parents and grandparents to the danger signals of hearing loss in infants while we continue our sometimes frustrating task of informing the physicians of the same thing. In my doctoral study, I found that both in Sweden and the United States it was not the physicians or the visiting nurses who first suspected the hearing loss, it was the mother and the grandmother! Perhaps our early detection efforts should be modeled after that adopted in the state of Massachusetts where each new mother in the hospital is provided with a kit of pamphlets which inform her about the danger signals of possible deafness in her baby. They also tell her what she should do if those signals appear when she goes home from the hospital with her child.

With respect to diagnosis, I will comment only briefly on the desirability of expediting the delivery of appropriate diagnostic services to families with young children. Also, since by no means are all otologists or audiologists qualified by knowledge, experience, and inclination to work with babies and young children, perhaps there should be an international directory of those centers and individuals who are known to have such competencies. We simply cannot assume as an act of faith that each person with an M.D. or a Ph.D. in audiology after his name is knowledgeable and capable of testing young children and guiding their parents.

There would appear to be every reason to encourage and support the work of men like Fourcyn, University College, London, in application of new phonetically based audiometric testing. Indeed, we can substantially improve our present diagnosis of hearing loss in young children by strengthening the medical school training and the in-service training of physicians, audiologists, and related professionals in how to test or where to get testing done promptly if they themselves are not prepared to do it.

From my experience, Davies gives far too much credit to the teacher of the deaf as a counselor and consoler of parents upon their discovery of a hearing loss in their child. It reminds me of my son-in-law who recently graduated from medical school and who admits that he has had no preparation for the task of preparing terminally ill patients for the inevitable moment of death which all human beings must anticipate. "I think one of my professors devoted part of a lecture to it once," he reported when I inquired. I would wonder, similarly, how much attention is given in the preparation of teachers of the deaf for the task of helping parents work through the trauma of discovering they have a deaf child?

I wish Dr. Davies had given us more insight and references to support her position on the use of binaural aids. In looking at the program to date, and that which is to follow, I fear that the critical issue of proper use of amplification for *which* children, at *which* time, may not be given the attention which most of us would attribute to it. So many programs today, in the developed countries at least, concentrate on the maximum use of residual hearing that I fear we will not adequately treat this subject in our discussions or in our proceedings when they are published. We cannot assume that those who plan and direct either oral or "total communication" educational programs throughout the world will have the same commitment as most of us to maximizing the use of any remnant of hearing which a child may have.

There are matters which I should like to see discussed in much more detail. The issue of aided audiograms is critical in my opinion. We assert and commend the use of residual hearing, yet we persist in showing parents and teachers pure-tone, unaided data on children and expect them to translate this into educational implications. Some have decried this practice (Fellendorf, 1978) and recommended emphasizing "what's left" rather than "what's gone," which is what we do when we refer to "hearing loss."

I would also commend our consideration and use of the idea of a quantitative measure of the improvement of the use of hearing over a period of time; i.e., the Acoustic Rehabilitative Acuity (ARA) of Borkowska (1975). We need to emphasize and publicize for that great army of uninformed public(s) with whom we and our deaf children must relate, the viability of the use of residual hearing.

In conclusion, may I endorse Dr. Davies' call for much greater collaboration and mutual respect between pediatricians, audiologists, and educators of hearing impaired children. We have models of successful efforts in achieving such cooperation and exchange which should be publicized and replicated. While we are all considered professionals in our respective fields and may thereby consider it "someone else's" responsibility to speak out in the press, on radio and TV and before other bodies, this responsibility indeed rests with each of us. We *know* the importance of early detection and assessment to the lives of young children and their families.

Can we do less than tell what we know to the public(s) which are as yet pitifully uninformed?

References

Borkowska, D. *Study on Hearing Impairment in Children in Poland*, Warsaw Research Institute of Mother and Child, 1975.

Fellendorf, G. W. *The Eduhealth Delivery Service Index: A Study of the Delivery of Education and Health Care to Young Hearing Impaired Children and Their Parents.* Washington, D.C.: The Alexander Graham Bell Association for the Deaf, 1974.

Fellendorf, G. W. An Editorial, *The Volta Review*, September 1978.

15

assessment of the speech of deaf children: a survey of available tests
andreas markides

We learn to talk and later to control our speech mainly by auditory feedback. It is obvious, then, that a hearing impairment will interfere partially or totally, depending on its severity, with this auto-corrective cyclical process. The severity of such interference varies from person to person and can be dramatically and positively illustrated by the multiplicity of disorders characterizing the speech of deaf children.

The purpose of this paper is (a) to present and describe major attempts to study the speech of deaf children; (b) to isolate and discuss both major error categories and major factors affecting the speech intelligibility of deaf children; and (c) to describe relevant procedures employed in the assessment of the speech of deaf children.

Major Studies Relating to the Speech of Deaf Children

Hudgins (1934) compared the speech coordination of 62 deaf and 25 hearing subjects through Kymographic tracings as they repeated phrases of nine, seven, five and four syllables containing voiced, unvoiced, nasal, and stop consonants. In comparing the speech of the two groups he concluded that the deaf had the following abnormalities:

(a) Extremely slow and very heavy, labored speech with inadequate chest pressure;
(b) Expenditure of an excessive amount of breath for each phrase;

(c) Substitutions and distortions of vowels and consonants;
(d) Abnormalities of rhythm;
(e) Excessive nasal emission;
(f) Improper functioning of either releasing or arresting consonants; and
(g) Production of inappropriate adventitious syllables.

He recommended that teachers of profoundly deaf children would be helped through understanding the speech coordination of normal children.

Two years later, Hudgins' experiment, with slight modifications, was replicated by Rawlings (1936). He compared the amount of breath consumed by deaf and hearing subjects while breathing quietly and while speaking. He found that the normal speakers used the same amount of air for speaking as for quiet breathing. Among deaf children he found that breath consumption while speaking depended on the degree of hearing loss: the greater the hearing loss, the greater the amount of air consumed. In fact, his results were similar to those of Hudgins, both experiments supporting each other and suggesting the need for teaching the deaf child a more economical and efficient management of breath control.

Voelker (1935), using the strobophotoscopic system, compared the speech and voice of 28 deaf children when reading 10 sentences with the speech and voice of their teachers and a group of normal children. His aim was to determine and measure the effects of the factors of intonation, pitch, and duration on the speech of the deaf. He found that, although some of the deaf children showed a tendency toward perseverated pitch patterns, the majority of them were capable of pitch changes as rapid and as extensive as in normal voices. He also stated that the deaf, on average, took almost four times as long and used three times as much phonation in saying a sentence as the normal speakers. In a later study Voelker (1938) reported on the rate of speaking of deaf and normal speakers when reading simple sentences. He found that the mean rate of utterance for normal speakers was 164.4 words per minute. The deaf children showed a wide range of scores with a mean of 69.6 words per minute. He concluded that in the oral education of the deaf the children should be helped to acquire normal rate of speaking by placing more emphasis on an increased rate of utterance.

A more analytical study of the speech of deaf children was reported in 1936 by Miller-Shaw. He included in his study 10 hearing impaired adolescents whose intelligence, according to their teachers, was average or above average. He investigated their speech accomplishments following three months of intensive speech training during which the 10 children were each given four 40-minute periods of speech teaching each week, using a high-fidelity amplifier which made it possible for the children (according to Miller-Shaw) to hear all the speech sounds! He pointed out, however, that although auditory stimulation played the predominant part in the correction technique employed, he also supplemented it by using visual, tactile, kinesthetic and, in fact, every technique known to him. He pointed out "as perhaps the most universal characteristic common to every one of the ten subjects" regarding their speech was the frequent reversal of consonants: /bets/ for /best/, /bakset/ for /basket/, /kate/ for /take/, etc. Moreover, he stated that none of the subjects pronounced /s/ or /z/

correctly in the three positions—initial, medial, and final—and seven of the ten children could not say correctly the voiced velar nasal consonant /ŋ/ as in /king/. Miller-Shaw was very reluctant to make any generalizations owing to the small sample studied and the relatively short training periods. However, he concluded that the marked improvement in the children's speech intelligibility, spontaneous speech, phrasing, and accent amply justified the time and effort expended on training.

Five years afterwards the implications of Miller-Shaw's study were taken up by Hughson, Ciocco, Whitting, and Lawrence (1941). Their sample of 366 deaf children was divided into two groups, one of which had been taught by the "auricular" method, the other by the "oral" method. The test administered to the children consisted of 26 words known to young deaf children. This list of words, according to the authors, included all vowels and consonants with the latter being tested in initial and final positions as far as was possible. The children were asked to read these words and their speech was recorded on 12" cellulose acetate discs. The same test was also administered to a group of hearing children whose speech was recorded for comparative purposes. The following speech characteristics were studied: articulation, explosiveness and audibility of the first and final consonants, holding or duration of vowels, syllable continuity, and expression. Their final evaluation indicated that children from "auricular" classes were superior in speech intelligibility when compared to children taught by "oral" methods. However, Dale (1958) considered their findings to be invalid on the grounds of lack of information regarding the sampling technique used to select the two groups of children and the omission of any information on the residual capacity of the children to hear. It is also pointed out that the above writers failed to give any precise definition of their "auricular" and "oral" methods of teaching speech.

There is no doubt that the most intensive study of the intelligibility of the speech of deaf children was conducted by Hudgins and Numbers (1942). They recorded speech samples of 192 deaf pupils from ages 8 to 20 with hearing losses ranging from a slight impairment to profound deafness. The pupils were drawn from two oral schools for the deaf. The test materials employed consisted of 1,200 unrelated simple sentences which were grouped in tens. Each pupil was provided with one group of sentences which he read after practice, his speech being recorded phonographically on either aluminium or acetate discs. The records were then played to groups of listeners who had some experience with the speech of the deaf. Each recorded sentence was replayed three times and the auditors were required to write on paper what they thought the child had said. The speech intelligibility scores were determined as follows: 10 points were given for sentences written correctly, no points being awarded for partially correct interpretations. Moreover, the records were also analyzed to determine the frequency and type of both rhythmic and articulatory errors committed and their relationship to intelligibility.

The sentences in the test were divided into three groups according to rhythm: Those spoken with normal rhythm (approximately 45 percent), those spoken with abnormal rhythm (approximately 35 percent), and those spoken without rhythm (approximately 20 percent). The chief characteristics of the sentences spoken with abnormal rhythm were the unusual groupings of the words and syllables in the sentence and the atypical stress patterns affecting both place and degree. The non-rhythmical sentences exhibited monotonous stress patterns with all vowel-like sounds in the sentence equally affected. They found a high correlation between rhythmic errors and poor intelligibility. Sentences spoken with normal rhythm were understood four times as often as those sentences spoken with incorrect rhythm. The writers also analyzed all rhythmic sentence categories according to degree of hearing loss and age. They found an increase in the number of sentences spoken with normal rhythm with increasing amount of residual hearing and a decrease in the number of sentences spoken non-rhythmically with increasing age.

The articulatory errors of the deaf children were assigned into two major error categories: errors involving vowels and errors involving consonants. The vowel errors revealed vowel substitution, nonfunctioning of the diphthong (splitting the diphthong, thus making two distinct vowels, and/or omitting one member of the diphthong, usually the final one), nasalization of vowels, neutralization and diphthongization of simple vowels. Among other consonant errors the deaf children failed to distinguish between surd and sonant consonants, they substituted consonants, they produced consonants with excessive nasality, they misarticulated compound consonants, and they failed to produce releasing and arresting consonants adequately.

The writers also analyzed all the articulatory errors according to degree of hearing loss and to age. In the first instance they found that as hearing loss increased, a greater number of errors occurred. In detail they stated that consonant substitutions and errors involving compound and arresting consonants were more numerous among the hard of hearing pupils than among the profoundly deaf. In the second instance they found that consonant errors increased with age while vowel errors showed very little change. They argued that, since frequency of articulatory errors and speech intelligibility scores were negatively correlated, the speech of the older pupils was less intelligible than that of the younger children. However, they made the above statement with some reservation mainly because the degree of hearing loss among the pupils of individual age groups was not the same. Nevertheless, their findings tend to agree with Haycock's statement (1933) that "It is commonly observed that the speech of deaf-born pupils becomes less intelligible as they advance from the lower to the higher classes in school."

Their general conclusion was that speech intelligibility depended considerably on the proper articulation of phonemes and on the rhythmic pattern of the sentence. They indicated that the speech errors of the deaf children may have been due to the analytical method of teaching speech used in the schools concerned. They recommended the use of syllables rather than isolated phonemes in the teaching of speech.

Following this study, Hudgins became very interested in the breathing habits of deaf children and in 1946 he reported on the relationship between speech breathing and speech intelligibility among deaf pupils. In this pioneer study he referred to five anomalous breathing habits characterizing the speech of deaf talkers:

(a) Short irregular breath groups often only one or two words in length with breath pauses interrupting the speech flow at improper points;

(b) Excessive expenditure of breath on single syllables resulting in breathy speech;
(c) False grouping of syllables resulting in the breaking up of natural groups and misplacement of accents;
(d) A slow methodical utterance resulting in a complete lack of grouping; and
(e) A lack of proper coordination between breathing muscles and articulatory organs.

He found a marked reduction in speech intelligibility due to poor breathing habits, thus emphasizing the importance of good and appropriate respiratory control.

In 1953 Clarke studied two similar groups of profoundly deaf children (N = 23 children in each group). The children in one group received two 45-minute periods of auditory training each week for a period of a school year. He concluded that at the end of the year the children who received his training showed statistically significant improvements in language development, speech perception, intelligibility, rhythm, and rate of speaking. Regarding speech intelligibility, he asserted that consonants were more important for intelligibility than vowels and that the total number of articulation errors gave the best predicted value of intelligibility.

Sanders' investigation (1961) concerning the progress made since entry to school by a group of 50 deaf children who received preschool training and early use of an individual hearing aid, contained information on the speech intelligibility and voice production of 41 of these children. He assessed their speech intelligibility during the testing period while they were describing a set of pictures. Assessment was done on a six-point scale. His results showed that he had little difficulty in understanding the speech of the majority of the children. In comparing the ratings of the speech intelligibility of the children with their hearing loss he found a definite relationship, i.e., the speech of the children with a slight hearing impairment was better than the speech of children with more severe hearing impairment. At the time of rating intelligibility he also made a subjective evaluation of the degree of impairment of each child's voice. This was done on the following four-point scale:

1. Normal voice
2. Voice slightly affected
3. Voice moderately affected
4. Voice severely affected

He found a definite relationship between the severity of the hearing loss and the degree of impairment of voice. He stated that children with hearing losses of less than 75 dB did not exhibit more than a slight impairment of voice quality while children with losses of 75 dB or over showed definite defects in voice quality. It is only fair to state, however, that Sanders himself was rather sceptical about the validity of his findings regarding this aspect.

The main aim of Johnson's study (1962) was to obtain information with regard to the educational attainments and social adjustment of hearing impaired children. Out of the 66 children studied, he reported that 54 had speech defects. He asserted that type of hearing impairment rather than degree of hearing loss was the main factor affecting speech intelligibility. He stated that children suffering from "perceptive" deafness nearly always develop defective speech. The results of his study led him to believe that hearing impaired children develop considerably greater fluency of speech in a normal school environment where they have the opportunity of mixing with hearing children rather than in a special school where this opportunity is lacking.

An interesting experiment was carried out by John and Howarth (1965) into the effects of time distortions on the intelligibility of speech of deaf children. Recognizing that many of the errors in the speech of such children may be described as those of abnormal time relationships, an attempt was made to improve the speech intelligibility of a group of 29 severely deaf children by focusing teaching on this aspect of their speech. The children were selected at random from three schools. Due to lack of information, only two factors which might have affected the children's speech intelligibility were examined statistically, namely hearing loss and age. Twenty-nine short spontaneous sentences, one from each child, were recorded on tape both initially, before any teaching was carried out, and finally, after three or four minutes' teaching designed to improve only the time aspect of the speech. The speech intelligibility of the children was judged by 20 university students who were required to write down as much as they could of the initial and final versions of the children's recorded speech. The judges' interpretations were scored in two ways, firstly on the number of words understood correctly and secondly on the recognition of the complete syntactic pattern of the children's speech. Using the first method of scoring, an improvement in intelligibility of 56 percent between the initial and final versions was found. When scoring on the second method the improvement noted rose to 203 percent. There was no statistical difference in improvement on the basis of either hearing loss or age. They concluded by stating that teaching which stressed the temporal aspects of speech, relying heavily on the auditory feedback of speech patterns as wholes, was a quick and effective means of improving speech intelligibility in deaf children.

Markides' (1967) study on the speech of hearing-impaired children contained information on the articulatory errors and overall speech intelligibility of 58 junior deaf children (hearing loss in the better ear averaged across the frequencies 250 Hz–4000 Hz, in excess of 80 dB HL) and 27 partially hearing children (averaged hearing loss less than 80 dB HL). The articulation test administered was specially constructed by the writer as none was available. The test consisted of 24 monosyllabic words which were represented pictorially on separate cards. The words were chosen to be within the vocabulary of the children involved and to test a representative number of vowels, diphthongs, and consonants in the English language. The speech of each child, elicited through a series of pictures, was put on magnetic tape and later assessed for intelligibility by separate panels of both sophisticated and unsophisticated listeners.

The articulatory errors of the children were dealt with in two major categories: errors involving vowels and errors involving consonants. With regard to the vowel errors it was found that the deaf children misarticulated nearly 56 percent of all vowels and diphthongs attempted while the partially hearing children misarticulated approximately 9 percent of all vowels and diphthongs attempted. Both the deaf and the partially hearing children had more difficulty with the pronunciation of diphthongs than with the pronunciation of simple vowels.

Vowel Errors

The vowel errors of the children were assigned to four categories:

1. Vowel substitution
2. Vowel neutralization
3. Vowel prolongation
4. Vowel diphthongization

Among the deaf children the most substitutions were made for the short vowel /I/ as in /pig/, followed by the vowel /a/ as in /bath/ and the vowel /ʌ/ as in /gun/. The substitutions were not limited to adjacent vowels or to vowels of a similar formation as in /i/ or /I/. For example, the back vowel /ɔ/ as in /ball/ was substituted for the high front long vowel /i/ and for the high front short vowel /I/. The most frequently neutralized vowels were /æ/ as in /cat/ and /ɛ/ as in /red/. Vowel prolongation among the deaf and partially hearing children occurred mainly with the back vowels /ɒ/, /ɔ/ and /u/ which accounted for nearly 90 percent of all errors in this category. Diphthongization of vowels was the least common mistake made by both deaf and partially hearing children. Among the deaf children diphthongization affected all vowels, the most commonly diphthongized being /ɒ/ as in /dog/ and /i/ as in /keys/. /ɒ/ was produced either as /ɔɪ/ or /oʊ/. /i/ was heard as /Iə/ and sometimes as /Iʊ/.

Both the deaf and the partially hearing children had most difficulty with the diphthongs /ɛə/ and /aɪ/. Their commonest mistake was to substitute the neutral vowel /ə/ for the diphthong, thus /aɪ/ as in /knife/ was heard as /ə/ /knəf/ and /ɔɪ/ as in /boy/ was heard as /ə/ /bə/. The next common mistake was to drop the second component of the diphthong, at the same time prolonging its first component. For example, /aɪ/ as in /knife/ was heard as /ə/ /na:f/ with or without the final /f/. Finally, the excessive prolongation, usually of the first component of the glide, resulting in the diphthong being heard as two distinct vowels, constituted the least diphthong mistake. For example, the diphthong /ɔɪ/ as in /boy/ was heard as /ɔ:ɪ/ /bə:ɪ/ or /ɛə/ as in /chair/ was heard as ɛ:ə/ /tʃɛ:ə/.

Consonant Errors

With regard to consonant errors the deaf children misarticulated nearly 72 percent of all consonants attempted while the partially hearing children misarticulated a little over 26 percent of all consonants attempted. Among the deaf children omission errors were more numerous, followed by substitution and finally by distortion. Among the partially hearing, substitution errors were more numerous, followed by omissions and finally by distortions. For both the deaf and the partially hearing children errors involving the final consonants were more numerous than errors involving the initial consonants.

The consonants in the test material were divided according to their manner of production into four groups and the errors made by the children were assigned to omissions, substitutions and distortions. The four groups were:

(1) Plosives.   /p, b, t, d, k, g/
(2) Nasals.   /m, n, ŋ/
(3) Fricatives.   /f, v, θ, s, z, ʃ/
(4) Others.   /tʃ, l, r, w, h/

Plosives

The most frequently omitted plosive consonants among the deaf children were /g/, /d/, and /k/. Among the partially hearing children the most frequent omissions in this category were /d/, /g/, and /t/.

Plosive consonants were mainly substituted for plosives. There was a tendency for the unvoiced plosive consonants to be substituted for their voiced cognates. For example, /p/ was substituted for /b/, /t/ for /d/, and /k/ for /g/. Substitutions involving changes both in the manner and in the place of articulation were also relatively frequent. For example, /m/ was produced in the place of /p/, /tʃ/ was produced in the place of /t/, the semivowel /j/ was produced in the place of /d/, /t/, /k/, and /g/.

The most frequently distorted plosive consonant was final /p/. When produced it was accompanied by excessive breathiness. For example, /p/ as in /ship/ was heard as /pʰa/ / ʃɪpʰa/.

Nasals

Only six deaf children produced correctly the final /ŋ/. The other 52 deaf children omitted it altogether. Omission of the other two nasal consonants was less frequent.

The most frequent substitution involved changes in the manner of articulation. For example, /p/ was produced in the place of /m/ and /t/ in the place of /n/. These substitutions show that although the closure of the oral passage was correctly placed for the production of the nasals /m/ and /n/, the second prerequisite for the production of these consonants, that is the dropping of the velum, was absent.

The most commonly distorted nasal consonant was /m/. This phoneme was mainly given as a strongly nasalized /m/ with some overtones of /b/, the words /farm/ and /moon/, for example, being heard as /fa:m^{ba}/ and /m^{b}un/ respectively.

Fricatives

Both the deaf and the partially hearing children found the sibilants /s/, /z/ and /ʃ/ most difficult to produce.

The plosive consonants /t/ and /p/ were the most frequently substituted phonemes for the fricative consonants. Another frequent substitution error was the interchange of the sibilants. For example, /ʃ/ was substituted for /s/ and /z/, /s/ for /z/, /ʃ/ and /ʒ/.

The three most frequently distorted fricatives were /s/, /ʃ/ and /θ/. Distortion of /s/ when tested initially was mainly due to intrusive overtones of the plosive consonant /t/. For example, the word /sun/ was heard as /stʌn/. Distortion of final /s/ was mainly due to excessive prolongation followed by a sudden release of breath. For example, /house/ was heard as /hausʲə/. Distortion of /ʃ/ was similar in nature. Distortion involving /θ/ was mainly due to a partial arrest of the continuous flow of breath required for its production. For example, /bath/ was heard as /batθ/. In some instances /θ/ was followed by an abrupt release of breath /batθə/. Amongst the partially hearing the most frequently distorted fricative consonants were /ʃ/, which was most commonly heard as /ʃʰə//ʃIʃʰə/, and /z/, which was heard as /tz//tzu/.

Others

In this category the most frequently omitted, substituted and distorted phoneme for both the deaf and the partially hearing children was the affricative /tʃ/. Distortions of this consonant, when tested in the initial position, were mainly due to an abrupt release of its plosive component. Thus the test word /chair/ was heard as /tə ʃɛə/. Distortion of final /tʃ/ was mainly due to excessive prolongation of its second component followed by a sudden release of breath. For example, /watch/ was heard as /wɒtʃːʰə/.

When all articulatory errors were analyzed, it was found that the deaf children, as expected, made more errors on average than the partially hearing. The difference was statistically significant at .01 level. No significant differences were found with reference to age, sex, and residential status. There were, however, wide variations between the average number of errors made by the children attending the different schools. Some of these differences were statistically significant (P = .01). The number of errors increased as hearing loss increased. The product-moment correlation coefficient between the number of errors made by the 85 hearing impaired children and their hearing loss was .78.

As expected, negative correlations between articulatory errors and speech intelligibility were reported: as the frequency of articulatory errors increased, the intelligibility scores decreased. The three highest ranking articulatory error categories affecting speech intelligibility were "total consonant, vowel and diphthong errors" ($r = -.89$), "total consonant errors' ($r = -.88$), and "final consonant errors" ($r = -.87$).

With regard to overall speech intelligibility it was concluded that the main factors which were found to influence intelligibility, apart from those inherent in the children (age of onset of deafness, degree of hearing loss and intelligence), were the speech environment and level of educational aspirations set by each school, the degree and efficiency with which hearing aids were used, and individual speech teaching.

Main Errors

Even the most casual analysis of the speech of deaf children reveals a wide variety of errors. Broadly speaking, these errors can be conveniently grouped under two major categories: errors involving the prosodic aspects of speech, and errors of articulation. Of course, such a classification is an oversimplification, since acoustically these two categories interpenetrate. Nevertheless the labels provide a useful framework within which the different errors can be presented and discussed.

Prosodic Errors

The most common errors affecting the prosodic aspects of the speech of deaf children relate to intonation, phrasing, pausing, rate of speaking, breath control, stress, overall rhythm and, of course, voice quality. Intonation is usually flat and monotonous and this, according to Angelocci, Kopp, and Holbrook (1964) and Mártony (1968), is due to the fact that deaf children cannot control and/or have very limited control over their voice frequency. Phrasing and pausing are usually inaccurate and tend to occur more frequently and at inappropriate locations. Breath control is defective, thus interrupting the natural flow of speech. Rate of speaking is generally slow and labored, with wrong stress patterns. These errors interfere primarily with the complex durational aspects of speech (speech rhythm), thus affecting speech intelligibility (Story, 1909; Bell, 1916; Voelker, 1935; Hudgins & Numbers, 1942; Calvert, 1964; John & Howarth, 1965; Hood, 1967; Hood & Dixon, 1969; Markides, 1978). In addition to these errors, many deaf children exhibit abnormal voice qualities which are detrimental to effective communication. The most common problems of voice quality encountered with deaf children include excessive breathiness, nasality, stridency, and harshness (Markides, 1970).

Articulatory Errors

The major articulatory errors characterizing the speech of deaf children have already been presented in detail. It is of interest to note that a considerable proportion of these errors is basically of durational character (Calvert, 1961, 1962). This clearly implies that teaching which stresses the temporal aspects of speech, both in absolute and relative terms, can bring about not only improvement in rhythm but also improvement in articulation. There still remain, however, a large number of articulatory errors which are brought about predominantly as a result of poor control over the manner and place of articulation. Improper control of the velum, for example, can cause nasalization of both vowels and consonants; ineffective closure in the production of plosives can bring about distortion and/or substitution. Similar articulatory errors can also be associated with incorrect placement of the tongue, especially in the production of fricatives.

With regard to the teaching of speech, Boothroyd, Nickerson, and Stevens (1974) found that methodologies of teaching speech to deaf children which emphasize solely the rhythmic aspects of speech have very little to recommend them. On the other hand, it is well known that undue emphasis on teaching individual phonemes has been found to obstruct rather than promote intelligible speech (Ewing & Ewing, 1938; Hudgins & Numbers, 1942). The overwhelming evidence available suggests a teaching methodology which puts emphasis not only on the prosodic features of speech but also incorporates basic articulatory work, with the balance of emphasis (rhythm vs. articulation) depending on the age, abilities, and needs of the child.

Main Factors

There is a plethora of factors which can affect the speech intelligibility of deaf children. Some of these factors (voice quality, rhythm, misarticulations, etc.) have already been discussed. Other major factors which need to be considered are the degree of hearing loss, use of residual hearing, educational environment, linguistic ability and, of course, speech teaching. This is by no means a comprehensive list of factors affecting the speech intelligibility of deaf children. Additional factors such as other handicap(s), intelligence, preschool guidance, caliber of teachers involved, the actual methodology employed in the teaching of speech, etc. can have considerable bearing on the speech of deaf children. Having said this, however, it needs to be stated that it is beyond the scope of this paper to evaluate all these factors; only the most important ones will be considered.

It is generally accepted that the degree of hearing loss is one of the most important factors affecting the speech intelligibility of hearing impaired children (Hudgins, 1934: Hudgins & Numbers, 1942; Sanders, 1961; Markides, 1967, Kyle et al., 1978). As hearing loss increases, articulation errors increase and overall speech intelligibility becomes worse. In 1962, however, Johnson, in his study on the educational attainments and social adjustment of hearing-impaired children in ordinary schools, asserted that type of audiogram configuration rather than degree of hearing loss was the main factor affecting intelligibility. Johnson's assertion was later on refuted by Markides (1979), who found that the speech intelligibility of three groups of children, representing three different pure-tone audiogram configurations but with similar average hearing levels, were very similar. Time of onset of deafness is, of course, an obvious factor affecting speech intelligibility. It is true to say that a hearing impairment acquired later on in life affects speech intelligibility differently from a hearing impairment acquired at birth or very early in life. In the first instance, the individual affected has already learned the auditory clues for speech perception through normal auditory channels and in most cases such a disability can, to a large extent, be overcome by simply increasing the intensity of speech through the use of a hearing aid. In the latter case, however, the individual affected has to learn to speak through faulty auditory channels which receive, comparatively speaking, very little stimulation. As a result of this he may come to rely on different and fewer auditory clues for speech perception and this may well render him more susceptible to extraneous interference due to such things as noise, reverberation, change of speaker, change of hearing aid, etc. In addition to these difficulties which arise either directly or indirectly from a hearing impairment, one must not overlook the possibility that whatever caused the hearing damage could also have caused further damage impinging on central processes in speech perception, i.e., integration problems, difficulties in selective attention, and short-term memory (Boothroyd, 1967). These disabilities are not easily detectable, especially when they are clouded by an obvious hearing impairment.

The provision of auditory experience for deaf children has been shown by Clarke (1952), Ewings (1957, 1958, 1964), and by many other workers to be important in furthering educational attainment. Markides (1967) found that the speech intelligibility of the deaf children who were making good use of their hearing aids was significantly superior to the speech intelligibility of the deaf children who were not making good use of their hearing aids. He also reported considerable differences between schools both in the amount of electronic equipment available and in the efficiency with which such equipment was used. It is true that a considerable number of schools for the deaf have inherited accommodation and physical conditions which are far from satisfactory for the proper functioning of hearing aids (John, 1957; Watson, 1964). What is even more depressing, however, is the fact that a considerable number of modern educational establishments for hearing-impaired children, especially units for partially hearing children attached to ordinary schools, have been designed without proper consideration pertaining to their acoustic environment (Markides, 1979), thus limiting the potential use of hearing aids.

Markides (1967) reported significant variations between the speech intelligibility of deaf children attending different schools. This ties in well with the results obtained by Murphy (1957), Wollman (1961), and Redgate (1964) with regard to educational attainments. It is generally accepted that educational environment affects achievement, especially in the case of handicapped children. Deaf children, for instance, because of their auditory handicap, are denied much of the incidental learning which is available to normal children both inside and outside the school. The special school has, therefore, to make good this deficiency and the degree of success in doing so depends mainly on the quality of education given in the school. Many of the schools for the deaf, apart from being geographically isolated from each other, have long and well-established traditions which might hinder communication of new ideas. Attitudes more suited to the 19th century possibly linger on, and the setting of a low level of aspiration may well be the reason for low academic standards. Both Markides (1967) and John (1975) considered the educational environment and educational aspirations set by each school as one of the most important single factors affecting speech intelligibility, so much so that the degree and/or type of hearing loss becomes of secondary importance.

Both Markides (1967) and John (1975) reported a significant relationship between linguistic ability and speech intelligibility. Those children who performed better in the linguistic tests also tended to have better speech intelligibility. It may well be that a child who has a clear picture of what he wishes to say and who knows the correct method of putting words together will be able to speak more fluently, his rate of speaking will be more normal, and thus his speech intelligibility will be better. Ignorance of the correct meaning and use of language may cause a child to be uncertain and halting in his speech, thus speech intelligibility will suffer as a result of poor linguistic ability. On the other hand, a deaf child with good speech intelligibility, because of his ability to communicate to others in an understandable manner, has an incentive to use his language and in the process of communicating he will naturally develop further his linguistic abilities.

As far back as 1933 Haycock, commenting on the poor speech intelligibility of deaf children, attributed this to "inadequate and insufficient training and preparation to meet a continually growing and expanding set of varied speech requirements." Hudgins and Numbers (1942) also thought that the speech intelligibility of deaf children was dependent on such factors as amount of time spent on speech training and the extent to which the habit of speech was cultivated. It was not surprising, therefore, to find (Markides, 1970) that the speech intelligibility of deaf children who were receiving systematic and consistent tuition on speech was significantly better than that of similar children who did not receive such training.

Speech Assessment

No attempt will be made in this paper to describe in detail the wide range of methods and procedures (ranging from simple rating scales to spectrographic analysis and more recently complicated computerized techniques) which can be used in the study of speech disorders relating to the voice quality, pitch, loudness, intonation, breath control, and rate of speaking of deaf children. This information has been well documented in books by Travis (1957) and by Ewing and Ewing (1964) and, among others, by Hudgins and Numbers (1942), John and Howarth (1965), Markides (1970, 1978) and Black (1971) in their special papers. Suffice it to state here that the most commonly used techniques in the assessment of the above-mentioned speech parameters of deaf children involved specially constructed rating scales and/or spectrographic analysis.

The function of rating scales is obvious; their reliability, however, is very poor. Markides (1970), for example, found a very high incidence of disagreement and very low test-retest reliability among normally hearing assessors, both sophisticated (teachers of the deaf) and unsophisticated (lay persons), in their ratings relating to voice quality, intonation, rhythm, etc. of deaf children's speech.

Spectrographic analysis is a much more objective technique and it gives valuable information on four basic physical dimensions of speech: (a) durational (horizontal axis of the graph), (b) frequency composition (vertical axis of the graph), (c) relative intensity of main frequency bands (variations of blackness of markings) and, (d) vocal cord activity or fundamental frequency (pitch) of the voice. These four physical properties of speech convey valuable information relating to the voice and articulation of the speaker. In other words, spectrographic analysis can give accurate information on the following: accuracy and distinctiveness of articulatory movements, absolute and relative duration of phonemes, the effect of adjacent sounds on articulation, differentiation between voiced and unvoiced phonemes, differences in frequency composition of phonemes, pitch control and its variations, intensity control and duration control of the prosodic aspects of speech.

It is true that spectrographic analysis gives extensive information on the articulatory abilities of the speaker, but it does not provide a detailed description of the whole event. In view of this the traditional way of assessing articulatory abilities whereby samples of speech—be it sentences, phrases, or individual words—are subjected to careful phonetic analysis, has considerable merit. A combination of the two methods, however, is preferable to either one.

At the end of the day, however, our main concern is with the overall speech intelligibility of the child. As such, this area will be treated more thoroughly. Methods of assessing the speech intelligibility of deaf children basically involve the use of a panel of assessors, whose function it is to listen and either (a) write down whatever they think the child has said for later assessment or, (b) rate the speech intelligibility of each child on a given scale, which usually ranges from normal speech to unintelligible or no speech at all. The assessment of speech intelligibility can be greatly affected by the way in which the speech material is elicited from the children, the relative sophistication of the assessors, and by the scoring procedures adopted.

Speech Elicitation

The assessment of speech intelligibility necessitates the elicitation of representative samples, in sufficient quantity, of the children's speech. To achieve this one needs to take into consideration (a) the provision of favorable conditions and (b) the test materials and methods to be used.

It is important for the researcher to avoid generating tension among the children because this tends to influence their speech production adversely. One way to remove the stress inevitable in face-to-face testing is to record the samples of the children's speech. This procedure has been followed by most of the researchers in the field (Hudgins, 1934; Rawlings, 1936; Hudgins & Numbers, 1942; John & Howarth, 1965; Markides, 1967, 1978). Recordings may be criticized on the grounds of limitations inherent in recording and reproduction and also as a factor affecting the spontaneity of speech, especially when the child is aware that his speech is being recorded. Recordings, however, provide a permanent record which can be evaluated at leisure later on.

With regard to the elicitation of speech from the children, two main methods have been followed in the past: the "oral reading" method and "picture description." The oral reading method involved the reading aloud of lists of words (Hughson et al., 1941), phrases (Hudgins, 1934), or sentences (Voelker, 1935; Rawlings, 1936; Johnson, 1939; Hudgins & Numbers, 1942; Conrad, 1976) while the picture description method involved the description of picture material (Sheridan, 1948; Sanders, 1961; Markides, 1967, 1978; John, 1975).

Clarke (1953), Silverman (1961), and Markides (1977) have criticized the oral reading method on the grounds that:

(a) Oral reading does not represent speech in a social context;
(b) Oral reading does not elicit representative samples of each child's speech;
(c) Oral reading artificially manipulates the linguistic structure of the children's speech;
(d) Oral reading interferes with the spontaneity of speech;
(e) Oral reading puts a heavier burden on the children, especially those children with reading difficulties;
(f) Oral reading interferes with the temporal aspects of the speech of deaf children; and
(g) Oral reading depresses the speech intelligibility scores of deaf children.

On the other hand, Kyle (1977) was of the opinion that picture description is not only a difficult and complex test of speech intelligibility but is also inaccurate. Conrad (1976) and his associates (1978) favored instead the oral reading method. Some of the reasons given in favor of the oral reading method were the following:

(a) It helps in "the practicalities of scoring which necessitate the identification of each attempted speech sound";
(b) It "reliably reflects articulation rather than the mood of the child"; and
(c) It presents a simple task both for the researcher and the listeners.

In view of this controversy Markides (1978) compared the relative efficiency of these two methods in assessing the speech intelligibility of hearing-impaired children. It was found that the speech intelligibility of the children elicited through picture description (mean intelligibility score 81.7 percent) was significantly superior ($p = .01$) to the intelligibility of their corresponding speech elicited through oral reading (mean intelligibility score 57.4 percent). It was concluded that picture description as opposed to oral reading provides a more realistic picture of the speech intelligibility of hearing impaired children.

When using pictures for elicitation of speech it is imperative to ensure that both the subject matter of each picture and the vocabulary required to describe each picture are within the abilities and interests of the children concerned. This method and/or the interview method, however, tends to interfere with the spontaneity of speech (albeit to a smaller degree than when reading lists of words, phrases or sentences) and also the speech samples elicited from each child when following these methods may be of widely different linguistic complexities. When using pictures it is necessary to employ several individual or groups of pictures and/or several picture sequences which need to be standardized, especially in terms of difficulty of description. The use of only one picture and/or only one picture sequence will almost inevitably interfere with the final assessment of speech intelligibility, mainly because of learning factors affecting the assessors. Silverman (1961) suggested that it would be helpful to capture the casual conversation of children for purposes of assessing speech intelligibility. In theory this is ideal; in practice it imposes formidable difficulties impinging on acceptable homogeneity of experimental procedures, and also it is a time-consuming undertaking.

Assessors

Regarding the selection of listeners to assess the speech intelligibility of deaf children, it is noted that previous writers used either people familiar with the children's speech (teachers of the deaf—sophisticated listeners) or people to whom the speech of deaf children was completely strange (laymen—unsophisticated listeners) or both sophisticated and unsophisticated listeners. There is general agreement, however, that a realistic assessment of the speech intelligibility of deaf children can only be reflected by the responses of unsophisticated listeners, mainly because teachers of the deaf, being accustomed to such speech, tend to over-estimate its intelligibility (Markides, 1967).

For comparative purposes it seems essential to use the same group of listeners in evaluating speech intelligibility. This may not be a crucial factor affecting the results, though, for previous workers such as Hudgins and Numbers (1942), Clarke (1953), John and Howarth (1965), and Markides (1967) have found little or no difference between the performances of different assessors within a group when assessing the speech intelligibility of deaf children. Both Hudgins and Clarke used as assessors a group of persons who had considerable experience with deaf children. John and Howarth used instead a group of lay people, while Markides used separately both lay people and teachers of the deaf.

Scoring

Methods of scoring speech intelligibility tests show wide variations. Johnson (1939) scored the speech intelligibility of deaf children by awarding 10 points to sentences understood correctly the first time, 5 points to sentences understood correctly the second time, and 2 points to sentences understood correctly the third time. Hudgins and Numbers (1942) scored speech intelligibility by awarding 10 points to sentences fully understood—no points were given for partially correct interpretations. John and Howarth (1965) scored speech intelligibility in two ways: first, on the number of words understood correctly; second, on the recognition of the complete syntactic pattern of the children's speech. Markides (1969, 1978) scored speech intelligibility on the average number of words understood correctly by the assessors expressed as a percentage of the total number of words actually produced by each child. Conrad (1976) scored speech intelligibility on the mean number of "target" words (two target words in each of 10 sentences read aloud by each child) correctly identified by a group of listeners.

It is clear that the methods of scoring used by Johnson and Hudgins and Numbers give an underestimation of the children's speech intelligibility because no consideration was given to the partial successes of the children. Conrad's method of scoring was restrictive for it was based solely on two target words within a sentence to the exclusion of the intelligibility of the rest of the words comprising each sentence.

Rating Scales

Johnson (1962) used the following four-grade scale in assessing the speech intelligibility of hearing impaired children.

GRADE A : No noticeable difference in his/her speech from that of other children.

GRADE B : Has slight but noticeable impairment of consonants, e.g., substitutions, omissions or distortions but not so as to make speech indistinct.

GRACE C : Very noticeably a child with defects of speech but intelligible to those familiar with his/her speech.
GRADE D : Speech seriously defective; difficult to understand what he/she is saying.

Markides (1967), in addition to assessing the speech intelligibility of 85 hearing impaired children on the number of words correctly understood by two separate panels of assessors (one panel being teachers of the deaf, the other lay people), also asked the assessors to rate the speech intelligibility of the children on the following six-point scale:

1. Normal
2. Very easy to follow
3. Fairly easy to follow
4. Rather difficult to follow
5. Very difficult to follow
6. Unintelligible.

Agreement between the ratings of the assessors in each group was high. Their ratings, together with the corresponding intelligibility scores of the children, are shown in Table 1.

TABLE 1

Speech intelligibility ratings and percentage scores

Speech Intelligibility	Teachers' Ratings and Scores N	Mean	Range	Laymen's Ratings and Scores N	Mean	Range
1	1	100.0	—	—	—	—
2	15	94.7	100-84	6	92.8	100-84
3	8	80.8	90-72	16	79.3	100-53
4	11	53.2	79-23	9	48.3	72-14
5	19	32.0	52-10	21	19.9	45-0
6	31	7.5	42-0	33	3.3	21-0

As expected, the results showed that the laymen found more difficulty in following the speech of the children than did the teachers. It is also obvious from the above table that rating scales provide only a crude estimate of the speech intelligibility of each child. (Note the wide range of percentage scores within each grade of the rating scale.)

Conclusions

It seems that the least objectionable method of assessing the overall speech intelligibility of deaf children entails:

(a) Elicitation of representative samples of each child's speech in sufficient quantities (50-100 words per child);
(b) The use of standardized groups of individual pictures and/or picture sequences, the content of which is within the experience of the children and the description of which is within the vocabulary abilities of the children;
(c) The recording of the children's response;
(d) The use of groups of unsophisticated listeners acting as assessors; and
(e) The scoring of speech intelligibility to be based on the average number of words understood correctly by the assessors expressed as a percentage of the total number of words produced by each child.

Future Research Needs

There is no doubt that at present we possess an enormous amount of knowledge regarding the speech of deaf children. Also, in the last two decades we have witnessed an unprecedented expansion of facilities in the relevant fields of education, medicine, and audiology. We have considerable access to highly sophisticated electronic amplifying equipment. Our special educational system is rapidly becoming more flexible and more versatile in meeting individual needs. In spite of all this progress, however, there still remains a large number of deaf children who leave school without an acceptable degree of speech intelligibility. This state of affairs may be partly due to our delivery system, that is, the interaction between child and the teachers and the methods and procedures employed in the teaching of speech to deaf children. It is the opinion of this writer that this particular area has not as yet been given the research attention it deserves.

References

Angelocci, A. A., Kopp, G. A., & Holbrook, A. The vowel formants of deaf and normally-hearing eleven to fourteen-year-old boys. *Journal of Speech and Hearing Disorders,* 1964, 29, 156–170.
Bell, A. G. *The mechanism of speech.* New York: Funk & Wagnals, 1916.
Black, J. W. Speech pathology for the deaf. In Connor (Ed.), *Speech for the deaf child: Knowledge and use.* Washington, DC: A. G. Bell Association for the Deaf, 1971.
Boothroyd, A. *The selection of hearing aids for children.* Doctoral dissertation, University of Manchester, 1967.
Boothroyd, A., Nicherson, R. S., & Stevens, K. N. *Temporal patterns in the speech of the deaf—a study in remedial training* (S.A.R.P. 15). Northampton, MA: Clarke School for the Deaf, 1974.
Calvert, D. R. *Some acoustic characteristics of the speech of profoundly deaf individuals.* Doctoral dissertation, University of Stanford, 1961.
Calvert, D. R. Deaf voice quality: A preliminary investigation. *The Volta Review,* 1962, 64, 402–403.

Calvert, D. R. An approach to the study of deaf speech. In *Report of the proceedings of the international congress on education of the deaf*. Washington, DC: Government Printing Office.

Clarke, B. R. *Auditory training of profoundly deaf children*. Doctoral dissertation, University of Manchester, 1953.

Conrad, R. Speech quality of deaf children. In Stephens (Ed.), *Disorders of auditory function II*. New York: Academic Press, 1976.

Dale, D. M. C. *The possibility of providing extensive experience for severely and profoundly deaf children by the use of hearing aids*. Doctoral dissertation, University of Manchester, 1958.

Ewing, A. W. (Ed.). *Educational guidance and the deaf child*. Manchester: Manchester University Press, 1964.

Ewing, A. W., & Ewing, E. C. *Teaching deaf children to talk*. Manchester: Manchester University Press, 1964.

Ewing, I. R., & Ewing, A. W. *The handicap of deafness*. London: Longmans Green, 1938.

Ewing, I. R., & Ewing, A. W. *New opportunities for deaf children*. London: London University Press, 1958.

Hallowell, D., & Silverman, S. R. *Hearing and deafness*. New York: Holt, Rinehart & Winston, 1961.

Haycock, C. S. *The teaching of speech*. Hill and Ainsworth, Ltd., 1933.

Hood, R. B. Some physical concomitants of speech rhythm of the deaf. *Proceedings of the International Conference on Oral Education of the Deaf*, 1967, *1*, 921–925.

Hood, R. B., & Dixon, R. F. Physical characteristics of speech rhythm of deaf and normal speakers. *Journal of Communication Disorders*, 1969, *2*, 20–28.

Hudgins, C. V. A comparative study of the speech coordinations of deaf and normal subjects. *Journal of Genetic Psychology*, 1934, *44*, 1–48.

Hudgins, C. V. Speech breathing and speech intelligibility. *The Volta Review*, 1946, *48*, 642.

Hudgins, C. V., & Numbers, F. An investigation of the intelligibility of the speech of the deaf. *Genetic Psychology Monographs*, 1942, *25*, 289–392.

Hughson, W., Ciocco, A., Whitting, G. E., & Lawrence, S. P. An analysis of speech characteristics in deafened children with observation on training method. *The Laryngoscope*, 1941, *51*, 868–891.

John, J. E. J. Acoustics in the use of hearing aids. In Ewing (Ed.), *Educational guidance and the deaf child*. Manchester: Manchester University Press, 1957.

John, J. E. J. *The linguistic imput to a hearing aid*. Paper presented at the second conference of the British Society of Audiology, Southampton, 1975.

John, J. E. J., & Howarth, J. N. The effect of time distortions on the intelligibility of deaf children's speech. *Language and Speech*, 1965, *8*, 127–134.

Johnson, E. H. Testing results of acoustic training. *American Annals of the Deaf*, 1939, *84*, 223–233.

Johnson, J. C. *Educating hearing-impaired children in ordinary schools*. Manchester: Manchester University Press, 1962.

Kyle, J. G. Audiometric analysis as a predictor of speech intelligibility. *British Journal of Audiology*, 1977, *11*, 51–58.

Kyle, J. G., Conrad, R., McKenzie, M. G., Morris, A. J. M., & Weiskrantz, B. C. Language abilities in deaf school leavers. *Journal of the British Association of Teachers of the Deaf*, 1978, *2*, 38–42.

Markides, A. *The speech of deaf and partially-hearing children with special reference to factors affecting intelligibility*. Master of education thesis, University of Manchester, 1967.

Markides, A. The speech of deaf and partially-hearing children with special reference to factors affecting intelligibility. *The British Journal of Disorders of Communication*, 1970, *5*, 126–140.

Markides, A. The teaching of speech to deaf and partially-hearing children. *Talk,* 1970, *57,* 24–25.

Markides, A. Ratings relating to the speech of deaf and partially-hearing children. *The Teacher of the Deaf,* 1970, *68,* 323–330.

Markides, A. Assessing the speech intelligibility of hearing-impaired children: Oral reading versus picture description. *Journal of the British Association of Teachers of the Deaf,* 1978, *2,* 185–189.

Markides, A. *Pure tone audiogram configuration and speech intelligibility.* Manuscript submitted for publication, 1979.

Markides, A. *The uses and abuses of speech training units and group hearing aids.* Paper in preparation, 1979.

Mártony, J. On the correction of voice pitch level for severely hard of hearing subjects. *American Annals of the Deaf,* 1968, *113,* 195.

Miller-Shaw, M. O. A study in the analysis and correction of the speech of the hard of hearing. *American Annals of the Deaf,* 1936, *81,* 225.

Murphy, K. P. In Ewing (Ed.), *Educational guidance and the deaf child.* Manchester: Manchester University Press, 1957.

Rawlings, C. G. A comparative study of the movements of the breathing muscles in speech and in quiet breathing of deaf and normal subjects. *American Annals of the Deaf,* 1936, *81,* 136–150.

Redgate, W. G. *Diagnostic tests of reading ability for deaf children.* Master of education thesis, University of Manchester, 1964.

Sanders, D. A. *A follow-up study of fifty deaf children who received pre-school training.* Doctoral dissertation, University of Manchester, 1961.

Sheridan, M. D. *The child's hearing for speech.* London: Methuen, 1948.

Story, A. J. The importance of the consonants in speech and speechreading. *The Volta Review,* 1935, *37,* 243.

Travis, L. E. (Ed.). *Handbook of speech pathology.* New York: Appleton-Century-Crofts, 1957.

Voelker, A. C. A preliminary strobophotoscopic study of the speech of the deaf. *American Annals of the Deaf,* 1935, *80,* 243.

Voelker, A. C. An experimental study of the comparative rate of utterance of deaf and normal speakers. *American Annals of the Deaf,* 1938, *83,* 274–283.

Watson, T. J. The use of hearing aids by hearing-impaired children in ordinary schools. *The Volta Review,* 1964, *66,* 741.

Wollman, D. C. *Some problems involved in the application of secondary modern education for deaf pupils with special reference to the institution of a leaving certificate.* Doctoral dissertation, University of Manchester, 1961.

reaction to 15

daniel ling

My first task is to respond to Markides' paper. It is more wide ranging than its title suggests, hence more interesting than a description of available tests of speech production. It contains an excellent survey of the literature on the speech of deaf children. The generally impoverished nature of their spoken language is shown to be more than adequately documented. Indeed, it shows that far more Ph.D's have been earned describing faults than in trying to do something to ameliorate them. Markides' analysis of the principal factors underlying poor speech provides excellent guidelines for future workers who wish to do research on the design, application, and evaluation of remedial procedures.

Markides, in reporting several of the studies undertaken to date, describes the range of evaluation procedures that are currently available. They include the sampling and analysis of elicited and spontaneous speech and the rating of intelligibility. Implicit in the paper is the notion that two distinct purposes are served by these procedures. Whereas sampling and phonetic analysis of elicited and spontaneous speech samples are the most appropriate means of obtaining guidelines for teaching, intelligibility ratings may be considered as the preferred tool for judging what has been achieved and how the achievements of one group compare with those of another.

Markides makes no reference to the many standardized, norm-referenced speech evaluation measures that are currently in common use with normally hearing children. I presume this is because, like me, he considers criterion-referenced tests, phonetic and phonologic evaluations, to be more appropriate in that they provide the range of fine-grained information necessary for effective teaching. Certainly, he implies that tests other than intelligibility ratings are required. Speech may be intelligible, but yet grossly abnormal.

Markides' analysis of the problems underlying intelligibility rating procedures shows that particular care must be taken in interpreting findings. Many factors can influence scores. Direct comparisons of the intelligibility scores reported in various studies are shown to be impossible and the need to standardize procedures is highlighted.

Of particular importance, both for phonologic analysis and intelligibility rating, is the selection of the topic on which the child speaks. Markides has contrasted picture description and oral reading and found the former to be superior. In my own work, I have sampled language from five areas of discourse for these purposes: narration, explanation, description, conversation, and question. I have found that the proportion of errors and the intelligibility of speech both differ significantly with the nature of the sample.

The fact that Markides and I have both been involved in speech evaluation, and that relevant research has recently been undertaken here at Sint Michielsgestel, in Germany, Sweden, Italy, and other countries, shows that what is said at this conference will be of international concern. On this account, I should like to join Markides in reiterating that if we already applied what is known about speech teaching, if teachers and researchers recognized the volume of others' work as well as their own, radical improvements in standards of spoken language would rapidly become a widespread phenomenon.

16

assessment of language: a survey of available tests

h. leslie owrid

This paper consists of two parts. The first is a brief discussion of aspects of language assessment and in particular of the problems which arise in the assessment of the language of children who suffer from extreme deafness from earliest life. The second part is concerned with means by which the language of hearing impaired children may be assessed. The procedure followed in the second section is to distinguish the chief components of spoken language and give some account of tests and other linguistic measures which may be regarded as representative in the particular area under discussion and which have been employed or have the potential for employment with children who are very deaf from earliest life. The section ends with a brief consideration of some composite scales of linguistic development. Here again the discussion is from the standpoint of their use with deaf children.

The main orientation of the paper is toward spoken language. Reading and written expression as independent topics will be excluded because of lack of space. However, the possibility of presenting test items in printed form and also of obtaining samples of language in written form may need to be borne in mind in relation to some of the tests and measures which are discussed.

SECTION I

Aspects of Linguistic Assessment and Problems Which May Arise in the Assessment of the Language of Hearing-Impaired Children

Roman Jakobson (1960), in his essay on linguistics and poetics, draws up a schema of the speech act which, I believe, is helpful when one is reflecting on the linguistic assessment of deaf children. Jakobson's schema comprises six factors arranged as follows: —

	Context	
Addresser	Message	Addressee
	Contact	
	Code	

Jakobson focuses on the dual or dyadic nature of the speech act, as Anthony van Uden insists, language, the speech act, especially where children are concerned, is an act of conversation. Of the six factors in the schema, three—Addresser, Message, Addressee—require no further elucidation. For the remaining three we may usefully add a little more from Jakobson's explanation. *Context* is that to which the Message *refers*. Loosely and perhaps rather inaccurately, it is the meaning of the Message. Code is the form in which the message is couched, and Contact is the channel which links the Addresser and the Addressee. I find the schema valuable in the way it highlights aspects which are not normally obtrusive when one is concerned with communication among the normally hearing, but which may assume crucial importance when imperfect hearing raises obstacles to ready communication. As instances I would cite the effects of different contexts on the comprehensibility of the Message for the Addressee who suffers from deafness, and the matter of the status of the code when the Addresser's code is almost wholly acoustic and the Addressee's mainly visual and proprioceptive. Jakobson goes on to link each of the six factors of language with a language function. The functions of language must be regarded as beyond the scope of this paper, although a comparative account of the ways in which language is used by hearing and hearing impaired children would make an interesting and valuable study.

The core of the topic before us now is the mastery of the code. Perhaps in deference to Alice in Wonderland's conversation with Humpty Dumpty[1], we shall say, rather than mastery, obedience to the code. The code which concerns us is verbal language, that is to say, the native language of the environment—the mother tongue and primarily in its original form: the language as spoken and as comprehended by eye and ear. (With apologies to our hosts I have to admit that the native language of the environment is in this case mainly that of my environment, hence English, but English sometimes in the American version.) My apology is restrained by the knowledge that whether the native language is Dutch, English, or Japanese the same manifestations in linguistic development, and the same needs in linguistic assessment are shown by deaf children.

Languages are normally studied from three aspects: sounds, meanings, and rules which link sounds and meanings[2]—the phonological, semantic, and grammatical aspects. The assessment of language in hearing impaired children needs, therefore, to take account of speech sounds—their comprehensibility when uttered by or when addressed to hearing-impaired children, to take account of the main carriers of meaning in lexis or vocabulary and to take account of the capacity to follow the rules of grammar both in comprehension and expression.

The intelligibility of spoken language is treated in another paper in the Symposium. The other aspect of contact (to use Jakobson's term) in which the deaf child is the Addressee involves principally the topic traditionally termed lipreading. Although this topic may reasonably be considered to be a part of my paper, pressure of space prevents it from receiving more than brief mention.

Problems in the Assessment of the Language of Hearing-Impaired Children

The assessment of language of children may give rise to problems whether the children concerned are normally hearing or not. In addition to general problems of this type there are, of course, problems which are specific to the assessment of deaf children. One of the most intractible problems in linguistic assessment is the status of the evidence on which the assessment is based. The problem arises even in expressive language since we may not be sure to what extent particular utterances are representative of the child's general spoken expression. In assessment of comprehension the difficulty is much more acute. Comprehension of spoken language, so we are convinced by our personal experience, often takes place without any readily observable changes in the behavior of the Addressee. Because of the very nature of comprehension we are driven to rely on indirect evidence of its presence. Such evidence is usually most informative when it is in verbal form—spoken or written responses. On occasion, however, we are unable or unwilling to rely on spoken expression as evidence of comprehension. To provide substitutes in the form of pictures which can be selected by the Addressee, or directions which he may carry out, demands much ingenuity from the test constructor and places strict limitations on the nature of the language which is to be considered.

The range and complexity of linguistic skills in normally hearing children is reflected in the outstanding achievement of many deaf pupils. Hence a very wide range of material may be required to assess deaf children's language to accommodate those children who have extreme difficulty in making verbal progress, and those whose language levels are similar to the levels of their normally hearing peers.

It must be recognized that most of the measures of language available for use with deaf children have been developed originally for use with normally hearing children. In relatively few cases have the authors of the tests been aware of the needs of linguistically handicapped children. Tests designed for the normally hearing often have the advantage of standardization on relatively large numbers of children. They also offer the means of making comparisons between linguistically handicapped children and their normally developing peers. On the other hand, they may well incorporate administration and scoring procedures which are not readily amenable to meeting the obstacles to comprehension and speech intelligibility which are created by deafness. Another feature of tests devised for hearing children which may be a marked weakness when a test is used with deaf children is the difficulty of gradation of the items. A coarse gradation in which there is a steep increase in item difficulty over a small range of items may result in the test failing to distinguish clearly between deaf children whose language levels are distinctly different, even though the differences may be relatively slight by the standards of language development in normally hearing children. An allied feature of many tests is that they do not provide sufficient simple or easy items either to make the test accessible to deaf children or to enable them to achieve sufficient success to gain confidence. There may, too, be a serious mismatch between the deaf child's cognitive and social maturity and the level of the test materials which is appropriate to the linguistic level at which the deaf child is functioning.

Tests of language which have been developed specifically with deaf children in mind are rather rare, especially in published form. It must be admitted, too, that because of the difficulties of assembling large numbers of deaf children and because of the variability of the children in the groups which may be assembled, in terms of important factors such as intelligence, it is extremely difficult to obtain well standardized measures which allow close comparisons between individual children.

Finally, in this selection from the problems of language testing, there is that of the circumstances in which the tests are administered. To make clear what is essentially an obvious point, one has in mind examples such as the scoring of responses in expressive speech by a teacher who is very familiar with a particular deaf child's speech and, on the other hand, a psychologist who has not had close contact with the child. The resulting scores from the two testers may be considerably different.

One or two of the problems which are most familiar to me have been outlined here. I am aware that there are several others which I have not raised. I do not think that the difficulties we encounter are sufficient to vitiate the results of linguistic assessment. We may regard these obstacles as cautionary rather than prohibitive.

SECTION 2

Linguistic Assessment: Tests and Other Measures

This section is divided into four parts. The first three parts are principally concerned with specific or homogeneous tests as contrasted with more general heterogeneous scales, although on occasion specific subtests from scales will be referred to. Part I consists of a brief note on assessment of lipreading. Part II is devoted to lexis or, as I prefer to say, vocabulary. Part III examines the area of words in combination, including the rules of combination—grammar. In Part IV brief comments on scales are made.

In considering the linguistic performance of children one needs to bear in mind the possible relationships between intelligence and language. In normally hearing children the relationship is generally thought to be very close in the case of vocabulary knowledge. L. M. Terman (1937) attributed high value to the vocabulary test, and such tests play an important part in most verbal intelligence scales. The Peabody Picture Vocabulary Test provides norms in terms of mental ages for scores on the test although the English adaptation (English Picture Vocabulary Test) is described as a measure of listening vocabulary with high correlation with more general measures of intelligence. When applying such tests with deaf children we would obviously regard them as poor indicators of general mental ability, though we would admit that it is not possible even in the case of deaf children to separate language functioning from the effects of intelligence.

It should be borne in mind that in the following sections a selection has been made especially where several measures of the same type exist. The selection is a personal one based partly on the evident applicability and usefulness of the tests, partly on possibilities of future use which seem to be inherent in some tests, and partly on the limitations and prejudices of personal knowledge.

Part I – Lipreading

For the purpose of simplifying and limiting my task I propose to regard the assessment of speech reception as an aspect of the assessment of hearing and, therefore, beyond the scope of this paper. The matter of lipreading, to use the traditional term, is rather more difficult to avoid, especially in considering children as deaf as those we have in mind in this seminar. I hope then to sidestep a fairly lengthy discussion by reference to the work of other people.

R. Conrad devotes a chapter to lipreading in his recent book *The Deaf Schoolchild* (1979). Within the limits of the chapter there is thorough discussion of the problems of assessing lipreading. Conrad's team developed a test based upon the Donaldson Lipreading Test (Montgomery, 1968). The modified test was treated as a test not solely of comprehension but of speech comprehension. American tests of lipreading are described in Herbert J. Oyer's chapter on the measurement of the dimensions of visual communication which is included in Singh's (1975) book on measurement procedures in speech, hearing, and language. Recently a test of lipreading for use with English deaf pupils has been devised by Andreas Markides. A full description of the test will be given in A. C. Markides' "Manchester Speech Reading (Lipreading) Test" (to be published). The test includes single words and sentences varying in length from two to six words. There are two parallel forms.

Part II – LEXIS (Vocabulary)

Where extreme deafness is present from earliest life the difficulties encountered by the child in the development of grammar are so prominent that the importance of the area of vocabulary is sometimes underplayed. Vocabulary assessment is, however, commonly employed with normally hearing children. The ease with which the tests may be administered doubtless plays a part in their frequent use, but it nevertheless remains that vocabulary measures are among the most sensitive indicators of level of linguistic attainment. I believe this to be the case for deaf as well as for hearing children.

Comprehension Vocabulary

Comprehension vocabulary tests in which a choice from a number of illustrations has to be made by the person tested in response to the spoken description have a venerable history in the United States. Subtests with a similar rationale are found in the Stanford-Binet Scale. Among independent tests the Van Alstyne Picture Vocabulary Test was published as long ago as 1929. The Ammons Full Range Picture Vocabulary Test is a later addition in the same field. The most recent test, the Peabody Picture Vocabulary Test, is by far the most widely used. It provides normative data for subjects from approximately 2 to 18 years with extrapolation to a level of 1 year, 9 months. It has been much used with hearing impaired children, the form of response avoiding problems which might arise were a spoken response necessary. It is particularly valuable in the extent to which early vocabulary is represented. The illustrations, clear line drawings, do not seem to have appreciable cultural bias, perhaps reflecting the trend for developed cultures to become more and more similar to each other. The vocabulary itself does contain a number of specific American usages even at relatively simple levels. The word "wiener" is not yet current in England, that is to say it has not yet replaced that other term which came to us when the silent screen became "the talkies," namely the "hot dog"! Since the test provides two parallel forms it is possible in most instances to sidestep this difficulty by substituting from the alternate form. In translation, of course, the problem would not arise. Our Dutch hosts have, I understand, translated and used with their deaf children the Peabody Picture Vocabulary Test. It will be valuable to have their views and information. Three aspects of the use of the test with deaf children may be noted, and the points made in relation to this test will be relevant in the application of other tests. Obviously, there is an effect of lipreading especially since the linguistic context of the item is very limited. Scores typically increase for older deaf children when the item is presented in written or printed form. Hence a score based solely on spoken language presentation is not a measure simply of word knowledge which may well be underestimated in such circumstances. The second point is the possibility that the deaf child being tested may have an expectation that the items are likely to take noun-object form. Although the inclusion of verb forms in the practice items should meet this problem, we may find the child at a loss unless it is made very clear to him that forms other than the noun will occur. The third point is the problem of guessing which may be more acute in the PPVT since the child has to reach a level of six failures in eight successive items before the test is discontinued.

The value of the PPVT is reflected in the amount of use made of it. In the United Kingdom Alan Brimer, then of the University of Bristol, took up the standardization of the test on English children. The result is now the Full Range English Picture Vocabulary Test. The FREPVT employs the same illustrations as the PPVT but the vocabulary has been selected to meet U.K. needs. The test has only one form and the norms range from approximately 3 years to 18 years. The effect of this difference is to lose an appreciable number of those easier items which are so much needed in testing deaf children. Inflation of the score by guessing is reduced in the EPVT by discontinuing when five errors in eight successive items are made.

A comprehension vocabulary test which is linked to the selection of objects rather than pictures is a valuable one for young deaf children. Such measures already exist within scales of language development such as the Reynell Scale, which will be discussed later. Clearly such a test becomes much clumsier in administration than a picture vocabulary test, and those which exist restrict themselves to a small number of items. The success of David Kendall's speech tests of hearing, in which the young child selects from a choice of toy objects according to the word he hears, indicates that a vocabulary comprehension test of this type could fill a gap at the level of the nursery and early primary school child.

An ingenious test of comprehension vocabulary forms one of the subtests of the Illinois Test of Psycholinguistic Abilities. In the Auditory Decoding Test the vocabulary item is presented as a question to which the child answers with a YES/NO response. Questions take the form "Do apples fly?"; "Do lanterns shine?"; "Do abrasions cogitate?" The ITPA is used with hearing impaired children, but a vocabulary test of this type may create difficulties of interpretation for the child which are beyond those of the simple difficulty level of the word meaning.

Expressive Vocabulary

The most frequently employed method of assessing expressive vocabulary is to present the child with a series of items of increasing difficulty for which he has to give the meanings in his own words. When the items are in the form of words, which they usually are, then the test obviously is one of comprehension as well as expression. The assumption is that the difficulty of comprehension will be less than that of expression, but with deaf children this may not be the case. Such tests are demanding for young children even when they have normal hearing. More accessible expressive vocabulary tests have been devised in which the child simply has to name an object presented to him. Such tests have long formed a part of scales for the assessment of intelligence in young children as, for instance, the Stanford-Binet. These subtests do not normally have sufficient items to act as independent vocabulary tests. A naming vocabulary test utilizing material from several earlier scales has been in use for some years in my own department.[3] The test is such that normally hearing children of 2 plus years can name about half of the 25 items. Norms are available for partially hearing and deaf children between the ages of 5 and 8 years. Reasonable discrimination is provided by the test for the deaf child and the younger partially hearing children, and data are available on normally hearing children between 2 and 5 years.

A. F. Watts published among several tests of language in his *The Language and Mental Development of Children* (1944), a vocabulary test for young children which was employed successfully with deaf children by Sir Alexander and Lady (Ethel) Ewing. The test contains 100 questions, the first 50 of which relate to what is seen and the second 50 to what is described. Watts had in mind normally hearing children between the ages of 3½ and 8 years, and provides normative data. Although sections of the material are outdated, the format is one which would usefully form a bridge between the vocabulary tests based on objects and pictures and those which operate wholly in the area of language without any visual support.

It may be noted here that the Peabody Picture Vocabulary Test has been used with cerebral palsied children as a test of naming vocabulary (R.J. Love), but so far as I know there is no published normative data on its use in this way.

Of the tests which present a word to the child for him to define, the series provided by J. C. Raven is best known to me. These vocabulary tests are designed to accompany the nonverbal Matrices tests which have themselves been very widely used with deaf children. The Raven series has an advantage over vocabulary tests provided in verbal intelligence scales, as for example, the Wechsler scales, in that Raven has constructed in the Crichton Vocabulary Scale a test aimed at an age range for normally hearing children of 5 to 11 years. The test contains 80 items and as a consequence includes a reasonable number of items which are easy for primary school children. Amongst Raven's more advanced tests for older children and adults are pencil and paper versions which include assessment of vocabulary by multiple choice from which selection of synonyms is to be made.

One measure which should be mentioned here because of its widespread use, although not a test as such, is the Type/Token ratio: the number of different words produced compared with the total number of words produced. Hence the TTR is a measure of diversity of vocabulary. John B. Carroll suggested a modification of the formula to make the resulting figure less dependent on the length of the sample. Carroll's formula is the number of different words divided by the square root of twice the number of words in the sample.

A matter which may usefully be touched on here—although the problem arises generally in the presentation of results of tests of linguistic attainment administered to linguistically retarded children—is the form in which the results are to be quoted. In tests which provide quotients, standardized scores or similar statistics, it frequently happens that the raw scores for deaf children do not reach the lowest ranges of quoted standardized scores. By examining the tables of norms to find at which age level the raw score obtained by the deaf child is an average score for the normally hearing population on which the test was standardized, one can offer the score in the form of a vocabulary age. Indeed, in some tests such as the PPVT it is possible to read off an age level from a raw score. There are several serious and very reasonable objections to such a practice. On the other hand the vocabulary or language age determined in this way may be the only generally meaningful way of offering an indication of the level obtained by the child on that test. It seems to me that, if the appropriate provisions are made, it is more profitable than not to make use of language ages where these are the only figures into which the raw scores can be converted.

Part III — Words in Combination

I should point out that, in this part, comprehension and expression are not separated into distinct sections.

> The 'combinability' of words . . . . seems to me the central problem in teaching a language to deaf children
> (A. van Uden)

In the immense flood of literature on child language which was released by Noam Chomsky's innovative ideas, consideration of grammar was pre-eminent, particularly in the earlier studies. It is not surprising, therefore, that attention was turned to the assessment of the grammatical knowledge of young children. Roger Brown's experiments in testing comprehension of linguistic constructions and Jean Berko Gleason's exploration of children's ability to apply grammatical rules to new material, have had much influence. There is also an older tradition stemming again from intelligence scales in which the ability of young children to follow out spoken directions is examined.

The Michigan Picture Language Inventory by Lerea, published in 1958, may be said to have anticipated the interest in syntax created by Chomsky. The MPLI includes assessment of vocabulary. The Northwestern Syntax Screening Test is limited to the investigation of grammar and assesses both comprehension and expression. The expressive scale depends on the fairly generally accepted view that normally hearing children do not imitate accurately, grammatical structures which are beyond their own grammatical grasp. The child is provided spoken descriptions of pictures which he is then asked to describe. Provided that he follows the correct grammatical form and makes no other grammatical error, the response is correct. It is hard to envisage the expressive scale of this test operating satisfactorily with many deaf children. The comprehension scale can certainly be employed with children with severe hearing losses and, with relatively slight modifications, I believe it would prove suitable with deaf children. The comprehension scale has 20 pairs of items. Each item matches one of four pictures to which the child points when the appropriate sentence is spoken. The test was standardized on normally hearing children between 3 and 8 years. A difficulty in such tests—and especially when used with hearing impaired children—is to know to what extent failure on particular items can be regarded as indicative of lack of knowledge of the construction in general. Similar tests which examine comprehension have been produced in the United States by Sister Elizabeth Carrow and in the U.K. by Arnold Spencer in Manchester. Spencer's test, prepared for a research study made in the Department of Audiology, was employed with deaf children.

Comprehension of spoken directions receives considerable attention in Reynell's scale, but perhaps the most extensive provision is that made by Coral Richards, a speech therapist, in her test of the understanding of the spoken word. The test consists of a series of directions of increasing length and complexity. The directions are followed out by the child in the manipulation of play material. The maturity level of the material is such that it would not be suitable for older children, and the standardization is that of a pilot study. Nevertheless, the test has been used successfully with young deaf children and could well be modified to make it satisfactory for older deaf children.

Tests of grammatical expression are found in forms such as the grammatical closure test of the Illinois Test of Psycholinguistic Abilities. The test uses pictures and statements which the child has to complete: *Here is an apple. Here are two _____* . An obvious problem in the use of tests of this type is the ability of the child to intelligibly produce forms such as the plural markers, which are in fact known to him. Written production could be borne in mind in this context.

The commonest treatment of grammatical expression has been by the analysis of and the application of formulae to samples of written expression. There are, nevertheless, several measures which can be fairly readily applied to samples of spoken language which have been recorded and transcribed. Two of these which have been in use for a very long time and have been applied to the language of both hearing and hearing impaired children, are the mean length of utterance and sentence complexity. Roger Brown regards mean length of utterance as a sensitive index of linguistic development in young hearing children, since increase in grammatical mastery is almost inevitably accompanied at this stage by increase in length. Provided that a deaf child's expression is such that the utterances can be distinguished in terms of combinatory units, the measure is an effective one. Brown employs an utterance length based on morpheme count which is likely to be more sensitive grammatically than the older word count which was used by McCarthy and Templin.

Classifications of sentence complexity are obviously applicable only at stages at which language production is fairly well developed. The Heiders carried out sentence classification in their pioneer studies of the language (in this case the written language) of deaf children. Lee's Developmental Sentence scoring has been applied by Presnall to the spoken language of deaf children.

Courtney Cazden has described indices of the development of the Noun Phrase and the Verb Phrase which are applicable with young normally hearing children. Joan Tough has employed them in analysis of language of English nursery school-age children. So far as I know these indices have not been applied to samples of language from deaf children. We should note too that there is a form for grammatical application (Hass) of the Type/Token ratio.

A recently published English account of a procedure for assessing expressive language development in linguistically handicapped children is that of David Crystal and coworkers (The Grammatical Analysis of Language Disability, 1978). In this procedure a very detailed analysis is made of a transcribed sample of spoken language. The analysis is made by successive scans which examine the material from different grammatical aspects. The analysis can be charted and the results compared with the grammatical progress of normally developing children at seven stages between the ages of 9 to 18 months at the earliest stage to 4½ plus years at the latest. The use of the procedure with children from a partially hearing unit has recently been described (Crystal, 1979), but the extent to which the analysis will be valuable with deaf children is not yet clear.

The grammar of deaf children's written expression has been extensively studied in recent years. In the United States there is the work associated with the names, among others, of Stephen P. Quigley, D. J. Power, and D. F. Moores, and in England of G. P. Ivimey. It would be inappropriate, too, to omit the name of one who earlier contributed much in this area—H. R. Myklebust.

Part IV — Scales of Language Development

Brief consideration is now given to two scales of language development which have been referred to previously.

The Reynell Development Language Scales provide for the assessment of verbal comprehension and verbal expression in children aged from 1 to 7 years. The comprehension scale is better developed than the expressive scale, which is a merit if we consider that the assessment of comprehension is unduly neglected. The scales begin with items scored on the basis of observation of the child. They continue through simple tests, some of which have already been mentioned, and at the highest levels they involve the completion of complex directions in comprehension and, in expression, creative use of language in the verbalization of thought. Joan Reynell has envisaged the use of the scales with deaf children and for many years has provided short courses to teachers of the deaf on the nature and administration of the scales. No standardization with deaf children has been attempted, but deaf children's language levels can be related to those of hearing children and different aspects of the child's linguistic abilities can be investigated. The author provides for the possibility of presenting the scales by means of the written language or by signs, and gives instructions about procedure. The different means would be kept distinct, spoken language being used first, then, in case of failure, written language and finally signing.

The Illinois Test of Psycholinguistic Abilities provides a number of subtests of verbal type as well as several which are nonverbal. A rather complex and perhaps superseded psycholinguistic theory underlies the scale, but the subtests may be considered in their own right as measures of different aspects of verbal functioning. The age range of the scale is approximately 2½ to 10 years. Psycholinguistic ages can be obtained from the subtests. The nonverbal tests applied with hearing impaired children may not provide greater or very different information from that gained from a nonverbal intelligence scale. Of the verbal tests several would be difficult to apply with deaf children. The Auditory Reception Test has been noted already. In the Auditory Closure Test the examiner utters part of a word which the child has to complete. Probably the most useful test for deaf children is the already mentioned Grammatical Closure Test.

Descriptive Schedules

Those who work with young deaf children, especially in research projects, have often needed to make some assessment of the beginnings of language in such children. The descriptive methods employed by Arnold Gesell, and in England by Mary D. Sheridan, have given guidance. But since these writers were concerned foremost with normal development, the linguistic items in their schedules are frequently not sufficiently detailed for the needs of the worker with deaf children. In my own department, schedules which set out the early stages of orientation toward comprehension of spoken language and of the beginnings of spoken expression have been drawn up. These have not been standardized. They are intended to be scored on the basis of the witness of an observer who is familiar with the child—the mother, visiting teacher of the deaf, or nursery class teacher. Estimates of the child's level in comprehension and expression of numbers of words or phrases form an appreciable part of the scales. The purpose of these schedules is to provide a bridge to the point at which the child is sufficiently mature, developmentally and linguistically, to be able to cooperate in the simplest tests.

Concluding Remarks

I am aware that many tests have been left out of this paper, of which one or two have been mentioned to me as suitable for linguistically handicapped children. I have attempted some remedy by including names of further tests with the list of references.

I have not sought to justify linguistic assessment against critics or to detail its several values. Instead I have assumed that usually it is a good thing. I appreciate that the tests have weaknesses, especially in respect to their standardizations, their sampling of subjects, and the normative data which is provided. In spite of their weaknesses I believe that most of them can serve a useful purpose when their limitations are recognized.

Many of the tests we have been concerned with allow for comparisons to be made between deaf and normally hearing children. It is my personal opinion that such comparisons must be kept in proper perspective and used, as they can be, in positive ways. Any permanent bilateral imperfection of hearing for speech, let alone profound deafness, is likely to be accompanied by some effect on a child's linguistic progress. On the other hand, normally hearing children of 3 and many of 2½ years are excellent conversationalists. A deaf secondary school child who can function at a similar level is not badly equipped for communication in the everyday world.

ADDITIONAL TEST MATERIAL

Bzoch, K. R. and League, R. (1978) Assessing language skills in infancy (The Receptive-Expressive Emergent Language Test). M.T.P. Press.

Ijsseldijk, F. J. W. Dutch translation and standardization of the Peabody Picture Vocabulary Test (Unpublished). Sint Michielsgestel.

Ling, R. H. (1977) Schedules of development in audition, speech, language, communication for hearing-impaired infants and their parents. Washington, DC: A. G. Bell Association for the Deaf.

Ling, D., (1978) Cumulative record for speech skill acquisition. Washington, DC: A. G. Bell Association for the Deaf.

assessment of language **405**

Moog, J. and Geers, A. Grammatical analysis of elicited language. Central Institute for the Deaf, St. Louis.
Moog, J. and Geers, A. Scales of early communication skills for hearing-impaired children. Central Institute for the Deaf, St. Louis.
Nakanishi, Y. Picture vocabulary comprehension test for use with deaf children. (Unpublished). Tokyo Gakugei University.
Salvia, J. and Ysseldyke, J. E. (1978) Assessment in special and remedial education. Houghton Mifflin.
(Includes list of publishers of American tests).

LIST OF TESTS

References for the formulae and analyses and for some of the tests are given in the list of references.
Published tests including those published in the U.S.A. are normally obtainable through:

> The N.F.E.R. Publishing Co. Ltd.,
> Darville House, 2 Oxford Road East,
> Windsor, Berkshire, SL4 1DF, England.

Vocabulary

Full Range English Picture Vocabulary Test (M.A. Brimer and L.M. Dunn).
Full Range Picture Vocabulary Test (R.B. and H.S. Ammons)
    (A short form of the FRPVT, the Quick Test is available)
Mill Hill and Crichton Vocabulary Scales (J.C. Raven)
Peabody Picture Vocabulary Test (L.M. Dunn)
Toy Vocabulary Test (H.L. Owrid. Unpublished)
Van Alstyne Picture Vocabulary Test (D. van Alstyne)
Vocabulary Test for Young Children (A.F. Watts)

Grammar and Word Combinations

Comprehension of Sentence Structure (A. Spencer: Unpublished. *See* Kitzinger, M.D. (1975) The Comprehension of Grammar by Hearing-Impaired Children. M.Sc. Thesis. John Rylands Manchester University Library)
Michigan Picture Language Inventory (L. Lerea).
Northwestern Syntax Screening Test (L.L. Lee)
Test for Auditory Comprehension of Language (E. Carrow) *also* Screening Test for Auditory Comprehension of Language (E. Carrow)
Test of Understanding of the Spoken Word (C.M. Richards) (*See* Richard's article of the same title. Brit. J. Dis. Comm. *v*, 2)

Scales

Illinois Test of Psycholinguistic Abilities (S.A. Kirk, J.J. McCarthy, W.D. Kirk)
Reynell Developmental Language Scales (J. Reynell)
Schedules for Assessment of Comprehension of Speech and of Expressive Speech. (H.L. Owrid. Unpublished)

Additional

Boehm Test of Basic Concepts (A.E. Boehm).
British Ability Scales (C.D. Elliott, D.J. Murray and L.S. Pearson)
Preschool Language Scale (I.L. Zimmerman, V.G. Steiner, R.L. Evatt)
Wechsler Intelligence Scales (Verbal Scales)

Footnotes

1. "When I use a word," Humpty Dumpty said, in rather a scornful tone, "it means just what I choose it to mean—neither more nor less." "The question is," said Alice "whether you *can* make words mean so many different things." "The question is," said Humpty Dumpty, "which is to be master—that's all." (*The Complete Works of Lewis Carroll.* London. The Nonesuch Press, 1939, p. 196. *Through the Looking-Glass*)
2. The person who has acquired knowledge of a language has internalized a system of rules that relate sound and meaning in a particular way. Noam Chomsky. *Language and Mind.* New York: Harcourt, Brace. 1968. p. 23.
3. Owrid, H. L. (1960) Measuring spoken language in young deaf children. *Teacher of the Deaf.* v. 58, pp. 24–34, 124–128.

References

Brown, R. *A first language.* London: Allen & Unwin, 1973.
Brown, R. Linguistic determinism and the part of speech. *Journal of Abnormal and Social Psychology,* 1957, 55.
Carroll, J. B. *Language and thought.* Englewood Cliffs, NJ: Prentice-Hall, 1964.
Cazden, C. B. *Child language and education.* New York: Holt, Rinehart & Winston, 1972.
Conrad, R. *The deaf schoolchild.* London: Harper & Row, 1979.
Crystal, D., et al. *The grammatical analysis of language disability.* London: Arnold, 1976.
Crystal, D. *Working with LARSP.* London: Arnold, 1979.
Gesell, A. (Ed.). *The first five years of life.* London: Methuen, 1963.
Gleason, J. Berko. The child's learning of English morphology. In S. Saporta, (Ed.), *Psycholinguistics.* New York: Holt, Rinehart & Winston, 1961.
Hass, W. A., & Wepman, J. M. Dimensions of individual difference in the spoken syntax of schoolchildren. *Journal of Speech and Hearing Research,* 1974, 17.
Heider, F. R., & Heider, G. M. A comparison of sentence structure of deaf and hearing children. *Psychological Monographs,* 1940, 52.
Ivimey, G. P. The written syntax of an English deaf child: An exploration in method. *British Journal of Disorders of Communication,* 1976, 11.

Jakobson, R. In T. A. Sebeok (Ed.), *Style in language*. New York: M.I.T. Press & John Wiley, 1960.

Kendall, D. C. Audiometry for young children (part II). *Teacher of the Deaf*, 1954, 52.

Lee, L. L. Screening test for syntax development. *Journal of Speech and Hearing Disorders*, 1970, 35.

Lee, L. L., & Canter, S. M. Developmental sentence scoring. *Journal of Speech and Hearing Disorders*, 1971, 36.

Lerea, L. Assessing language development. *Journal of Speech and Hearing Research*, 1958, 1.

Love, R. J. Oral language behavior of older cerebral palsied children. *Journal of Speech and Hearing Research*, 1964, 7.

Markides, A. C. *Manchester Speechreading (Lipreading) Test*. (To be published.)

McCarthy, D. *The language development of the pre-school child*. Minneapolis: University of Minnesota Press, 1930.

Montgomery, G. W. G. A factorial study of communication and ability in deaf schoolleavers. *British Journal of Educational Psychology*, 1968, 38.

Moores, D. F. *An investigation of the psycholinguistic functioning of deaf adolescents*. Washington, DC: Department of Health, Education and Welfare, U.S. Office of Education, 1971.

Oyer, H. J. The measurement of the dimensions of visual communication. In S. Singh (Ed.), *Measurement procedures in speech*, 1975.

Pressnell, L. M. Hearing-impaired children's comprehension and production of syntax in oral language. *Journal of Speech and Hearing Research*, 1973, 16.

Quigley, S. P., et al. *Syntactic structures in the language of deaf children*. Urbana, IL: Institute for Child Behavior and Development, 1976.

Sheridan, M. D. *The developmental progress of infants and young children*. London: Her Majesty's Stationary Office, 1968.

Templin, M. *Certain language skills in children*. Minneapolis: University of Minnesota Press, 1957.

Terman, L. M., & Merrill, M. A. *Measuring intelligence*. Boston: Houghton Mifflin, 1937.

Tough, J. *The development of meaning*. London: Allen & Unwin, 1977.

van Uden, A. *A maternal reflective method of teaching an oral mother tongue to deaf children*. Sint Michielsgestel: Institute for the Deaf, 1968.

Watts, A. F. *The language and mental development of children*. London: Harrap, 1944.

reaction to 16

daniel ling

I have already reacted to chapter 15. My second task is to review the paper by Owrid. Owrid's approach is to view language in terms of Jakobson's (1960) schema which comprises six factors: Addresser and addressee, context, message, contact, and code. It is a refreshing exercise to relate this schema both to work with hearing impaired children and to modern developments in linguistics. The exercise is, of course, too extensive for a short paper and perhaps too long for the discussion period allotted for this Symposium.

Owrid has presented many of the tests that are currently in use in the U.S. and in Britain. The Manchester work, in which Owrid has played a significant role, will be of interest to many from other countries. It is important to stress that, whereas language development and related tests may be applicable from one English-speaking country to another, speech reception tests are not. Thus many of the speech tests of hearing and measures of lipreading skill can not, for reasons relating to dialect, be used without considerable adaptation in the U.S. and Canada. As with speech evaluation procedures, language tests can be carried out for two main purposes—comparison, as with tests based on normative data—and as a guide for identifying the child's stage of development with a view to providing a systematic approach to further language learning.

I find Owrid's paper quite different from papers with similar titles written in North America. In the U.S. and Canada, language is currently considered almost exclusively in terms of context, message, and code. This is shown by yesterday's papers. Furthermore, although Crystal's work is well known in North America, more emphasis would be given to other evaluation tools. Current work in the U.S. is also concerned with elicited language as well as with the analysis of spontaneous samples. Perhaps with meetings such as this an international perspective will emerge.

In personal discussions with Owrid, we have considered future work. It seems to us that a greater emphasis in work with hearing impaired children should not be simply on language, but on the effectiveness of speech communication. In this rapidly growing area of interest, it might well repay us to discuss in some detail how international collaboration can help us both gather and apply the information we need for more effective language teaching and communication development in hearing impaired children.

17

psychological and educational diagnosis and assessment

m. l. h. m. broesterhuizen,
jan p. m. van dijk, and
frans j. w. iJsseldijk

Introduction

It is a false assumption to suppose that all hearing people can learn to talk. There are a great many people who, despite having a normal audiogram for pure tones, have difficulties in articulating words and sentences fluently.

Reasons for failure in oral communication are diverse. Neurological factors can play a role, as in aphasic problems as well as factors such as emotional disturbance (e.g. elective mutism, childhood schizophrenia). It is interesting to notice that sometimes a severely mentally retarded person, without neurological damage or emotional problems, still functions relatively well on the level of oral communication. It is also known that a normally hearing person's ability to converse orally, is dependent on hereditary factors, but not on these exclusively. If it is true that, for a person with normal hearing, the development of speech is quite an accomplishment, then it is infinitely more so for a hearing impaired person.

The purpose of this paper is to give an overview of the factors which are involved in the development of speech, and the other skills which play a role in oral communication. In this study the many factors which are involved in the process of learning to converse orally, and developing an oral mother-tongue will be discussed. It is not possible to predict the exact weight of every factor in its relationship to oral ability. The field of differential diagnosis has not yet reached this level of sophistication.

When research done at the school for the deaf in Sint Michielsgestel is referred to, the pupils are mostly Caucasians, come from all parts of the country, from mostly Catholic parents. Since Sint Michielsgestel has a rather extensive service for multihandicapped deaf children, other schools or agencies refer a great many of these youngsters to Sint Michielsgestel. Thus the number of "deaf children with other handicaps" is somewhat overrepresented in our population.

We have organized this paper as follows:

Part I; A discussion of etiological factors and their possible relationship with learning an oral mother tongue.
Part II; A discussion of the other factors: hearing-loss (2.1), intelligence and memory (2.2), motor development (2.3), sensorimotor integration (2.4), and emotional and personality factors in their relationship to learning (2.5).
Part III; The philosophy and educational methods of the school and the influence of these on the final result of the child's education.

Where statistical data are available they will be used in our discussion. However, phenomenological analysis, as well as statistical methods, can also give us insight into the problems of acquiring a mother tongue.

Part 1. Etiology of Deafness and Its Relationship to Communicative Competence

In his study on 3,535 individuals with severe hearing loss, Frazer (1976) draws two conclusions:

1. Neither the degree nor the age of onset of the hearing loss is defined (in the studies he refers to) in a biologically objective manner and
2. It is hard to establish whether the educational difficulties are due to damage to the peripheral auditory apparatus or to more central causes. Because of lack of objectivity in medical diagnosis, it is impossible to compare the outcome of etiological studies.

The greatest difficulty is that in many instances the cause of deafness is unidentified; sometimes this percentage is as high as 40 percent of the population of deaf people (Frazer, 1976). Even when the cause is "known" one should be very careful. In preparing a study on rubella hearing-impaired children, van Dijk received 112 names of so-called rubella children from referring agencies. After careful screening, 30 children had to be eliminated because they did not meet the strict criteria for intrauterine rubella (Hardy, 1973).

van Dijk's study, currently in preparation, has given us insight, despite the exclusions mentioned before, into the importance of the etiology and its effect upon factors influencing the development of the child.

1.1 Prenatal versus postnatal causes

The most important prenatal causes of deafness are rubella, syphilis, and toxoplasmosis; these can damage the embryo during certain periods in pregnancy (rubella up to 31 weeks).

The time of infection can be a crucial factor in determining the variety of handicaps incurred. If the invasion of the rubella virus coincides with the period of development of the lens (during the fourth through eighth weeks), the child might develop cataracts. In all cases, early infection prevents a normal development of the embryo. Very often the rhythm between mother and child is disturbed, and this can cause problems in basic processes such as feeding and sleeping.

Early infections can cause damage to the brain (e.g. toxoplasmosis) and also prevent normal growth of brain cells. Moreover, the neural connection can be poorly developed in these cells. If this is the case, then it is likely that the integration of different parts of the brain is hampered, and this may lead to severe learning problems. Furthermore, because of early neurological involvement, the integration system of the brain (the reticular formation) is poorly organized. This can influence the child's perception, for example, he might be overselective with regard to visual stimuli, while disregarding other stimuli—hearing for instance (Lovaas & Buckner, 1977). When a child with such a complicated history is born, often with a very low birthweight, the relationship with his mother is easily threatened by his failure to thrive, or by the way he reacts to stimuli.

Even with rubella children who later turn out to be good students, difficulties in the early years are reported. Such a history may lead to emotional deprivation and henceforth to problems in later life in children who have suffered from early infection (Chess, Korn & Fernandez 1971). Because of the neurological disorders described earlier, infantile autism might also occur. Stereotyped behavior is almost always present in the first years after birth. This sometimes disappears spontaneously, but in other cases preference for a specific modality exists throughout life and may result in good performance in this area. This is especially true for the rubella child whose performance on visual tasks is significantly better than that of the nonrubella child (van Dijk, work in preparation).

In this paper, visual-motor-integration is considered to be one of the factors influencing learning and speech. The child with an early traumatic history is always liable to have difficulties in this area. If the child's hearing is severely impaired as well, it is highly probable that fluent speech and lipreading will not develop easily. Although van Uden, in his research on language disorders, did not include etiology as a controlled variable, later analysis showed that 8 children in his sample were diagnosed as rubella; 7 of them belonged to the group of dyspractic children.

The number of children who are deaf due to prenatal causes is unknown. Since rubella is easily confused with other viral diseases or frequently overlooked, we estimate that the number is higher than the literature reports. Today, because of effective medical intervention, congenital syphilis is a less important cause of deafness than in the past. It is difficult to assess the importance of toxoplasmosis as an etiological factor because laboratory tests are not always reliable. The figure of 10–20 percent mentioned in Theissing and Kittel's research (1962) seems to be far too high.

1.2 Postnatal causes of deafness

Meningitis and encephalitis are the best known of postnatal causes of deafness, accounting for about 10 percent. The deafness is acquired after the child has adapted himself to extrauterine life conditions, about one month after birth. Deafness is often a result of the disease itself or of the medication,for example, streptomycin, gentomycin. It is generally agreed that the earlier the infection is incurred, the more likely it is that the child will have additional handicaps, such as overt brain damage—spasticity, epilepsy. Minimal brain damage symptoms such as hyperactivity can be noticed often in this etiological group.

The final educational outcome of these children seems somewhat dichotomous. Vernon (1969) found groups of children who did well in academic achievement and groups of children with severe communication problems. Recently, studies have given us more insight into the early neurological development of children and animals. It becomes more clear that any period of abnormal circumstances immediately following birth can be decisive for the child's development. Early hospitalization and consequent deprivation of stimulation can cause emotional problems later in life. We are finding more and more children who were hospitalized in the eighth or ninth month of life now suffering from anxiety (Rutter & Hersow, 1977).

1.3. The perinatal etiology group

Dysmaturity (birthweight under 2500 grams but with normal fetal age) or prematurity (the period of gestation significantly reduced) become more important since they play an increasing role in the cause of deafness.

Dysmature and premature children are easily prone to diseases such as jaundice, respiratory difficulties, and infections, but apart from these such births may have been complicated by mechanical trauma or anoxia. With neurological diagnosis improving one finds more and more children with typical damage due to lack of oxygen during or immediately after birth.

Apart from the typical symptoms of brain damage (cerebral palsy and athetosis), one also finds finer neurological defects (perceptual problems, hyperactivity). We are becoming more aware of the slow maturation of these children. Even in cases where the child, neurologically speaking, is "normal," one often finds a delay in the young child's motor functioning which is important for subsequent learning. It is quite possible that these perceptual problems are associated with the early lack of stimulation (humidity crib, incubator, hospitalization) and the delay in motor development. This is particularly true for the pre- and dysmature child with ocular problems: myopia, hemianopsia or lens-involvement (Harcourt & Wybar, 1969). This demonstrates how important good ophthalmological services are for deaf children. Very early intervention is needed for all deaf children, but particularly for this group.

The perinatal causes of deafness account for 10–12 percent as a beginning cause of deafness in general.

1.4. The genetically determined group

Of the identified causes of deafness, the group whose deafness is *genetically determined* is almost 50 percent (Frazer, 1976). Inheritance can be differentiated in its origin (autosomal recessive, autosomal dominant, or x-linked). Although the body of knowledge relating to the laws of genetics is growing rapidly, it is still uncertain how genetics affect the body system. Different patterns of deafness may exist within one family. If we can take a syndrome (e.g., Usher's syndrome, deafness with retinitis pigmentosa) the family patterns may give indications of the patient's future, but it should be stressed that other cases of Usher's syndrome may develop in quite a different way (Kloepfer et al., 1966). Much of the literature on hereditary deafness focuses on cases where Mendelian laws of inheritance count. In these cases, one is rather optimistic about the person's future, because no brain damage is involved.

It is beyond the scope of this paper to discuss the syndromes which are not inherited in a simple manner, such as Klinefelder's syndrome, etc. In these instances the handicap is inherited, but are the patients not the "good achievers" of the study of "deaf children from deaf parents" (Stuckless & Birch, 1966). The last group is growing; more and more deaf people are marrying each other.

As Brill already stated in 1960, the deaf child from a home or family where one is used to dealing with deafness is either well accepted, and therefore doing rather well, or completely rejected, which means maladjustment.

In another research study it was found that the number of children from deaf parents or from families with more deaf siblings, with a reading level of 4.9 grade or higher, was significantly higher than the relative number of the other deaf children who reached the same level. The reason for this is somewhat obscure; it cannot be accounted for by manual communication in the early years, as there is no such thing as manual communication in Holland. Moreover, studies from other oral schools reveal that deaf children of deaf parents are the best achievers in "oral ability" (van Uden, A., 1977). There might be less neurological damage, and the IQ of this "heredity group" might be higher, but it is nonetheless a surprising finding. Perhaps emotional balance and motivation may be the solutions to this problem.

To conclude this part

In predicting a deaf child's future, one should take the cause of his deafness into consideration because it can give indications of the degree to which his body systems and organs are damaged. To what extent the damage actually influences physical and psychological development is largely dependent on "surviving" factors in the child, the degree of damage to the auditory system or to other systems (e.g., visual-motor), and—last but not least—on the influence of the environment. It seems appropriate to consider these individual differences in the next part.

PART II
2.1. Hearing loss

In searching for the predictors of successful oral education hearing loss plays a very important role. Researchers such as Hudgins (1948), Sanders (1968), Erber (1972), and Eggermont (1964) have already shown that the deaf students who used their residual hearing best scored 5 to 15 percent higher in lipreading than children who did not use their residual hearing. Donolly (1969), who investigated 249 students from Gallaudet College, in whom he measured the influence of 30 variables on the process of lipreading, found that hearing loss was the most significant factor. Research by Smith (1975) and Ahlstrom (1970) showed important significant relationships between speech, intelligibility, and hearing loss. In a research project in which IJsseldijk (1977), investigated the ability of deaf children to perceive speech auditorily, it was found that the results of all tests (recognition, identification, and discrimination of words) correlated significantly with the degree of hearing loss. All of this research shows that, even in the most profoundly deaf student, the use of residual hearing is important in the development of learning speech and lipreading. No other channel of information can process speech as rapidly as the auditory sense.

Aside from the speed of information processing, the rhythmic character of the auditory sense enables one to preceive more bits of information than is possible by means of the sense of vision or the sense of touch.

In order to help deaf children use their residual hearing, the following distinctions are important. Most children enrolled in a school for severely hearing-impaired children can be grouped into four categories:

    a. Hard-of-hearing children
    b. Descant deaf children
    c. Deaf children with useful residual hearing
    d. Vibration-deaf children.

a. *Hard of hearing children* are those who, with the help of a hearing aid, are able to perceive language mainly through hearing. Additional information is obtained by the visual and articulatory channels. Therefore children in this group differ in their speech and language education from those in groups c and d, who, even with the best auditory training and the best available hearing aids, have to rely mainly on lipreading as a means of understanding speech.

Students of categories c and d have a worse audiogram than this one:

125	250	500	1k	2k	4k Hz
60	60	90	90	90	90 dB

The students from category *a* normally have a better audiogram than the above.

In Holland a distinction is made between the group of children who are able to develop speech and language via the auditory channel, and the groups of those who, because of their hearing loss, are unable to do this. In the past, schools for hard-of-hearing children and schools for deaf children were founded as separate institutions.

It is believed that this differentiation in school organization is of benefit for both groups of children. When these groups are mixed, and history has shown this very clearly, it is very likely that all sorts of esoteric forms of communication are invented by the children, mainly by those who are hard of hearing. If this kind of communication develops, true oral education is endangered. A distinction between hard-of-hearing children and deaf children is, however, not completely dependent on the hearing threshold mentioned previously. There are always exceptional cases where, for different reasons, enrollment in a school for deaf children is advised.

b. *Descant deaf students* represent a rather typical group of the authors' students. These are pupils who profit mainly from the lower frequencies 125, 250 and 500 Hz; they do not follow the pattern described above. Typically, these pupils function initially as deaf children. Through intensive auditory training and good language teaching, they start using their residual hearing more. This has a marked effect on speech and language development as the child grows older. These students are mostly the good oral and lipreading children among the group of deaf students.

An illustrative sample of descant deaf children is given in Figure 1.

These pupils are able to recognize, without hesitation, listed words from which they have to make a choice. When one offers these students spondaic words, they are able to discriminate 90 percent of these words through hearing only (IJsseldijk, 1978). The so-called Fletcher Index is not a reliable measure in these cases.

This descant deafness is intriguing because it demonstrates the importance of the lower frequencies, 125, 250 and 500 Hz, especially for the rhythm of speech. What role do these frequencies play in the process of hearing and language? Research by one of the authors (IJsseldijk, 1976) with deaf children showed that residual hearing at 125 and 250 Hz has the same importance as residual hearing at the 1000 and 2000 Hz level. Smith (1975) came to the same conclusion.

From this discussion it may be concluded that, in deaf children, residual hearing in the lower frequencies is very important for hearing and learning to speak.

c. and d. These are the main categories of students in Dutch schools for the deaf. The differentiation between deaf students with useful residual hearing (80 to 90 percent of all deaf children according to research by van Uden, 1974 and

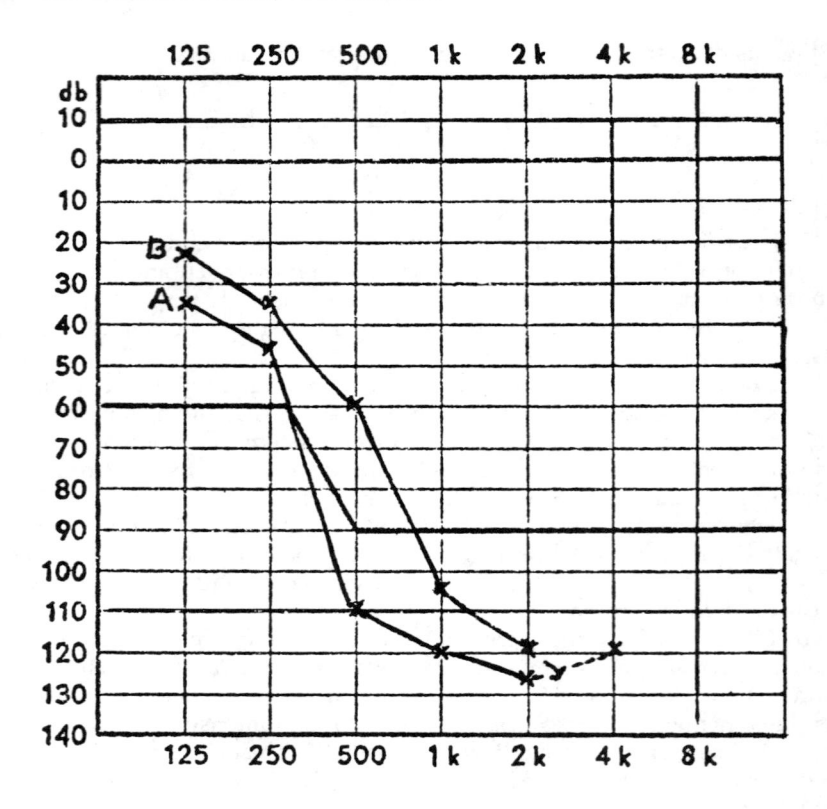

FIGURE 1. THE AUDIOGRAM OF TWO DESCANT
DEAF CHILDREN (BEST EAR).

Boothroyd, 1970) and the vibration-deaf students (according to the same research, 5 to 20 percent) is of great importance. "Vibration-deaf" refers to those pupils who respond to sound only by means of vibration.

Bayne (1970) drew *for this reason* the following curve:

125	250	500	1k	2k	4k	Hz
75	80	90	110	—	—	dB

This figure shows that reaction to vibrations can only be felt up to 1000 Hz. It is still a problem as to how we interpret the behavior of vibration-deaf children who respond to "sound" at the 2000, 4000 and 8000 Hz-levels. Research to gain insight in the diagnosis of vibration-deaf children is still necessary.

From experience it is concluded that this group of children includes many students who have severe lipreading-speech difficulties and whose language-acquisition is slow. The development of alternative aids for sound perception is desirable for this group of children.

2.2. Intelligence and memory

The intelligence test is the most used instrument in the psychological diagnosis of deaf children. Intelligence testing is done so often because it can serve different purposes:

1. The intelligence quotient of the child gives some indication of the child's learning ability and learning aptitude.
2. The intelligence test helps determine the strengths and weaknesses in the child's learning ability. The profile indicates certain psychological dysfunctions which can be used to predict or explain learning disorders.
3. The psychological test is a standardized instrument for the observation and assessment of the subject's cooperativeness.
4. In testing the child, the psychologist is able to observe the student's learning attitude, motivation, concentration, and anxiety about failing. Moreover, the way in which the subject handles the material, shows the psychologist many of his emotional and social attitudes. These impressions have only a limited value because they are not representative of the child's total behavior.

Measurement of intelligence still has many theoretical problems.

1. What is the relationship between intelligence as ability and learning as achievement?
2. How is intelligence structured in the different stages of development?
3. What is the influence of inheritance on the one hand and the influence of environment on the other?
4. To what extent is it possible to influence the level of intelligence?

It is not the purpose of this article to discuss these problems in detail. The value of measuring the intelligence of deaf people is very dependent on the experience of the psychologist. In testing deaf subjects, good instructions and motivation of the subject pose specific problems.

One should always be aware in what way "intelligence" in a certain test is operationalized, and the way in which a test is validated and standardized, e.g. is this test standardized on a hearing and/or deaf population? Another intriguing question is whether a nonverbal IQ test is really independent from cryptoverbal subtests. Examples of "crypto-verbal subtests" are the visual memory for numbers (Hiskey), and the WISC Picture Arrangement subtest. A subject's language ability might influence results of these kinds of subtests, and the IQ is therefore not an accurate assessment of non-verbal ability.

From our experience and the literature on testing deaf children, the following insights into the value of intelligence testing have been gained. First of all, consider the IQ scores:

1. A nonverbal IQ gives an indication for the prediction of success of deaf children in arithmetic, reading, speech, and lipreading. These skills are listed in order of accurate predictability of success. With regard to arithmetic, we believe that deaf children with normal intelligence and a certain verbal language and coding-level skills can reach a normal level of attain-

ment. However, this achievement only can be attained when the subject's spatial perception and memory for numbers are normally developed and good arithmetic methods are used. Bannatyne (1971) explains the relationship between the non-verbal IQ and arithmetic by pointing out that a non-verbal test and quantitative and mathematical thinking both refer to the function of the right hemisphere. The left hemisphere is largely responsible for the processes of learning a language. The relationship between arithmetic difficulties and problems in visual/spatial perception and organization has been frequently demonstrated in hearing subjects (Borghouts, 1978, Bannatyne, 1971).
2. The relationship between IQ score and learning verbal language, as opposed to esoteric sign language, is much more complicated. First, there is no direct significant relationship between these two. Other variables play a role in this matter, such as supervision of the teachers, parent guidance, and philosophy of education implemented.

Another point worth mentioning is that the outcome of a non verbal test is not directly related to functions on which language and speech of deaf children are built. All non verbal tests require the subject to have a certain skill and ability within a concrete surveyable space. Language, on the other hand, can be considered as a successive process which has a strong relationship with hearing, and is therefore more difficult to perceive visually. A performance IQ indicates to what degree a deaf student is able to absorb experiences, to see the relationships between events, and to draw conclusions. The performance IQ lends support to the assumption that deaf and hearing children have equivalent abilities in cognitive and learning skills.

These functions influence learning of language also. Experience leads to the conclusion that to learn a verbal language, deaf children should have no less than an intelligence quotient of 70. The Instituut has a department (Mariëlla-Paviljoen) for deaf students with sub-normal intelligence. These pupils cannot reach the level of verbal communication because their cognition is too low and, often, severe neuropathology is involved. These students need esoteric signs in addition to speech and lipreading in order to develop communication skills. This category of children accounts for 13 percent of all students of the Instituut. The number is so high because in Holland there are only very limited schooling possibilities for these youngsters. Therefore the Instituut has more "iconic" children than other schools and institutions. Testing these children indicates that their IQ is almost always lower than 70. Investigations (Dunn, 1978) with the Peabody Vocabulary Test (with 28 students 9 to 18 years of age) showed that 50 percent of the pupils scored the lowest test norm for hearing children: under 2.6 years.

The other 50 percent gained a score between 2.6 and 5.0 years, on norms for hearing children. In this test the child has to make a choice out of 4 pictures which are presented to him. This presentation was done both in writing and verbally. Analysis of the test results showed that the students had better results with words which referred to a concrete object. However, difficulties arose when they had to select more abstract words or generic terms such as "insect," "vegetables," "food," etc. A reading test showed that none of these subjects between 9 and 18 years of age were able to read at second grade level on norms for hearing children. This Dutch reading test presents the child with a picture and a printed sentence. He is asked to carry out a certain task. For example, one of the pictures shows several dolls; the sentence the child has to read is: "Draw a checkmark above the head of the doll which has the least hair."

The conclusion of reading tests is that these children with sub-normal intelligence stay at the level of ideo-visual reading (van Uden, 1976). This result shows sufficiently that, in order to develop communication, most of these children need additional esoteric signing. Our research on reading demonstrates this. For 4 years the development of reading of deaf children was followed at the Instituut (except the students of the Mariëlla-Paviljoen). On the basis of this longitudinal study 4 types of readers have been determined.

One group consisted of students who, despite 4 years of being taught reading, did not reach a level of comprehension reading on any test form (10 to 15 percent of our students). In contrast to this group we found a type of deaf child who, in comparison with hearing children, did not reach the 4th grade level of comprehension reading (25 to 35 percent). These two groups could be differentiated according to a number of variables.

1. The mean performance IQ of the subject of these groups was computed with the following results:
    Readers: mean performance IQ   120 (n = 26, SD = 9.8)
    Nonreaders: mean performance IQ 95 (n = 14, SD = 18.4).
   The difference in performance IQs between both groups of children is very clear, but it is not the only variable involved (IJsseldijk, 1978).
2. In these 26 prelingually deaf children who did reach the level of comprehension reading, there was one student with a performance IQ of 94 and one of 100. Among the nonreaders two students had a performance IQ higher than 120. These results show once again that a good intelligence is significant in language development. It shows at the same time that a high performance IQ is no guarantee that the student actually will reach the level of true reading. The opposite can be true as well.
3. After this discussion it might be clear that the IQ test scores have their value, but for the purpose of diagnosis the *profile* of intelligence is more important. It is proven that two types of memory subtests are useful. Here we refer to the test for simultaneous visual memory and the test for nonverbal successive memory.
4. Apart from what has been mentioned previously about the "different memories," the mean scores on memory items are important. The memory of some deaf children might be so weak that it can be considered a genuine explanation for learning difficulties.
5. In studying the test profile, we are aware that some children have problems in visual and spatial organization. This problem must be seen in relationship to a weak memory and also to dyspraxia. Its influence on arithmetic is obvious (see Borghout, 1978; Bannatyne, 1971; van Uden, 1977).
6. In diagnosis special attention is given to tests which investigate figure-ground perception, for example, ITPA, visual closure, Benton, form

ognition, and Frostig tests. Do the problems in figure-ground perception have some relationship with visual analysis and synthesis in the early stages of learning the basic skills of reading? When the examiner observes these problems, he informs the teacher that visual figure/ground difficulties in teaching the child might be encountered. The validity and prediction of this kind of test in relation to reading is still a matter of research.
7. Finally, the performance IQ sometimes is an important factor in discussions with parents. The performance IQ generally shows the positive nonverbal cognitive ability of the deaf child. This knowledge might support the acceptance process and positive attitude of the parents towards the child.

2.3. Motor development

Motoric skills play an important role in the diagnosis of oral communication and learning disorders in deaf children. The relationship between fine motor-control and learning how to speak and to lipread is very important. In this section we will not discuss general sensorimotor delay and its relationship to thinking and social maturity. Nor will we discuss the relationship between motoric ability and social-emotional development (acceptance, popularity in the group, leadership and self-image).

From the research of Myklebust (1966) and Wiegersma (1977) there are sufficient indications to assume that deaf students are more endangered than their hearing peers in their general motoric ability. Early diagnosis and observation and good training programs are obviously very important.

The importance for language of motoric training programs must be stressed. The fine motoric component is essential for the development of speech. Learning how to speak demands a complicated coordination of tongue, jaw, and lip movements. If there is little or no auditory feedback, as is often the case in deaf children, they have to base their feedback process more on the fine kinesthetic sense. Disturbance of this sense will adversely influence speech and lipreading.

A distinction must be made between motor disorders which are related directly to neurophysiological damage (e.g. spasticity and dysarthria), and motor dysfunctions, such as poor coordination of limbs, integration, and automatization of movements. Overt neurological damage has a clear relationship with the motor system. We refer to disorders such as athetosis and chorea which have a direct influence on speech production (e.g., dysarthria). These students have difficulties in articulating phonemes such as /p-m-b/, /t-d-n/ and /k-g-ng/ where fine differences are essential. It should be noted that in some deaf children these problems are difficult to observe but still affect the quality of articulation. Sometimes observation while the child is drawing, stringing beads, or building with blocks, can be helpful; sometimes the child is asked to keep his lips closed for a period of 15 seconds.

The way Touwen and Prechtl (1970) assess motor ability is also useful for this purpose. The child is asked to stand up straight, to put his arms forward, and to spread his fingers. In the case of chorea one will see many involuntary movements in the fingers. If this is the case, then one may expect dysarthric speech problems.

The coordination, integration and automatization of fine motor activities are very important factors in the process of learning to speak. The Instituut refers to these concepts as eupraxia and eurhythmia.

Eupraxia can be described as planned motoric behavior, behavior according to planned movements. It means being able to find and to coordinate one's limbs quickly and correctly, being able to steer, retain, and reproduce movements. This planned motoric behavior not only concerns gross movements but includes particularly fine motor movements (articulo-motor). A disturbance of eupraxia is called dyspraxia.

One aspect which plays a role in total eupractic behavior is eurhythmia, which can be described as imitating, remembering, and reproducing rhythmic movements. Any automatized motor planning includes a form of eurhythmia, (for example, in driving a car). Eurhythmia not only refers to the execution of movements, but includes memory of movements as well. For memory and reproduction of successive data such as speech, rhythm plays a supportive role. van Uden's research (1974) has shown very clearly a significant positive correlation between eurhythmia and eupraxia on the one hand and speech and lipreading on the other.

This research has made it possible to recognize and to categorize speech problems in deaf children. It has laid the foundation for special programs for these youngsters and the establishment of different centers at the Instituut according to the needs of different types of children. This is the reason this research has been detailed. (See Appendix A for composition of research groups, B the 15 tests and C correlation matrix, and the mean score of the test).

In his experiments with deaf children, van Uden found that, aside from residual hearing and intelligence, there were among the 15 tests some which had a high correlation with the development of speech (see Appendix C). The question was whether these 15 tests related to each other. In order to formulate the problem as clearly as possible, van Uden included in his research project only prelingually deaf children with normal intelligence and without additional handicaps. The children were 7 to 11 years of age. Eighty-three children were carefully selected. Children who were of low intelligence, whose Fletcher-index was below 90 dB., who had not had hometraining, or who were enrolled too late were excluded from the sample. The group of children was divided into 4 age-groups ranging from 7 to 10.11 years. They were assessed by one person, van Uden, on speech and lipreading ability, and with the 15 tests mentioned.

The question was, which factors were most significant in the results of these tests, and were there any differences among the 4 age-groups with regard to the importance of these factors? For these purposes the INDSCAL-analysis was used. van der Sanden (1973) showed how this method can be used for simultaneous analysis or for correlating matrices which are obtained from different groups of subjects. This INDSCAL-analysis made it possible to use a 3-factor model. For the diagnosis of eupraxia/dyspraxia and eurhythmia/dysrhythmia, the result of the first factor is the most important. This factor was composed as follows: (Figure 2)

422 oral education: today and tomorrow

Factor I Scheme of the loadings in steps of 5.

Range: +40 +35 +30 +25 +20 +15 +10 +5 0 −5 −10 −15 −20 −25 −30 −35 −40

3-Factor analysis.

(10) Putting the fingers in a certain position according to an example.	+ 0.350
(14) Lipreading with sound-perception and repeating.	+ 0.323
(15) Speaking correctly repeated words again.	+ 0.318
(12) Repeating rhythmically spoken syllables.	+ 0.304
(11) Imitating shown finger-movements from memory.	+ 0.293
(2) Imitating seen successive folding movements.	+ 0.274
(4) Remembering successively presented pictures.	− 0.028
(9) Tapping four cubes in a shown order.	− 0.033
(5) Repeating spoken series of numbers.	− 0.053
(1) Remembering simultaneously presented coloured rods.	− 0.196
(13) Speaking as many words as possible within 2 minutes.	− 0.239
(3) Remembering simultaneously presented pictures.	− 0.245
(8) Identifying simultaneously presented geometrical figures from memory.	− 0.287
(7) Copying simultaneously presented geometrical figures from memory.	− 0.287
(6) Simultaneous number/symbol association.	− 0.304

Importance of this factor, deduced from the weights to the four age-groups:

7 year olds 3.991
8 year olds 2.700
9 year olds 4.590
10 year olds 6.662

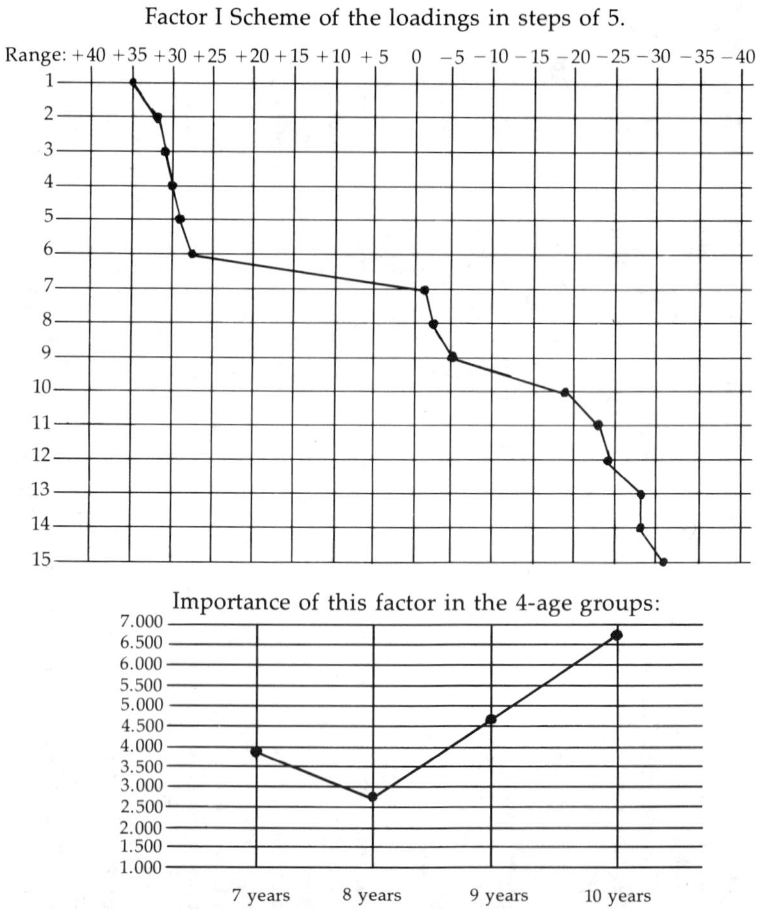

Importance of this factor in the 4-age groups:

7 years   8 years   9 years   10 years

FIGURE 2

We can see that this factor can be considered a polar factor. In the plus-loadings are those tests which are related to the fine motor movements of fingers and mouth. Therefore, eupraxia of the fingers can be considered as being related to vocal-movements. Children who could use their fingers well had well coordinated speech, whereas clumsy speakers were the children with clumsy movements of the fingers. Eupraxia also showed a relationship with rhythmic movements, this points to a common factor. In the minus loadings, all tests which play a role in memory for simultaneous visual data were computed. Examining the polarity of factor I, it becomes clear that subjects who are less fluent in motor behavior had better results in those tests which were related to data for simultaneous visual memory. Again, the opposite was also true.

The research shows too that the importance of this factor increases with age: Older children who are motorically less able seem to compensate for their motor problems by using the visual mode to its utmost. This last finding is an important indication for the education of the children. In teaching these youngsters, one should be aware that the development of speech should be based upon graphic [written] conversation.

Again, in this investigation of motor planning, it is clear that fine motor behavior—especially in the fingers—seems to be associated with the articulation processes of deaf children. van Dijk, who carried van Uden's research further with rubella children, came to the interesting conclusion that good oral behavior is related to imitations of arm and hand movements (van Dijk, in preparation).

It is an intriguing question whether motor planning behavior of daily life activities is a predictive factor in the development of speech in deaf children. A distinction between transitive and intransitive movements is therefore important. Transitive movements are those in which an object is involved, e.g., dressing oneself or building. Intransitive movements are those in which no material can support the movements. According to van Uden, observations during activities like building, dressing, and drawing give too little information about the quality of the intransitive movements and therefore have less value in diagnosis of speech problems. Only in very dyspractic children can observations such as those mentioned above be valuable.

This finding can be supported again by the information from the rubella research. Items such as paper folding did not correlate with a weak successive memory because the visual ability of the rubella children was so strong that it compensated for a poor performance of intransitive tasks.

How does dyspraxia influence speech? It is different from the case with dysarthric speech problems. In the case of dyspraxia, the child has difficulties in finding and executing the speech movements. When he is asked to produce rhythmic speech, he is unable to find quickly the appropriate mouth positions needed for articulating a certain phoneme. With these children, the automatization of speech patterns develops very slowly, and therefore their memory for spoken words can be hampered. In the speech of dyspractic children, one often finds perseverations, substitutions, abbreviations; these children easily forget the way words are articulated (poor memory for speech).

It is obvious, therefore, that these children have tremendous difficulties with lipreading and using their residual hearing. For deaf children lipreading and perception of speech are considered as a sensorimotor process. The discovery of dyspraxia and dysrhythmia as one of the most important sources of speech and lipreading difficulties has led to the following group differentiations in Sint Michielsgestel.

1. 10 percent of the children have this disturbance to a mild degree. With special help they can be placed in classes of normal deaf children.
2. Another 10 percent can only be educated by the oral method if they are placed in classes of three or four children. Their education is intense and they get extra speech lessons. Their language acquisition is mainly based upon graphic communication.
3. Another 10 percent suffer so much from the dyspractic syndrome that oral education, in its strict sense, is no longer possible. Their strong memory for simultaneous data is used for language and speech development. The basis for language acquisition is writing, and superimposed fingerspelling is used.

2.4. Sensorimotor integration

In Part 1 and in 2.3 we discussed etiological factors and their possible influence on communication in general, and oral communication in particular. In Part 2.3 we spoke about specific learning problems in deaf children. We focussed on one of the main underlying factors of communication problems in deaf children, dyspraxia. In this section we would like to call attention to perhaps one of the most overlooked problems in learning: the integration of sensory modalities.

There is a category of deaf students whose progress in language development and reading is slow. The research and experience of van Uden suggest that, apart from eupraxia, there is another factor contributing to language development: the level of integration of sensory modalities.

What does "integration of sensory modalities" mean? Sensory experiences are not fragmented; they form a sensory motor gestalt. Knowledge of an object includes touching, smelling, manipulating, seeing, and hearing it. The whole spectrum of sensory modalities plays its part in this experience. The word refers to this gestalt and its symbolization. In hearing persons, the word penetrates the experience, and helps to integrate the whole experience in one gestalt. In the deaf child, this process is more difficult. The symbol does not directly integrate with the experience. Therefore the development of symbolization and symbol consciousness in deaf children does not develop as easily as in hearing children. The deaf child's attention is distracted from the direct experience because he has to watch the face of the person who wishes to give him the word for that experience.

Studies of linguistic abilities of adults with acquired aphasia suggest that sensory information plays a role in matters such as word retrieval, word recognition and word retention: the scope and the nature of sensory information determine the strength of the connection between the symbol and the experience.

Marshall & Newcomb (1973) and Shallice & Warrington (1975) report that patients with acquired aphasia and with dyslexic problems caused by a disturbance in the use of phonemic-graphic analysis were only able to read very picturable words. These are words which refer to a specific image (chair, table, etc.). In contrast with these are the abstract in nonpicturable words which are learned through the context of the sentences in which they are heard, rather than by learning associations between words and visual referents (Goodglass, Hyde & Bloomstein, 1969). This type of word was the hardest for the patients. Halpern (1965) noticed that when an aphasic person has to read words aloud, he has a tendency to make more mistakes in those words which are of high and medium abstraction, e.g., "friendship."

Gardner (1973) assumes that the kinesthetic sense, more than the picture quality of the words, plays a role in word finding. He developed several series of 4 pictures with so-called operational objects. These are objects which can be manipulated and have a rather free access to the different sensory modalities, e.g.: "screwdriver," "book," "finger," etc. Apart from this group of pictures he designed pictures which referred to more figurative objects like "cloud" and "wall." In his test on word finding, he found that both frequency and "possibility of handling the object" had a significant effect on the ability to find the right word for the picture. "Operative elements" seem to be more resistant to aphasia than elements such as colors, letters of the alphabet, and the printed word, which do not directly refer to sensory associations. Gardner (1974) did the same kind of research with normal children (aged 3 and 4 years old). He found that they also responded better to words which were more operative in their quality and more frequently used in their experience. In their discussions on word frequencies, Riegel & Riegel (1961) put forward the notion that the frequency of words, as such, does not influence the naming process, but the degree to which the subject has experience with the object *does* have such an influence. They suggest that the ability to retrieve words in aphasic patients is connected with sensory impressions which are aroused when one tries to recall a word.

A study quoted by Lesser (1978) suggests that aphasics were helped in word finding by permitting them to smell an object, rather than only see it. The role of the factors mentioned, such as operational ability, picturability, and the capacity of arousing multisensory associations in the naming process is, according to Geschwind (1965), connected with the function of the parieto-temporo-occipital area of the dominant hemisphere, the so-called association areas, in which the integration of the sensory modalities takes place.

Is it correct to assume that a great variety of sensory information facilitates the association of the symbol to the referent? Gardiner & Brookshire (1972) questioned this. In their research they found, however, that the variety of sensory information did not support the naming process in all persons. It is not only the quantity of sensory information, but the simultaneous synthesis, which is crucial in the naming process (Luria, 1973). So one may conclude that it is not only the amount of sensory information that facilitates the formation of a link between the symbol and its referent, but also the ability of the person to integrate the several sensory modalities into one experience.

Another aspect of language research which is relevant with regard to this subject is the discussion on asymbolia (Plank, 1978). In this discussion the problem is: Does a relationship exist between aphasia and asymbolia? The latter refers to the inability to understand verbal and nonverbal symbols. In this kind of research one is interested if a special element of speech and/or language is more easily disturbed than another. This question should be solved by studying the level of abstraction of the code and iconicity. The "level of abstraction" refers to the arbitrary relationship between code and referent, while in iconic codes there is a clear analogy between code and referent, for example, in the sign for "house" and the referent: the mental image of house. Plank refers to a number of research findings on asymbolia. All show that aphasic patients have more difficulty than non-aphasics in handling non-iconic symbols. Plank refers also to studies in the U.S.A. which show that sign language is more aphasia resistant than fingerspelling, although, according to Plank, "It should not be overlooked that in some of the American sign language systems one has to do with a rather abstract non-iconic system."

From the research on aphasic subjects one may draw the following conclusions:

- In children who suffer from learning difficulties, one often finds a retardation in the development of intersensory learning.
- In the case of semantic learning difficulties such as word finding, attaching meaning to words, one often finds difficulties in the simultaneous synthesis of sensory stimuli.
- In the case of deterioration of language one finds, according to Plank, a de-symbolization and re-iconization of words because the iconic aspects of language are most resistant. Plank considers the development of language, therefore, as symbolization on the one hand, and de-iconization on the other—an approach which has proved its value in the development of language in deaf/blind children.
- Operative and picturable elements, and elements which are capable of arousing multi-sensory associations, are the most resistant to aphasia.

Difficulties with the simultaneous integration of sensory experiences in deaf children may cause difficulties in the development of symbolization. What are the consequences of these difficulties?

1. At first a noticeable number of behavior characteristics can be observed:

    - The experiential situation for such a child is fragmented. The child is less embodied in the situation in which he lives. He will be easily distracted by environmental stimuli. His behavior will be more or less chaotic and incoherent.
    - Abilities which require integration of kinesthetic experience, like grasping small objects or modeling with clay, do not develop easily in these children. There is a kind of sensory dyspraxia which should be distinguished from motor dyspraxia.
    - Since the child does not understand the situation immediately, he may imitate in a meaningless way. He may behave in a way not appropriate to the situation in which he lives.

2. It is not only in a child's behavior that one may observe the symptoms of disturbance of intersensory integration; one also finds them at the level of symbolic behavior:

- There is difficulty with the association between experience and symbol in its different forms (written, spoken, etc.). This may lead to a variety of difficulties:

    (a) The symbol remains without any meaning: the child repeats a word, a question, without grasping its meaning (echolalia). (b) Words acquire a general meaning only with difficulty. Meaning is too much attached to one concrete situation. (c) Learned words are easily forgotten. (d) Word retrieval difficulties occur.

    In a naming task the child may prefer making a sign or gesture (e.g., a shooting movement) rather than saying the *word* "ball". If one still asks him to name the picture, he often says other words, like "tree" instead of "flower," though he understands the word passively.
- There is difficulty in the association of the various modalities of one word. Graphemes do not integrate with phonemes; the written word does not integrate with the spoken word. These are not caused by problems in the basic reading skills or in visual perception. It may also happen that the child, having mastered the basic skills, reads correctly "tree" and then spontaneously says "flower" and points to a flower. Other typical behavior is the inclination to look to the teacher's face even when the child is reading. Such children do not seek information in the written word. They seldom ask the teacher to write something down. When they are not understood, they will not spontaneously use writing as a means to express themselves. When writing the child may not produce the written word correctly; he makes orthographical errors because he relies too much on his articulation.

At the base of his hypothesis van Uden has developed an inventory for clinical use consisting of three parts:

List A: meant for all children. It is a list in which 27 questions are asked relating to the child's behavior. Questions are asked about matters such as the ability to see coherence in situations; echolalic and imitating behavior, sensory eupraxia, and grasping the clues of situations without using words.

List B: for children older than 5.6. A list with 31 questions about symbolic behavior.

List C: a complementary list for children older than 8.0. Lists B and C contain questions about symbolic behavior, interpretation of words and signals (lipreading, hearing, sound-signals, reading), the integration of the written word and the spoken word, word retrieval difficulties, the understanding of the meaning of words, and the understanding of music-symbols. Finally, a number of questions concern arithmetical abilities.

In order to get an impression of its value, this inventory has been completed for 70 pupils of the "Eikenheuvel," a department for dyspraxic deaf children, and on 19 children in the preschool, aged 4 to 6. First of all, it has been checked whether there was a relation between sensorimotor integrative behavior (list

TABLE 1. LEVEL OF ARTICULATION OF THE CHILDREN FROM EIKENHEUVEL
N = 70

Age	Number of children	Undifferentiated articulated sounds	A few single phonemes	All Dutch single phonemes	Connections of C-V or V-C	Connections of C-C-V	Phrases	Sentences
4–4;11	1	1	1	a few	a few			
5–5;11	0							
6–6;11	4	3	3	2 × a few	3 × C-V only			
7–7;11	3	3	3	1 1 × a few 1 × -r/-ee	2 1 × C-V only	1	1	1
8–8;11	7	7	7	2 1 × -r 1 × -r/-h/-ie -uu 1 × -r/-ng -ie/-uu -ee	5 2 × C-V only a few	4 1 × a few	4 1 × a few	4
9–9;11	4	4	4	3	3	3	3	2
10–10;11	4	4	4	2	2	1	1	1
11–11;11	2	2	2	2	2	1	1	1
12–12;11	1	1	1	1	1	1	1	1
13–13;11	4	4	4	3 1 × -r/-ee	4	4	4	4
14–14;11	8	8	8	8	8	8	8	8
15–15;11	6	5	6	5	5	5	5	5
16–16;11	7	7	7	5	5 1 × a few	5	5	5
17–17;11	9	9	9	6 1 × -ng 1 × -g 1 × -h/-ng	9	9	9	9
18–18;11	5	5	5	5	5	5	5	5
19–19;11	4	4	4	4	4	4	4	4
20–20;11	1	1	1	1	1	1	1	1
4–20;11	70	68	69	48 4 × a few 5 × -r 3 × -ee 3 × -ng 2 × -h 2 × -ie 2 × -uu 1 × -g	56 4 × C-V only 2 × a few 2 × C-V only a few	52 1 × a few	52 1 × a few	51

A) and symbolic behavior (list B). These lists have been filled out twice for each pupil; once by the teacher and once by the house-parents.

The following are the product moment correlation coefficients:

Preschool (n = 19)
List A (class) × list B (class): r = .70
List A (group) × list B (group): r = .55
List A (group) × list B (class): r = .23

Eikenheuvel (n = 70)
List A (class) × list B (class): r = .69
List A (group) × list B (group): r = .74
List A (group) × list B (class): r = .35

Only the correlations between list A, filled out by the houseparents, and list B filled out by the teacher, were not significant in the preschool group. This is understandable because list A contains many behavioral items, which are also determined by the different context in which the observers are familiar with the child. Dyssymbolic behavior in the group shows itself somewhat different from dyssymbolic behavior in the classroom.

In order to test the hypothesis that eusymbolia and sensorimotor integration influence the development of vocabulary and language, we compared the judgments of the pupils on the lists A, B, C and their scores on the Peabody Picture Vocabulary Test and the Metropolitan Reading Test. For the list A we took the judgment of the pupil by the houseparents, and for the lists B and C we took the judgment by the teacher.

We found the following results:

	Peabody (N = 70)	Metropolitan (N = 15)
List A	.83	.68
List B	.49	.72
List C	.80	.82

This correlation matrix, in which all correlations are very significant, indicates the validity and usability of these lists. Factor analysis was computed between the following variables: age, time of enrollment, scores on list A, B, C, vocabulary. Five factors explain 69 percent of the variance, or 84 percent of the total variance. On the basis of loading, the most important factor is eusymbolia in relation to vocabulary. The high loading of the behavior list A was unexpected, and shows the relationship between age and eusymbolia. This shows the usefulness of the lists for predicting the language development of the deaf child.

2.5. Emotional and personality factors in language development

Every clinician knows that emotions have an enormous influence on language development. A child who has an aversion to his teacher will accomplish very little in the classroom. An adolescent boy with sexual problems might suddenly show reading problems by suppressing his feelings which are associated with words or letters with a sexual character (Prick & Calon, 1967). In this chapter the role of emotions in learning will be approached by using the psychoanalytic model which is one of the possible ways to gain insight into the relationship between the emotional status of the child and his communicative competence.

The development of language in children, according to psychoanalytic authors (Anna Freud, 1973; Brenner, 1972) is not a phenomenon in itself, but it is, as it were, embedded in the total psychosexual development. Language and speech are ego functions the development of which, like other ego functions, must be seen in the relationship between the child and his most important caretakers. More than in any other function this is true for language imitation: the child likes to identify himself with his most important "love objects." The child learns language as the language from his parents, by means of imitation and identification.

In the psychoanalytic approach, psychopathology of language and speech is at the same time psychopathology of the relationship of the child with his most important love objects. In the early development of the child the following critical moments should be mentioned:

1. In some children no object relationship is developed at all. Here libido can be considered as narcissistic libido. The relationship between the child and his environment is broken. There is no imitation and communication, even "gaze aversion" can often be observed. The child's own ego functions are very strongly cathexed upon with libido. In the case of hearing children, no language development will occur.
2. It is possible that the child develops a relationship with an object, but this relationship is defective. If the contact with the mother or a mother's substitute is endangered, a very fundamental lack of trust can be the result. Moreover, the child stays at the level of a rather strong narcissism. In cases where the intense biological interrelationship between mother and child (Bowlby, 1974) is disturbed, one may often observe the so-called desolation syndrome: the child lacks the fundamental trust, he is seeking for security, and he overemphasizes his tactual sense. Sometimes he may show moments of aggression and pseudo delinquency. On the whole, the child has a rather strong autoerotic attitude (Bowlby, 1974; Rutter, M., 1978). According to observation of psychoanalytic authors, this might lead to a delay in the development of the ego functions which play a role in the developmental stages to come (Erikson, 1963).

   Titchener (1967) points out that if the preverbal communication between parents and child is disturbed, the child does not develop trust in verbal communication. It is Vygotsky's opinion (1956, 1960) that a disturbed mother-child relationship has its influence on language development until adolescence. Research relating to the early mother-child interaction shows that the development of vocalizations, speech, and language, is influenced by the way in which a child and mother communicate at an early age (Dunn, 1978; Ciba Symposium, 1975).

   Riksen-Walraven (1976) wonders if, in the case of a disturbance in early interaction of the child with the environment, the cause might be that the child has received too little stimulation, especially if the environment has not been responsive enough to the child's initiative. For the purpose here the research findings of Greenstein, McConville & Stellini (1975) are interesting. They investigated factors upon which the receptive and expressive oral language of deaf children aged 20 to 40 months are built. The researchers found a significant correlation between receptive/expressive language and the way in which the mother had accepted the child and was sensitive to his needs. Flexibility in her relationship with the child, the way she enjoyed the child, and her expression of warmth and affect were significant factors as well. These are all factors which stimulated the child in his language development. Mothers who show all these traits had, at the same time, more significant visual interactions with the children. It is obvious how important visual interaction is in deaf children for the development of lipreading.

3. In the second year of life the child discovers, according to the psychoanalytical scientists, his ego functions, such as motor abilities. Depending upon the reaction of the parents, the child develops an autonomy or shame about his own behavior (Erikson, 1963). It is interesting to see that the psychoanalytical theory can be compared with research data acquired in the assessment of hearing and deaf children.

Clarke-Stewart (1973) found that the amount of maternal attention and looking influenced the child's later performance on intelligence tests, and that the child's activity and exploration were also negatively affected by maternal restrictiveness. Nelson (1973) found that a non-directive parental attitude facilitated the child's language acquisition. This was the case in verbal and nonverbal language development. A less restrictive attitude was also found in deaf parents towards their deaf children (Schlesinger & Meadow, 1972).

Greenstein (1975) found a negative correlation between proximal behavior of the mother (physical coercion and touching) and receptive and expressive oral language in deaf children aged 20 to 40 months. A mother who showed more proximal behavior was less able to communicate with the child, and had not as much understanding of his needs. These children received a low judgment on the quality of their receptive and expressive oral language. By the same token, Greenstein found a high negative correlation between negative and criticizing remarks of the mother and the language competence of deaf children.

Characteristics of early interaction between mother and child influence the language development of the deaf child. In his study on deaf children, Greenstein found that deaf mothers (in his observation scale) were rated as warmer, and the flow of communication between mother and child as easier. The children from deaf families did better in ratings and tests of language competence, but the children of hearing parents who were rated as warmer and more sensitive to their child tended to do as well. Deaf children of deaf parents were significantly better directed towards the face, and children of hearing parents rated as interactionally closer and warmer. They also maintained more eye contact.

Greenstein also found an oral linguistic superiority in deaf children of deaf parents, and assumes that the linguistic superiority deaf children of deaf parents displayed to Vernon and Kok (1970, 1971) was largely due to the greater acceptance of the deaf mother at the discovery of the child's handicap. It seems, therefore, that the quality of the early interaction between mother and child is more crucial than the mother's hearing status.

The relationship between mother and child does not start with the birth of the child. Speaking about premature birth Caplan (1964) points out that in the case where there is no "psychological pregnancy" (i.e., the mother has fantasies about the birth of the child, imaginary talks to the child, touches the moving child in her body, etc.) an emotional crisis and a disturbance in the mother-child relationship after delivery may result.

Moss and Robson (1968) found that the extent to which the pregnant mother experienced her future baby as gratifying, pleasant and nonburdensome served as predictors of mutual visual regard and eye contact when the baby was one month of age.

Vernon (1978) warns us that one should not confuse in research the mother-child interaction and responsiveness of the mother since many individual differences can be observed. Some children evoke more response than others.

A disturbance in the parent-child relationship is not always because of some typical characteristics of the mother. Traits in the child himself, life-events, characteristics of the family and family relation, as well as socio-economic factors, may play a role too. Factors which are dependent on the child himself are:

- A severe form of contact disorder originating from an organic damage. If this is the case, many learning problems are often accompanied by emotional problems.
- Neurological disorders of the child may lead to behavior problems such as in hyperactivity.
- Deafness, as such, can also be a factor which influences parent-child interaction.
- The responsive deaf child seems to get more easily involved in conversation. In testing the vocabulary of preschool children, there was a positive significant correlation between the score on vocabulary and the "level of extraversion" measured with an observation list.

Life events which are of influence on the parent-child interaction are:

- Prematurity followed by a long period in the *humidity crib,* incubator. This makes a good relation between the mother and the child impossible (Kaplan & Mason, 1965).
- Hospitalization during the first years of life (Ciba Symposium, 1975).
- "Medical shopping," so often seen in the history of a deaf child.
- The way in which the cause of deafness is discussed between the parents and how it influences their relationship, for example, in blaming each other.
- Temporal or definite separation of the parents.
- Death of one or both of the parents.

In diagnosing a child's oral ability one has to include the socio-emotional development of the child, as described above. As a special aid to this purpose Sint Michielsgestel uses the observation lists, which are, however, still in an experimental stage.

Part 3. School Philosophy and School Organization

In the previous parts many variables have been discussed which may have a relationship with learning in general and development of an oral mother tongue in the child in particular. In some instances, correlation quotients and factor analyses were put forward to support our arguments. It is a fact that all variables involved have their influence on the final results: the child's cognitive and emotional level of functioning. Perhaps more important than all the data put forward is the school itself; its organization, its teachers, and the parents' involvement. It is difficult, and perhaps impossible, to assess the weighting of these factors in statistical terms. However, the way in which the school approaches a deaf child might be crucial for his future. Perhaps one of the most important factors in a school philosophy is the influence of the following:

3.1. Educational pessimism versus educational optimism

Does a teacher of deaf children who is struggling day after day to get something across really believe in a deaf child's ability? So often it is heard—even in the so-called sophisticated research—"The deaf cannot do this, they cannot do that. . . ." If this belief pervades a school one is fighting a losing battle. Gradually, the teacher will lower his educational goals and not try to make the impossible come true.

In order to prevent this fallacy, it is important that the school has a solid philosophy of education. The essence of such a philosophy is the strong belief that a deaf person can be made free from the imprisonment of his handicap: lack of language and be able to make fundamental decisions in his life. To convince teachers that this is a realistic goal, they should have intensive contact with the alumni of the school. Then they can see the results of the school's philosophy and educational strategies. It must be said that the educational results of a school are sometimes rather poor. If the number of alumni who are actually able to participate fully in the culture of their country is only a minority of the school's former pupils, it is almost impossible for young teachers to have faith in the school's educational objectives. The reasons why the educational outcome is so poor in some places are manifold. This paper stresses again the importance of another factor.

3.2. Differential diagnosis

In previous parts this theme was discussed in depth. If children with severe learning and behavior problems are taught together, one can be sure that the level of teaching will be directed towards the lowest functioning child. We have clear indications of the "leveling down" phenomenon. That is, when a class of 5 or 6 children is formed at the beginning of a year, there is always a difference in language competence between the best child and the poorest one. It can be predicted that, by the end of the year, the gap between the two has narrowed. The lowest child has made progress at the expense of the better child. The best one is slowed down in the process.

In cases where there are two children in the classroom with undiscovered learning problems, one can almost predict that none of their classmates will make the maximum progress. More clearly than anywhere else in education it can be demonstrated that homogeneous grouping is crucial in the organization of a school for deaf children. It is the task of the school psychologist to bring to the attention of the school cases where a specific class is slowing down because of incorrect grouping of children. The child with learning and/or emotional problems should be given a fair chance in another setting.

In some instances alternative communicative methods have to be used, but not necessarily signing, as suggested by Ling. During the last ten years Sint Michielsgestel has tried to establish separate schools to allow every deaf child an equal chance for optimal development.

FIGURE 3. SCHOOL ORGANIZATION OF THE
PRESCHOOL AND THE ELEMENTARY SCHOOL
Sint Michielsgestel

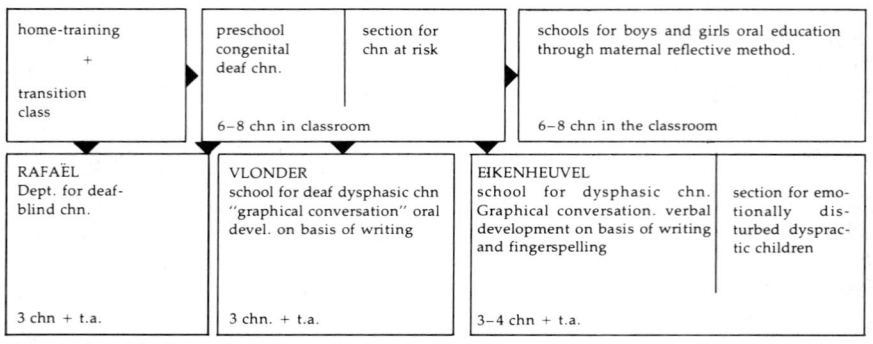

home-training + transition class	preschool congenital deaf chn.	section for chn at risk	schools for boys and girls oral education through maternal reflective method.	
	6–8 chn in classroom		6–8 chn in the classroom	
RAFAËL Dept. for deaf-blind chn.	VLONDER school for deaf dysphasic chn "graphical conversation" oral devel. on basis of writing		EIKENHEUVEL school for dysphasic chn. Graphical conversation. verbal development on basis of writing and fingerspelling	section for emotionally disturbed dyspractic children
3 chn + t.a.	3 chn. + t.a.		3–4 chn + t.a.	

*t.a. = teachers aid

We have shown in Part 2 that many children who are (initially) oral failures still can be educated in Dutch through writing and fingerspelling and that many of them are able, despite severe learning problems, to acquire basic skills in speech and lipreading. Compare results of the dyspractic children of Eikenheuvel in Figures 4 and 5.

3.3. Method of education and teachers' ability

In assessing why children fail in school, poor teaching is often overlooked. This is called *dyspaedagogia* (Coles, 1978). Because of the teacher's lack of knowledge of linguistics a number of children do not learn to read. By the same token, some children do not learn to speak because the teacher lacks the quality to carry out the *art*. Sometimes teacher training programs can be blamed, sometimes the blame can be put on the school's supervisors who are unable to support their poorly trained staff.

psychological and educational diagnosis and assessment **435**

FIGURE 4. RESULTS: TEST FOR LIPREADING-SPEECH- AND HEARING PERFORMANCE.

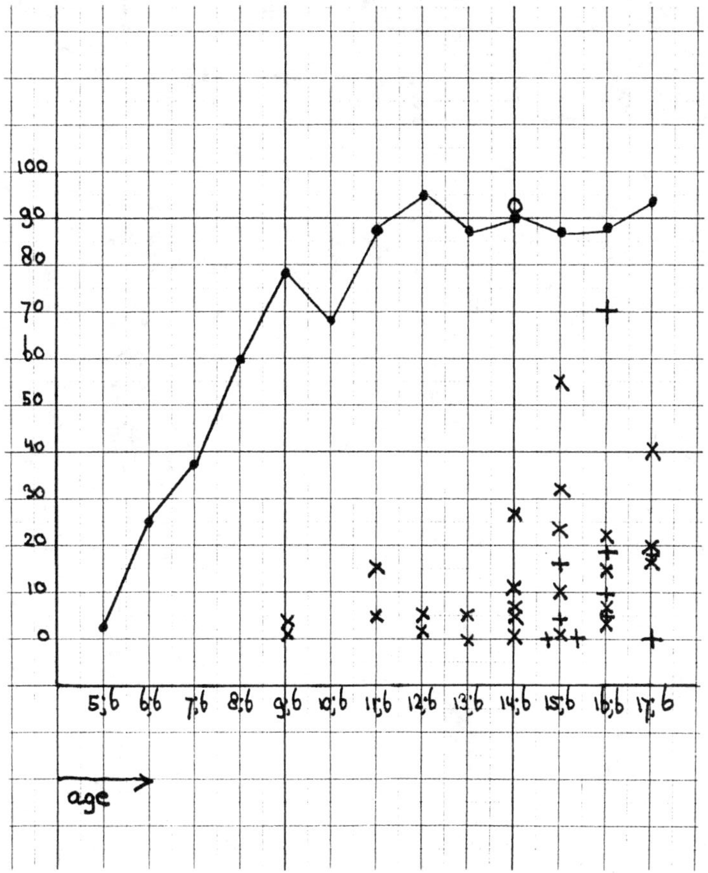

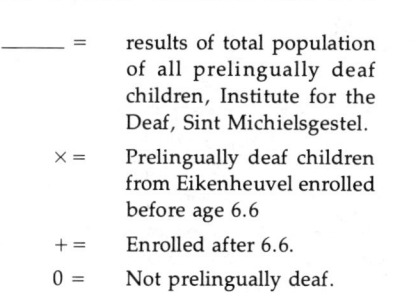

436 oral education: today and tomorrow

FIGURE 5. PEABODY VOCABULARY TEST

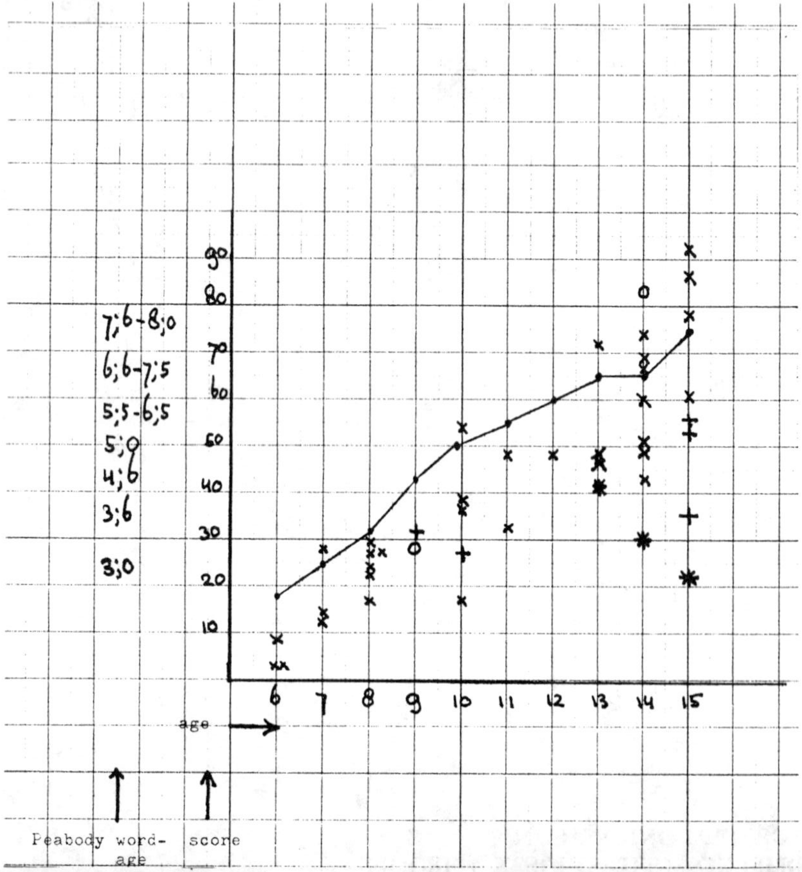

x = Score of the total population prelingually deaf children, Institute for the Deaf, Sint Michielsgestel

+ = Individual score of Eikenheuvel students enrolled before the age of 6.6

0 = Enrolled after the age of 6.6

* = Not prelingually deaf children

If a teacher feels incompetent he will look for help. Often he thinks that he can find this in the so-called language programs, full of pictures and "baked" sentences (van Uden, 1977). Simple stilted language will be taught: that is to say the teacher talks and the child repeats (the imitative method). These types of methods are more teacher centered than child centered. Ample research has shown that teaching methods in which the child gets the opportunity to express himself, and is not interrupted again and again by the teacher, are the most effective methods. The child's sentences will be longer and more complex, and his drive to communicate stronger. In child-centered methods the students get the opportunity to discover the structure of the subject themselves, e.g. the structure of language. This is an active way of learning and therefore more effective.

In many schools for the deaf, especially the schools with the "pre-fab" language method, the child is talked to all day long, the teacher doing the talking. Where this is the case, the child will not get the opportunity to train functions such as memory, upon which subsequent language is based. The child will get little opportunity to practice his oral skills and because of this, his speech will not become fluent and automatized.

This can be prevented by using the maternal reflective method (van Uden, 1977), which is more than merely *a method*. It is a way of approaching the human being. It is a method of hope because it believes that the nature of a deaf child is strong enough to build up, through proper teaching, his *own* language. A deaf child may suffer from learning problems; nobody can be blamed for this. A deaf child may be the victim of the educator's ignorance; this is intolerable.

Judging from the *results* of deaf education, one might conclude that quite a number of deaf children are really failures because the teacher did a poor job, the school was not well organized and, last but not least, learning problems were undiagnosed.

References

Ahlstrom, K. On evaluating the effects of schoolings, in *Proceedings of the International Congress on Education of the Deaf*, Washington, D.C.: A.G. Bell Association, 1970.

Bannatyne, A. *Language, reading and learning disabilities*. Springfield, IL: Charles C Thomas, 1971.

Boothroyd, A. Vibrotactile thresholds in pure tone audiometry. *Acta Otolaryngologica*, 1970, 381–387.

Borghouts-van Erp, J. W. *Rekenproblemen: Opsporen en oplossen*. Groningen, the Netherlands: Wolters-Noordhoff, 1978.

Bowlby, J. *Attachment and loss*. London: Hogarth Press & the Institute for Psychoanalysis, 1974.

Brenner, O. *Grundzüge der psychoanalysis: Erweiterte neuausgabe*. Frankfurt am Main, West Germany: S. Fischer Verlag, 1972.

Caplan, G. *Principles of preventive psychiatry*. New York: Basic Books, 1964.

Chess, S., Korn, S. J., & Fernandez, P. B. *Psychiatric disorders of children with congenital rubella*. New York: Brunner/Mazel, 1971.

Ciba Symposium. *Parent-infant interaction*. Amsterdam: Elsevier-Excerpta Medica, 1975.

Clarke-Stewart, K. A. Interactions between mothers and their young children: Characteristics and consequences. *Monographs of the Society for Research in Child Development,* 1973, *38* (Serial no. 153), 6–7.
Coles, G. S. The learning-disabilities test battery: Empirical and social issues. *Harvard Educational Review,* 1978, *48* (3), 313–340.
van Dijk, J. *Hearing impaired rubella children* (in preparation).
Donolly, K. An investigation into the determinants of lipreading of deaf adults. *International Audiology,* 1969, 501–508.
Dunn, J. De vroege relatie tussen moeder en kind: Individuele verschillen en hun gevolgen, *In:* F. J. Mönks & P. G. Heymans (Eds.), *Communicatie en integratie bij het jonge kind.* Nijmegen, the Netherlands: Dekker en Van de Vegt, 1978.
Eggermont, J. *Taalverwerving bij een groep dove kinderen,* Groningen, the Netherlands: J. B. Wolters, 1964.
Erber, N. P. Auditory, visual and auditory visual recognition of consonants with normal and impaired hearing. *Journal of Speech and Hearing Research,* 1972, 413–422.
Erikson, E. *Childhood and society.* New York: W. W. Norton, 1963.
Frazer, G. *The causes of profound deafness in childhood.* Baltimore, MD: Johns Hopkins University Press, 1976.
Freud, A. *Normality and pathology in childhood.* London: Hogarth Press & the Institute of Psychoanalysis, 1973.
Gardner, H. The contribution of operativity to naming capacity in aphasic patients. *Neuropsychologia,* 1973, *11,* 213–220.
Gardner, H. The naming of objects and symbols by children and aphasic patients. *Journal of Psycholinguistic Research,* 1974, *3,* 133–149.
Gardiner, B. J., & Brookshire, R. H. Effects of unisensory and multisensory presentation of stimuli upon naming by aphasic subjects. *Language and Speech,* 1972, *15,* 342–357.
Geschwind, N. Disconnexion syndromes in animals and man. *Brain,* 1965, *80,* 237–294; 585–644.
Goodglass, H., Hyde, M. R., & Blumstein. Frequency, picturability and availability of nouns in aphasia. *Lentex,* 1969, *5,* 104–119.
Greenstein, J. M., McConville, K., & Stellini, L. *Mother infant communication and language acquisition in deaf parents.* Northampton, MA: Lexington School for the Deaf, 1975.
Halpern. Effect of stimulus variables on dysphasic verbal errors, *Perceptual and Motor Skills,* 1965, *21,* 291–298.
Harcourt, B., & Wybar, K. Congenital cataracts. *Proceedings of the Royal Society of Medicine,* 1969, *62,* 689–693.
Hardy, B. Clinical and developmental aspects of congenital rubella. *Archives of Otolaryngology,* 1973, *98,* 230–236.
Hudgins, C. Speech perception in present-day education for deaf children. *The Volta Review,* 1948, *50,* 449–456.
IJsseldijk, F. *The capability of strictly orally educated deaf pupils to understand speech by hearing.* Sint Michielsgestel, The Netherlands: Instituut voor Doven, 1978.
IJsseldijk, F. *A longitudinal research into the reading results of deaf pupils at the Institute for the Deaf at Sint Michielsgestel.* Sint Michielsgestel, the Netherlands: Instituut voor Doven, 1979.
Kaplan, D. M., & Mason, E. A. Maternal reactions to premature birth viewed as an acute emotional disorder, In H. J. Pard (ed.), *Crisis intervention.* New York: Family Service Association of America, 1965.
Kloepfer, W., Laguarte, J. K., & McLaurin, J. W. The hereditary syndrome of congenital deafness and retinitis pigmentosa. *Laryngoscope,* 1966, *86,* 850–862.
Lesser, R. *Linguistic investigations of aphasia.* London: Edward Arnold, 1978.
Lovaas, O., Scheibman, L., Koeger, R., & Rehm, R. Selective responding by autistic children to multiple sensory input. *Journal of Abnormal Psychology,* 1977, 211–222.

Luria, A. R. *The working brain: An introduction to neuropsychology.* London: Allan Lane, the Penguin Press, 1973.

Marshall, J. C., & Newcombe, F. Patterns of paralexia: A psycholinguistic approach. *Journal of Psycholinguistic Research,* 1973, *2,* 175–199.

Moss, H. A., & Robson, K. S. Maternal influences in early social visual behavior. *Child Development,* 1968, *39,* 401–408.

Myklebust, K. P. *The psychology of deafness.* New York: Grune & Stratton, 1966.

Nelson, K. Structure and strategy in learning to talk. *Monographs Bulletin of the British Psychological Society,* 1973, *27,* 251–257.

Plank, F. Ueber asymbolie und ikonizität. In G. Peuser (Ed.), *Brennpunkte der patholinguistik.* München: Wilhelm Fink Verlag, 1978.

Prick, J. J. G., & Calon, P. J. A. *Een schets van intelligentie en Dementie.* Amsterdam, The Netherlands: 1967.

Riegel, K. F., & Riegel, R. M. Prediction of word recognition thresholds on the basis of stimulus parameters. *Language and Speech,* 1972, *15,* 342–357.

Riksen-Walraven, J. *Stimulering van de vroegkinderlijke ontwikkeling: een interventieexperiment.* Amsterdam, The Netherlands: Swets & Zeitlinger, 1976.

Rutter, M. *Maternal deprivation reassessed.* London: Penguin Modern Psychology, 1971.

Rutter, M., & Hersov, L. (Eds.), *Child psychiatry.* Oxford: Blackwell Scientific Publication, 1977.

Rutter, M. Diagnosis and definition. In M. Rutter & E. Schopler, (Eds.), *Autism: A reappraisal of concepts and treatment.* New York: 1978.

Sanders, D. Auditory training within a communication framework. *Proceedings of the 43rd Meeting of the Convention of American Instructors of the Deaf.* 1968, 251–258.

Schlesinger, H. S., & Meadow, K. P. *Sound and sign: Childhood deafness and mental health.* Berkeley: University of California Press, 1972.

Shallice, T., & Warrington, E. K. Word recognition in a phonemic dyslexic patient. *Quarterly Journal of Experimental Psychology,* 1975, *27,* 187–199.

Smith, C. Residual hearing and speech production in deaf children. *Journal of Speech and Hearing Research,* 1975, *18,* 795–811.

Stuckless, E. R., & Birch, J. W. The influence of early manual communication on the linguistic development of deaf children. *American Annals of the Deaf,* 1966, 452–460; 499–504.

Theissing, G., & Kittel, G. Die bedeutung der toxoplasmose in der aetiologie der connatalen und früh erworbenen hörstörungen. *Arch. Ohr-, Nas-, und Kehl-Heilk.,* 1962, 180–219.

Titchener. The epigenesis of the ego in the family system, In G. H. Zuk & I. Boszormenyi-Nagy, *Family therapy and disturbed families.* Palo Alto, CA: Science and Behavior Books, 1967.

Touwen, B., & Prechtl, H. *The neurological examination of the child with nervous dysfunctions.* London: Clinics in Developmental Medicine, 1970.

van Uden, A. *Dove kinderen leren spreken.* Rotterdam: Universitaire Pers, 1974.

van Uden, A. Methodische overwegingen over het leren lezen door prelinguaal doven. *Het Gehoorgestoorde Kind,* 1976, *4.*

van Uden, A. *A world of language for deaf children.* Amsterdam: Swets & Zeitlinger, 1977.

Vernon, McCay. *Multiply handicapped deaf children.* Washington, DC: Council for Exceptional Children, 1969.

Vernon, M., & Kok, S. D. Early manual communication and deaf children's achievement. *American Annals of the Deaf,* 1970, *115,* 527–536.

Vernon, M., & Kok, S. D. Effects of oral preschool compared to early manual communication and education and communication in deaf children. *American Annals of the Deaf,* 1971, *116,* 564–574.

Vygotsky, L. S. *Selected psychological investigations*. Moscow: Publication of the Academy of Pedagogical Sciences of the R.S.F.S.R.
Vygotsky, L. S. *Development of the higher mental functions*. Moscow: Publication of the Academy of Pedagogical Sciences of the R.S.F.S.R.
Wiegersma, P. H. De ontwikkeling van lichamelijke vaardigheden bij ernstig gehoorgestoorde kinderen. *Van Horen Zeggen*, 1979, 20 (1), 3–6.

APPENDIX A

The Composition of the Research group.

Group	Age	Total	Boys	Girls	Hearing loss in dB.	WISC HAWIK Performance IQ	Hiskey derived IQ
I	7.0– 7.11	20	12	8	100.1 ± 11.3	106.4 ± 9.4	108.5 ± 14.9
II	8.0– 8.11	18	8	10	108.8 ± 10.5	106.3 ± 12.5	108.4 ± 10.7
III	9.0– 9.11	23	14	9	108.9 ± 10.5	107.0 ± 10.6	104.0 ± 12.3
IV	10.0–10.11	22	12	10	110.0 ± 9.3	108.7 ± 12.8	104.3 ± 12.3
I–IV	7.0–10.11	83	46	37	108.5 ± 10.3	107.1 ± 11.2	106.1 ± 12.6

APPENDIX B

The Instituut Test Battery.

(1) *Remembering simultaneously presented colored rods* (Hiskey's test 1966). Abbreviated to *Si.C.*

(2) *Imitating seen successive paper folding movements* (Hiskey's test 1966). Abbreviated to *Su.Fo.*

(3) *Remembering simultaneously presented pictures* (Hiskey's test 1966). Abbreviated to *Si.Pi.*

(4) *Remembering successively presented pictures* Abbreviated to *Su.Pi.* (same pictures as in test 3).

(5) *Repeating spoken series of numbers* (test WISC-HAWIK, 1966). Abbreviated to *Rep.N.*

(6) *Simultaneous number/symbol association* (test WISC-HAWIK, 1966). Abbreviated to *N.Sy.*

(7) *Copying simultaneously presented geometrical figures from memory* (Benton's test, 1963). Abbreviated to *Bt.C.*

(8) *Identifying simultaneously presented geometrical figures from memory* (Benton's test, 1963). Abbreviated to *Bt.Id.*

(9) *Tapping four cubes in a shown order* (Knox's test, 1914, and Snijders-Oomen's 1970). Abbreviated to *Knox*.

(10) *Putting the fingers in a certain position according to an example* (Bergès's and Lézines's test, 1963). Abbreviated to *Bergès*.
The experimenter puts his fingers in a certain position and keeps them like that, until the child has imitated him. We refined the original scoring as follows: one hand is not allowed to help the other. When the child cannot imitate the position of the fingers without some help, the score is 0. When the child does not put his fingers in the correct position within 5 seconds, but puts it right finger by finger, the score is ½. When the child manages to get it right within 5 seconds, the score is 1. Maximum score: 16.

(11) *Imitating shown finger-movements from memory*. Abbreviated to *Fi.Mov.*
The experimenter, with eyes closed, puts his hand up. He then touches the tip of his thumb with the tip of his index finger three times. The child is asked to imitate this without looking at his fingers. Next the experimenter does the same with the middle finger, then with the ring finger and the little finger; then all the fingers in a row, at first in a tempo of 1 second per touch, then of ½ a second, then of ¼ a second. The score is 0 when the child uses the wrong fingers, 1 when he touches the right finger but not the finger tip, 2 when both aspects are correct. Maximum score: 42.

(12) *Repeating rhythmically spoken syllables*. Abbreviated to *Rhythm*.
The experimenter first says the following rhythmic pattern: ba-babà. The child has to repeat this. The score is 0 when the pattern is unrecognizable, 1 when it is recognizable but when the meter is not quite correct, 2 when everything has been repeated correctly. This is repeated once again. After this the child is asked to repeat the pattern five times without any help. Each time the scoring is worked out in the same way. The rhythmic patterns increase in difficulty, for example baba-bababà, babababà, etc. There are 15 items. *Appendix C & D, 11*. Maximum score: 210.

(13) *Speaking as many words as possible within 2 minutes*. Abbreviated to *Or.Fl.* (oral fluency).
The child is asked to speak different words, as many and as quickly as possible. They need not be correctly articulated, provided they are understandable to the experimenter. See *appendix C & D, 10–2*. Maximum score: ± 90.

(14) *Lipreading with sound-perception and repeating*. Abbreviated to *Lipr*.
The test consists of 50 words, varying from one syllable up to and including 5 syllables. The scoring is as follows: when the child repeats the word in the correct rhythm after having heard it once, he receives 4 points; when he repeats all the speech-sounds, in however a less correct rhythm, he is awarded 3 points; when the experimenter only has to say one syllable again and when the child then repeats it correctly, he scores 2 points; should the experimenter have to analyze the word further and the child manages to repeat the word correctly after that, he receives 1 point; in all other cases no points are awarded. Maximum score 200/2 100. See *appendix C & D, 10*.

(15) *Speaking correctly repeated words again.* Abbreviated to *Spe.rep.*

This is the second phase of test (14): when the child has repeated a word correctly, he is asked to repeat this word up to five times. The experimenter writes down the correct speech sounds. The score is expressed in percentages of correct speech sounds.

APPENDIX C
Correlation Matrix of 15 Selected Variables

N = 83

	1 Si.C.	2 Su.Fo.	3 Si.Pi.	4 Su.Pi.	5 Rep.N.	6 N.Sy.	7 Bt.C.	8 Bt.Id.	9 Knox	10 Bergès	11 Fi.Mov.	12 Rhythm.	13 Or.Fl.	14 Lipr.	15 Spe.rep.
1 Si.C.		+0.19	+0.81	+0.64	+0.46	+0.62	+0.70	+0.68	+0.31	+0.08	−0.03	+0.19	+0.60	+0.25	−0.13
2 Su.Fo.	+0.19		+0.03	+0.62	+0.68	+0.17	+0.04	+0.12	+0.75	+0.72	+0.67	+0.68	+0.49	+0.80	+0.79
3 Si.Pi.	+0.81	+0.03		+0.54	+0.39	+0.61	+0.78	+0.68	+0.20	−0.03	−0.15	−0.01	+0.50	+0.08	−0.30
4 Su.Pi.	+0.64	+0.62	+0.54		+0.76	+0.54	+0.55	+0.56	+0.60	+0.52	+0.29	+0.63	+0.69	+0.63	+0.38
5 Rep.N.	+0.46	+0.68	+0.39	+0.76		+0.37	+0.41	+0.39	+0.64	+0.63	+0.50	+0.62	+0.67	+0.70	+0.51
6 N.Sy.	+0.62	+0.17	+0.61	+0.54	+0.37		+0.63	+0.67	+0.35	+0.03	−0.06	+0.13	+0.51	+0.06	−0.08
7 Bt.C.	+0.70	+0.04	+0.78	+0.55	+0.41	+0.63		+0.79	+0.23	−0.03	−0.18	+0.01	+0.53	+0.01	−0.25
8 Bt.Id.	+0.68	+0.12	+0.68	+0.56	+0.39	+0.67	+0.79		+0.31	+0.03	−0.06	+0.02	+0.57	+0.05	−0.17
9 Knox	+0.31	+0.75	+0.20	+0.60	+0.64	+0.35	+0.23	+0.31		+0.55	+0.52	+0.52	+0.55	+0.57	+0.59
10 Bergès	+0.08	+0.72	−0.03	+0.52	+0.63	+0.03	−0.03	+0.03	+0.55		+0.52	+0.76	+0.43	+0.75	+0.72
11 Fi.Mov.	−0.03	+0.67	−0.15	+0.29	+0.50	−0.06	−0.18	−0.06	+0.52	+0.82		+0.56	+0.30	+0.66	+0.72
12 Rhythm.	+0.19	+0.68	−0.01	+0.63	+0.62	+0.13	+0.01	+0.02	+0.52	+0.76	+0.56		+0.43	+0.76	+0.66
13 Or.Fl.	+0.60	+0.49	+0.50	+0.69	+0.67	+0.51	+0.53	+0.57	+0.55	+0.43	+0.30	+0.43		+0.50	+0.32
14 Lipr.	+0.25	+0.80	+0.08	+0.63	+0.70	+0.06	+0.03	+0.05	+0.57	+0.75	+0.66	+0.76	+0.50		+0.76
15 Spe.rep.	−0.13	+0.79	−0.30	+0.38	+0.51	−0.08	−0.25	−0.17	+0.59	+0.72	+0.72	+0.66	+0.32	+0.76	

Level of significance: .21 $p < .05$
.27 $p < .01$

psychological and educational diagnosis and assessment **443**

APPENDIX D The Averages per Age-group on the 15 Tests. "Rough scores."

	1 Si.C.	2 Su.Fo.	3 Si.Pi.	4 Su.Pi.	5 Rep.N.	6 N.Sy.	7 Bt.C.	8 Bt.Id.	9 Knox	10 Bergès	11 Fi.Mov.	12 Rhythm	13 Or.Fl.	14 Lipr.	15 Spe.rep.
Group 7.0–7.11 N 20	13.8 ±1.0	5.9 ±1.3	8.4 ±1.0	6.3 ±1.4	3.5 ±1.9	32.3 ±7.5	3.3 ±1.3	5.5 ±1.6	8.7 ±1.7	12.0 ±1.8	27.6 ±5.9	120.1 ±24.0	38.3 ±12.8	49.7 ±15.7	87.8% ±13.0%
Group 8.0–8.11 N 18	14.8 ±0.8	6.3 ±1.4	9.2 ±0.7	7.6 ±1.3	4.8 ±1.8	27.4 ±5.2	4.1 ±1.3	6.3 ±1.7	9.0 ±2.4	13.3 ±1.7	31.8 ±4.7	129.4 ±20.0	48.6 ±11.2	68.3 ±15.3	91.2% ±12.1%
Group 9.0–9.11 N 23	15.1 ±0.8	6.8 ±0.9	9.4 ±0.8	8.3 ±1.3	5.5 ±1.0	31.6 ±5.5	4.2 ±1.1	6.3 ±1.9	9.4 ±1.8	13.9 ±1.5	31.3 ±3.7	146.3 ±29.0	55.0 ±13.9	75.2 ±9.2	93.1% ± 7.0%
Group 10.0–10.11 N 22	15.8 ±1.0	7.3 ±0.8	9.7 ±0.8	10.5 ±1.1	6.9 ±0.9	38.8 ±6.8	5.5 ±2.5	7.5 ±1.7	10.5 ±1.3	15.0 ±1.6	32.0 ±4.5	187.5 ±39.0	66.2 ±10.8	82.3 ±10.9	95.6% ± 5.8%
Total children N 83	14.9 ±1.1	6.6 ±1.2	9.2 ±1.0	8.3 ±2.0	5.2 ±1.9	32.7 ±7.4	4.3 ±1.8	6.4 ±1.9	9.4 ±1.9	13.6 ±1.9	30.7 ±5.0	147.2 ±37.7	52.6 ±15.8	69.4 ±17.5	92.1% ±10.0%
Maximum:	19	9	16	16	17	57	10	10	15	16	42	210	±90	100	100%

APPENDIX E

CASE I   J.J. van Put; born 10/16/66   (fingerspelling-department)

1. *Audiogram* d.d. February 1979

	125	250	500	1k	2k	4k	8k	Hz
Right ear	65	85	100	90	80	100	↘	dB
Left ear	65	90	110	120	125	130	↘	dB

There are good residual hearing possibilities present. Not typically deaf. The audiogram is since discovery almost the same.

2. *Anamnestic data.*

Cause of deafness: Rubeola, deafness discovered at 0.2 years.
First hearing aid: 0.7 years.
On preschool when he was 3.8 years.
There was hometraining service given.
At 6.6 years he has been transferred to a department whch used fingerspelling.

3. *Psycho-diagnostic data.*

At 4.6 years: HISKEY Performance IQ; 105.
                There was a serious dyspraxia. Bergès-Lézine test and Rhythm-test were not possible to score.
                Behavior: slightly autistiform behavior.
                          emotional some signs of desolation.
At 11.5 years: WISC-R Performance IQ: 117;
                Verbal (written form): 62.

CASE II   R. Westerik; born 8/12/65   (oral department)

1. *Audiogram* d.d. 08.06.1978.

	125	250	500	1k	2k	4k	8k	Hz
Right ear	90	90	95	105	120	130	↘	dB
Left ear	85	80	95	110	125	130	↘	dB

The audiogram is since discovery almost the same.

2. *Anamnestic data.*

Cause of deafness: Unknown, discovered at 1.0 year.
First hearing aid: 2.4 years.

On preschool when he was 3.8 years.
There was hometraining service given.

3. *Psycho-diagnostic data.*

At 5.6 years: Normal non-verbal intelligence quotient: SON
Good simultaneous memory.
At 7.4 years: SON IQ: 105.
There is some restlessness in his behavior.
He reacts impulsively to the situation.
Global perception of the situation.
Speech Behavior is below the mean of his age.
At 11.4: WISC-R Performance IQ: 96, with time-correction:
± 105; Verbal I.Q. (written form): 72.
A light form of dyspraxia and a light form of integration difficulties (oral and written word image).
There are arithmetic problems.
Behavior: extrovert, expansive, and impulsive.

CASE I   J.J. van Put

4. *Learning results*

	test age	score	word age hearing	deaf children
Peabody Vocabulary test	10.6	52	5.11	11.0
	11.5	56	6.5	11.6
			reading-age	
Metropolitan paragraph reading	12.0	22	8.0	13.0
Brus-van Bergen written tasks	12.0	19	7.6	—

Test results, October 1979 (video) communication test.

1. *Tests for eupraxia:*
   a. Bergès-Lézine   (max. 16): 14 (below age-norm)
   b. Finger test van Uden   (max. 42): 28 (10 years deaf ch.)
   c. Bruininks-Oseretsky test: below age-norm
   d. Rhythm test first presentation   (max. 30): 6–8 (7 years, norms for deaf children)
   e. Nonverbal successive memory, KNOX: 10 (10 years age-norm)

   Conclusion:
   There is a serious dyspraxia present. Because of the continuous use of fingerspelling, there is some compensation on finger-eupraxia tests. There are some visual corrections.

2. *Intelligibility of speech:* very difficult to understand.
3. *Lipreading test;* van Uden (25 words): too difficult; ± 5 percent correct.
4. *Memory for sentences* (only by lipreading): too difficult.
5. *Vocabulary and reading:* See 4 (above).

CASE II R. Westerik

4. *Learning results.*

	test age	score	word age hearing	word age deaf children
Peabody Vocabulary test	10.0	46	5.0	10.0
	12.0	73	8.0	13–14
			reading-age	reading-age
Metropolitan paragraph reading	12.10	17	7.6	11.6
Brus-van Bergen written tasks	12.10	22	8.0	—

Test results, October 1979 (video) communication test.

1. Tests for eupraxia:
   a. Bergès-Lézine   (Max. 16): 15 (too easy, not a max. score)
   b. Finger-test van Uden   (max. 42): 35 (lightly below age-morm)
   c. Bruininks-Oseretsky test: according with his age
   d. Rhythm-test first presentation   (max. 30): 20 (lightly below age-norm)
   e. Non-verbal successive memory, KNOX: 13 (13.6–16.6 years)

   Conclusion:
   There is still a light form of dyspraxia present.

2. *Intelligibility of speech:* mean results.
3. *Lipreading test;* van Uden (25 words): ± 80 percent correct (mean score for deaf children).
4. *Memory for sentences* (18 syllables): ± 14 syllables (mean score for deaf children).
5. *Vocabulary and reading:* See 4 (above).

APPENDIX F

Current Research

One session of the Symposium was spent on the presentation of current research including the following studies:

1. IJsseldijk F.:	The capability of strictly orally educated deaf pupils to understand speech by hearing.
2. IJsseldijk F.:	A longitudinal research into the reading results of deaf pupils at the Institute for the Deaf at Sint Michielsgestel.
3. Löwe A.:	Oral education of deaf children in a speaking environment. A comparative study of the linguistic competency of deaf and hearing children.
4. Povel D.J.:	Development of a Vowel Corrector for the Deaf. (This study is published in *Psychological Research, 37*, 51–70 (1974) by Springer Verlag 1974).
5. Povel D.J.:	Evaluation of the Vowel Corrector as a Speech Training Device for the Deaf. (This study is published in *Psychological Research, 37*, 71–80 (1974) by Springer Verlag 1974).
6. Schulte K.:	The Phonemetransmitting Manual System (P.M.S.).
7. Smale T.G.:	Assessment of speech intelligibility at Sint Michielsgestel. Institute for the Deaf - Sint Michielsgestel.
8. Uden A.M.J. van:	Reading.—How to teach deaf children to read? Institute for the Deaf, Research Center, Sint Michielsgestel.
9. Uden A.M.J. van:	Congenital Deafness and Disturbed Psychomotor Development. Institute for the Deaf, Research Center, Sint Michielsgestel.
10. Uden A.M.J. van:	Does seeing oneself speak benefit lipreading? Institute for the Deaf, Research Center, Sint Michielsgestel.
11. Uden A.M.J. van:	Composition work—written approximations of Dutch. Institute for the Deaf, Research Center, Sint Michielsgestel.
12. Veeger L.M.:	Some neurological disorders in deaf children. Institute for the Deaf, Sint Michielsgestel.

reaction to 17

helen s. lane

It was with sincere regret that I had to cancel plans to be with you personally, but I appreciate the privilege of sharing in this International Symposium on Deafness via videotape. I was invited to react to the paper entitled, "Psychological and Educational Diagnosis and Assessment" written by Drs. M. Broesterhuizen, J. van Dijk, and F. IJsseldijk. (Please excuse me if I have mispronounced your names. I could not find a Dutch scholar to guide me on short notice and feel like one of our deaf students who said, "Sometimes I put the accent on the wrong syllable".)

The authors' presentation was so well organized, so comprehensive in the discussion of the variables that influence the the development of language and speech of the deaf child and so much in accord with my personal observations and opinions that it was stimulating, informative, and enjoyable to read.

Part I deals with the etiology of deafness. Examination of the applications for admission to the Central Institute from 1914 to the present date shows the same consistent report of causes of deafness as unknown for the same high percentage of the children as reported in this study. With my knowledge of case histories, a few of the unknowns could have been placed in the category of hereditary deafness.

As the authors suggest, deafness due to prenatal infections (maternal rubella), post-natal infections (meningitis), dysmature and premature births, give us reason to suspect central nervous system problems. It is now possible, by using early diagnostic tests, to get information about hearing impairment, visual problems, and developmental abnormalities, which makes appropriate referrals possible. However, diagnostic teaching over a period of time is necessary in order to refer the child to the educational program best suited to his needs.

Part 2 is concerned with individual differences, and the first of these is hearing loss. The authors list four categories of hearing-impaired children. One of these is called descant-deaf and refers to those children who profit from auditory training from residual hearing in the lower frequencies. Today, in some schools in the United States, decisions concerning the oral education of a hearing-impaired child are based on the audiogram, and often on the average of the three speech frequencies in the better ear. The inclusion of the lower frequencies would give many of these children the opportunity for oral education. If responses to 250 Hz are included in the average, there would be a shift of many children in schools for the deaf from the classification of profoundly deaf (average loss > 96 dB) to severely deaf (average loss 76–95 dB).

Individual differences in motor development are discussed next, as they are related to speech and lipreading. In psychological testing of preschool age deaf children, motor coordination can influence the scores in cutting, block building, paper folding, drawing, bead stringing and tapping. In cutting, this may be a learning problem if mother has not permitted the child to use scissors. In block building, some children have not developed preferential handedness. When the task requires memory for a pattern, as in bead stringing, lack of motor skill interferes with memory of the pattern.

Dr. Max Goldstein, founder of Central Institute, said that speech required the highest coordination of the muscles involved and felt that training of the gross muscles would lead to better coordination of the finer muscles required for speech. He therefore stressed a rhythm program for all the children, starting with the interpretation of rhythmic and temporal patterns as they felt the vibrations on the piano, to group rhythmic recitations of the older children. At present there is a Physical Education program for all the children, with a curriculum planned to improve motor development and coordination.

My first knowledge of the work at Sint Michielsgestel was of the excellent rhythm program there. When I have had the opportunity to hear Dr. van Uden speak, I have been impressed by his studies of the relation between eurhythmia and eupraxia in the development of speech, and the value of the rhythm program in the education of the deaf. We shall all be interested in the present research of van Uden and his associates who collaborated in this paper, in which they used fifteen motor test items that were related to speech and lipreading. The research seems to indicate a relation between fine motor behavior, especially from the fingers and the articulation processes in deaf children.

Additional research indicates the importance of the motoric factor with age. We are all aware that any motor skill requires practice in order to maintain adequate performance, whether it is playing a musical instrument or participating in a sport. Yet we fail to stress the need for practice in using speech for deaf students leaving the special school. Those who continue in a hearing world academically, vocationally, and socially show improvement in the intelligibility of their speech; those who rely on manual communication for continued education, on the job, and with friends and family, lose some of their speech skills.

For the speech of dyspractic children, as described by the authors, there is a need for a more structured method of teaching—a breaking down of speech instruction into smaller units.

Part 2.4 directs attention to those children with problems of the integration of sensorimotor modalities.

Myklebust (1964) stated that sensory deprivation limits the world of experience, and because total experience is reduced, there is imposition on the balance and equilibrium of all psychological processes. Experience is constituted differently and the world of perception, conception, imagination, and thought has a new configuration. The configuration may differ for the hearing impaired, but the majority adjust to the imbalance of their psychological processes. In a few there have been severe learning problems in the acquisition of speech and language.

Mildred McGinnis, teaching adult aphasics following World War I, noted similarities of these adults to deaf children of good intelligence who had severe learning problems. This suggested to her the possibility of a congenital condition similar to that of the adult whose speech and language disturbance was the aftermath of a head trauma. In order to teach these children she developed an Association Method in 1968, so named because in its application there is a close association of the essential processes of learning which are attention, retention, and recall. Aphasic children cannot follow rapid speech patterns either in lip-reading if they are deaf or in imitation of the oral pattern if hearing is normal. The method is a very structured breaking up of speech into single elements and subsequently combining them into syllables and words. The child feels the sound, sees it on the lips, hears it, writes it, repeats it from imitation, from the written symbol, and then from memory. As sounds are combined to make words he sees the object, may feel it, sees a picture, and hears it pronounced by the teacher. Every sensory and kinesthetic approach is associated with the object or concept. Some of these children with normal hearing go into classes for the hearing, some with hearing impairment into classes for the deaf, and some are placed in vocational training programs. The Association Method is in use in many programs for the hearing and speech handicapped in the United States, and has been successful for children with problems of integration of the sensori-motor modalities.

Earlier identification of these children may be possible by use of the lists of van Uden that were filled out by house-parents and teachers. If school administrators can change the child to a different method of instruction, they may be able to prevent the frustration of continuous failure the child must feel in a class of "just deaf" children.

Part 3 deals with school philosophy and organization. Dr. Richard Silverman (1978), Director Emeritus of Central Institute tells "How we go about educating deaf children is related to the goals we have set for them, and these goals in turn are determined by what we consider to be the overall educational, psychological, and social potential of deaf persons."

In the United States, there has been such widespread publication of the low reading level of deaf students (3rd grade) that in some schools this is accepted as the maximum reading grade. Wrightstone, Aranow, & Moskowitz (1963) published an article with results based on reading scores on the Metropolitan Achievement test, showing that deaf students between the ages of 10 and 16 showed only 8 months improvement in this period.

Dorothea Baker French (1974), as a graduate student at Central Institute, studied the progress of Central Institute students of the same chronological age range over a 4-year period. Their reading scores indicated a gain of 2.5 grades and a reading level of grade 6.2 when they graduated. The curve showed no plateau and had not reached asymptote.

Student teachers should always be given an opportunity to meet and talk to deaf alumni. In their practicum they should teach or observe classes achieving academic success in preparation for "mainstreaming."

Homogeneous grouping is essential for good instruction but not possible in some school systems where there had been only 2 or 3 classes for deaf children in a public school for the hearing. In such programs "differential diagnosis" cannot be accomplished.

We, too, have examples of the teacher who does all the talking with little or no response from the children. With such an inexperienced first year teacher the guidance of a good supervising teacher helps correct the problem. In the United

States, many educators of the deaf are concerned about the number of day classes where there is no supervising teacher of the deaf, where homogeneous grouping is not possible, and where deaf children sit in classes for the hearing before they are ready.

In Part 2.2, the authors discuss intelligence and memory. If intelligence is defined as the ability to do abstract reasoning, a verbal test must be used and either the deaf are judged as defective mentally or we must conclude that their intelligence cannot be measured. If intelligence is defined as the ability to see relationships and to use past experience in new situations, a performance test can be selected. Care must be used in test selection to insure that the test is non-verbal in both instruction and response. If a test instruction requires the examiner to say "Watch me carefully and do as I do," the deaf child may not understand the task.

Recent test results of the intelligence of the deaf show a normal distribution of scores and a normal IQ. However, some investigators insist that this is a quantitative comparison and the deaf differ from the hearing in qualitative measures. How can these be measured?

The authors point out the seeming advantage the child has who can verbalize the task. I have noted this advantage in tests of memory span for numbers, for colors, and for pictures in the Hiskey test.

Wechsler, who believes intelligence is a global capacity, includes verbal and performance sections in his tests. The hearing child usually scores equally well in both parts. The deaf child is usually tested on the performance section only, assuming that if he had normal hearing and language he would perform at the same level on the verbal scale.

Before deaf children leave Central Institute to be placed in a hearing school, we give the Full Scale WISC-R. This is an index of his readiness for hearing classes. If it is within the normal range, there is no reason for anxiety. There is really not much difference between the verbal and performance scores. However, the verbal score improves with academic success in high school and college. On the vocabulary test, the deaf do not follow the order of difficulty of the words, they define correctly more difficult concrete nouns and miss easier abstract words.

The authors have studied the relation of performance test scores to school subjects. Performance tests are not predictors of academic achievement; the closest relation was in arithmetic.

We measure educational progress by using achievement test batteries that are written group tests, standardized on the national population of children in public schools. Such test scores give us the amount of educational retardation in school subjects from grades 2 through 9. Deaf children have the lowest scores in reading and in arithmetic reasoning or problem solving and the best in arithmetic computation where the language difficulties are at a minimum. Therefore, the reading tests and the arithmetic reasoning tests are important in evaluation and in determining readiness for placement in hearing classes.

A number of variables that defy objective measurement are discussed in the final section on emotional and personality factors. The first of these is the mother-child relationship, which is discussed in detail by Dr. Simmons-Martin in her paper for this Symposium. However, she does not mention the construction of a rating scale of parent behavior. We plan to use—and hopefully to standardize statistically—to determine affective behaviors of parents who establish a good relationship to the deaf infant and to guide other parents into such a relationship.

Life events that influence parent-child interaction are listed by the authors with the promise of an observation list—now in the experimental stage—that should help all of us study the important emotional and social behavior patterns.

The presentation of Drs. Broesterhuizen, van Dijk, and IJsseldijk has given us a comprehensive discussion of problems in psychological and educational assessment of deaf children. Well documented by research at Sint Michielsgestel and by other investigators. I have attempted to insert a few personal reactions based on my experience.

In conclusion, I would like to quote from Dr. Silverman's report at the conclusion of the Fiftieth Anniversary of Central Institute (1965).

> Central Institute for the Deaf, since its founding, has been dedicated to breaking down the barriers to free communication. Its goal has always been to develop natural means of conversation—expression through speech, and understanding through lipreading, and hearing where possible. Its rule of measurement has been in terms of the human product—its success in producing well adjusted individuals able to find self-expression and happiness in the environment of their times.

As I read the program of the Symposium and the papers sent to me, I felt the same goal exists for those attending this meeting on Oral Education Today and Tomorrow. Best wishes for success at the meeting and in your work for oral education for deaf children when you return to your schools.

References

Davis, H., & Silverman, S. R. *Hearing and deafness.* New York: Holt, Rinehart & Winston, 1978.

Lane, H. S., & Baker, D. Reading achievement of the deaf: Another look. *The Volta Review*, 1974, *76*, 489-499.

McGinnis, M. A. *Aphasic children: Identification and education by the association method.* Washington, DC: A. G. Bell Association for the Deaf, 1963.

Myklebust, H. R. *The psychology of deafness.* New York: Grune & Stratton, 1964.

Silverman, S..R. *Central Institute for the Deaf News Notes,* Summer, 1965.

Wrightstone, J. W., Aranow, M. S., & Muskowitz, S. Developing reading test norms for deaf children. *American Annals of the Deaf*, 1963, *108*, 311-316.

part V

social and
emotional development of
prelingually deaf persons
during school life
and afterward

18

the effect of oral education on the attitudes of deaf persons toward the hearing environment
george w. fellendorf

Abstract

A questionnaire on attitudes toward the hearing environment was mailed to 291 members of the Oral Deaf Adults Section of the Alexander Graham Bell Association for the Deaf. A total of 201 (69 percent) responses were received. A substantial majority of respondents reported strong positive feelings of acceptance as equals and comfortableness toward persons with normal hearing. Many attributed these attitudes to their oral educational training, but a large number credited their parents as the major source of their expectation levels and their orientation to the hearing environment. Attitudes toward the non-oral deaf environment were considerably less positive. The conclusion is that oral training, if the family is included, can help deaf children develop positive attitudes toward the hearing environment.

Few authorities, deaf persons, and parents of deaf persons in any country of the world would deny the desirability of articulate speech to deaf and profoundly hard-of-hearing individuals. There would be little argument in this field if it had been demonstrated consistently over the years that all deaf children and youth could develop adequate communication skills and the accompanying language through what is generally referred to as an oral education.

The issue that has separated the experts and deaf persons themselves into groups of "oralists," "manualists," and now "total communicators" arises from the fact that over the years not all of those exposed to even excellent oral educational programs seem to have progressed uniformly to similar levels of achievement of their potential. Thus the question, "Is it worth the tremendous effort and the investment of money, time, and talent if there is always a certain percentage who do not achieve communication skills sufficient to function comfortably in the hearing environment?"

Another question less often asked is, "What is the effect of the hard work to learn to speak on the attitudes of adult deaf persons toward the world of the normally hearing?" It would appear to be of great importance to begin to ask this question of adult deaf persons themselves.

This paper reports the results of such an investigation. More specifically, it was designed to test two hypotheses:

> **Hypothesis I**—An oral education leads deaf persons to attitudes of acceptance, tolerance, confidence, and comfortableness toward most hearing people and the hearing environment.

This hypothesis speaks to the very nature and *raison d'être* of oral education of deaf children. The purpose of such an educational approach is to give hearing impaired children the language and communication skills to function independently and to the fullest extent of their God-given capabilities. One who has achieved academic success and then finds that he is neither accepted nor comfortable in the society of those with whom he expected to live and work might tend to question the validity of the educational choices of his parents. The alternative might be to adopt the non-oral emphasis which is today popularly rephrased "total communication," and aim for proficiency in an atmosphere where articulate speech and listening capabilities are not so vital as in the normally hearing world.

This leads to the second hypothesis:

> **Hypothesis II**—An oral education leads deaf persons to attitudes of acceptance, tolerance, confidence, and comfortableness toward nonoral deaf adults and the deaf environment.

This hypothesis seeks to determine if the emphasis on the development of oral communication skills in children leads to acceptance of that group of adult deaf persons who do not have such highly developed oral communication skills and tend to function more comfortably in what is referred to as the deaf world or the deaf environment.

Review of the Literature

The English language literature is sparse on the subject of attitudes of deaf persons, oral or manual, toward the hearing environment. Considerably more appears in the journals and research reports on the attitudes of nonhandicapped persons toward those who are handicapped (Murphy et al., 1960). To date few investigators have undertaken any formal research into how the handicapped person feels toward the environment in which he was allegedly prepared to function by his parents and teachers.

The earliest references to the attitudes of deaf people are based upon observations by individual deaf persons about their own experiences (Balis, 1901, Boyd, 1901). One author would relate his or her experiences and feelings about them and then be challenged or supported by subsequent authors in a later issue of the same journal. Before the advent of electronic hearing aids, there were many references to lipreading and the strain which it placed upon one's whole system after a day of searching for meaning in the lips and faces of hearing contemporaries. One deaf writer states that upon occasion it was a positive relief to run away from everybody and find other amusement or occupation than conversation (Balis, 1901). Seeking temporary relief from the strain of oral communication was not so much a rejection of this communication mode or an interest in the hearing environment, as it was a behavioral reaction to the exhausting effects of lipreading upon an intelligent and inquisitive hearing impaired person in the presence of hearing persons.

Claims have been made for the value of an oral education in preparing deaf children for satisfactory integration into the hearing world, but the emphasis has most often centered on academic and speech training as compared to attitudinal and social development. Equally important, however, but less well understood, are the effects of deafness on the personality and social development of the individual (Heider, 1940).

In a monumental survey of 731 graduates and leavers of the Central Institute for the Deaf from 1914 to 1969, Lane felt it was impossible to measure social success from her data. Thus, she focused her attention on the achievement of integration into a hearing high school. She asserts that the many variables that influence social success prevent any reliable conclusions in this area of behavior (Lane, 1976).

After justification of the use of speech as compared to signs, some sweeping claims have followed: "Deaf children orally taught in oral schools lead happy and joyous lives" (Crouter, 1911). These remarks reflect an attempt to compare and justify the use of speech and lipreading instruction as compared to manual instruction in schools. The issue, one might suspect, is more of comparisons than absolutes. Thus, "Is the orally taught youngster more happy and joyous than the manually taught child?" The unasked and unanswered question is— "Is the orally taught child more happy and joyous than a hearing child?"

The relationships between attitudes and accomplishments of deaf persons are often framed and perhaps obscured by references to methodology. After many years as superintendent of the world famous Lexington School for the Deaf in New York City, O'Connor states that under the natural or "oral" language atmosphere, the best of the deaf will do better and the poorest will do no worse than under a manual or simultaneous system of instruction (O'Connor, 1957). He appears to be referring to academic accomplishment, however, rather than attitudes of an adult deaf person toward the hearing environment and in achieving what might be labeled social success.

On the occasion of the 50th anniversary of the American Association for the Promotion of the Teaching of Speech to the Deaf in 1940, the theme of the summer meeting in Providence, Rhode Island, was "The Adjustment of the Deaf to their Hearing Contemporaries." It was pointed out that in the years before the Association had been founded, neither in childhood nor in adult life was the deaf person expected to be adjusted to his hearing contemporaries in the sense of being one of them. Rather, education was directed toward making him a "good deaf man" (Gruver, 1945).

The intrinsic nature of the oral movement, indeed the ultimate goal of the teaching of speech and lipreading and imparting language using these modes of communication, was to lead deaf children into functioning as close to normal as possible. The oral school was not to just make a "good deaf man" but to try to make a deaf child into an almost normally functioning hearing adult. The school years in residential settings were no longer viewed as miniature models of the adult world in which the deaf person would function, that is, surrounded by other deaf persons, but they became a necessary means by which sufficient language, speech, and lipreading skills were to be imparted so the graduate could escape from the deaf world (van Uden, 1977).

The issue of an oral education in a residential school versus a day situation may be considered by some to be academic since the historic comparison has been between oral and manual forms of instruction in the classrooms. For others, however, the issue of the setting in which the oral instruction is received is critical. Alexander Graham Bell is quoted as saying to associates that the best school for the deaf is the school with only one deaf child in it (Deland, 1923). Other authorities of Bell's era, though not necessarily associates or followers of Bell, made similar references to the merits of maintaining regular contact with the family and with hearing peers. In discussing the need for education of the deaf for life in human society, a German educator stated that the first aim of education must be to give to the deaf the speech of that world, not the speech of books but the speech of life, of daily intercourse (Danger, 1901). The second most important aim is "to strengthen a love of home, a love of the family, be that family high or low." Danger states that the physical surroundings in a school for the deaf may be so far above that of the home from which a pupil came that adjustment to the life and the people in that home may be extremely difficult when he returns. Thus, there is an implication that while the school for the deaf may offer a quality of formal education not available in the local school or in the home, the attitudes toward the home and his village may be distorted by the different climate and culture of the residential setting (van Uden, 1977).

Fritz and Grace Heider point out that the social effects of the handicap of deafness, including the problems of adjustment, are less important to the child while attending a residential school because he lives most of the year in a situation that is tuned to his special needs. When he leaves the school for the deaf, he begins to really become aware of what it means to be deaf. The child does not feel the full impact until he leaves the security of school (Heider & Heider, 1943a).

In the Heiders' study of 82 school graduates or leavers from five schools for the deaf, few respondents reported the loss of sound *per se* as a problem. It was the lack of adequate communication resulting from the lack of hearing which surfaced as the major problem (Heider & Heider, 1943a). The resulting experiences created attitudes of resentment:

The hearing do not bother to include the deaf in their conversation.
They talk down to me.
They won't take the time to explain.
People answer me politely, then go back to their own absorbing conversation.
I was treated like a piece of furniture.

Resentment also seems to have been created and nurtured by teachers whispering in front of deaf students and talking about them to other hearing teachers as though the children did not exist.

The attitudes and practices of the deaf student when he is thrust into the world of the hearing can be either one of *withdrawal* or *active adjustment*. The first involves pulling away from the larger social group of hearing people and simply avoiding the problem of social intercourse. The second involves the attempt to compensate for the specific limitations of a situation while staying in contact with the larger group (Heider & Heider, 1943a). These two prominent psychologists recommended that some of the withdrawal and adjustment problems and frustrations which they found in young deaf persons upon leaving the school for the deaf could have been avoided, or solved more easily, if adult experiences could have been passed along to the deaf children and to the hearing parents and teachers earlier.

Feelings of success, including social acceptance sought by all persons including the deaf child, are heavily influenced by the individual's level of aspiration (Heider & Heider, 1943b). The level of aspiration is defined as the goal a person has set for himself and the measure of what he expects to accomplish. If the aspiration level is too high, the person consistently fails to achieve, and attitudes of failure and unhappiness result. For the deaf child, it is important that he be helped to understand the situation objectively and to attribute at least some of his limitations to the right source; that is, to a pair of ears which fail to transmit sound properly. Adjustment has no meaning in itself. It is always adjustment to a specific situation (Heider & Heider, 1943a).

With fluctuating aspiration levels and varying degrees of success in achieving them, it should not be surprising that some deaf leaders and journal contributors look back to the "good old days" when it was okay to be a "good deaf man." The emphasis on normalcy and integration apparently has tended to lead away from the deaf world some of the more talented graduates, leaving behind those who could not pass and/or function as hearing persons (Stewart, 1943). Pintner is quoted as saying that "the aim of the education of the deaf child should be to make him a well integrated, happy deaf individual and not a pale imitation of a hearing person" (Stewart, 1943).

In a study of graduates of three Midwestern schools of the deaf, only one of which was a residential school, Frackelton found two distinct attitudinal groups. Of 38 respondents, 18 were in the age range from 15 to 25, while the balance ranged in age from 26 to 68. Among the younger group, she found considerable resentment and regret toward the hearing loss and the limitations which it imposed. On the other hand, the older group of respondents evidenced a strong sense of resignation to their hearing loss and all that it implied (Frackelton, 1944). Another investigator 20 years later explained that the distorted perceptions in younger persons slowly diminished in adulthood, suggesting a delayed period of maturation in deaf persons as compared to those with normal hearing (Neyhus, 1964). The adjustment of aspiration levels and developing coping mechanisms as one grows older would appear to account for the reported attitude of resignation that characterized the older subjects in the Frackelton study.

A large percentage (80 percent) of respondents in the Frackelton study reported that they were afraid of being alone. This is in marked contrast to the Heiders' observation that deafness naturally involves a lot of occasions of being alone. The conclusion might be drawn that while deaf people are often alone, they don't like it!

An interesting indication of deaf persons' attitudes toward the hearing environment may be found in the marriage statistics. It is well known that the majority of deaf persons tend to select other deaf or hard-of-hearing persons as mates, perhaps revealing thereby evidence of the feelings of acceptance and comfortableness which are sought and usually characterize a happy marriage. In a group of adolescents attending special schools for the deaf, apparently there was no expectation by most of the students that they would ever marry anyone but another deaf person (Rodda, 1966). Rodda's data also were interpreted to indicate that girls were better adjusted than boys.

The most recent effort at examining the attitudes of deaf adults who have received an oral education is found in the doctoral study of Ogden at the University of Illinois (Ogden, 1979). He begins with a definition of attitudes as "a learned predisposition to respond in a consistently favorable or unfavorable manner with respect to a given object or situation." Further, he defines an oral school as one in which signs are forbidden in class, in the home, or elsewhere. His focus is not so much on attitudes toward the hearing environment as it is toward their own education in an oral school and toward certain experiences which occurred during their years of school attendance.

Ogden's subjects were drawn from the graduates or school leavers of three internationally recognized oral schools for the deaf, i.e., Central Institute for the Deaf, Clarke School for the Deaf, and St. Joseph Institute for the Deaf. Of the 1,102 questionnaires mailed and received by potential respondents, 637 were returned, a 58 percent response. Of the 113 questions asked, 58 were informational and 55 were scaled items dealing with attitudes. The questions to which the researcher sought answers were:

1. Are you glad you attended an oral school? Why?
2. Do you have special problems because you are an oral deaf person?
3. How can these problems be eliminated by the efforts of the schools?
4. How can you eliminate or decrease these problems?

A large number of tables reveal the responses to the questions asked, and only a few which appear to represent attitudes toward the hearing environment, are reported at this time.

In Table 1, respondents emphasized communication problems as their most prominent. In Table 2, subjects reported the general problems which they experienced as a result of their hearing loss. In an effort to determine any constructive suggestions as to how oral schools for the deaf might help to solve some of the problems which they were now experiencing as oral deaf adults, the respondents reported in Table 3 as most significant, the ability to speak and lipread.

Table 1
(Ogden's Table 75)
Subjects' specific problems as oral deaf adults.

16.4%	People had difficulty understanding their speech.
16.4%	They had difficulty lipreading others.
16.6%	In groups of hearing people, they had difficulty in following the conversation of others.
7.0%	Had feelings of isolation resulting from not fitting into hearing or deaf worlds.
6.8%	Inability to communicate with deaf people who only sign.
5.9%	Inability to control the volume or pitch of their voice.
5.7%	Impossibility of lipreading 100% of what is said.

Table 2
(Ogden's Table 77)
Subjects' general problems as deaf adults.

33.2%	Public's lack of understanding of deaf people.
23.8%	Cannot use the telephone.
18.7%	Cannot understand movies or TV.
8.9%	Difficulty in finding employment.

Table 3
(Ogden's Table 79)
Subjects' recommendations on how oral schools could help solve problems.

16.3%	Make every effort to teach good speech and lipreading, improve the teaching methods for oral skills, and increase the amount of training in speech.
14.0%	Make more contacts with hearing children and have more experiences in the hearing world.
12.3%	Use total communication.

It is interesting to find that more than 10 percent of the respondents mentioned that training in the use of signs and fingerspelling might contribute to the resolution of some of the problems they were experiencing as oral deaf adults. In a related question, subjects were asked if they would send their own deaf child to a total communication school. Thirty-eight percent responded "Yes," while 50.5 percent indicated an oral school would be their choice if their child had a hearing loss.

In explaining the conflict between several sets of questions relating to where they would send their own deaf child, Ogden suggests that many respondents would select a total communication school for their child if they could be sure that the superior quality teachers and the emphasis on speech training which characterizes oral schools would be found also in the total communication schools. In fact, Ogden surmises that most of the respondents felt that the so-called total communication schools focused primarily upon the teaching and use of manual communication and that speech was taught poorly, if at all. Thus, while they could see some advantages in manual communication skills for their own deaf children, they would not sacrifice the oral skills that they had reason to expect would not be developed in a total communication environment.

While all of the respondents had attended oral schools for the deaf where sign language and fingerspelling were forbidden in the classrooms and in the dormitories, 67 percent of Ogden's respondents reported that as of the date of the survey they knew and could use sign language. In general, as a group, the respondents seemed to be disposed toward the oral education for themselves, but were more lenient with respect to their own deaf children learning manual communication in childhood.

Attitudes toward one's own family are the source of attitudes toward the hearing environment in general. van Uden has stated that one can expect integration into the hearing society only through integration into one's own family, and he states also that a deaf child can live in a kind of ghetto even within his own family. At his school, van Uden reports that often children complain that at home they are very lonely, that father and mother never talk to them, and that they are not allowed to join in with brothers and sisters (van Uden, 1977).

The Subjects

The subjects in this study were the entire membership of the Oral Deaf Adults Section (ODAS) of the Alexander Graham Bell Association for the Deaf as listed in the 1978 membership directory published by the Association.

The ODAS is a voluntary service organization founded in 1964. Membership in the ODAS is open to hearing impaired persons 21 years of age or over who show satisfactory educational, occupational, and social adjustment among the hearing through the use of oral communication (speech, speechreading, and wherever possible, residual hearing). A membership application must be filed with the ODAS Membership Committee and must include at least three references who will certify to the applicant's qualifcations to meet the membership requirements. If the membership application is approved by the Committee, the individual is accepted into ODAS. No additional dues, beyond the A. G. Bell membership fee, are required.

Procedures

Data were collected by means of a questionnaire mailed to a group of oral deaf adult persons in the United States during the late summer of 1979. The responses were entered into a data processing system at the Office of Demographic Studies, Gallaudet College, and then analyzed.

The Instrument—The instrument used in this study was a questionnaire of 29 questions; eight were descriptive and 21 related to attitudes and experiences of the respondents with regard to the hearing environment. Three questions called for open-ended responses; the rest were multiple choice (See Appendix).

The questionnaire was pretested in August, 1979, when it was reviewed by six oral deaf adults and by seven members of the Educational Advisory Committee of the Hearing, Educational Aid and Research Foundation, Inc. The statement of possible hypotheses and research questions was also shared with the members of the Educational Advisory Committee. A number of constructive suggestions were received.

The Procedures—The questionnaires were mailed to 291 members of the Oral Deaf Adults Section. Only two weeks were given for responses to be mailed back in a stamped return envelope. Respondents were requested not to place their names anywhere on the questionnaire or on the return envelopes in order to preserve complete anonymity.

The data analysis was limited to frequency distributions and a series of cross-tabulations. The size of the sample and its highly selective nature, coupled with the limitations of time, limited further analysis currently.

The Results

Questionnaires were sent out to 291 oral deaf adult persons via first class mail. All can be presumed to have been received, since none were returned by the post office. Of these, 209 (72 percent) were returned, but only 201 (69 percent) were received by September 10, the deadline for being included in the data analysis.

The frequency distributions are shown in Appendix A directly on a copy of the questionnaire. The following observations will serve to highlight those areas which might be considered of special significance to the hypotheses that were to be investigated.

Hearing Loss and Age of Onset—Ninety-six percent of the respondents reported a hearing loss to be severe or profound. Seventy-four percent indicated that their hearing loss occurred before the age of 2 years. There is little doubt that the respondents can be considered deaf, both from the standpoint of the degree of hearing loss at the time of the survey and the age of onset.

Oral Education, Training and Family—Very few of the respondents had educational experiences outside the strictly oral schools for the deaf or a hearing school where they were integrated totally or partially with non-hearing-impaired students. Almost 50 percent reported attending graduate school with hearing peers.

In the childhood homes of the respondents, almost 25 percent said there were one or more hearing impaired persons.

The number of unmarried individuals (46 percent) is considerably higher than the national figure reported for the total population of the U.S. in the 1974

Almanac, which showed 35.5 percent of U.S. citizens as single, widowed, or divorced.

Attitudes Toward the Hearing Environment—The questions which sought information about respondents' attitudes toward the hearing environment revealed a general satisfaction with their present relationship to hearing persons. Also, most of their time is spent in the company of hearing persons. None of the respondents reported that they spent most or all of their time with other deaf people, excluding those in their immediate family. There was little indication that respondents wanted to change their present social or business life and move in the direction of more contact with deaf people. Ninety-six percent of the respondents said they felt comfortable in communicating on a one-to-one basis with most hearing people with whom they came in contact, and similar percentages said they felt they could understand and be understood by most of those with whom they had contact.

When asked to select the terms that best described their attitudes toward hearing people and the hearing world, 84 percent of the respondents indicated feelings of acceptance as equals and tolerance. Few reported resentment, jealousy, or impatience. As to their expectations about participating in the hearing world, there was an indication of exaggerated expectations on the part of both parents and teachers which were not fulfilled when the children became adults. The parents, not the school, were found to be the major sources about expectation, with 76 percent of the respondents saying that it was their parents who gave them their information and perceptions about being a part of the hearing world when they became adults.

The respondents' perceptions of the attitudes of hearing people toward them also showed feelings of acceptance as equals and tolerance. In order to offer the respondents an opportunity to express their attitudes in an unstructured manner, Questions 28 and 29 of the questionnaire were open-ended inquiries into attitudes toward the hearing and the deaf world. Here again, the attitudes toward the hearing world were strongly positive, but it is not so clear that these attitudes were inculcated through the formal educational process in school. In fact, in 15 percent of the cases, some source other than oral school, teachers, or therapists was mentioned specifically as the primary source of the attitudes toward hearing people.

With respect to attitudes toward non-oral deaf people and their world, far less acceptance and comfortableness was expressed. Fifteen percent of the respondents felt negative toward those who communicate primarily through signs and expressed that feeling by reactions of discomfort in the presence of signs and/or an actual rejection of this mode of communication and those who use it. Another 15 percent were sympathetic toward those who functioned primarily through sign language, often noting that it was a "shame" that these individuals apparently did not have the same opportunities for development of oral communication skills as they had had. Indeed, there were many expressions of pity among these respondents who appeared willing to accept non-oral deaf people as friends but found it difficult to communicate with them. Not only was a lack of communication skills deplored, but there was among some respondents a feeling that the language skills and the range of interests of the non-oral deaf persons prevented true friendships and commonality of interest.

Conclusions and Observations

The purpose of this study was to test two hypotheses, one relating to the effect of an oral education on deaf adults' attitudes toward the hearing environment, and the other relating to their attitudes toward the deaf environment.

The data would appear to support Hypothesis 1, at least in part. There is substantial evidence that the oral deaf adults who responded to this questionnaire have positive attitudes toward the hearing environment, are tolerant of their hearing peers, and feel comfortable in their company. If the term "comfortable" can be considered an acceptable way of expressing a relationship which reflects equal treatment, tolerance, confidence and general well-being, then the oral deaf adults in this study would appear to be comfortable in their relationships with the hearing environment.

On the other hand, there is no clear evidence that the attitudes can necessarily be attributed to the oral educational process *per se*. At issue may be the definition of "oral education." Where does it take place, i.e., in a special oral school, in a regular school with special help, in a regular school with no special help, or in the home? If attitudes tend to develop early in life, then there would be a tendency to feel that the parents and family members are indeed the sources of attitudes toward the hearing environment and perhaps the deaf environment as well.

The data do not support Hypothesis 2. It is true that a small number of respondents expressed an interest in spending more time in communication with deaf people, but the same percentage also would like to spend more time with those who can hear normally. Only about 15 percent of the respondents indicated that they currently communicate equal amounts of time with deaf and hearing people, but this question did not ask them to differentiate between oral or non-oral deaf persons.

Oral training in its broadest definition, which includes family and school, did not appear to have prepared deaf students for what might be termed the inevitable confrontation with the non-oral deaf world. There was a substantial "No Response," however, to Question 29 concerning attitudes toward the non-oral world. An in-depth analysis of these individuals might reveal further information which would qualify this observation. In assuring anonymity of responses, there was a conscious effort to encourage respondents to report their true feelings, some of which might not be considered acceptable by their peers in the Oral Deaf Adults Section. Even with this assurance, there is at least a possibility that the "No Responses" to Question 29 might reveal a more positive attitude toward the non-oral environment.

One might question the need to prepare oral deaf children for a more comfortable relationship with the non-oral world; especially the well-prepared oral deaf adult who neither seeks nor needs such a relationship. As this question is broached, it is important to reiterate that the population in this study is the "cream of the crop" among orally trained individuals in the United States. They are by no means the ordinary deaf adult who has had all or some of his educational preparation in a strictly oral school. The unanswered question with respect to both Hypothesis 1 and 2 is, "What would be the responses if another population were surveyed?"

In conclusion, then, Hypothesis 1 tests out positively for the population reached through this investigation, but has not been proven true with any other population of oral deaf adult persons in the United States. It should be gratifying and encouraging to parents and teachers who endorse the oral philosophy of education of deaf students to learn that for those who have an early start, interested parents, and a sound educational program which focuses on listening, lipreading, and speech, positive social attitudes can be anticipated among the great majority of orally trained deaf individuals.

In the literature, those few surveys reported that are somewhat similar to this one, did not reveal the same homogeneity of respondents nor the same degree of satisfaction with their lifestyle among hearing people. It is difficult to compare because most of the studies were conducted many years ago when a number of conditions were different, especially the use of hearing aids, early detection and intervention, and parent counseling. Furthermore, the current wave of interest by government, as well as society in general, in the human rights of individuals who are disabled or from minority groups would appear to have enhanced the attitudes of the hearing environment toward the hearing impaired, and quite possibly thereby improved the attitudes of the hearing impaired toward the normally hearing.

The test of Hypothesis 2 would appear to be negative for this population. The combination of guidance from parents and teachers, coupled with the oral deaf individuals' own personally developed attitudes, does not appear to have led to acceptance, tolerance, or comfort in the non-oral environment. Thus, it would appear that for those who have the best oral training and appear to have succeeded in their relationships with the hearing environment, a price has been paid with respect to their relationships with other deaf people who are not so successful, for whatever reasons, with oral communication.

The response to the observation on Hypothesis 2 as given in the previous paragraph may be "So what?" After all, isn't the goal of oral training the preparation of deaf children and youth for independent life in the hearing environment rather than the deaf environment? Indeed, Heider and Heider (1943b) make a point of the fact that children attending an oral school for the deaf don't really face the implications of their deafness until they leave the school and face life in the hearing world. It is then that they find out how well they have been prepared with language, social skills, and communication skills to be independent of special teachers and an environment that is finely tuned to their special needs.

One may conclude from this study that an oral education which includes both the home as well as the school has indeed led to positive and healthy attitudes toward the hearing environment by a selected group of oral deaf adults in the United States. There is reason and logic to support the statement that if your hearing impaired children are given the same opportunities and treatment as those in this sample, many will achieve similar attitudes and acceptance with respect to the hearing environment.

With respect to the so-called deaf world, the same approach which appears to have succeeded with the hearing environment tends to produce a diametrically opposite effect for children and youth given an oral education.

Of considerable interest to educators and parents as well as to future generations of deaf persons must be the questions, "Does a positive attitude toward the hearing environment necessarily result in a negative attitude toward the deaf environment?" "Must deaf children graduating from an oral school for the deaf or from a mainstreamed public school program leave with a feeling that they must choose which world they will live in or be comfortable in?"

Recommendations

Some recommendations that surface when examining the results of this study relate to the extension of the benefits of a true oral education to far greater numbers of hearing impaired children to take advantage of the potential for comfortable relations with the hearing environment. Furthermore, in view of the realism of life as it is, rather than as we might like it to be, other recommendations deal with the considerably larger number of deaf children and youth who to date have not achieved the degree of success indicated by the respondents in this study.

Recommendation 1: Continue to strengthen and expand parent counseling and support since it appears that this is the source of attitudes, even though parents may be a little too optimistic at times.

Recommendation 2: Impress upon teachers, school authorities, and especially student teachers, the importance of the family in developing positive attitudes toward the world in which the children will live as adults. Include in teacher preparation curricula more intensive relationships with parents, and clearly indicate to student teachers that which can be learned from parents, as well as that which can be taught to them.

Recommendation 3: Assure that parents, elected officials, school authorities, and especially those professionals who have recently "discovered" deafness are made aware of the indicated levels of acceptance achievable through an oral education emphasis in a variety of educational settings. Impress upon all that this opportunity must not be denied to any hearing impaired child because of allegations that it is not possible unless an extraordinary set of preconditions are met in full.

Recommendation 4: Carefully design, pretest, and assist in implementing an "Orientation to the Non-Hearing Environment" as an elective course for hearing impaired children and youth who are preparing to leave an oral educational setting to enter the mainstream of education or are leaving school for the world of work. The purpose would be to acquaint the children with the fact that they have had a wonderful opportunity which may not have been possible for all other hearing impaired children and that they will very likely find themselves in the company of such individuals. Included in the curriculum would be an effort to understand the reasons for differing educational treatments, the strengths and weaknesses of each, how one can improve relationships with those who may be different from themselves, and how they can serve as models for parents of young hearing impaired children.

Recommendation 5: With necessary modifications, offer the same course, "Orientation to the Non-Hearing Environment," to students preparing to leave "total communication" and other manually oriented programs. As was proposed in Recommendation 4, the goal should be less tension and greater understanding among persons sharing a common disability.

Recommendation 6: Replicate this study with other populations of deaf adults, including graduates and school-leavers from oral programs who may not be members of the Oral Deaf Adults Section, graduates and school-leavers from total communication programs, and oral deaf adults from countries other than the United States.

In conclusion, it is hoped that this brief investigation of the attitudes of oral deaf adults will be the beginning of a series of studies designed to assess the social implications of one of the most severely disabling conditions; i.e., profound prelingual hearing loss. Of vital importance to the authenticity of any such studies will be honest input from deaf persons themselves.

APPENDIX A QUESTIONNAIRE

SURVEY OF ORAL DEAF ADULTS

George W. Fellendorf, Ed.D.
September 1, 1979

PLEASE *DO NOT* SIGN YOUR NAME OR IN ANY WAY IDENTIFY YOURSELF.

IF YOU FIND YOU CANNOT ANSWER ALL THE QUESTIONS, COMPLETE ALL YOU CAN.

IF YOU DON'T WANT TO PARTICIPATE AT ALL, PLEASE RETURN THE QUESTIONNAIRE ANYWAY.

Note: Numbers typed in for each response are percent responses of the total number of responses received as of Sept. 10, 1979

1. I am (45.8) male; (54.2) female.

2. My age is (35.3) 21–30; (20.9) 31–40 (13.4) 41–50; (14.9) 51–60 (14.9) over 61. (0.5) NR

3. I estimate my hearing loss is (1.5) mild; (1.0) moderate; (15.9) severe; (80.1) profound.   (1.5) No Response

4. As far as I know, my hearing loss occurred
   (55.7) at birth.
   (18.4) before age 2.
   (23.4) after age 2.
   (2.0) don't know.
   (0.5) NR

I attended the following schools (Check all that apply):

	Strictly oral school for deaf	Combined method school for deaf (signs, etc.)	School for hearing: public or private	Other (Specify)	Did not attend	NR
5. Preschool	(45.3)	(0.5)	(25.4)	(3.0)	(8.0)	(17.9)
6. Elementary	(47.8)	(2.0)	(45.3)	(1.0)	(—)	(4.0)
7. Junior high	(17.9)	(2.0)	(64.3)	(1.0)	(2.0)	(12.9)
8. High school	(5.5)	(1.0)	(88.6)	(4.5)	(0.5)	(4.5)
9. Vocational/ business	(1.0)	(0.5)	(22.4)	(0.5)	(13.4)	(62.2)
10. Undergrad	(2.0)	(4.5)	(67.7)	(—)	(2.5)	(23.4)
11. Graduate	(3.0)	(0.5)	(48.8)	(—)	(—)	(39.3)

12. The title of my present job is _____
 write title or brief description
 (44.3) Professional
 (5.5) Managerial
 (7.5) Clerical
 (16.9) Craftsman
 (0.5) Operative
 (1.0) Laborer
 (15.4) Unemployed, student or retired
 (9.0) No Response

13. I am able to understand most hearing people
 (58.2) very well
 (40.3) fairly well
 (1.0) poorly
 (0.5) no response

14. I believe most hearing people find my speech
 (33.8) excellent   (12.9) fair
 (52.2) good   (0.5) poor
                     (0.5) No Response

15. When I was young, the following members of my immediate family had hearing losses:
 (1.5) mother
 (2.5) father   (4.0) Two or more deaf relatives
 (8.5) brother/sister (2.0) no response
 (7.0) other nearby relative (74.5) none of these

16. My husband (or wife) is deaf too: (24.4) Yes (24.9) No (46.3) Unmarried
 (4.5) no response

17. In a normal week, I communicate (excluding those in my family)
 (41.8) all the time with hearing people
 (41.8) mostly with hearing people and a few deaf people
 (15.4) about half hearing and half deaf people
 (—) mostly with deaf people and a few hearing people
 (—) all the time with deaf people
 (1.0) no response

18. I wish I could spend
    (12.9) more time with deaf people
    (70.6) no change
    (13.9) more time with hearing people
    (2.5) no response

19. In general I feel comfortable in communicating on a one-to-one basis with: (Check all that apply.)
    (2.5) deaf adults who speak and lipread only
    (10.4) hearing people who only speak and don't sign
    (2.5) deaf adults who speak and sign simultaneously
    (—) deaf adults who only sign
    (1.0) don't feel comfortable communicating with anyone
    (10.4) Checked all
    (43.8) Checked 1 & 2
    (27.4) Checked 1, 2, 3

20. I feel I have adequate success in communicating on a one-to-one basis with:
    (29.9) all hearing people
    (66.2) most hearing people
    (3.0) only a few hearing people
    (—) don't feel adequate with any hearing people
    (1.0) no response

21. At the present time I participate generally in the same activities as hearing people of my own age:
    (40.3) completely
    (44.8) almost completely
    (13.4) somewhat
    (0.5) not at all
    (1.0) no response

22. When I was young, I expected that when I was an adult I would be able to participate generally in the same activities as hearing people:
    (37.8) completely
    (48.3) almost completely
    (9.0) somewhat
    (3.0) not at all
    (2.0) no response

23. My expectations about participating in the hearing environment were based largely upon information and perceptions instilled in me by: (Check the *most* important one.)
    (76.1) my parents and family
    (7.5) my teachers or therapists
    (0.5) other deaf students
    (1.5) deaf alumni
    (5.5) someone else _____
    (2.0) no response   specify
    (7.0) no one else

24. I now feel that they were:
    (8.5) much too optimistic
    (27.9) optimistic
    (54.2) just about right
    (2.5) pessimistic
    (1.0) much too pessimistic
    (1.5) don't know   (4.5) no response

25. At the present time I think the following statements best describe my attitudes toward hearing people and the hearing world: (Check all that apply.)

(64.2) I accept them as equals mostly.
(6.5) I tolerate them.
(2.0) I am impatient with them.
(0.5) I resent them.
(1.0) I am jealous of them.
(3.0) other (specify) _____

(3.5) Checked all answers
(15.9) Checked 1 & 2
(1.5) Checked 3, 4, 5
(2.0) No Response

26. I feel comfortable in communicating through speech with hearing members of my immediate family:
(21.5) all the time
(6.5) some of the time
(0.5) never
(1.5) no response

27. At the present time, I think the usual attitudes of most hearing people toward me are:
(69.2) They mostly accept me as an equal.
(14.4) They tolerate me.
(5.0) They are condescending toward me.
(2.5) They are impatient with me.
(1.0) They ignore me.
(2.5) other (specify) _____

(3.0) Checked 1 & 2
(2.5) No Response

28. Please write below any comments you would like to add about how your oral training influenced your attitudes toward hearing people and the hearing world in general.
(34.3) Strong positive attitudes directly attributed to schooling.
(22.9) Strong positive attitudes, but no specific mention of schooling.
(3.0) Already had strong positive attitudes before schooling began.
(11.9) Strong positive attitudes, but gained at other than oral school.
(1.0) School set too high goals—should have been more realistic.
(0.5) Regular school pointed out limitations earlier.
(1.0) Shared a desire to hide hearing loss—wanted to deceive others.
(1.5) Expressed resignation to loneliness.
(1.5) Did not credit oral education with any attitudes.
(22.4) No Response

29. What was the effect of your oral training on your attitudes toward non-oral deaf adults and the deaf world?
(4.0) Strongly oral—nothing negative about non-oral or signs.
(19.4) Strongly oral—willing to accept non-oral and signs; comfortable with them.
(13.9) Strongly oral—uncomfortable with non-oral deaf persons and signs.
(12.4) Strongly oral—dislike and/or rejection of non-oral deaf persons and signs.
(1.5) Comfortable with non-oral deaf persons and signs.
(15.4) Sympathetic and/or sorry for non-oral deaf persons; expressed pity.
(6.0) Strongly positive toward non-oral deaf persons and signs.
(2.0) Little or no contact with non-oral deaf persons—no attitudes expressed.
(1.0) Definite feeling of superiority over non-oral deaf persons.
(24.4) No Response.

Many thanks for your cooperation. If you would like a copy of the report of this study, send me a card and I'll be glad to mail you a copy in early December.

George W. Fellendorf, Ed.D.
Box 32054
Washington, D.C. 20007

References

Balis, S.C. The deaf and their social relations with the hearing. *The Volta Review*, 1901, 3, 141–144.

Boyd, H. The deaf and their social relations with the hearing. *The Volta Review*, 1901, 3, 227–236.

Crouter, A.L.E. The possibilities of oral methods in the instruction of deaf children. *American Annals of the Deaf*, 1911, 56, 390–407.

Danger, O. The education of the deaf for life in human society. *The Volta Review*, 1904, 6, 101–108.

Deland, F. An ever continuing memorial. *The Volta Review*, 1923, 25, 90–99.

Frackelton, B.P. Adjustments of the deaf. *American Annals of the Deaf*, 1944, 89, 173–181.

Gruver, E.A. The adjustment of the deaf to their hearing contemporaries. *The Volta Review*, 1945, 47, 69–71; 112–116.

Heider, F. Adjustment of the adult deaf. *Psychological Abstracts*, 53, 242.

Heider, F., & Heider, G. The adjustment of the adult deaf. *The Volta Review*, 1943a, 45, 325–328.

Heider, F., & Heider, G. The adjustment of the adult deaf II. After school problems as the psychologist sees them. *The Volta Review*, 1943b, 45, 389–391.

Lane, H.S. The profoundly deaf: Has oral education succeeded? *The Volta Review*, 1976, 78, 329–340.

Murphy, A.T., et al. Acceptance, rejection and the hearing handicapped. *The Volta Review*, 1960, 62, 208–211.

Neyhus, A.I. The social and emotional adjustment of deaf adults. *The Volta Review*, 1964, 66, 319–325.

O'Connor, C.D. Benefits of an oral climate for all deaf children. *The Volta Review*, 1957, 59, 335–337.

Ogden, P.W. *Experiences and attitudes of oral deaf adults regarding oralism*. Unpublished doctoral dissertation, University of Illinois, 1979.

Rodda, M. Social adjustment of hearing impaired adolescents. *The Volta Review*, 1966, 68, 279–283.

Stewart, H.L. The social adjustment of the deaf. *American Annals of the Deaf*, 1943, 88, 127–130.

Van Uden, A. *Should parents play the principal or a supporting role in the education of deaf children?* Lecture given to Federation of Parents' Associations in Schools for the Deaf, Utrecht, February 5, 1977.

19

the effect of oral education on the attitudes of the family and the environment toward deafness

edgar l. lowell

The title of this paper, "The Effect of Oral Education on the Attitudes of the Family and the Environment Toward Deafness," should be viewed as a companion piece to the preceding paper, "The Effect of Oral Education on the Attitudes of Deaf Persons Toward the Hearing Environment." The earlier paper is concerned with the attitudes of deaf persons, whereas this paper is concerned with attitudes of society toward the deaf person, and more particularly the effect of oral education on those attitudes. I am assuming that the term "society" is fairly close to what the organizers meant by "the family and the environment."

I shall deal first with the attitudes of society toward the deaf person, and then with the effect of oral education on those attitudes. It is appropriate at this point to concede that this is an extremely challenging task because of the wide range of meanings that can be attached to two of the terms used in the title of this paper, and the misunderstandings that can result therefrom.

When we speak of an "oral education," at least in the United States, we may be describing educational programs that differ widely in their quality. There are a number of programs that represent very poor oralism. I regret I cannot cite the research evidence to document my statements, I can only speculate on some of the possible causes.

One cause for poor teaching, be it oral or total, may have had its roots in our government's program to stimulate the training of more teachers of the deaf by financially supporting teacher training programs. In 1960–61 we had 25 programs and prepared 177 teachers. The need at that time was estimated at 500 teachers per year. The federal legislation (P.L. 87–276) to financially assist teacher preparation programs was passed in 1961, and by 1964 the number of training programs had increased from 25 to 51 and the number of graduates increased from 177 to 559. The only problem was that there simply were not enough qualified and experienced faculty to adequately staff all of the new programs. The inevitable consequence was that the quality of the training programs suffered, with the further result that some of the educational programs where the graduates of these programs were employed also experienced a decline in quality. I have heard many arguments about oralism and manualism, where examples of poor oral programs were used as a representation of oralism. I do not wish to belabor this point, but I should make it clear that in this discussion I am talking about "good" oral programs.

The term "deafness" also deserves some comment. Although the organizers have provided us with a decibel definition of deafness, it is difficult to accurately characterize "deafness" or "the deaf." We use these terms for convenience, but it is well to keep in mind that they are overgeneralizations, that all deaf people are not alike. Attitudes about individual deaf people will be influenced by many other personal factors which would vary from individual to individual. For convenience in this paper, I will continue to speak about "the deaf" and try to deal with some of the more general factors influencing attitudes toward all deaf people.

Deviance

In considering society's attitude toward deafness, it may help us to start with the concept of deviance (Rhodes & Tracy, 1974). In contrast to the concept of disability which designates a defective organism as the central problem, deviance is culturally defined. It usually refers to a specially identified or labeled group such as "the deaf" and views their problem as a product of the encounters between the labeled group and the dominant culture. There are usually three components to deviance; rule breaking by specific individuals or groups (in this case, the deaf), negative evaluation by others (in this case, society), and punishment.

Rule Breaking

For the deaf, the rule breaking is in their failure to communicate in a normal and expected fashion—that is, the way other members of society do. There are several lines of reasoning that support the view that failure to communicate in a normal and expected fashion is construed as rule breaking and is the basis for labeling the deaf as deviant.

First, society has a great many social rules, ranging from explicit and public rules, such as published laws, to much more subtle and implicit but nonetheless important rules. As Scheff (1966) has pointed out, there are many examples of these subtle and implicit types of rules. One example is the norms governing eye contact during conversation. "A person engaged in conversation is expected to face toward his partner, rather than directly away from him and to stand at a proper conversational distance, neither one inch away nor across the room." We have similar rules about communication. We expect other people in our society to use our language and to use speech that approximates our own. When they do not, they are breaking the rules.

Second, the rule breaking of the deaf in the area of communication is an example of behavior which does not conform to our expectancies. It is easy to overlook the power of our expectancies; the extent to which expectancies control our behavior, and how upset we are when our expectancies are not confirmed. I expect that when I turn the key in the ignition, my car will start. If it does not, I am upset. When I drive the car to work, I expect that people will drive on the proper side of the road, will stop at stop signals, and will signal before they turn. If my expectations fail, I will be upset, or possibly injured.

Expectancies explain why we are more comfortable with old friends than with strangers. We know what to expect from old friends and do not have to be attentive to a "new" situation. When the deaf person does not communicate as we expect another person to, our expectancies are not confirmed, and we are upset. This is a very real experience. If I were to suddenly sit on the floor and continue reading this paper, it would produce an uneasy reaction from many of you. I am certain that the chairman would be disturbed, and the rest of the audience would become much more attentive as you prepared to cope with this "new" situation. After all, one does not expect to have a paper delivered by someone seated on the floor.

It is very likely that the degree of unrest or distress resulting from the failure to confirm expectations is a function of the viewer's own state of adjustment or self-confidence. The uncertain, insecure individual is likely to be more uncomfortable or upset than the well-adjusted, self-confident person. The naive hearing person—if uncertain and insecure—who does not understand the communication attempt of the deaf person may wonder whether the failure to communicate is his own fault.

Still another argument for failure to communicate in a normal fashion as the "rule breaking" which sets the deaf apart, is that this is the major dimension of difference between the hearing and deaf person. There is no other visual stigmata associated with deafness that could explain the consequences we will be discussing.

Negative Evaluation

Rule breaking automatically includes a negative evaluation. If rule breaking is not negatively evaluated, then the social and cultural values supported by the rules are in jeopardy. There are many examples of this negative evaluation. The deprecatory labels "dummy" or "deaf and dumb" are classic examples.

Another example of this negative evaluation is seen in Blood et al.'s (1977) study about observers' impressions of children with and without hearing aids.

Observers rated slides of normal-hearing children with and without hearing aids and heard recordings of the children's speech. To avoid bias, the situation was structured so that observers did not rate the same child both with and without hearing aids. Observers rated each child on a semantic differential scale regarding intelligence, achievement, personality, and appearance. More negative ratings were elicited by the children wearing hearing aids.

Punishment

The third component of deviance, along with rule breaking and negative evaluation, is punishment. It is clear that the deaf are punished by society. A catalogue of these punishments is contained in the cases handled by our National Center for Law and the Deaf which has been using legal action to ensure the rights and privileges guaranteed to all citizens by our Constitution, but which have in the past been denied the deaf, at least in part, because of their deafness.

There are other examples of punishment or discrimination. Vernon (1970) reports discrimination against the deaf individual in opportunities to enter teacher training programs and discrimination in hiring practices in school systems. When the deaf person is hired as a teacher of the deaf, Vernon reports that they are often assigned more extra duties than hearing teachers, are assigned classes of slow and multiply handicapped children, and develop feelings of hopelessness and frustration regarding their own future as professionals.

In the nationwide survey of deaf people by Lunde and Bigman (1959) it was found that deaf persons were consistently underemployed as compared with the hearing population. So it would appear that there is negative evaluation and a form of punishment or discrimination against the deaf for their deviance.

So far, it has been proposed that society's attitudes toward the deaf can at least be partially explained in terms of a sociological concept of deviance which proposes that the deaf break certain societal rules by failing to confirm society's expectation about how communication will take place. This deviance is negatively evaluated, which is the basis for the formation of negative attitudes toward the deaf.

Learning Theory

There are other types of analysis that might have been employed. The learning theorist might argue that on an individual basis, attitudes toward the deaf might be formed, or at least largely influenced, by the hearing person's experience in social interaction with the deaf person. This line of argument suggests that reinforcement in social interaction will occur when the interaction is satisfying or pleasant for both parties, and that when reinforcement occurs it is likely that the social interaction will be continued and repeated. Conversely, when the interaction is unsatisfactory, or unpleasant, there will be no positive reinforcement, and it is likely that the social interaction will be terminated and will not likely be reinstituted.

Unless one is masochistic, I believe that this analysis applies rather generally. I know that if I am in a social gathering where English is not the primary language being spoken, I will gravitate toward those individuals who speak English. I would find it fairly nonreinforcing to spend a social hour with a group of non-English speaking persons. If the discussion was purely social, I would probably find some excuse to leave the group. If they were discussing information that it was important for me to have, I would probably find the experience frustrating and unpleasant. This is a sad commentary on my poor linguistic ability, but I believe such a situation would put me in the same situation as the deaf person. If communication cannot take place, or does so only haltingly or imperfectly, it will not be a pleasant situation and generally unfavorable attitudes toward such interaction will develop.

Subculture

Another concept which deserves some mention in this discussion of attitudes toward deafness is that of the subculture. In some respects the deaf do behave like a subculture. In a study of 10,101 deaf persons in the United States, Lunde and Bigman (1959) reported that of the 6,745 who were married, 93.9 percent were married to deaf or hard-of-hearing persons. The authors went on to point out that the population covered by their survey was probably "the deaf community," those who identified themselves primarily as deaf and associated primarily with other deaf persons.

It is likely that the means of communication is the agent that binds this group together. Those who choose manual communication will communicate more readily with others who use manual communication.

If the deaf are identified and labeled as a subgroup, they run the risk of engendering the negative attitudes that grow up about other minority subcultures.

The title of this paper referred to both the family and the environment, which I have referred to as "society" during much of this discussion. It may be appropriate to say a few words about some of the obvious distinctions between the reactions of the family and the rest of society.

I think it is safe to characterize society's attitude about the deaf as disinterest. The vast majority of the hearing have little knowledge of deafness, no contact with deaf people, and consequently very little interest in deafness. When there is contact, it is apt to be minimal and for reasons discussed in this paper quite likely to lead to negative attitudes.

The family, on the other hand, is understandably very personally and deeply concerned about deafness. From our experience at the John Tracy Clinic, I think it is difficult to attempt to generalize about parental attitudes toward deafness. Each individual copes in whatever way he can. It may be useful to distinguish between the attitudes at the time of discovery of the deafness, and their attitudes later on. Altschuler (1974) argues that:

> Parental reaction to the discovery is inevitably depression. Nothing quite matches the creative scope of giving life, and it is imbued with all the unresolved fantasies

and wishes of one's own early development. To the mother it is often a fulfillment, a restoration in wishful disproof of any previous deficiencies . . . for the father it is also an extension of self and a demonstration of primeval potency. The presence of a defect is a blow to such aspirations and it is reacted to in proportion to the intensity with which they are present . . .

Others have described the impact of the discovery of a deaf child in the family in terms of mourning and grief reactions.

Regardless of the explanatory concepts we use, it is clear that the birth of a deaf child has a profound and personal impact on the family, and the attitudes that develop toward the deaf child and deafness in general are undoubtedly the result of many factors which may vary from family to family.

It is sometimes useful in attempting to understand different parental reactions to invoke the concept of psychological strength. Some families who discover their child is deaf have great psychological strength and are able to marshal their energies and apply them to a constructive educational program for their child. Others, possibly because of other stress, are not so psychologically strong, and are completely devastated by the discovery. The reactions cover the entire gamut between these two extremes.

It is very likely that the normal affective bonds that are formed between the mother and infant that are mediated by verbal communication are going to be different. The degree of difference is difficult to predict, but just as we know that having a deaf child will inevitably change some aspects of the family's life, we also know that the affective relations will be different.

Even the parent's expectations will be shattered. As Luterman (1979) has pointed out:

> The parent, when the child is very young, goes to the professional with many expectations. Many of those expectations are violated, albeit through no fault of the professional.
>
> The major violated expectation that most parents have had is the very reasonable one that they will have a normal child. The next expectation is that the professional will take care of them.
>
> The most pervasive and perhaps deadliest expectation concerns what the parents expect of themselves and of the child. That expectation is the anticipation that they will conquer the deafness with absolute aplomb and grace, never feeling despair or anger. They want their family to be a loving and cooperative team with everyone pulling together to produce a super deaf child.

From any point of view, deafness creates a special situation for the family. There are special stresses which each family deals with in its own way, and each family develops its own attitudes toward deafness. These attitudes are likely to be not the same as those of the rest of society, because being familiar with deafness they do not view deaf communication as deviant. They are likely to be more positive and empathetic not only because of the family bond, but because of daily living with deafness, they have a better idea of the special challenges facing the deaf child.

We now come to a consideration of the effect of oral education on the attitudes we have been discussing. Central to what has been said here is the assumption that a good oral education will lead to a deaf person with good oral communication skills.[1]

If negative attitudes develop about the deaf because their communications are judged deviant by the larger society, it follows that the less different from the "normal" their communications are, the less negative will be the attitudes. It seems self-evident that an oral education will produce a person who is able to communicate more "normally" than one who has received a manual education. This is not a judgment about manual communication; it is merely a statement that oral education is more likely to produce a person who can communicate normally, than does manual education.

For the family, the situation is somewhat different. If it is a successful oral education, it must almost invariably involve the cooperation and participation of all other family members. This is why our program at the John Tracy Clinic emphasizes the education of parents so that they can participate more effectively in their child's education. We believe that such a program must have two components: one dealing with the cognitive aspects of developing language and speech, while the other deals with the affective component in which we attempt to help the parents deal constructively with the feelings and attitudes that may have been developed in connection with their child's deafness. The fact that this work is carried on by skillful psychologists and is done in a group of parents who are all sharing the same experiences helps to develop more positive attitudes. In the final analysis, we find it is how the parents feel about themselves that is the most important determiner of how they feel about their deaf child. It is a challenge, but I believe a realistic requirement, if we are to achieve a good oral program.

As a final comment, if things are as bleak as I have presented them, and if the clear-cut prediction is negative attitudes toward the deaf, how is it that I have good, positive, and I hope mutually reinforcing relationships with so many deaf people, particularly in view of the fact that my manual communication skills are practically non-existent. On reflection, I have to admit that many of my positive relationships with deaf people are with those who can communicate with me. But there are enough of the others, that is, those who do not have good oral communication skills, yet with whom I have what I believe to be a very positive and mutually rewarding relationship. I suspect the answer is in part because there are some very remarkable deaf people. Individuals who can persist despite all the problems that have been discussed in this paper and yet still develop positive relationships with hearing people. Truly remarkable!

---

[1]We know that this is not always the case. For reasons which we are just beginning to understand, there are some who do not seem to benefit from oral education. This raises an interesting point. Do we blame our oral failures on the system, that is, on oralism, or on an imperfect application of oralism? From what I have said earlier about poor oral education, you might guess that my preference would be to first blame the application rather than the system. I feel that too often it may be easier to "give up" on oralism than to put forth the effort it clearly requires.

References

Altschuler, K. Z. The social and psychological development of the deaf child: Problems, their treatment and prevention. *American Annals of the Deaf*, 1974, 4, 119.

Argyle, M. *Social interaction*. New York: Atherton Press, 1967.

Blood, G. W., Blood, I. M., & Danhaver, J. L. The hearing aid "effect." *Hearing Instrument*, 1977, 6, 28.

Lunde, A. S., & Bigman, S. K. *Occupational conditions among the deaf*. Washington, DC: Gallaudet College, 1959.

Luterman, D. *Counseling parents of hearing-impaired children*. Boston: Little Brown, 1979.

Rhodes, W. C., & Tracy, M. L. *A study of child variance, (Vol. 1, conceptual models)*. Ann Arbor: University of Michigan Press, 1974.

Scheff, T. *Being mentally ill*. Chicago: Aldine, 1966.

Vernon, McCay. The role of deaf teachers in the education of deaf children. *The Deaf American*, 1970, 22.

reaction to 18 and 19

david manning

The theme of today's meeting—"The Social-Emotional Development During School Life and After"—is of particular interest to me because I am the parent of a deaf teenager, and because my responsibility as Mainstream Coordinator at the Clarke School is to follow up on its graduates as they complete their education with hearing students.

Listening to the two papers that have just been given, I was aware of their contrasting tone. Dr. Fellendorf, in speaking about the attitudes of deaf people toward hearing people, has used words such as: satisfaction, comfortable, acceptance, tolerance, positive, confidence, and well-being. Dr. Lowell, on the other hand, spoke of the hearing environment using words such as: deviant, rule-breaking, negative evaluation, punishment, and disinterested. I find this contrast in attitudes very interesting, and I would like to speak about this in relation to my work in mainstreaming because it applies there. The teenagers I follow are not included in Dr. Fellendorf's study, but they are enrolled in one of the schools involved in his study, and will one day be oral deaf adults. Right now, they are going through a series of very challenging social and emotional events which will affect how they feel as adults.

Dr. Fellendorf has reported that the oral deaf adults in his study have "positive attitudes toward the hearing environment, are tolerant of their hearing peers, and feel comfortable in their company." The experience I am having with high school students in New England presents a view of life that is more complicated than this. Perhaps in the future, they will develop the attitudes described by Dr. Fellendorf, but I strongly believe their feelings about the hearing environment will be more complex than those reported in his study.

Most of our deaf graduates now attend regular public high schools that are large regional facilities with enrollments of up to 3,000 students. They are complex environments with layers of administrative officials; guidance counselors with case loads of 300 to 400 students; computers that arrange all schedules; and unions that impose restrictions on the tasks the teachers are asked to perform. The enrollments in these schools are so large that students often know only a small number of their peers, and they know only those teachers with whom they come in direct contact. It is essential in an atmosphere like this that the students understand the workings of the system in order to be able to negotiate with it so that it will work for them.

This kind of educational environment presents a great many problems to a deaf youngster, even though he is oral. And experience has shown us that it is too complicated a system to expect most students to handle entirely on their own. Thus a closely coordinated support system is recommended through Public Law 94-142 that will insure the provision of a variety of academic services to the student to help him succeed.

As he enters this kind of school, the deaf student has to wrestle with a new reality: being deaf in a normal school. He has to adapt to the teaching style of an instructor who has never taught a deaf person before. He has to learn to speak up when he is confused, even though the teacher might not understand him. He has to try to make friends with students who perhaps have never known another deaf person. He has to keep gathering information about the activities and duties in the school each day so that he will know which ones he is being held responsible for. He has to keep checking to be sure that a problem is not developing and, in the event one does, he must learn how to go about solving it. He has to learn how to pull all of the loose ends together so that he can be as self-sufficient as possible.

The greatest challenge this youngster has to cope with, in my opinion, is the feelings he has about his deafness and the way others relate to him. He is the product of an oral educational program and home life that Owrid (1972) points out has a strong belief in the value of spoken language; has people trained and interested in talking to him all of the time; is understanding of his disability; and provides companionship. This all leads to what Reeves (1977) has called an "optimism" about himself, the world, and his future.

What this student finds when he enters the large public high school is a very different educational environment; one which has a different understanding of him and his disability, and one that will not provide the same quality of support he is accustomed to. He has to learn to live with the fact that most people don't know very much about his deafness. He has to learn to handle people who want to help him, but talk down to him; people who want to think for him, or who think of him in stereo-typical ways. He has to try to understand the reasons some people will not make the effort to engage in normal and satisfying conversation with him. All of these efforts to cope with this new environment bring him to a new understanding of himself, his deafness, and how effectively and independently he can function in the everyday world. And this is in addition to the normal adolescent adjustments he has to make. Every time he changes to a new set of courses, he will go through these adjustments again because the integration he is attempting is a process, not a one-time thing.

My observation of our students as they have moved through their various schools is that the element that remains constant during this time of change in their lives is the family. My contacts with a large number of parents have shown me that they are the ones who play the major role in helping their child learn to cope with his disability and develop positive attitudes toward life. The parents' ability to deal in a tolerant fashion with the problems that accompany deafness, while at the same time showing their child respect, encouragement, and acceptance, helps the child learn to do the same. But the family's ability to do this depends on the experience their child is having at any one time, and for this reason there is a great need for help and guidance for the parents and the child on a long-term basis.

Most of the students with whom I work have parents who give them strong support at home and, therefore, do not let their problems dominate their lives. They are able to enjoy most activities in their schools and are able to make up for the things they miss through outside activities. The optimism Reeves referred to is apparently not lost, though it is moderated. It is not surprising to me to see that the value of this parental support is recognized by the oral deaf adults in Dr. Fellendorf's study.

So even though it has been my impression that most of the adolescent people with whom I work have a generally positive attitude toward the hearing environment, it has been made clear to me repeatedly that these people also have some specific attitudes that are less positive about their interactions with hearing people. This is where I run into difficulty with the Fellendorf study we have just heard. It is surprising to me that the adults who were questioned had nothing to say about the social and emotional pressures they feel each day and how these affect their attitude about the world and themselves. Are they really this positive about all parts of their lives with hearing people?

It appears to me that Dr. Fellendorf's study might present a more complete picture of a deaf person's point of view if, in addition to their comments about being able to communicate with hearing people, there was information from them regarding their feelings. This would be very helpful information for all of us, especially for those younger people who are just beginning the struggle to find a place for themselves in their communities, and who need advice on possible ways to cope.

I am in strong agreement with the recommendations in Dr. Fellendorf's paper, particularly with regard to parent and student counseling on the secondary level. Clarke School has recently added to its staff a guidance counselor who is a former Clarke School student. He went through an ordinary school and understands what it is like. He is now working with our students who are preparing to graduate, trying to help them understand what they are facing. He is also doing the same thing with their parents.

Dr. Lowell has said that the hearing environment is indifferent to deafness. I think we should mention here, however, the increasing interest the United States government has been taking during the last ten years or so on behalf of all disabled people. P.L. 94-142 and Section 504 of the Rehabilitation Act of 1973 are two examples of this. It remains to be seen what the long-term effects of this governmental action will be, and how it will affect the attitudes of hearing people.

In conclusion, Clarke School graduates have been completing their education with normally hearing students in ordinary schools since 1875. That's 104 years. This was not a decision that was made by Clarke School. It was a choice that was made by the graduates and their families. Oral education made that choice possible.

References

Owrid, H. L., Education and communication, *Volta Review*, 1972, 74, pp. 225–234.
Reeves, J. K., Scope for oralism, *Volta Review*, 1977, 79, pp. 43–54.

20

a perspective on the mental health of young deaf adults in modern society
d. robert frisina

What I have to say about the mental health of young deaf adults in modern society comes principally from the experience of nurturing the first decade of growth in the National Technical Institute for the Deaf (NTID) in the U.S.A. The setting for the spawning of NTID has been the Rochester Institute of Technology, a 10-college institution for hearing students currently in its 150th year. The rationale for the establishment of NTID lay in the reality that only a handful of deaf persons completing secondary schools were qualified for entrance to a regular college or university. As a consequence, in a time of advancing technology, deaf people found themselves at a severe disadvantage. This disadvantage resulted from the lack of preparation needed to enter the economic mainstream on a par with their hearing peers. NTID came into existence as a hope for reversing this negative outcome for young deaf adults.

Profound deafness from birth or early life, as we are all painfully aware, is an enduring challenge. So many correct and timely events and actions must occur in order to overcome the obstacles placed in the paths of the individual, the family, and those who study and teach on their behalf. This circumstance is no less so for the students for whom NTID was intended: a target population broad-gauged in terms of educational attainment levels. NTID serves a group of deaf students whose educational levels upon completion of a secondary (high school) experience range from the eighth grade and above. In truth the reading levels of these students and their overall educational achievement levels are skewed toward the eighth grade end of the continuum; this in spite of an average of 14 years of instruction and training prior to entrance to NTID; this in spite of their average age at entrance to NTID of 19.5 years with 28 percent between 17.0 and 18.0 years, 63 percent between 18.1 and 22.0 years, and 9 percent over 22.1 years of age.

They tend to be fragmented and limited in their understanding of the world around them and somewhat unfinished with respect to their personal strengths and abilities to advance themselves independently. This is partly because they are young people in a modern society, and partly because they are deaf, and have been so since they were born or very shortly thereafter.

Their communication skills vary one to the next and as a group they still have room for improvement in all the expressive and receptive modes of communication and language. They come to us, some with a curious blend of hope and wonderment and pristine innocence, some with great enthusiasm and sense of direction, and a few with sordid histories and irrevocable scars. These are our young people, unfinished perhaps, but our future and our mutual responsibility.

As a consequence, it would not be far-fetched to say that NTID, as we consciously fashioned it, is an educational system devoted to improving the mental health of young deaf adults who are destined to live in a modern society; a support system dedicated to getting their lives under their own control.

Dimensions of Mental Health

Theories of personality, theories of learning and of behavior, tests of psychological functioning, and psychotherapeutic methodologies are many and diverse. All of these are subsets to what we might call "mental health." Qualifiers to the term "mental health" generally refer to the state of one's relation to self and/or the quality of one's relationship with others. That is, status, conditions, or descriptions of one's mental health generally relate either to intra-individual strengths and weaknesses or to one's success or failure in interpersonal relations. Irrespective of diversity in theory and methodology down through the years, descriptions of the state of one's mental health are surprisingly similar. As we concern ourselves with the subject of mental health of young deaf adults in modern society, it might be well to set before us examples in common use.

Conditions or Traits that Connote a Healthy State

- good sense of own identity
- realistic self-regard
- feelings of self-worth
- confidence in one's own abilities
- ability to accept a range of emotions
- seeing oneself as growing in important ways
- feelings of belonging to a world larger than self and family
- ability to cope
- ability to deal with stress
- ability to deal with distress
- ability to distinguish reality from perception

- ability to assess the self realistically
- ability to tolerate human differences
- ability to learn self-management
- sensitivity to the feelings of others
- commitment to some form of work or vocation
- ability to work toward goals
- ability to trust oneself as well as others
- ability to deal effectively with feelings and attitudes about people and events
- others

Suspended Adolescence

This paper recognizes that modern societies become so, and remain so, on the bases of their advanced technology, well-established industry and commerce, and extensive educational systems. Consequences of "modernizing" a society, particularly as experienced in open societies, include:
- a higher standard of living, i.e., a broad array of consumer goods and appliances
- affluence
- job mobility
- geographic mobility
- diversified work force
- requirement of more education and training of its workers and citizens
- mass communication networks
- decline in traditional work ethic
- breakdown in stability of the family
- virtual elimination of the extended family structure
- change from an attitude of saving to one of consuming
- an increased emphasis on "I and me" and less on "thee"

In aggregate these tend to create a period of "suspended adolescence." Under these conditions, moving from a dependent status to one of assuming full responsibility for self, and shortly thereafter responsibility for others, constitutes a challenge for any young person deaf since birth or very early in life. Making it through successfully is indeed a remarkable achievement. It is not surprising that the period of suspended adolescence tends to be prolonged in deaf people whenever suitable educational and experiential opportunities are not made available on a par with those who hear.

Comprehensive View of Mental Health for Young Deaf Adults

Mental health as used in this presentation is best achieved and exemplified when one's life is under one's own control. Achieving this goal and maintaining it in an industrial society challenges the best in each of us. The NTID experience suggests that in order to get there, and to stay there, six personal accomplishments are necessary.

1. **A Marketable Skill.** It is difficult to be a competent generalist in a highly specialized world. A special talent or area of competence is essential to begin the process of making it on one's own as an adult. Whether it be in engineering, in art or in philosophy, a negotiable technical competence that society values and rewards is essential. With experience and further knowledge one's technical competence and career options become broader. One's sense of self-worth is enhanced as a marketable skill is developed. It is the true beginning of getting one's life under one's own control in a modern society.

2. **Personal Maturity.** Self-esteem development is a process very much alive in the young adult who is striving for independence, for confidence in one's own abilities, for a good sense of one's own identity, and for the spiritual dimensions of one's life. It is at this juncture in one's life that the learning of self-management is so critical. Getting one's emotions under reasonable control marks the movement from a self-oriented person to one who becomes sensitive to the feelings of others. Personal maturity assumes the ability to trust oneself with a quality that enables a display of trust in others. This characteristic is essential for becoming a reliable member of a group, and with experience to become a leader whether at work or in one's community. Until an adult-like level of personal maturity is achieved it is unlikely that social maturity can be attained.

3. **Social Maturity.** Losing oneself in others is probably the highest form of social maturity, the essence of which is to take on responsibility for others. Marriage and family, supervision in the work place, and leadership in the community are all manifestations of this personal quality. Successful dealings with others are founded on seeing the self as growing in important ways and an emerging realization of belonging to a world larger than self.

4. **Communication Proficiency.** The ability to use one's native language in its variety of forms is of real significance in attaining one's personal and economic goals in a modern society. By and large the modern work force is an information-based work force. Data bases in large measure lie beneath critical decisions made in the work place. Linguistic competence and communication abilities are significant to upward mobility. Failure to advance according to one's aspirations and expectations because of communication and/or linguistic deficiencies can be personally defeating. A modern society is fraught with this danger, and especially when one's language and/or communication skills are somehow limited.

5. **Perspective.** One who has developed a measure of personal and social maturity, a marketable skill, and a reasonable communication and language fluency is well on the way to becoming a psychologically healthy person. Yet in today's world more is needed. Because there are few quick and simple solutions to complex problems, the attitude of "absolutes mentality" is rarely germane. The ability to tolerate shades of gray requires a deeper understanding of history, cultures, economic systems, political systems, and general knowledge that is cumulating at a quickened pace. The ability to view current situations, activities, or events in some larger context is an attribute of great personal and psychological value in a rapidly changing world.

6. **Self-Generated Learner.** The goal of educators must certainly be to have their charges become self-generated learners. The oft repeated statistic that scientists alive today exceed the cumulative number in history is, of course, significant. Knowledge is cumulating at a pace that tends to render obsolete many in the work force. Continuing education in a modern society is becoming commonplace. Life-long learning, once a fresh concept, is fast becoming a necessity. The mature adult and psychologically secure individual is one who has developed a commitment to self-improvement and one who thereby maintains confidence in his own abilities to the extent that assures that one's life is under one's control.

These six personal characteristics are nurtured within both formal and informal arrangements. Career choices at RIT exceed more than 150 in all, ranging from engineering to art. The significance of a marketable technical competence is basic and has been emphasized. Some of the ways in which the other five target areas are approached are suggested next.

Culturally Enriching Courses
- Language and literature
- Social sciences
- Humanities
- Personal development

Students Learn About Themselves and Others
- Psychology
- Sociology
- History
- Philosophy and religion

Personal Growth
- Experimental educational theater
- Human sexuality
- Personal finance
- Leadership development

Social Awareness and Self-Confidence
- Work-study programs
- Volunteer work in community

Independent Learning
- Learning centers in math, physics, English, general education, and science

Career Exploration
- Summer vestibule program for learning, testing, exploring, choosing

These are simply illustrative of institutional efforts supporting the growth and development of its students. Anything but a comprehensive approach to this type of student population is likely to fall far short of the mark. We are encouraged by our placement record that shows 97 percent placed in jobs; 93 percent placed in employment situations commensurate with their level of training and education; 80 percent employed in private industry and business; 12 percent employed in government; 8 percent working in educational environments. It is especially noteworthy that the range and types of work and the sector of the economy to which the graduates distribute themselves are consistent with their fellow Rochester Institute of Technology graduates who are not deaf.

Dimensions of Consequence in a Modern Society

Industrialization. Modern societies are industrialized societies. Industrial nations have work forces that reflect high levels of technology and professional services. High levels of technology and professional services require more, not less, education. Whether deaf adults are included as *bona fide* participants in the economic mainstream depends upon their opportunities and abilities to obtain the education necessary to compete successfully in the open marketplace. That is, unless extreme egalitarianism or hereditary privilege determines what happens to whom. In those modern societies where performance dominates as precursor to economic rewards and status, genuine opportunities are *sine qua non*.

Work force requirements of a modern society have characteristics that will continually challenge young deaf adults and all who care about them. The personal and social skills required to move successfully within a modern society continue to increase in their complexity. Communication proficiency and linguistic competence influence choice and place in the work force. Technical skills, managerial abilities, and professional talents are highly valued and rewarded. For the type of persons focused on at this conference, failure to gain experience and attain levels of education that prepare them for successful employment is likely to have a deleterious effect on their mental health.

Comparative Risks. The implications for mental health in young deaf adults are not equal in all industrial societies. It is true that the professional and technical competencies required to support a modern society are somewhat similar in the open and closed society. One the other hand, the personal, social, and managerial requirements vary dramatically in accordance with political and economic systems practiced. Centrally controlled governments and stratified societies are similar in terms of their possible influence on the mental health of their citizens. Since opportunity is limited, expectations are limited. Personal risk-taking for status and economic reward is limited. In the free and open society where performance is a major criterion for status and advancement, the risk to one's self-esteem and mental health can be seen to be greater. Gardner (1971) captured the essence of this concept in the following:

> In a society of hereditary privilege, an individual of humble position might not have been wholly happy with his lot, but he had never had reason to look forward to any other fate. Never having had prospects of betterment, he could hardly be disillusioned. He entertained no hopes, but neither was he nagged with ambition. When the new democracies removed the ceiling on expectations, nothing could be more satisfying for those with energy, ability and emotional balance to meet the challenge. But to the individual lacking in these qualities, the new system was

fraught with danger. Lack of ability, lack of energy or lack of aggressiveness led to frustration and failure. Obsessive ambition led to emotional breakdown. Unrealistic ambitions led to bitter defeats.

In a questionable sort of way, young deaf adults in closed societies are also being "protected" from these risks.

Insights from the NTID Experience. Experience with nearly three thousand young deaf adults suggests that the great majority of deaf children upon whom this conference is centered can succeed in a modern society—provided that many "correct" things are made to happen along the way. Experience suggests, also, that my colleagues at this conference have for a long time helped these "correct" experiences to accrue in many deaf children on their way to young adulthood. Much unfinished business, however, still remains.

Experience suggests, too, that only a very small percentage of young deaf adults in modern societies are receiving educational and training preparation that truly fits their personal and social needs for gaining access to the socioeconomic mainstream on a par with their hearing peers.

Four observations emanating from the NTID experience are offered for your consideration and discussion:

- The mental health status of young deaf adults is not developed to the level that qualifies them for jobs in the open marketplace on a par with hearing peers of similar chronological age.
- Conventional secondary education as terminal formal education is insufficient preparation for an increasing number of jobs in a modern society.
- Information and knowledge pertaining to the personal, social, and professional/technical requirements in the workplace are not well understood by young deaf adults themselves and many with whom they have contact.
- When provided genuine learning opportunities, young deaf adults can develop the necessary personal, social, technical, and linguistic skills to compete successfully in the open marketplace of a modern society.

Mental Health Trends and Realities

New Interest. When NTID opened its doors to students in 1968, postsecondary opportunities were being utilized by only a handful of deaf students except for the several hundred attending Gallaudet College. Likewise at that time it was unusual to find professionals trained in psychology or psychiatry and who had a working knowledge and experience with deaf people. During the past decade a welcome change has taken place in the general interest level on the part of social workers, counseling psychologists, and psychiatrists. Community interest has heightened, and hospital units to accommodate deaf persons on an in-patient basis have become available in at least a dozen locations. One of the outcomes of the past decade has been a consensus that to satisfy the counseling needs of deaf people, (1) straight educational training is not sufficient, (2) straight counseling or psychological training is not satisfactory, (3) rather, the combination of professional training in psychology with a knowledge base in deafness is essential. NTID currently has 20 full-time professionals with dual training.

The Educational Milieu. During the late '60s and early '70s campus life in colleges and universities was suffering from a permissiveness and a form of "organized chaos." It was not the most propitious time to begin a new program—particularly within the context of an existing university. The concept of *in loco parentis* had been challenged in the courts, the results of which placed the universities in a tenant-landlord posture as opposed to viewing residence living as a significant part of the educational process. There are signs now visible that a new version of *in loco parentis* is likely to emerge: one that contains expectations on the part of students to respect the rights and choices of others relative to the conditions and mores of residence life. The students themselves are asking for public calmness and quiet and the respecting of one's privacy. At the same time, parents are beginning to exert more influence on students and their choice of universities. In association with the steadily rising costs of education, parents and students alike are becoming more attuned to the concept of "economic return on investment." They are beginning to ask aloud what employment options are likely to result from a degree from this or that college.

General Counseling Needs of NTID Students. Threads of continuity from the larger society are apparent in the psychological makeup of NTID students overall.

The mobility associated with living and working in a modern society has resulted in a marked decline in the extended family. Add to this high divorce rates, chemical dependency, and child abuse in the general population and it is apparent that these manifest themselves in the behavior of a small but significant number of deaf students. Upon closer look it appears that the past two decades have popularized a range of childrearing practices. There has been a corresponding emphasis on parent education. It appears to us that these efforts at parent-child relations may not have resulted in a comparative degree of usefulness to deaf children, at least those who are represented at NTID. These observations, for example, stem from case studies of students in counseling who often unknowingly were victims of child abuse. In comparing notes with their classmates they came to the realization that what they had been carrying in their heads as something common to all fearfully emerged as something anomalous, distasteful, and troublesome.

Mental Health Service at NTID

The psychological services offered at NTID result from the demonstrated needs of its students. Twenty professional counselors plus chaplains are involved with 900+ students on roughly a 50:1 ratio. These special services are organized around three distinct student needs: namely, developmental tasks, situational stress, and psychopathology.

Developmental Tasks. Eighty to 90 percent of the students receive counseling in tasks identified as developmental. The nature of the counselor-student relationship is one characterized as an interactive process of problem solving and/or decision making. The two main spheres of activity relate to (1) career problems and decisions and (2) personal problems and decisions.

It is in these sessions, some group and some individual, that (1) the basis for personal independence is established, (2) career goals are identified, (3) educational program directions are selected, (4) the working and social identities of the person are developed, and (5) psychological impediments to embarking on career preparation are dealt with.

Situational Stress. The educational and personal/social distance between an entering student and eventual entrance to employment as an independently operating educated person is indeed great. Nevertheless, they do succeed in large numbers.

1. *Stress as a function of the college environment* itself constitutes a stress that is common to all students, deaf and hearing.
Examples:
   a. Adjustment to absence from home
   b. Adjustment to living with roommate(s)
   c. Anxiety associated with realization that all other students are equally as capable (as differentiated from high school peers)
   d. Fear of academic failure
   e. Coping with failure
   f. Examination week anxieties
   g. Letting off steam before vacations
   h. Anxiety before graduation

2. *Stress Unique to the Student.* Psychological problems occur that are related specifically to the student. The most prevalent would be those reactions to the *college environment* (listed above) that are not resolved and are suggestive of deep-seated problems in an individual. Boyfriend-girlfriend misunderstandings and quarrels can be disruptive to one's adjustment and responsiveness to the educational demands at RIT. Divorce in the family is another cause of problems in students who require counseling. Chemical dependency including alcohol and drug abuse are problems associated with individual students.

3. *Adapting to a Second Disability.* Students who discover a second disabling condition undergo considerable stress in attempting to adjust to the new condition. Cases of recently manifested retinitis pigmentosa can be a terrifying threat to one's hopes and aspirations regarding career development. Two cases of Von Recklenhausen's Disease have been discovered. This appears to be a genetically determined degenerative CNS disorder that combines early deafness with later visual, fine and gross motor defects and is terminal.

Psychopathology. Students with psychopathology are those who require personality restructuring under the direction of a clinical psychologist or a psychiatrist. The causative agents appear to be extensions from general society and would include the scars of child abuse, reaction to divorce in the family, drug abuse and alcoholism.

Examples of behavioral manifestations in this group include severe hypochondria, severe isolation, severe dependency, fantasy career and life goals, degenerative CNS disorder, severe family conflicts, and suicidal threats.

Experience has demonstrated that 80–90 percent of NTID students take advantage of career counseling associated with *developmental tasks*; 80–90 percent are likely to seek help regarding personal problems that respond to *supportive therapy of brief duration;* 5–10 percent of the population are in need of *reconstructive therapy* under the direction of a psychiatrist or clinical psychologist.

Are these demonstrated needs of young deaf people peculiar in their nature and frequency? A recent article concerning students in the college setting is somewhat illuminating in this matter.

Excerpts from an article titled "College Blues" (Beck & Young, 1978) vividly protray some special characteristics and psychological circumstances confronting college students generally:

> Over the next nine months, as many as 78 percent of the 7,500,800 students enrolled in American colleges may suffer some symptoms of depression—roughly a quarter of the student population at any one time. . . .
>
> Triggered by traditional student pressures—including failure to meet personal academic standards, the need to define goals for life and career, and the lack of support systems to fend off lineliness—the depression will be mild or subclinical for about a third of the students who get the campus blues. But for 46 percent of them, however, the depression will be intense enough to warrant professional help. Campus depression will play a role in as many as 500 suicides, which are 50 percent more frequent among college students than among non-students of the same age.
>
> Despite the amount of depression around them, however, depressed students often perceive themselves to be alone. One result is that they often have trouble evaluating the seriousness of their problems and whether or not they should consult a psychiatrist or psychologist.

These observations are essential for understanding and perspective. They also lend credence to the special nature of the college experience, complete with its tensions, challenges, and triumphs.

Closing Comment

In closing let me say that nothing short of a multifaceted approach to mental health is likely to produce desired results in the type of population we are serving and the nature of the society and the work force into which they must fit. We need our young people and what is best in them—and nothing spurs them on better than for them to realize that this notion is genuine. Part of the tonic at NTID is (1) to raise their levels of aspirations, (2) to help them attain worthy personal, educational, and career goals, and (3) hope they see their place and value in the larger society. We have provided the environment and the opportunity and they have responded—who could ask for anything more?

References

Beck, A. T., & Young, J. E. College blues. *Psychology Today*, September 1978, 80, 85–86, 89, 91–92.

Gardner, J. W. *Excellence, can we be equal and excellent too?* New York: Harper & Row, 1971.

reaction to 20

irene w. leigh

I had lost track of a brilliant young deaf oralist. Years later I encountered a mutual deaf acquaintance and inquired as to the whereabouts of this long-lost person. The reply was, "He's either isolated or cracked-up. . . ."

I cannot accept this as a stock answer. But I believe it represents the inherent assumption among many deaf people in the United States that, while efforts need to be made to relate to the society at large, a price is to be paid for attempts at "assimilation." As you have heard all week, there are positive gratifications for the aural/oral deaf adult whose oral communication skills *facilitate* entry into the mainstream of society. In my response to Dr. Frisina's paper, I shall attempt to delineate my perspective of the mental health of the young deaf adult in today's society. It is a perspective taking into account information based on research as well as my professional experience in education and counseling of the deaf and my phenomenological set as a deaf adult in daily contact at home and outside with cross-sections of both deaf and hearing populations.

During the process of development, children increasingly engage in the world around them. Concomitantly, as their self-concept evolves, it is modified by perceptions of the vicissitudes of ongoing experience which occur as a consequence of interactions with significant adults and with their extended environment. Though generalizations are often made, by its very nature, the self-concept can never be a static concept. Research attempts to define the self-percept of deaf individuals have to date failed to produce truly valid conclusions as a consequence of problems arising from linguistic limitations and inadequate test instrumentation. Indications, however, point to deaf self-percept as being more negative in relation to the hearing percept of deafness. For a review of the literature, the reader is referred to articles delineated with an asterisk in the bibliography following this paper. With regard to oral aspects specifically, Sussman in a study concerning the relationship between the self-concepts of deaf adults and their perceived attitude toward deafness found positive correlation between self-rating of oral communication ability and the self-concept. He also found a positive correlation between self-rating of oral communication ability and the deaf adult's perception of hearing people's attitude toward deafness. (23) Substantiating these findings is Fellendorf's research reported here at the Symposium which indicates that for his limited oral deaf adult sample, the percept of the hearing environment is comfortable, having developed as a reaction to "successful oral education" and/or familial support (6). The results imply that those who feel more "oral" also feel less "deviant" in terms of society's parameters of normality.

Dr. Lowell with his presentation has saved me the effort of delineating society's general attitude toward deafness. To reiterate, his ultimate generalization is described as *disinterest,* with propensity towards negativeness (14). Both this description and the research indications cited above imply that hearing people do not understand basically what it means to be deaf. Emerton and Rothman's review of the general research and their study done at NTID capture the essence of this attitudinal description with results revealing a downward trend from initial mildly positive attitudes on the part of hearing college students after some interaction with a deaf "subculture." Interestingly, positive regard seemed to center about one-to-one relationships while negative regard developed as a reaction to certain mannerisms exhibited by the deaf as a group (5). Apparently, individuals who are deaf do not project deviation from society's norms as clearly as the "collective" does, and it is the collective aspect that reinforces negative stereotypes.

Having made an attempt to provide a frame of reference, I shall now respond to specific points in Dr. Frisina's presentation.

Dr. Frisina attributes the causal factors of the tendency toward "fragmentation and limitation" in understanding the world and the unfinished nature of the typical NTID entree to: (1) living in a modern society and (2) deafness. I do not accept the premise that deafness in this particular aspect necessarily reflects definition as a causative factor. To quote Anna Freud: "Heredity factors depend for their pathogenic impact on the accidental influences with which they may interact. Organic defects give rise to the most varied psychological consequences according to the environmental circumstances and the mental equipment of the child." (7) Students are fragmented and limited not because of the deafness but because of inadequacy in terms of evolved communication pathways within familial, educational, and societal settings which result in limitation of environmental input, diminishing utilization of innate abilities, and leading to the creation of stressful intrapersonal development. To view deafness per se as a causative attribute is merely to reinforce a stereotype of deafness as the excuse for limited functioning, thereby reinforcing a negative self-concept for the deaf population. We are meeting this week to explore ways to minimize the pervasive impact of deafness, and in so doing we implicitly acknowledge that deafness does not have to become automatically equated with emotional, social, and educational maladaptation if handled in an optimum manner, depending on individual attributes.

I would like to emphasize that the typical NTID achievement levels are high as contrasted with reports defining national mean grade level achievements for those deaf exiting from educational systems at roughly fourth to fifth grade levels (16). The task for deaf education is self-evident. Even though hundreds of deaf students from the mainstream of public or private education do go on to successful attendance at hearing colleges in the United States, a significantly large number end up selecting postsecondary programs with support systems for the deaf where they join graduates emerging from day and residential schools for the deaf. Not only may the reasons be based on educational inadequacies and lack of experiental input, but also on attributes related to one's sense of adequacy/inadequacy within hearing or deaf social settings or, in other words, one's sense of isolation/non-isolation, his definition of this sense and the degree of acceptance of this sense. To put it simply, if you cannot accept the nature of your participation, you try to search for compatible compromises. Let me quote from a successful product of mainstreaming:

> I think mainstreaming is both a triumph and a challenge . . . In one sense it is good experience. School can be a microcosm of the real world the child must face upon leaving the security of home. But it can also mean a lot of hard knocks at a tender age. (22).

In view of the general disinterest on the part of society and the known tendency of many children/adolescents not attuned to acceptance of individual differences to be unwittingly insensitive and/or cruel to those who do not totally conform to popular modes of interpersonal relationships, one begins to sense the possible price to be paid as the mainstreamed deaf person strives for acceptance. Those who survive the stressful experiences are rewarded by increasing self-esteem.

Erikson describes the adolescent stage as involving a search for identity, with a certain amount of time necessary for one's internalization in a complex environment. There is a significant pause before a separate sense of identity is confirmed. Those from schools for the deaf often need help in separating their identity from that of their school and in establishing patterns of adjustment to deafness that aid in independent functioning (20). An added variable includes the linguistic limitations imposed by deafness which may compound the adolescent's communication problems resulting in alienation from the parents that seems part of the American adolescent's search for identity (4). I suggest that those in the mainstream who are successful often have to work through dependency patterns based on parental guidance and intervention, though I am not denying the need for that guidance and intervention. If the task of identity definition is incomplete, fixation in or regression to patterns of dependency in various manifestations is likely to occur.

I have expounded on adolescence in order to elaborate on Dr. Frisina's usage of the term "prolonged suspended adolescence" in application to deaf individuals. This term serves to reinforce various research studies which among other characteristics cite the immaturity, poor social judgment, and fragmentation due to the deaf individual's distorted perception of reality. (11,17,20) Considering the extent of the impact developmentally from social, educational, and career perspectives, I appreciate Dr. Frisina's view of the prolongation from the mental health perspective as a healthy adjustment rather than "a failure coming out of the educational system." It institutionalizes normalization of the need for extra time to navigate the transition from the protected home/school environment to society at large, depending on the level of the deaf individual at secondary school completion. The utilization of comprehensive services during this transition facilitates maximization of opportunities to complete the adolescent phase psychologically, and psychic damage from reinforcement of incompetency is minimized. I must applaud the foundations NTID has laid in fulfilling its goal to make the transition of the young deaf adult to the extremely competitive American society. Some programs as comprehensive as NTID's and some even more so utilize very individualized support services for those less advanced than NTID's population. They are beginning to emerge in the United

States as a reaction to the inherent fact of the deaf population's difficulty in achieving competitive status in an increasingly automated society. Nonetheless, young deaf adults being made aware of these programs need to comprehend the ultimate goal of independent functioning and problem-solving postures apart from the family and/or school setting that nurtured them.

Referring to the observations emanating from the NTID experience, I would like to take a moment to focus on the fourth one:

> When provided genuine learning opportunities, young deaf adults can develop the necessary personal, social, technical, and linguistic skills to compete successfully in the open market place of a modern society.

I see before me the proverbial question, "What comes first, the chicken or the egg?" A modicum of mental health is required to ensure receptivity of learning. If one is depressed or distracted by personal problems, genuine learning opportunities become under utilized. The Mental Health Department at the Lexington School for the Deaf came into existence in reaction to the rise of emotional problems that increasingly had an adverse effect upon classroom learning. Annually, 10–15 percent of the total school population are referred for some form of mental health intervention (13). This is where the area of preventive mental health can come to the fore as parents work through the initial mourning reaction to diagnosis of their child's deafness to maintain as much as possible the development of a solid foundation based on accepting parent-child interaction as a precursor to and concomitant with emotional readiness for formal learning. Controlled research focusing on the relationship of early intervention and the quality dimensions of the parent-child emotional bond to the educational process of the deaf child is still in its infancy, although it is generally accepted that supportive parental attitudes and adjustment together with readily accessible communication input have implications in terms of facilitating the rearing of deaf children.

I feel impelled to react to Section C by saying we need to view dimensions of mental health as variables rather than as absolutes, reflected by the varied stress factors of the relevant society that nurtures them and sets for them the boundaries of patterns for adjustment. Unquestionably, competition is a factor in modern society, made inherent by the pressure of population growth. It is a struggle for all of us to move through Maslow's hierarchy of needs from physical need satisfaction to the self-actualizing level. But permeating through all the risks/requirements inherent in each society is that of its general attitude toward deafness. Here I am tempted to paraphrase Dr. Frisina's quotation of Gardner, namely: "Unrealistic ambitions led to bitter defeats," and say that: Realistic ambitions can lead to bitter defeats if society does not moderate the limits it defines for deafness. The pervasive influence of "handicapism" has its effect on the deaf population. To be more specific in terms of our society, stories detailing underemployment conditions, discrimination, and social isolation within hearing groups are legion and too often well-founded, even for oral deaf adults, a number of whom have had fantastic inner resources to spur them on. NTID's entry-level employment results are indeed encouraging, reflecting as it does the provision of genuine learning opportunities, but these results are also undeniably a product in part of intensive employer/community contact within local and national environs. NTID's recent establishment of a National Center on Employment of the Deaf is significant testimony to the necessity of ensuring upward job mobility for the deaf, the perennial albatross of employed, qualified deaf adults. We now have a National Center for Law and the Deaf which focuses on discrimination, namely the denial of equal opportunities to compete for a job or equal access to government services and benefits solely because of deafness (1), which was organized in response to documented needs. Modern American society is being increasingly inundated with information on deafness via the mass media with the seemingly apparent and hopeful result that this insiduous "benign neglect" on the part of society is being invaded by "conditional regard" toward the deaf, thus encouraging greater willingness to include the deaf in the mainstream of occupational mobility provided that their qualifications meet actual job descriptions. Definitely encouraging is the success of deaf adults in a wide variety of diverse and sophisticated occupational fields.

Within the field of deafness, it has been only during the last two decades that great strides have been made in our country regarding inclusion of deaf input into the organization and functioning of facilities geared to meet the varied needs of deaf individuals. Here are a few examples . . . A bill covering a Pilot Mental Health Program for the Deaf presently pending before a state legislature stipulates among its provisions that the advisory committee be at least 50 percent hearing impaired, drawn from a cross-section of professionals, parents and consumers (deaf adults) (15). The Alexander Graham Bell Association for the Deaf recently had its first deaf president at the helm. Some deaf individuals have advanced to administrative level positions in a wide variety of educational settings and governmental institutions. These recent trends obviously have implications in terms of expanding the potential of young deaf adults and in providing them with the opportunities to function effectively in policy-making arenas.

The tendency of deaf adults to gravitate toward each other for socialization is well documented. I view it as a basic enhancement to mental health. Social life with hearing individuals is of course to be encouraged, and many young deaf adults attempt to pursue this goal to varied degrees. I, however, do not recommend that this goal be viewed as the ultimate achievement on the path to self-actualization after having seen a number of deaf adults coming from the society at large, hungry for at least minimal contact with deaf peers on comparable educational and social levels. Rather, this goal should be on a par with the ability of the individuals involved to engage in personal enrichment interaction.

Despite potential possession of the six personal accomplishments listed by Dr. Frisina as necessary to get one's life in control, there are life stresses that make this control difficult. The consequences of being deaf obviously add to the stress factor in daily life, and no one can totally escape some negative reflection of that deafness. Efforts to compensate for the deafness and minimize "deviation" can be exhausting, depending on individual capacities. Based on experience rather than on definite evidence, I wish to state my belief that, in psychological terms, repression as a defense mechanism recurs in the process of maintaining an equilibrium in this complex society as coping mechanisms come to the fore. Whether this is a healthy adjustment is subject to debate, but the reasons causing this process do exist. To illustrate, a successful oral deaf adult who graduated from Harvard University and received his doctorate in clinical psychology from Boston University was unexpectedly confronted with deafness in his offspring. In the process of working through his confrontation, he realized increasingly that he had never fully accepted his own deafness . . . "All the hidden frustrations, anger and resentment over being deaf and the consequences that came as a result of being deaf in this hearing-oriented society came to realization." (24). When the rewards of mainstreaming into the society at large become real for the ready and prepared person, the negative experiences encountered in relating to that same society fade. These negative experiences, however, serve as evidence that equating assimilation with self-actualization or self-esteem may have vast implications for the mental health of many deaf adults if inadequately dealt with.

Dr. Frisina outlines the development of mental health delivery systems for the deaf as a sign of new mental health trends in our country. This growth is truly encouraging, especially as it exposes the absolute minimum of services in the past and takes into account the recognition of the right of deaf citizens to participation in life's mainstream, partaking of services generally available to the population at large. The projected need of the deaf adult for mental health services is large. A higher percentage of deaf adults have difficulty in coping with life stresses than the percentage reflected for the hearing population (10,13,17,19). Also, the rate of emotional disturbance in deaf children continues to be documented as higher than that for their hearing peers (11,13,18,20). Specific figures for those who perceive themselves as oral deaf adults have not been documented. Many referrals to existing facilities are declined on the basis of the agencies' inability to deal with the deafness (13). There are no specific mental health programs for the adult deaf in large sections of the United States, and this is a glaring omission in view of the rise of modern stresses paralleling those inherent in the society at large (10). Many deaf adults are unaware of what services are potentially available to them.

In a study researching perspectives on the need and acceptance of counseling services, Chough presents an arresting conclusion: *only* 27 percent of his subjects (Gallaudet College students) regarded their mental health as good. Speaking of college blues, there you have it! . . . 81 percent indicated they would seek vocational or educational counseling; 61 percent would seek help for personal problems, with many preferring to seek help from family or friends first (3). Another survey, this time of deaf members of a state association for the deaf, revealed some disinterest in using counseling services because of feelings of shame, public stigma, or disbelief in counseling effectiveness (2). Institutionalization of counseling/mental health services such as those provided by NTID is helpful, but we need to know more about the measured effectiveness of counseling—the quality and nature of the changes occurring during counseling, using measurements other than description of positive or negative movement. This is essential for the enhancement of counseling as a mental health and educational tool for the deaf population.

To conclude: "The inner well-being of deaf individuals is subject to the same psychological principles that govern the well-being of all mankind . . ." (12)

... This concept has clearly been elaborated on by Dr. Frisina in his presentation. In essence, with the development of adequate coping mechanisms through education and experience as well as selective repression, many young deaf adults learn how to adapt and adjust well to frustrating situations, thus presenting a picture, at least on the surface, of satisfactory adjustment and basic life satisfaction. As a whole, they are to be commended for the way they attack the task of getting their daily lives under their control, with or without support services. Mental health professionals can help with the complex struggles ensuing from a rigid society. It is imperative that those professionals have true empathy for the implications of deafness in addition to professional training in counseling/psychology and deafness. Ultimately, if young deaf adults have received optimum familial/educational/social support which related to their unique individual needs, they will develop the psychic strength to fight for self-gratification as functioning members of society, and they will perceive their struggles as worthwhile when society allows the feasibility of rewards.

In this reaction, I hope I have added an extra dimension to your empathy of what the deaf person/adult experiences in daily life as you help to prepare deaf individuals for adult life with all its implications. If so, I consider this an accomplishment. There is no simple answer to mental health, involved as it is with the infinite variability of individual differences and life stresses.

References

1. Charmatz, M. Working against discrimination. *The Broadcaster*, 1979, 1 (6), 6.

2. Chough, S. The mental health needs of the deaf community: Implications for advocacy. *Mental Health in Deafness*, 1977, 1, 13–19.

3. Chough, S. *Perspectives on the need and acceptance of counseling services reported by deaf college students.* Unpublished doctoral dissertation. Columbia University, 1978.

4. Cohen, O. The deaf adolescent: Who am I? *The Volta Review*, 1978, Vol. 80 (5), 265–274.

5. Emerton, R. G., & Rothman, G. "Attitudes towards deafness: Hearing students at a hearing and deaf college." *American Annals of the Deaf*, 1978, 123, (5), 588–593.

6. Fellendorf, G. *The effect of oral education on the attitudes of deaf persons towards the hearing environment.* Paper prepared for The International Symposium on Deafness, The Netherlands, November 1979.

7. Freud, A. *The writings of Anna Freud (Vol. 6, Normality and pathology in childhood: Assessments of development).* New York: International Universities Press, 1965.

*8. Garrison, W., & Tesch, S. Self concept and deafness: A review of research literature. *The Volta Review*, 1978, 457–466.

*9. Garrison, W., Tesch, S. & DeCaro, P. An assessment of self concept levels among post-secondary deaf adolescents. *American Annals of the Deaf*, 1978, 123 (8), 968–975.

10. Goulder, T. Federal and state mental health programs for the deaf in hospitals and clinics. *Mental Health in Deafness*, 1977, 1, 13–19.

11. Harris, R. Impulse control. *American Annals of the Deaf*, 123 (1), 52–67.

12. Levine, E. S. *The psychology of deafness: Techniques of appraisal for rehabilitation.* New York: Columbia University Press, 1960.

13. *Application for operating certificate for the Lexington Center for Mental Health Services.* January, 1979, Lexington School for the Deaf.

14. Lowell, E. *The effect of the oral education on the attitudes of the family and the environment towards deafness.* Paper prepared for The International Symposium on Deafness, The Netherlands, November 1979.

15. *Maryland Mental Health Bill.* Proposed by the National Center for Law and the Deaf to the House of Delegates, #9141170, No. 2401-05900, Delegate Beck.

16. Mindel, E. & Vernon, M. *They grow in silence: The deaf child and his family.* Silver Spring, MD: National Association of the Deaf, 1971.

17. Rainer, J., Altschuler, K. & Kallman, F. *Family and mental health problems in a deaf population.* New York: New York State Psychiatric Institute, 1963.

18. Schein, J. D. Deaf students with other disabilities. *American Annals of the Deaf,* 1975, *120,* 92–99.

19. Schlesinger, H. Panel presentation, special mental health needs of deaf adults. *Journal of Rehabilitation of the Deaf,* April 1979, Vol. 12 (4), 82.

20. Schlesinger, H., & Meadow, K. *Sound and sign: Childhood deafness and mental health.* Berkeley: University of California Press, 1972.

*21. Schroedel, J., & Schiff, W. Attitudes towards deafness among some deaf and hearing populations. *Rehabilitation Psychology,* 1972, *19* (2), 59–70.

22. Scopaz, V. Living with a hearing loss. *Hearing Rehabilitation Quarterly,* Winter 1968, 11–13.

23. Sussman, A. E. *An investigation into the relationship between self-concepts of deaf adults and their perceived attitudes toward deafness.* Unpublished doctoral dissertation, New York University, 1973.

24. Thompson, R., Thompson, A., & Murphy, A. Sounds of sorrow, sounds of joy: The hearing impaired parents of hearing impaired children—a Conversation. *The Volta Review,* 1979, *81* (5), 341.

21

a panel of young deaf adults: experiences with oral education

toos verdonschot-kroëf, bart bosch, p.m.a.l. hezemans, and w. noom

toos verdonschot-kroëf

So interwoven is my life with that of the people who can hear, that it is difficult for me to speak about my experiences related to my deafness. Not being able to hear is something which I have come to take for granted. Before I started primary school at the Institute for the Deaf, I had no idea I could not hear let alone speak. To me it was normal to learn to both read and speak words at school. I can remember being glad to be at school and enthusiastically taking in every word.

Looking back at the past I now find that at primary school my knowledge of language was too limited to be able to express my emotions. For this reason I often felt myself expressionless and above all helpless. Until I was about 15 years old I had no insight into the logic of grammar. My thoughts were primitive and due to the institutional way of life too protected from the outside world. This is obvious from the following fragment taken from one of my essays. I was then 11 years old.

> ... Very coincidently two drunkards meet each other on the street. One of the drunkards steps out of the car and goes to the other drunkard. He asks: "Do you very much want to make accident so that the police will be unhappy because you

have caused them a lot of trouble by having to make them chase all the people away." "Good", says drunkard. One drunkard steps into the car again. He drives to another drunkard. "Bom", says the car. Two drunkards fall out the back. . . . .

With my parents I led a very secure life. I did not hear the pleasant or unpleasant words which were exchanged between the people who could hear. At home I was accepted; but in someway or another I noticed that they did not find it pleasant that I was deaf and that they were frightened that later on I would remain behind compared with my brothers and sister. In the holidays, home on the farm, I was able to lead a normal daily life: helping in the household, gradually being able to do the shopping on my own, and taking the responsibility of collecting and packing eggs. My sister was one of the few people of my own age who was able to get on with me in a skillful way. She could understand me and play with me.

Through continuously analysing language I began to catch on to the logic of grammar. After this I made rapid progress. Gradually my naive thoughts and helpless feelings became less. By doing lots of reading I gained access to the outside world. Through this I learned of all sorts of situations and emotions and therefore also learned to know myself. I could more easily place myself into the outside world. I became more sociable and began making less and less use of sign language. Although the school forbade sign language, I occasionally still used it when speaking with deaf people partly because it was easier and often it was necessary. Along with the gradual growth in my development there was also a change within the Institute. The educational level was improved; male teachers were introduced and this had a positive influence on my adolescence. During this phase I had to overcome problems related to my deafness. Compared with my sister I felt that I could not get on well with people who could hear. One of the effects this had was to stimulate my ambition for further study.

I can now place myself objectively in a hearing society. I attended a normal secondary school and then the Agricultural University in Wageningen where I completed the study in food-chemistry. Naturally I could not follow lectures. I gained all my knowledge from lecture notes, and the notes fellow students made in their text books etc. I learned to apply this knowledge during my doctoral phase. At the moment I am working with the same professor for whom I completed my doctorate. Since I have started working, the drawbacks, due to my deafness, have become clearer. It is difficult for me to take part in work discussions. I can not personally follow readings and conferences. I do, however, get to see the reports of these. I also do not know what is being said in general conversation. This way I have little chance to get to know the train of thoughts of different people. Because of this there is a danger that my knowledge becomes too one sided. I have never got myself too worked up about these drawbacks.

When you accept your deafness, orient yourself as openly as possible, do not make yourself unpopular through self-pity, and have enough intuition, it is easy to make contact with people who can hear, even if you can not lipread fluently or speak clearly. During the conversation the problems surrounding the method of conversing will nearly disappear. When the articulation is poor, pen and paper are still necessary. There are certain thoughts and feelings which I can only express when the person to whom I am speaking is truly interested in me and willing to listen. True contact with my fellow man is for me the greatest thing on earth. As a small child I was handed over to my educators with their ideas concerning the communication of thoughts. That is why I think I am lucky in having been to an Institute where learning to speak was top priority.

Curriculum vitae

She was born on February 25th, 1946. At the age of 2 years, it was discovered that she was totally deaf. At the age of 4 years she went to Sint Michielsgestel, which is an institute for the deaf. When she was 21 she passed the examination for Mulo-B (secondary school) at Sint Michielsgestel. After this she went to a public H.B.S. which she finished in 3 years. She went to the Agricultural University in Wageningen. After 7½ years, in March 1978, she graduated with a doctorate. Her specializations were food-chemistry and microbiology. In the meantime she has married and has one child of 1½ years. Since February this year she has a temporary job at the Agricultural University.

bart bosch

ORAL EDUCATION.

1. Introduction.

The Institute for the Deaf asked me to give my own opinion about oral education as it is used by the Institute to educate deaf children. I agreed with it because I think it is a very important matter for deaf children to have a chance to learn to speak and lipread. Because I was one of those children who got such a chance, I am allowed to give my opinion about oral education.

2. The Importance of Oral Education in the Society

I am telling you: I can talk to anybody in my own language. The result is that I come into contact with hearing people which is the basis to start real human relationships. If you speak, you are capable of giving your own opinion about several subjects and discussing with other people. You can have interesting discussions together. The fact is the society is based on hearing people. Most of the communication is oral, so the deaf people have to adjust themselves to oral education. In this way they can take part in the society. Only then they can be accepted by hearing people. The above statement means: If a deaf person cannot talk with hearing people, there will be no relationship between them. It is a disadvantage for a deaf person that a hearing person easily comes into contact with other hearing persons. Only his equals can understand him. The consequence is "Alienation from the hearing society." In a hearing society a deaf society will develop, deaf people won't integrate in this society. It will mean that deaf people develop their own communication like sign language or finger language that only a few hearing people understand. So my opinion is that oral education stimulates integration of deaf people into a hearing society.

3. My private opinion.

After my study in the Institute for the Deaf I went to hearing school. Why? Because I wanted to prove myself in society. I wanted to use all possible chances. By trying, you can afterwards say: "I tried." Has it been a success, you were lucky, if it wasn't a success, you have had bad luck. By saying "It will fail" people show traces of doubt. For me it is a challenge to try everything that is possible for me. Because I was a good pupil at the Institute for the Deaf, it was possible for me to study further. It gave me all courage and faith to try. What would have happened to me had I not learned to talk? Then I would be dumb and I could not have developed into the situation I am in today. Hearing people and even my own family would not have accepted me as a full person with my own opinions. They would have considered me a reject, as a defective. Not to express your feelings is the most important aspect. If you express your feelings the other people will know you better. Hearing people will respect speaking deaf people more than mutes. If you cannot express your feelings, people cannot understand you. Other people will decide everything for you to do. They know what is best for you. Hearing people will carp on you. Your own feelings and opinions are worthless to them. You will be a cipher, a problem for society. Look at the rejects, defectives. You don't meet them often. If people don't want to isolate deaf people from hearing society, it is important that deaf people can express themselves and show their own feelings and express opinions in the same language as hearing people. So my conclusion is: Oral education is the best way. Other people may have other opinions. But they cannot talk about my own speaking knowledge. I learned to speak. I am very proud of myself that I can make my own decisions about my own life and that I can express myself about what I feel and mean. I am sure that this is the most important goal of oral education. The Institute uses this motive to give all possible chances to deaf children. If deaf children get all chances to develop themselves, they can choose the profession they like.

In my case this means: a technological school certificate with a bachelor of science in civil engineering and a job as a designer in civil engineering in "concrete". And I am still learning in my profession. I often talk and discuss with my colleagues concerning practical problems. All this would never have been possible if I had never learned oral education.

4. Finger language

I want to tell something about finger language. Maybe this is not right but I'd like to give my opinion. If I had learned finger language instead of oral education, who would communicate with me? Only a small group of people who know finger language. In general, hearing society doesn't accept finger language. And they would think it is a mad show of a reject. You cannot come into contact with hearing people with finger language. The same is true of sign language. Because people in society never learned this. Once I saw a program for deaf people on TV, a deaf person using finger language to deaf people. It was so ridiculous to me. If I should think so, hearing people would also think so. Oral education in Holland is very good, I think other communication languages are not allowed in general use. Only in special cases for speech defectives who can learn special languages. These people have a double handicap so the special languages can help them to utter their feelings.

5. Talking—curse or blessing

From my own knowledge of life I must confess that talking is a blessing. I am happy with my life I can talk and express myself. I can not imagine what it would be like to be a reject living in an institution while I had good brains which I could not use because I could not talk. If people give up oral education deaf people will go back to the days of shoemakers and tailors, which was the only possible work for them. Were deaf people happy then? In my opinion deaf people are happier now, because they have a chance to make their own choices in life. At the Institute, oral education is successful. I am very happy that the Institute will use the oral education from now on. In other places in the world oral education is not so successful. Because they aren't able to give all their energy to the welfare of the deaf. It depends on the mentality of hearing people and how they grasp the problems of oral education. It is especially a matter of good guidance and development in the oral education, adapted to the mother language. Thus oral education has its specific problems in each language. If people want oral education to become a success, they have to solve these problems. The issue of 100 percent is important to preserve so that oral education will be successful. The result will come, that is sure.

6. Experience with lipreading

What is lipreading and what is the connection with oral education? If a deaf person wants to learn lipreading, he has to learn to speak, too, because he has to lipread himself to know what other people are talking about. When you can observe recognizable words on the lips, you also are able to recognize sentences. If you know lipreading, you are able to follow a discussion with other people. Of course the learning period takes 10 to 15 years at a low speed. After which one is able to come into contact with hearing people. How deaf students will do it, depends on their character and talent. Nobody realizes the value of the time which is spent. If deaf people leave the Institute they only think "time went by so quickly." I learned oral education at the Institute like the other deaf people. I never realized that oral education was so special. Because my parents and sisters could talk, it was also logical that I should be able to talk. Now because I have to write my own opinion about it I have deep thoughts about oral education. Yes, I admit that oral education is wonderful. Hearing people can understand my speech. I am grateful to the Institute for teaching me the oral education. Also to my parents and my sisters who helped to teach me the language.

7. Conclusion

Continue oral education. Give all possible chances to deaf children to develop themselves. Persevere in the welfare of deaf children. Work hard so that you will be able to help other people in the world to make oral education popular. Later if oral education becomes generally used, you will see results which will make you proud. I am sure the following generations of deaf people will be very grateful to us that they will be able to develop themselves further than it was possible for us. I am very grateful to give you my opinions and I thank you.

Curriculum vitae

- Born on September 7th, 1954.
- Attended pre-school, elementary school and secondary school at the Instituut voor Doven until 1970.
- Attended 2 years Mavo-4, a secondary school at "Ruwenberg", a school for the hearing.
- 5 years H.T.S.-WW, higher technical school, inclusive of a preparatory year.
- Afterwards has been for 1½ years working for the Heide Maatschappij Nederland, a moorland reclamation society as H.T.S.-designer in civil-technical projects.

p. m. a. l. hezemans

Autobiography or "food" for Psychologists and Psycholinguists

1. Social Background

My name is Peter Marie Albert Louis Hezemans, I was born February 21, 1934 at Rotterdam. My father came from Eindhoven and rose from butcher to manager of the Zwanenberg-Organon factory; a self-made man who retired from business 20 years ago. My mother, from Rotterdam, was a charming woman, beloved by friends and acquaintances, she used to do everything for the career of her husband. I only have one brother, who followed my father's footsteps. He now is manager of a meat factory in Las Palmas on the Canary Islands. He is also since 1976 Honorary Consul for the Netherlands in Las Palmas. At the time of the airplane-crash at Tenerife, he helped the Dutch victims and their families and was knighted for this. He received the order of Orange-Nassau. At the age of 36 I married a hearing woman and I am the father of a hearing child.

2. Deafness

The cause of my deafness is encephalitis which was the result of a negative reaction to a cow-pox vaccination. There are other side effects, such as mild disturbances of equilibrium, poor regulation of the body temperature (perspiration), certain motoric disorders like mistakes in speaking and writing and irregular respiration.

3. Experiences with speech-training and articulation-lessons.

I remember my former speech lessons at the school for the deaf as follows. Initially in my pre-school period, I had no difficulties with the so-called phonetic vowel-triangle:

```
      ie ─────── uu ─────── oe
           ee ── eu ── oo
                 aa
```

but there were problems with the consonants: p-b-m; t-d-n; l-d; s-z; f-v; rt-r.

The aids which were used during the articulation lessons were classical: spatula, fingertips and mirror. I still remember how the guttural "f", on which I had worked very hard, was very much appreciated. And how the blowing exercises, (blowing out a candle from a distance) took a lot of effort.

In puberty the problems with the phonetic triangle increased especially the many nuances between *ie, uu, oe, ee, eu, oo* and *aa* and also with consonants. At the same time I learned to talk in "syllables." Subjects for tuition were the names of the teaching-brothers, Celestinus, Theobertus, Bonaventura, Ignatio, Firminius, and Leodulf.

At the age of 11, it became evident that my voice outside an intimate circle was hardly intelligible. It was monotonous and had no variety or pitch. This was likely due to a wrong way of breathing during speaking; I lack the technical ability to lower the pitch at constant expiration. Further I was aware that I put the stress at the wrong places and that I had the inclination to interchange syllables.

Although in the course of the years my speech improved, because of my relationship with hearing people, I have to admit that it takes a lot of energy to make myself clearly understood, especially with people whom I meet for the first time. I prefer to speak rather briefly, in popular terms: in telegram style. By only saying what is important I avoid misunderstandings. When I talk more than one hour, my vocal cords get tired.

Despite all these obstacles which I encounter while speaking, I am grateful that I learned how to speak at the Instituut voor Doven. This has greatly contributed to the fact that I am appreciated and fully accepted at my work. Because of my deafness I still have to overcome many obstacles which are still a challenge to me.

4. Problems with lipreading.

Lipreading is my weakest point. With my vocabulary growing, I get more difficulties in lipreading. This is understandable, because a slight change of the mouth and tongue position brings a big change in sound, in words like pet/pit and leg/lek.

When I am tired, it is hard for me to concentrate, with the result, that I understand less and less. If I get emotionally involved in a conversation, it is almost impossible to follow the others. My conclusion is that for good lipreading there is no necessity to be intelligent. From my own experience I can say, that I am only able to follow directly 30 percent of a normal conversation. In order to compensate for the other 70 percent, my procedure is as follows:

1. **Notes.** In discussions and meetings with hearing people, one uses notes. Often they are just a few sentences. Professor Schlösser, my boss, sometimes writes notes for two hours in telegram style.
2. **Guessing.** I often guess intuitively what it is all about. To me this is a matter of intelligence. As the saying goes "a word to the wise is enough."
3. **Reading minds.** Sometimes I catch myself knowing beforehand what somebody is going to say. Some colleagues even think that I am simulating deafness.

4. **Supporting gestures.** These to emphasize the spoken word. Although I did away with sign language for the deaf after I left school purposefully and demonstratively I still find that supporting gestures are indispensable to clarify the spoken word. I mean by "gestures" those signs which are used and understood by deaf as well as hearing people. In his book "Man Watching," Desmond Morris gives similar examples.

5. Language development.

At the age of 9, I discovered that the sentence construction occurred according to rules—I became acquainted with grammar. This happened when brother Bonaventura, the Superior of the brother-teachers, broke through the classical pattern of language teaching: after having seen an educational film, and we were "forced" by way of an experiment, to write an essay about what we had seen on the screen. This was in contrast to the conventional method in which story writing was "pre-fabricated" by the teacher. I remember that I was the only one of my 15 classmates who handed in his paper. After this, my interest in grammar grew gradually.

The most important reason, why I dissociate from sign language for the deaf, is it's disastrous—read: restraining—influence on language development. As you know, deaf people conversing in sign language use a type of language which in its morphology and structure differs from the language of their hearing environment. Learning sign language in my childhood came about through visual perception in which the "manual" description of objects and actions—which can easily be imitated—served as a basis. In essence signs are polyinterpretable, therefore the transition from "signs" to "speech" is a laborious process. This is obvious, because I had to change my ability to express myself in signs to the ability to express my thoughts in words. In making the oral language my own I recognize the following problems:

   a. I do not converse in smooth sentences, but I use a telegram style, as brief as possible. My vocabulary consists of active words, this means words I daily use, and a passive vocabulary, these are words which I read and understand.
   b. In using articles I often gamble. I am never sure whether it should be "de" or "het". I also mix up the words "hij" (he) and "zij" (she), "hem" (him) and "haar" (her) and "dit" (this) and "dat" (that).
   c. Being deprived of the positive influence of sounds on my language development, it is likely that this is the reason why I do not have the ability to rhyme. To compose a good story is easy for me, but wording my thoughts in smooth sentences is a tiring business. By reading a lot, this means the daily newspapers and weekly magazines, and a good book during the holidays, I try to improve my language competence. I am convinced that this would have been a lot easier if I had been a hearing person.

It is obvious to me that insight in grammar could not have unveiled all secrets of a language to me, but would have given indications where to go. I am convinced that one needs more, namely to become familiar with the phonetic world at an early age. Alas I was born too early; in 1936 oral education was not yet that advanced.

6. Communicative ability

First an introductory story from my early years: the most positive and fruitful contribution for communicating with others, was the active dialogue during the religion class at the school for the deaf. This was given by an alert priest who articulated very well. For me, this was a solid foundation to help me formulate my thoughts into words.

Lipreading at the school for the deaf was not very hard, because every day we saw the same faces. However, in society, with so many faces, so many characters and so many different shapes of the mouth, lipreading is not so easy. When people stick to the same subject during a conversation I have little trouble following it, but as soon as one rambles from one subject to another, I am lost. Good lipreading to me is:

- Understanding of the word.
- Understanding of the sentence.
- Having an insight in the meaning of the sentence.

Although the latter is essential for mutual understanding, I not only miss a certain type of humor, but also miss changes of intonation, phonetic puns, allusions, or turning of phrases.

Not everyone understands me upon meeting for the first time. Most people get used to it rather quickly. However, starting a conversation for the first time, I immediately sense whether we are on the same wave length. If so, this means a basis for permanent contact in the future. As I said before, I prefer to speak in telegram style, this implies that I think more in logistics than in linguistics. Syllogistic reasoning is not strange to me and I am also trained in the use of certain discussion and reasoning methods. Sometimes I feel inhibited while speaking, especially in the beginning, but once caught up by emotion, everything goes smoothly.

To me communication means expressing my thoughts and understanding intentions and purports of others, obviously it is more than speaking and understanding alone. In the previous paragraphs I mentioned my shortcomings in oral communication, therefore I do not hesitate to use the following aids:

1) Paper and pencil,
2) Blackboard and chalk,
3) Overhead projector,
4) Interpreters (colleagues and friends who function as such for strangers),
5) Technical signs, such as explaining with my hands how, for instance, a petrol engine works,
6) Practical psychology—for instance before starting a conversation with somebody I try to find out the level of conversation by enquiring after interests, hobbies, favorite topics, specialities etc.

I owe my ability to communicate to the following facts: intelligence, intuition, continuous interest, getting along with people, psychological insight in personal, social and power structures, environment, and last, but not least, my wife. The communication with other people gradually improves because of acceptance and respect and, since I learned how to react carefully in certain situations, to think in nuances and to have a neutral or mild opinion. Moreover

I learned to express myself carefully and to act diplomatically. It is my strong conviction, that, if I had been acquainted in the past (that is immediately after my deafness manifested itself) with the phonetic world by means of speech and auditory training, (which should not be confused with the former speech exercises) I would have made more progress, because: speaking presupposes hearing!

7. Integration in the "hearing" society

When I left the school for the deaf in 1950, I was enrolled at "Philips Bedrijfsschool". I felt this transition as a leap into the darkness. Although I was together with other deaf classmates at this school, I refused to communicate in sign language. I did not want to be different and thus become isolated. Since I wanted to make a career for myself, I could not afford such social isolation.

After I graduated from "Philips Bedrijfsschool", I worked a few years at Philips Science Laboratory. In 1956 I entered the "Higher Technical School" at 's-Hertogenbosch, where I studied Mechanical Engineering. During this period a process of social awareness developed inside of me and I learned to get emotionally involved. I was nominated as the Editor-Treasurer of the school magazine.

After I got the certificate of the "H.T.S." in 1961, I accepted a job as "literature researcher" at the Technical University at Eindhoven. It was my task to read about fifty Dutch and foreign magazines per week and to draw the attention of the professors to the technical developments in their fields. In this period I carried my reading to a high level which improved my reading ability. For this work I had to acquire knowledge of several fields of study and technical disciplines. Because of this my insight in the coordination of the technical sciences augmented. This insight proved to be one of the most important cornerstones of the career I was going to make.

In 1964 Professor Schlösser invited me to work in the area of propulsion technique. After having kept myself for three years in the background, I received a task, which for me as a deaf person, was a big challenge. I was asked to give a lecture on the reliability of machines, with which the physical model of the failure of these machines was set up. This lecture was given with the help of an overhead projector and made a good impression on the "public." Because of this success Professor Schlösser asked me to give every year three lectures, for a total of six hours, for a group of twenty-five students. The subject of these lectures was fluidica, which can be considered as an equivalent of electronics, on the understanding that instead of electric currents, one works with fluidic currents. The notes of these lectures were completed and published in book form. The interest for fluidica decreased and because of this the lectures came to an end.

In 1975, an educational committee of the department of mechanical engineering asked me to participate on a committee which was to introduce the "science of systems" into a new curriculum of the department of mechanical engineering. After half a year of discussions we did not reach an agreement because of different opinions and ideas, we even did not come to a "majority" report. I then took it upon myself to write a report entitled, "Philosophy on the Systems and Methodology of the System Techniques" and submitted it to the educational committee where it was received positively. To my big surprise I received from the committee an informal lecture assignment: teaching the science of systems to undergraduates. To elucidate this—the science of systems is the science which keeps itself busy studying, realizing and optimalizing systems, which are physically different on the basis of analogy of consideration and approach. These lectures take twenty-nine hours and are attended annually by about one-hundred students. Because of the fact of my handicap, not everyone can understand me properly, Professor Schouten is willing to present my lectures. I have the supervision of the lectures as well as the exams and preliminary exams. Recently I wrote a collection of notes in three parts, "Introduction to the Technical Science of Systems."

In addition to this I give annually, on the authority of Professor Schlösser, a 10-hour lecture in my field of study for doctoral students. This deals with the technique of controlling the mechanical, electric, hydraulic, and pneumatic propulsions. These students, in their last year of studies, understand me better, therefore I can permit myself to give oral lectures.

After I was admitted to the Scientific Staff of the University I got the job of aiding students in their last stage of study, this requires a rapid and intensive interchange of thoughts, orally or in writing.

As far as my appearances in public are concerned, I have to receive foreign guests and show them around, I do this with another colleague, who functions as interpreter. More than a month ago, I had to replace my boss, Professor Schlösser, who went on a study trip to Japan, at an official meeting of the University. On his behalf, I had to enter the auditorium in the company of professors in robes and during this academic ceremony, I had to present a certificate to one of the graduates. This was accompanied by a speech, written by me and read by the Dean. I could not have done all this without a good communicative ability.

8. Epilogue

In 1976 I joined the Advisory Board of the Magazine "Aandrijftechniek." In this I hope to publish one of these days an article called, "Insight in the Approach of Sound Abatement in Axial-Plumber Pumps." It is hard to believe that this should be in the hands of a deaf person. Needless to say, I did not analyze the problems of sound, physiologically, but physically, or more accurately: technically, with which the causes of sound in the pump were systematically searched and different methods were presented in order to get these eliminated. As study material I used Lord Raleigh's book (1877) "Theory of Sound." The first sentences of the first chapter intrigue me. They read:

> The sensation of sound is a thing *sui generis*, not comparable with any of our other sensations. No one can express the relation between a sound and a color or a smell. Directly or indirectly, all questions connected with this subject must come for decision to the ear as the organ of hearing—from it there can be no appeal.

With this I would like to emphasize that for the language development of a deaf person phonetic experiences during the years of childhood are indispensable. They comprise the beauty of a language which can hardly be put down to rules, and with which one can tell a story in "all its shades and peculiarities." The fact why the blind have a richer linguistic feeling than the deaf, speaks for itself. It therefore is a matter of great importance to bring the deaf child as early as possible into contact with the phonetical world, by means of speech and auditory training with hearing aids.

The axiom "deaf is deaf" is unproven and even an outdated fact, since now has been shown that only a very small percentage of the deaf are really deaf. In my opinion any residual hearing, amplified with a hearing aid, must be mobilized immediately in order to serve as a support for lipreading, for voice-volume-control, for regulating voice-rhythm and to reduce the psycholinguistic problems. The only right method for this is so-called "oral education" based on speech and auditory training, which is being practiced with such good results at the Instituut voor Doven at Sint Michielsgestel. Thank you!

Curriculum Vitae

- Born at Rotterdam   21 February 1934
- Admission "Instituut voor Doven" (Institution for the Deaf) at Sint Michielsgestel, kindergarten   1937
- B.L.O. (private-elementary education) there, boys' school   1940–1950
- "Philips Bedrijfschool" (Philips' Technical School) at Eindhoven   1950–1954
- Certificate Glass instrument maker and mechanical instrument maker   August 1954
- Employed at "Natuurkundig Laboratorium Philips" (Philips' Research Laboratory) as analytical chemist   1954–1956
- Passed entrance examination at "Hogere Technische School" (H.T.S.) (Technical College)   June 1955
- "IndustrieAvondschool" (evening school of Technical College) at Eindhoven, education: mechanical engineering   1955–1956
- H.T.S. at s'Hertogenbosch (day-school of Technical College), including transitional class, education: mechanical engineering   1956–1961
- Diploma Mechanical Engineering H.T.S. (Technical College)   June 1961
- Entered "Technische Hogeschool" at Eindhoven (Technological University, Eindhoven) Department Mechanical Engineering   October 1961
- Admission to the scientific staff members "Technische Hogeschool Eindhoven" (Technological University Eindhoven)   April 1976

- Teacher for system-engineering at
  Technological University, Eindhoven   June 1976
- Married and father of one child.

w. noom

A little over ten years ago I left the boarding school at Sint Michielsgestel where, for fourteen years, I followed deaf education via the oral method. I now have the feeling that I achieved a place in society. With the help of oral communication I now can get along with everybody; I have more contacts and have the courage to become involved in discussions. I even give lessons in the field of sports.

I still am very grateful to the boarding school, especially for the oral education. I am happy and wonder how I later on could have been able to follow all those courses and all that training without the education at Sint Michielsgestel.

I happened to meet a colleague in Deventer. This was after the Symposium. It also seemed strange to him that people who can talk rather well still use manualism.

Every day I am grateful that I am in a position to teach people who can hear. My lessons are mainly concerned with the world of sports. I not only teach how to play volleyball, I am also busy with massage, training, recreation and managing. All this gives me many more contacts in society and that is very important to deaf people. Moreover, I have no problems in my marriage with a wife and children who can hear. The hearing aid helps a lot to understand people and to be understood.

At the same time I work as a surveying clerk at the land registry where I have a normal verbal contact with all my colleagues.

Curriculum vitae

- Born on November 3rd, 1950 in Alkmaar.
- My deafness came at 3 months as a result of meningitis.
- I stayed at the Instituut voor Doven from 1954 until 1968. I finished pre-school, elementary school and UDO (secondary deaf education).
- From 1968 I attended for 2 years MULO-B (secondary school for the hearing) and graduated.
- After that, I started to work and study at the Office of the Land Registry.
- In 1972 I graduated as a civil servant in geodesy.
- In March 1980 I will take an exam to become a civil servant A.
- In 1975 I married Toos Janssen from 't Zand, a hearing person.
- We have two children; one 2½ years old and one 6 months old.

22

human values and idealism
john p. hourihan

History attests to the fact that the development of the human race is not a steady, smooth, even process (Clark, 1969). For some mysterious reason, at given points on the historical continuum, humanity makes a leap forward at the least expected times. Examples of this phenomenon are seen in Egypt and Mesopotamia 5,000 years ago when, quite suddenly, an advanced civilization appeared. Greece in the 6th century B.C., with its philosophy, science, art, and poetry culminating in development that was not to be seen again for centuries, is another example. Mankind witnessed it again in the 13th century, which is referred to as "the greatest of centuries," when leaders—both political and spiritual, saints and scholars—were giants in the "personae dramatis" of history.

Confidence and enthusiasm, as well as strength of intellect and will of the leaders of that age, made for a quantum leap that will be surpassed only in the development that we are witnessing in our own time. Toffler (1970) described this phenomenon in terms of the lifetimes of man.

> It has been observed that if the last 50,000 years of man's existence were divided into lifetimes of approximately 62 years each, there have been about 800 such lifetimes. Of these 800, fully 650 were spent in caves. Only during the last 70 lifetimes has it been possible to communicate effectively from one lifetime to another—as writing made it possible to do. Only during the last 6 lifetimes did masses of men ever see a printed word. Only during the last 4 has it been possible to measure time with any precision. Only in the last 2 has anyone anywhere used an electric motor. And the overwhelming majority of all the material goods we use in daily life today have been developed within the present 800th lifetime. (p. 15)

A Time For . . .

A parallel may be drawn with the history of the education of the hearing impaired. For almost 770 lifetimes the deaf existed in the caves of social ignorance before Christ cried out "Ephphatha" and proved that they were intelligent and could speak. Only during the last seven lifetimes have the deaf received an education. Only in the last four has free education been available. It is only within the present 800th lifetime that we have seen the research and technology which enable those who work with the visual-oral and the auditory-oral approaches to make the strides that are now possible to integrate the hearing impaired with society in general.

The history of educational programs for the hearing impaired, not unlike the history of civilization, has been one of uneven development (Flint, 1979). It is a history of leaps forward. The first great thrust was in the 16th century when a rare combination of professionals—teachers, doctors, and clergy—made outstanding contributions to the field. Cardano, Ponce de Léon, and Bonet are but a few of the great names of that period. The next great leap came in the 18th century with de l'Epée and Heinicke. The time between these phenomena has progressively lessened so that only a century later we have the developments resulting from the work of Thomas Gallaudet and Alexander Graham Bell.

Now the 20th century sees the field experiencing a development due to the explosion of knowledge in so many related fields—medicine, physics, biology, psychology, etc.—that those in the field could experience future shock. This rapid development of knowledge, as well as the radical changes in society, can be overwhelming. It is therefore significant that those leaders who espouse the auditory approach pause and reflect on the events of this 800th lifetime.

This symposium is most timely, giving all who attend the opportunity to review whence the profession has come and where it is going. It is a time for renewing commitment to the education of the hearing impaired; a time for renewing the spirit in order to accept the challenge of the future; a time to reflect; a time to contemplate professional ideals and values.

Idealism

A discussion of idealism and human values is a journey into the mind and brain of man that presents a challenge far greater than a journey into space. A journey into space is dependent upon the operation of the mind and only discovers facts that enable the mind to ascertain the purpose of the cosmos and man's role in it.

The challenge of a journey into the realms of reasoning is more important than a journey into space. A journey into space is just a journey with a beginning and an end. A journey into the mind and brain has no end. It is an unending series of new discoveries ever leading humanity to its destiny.

A Positive Philosophy

"We aspire to the unattainable ideal in order to achieve the highest levels." This statement, made by Sister Theresia at Sint Michielsgestel in 1934, was quoted by van Uden (1970) and can be said to sum up all that will be stated about "Idealism and Human Values."

Educators of the hearing impaired have achieved so much because they embraced an idealism which flows from a philosophy of life that is based on their faith in *homo sapiens* deprived of hearing. This philosophy, which was expounded earlier in this conference by Dr. Mulholland, sees the hearing impaired child or adult in terms of his abilities, and not his disabilities. It presents a positive view of human nature endowed by the Creator with unique powers which differentiate it from the rest of creation. This philosophy is an optimistic expression of the belief that the deaf child or adult can achieve, and in so doing, make his own contribution to the society in which he lives.

Ideals

An ideal is a mental model. It is that which is thought of as perfect or as a perfect model. When one strives to achieve his ideals, it is called idealism. Idealism, then, is behavior or thought based on a conception of things as they should be or as one would wish them to be. They become concretized in persons, places, things, or situations which one judges to be close to or identical with the idea in one's mind.

What is ideal for one may not be ideal for another. (This is obvious in the selection of a spouse.) It may explain why there are and always have been different approaches to the education of hearing impaired children. If in the mind of one educator the ideal is to have deaf children integrated into the society of their environment so that their primary language is the language of their environment, there will be one approach to their education. If in the mind of another educator the ideal is to have deaf children move, as adults, into a subculture with a language structure different from that of society at large, there will be another approach. If the ideal is to have the child become an adult functioning with two languages, one primary and the other a second language, so that they are citizens of two worlds, there will be still another approach.

Idealism, to be operant, must have some relationship with reality. The person with ideals related to reality is an achiever. Such a person is comparable to those whose feet are firmly planted on the earth but whose head (with a nod to Plato) is in the heavens. The person whose ideals are unrelated to reality is comparable to those with head and feet in the clouds. Reality is the realm in which ideals come alive.

Principles

Ideals, as abstractions, are similar to principles. Principles are fundamental truths or motivating forces upon which other things are based. They are concerned with the attainable and not necessarily with perfection. They, too, take form in reality, but they can come alive in different ways depending upon the situation in which they are applied. There may be a half dozen applications of a given principle in a certain situation. Each application may be different from the other. One may be the best application; one may be the worst, but still preserves the principle. In this situation, the principle is preserved without compromise. There is, however, compromise in its application. Good politicians and diplomats have made an art out of compromise of the applications without doing violence to their principles.

An example of this was seen in an interdisciplinary diagnostic center where the board of directors became antagonistic toward psychologists for political reasons and dismissed the psychological staff. Dealing with an unreasonable situation, the administrator of the center, who needed psychologicals on the children if the interdisciplinary principle was to be preserved, settled for psychological services one day a week. This was the least that could be done to preserve the principle. It certainly was not the best, but it kept the diagnostic center in operation until the political climate changed, emotions subsided, and reason once again predominated.

Implications

Inasmuch as ideals are concerned with perfection, there is a danger that some professionals may not act unless they think the ideal is attainable. Professionals with such a mental block are similar to those who are paralyzed when not able to apply a principle in the best way. As the latter do not understand the art of compromise, so the former do not understand reality. Idealism, as with marksmanship, requires that we raise our sights in order to hit the mark, to "achieve the highest level" in reality, as Sister Theresia noted.

Just as it is necessary in the light of reality to compromise on the application of a principle, so with ideals it is necessary to settle for less than the ideal in a real situation and thereby achieve the highest level possible. The highest levels will never be achieved if, before acting, teachers are waiting for the ideal child, or the ideal parents, or the ideal school, or the ideal world.

Those whose ideal it is to give deaf children an appreciation of music will strive to use all the amplification and technology available. They can be proud and pleased if the child, not getting the melody, does get the rhythm. Unless the teacher has the ideal, the child might never reach the highest level possible in the situation, namely, a sense of rhythm. On the other hand, if when all that she has is a drum she waits for an ideal situation with sophisticated electronic equipment, the child might never achieve his potential—a sense of rhythm. Another example is the idealist who maintains in the light of contrary evidence, that absolutely all deaf children will be aided by the auditory method only. Such a professional, who becomes rigid as a result of an idealism which goes contrary to reality, will work an injustice to those children who should be moved into programs using other methods as ongoing evaluation indicates. Or again, the idealism of people who believe that a deaf child should be taught signs as his primary language system—because in their ideal world they expect hearing citizens to learn signs as their second language—is an idealism with its head and feet in the clouds.

Beware of professionals who are inflexible personalities; many have difficulty compromising on the application of principles. Those who are dreamers may not be able to settle for less than perfection in an imperfect world. Most of all, beware of the professionals who are without principle or ideals. Such people think they have them, yet in reality they appear to operate from a policy of expediency. These professionals are those who rationalize that they are doing things for the deaf, when in reality they are primarily concerned with themselves. They are the professionals who, like reeds in the wind, sway to and fro with each new fad. They are the ones who reject constructive and creative conflict for fear that they must give up those positions with which they feel secure.

Any one or all of the above, instead of being professionals open to the explosion of new knowledge, can become professionals with closed minds, fanatics who operate more from emotion than reason, demagogues who seek positions of power, not to advance the cause of all deaf individuals but to use their power to force others to accept their own views.

The professional who is an idealist ignoring reality will find himself frustrated and disillusioned, grasping at straws and working an injustice upon the deaf child for whom he has responsibility. It is only the professional who is a realist, with ideals and principles flowing from a philosophy to which he is committed, who will be effective in achieving results. To be moved to action, such a one needs strong values.

Human Values

Philosophy as the love of wisdom has many branches, one of which was at one time psychology. Psychology broke away from its philosophical home and became what it is today, the science of behavior. Both disciplines are concerned with thought processes in man. Philosophy is concerned with how well we think; psychology is concerned with the way we think. Both fields of knowledge are continuing to make great contributions to our understanding of man as man distinct from other animals. Large numbers of psychologists are using a variety of scientific methods to unravel mysteries of the mind, while at the same time philosophers are constantly evaluating the quality of its thought.

Values are products of the thought processes in men and women and are related to other products of the mind: philosophy, principles, and ideals. To understand the relationship of all four concepts, one might compare them to a journey. Ideals are the preconceived image of our destination; philosophy is the map that we follow; principles are the guard rail keeping us on the highway; and values are the vehicle moving us along.

The word *value* is derived from the Latin *valere* meaning "to be strong." For something to be of value means that it has a strength or a power to do some specific thing. Whatever it is that has this virtue or power, then, is desirable to us and so can trigger an urgent need or demand for us to have or possess it.

Satisfying this demand is worth expending time, energy, money, and even life itself. People are attracted to whatever has a high value or is dear to them. Conversely, they have little interest in things they regard as having no value. Only things of value release the energy of will and passion required to give or sacrifice what is required to possess them.

The concept of values is moving to a central position in many sciences—education, medicine, political science, psychology, sociology, and theology to name a few. It is a concept similar to the concept of language in that it is uniquely attributed to man. Some authors refer to the concept as human values, but in the context of being peculiar to the human race the term human is not required. Certainly the literature dealing with values has not considered the concept as relevant to animals other than rational animals.

To reflect on values is fascinating, for values are related to so many other concepts that are unique to man: ideals, principles, attitudes, traits, and interests. A discussion of values can take many exciting paths. In fact, the temptation is to get off to a lively start by paraphrasing the classic question asked in audiology: "When a tree falls in the forest and there is no one present, is there sound?" One can ask, if there were no people on earth would a value exist? The discussion could become very sophisticated by exploring the relationship of values to language. Recognizing the relationship of thought and language in the formulations of Vygotsky (1962), Whorf (1956), and others, one could raise fascinating questions about the influence of language on values in the light of the linkage between a culture's philosophic vision, its language, and its thought.

These temptations will be avoided. So will the temptation to talk about the values needed in society today. The focus of this discussion will be on values as they relate to oral education.

Definition

The precise definition of the concept varies among professionals. Some view it objectively and some subjectively (Baier & Rescher, 1969). Objectively, a value is the capacity of objects to make some sort of favorable difference in the lives of individuals. Subjectively, it is the tendency to devote time, energy, and money to the attainment of the ends that are believed to have positive effects on the quality of one's life. Allport's (1961) definition clarifies a value as "a belief upon which a man acts by preference" (p. 454). For Rokeach (1973) a value is "an enduring belief that a specific mode of conduct or end-state of existence is personally or socially preferable to an opposite or converse mode of conduct or end-state of existence" (p. 5). It is this latter definition that is the basis for this second section of the paper. Rokeach did not indicate any contact with the disabled nor any research into their value systems, so it is assumed that there were no hearing impaired persons in the study that led to his theoretical approach to values. Yet his theoretical model appears to be an appropriate framework for our present considerations. This model could be used for a discussion of values emanating from the other philosophies of education of the deaf inasmuch as many of the values of the various philosophies will be similar; only their priorities will differ.

Concept of Value

A value is a belief. Beliefs can be distinguished as those capable of being true or false (e.g., believing that deaf people cannot talk); those concerned with morality and ethics (e.g., believing that a fetus suspected to be deaf should be aborted); and believing that something is desirable (e.g., developing the gift of voice). It is the last category that is the basis of the definition.

That this kind of belief to be a value must be an enduring one does not mean that it cannot be changed. If this were so, there would be neither social progress nor personal development. It has been suggested that the stability of individual values arises from the fact that they are learned in isolation from others in the environment. Over a period of time some values can change, at least in priority, as a child matures and deals with a changing world. An example of this might be the oral individual who eschewed sign language during his education because it would have been detrimental to his acquisition of his parents' language system, but who as an adult, realizing he should not discriminate against the deaf subculture, found sign language to be desirable.

When values refer to "end-states" or "modes of conduct," they are distinguished as terminal or instrumental. Rokeach emphasizes that this is an important distinction since there is a functional relationship between both types and since several instrumental values can be related to a single terminal value. Both terminal and instrumental values are further subcategorized into those that are society-centered (interpersonal) and those that are self-centered (intrapersonal). Finally, as a cognitive product, values are viewed as a concept of what is personally or socially preferable. This implies the intelligence to compare one value with another in one's system of values and to prefer one over the other. An example of this would be parents who value ease of communicating with their deaf child during his early years and who, at the same time, value the language system of the family as the basis for the communication mode. When faced with the fact that the systems of signs will make communication easier in the early years but will be detrimental to the development of the family's and society's language system, eventually forcing the child into a subculture life, the parents may find the oral approach, though slower and more difficult for the child and themselves, to be preferable.

Value Systems

People function under the influence of many values—religious, political, cultural, etc. A person's particular act is more often than not influenced by a cluster of values. Such a clustering is the result of an organized system wherein each value is ordered in priority with respect to other values. The reordering of these priorities is the basis of the change of values referred to previously. Variations in the circumstances of an individual's life not only beget different value systems, but also changes within a system. An example of different value systems is illustrated if one studies the different philosophies of educating deaf children. Adherents of the oral philosophy place a high value on integrating the deaf child into society in general by developing the language of that society as the child's first language. Proponents of the manual philosophy place a high value on an easy means of communication which develops a linguistic system at variance with that of the larger society. No one can say that one approach is better than the other; the only statement that can be made is that the adherents of one system prefer one mode of conduct or an end-state to that of the other. One might consider a change within a value system, for example, the situation in an oral approach where high value is placed on auditory-oral modes but a given child, due to intrinsic factors, is not progressing, not learning. This technique might be given a lower priority by the school, and a visual-oral technique such as Cued Speech might be accorded a higher priority within the oralist teacher's system of values.

Within the several value systems that people embrace there is a relatively small number of values to deal with the many complex and varied situations in which people find themselves. Rokeach (1973) states:

> On various grounds—intuitive, theoretical, and empirical—we estimate that the total number of terminal values that a grown person possesses is about a dozen and a half and that the total number of instrumental values is several times that number, perhaps five or six dozen. (p. 11)

This appears to be verified when viewing the values espoused by advocates of oralism. For them, integration and independence are terminal values, the former being a social terminal value and the latter being a personal terminal value. There are seven instrumental values: three personal (cognitive, linguistic, and reading competencies) and four social (auditory, speech perception, speech production, and writing competencies).

There are interlocking relationships between all of the instrumental values and the terminal values. It would be a mistake to simplify the interconnections by seeking to design a schema indicating a one-on-one correspondence. One instrumental mode, such as language competency, may relate to both terminal values; several modes, such as speech perception, speech production, and audition, relate to integration as a terminal value.

Principles as well as beliefs are constituents of the value system that is learned by a child. With these he is aided in his choice between alternatives, in his resolution of conflicts, and in making decisions. This does not mean that one's whole value system is employed each time a decision has to be made. Rather, only that portion of the system required by the situation is activated. There is not, then, a denial of the other values in one's mental structure but rather a particular focus for a particular end. Thus a focus on auditory training does not lessen the value one has for linguistic competency.

It is obvious that value systems have cognitive, affective, and behavioral components. A comment must be made about their motivational elements. Instrumental values motivate when their modes are understood to be closely related to the desired terminal value. The reward for fidelity to instrumental values is the terminal goal which is highly valued. Terminal values perceived as urgent have strong motivational power. This points up the need for the home and the school constantly to reinforce the importance of integration and independence in the mind of the student. These must be presented as super goals that will bring special benefits. These terminal values as conceptual tools are what the deaf person needs to fashion his future life as a member of a hearing world. When they are cherished by the student, he has the motivation to keep working with the day-in, day-out tasks associated with the instrumental values.

A Wonderland

Our profession is a wonderland. In a sense the deaf children are like Alice, of Lewis Carroll's story (1976 ed.). Do you remember how Alice went through the looking glass? She picked up a book and she said, while trying to find a part she could read, "—for it's all in some language I don't know" (p. 153).

JABBERWOCKY

'Twas brillig, and the slithy toves
Did gyre and gimble in the wabe:
All mimsy were the borogoves,
And the mome raths outgrabe.

When she realized it was a looking-glass book, she held it up to the glass and read:

JABBERWOCKY

'Twas brillig, and the slithy toves
    Did gyre and gimble in the wabe:
All mimsy were the borogoves,
    And the mome raths outgrabe.

"Beware the Jabberwock, my son!
    The jaws that bite, the claws that catch!
Beware the Jubjub bird, and shun
    The frumious Bandersnatch!"

He took his vorpal sword in hand:
    Long time the manxome foe he sought—
So rested he by the Tumtum tree,
    And stood awhile in thought.

And, as in uffish thought he stood,
    The Jabberwock, with eyes of flame,
Came whiffling through the tulgey wood,
    And burbled as it came!

> One, two! One, two! And through and through
> The vorpal blade went snicker-snack!
> He left it dead, and with its head
> He went galumphing back.
>
> "And hast thou slain the Jabberwock?
> Come to my arms, my beamish boy!
> O frabjous day! Callooh! Callay!"
> He chortled in his joy.
>
> 'Twas brillig, and the slithy toves
> Did gyre and gimble in the wabe:
> All mimsy were the borogoves,
> And the mome raths outgrabe.

When she finished reading, she concluded that

> It seems very pretty, but it's rather hard to understand. Somehow it seems to fill my head with ideas—only I don't exactly know what they are! However, *somebody* killed *something*: that's clear, at any rate.

Deaf children are like Alice when she could not understand the language of the book. Parents and professors working with the deaf have to hold up the mirror of oral education to help them to understand the language of their society. Even then they may not understand it perfectly, but if the children learn from their homes and the school the ideals and values of those who are committed to oralism, the day will come when even "toves" and "borogoves" will have meaning for them.

May the profession always be filled with men and women who dream dreams but are not dreamers. May it be blessed with people who have principles flowing from a philosophy that allows a compromise of the application of a principle without a compromise of principle. May it be overflowing with professionals who are committed to ideals that are related to reality and who respect others who have different ideals flowing from a different philosophy.

References

Allport, G. W. *Pattern and growth in personality.* New York: Holt, Rinehart & Winston, 1961.
Baier, K., & Rescher, N. *Values of the future.* New York: Free Press, 1969.
Bern, D. *Beliefs, attitudes and human affairs.* Belmont, CA: Brooks/Cole, 1970.
Carroll, L. *The complete works of Lewis Carroll.* New York: Random House/Vintage Books, 1976.
Clark, K. *Civilization: A personal view.* New York: Harper & Row, 1969.
Coleburt, R. *The search for values.* New York: Sheed & Ward, 1960.
Flint, R. History of education of the hearing impaired. In L. Bradford & W. Hardy (Eds.), *Hearing and hearing impairment.* New York: Grune & Stratton, 1979.
Hawley, R. *Human values in the classroom.* Amherst, MA: Education Research Associates, 1973.

Raths, L., Harmin, M., & Simon, S. *Values and teaching: Working with values in the classroom.* Columbus, OH: Chas. E. Merrill, 1966.
Rokeach, M. *The nature of human values.* New York: Free Press, 1973.
Scharf, P. (Ed.). *Readings in moral education.* MN, Minnesota: Winston Press, 1978.
Toffler, A. *Future shock.* New York: Random House, 1970.
van Uden, A. *A world of language for deaf children: Part I, basic principles.* Rotterdam: Rotterdam University Press, 1970.
Vygotsky, L. S. *Thought and anguage.* Cambridge, MA: M.I.T. Press, 1962.
Whorf, B. L. *Language, thought and reality.* Cambridge, MA: M.I.T. Press, 1956.

reaction to 22

jan j.m. van eijndhoven

I thank you very much for your inspiring lecture. Allow me to make some remarks.

You will agree with me that deaf children are more dependent on their educators than any other child. For example: hearing children can remain illiterate but they still have language and can come into conversation with others. Deaf children cannot develop a language by themselves, cannot come into conversation with others without special education. Also, in a developed country deaf children are always in the position of having poor opportunities.

Mr. Campbell, in his lecture this week, said: "One might give the deaf person the opportunity to choose freely whether or not he wants to learn and improve his ability to use the actual language usage of hearing people." I think we must say: deaf children don't have the opportunity to choose freely. The deaf pupils of the school in Sint Michielsgestel, educated manually from 1840–1900, could not choose freely to use the spoken language of hearing people. They could not free themselves from the manual language learned in childhood. That means: deaf children are terribly dependent on their educators.

Therefore, I can't fully agree with what you said on page 13 of your paper: "No one can say that one approach is better than the other." You know: Christopher Columbus grew up believing the earth to be flat, as did everybody in the 15th century. But Columbus changed his ideas and began to work with the belief that the earth was round. His new belief affected his behavior and he set sail westward and discovered a new country, America. His philosophy, his belief, his idealism were related to reality. He was a true professional while his belief was based on real assumptions. Without the belief of Columbus, Mgr. Hourihan probably would not be a lecturer today. Without the good research done by Columbus, America probably would not be a country open to people coming from Europe.

Research and evaluation must teach us, and so-called ideals of educators must be submitted to research and evaluation, in order to find out and understand what idealists are doing.

There is a big difference between professionals and professionals. I gather that too many people who are working in the field of the education of the deaf call themselves professionals. You know that they are but too many amateurs. A director of a school for the deaf, a psychologist, a linguist, etc. who cannot converse with deaf children is not a professional in the education of the deaf, and yet they often "boss the show."

It is a great honor to us that Mr. Hermes, State Secretary, as well as members of Parliament are here and are willing to listen to us. They are professionals as politicians, not professionals in the education of the deaf. But I can say that they, as well as the State Secretary and his colleagues, are good listeners, confident of the fact that we are professionals. Now I have the opportunity to say: "Thank you" for your willingness to listen to us now, in the past, and in the future.

A big problem is that the ideals of educators of the deaf are not the ideals of deaf children. At first deaf children cannot formulate their ideals. In my opinion, if a deaf child had the opportunity to formulate his ideal, he would say: "Help me to become a real partner in conversation, help me to become a personality who can converse with others and to whom others will listen." If educators of the deaf have as an ideal to have deaf children move, as adults, into a subculture, then deaf persons will be hampered in developing their ideals, which they could not formulate at first. The schools for the deaf in The Netherlands have chosen an oral education for a large majority of deaf children. They are convinced that this way is an open way. Deaf children educated in that way get the opportunity to freely choose their education depending on whether they want to go into a subculture or into the normal environment.

On page 522 you said: "Adherents of the oral philosophy place a high value on integrating the deaf child into society in general by developing the language of that society as the child's first language." Here, I would like to ask you: "What do you understand by 'oral philosophy' or by 'an oralist'?"

I can say that I am an adherent of the oral philosophy. But I explain the oral philosophy as follows:
1. A good professional in oral education sees oral education only as oral education if that oral education is *purely* oral.
2. A professional in oral education is one who has based his language education on language as an act of conversation by discovery-learning.
3. A professional in oral education sees each deaf child as an individual and he knows that purely oral education is not possible for all hearing impaired children.
4. He knows that purely oral education presupposes good diagnosis by several experts in the field of the education of the deaf.
5. He knows that purely oral education is only possible if schools for the deaf get the opportunity to organize their education in a way that is more freely adjusted to the needs of each individual child.
6. He knows that continual evaluation of the results of education is a necessity; research must be done, but by highly qualified professionals.
7. He knows that each class must have the opportunity of becoming a model class adapted to the potentialities of the children.

Education of the deaf is still at an early stage. I hope that all persons present in the Hague and responsible for the education of children will give every opportunity to the education of deaf children, a group of children with poor chances. I am convinced that they will help us so that we can carry out our responsibility to the benefit of the best people in the world, our deaf children.

part VI

summary and conclusions

23

an oral education of the deaf

jan j.m. van eijndhoven

Several methods of education and communication have been used during the history of schools for the deaf. In Sint Michielsgestel deaf children were educated manually or by means of total communication from 1830 to 1900.

On the strength of their experience with oralism and manualism in the past as well as at the present time, the board of trustees, principals, and staff of the Institute are convinced that the pure oral way of education is and will remain the ideal for the vast majority of prelingually profoundly deaf children. Many other schools in the world have the same conviction.

Every year many visitors from foreign countries visit the school in Sint Michielsgestel. We discuss with them, we make friends, we exchange thoughts. However these contacts are mostly too short for searching discussions. Therefore we felt a need to bring together international specialists: to confer on oral education for deaf children; to share the results of research and of practice as perceived from the point of view of sociology, psychology, speech science, education, anthropology; and its role in personal and vocational fulfillment; to describe the state of the art internationally and to determine areas of needed research; to publish the papers presented and to provide needed information for educators and parents of the deaf world-wide.

A final objective was to have a positive effect on the oral language of deaf pupils internationally.

An organizing committee was selected representing the United States, The Netherlands, England, and West Germany. The international committee invited selected participants from leaders in the field in the United Kingdom, The United States, The Netherlands, West Germany, Switzerland, Canada, Ireland and Hungary. A group of 40 participants came together and held discussions for a week in a conference center in Nüland.

The Bureau of Education for the Handicapped, Dr. Edwin Martin, Director, U.S. Office of Education, Washington, D.C., partly supported the costs of the

Symposium by a grant of $21,000. Many thanks to Professor Ann Mulholland of Columbia University, who made arrangements for that funding.

The participants of the Symposium have worked very hard this week. I must say it was not always easy to understand each other, but, as you will hear from Dr. Kopp we came to a number of conclusions and recommendations.

Is an oral education a good approach? I am convinced that we can say "Yes:"

- If the methods used in oral education are not teacher-centered but child-centered;
- If in child-centered methods the pupils get the opportunity to discover the structure of the subject themselves;
- If the method is a way of approaching the deaf child as a human being with the belief, he is strong enough to build up his own language by spontaneous discourse between himself and his caretakers;
- If research is a daily task for a group of scientific staff in each school. I am sure that schools for the deaf must create more opportunities to build up such a staff;
- If the schools have more freedom of organization;
- If the role of the parents in the education of their own child is really understood both by the parents themselves and by the child's other caretakers;
- If continuing education is recognized as an absolute need for deaf pupils.
- If group leaders or houseparents in a residential school are given better status as educators on the same level and with the same importance as teachers, and as such get salaries corresponding to that status;
- If pupil-scales in schools are more adapted to the specific handicap of deafness at each age level and to the development of each individual child;
- If in the schools there is only a small fluctuation within the staff of teachers and educators;
- If in schools there is a homogeneous method of teaching language;
- If teachers and other educators are well prepared for their special task by training courses.

We discussed many topics during the week. We did not always agree with each other, but we tried to understand each other by information and confrontation about the different aspects of the approach in an oral education. The initiative to organize the Symposium "Oral Education Today and Tomorrow" has been taken in Sint Michielsgestel. We have opened the door and given others the opportunity to see what we are doing. Our continuing task will be further study.

24

oral education defined

To ensure consensus in the use of terminology currently used to describe the focus of the Symposium, a Subcommittee was appointed to formulate a definition. While a number of terms are used to reflect the processes involved, it was agreed that the term "oral education" would be maintained as the descriptor most acceptable. After considerable discussion in committee and in plenary sessions, the participants approved the following:

> The International Symposium on Deafness "Oral Education Today and Tomorrow", convened at Nuland, The Netherlands in November 1979, reaffirms the belief that deaf persons have the right and the ability and should have the opportunity to integrate into the social and economic mainstream of society. History and experience have demonstrated the validity of the oral approach to the education of hearing impaired children including those who are prelingually deaf. The essential characteristics of oral education are:
> 1. A communicative system that uses speech, residual hearing, speechreading, and/or vibrotactile stimulation in spontaneous discourse.
> 2. An educational system in which instruction (teaching) is conducted exclusively through spoken and written language.

Father van Uden of Sint Michielsgestel, dissenting, later suggested the following amended version of "the essential characteristics of oral education:"

> 1. A communicative system that exclusively uses speech, residual hearing, speech-reading, and/or vibrotactile stimulation with or without normal gesticulation in spontaneous conversation.
> 2. An educational system in which the teaching of language and of all subjects involved in language is conducted exclusively through its spoken and written forms.

His explanation for these suggested amendments follows:

> I must confess, that I have four objections to the definition of "oral education," issued by the Symposium, three of which are in my opinion essential:
> - There are many schools for the deaf, calling themselves oral schools, in which the instruction in the classroom is purely oral indeed, but the children use a lot of signs mixed with speech in free time. A director of a school for the deaf once thematized this by saying, that such signs used in the free time are not harmful

to the teaching of language. I am sure that no member of the Symposium would accept such a philosophy. Yet this philosophy is supported by the definition given. All of these schools can use this definition in order to prove that they are real oral schools.

- There are teachers of the deaf who are so strict in their way of teaching, that they teach deaf children "with their hands in their pockets," and exclude every gesture, even pointing. I have met several such teachers. I don't think that the members of the Symposium would support such an extreme point of view.
- The term "discourse" seems to be too general. I prefer "conversation", defined by the Oxford dictionary as "informal exchange of ideas by spoken words".
- Less essential, but important enough: It is not acceptable to put a bracketed explanation into a definition, such as "Instruction (teaching)." Further, one might ask, "Instruction, teaching of what?" The answer to this question seems to be, the teaching of language and of all subjects involved in language.

This minority report was accepted, but no further action was taken on the suggested amended version.

a.m.m.

25

conclusions and recommendations
harriet green kopp

It is both a privilege and a responsibility to have been invited to summarize the papers and the week-long discussions of this conference. It is particularly appropriate that this first International Symposium on Deafness, focused on Oral Education, has been convened here at Sint Michielsgestel recognized as a fortress of oral education, the professional home of Father van Uden and his colleagues, who are renowned for the strength of their commitment and dedication to oralism and the excellence of their instructional programs. Their hospitality and that of their Board of Directors; the expertise of the Chairman of the Program Committee, Ton van Hagen, and his indefatigable and driving committee, combined with the vigor and high professionalism of the participants and observers have resulted in an extraordinary week. Although the contributed papers provided a significant focal point for the discussion groups, the scheduled and unscheduled discussions resulted in an interchange of ideas, a sharing of ongoing research, a search for definition and redefinition of terminology which will help us to understand future papers, publications, and research. Perhaps we are closer now to a common language or, at least, a professional vocabulary than we were a week ago. The papers will speak for themselves in the proceedings, as will the fine and thoughtful critiques of the reactors. What I hope to bring to you today, is a summary of some of the dominant issues, recommendations, and concerns that were expressed. It is obvious that all issues covered in a week's deliberations cannot be addressed in a summary. I trust that the discussions and papers as filtered through my cognitive structures and perceptual systems will be representative of the perceptions of the participants.

Historical Perspective

In considering the complex, cyclic historical development of instructional systems and models designed to promote the education of the deaf, including reception and expressive language, it is apparent that although change is inevitable over time, it is not always equated with progress. Ideally, we retain the best. In reality, increments of growth, ideologically as well as cognitively, tend to be more spiral than vertical. It is helpful, in periods of methodological regression, to remember that the beauty of the pearl arises from its absorption and incorporation into its "center" that which is a focal point of irritation. Although some of our discussions were disturbing, it was evident that dissonance may ultimately be beneficial. We do not learn as much from these who agree with us as from those who argue dispassionately and logically, provided we are open to change and not "fossilized." The overriding characteristic of youth is growth. The glory of age is the ability to encourage and to accept change; to let go of cherished convictions in the light of new data; and to encourage the independent activity and professional innovation of the young. Those who, by experience and professional contribution have assumed the role of "mentor," accept responsibility for assisting the next professional generation to move through the present, into the future, in light of the past. The mixture of generations, cultures, professional specializations and disciplines among the Symposium participants provided an exciting and challenging interplay of ideas, experiences, and research findings. That consensus was reached on some issues is significant. That different points of view were elucidated, helped to define issues for future discussion and research. Perhaps the single, most significant achievement of the symposium was the adoption of a definition of oral education, by unanimous vote of all the participants.[1] The carefully framed definition was derived from lengthy, vigorous discussion of each concept and word. It is a positive statement which reflects an amalgam of the various positions held by individual participants and represents only those points on which unanimous agreement was obtained.

Organismic Model

The Symposium Papers and discussions were organized to view the oral education of deaf individuals from a variety of perspectives. If we consider the human being, deaf or hearing, as a total organism in the framework postulated by George Adams Kopp in 1932, we recognize how difficult it is to isolate and to control the multiple variables in the complex interactive systems responsible for human learning, for memory, for acquisition and use of language and speech, for motor competency, for neuro-physiologic integrity, for cognitive processing, for emotional stability, for the multiplicity of feedback systems by which our autonomic, cognitive, and affective behavior is controlled. An additional complication results from the need to make spoken language, which is an acoustic/auditory function, accessible to those who cannot hear. The participants appear to share the conviction that communication through language cannot be taught, but must be learned by the communicator.

It is useful to think of language, and particularly spoken language, as a transaction which results in the communication of knowledge and emotion. The

[1]See chapter 24.

participants have expressed a strong consensus concerning the need to seek, in the deaf child, a recapitulation of the normal progression of communicative, linguistic and cognitive developmental stages found in all children. We have discussed the varying nature of these communicative-linguistic transactions at levels from pre-school to young adult with particular concern for the learning problems resulting from neuro-physiological deficits. We have had our attention directed to the egocentricity of the young child and have heard papers, seen video-tapes, and experienced live demonstrations at Sint Michielsgestel, of various methods through which advantage can be gained by using natural, developmental stages in helping the child to generate the rules of language and phonology. It has been stimulating to perceive that it is possible to reach the goal of communicative competency in prelingually, profoundly deaf individuals by various routes, using interactive, transactional approaches involving child-parent, child-teacher and child-child engaged in spontaneous discourse. We have been challenged, particularly by our Dutch colleagues, to observe the child at play with other children for evidence of success in the attainment of these objectives. We must remember that a transaction implies direct reinforcement within the situational context. Communicative success is the ultimate reinforcement and, when achieved, provides motivation for future communicative transactions.

We have been reminded of the need for repeated opportunities for learning to take place and have been concerned by the level of skills demanded of the teacher, the family, and the parent educator, in developing situations in which language may be acquired naturally, linguistic and phonological rules generated by the child, and developed to the level of automaticity in decoding and encoding through frequent application and use in natural contexts. We regard over-generalization of rules as a natural and desirable stage of development. In illustration of the delightful and normal signs of learning, I recall the little deaf girl who stopped me in the hall of the Detroit Day School for the Deaf one day. I was principal of that school and had brought my new puppy to school rather frequently, partly to provide the younger children with language experiences. She asked, "Dr. Kopp, why is your dog so frisk and my dog so unfrisk?"

We appear to have reached agreement that effective receptive and expressive language cannot be acquired didactically through the direct classroom application of language patterns or drills as manifested in what I term the regurgitative method in which the child echoes, from short term memory, the teacher's stimulus. However, we expressed awareness of the need for an underlying developmental structure approached through consistency, continuity, and much ingenuity. It was agreed generally, that learning by generation of rules and concepts may not achieve all necessary skills without recourse to specialized instruction focused on particular problem areas.

Different degrees of emphasis were accorded by various participants to the curricular content of the situations in which language may be acquired. The experiential content of lessons related to science, social studies, and other curricular subjects was raised in some of the group discussions. It seems of great significance to me, that we recognize that neither language nor speech can be developed in a cognitive vacuum. That is, language as the ability to internalize or externalize concepts, ideas, information, and feelings should be acquired and practiced in the course of the acquisition of curricular and social knowledge and skills. It is my deep conviction that it is more productive, in the education of the deaf child as an organismic whole, to provide language experiences in the science class where he is also exposed to the cognitive processing requisite to the formulation of hypotheses or questions; to the independent development of procedures appropriate to the testing of hypotheses in seeking answers to questions and in solving problems; and to the understanding of the implications of formulating inferences and testing conclusions, than in a continued language lesson. Sometimes unusual situations do occur. Perhaps I can share with you a true story. As principal of the Detroit Day School for the Deaf, one of my less pleasant duties was the appellate function of disciplinarian. One day, an angry second grade teacher came to the office with three small boys. They had been late in returning to the classroom from the bathroom and when she had gone to find them, they had been engaged in what she plainly regarded as highly undesirable behavior. In questioning the three, by then, frightened youngsters, I discovered that the teacher had been developing a curricular unit on linear measurement. Since we stressed the discovery method and an experimental approach, the children had been measuring desks, chairs, arms, legs, noses, feet, fingers. The boys had been continuing the learning situation by applying their new measurement skills to their proudest possessions. The teacher was to be congratulated for having generated a vivid learning experience; the boys counseled on the social dangers of carrying a little learning too far in a direction counter to social customs in our culture.

Reading and writing were discussed as supportive in developing linguistic competencies. However, these subjects were not treated in great detail in the program or in the group discussions.

CONCLUSIONS AND RECOMMENDATIONS

Collaborative Research

Recognition of the heterogeneity of the deaf population of the diverse methods and systems of education led the participants to recommend the encouragement of collaborative research providing a wider data base, especially where the population of deaf individuals in a particular category is limited in number. For example, concern was expressed for the paucity of research data on the multihandicapped and the gifted. There was disagreement expressed on the criteria used for prediction of success in oral education programs. The need for extensive research here is evident especially with respect to the stages of language, readiness and the effect of diminishing cortical plasticity. The use of the 'age five' was a focal point of dispute, some feeling it is too early, others, too late. Another major area discussed was that of quantitative/qualitative measures of status and of progress. It is recognized, that only through longitudinal research may we delineate the milestones and rate of progress to be expected in deaf students.

Specific questions that are considered to be critical are:

- Where are the plateaus?;
- What should be our expectation of variation in progress?;

- What is the effect of variables of teaching, of intelligence, of degree of hearing loss, of added handicapping conditions, of family/home/environment, of day versus residential settings, of controlled language exposure at school and home/dormitory, of cultural and ethnic differences?

We are not in agreement on criteria for assessment of competencies and expectations in language, speech, and school subjects including reading/writing. A significant lack is evident, also, in diagnosis of deaf individuals, including early identification and the assessment of specific variables (neurological, psychological, social, communicative, cognitive). Much discussion centered on problems surrounding the development of initial diagnostic inventories to be followed by longitudinal assessment.

Integration

The focus of discussion here was on the family-school-culture triad and on the criteria for assessing success/failure rates related to social-psychologic-economic variables. Three central issues were discussed with recommendations for research. The relationship of diagnosis and educational assessment to success in placement and the influence on these decisions of parental/community/cultural/school expectations was viewed as an urgent area for research. Criteria for selection of appropriate support services, use of diversified programming, the range of programs needed, ways of financing such services, and criteria for cost effectiveness were issues recognized as critical to mainstreaming with minimal data available. The importance of curricular content and of independent learning was stressed as a base requirement, if children are to be integrated successfully, with consequent demands for early acquisition of reading/writing competencies. Identification of these issues as essential research questions and recognition of the diverse solutions in process in various countries may provide focal points for relevant research.

The definition of oral education centers on the ability of deaf individuals to become part of the mainstream of society, thus solutions to these questions must be viewed as particularly urgent.

Acquisition and Correction

The Kopp organismic model referred to earlier, emphasizes that habits once acquired are not erased; cognitive traces remain and new habits must be superimposed on the old. Old habits are subject to recall, sometimes involuntarily under stress conditions. Thus, how we acquire language, speech, and motoric competencies is significant, and we must differentiate strategies for acquisition from those for remediation of established patterns. Research issues were discussed in relation to methodologic points of view included in the papers. At what stage is the conceptual base strong enough to permit corrective procedures which may be analytic, without disturbing the ability of the individual to continue to generate, from experience, rules, concepts, and skills?

There were many strong differences expressed with regard to how these experiences may be provided most efficiently and whether the order or system of presentation and the organization of experiences influences the internal cognitive processing of these experiences. We appear to have little knowledge about how the deaf individual stores and retrieves experiences or how we can improve the efficiency of his cognitive processing. Is it like that of the hearing or is it different at particular developmental stages? Although the terms used varied widely, much discussion focused on problems relating to closure as basic to encoding/decoding. Questions were raised as to how we can increase the rate and efficiency of closure in reading, in audition, and in speech. There was concurrence on the significance of audition in the development of communication, but much question on assessment criteria and on the most effective strategies for providing maximal use of audition.

Teacher Preparation

Considerable argument revolved around the goals and content of teacher preparation programs with recognition given to the increased rigor required of programs preparing teachers in oral education modes. There was agreement reached that we must insist on competences in teaching academic content subjects as well as communication/language knowledges and skills. Two major resolutions were proposed:

> **International Exchange** of teachers, administrators, supervisors, support personnel and teacher-educators was viewed as the most effective means of providing interchange of ideas, methods, learning models, diagnostic, and research competencies. An externship/fellowship program was proposed, with funding to be sought from each of the governments with members in attendance at the Symposium and from appropriate professional associations and private foundations.
>
> **Material Interchange** of teaching and diagnostic materials and research data was recommended as essential to maximum use of available international resources. It was resolved that one or more Resource Centers should be established in each of the countries represented, with funding to be sought from government, school, and agency sources. Such exchange was viewed as critical for progress in research, for improvement in teacher preparation, and in management and implementation of educational programs for deaf individuals.

Continuing Education

In general, the participants expressed concern for the lack of adequate support for secondary and post-secondary education especially in relation to the goals of integration. In all countries there were inadequate support services available. Legislation, such as the United States P.L. 94-142 and Section 504, was viewed as desirable in mandating the use of support services although the provision of funding in inflation economies was seen as either inadequate or difficult to obtain. Vocational/job counselors, personal counselors, social workers, psychologists, and secondary resource teachers were all considered to be critical to the support system required of the deaf individual, his family, and the community if integration is to be achieved. Accessible, on-going instruction in language, speech, and use of audition, in addition to continued academic/vocational/social/emotional development, is essential if deaf adolescents and adults are to reach their potential. Research data are critical to the decision-making process and to the choice of educational/vocational alternatives. We have little hard data or follow-up of vocational success/failure; employment levels related to level of communication skills and preferred mode (manual/oral); and social/emotional status (integrated/segregated). Consensus was obtained on the need for increased participation by qualified deaf adults in the areas of decision making, service delivery and, particularly, as counselors, educators, and role models.

Mental Health

On this issue, two major concerns were expressed. Insufficient attention is given in most countries to the mental health of children both in preventive and treatment aspects. Parent education and counseling programs, parental awareness of realistic expectations and problems, and parental acquaintance with deaf adults are critical at the earliest stages and throughout preschool and school years.

Development of appropriate affect in and provision of counseling for all those who impact upon the deaf child and adult and their families is seen as essential. Research data are needed on the assessment of mentally healthy as well as troubled deaf individuals. Milestones must be identified for crisis periods, stages when problems are apt to occur, or periods of change when assistance may be most beneficial.

Lingual-Cultural Pluralicity

It was agreed that the problems of the deaf child educated in a linguistic/cultural setting different from that of the home were being addressed sporadically in only a few educational settings. The educational/linguistic/social problems manifested in the United States, particularly on the East and West Coasts, have resulted in diverse solutions related to similar concerns for the hearing bilingual/cultural population. Common Market countries may be able to take advantage of these early experimental approaches. Research data are not available for the deaf, and little hard data are available for the hearing, on the effect of various methods and learning models on the child or adult and the home; on educational achievement; on social-psychological-economic status; and on language learning and communicative competencies.

Assessment criteria have not been validated nor have learning strategies. Here, there is an opportunity to prevent serious problems if resources and energy can be channeled into defining questions and testing solutions before crisis management becomes an overwhelming need. Advantage should be taken of the experiences and educational strategies found useful in countries where bilingualism and multilingualism are common in educational/social/cultural practice.

Effect of Legislation on Deaf Individuals

Much discussion centered on the effect of recent U.S. legislation on the education and social progress of the deaf. Mandated services and explicitly legislated rights were viewed as the optimal route for provision of early identification and diagnosis and appropriate educational placement with integration, when it is appropriate, made accessible by adequate support services. The discussions that led to the definition of oral education accepted by this Symposium were deeply concerned that the deaf individual be provided with both the ability and the opportunity to integrate into the mainstream of society. Both must be assured by legislation and implemented with funding and other resources if this goal is to be attained by the many as well as the few.

Leadership

There was strong consensus concerning the need to assure the on-going development of leaders with commitment to the education of the deaf. It was recognized that missionary zeal must be tempered by broad educational and service qualifications and by specialized knowledges and skills at the highest levels, if lasting progress is to be achieved. The panacea approach producing instant albeit questionable results of dubious validity, is to be avoided and demands our watchful alertness. Our leaders must accept their responsibility as mentors. We must provide resources that enable young, highly qualified interns to assume apprenticeships to work directly with acknowledged leaders in positions of increasing responsibility in varied settings. We must recognize that academic degrees are only a part of the baggage of the leader. Dedication, energy, vigor, intellectual rigor and honesty, scholarly attitudes, the affect of the helping professional can be recognized and encouraged but cannot be taught. We need to seek out potential leaders, provide them with the experiential and academic resources needed and place them with role models. They rise, like cream, only when they are not forced into a homogenized program. This is an old, not a new concept. We must give it more than lip-service. If oral education of the deaf is to be a reality that achieves full potential for those deaf individuals desiring integration into the mainstream of society as oral deaf adults, leaders must be provided in research, education, social/psychological/vocational services, and legislation who combine the highest level professional and personal qualification with commitment to this goal.